ZINN AND THE ART OF
MOUNTAIN BIKE
MAINTENANCE

ZINN AND THE ART OF MOUNTAIN BIKE MAINTENANCE

5th EDITION

LENNARD ZINN

Illustrated by Todd Telander

VELO press

BOULDER, COLORADO

1830 55th Street

Boulder, Colorado 80301-2700 USA

(303) 440-0601 · Fax (303) 444-6788 · E-mail velopress@competitorgroup.com

Distributed in the United States and Canada by Ingram Publisher Services

A Cataloging-in-Publication record for this book is available from the Library of Congress.
ISBN: 978-1-934030-59-2

For information on purchasing VeloPress books, please call (800) 811-4210 ext. 2169
or visit www.velopress.com.

This book is printed on 100 percent recovered/recycled fiber, 30 percent postconsumer waste, elemental chlorine free, using soy-based inks.

Cover and interior design by Erin Johnson

Composition by Erin Johnson and Jessica Xavier

Cover photo by Brad Kaminski; bike built by Lennard Zinn

Custom paint job on cover bike by Spectrum Powder Works, Colorado Springs, CO

Title font Sign Production JNL; body text Caecilia Roman

10   11   12 / 11   10   9   8   7   6   5   4   3   2   1

To Sonny, my wife,
without whose support this book
could not have been written;
or at least a few more decades
would have passed before
it got done.

A TIP OF THE HELMET TO . . .

My heartfelt thanks go out to Todd Telander, for producing illustrations that make the procedures more intelligible and beautiful; to my editors and in-house support system, Charles Pelkey and Mark Saunders, for separating the wheat from the chaff and adding more wheat when necessary; to Terry Rosen, for bugging me to write this book for so many years; to Mike Sitrin, formerly of VeloPress, for doing the same and promising to publish the first edition when I did; to Felix Magowan and John Wilcockson, for sharing their vision, extending financial support, and giving encouragement; to John Muir and Robert Pirsig, for writing such great books to encourage this effort. Special thanks to everyone at VeloPress for the countless efforts to improve it.

For technical assistance with the details, thanks to Wayne Stetina, Steve Hed, JP Burow, Ken Beach, Portia Masterson, Charlie Hancock, Sander Rigney, Doug Bradbury, and Chris DiStefano and to Scott, John, and Rusty at Louisville Cyclery (Louisville, Colorado) as well as to folks at Shimano, SRAM, RockShox, Pedro's, Effetto Mariposa, NoTubes, Manitou, Cane Creek, Fox, FSA, Park Tool, Hayes, Avid, ITM, 3T, Cinelli, Deda, Easton, Salsa, Mavic, Selle San Marco, Cannondale, and Ritchey.

I also want to thank my entire family for support and inspiration: Emily and Sarah, my daughters, for showing me that books can be written, completed, and published at a prolific rate; Dad and Mom, for encouraging me my whole life; Rex and Steve, for offering suggestions; Kai, Ron, and Dad, for being authors themselves and an inspiration to me; and Marlies, for taking the kids when I needed it. Thanks, Sarah, for proving Groucho Marx right.

CONTENTS

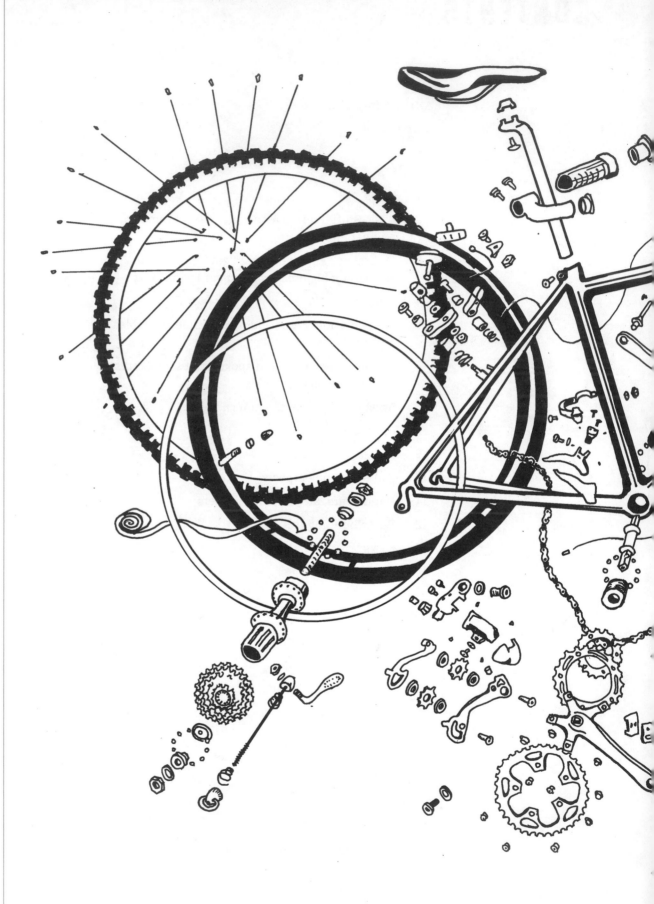

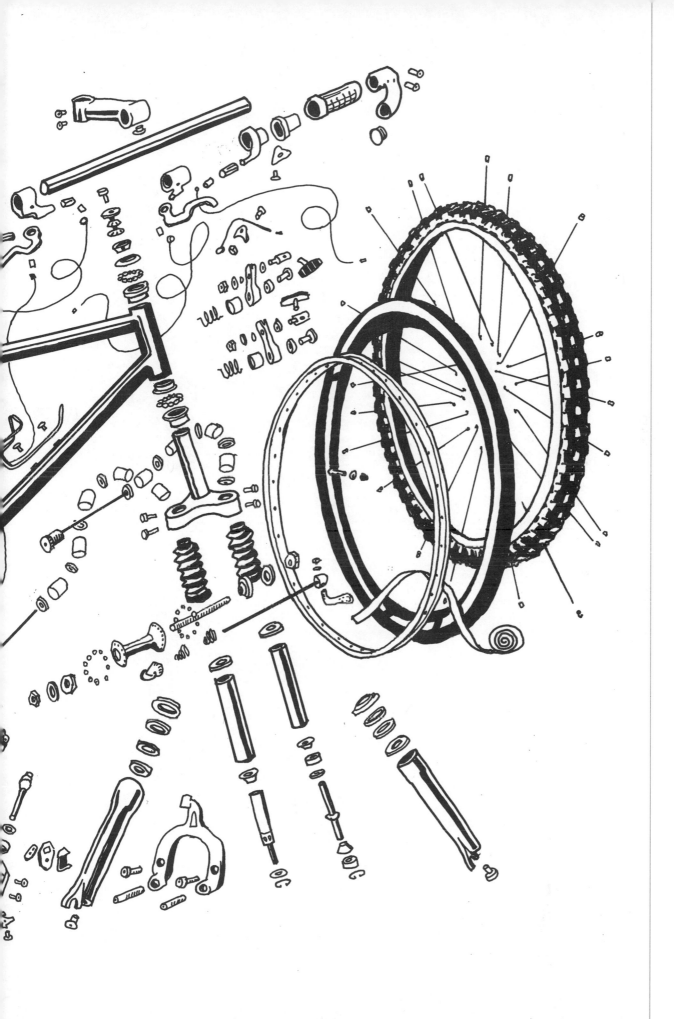

INTRODUCTION

Peace of mind isn't at all superficial, really. It's the whole thing. That which produces it is good maintenance; that which disturbs it is poor maintenance. What we call workability of the machine is just an objectification of this peace of mind. The ultimate test's always your own serenity. If you don't have this when you start and maintain it while you're working, you're likely to build your personal problems right into the machine itself.

—Robert M. Pirsig,
Zen and the Art of Motorcycle Maintenance

ABOUT THIS BOOK

This book is intended for people who have an interest in maintaining their own mountain bikes. I have written it for mountain bike owners who do not think they're capable of maintaining their own bikes, as well as for those who do and who want the how-to details at their fingertips. In *Zen and the Art of Motorcycle Maintenance*, Robert Pirsig explores the dichotomy between the purely classical and purely romantic views of the world, a dichotomy that also applies to mountain biking. Riding a mountain bike is generally a romantic experience of emotion, inspiration, and intuition, even when solving the complex physics of how to negotiate a technical section of trail without putting your foot down. Mountain bike mechanics, however, is a purely classical structure of underlying form dominated by reason and physical laws. The two practices—bike riding and bike maintenance—fit eloquently together. Each is designed to function in a par-

ticular way, and to have one without the other would be missing out on half the fun.

The romantic can appreciate how success at bike mechanics requires that the procedures be done with love, without which the care you imagined putting into your mountain bike would be lost. And even the pure romantic can follow the simple step-by-step procedures and "exploded" diagrams in this book (of which Fig. I.1 is an extreme example and is the only one not intended to be simple and clear!) and discover a passion for spreading new grease on old parts.

Zinn & the Art of Mountain Bike Maintenance is organized in such a way that you can pick maintenance tasks appropriate for you. The repairs in these pages require no special skills to perform; anyone can do them. It takes only a willingness to learn.

Mountain bikes are admirably resilient machines. You can keep one running a long time just by changing the tires and occasionally lubricating the chain. Chapter 2 is about the most minimal maintenance your bike requires. Even if that is the only part of this book you end up using, you'll have gotten your money's worth by avoiding some unpleasant experiences out on the trail.

This book was originally intended for home enthusiasts, not shop mechanics. For that reason, I have not included the long and precise lists of parts specifications that a shop mechanic might need. Nonetheless, when combined with a specification manual, this book can be a useful, easy-to-follow reference for shop mechanics, too.

WHY DO IT YOURSELF?

There are a number of reasons why you would want to maintain your own mountain bike. Obviously, if done right, it is a lot cheaper to do yourself than to pay someone else to do it. This is certainly an important factor for those riders who live to ride and have no visible means of support. Self-maintenance is a necessity for that crew.

As your income goes up and the time available to maintain your bike goes down, this becomes less and less true. If you're a well-paid professional with limited free time, it probably does not make as much economic sense to maintain your own bike. Yet you may find that you enjoy working on your bike for reasons other than just saving money. Unless you have a mechanic whom you trust and to whom you take your bike regularly, you are not likely to find anyone else who cares as much about your bicycle's smooth operation and cleanliness as you do. You may also need your bike fixed faster than a local shop can do during its busy season. And you need to be able to fix mechanical breakdowns that occur on the trail.

It is a given: Breakdowns will happen, even if you have the world's best mechanic working on your bike. For this reason, it takes away from my enjoyment of a ride if I have something on my bike that I do not understand well enough to know whether it is likely to last the ride or how to fix it if it does not.

There is an aspect of bicycle mechanics that can be extremely enjoyable in and of itself, almost independent of riding the bike. Bicycles are the epitome of elegant simplicity. Bicycle parts, particularly high-end components, are meant to work well and last a long time. With the proper attention, they can shine both in appearance and in performance for years to come. There is real satisfaction in dismantling a filthy part that is not functioning well, cleaning it up, lubricating it with fresh grease, and reassembling it so that it works like new again. Knowing that I made those parts work so smoothly—and that I can do it again when they get dirty or worn—is rewarding. I am eager to ride hard to see how they hold up rather than being reluctant to ride for fear of breaking something.

Also, if you share my stubborn unwillingness to throw something out and buy a replacement simply because it has quit working—be it a leaky Waterpik; a torn tent; a duffle bag with a broken zipper; or an old car, dishwasher, clock, or chainsaw that is no longer running well—then this book is for you. It is satisfying to keep an old piece of equipment running long past its time, and it's a great learning experience!

There is also something very liberating about going on a long ride and knowing that you can fix just about anything that might go wrong with your bike out on the trail. Armed with this knowledge (which begins with learning to identify the parts of a mountain bike, shown in Fig. I.2) and the tools to put it into action, you will have more confidence to explore new areas and to go farther than you might have otherwise.

To illustrate, an experience from way back in 1995 comes to mind, when I took a day to ride the entire 110-mile White Rim Trail loop in Utah's

Canyonlands National Park. It is as desolate as you can imagine out there, and I was completely alone with the sky, the sun, and the rocks for long stretches. I had a good mileage base in my legs, so I knew I was physically capable of doing the ride during the limited daylight hours of late October. I had checked, replaced, or adjusted practically every part of my bike in the days before the ride. I had also tried out the bike on long rides close to town. Finally, I added to my saddlebag tool kit a few tools that I do not ordinarily carry.

I knew that there was very little chance of anything going wrong with my bike, and with the tools I had, I could fix almost anything short of a broken frame on the trail. Armed with this knowledge and experience, I really enjoyed the ride! I stopped and gawked at almost every breathtaking vista, vertical box canyon, colorful balanced rock, or windblown arch. I took scenic detours. I knew that I had a good cushion of safety, so I could totally immerse myself in the pleasure of the ride. I had no nagging fear of something going wrong to dilute the experience.

Confidence in your mechanical ability allows you to be more courageous about what you will try on trails. And armed with this confidence you'll be more willing to share your love of the sport with less experienced riders. Bringing new people along on rides is a lot more fun if you know that you can fix their bikes and they won't be stranded with an old junker that won't roll.

HOW TO USE THIS BOOK

Skim through the entire book. Skip the detailed steps, but look at the exploded diagrams and get the general flavor of the book and what's inside. When it is time to perform a particular task, you'll know where to find it, and you'll have a basic idea of how to approach it.

Illustrator Todd Telander and I have done our best to make these pages as understandable as possible. Exploded diagrams are purposefully used instead of photographs to show more clearly how each part goes together. The first time you go through a procedure, you may find it easier to have a friend read the instructions out loud as you perform the steps.

Obviously, some maintenance tasks are more complicated than others. I am convinced that anyone with an opposable thumb can perform virtually any repair on a bike. Still, it pays to spend some time getting familiar with the really simple tasks, such as fixing a flat, before throwing yourself into complex jobs, such as building a wheel.

✹ LEVEL 1

✹ ✹ LEVEL 2

✹ ✹ ✹ LEVEL 3

Tasks and tools required are divided into three levels indicating their complexity or your proficiency. Level 1 tasks need level 1 tools and require of you only an eagerness to learn. Level 2 and level 3 tasks also have corresponding tool sets and are progressively more difficult. All repairs mentioned in this book are classified as level 1 unless otherwise indicated. Tools are shown in Chapter 1. The section at the end of Chapter 2, "Performing Mechanical Work: A General Guide" (§ii-17), is a must-read; it states general policies and approaches that apply to all mechanical work.

Each chapter starts with a list of required tools in the margin. If a section involves a higher level of work, there will be an icon designating the level and tools necessary to perform the tasks in that section. Tasks and illustrations are numbered for easy reference. Section references use the symbol "§." For instance, "§iii-6" means "see Section iii-6 in Chapter 3." Illustrations are referred to as "Figures," for instance, "Fig. 3.3."

I.2 See? There it is, all back together!

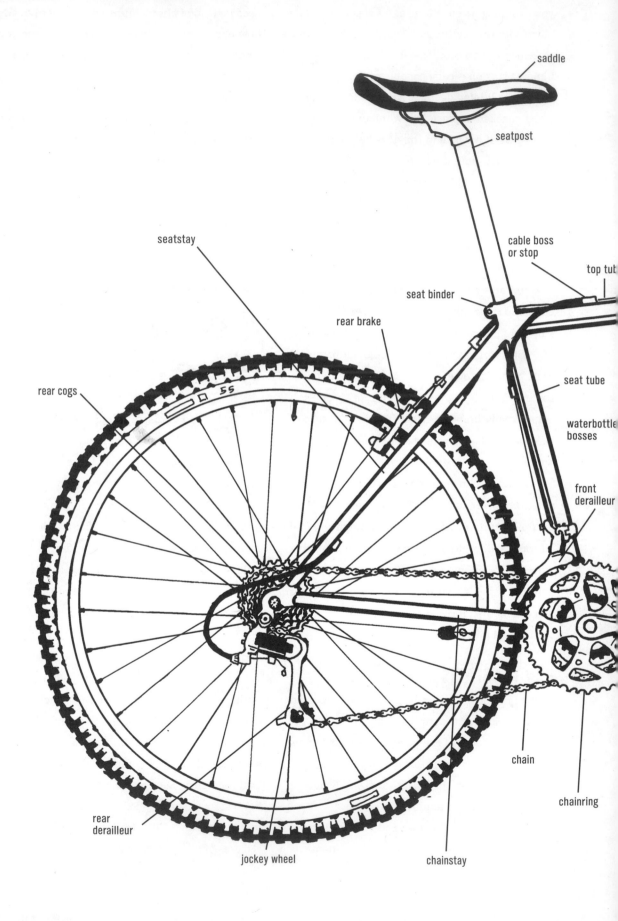

saddle

seatpost

cable boss
or stop

top tub

seatstay

seat binder

top tub

rear brake

seat tube

rear cogs

waterbottle
bosses

front
derailleur

chain

chainring

rear
derailleur

jockey wheel

chainstay

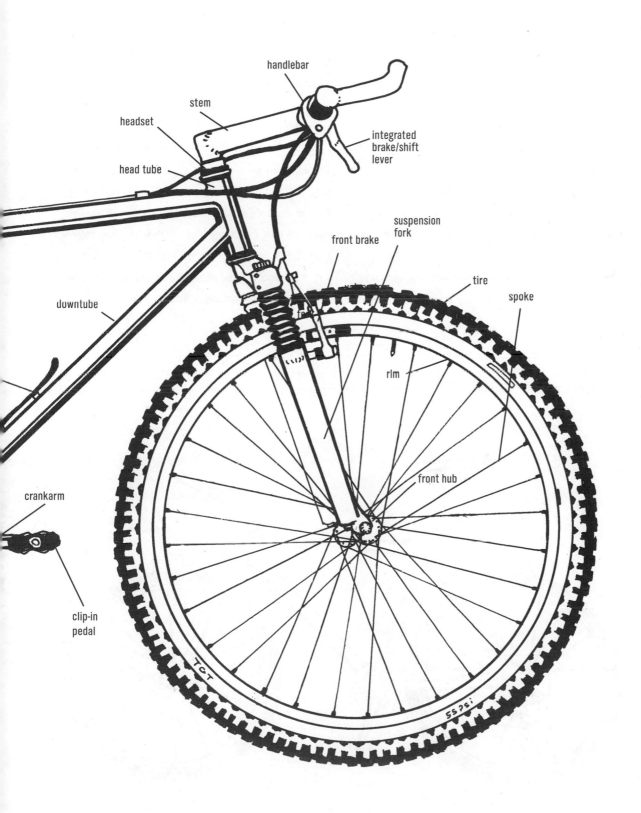

handlebar

stem

headset

head tube

integrated
brake/shift
lever

suspension
fork

front brake

tire

downtube

spoke

rim

front hub

crankarm

clip-in
pedal

At the end of some chapters there is a trouble-shooting section. This is the place to go to identify the source of a certain noise or particular malfunction in the bike. There is also a comprehensive troubleshooting guide in Appendix A.

There is a wealth of other valuable information in the appendixes. Get used to using the appendixes; many tasks will be simplified.

Appendix B has a complete gear chart and includes instructions on calculating your gear with nonstandard-size wheels. Appendix C is an extensive section on selecting the properly sized bike and positioning it to fit you. Appendix D lists the tightening specifications of almost every bolt on the bike in the Torque Table. As bike parts become ever lighter and made out of ever more exotic materials, tightening them to the recommended torque spec becomes ever more important. The glossary is a comprehensive dictionary of mountain bike technical terms. There is a separate index listing the illustrations in the book if you want to quickly check and see what something looks like.

THE MOUNTAIN BIKE

This (Fig. I.2) is the creature to which this book is devoted (in this case, a "hardtail" with cantilever brakes). All of a mountain bike's major parts are illustrated and labeled here. Take a minute to familiarize yourself with these parts now, and refer back to this diagram whenever necessary.

The mountain bike comes in a variety of forms, from models with rigid frames and forks (Fig. I.3), to hardtails (front suspension only—Fig. I.2), to models with front- and rear-suspension systems (Fig. I.4). They can come with rim brakes (Figs. I.2, 3, and 5) or disc brakes (Fig. I.4).

A mountain bike generally comes with knobby tires in a 26-inch diameter, although larger 29-inch

I.3 Fully rigid

I.5 Hybrid

and 650B (27.5-inch) tires and wheels are gaining favor, particularly for tall riders. Smaller 24-inch wheels and tires are found on small mountain bikes. Tire widths and shapes vary and include everything from studded snow tires to smooth street tires. This book also covers "hybrid" bikes (Fig. I.5), which are a cross between road bikes and mountain bikes.

No matter how a mountain bike is configured, even those who see themselves as having no mechanical skills will be able to tackle problems as they arise if they study the steps necessary to properly maintain and repair their bike. With a little bit of practice and a willingness to learn, your bike will transform itself from a mysterious contraption seemingly too complicated to tamper with to a simple, very understandable machine that can be a genuine delight to work on. Just allow yourself the opportunity and the dignity to follow along, rather than deciding in advance that you will never be able to do this. All you have to do is follow the instructions and trust yourself.

So, set aside your self-image as someone who is "not mechanically oriented" (and any other factors that may stand in the way of your making your mountain bike ride like a dream), and let's start playing with your bike!

Behold, we lay a tool here and on the morrow it is gone.
—The Book of Mormon

You can't do much work on a bike without tools. Still, it's not always clear exactly which tools to buy. This chapter clarifies the tools you should consider owning on the basis of your level of mechanical experience and interest.

As I mentioned in the Introduction, the maintenance and repair procedures in this book are classified by their degree of difficulty. Nearly all the repairs in this book are classified as level 1, unless otherwise indicated. The tools for levels 1, 2, and 3 are pictured and described in the following pages. Lists of the tools needed in each chapter are shown in the margin at the beginning of each chapter.

For the uninitiated, there is no need to rush out and buy a large number of bike-specific tools. With only a few exceptions, the Level 1 Tool Kit (Fig. 1.1A) consists of standard metric tools. This kit is similar to the collection of tools I recommend later in this chapter to carry with you on rides, though in a more compact and lightweight form (Figs. 1.5–6). The Level 2 Tool Kit (Fig. 1.2) contains several bike-specific tools, allowing you to do more complex work on the bike. The tools in the Level 3 Tool Kit (Fig. 1.3) are extensive (and expensive), and they ensure that your riding buddies will show up not only to ask your sage advice, but also to borrow your tools.

And if you really want to go all out and be set up like a pro (and even have mechanics wanting to borrow your tools), you can splurge on the set shown in Figure 1.4. If you loan tools, you might consider marking your collection to help recover those items that might otherwise take a long time finding their way back to your workshop. It wouldn't hurt writing down the details about which tool you lent to whom and on what date. You would be surprised how easy it is to forget who has one of your seldom-used tools such as snapring pliers or a metric tap.

i-1
LEVEL 1 TOOL KIT

LEVEL 1

Level 1 repairs are the simplest and do not require a workshop, although it is nice to have a good space to work. You will need the following tools (Fig. 1.1A):

- **Tire pump** with a gauge and a valve head to match your bike's tubes (either Presta or Schrader valves—see Fig. 1.1B; most good pumps will fit both). A spare rubber valve-seal insert for the head is a good idea; these wear out.
- **Standard screwdrivers:** small, medium, and large (one of each).
- **Phillips-head screwdrivers:** one small and one medium.
- Set of three plastic **tire levers** (Figs. 6.5–6).
- At least two **spare tubes** of the same size and valve type as those on your bike.
- Container of regular **talcum powder**. It works well for coating tubes and the inner casings of tires. Do not inhale this stuff; it's bad for the lungs.
- **Patch kit.** Choose one that comes with sandpaper instead of a metal scratcher and patches with soft orange rubber backing to the black rubber (Fig. 6.11). At least every year and a half, check that the glue has not dried up, regardless of whether the tube has been opened or not. On rides, you might as well take a little packet of glueless patches; they don't work as well as standard patches, but if the glue has dried up, you'll be glad you have them.
- One 6-inch **adjustable wrench** (aka "Crescent wrench").
- **Pliers:** regular and needle-nose.
- Set of **metric hex keys** (aka "Allen wrenches" or "hex wrenches") that includes 2.5mm, 3mm, 4mm, 5mm, 6mm, 8mm, and 10mm sizes. Folding sets are available and work nicely to keep your wrenches organized but are not strong enough or long enough in the big sizes (6mm and up); big bolts require more leverage. I also recommend buying extras of the 4mm, 5mm, 6mm, and 8mm sizes.
- Set of **metric open-end/box-end wrenches** that includes 7mm, 8mm, 9mm, 10mm, 13mm, 14mm, 15mm, and 17mm sizes.

1.1A Level 1 Tool Kit

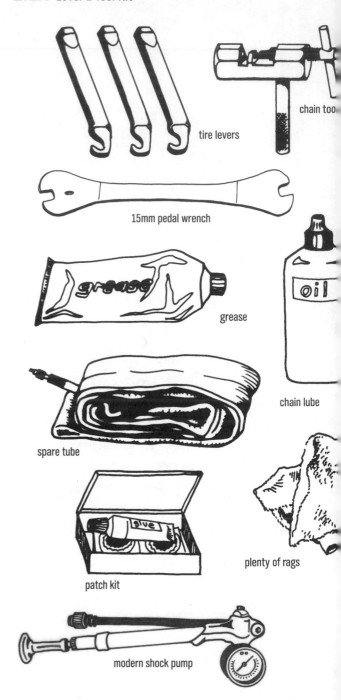

tire levers

chain tool

15mm pedal wrench

grease

chain lube

spare tube

patch kit

plenty of rags

modern shock pump

- 15mm **pedal wrench**. This is thinner and longer than a standard 15mm wrench and thicker than a cone wrench (Fig. 9.3). Your bike's pedals may accept only a 6mm or 8mm hex key (Fig. 9.4), so you may not need this tool.
- **Chain tool** for disconnecting and reconnecting

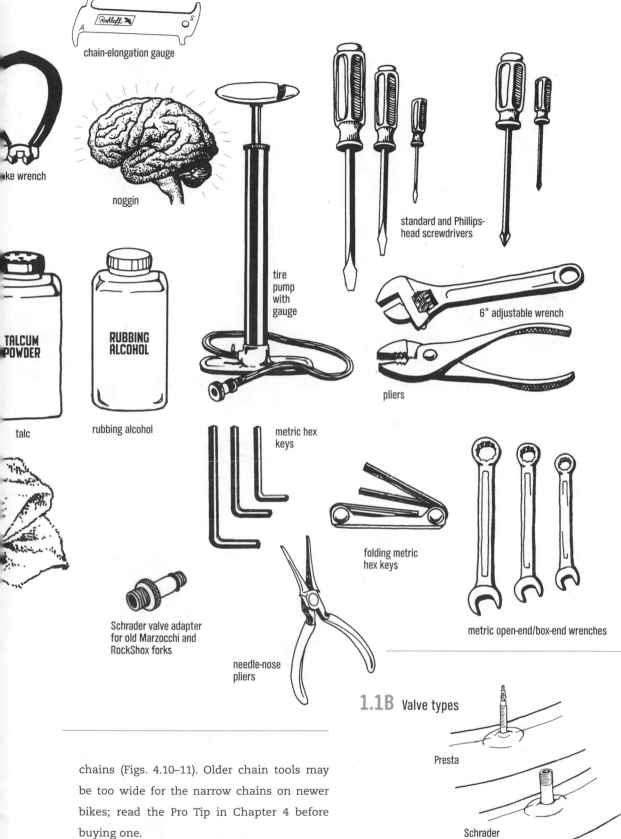

chain-elongation gauge

...ke wrench

noggin

TALCUM POWDER

talc

RUBBING ALCOHOL

rubbing alcohol

tire pump with gauge

standard and Phillips-head screwdrivers

6" adjustable wrench

pliers

metric hex keys

folding metric hex keys

metric open-end/box-end wrenches

Schrader valve adapter for old Marzocchi and RockShox forks

needle-nose pliers

1.1B Valve types

Presta

Schrader

chains (Figs. 4.10–11). Older chain tools may be too wide for the narrow chains on newer bikes; read the Pro Tip in Chapter 4 before buying one.

- **Chain-elongation gauge** to monitor the condition of the chain (Figs. 4.5–6).

- **Spoke wrench** to match the size of nipples used on your bike's wheels.

- Tube or jar of **grease**. I recommend using grease designed specifically for bicycles; however, standard automotive grease is okay, except in suspension forks and twist shifters.

- Drip bottle or can of **chain lubricant** (Fig. 4.1). Please choose a nonaerosol; it is easier to control, uses less packaging, and wastes less in overspray.

- **Rubbing alcohol** for cleaning disc-brake pads, rotors, shocks, and internal parts and for removing and installing handlebar grips.

- A lot of **rags**!

  Other useful items:

- If you have an air-sprung suspension fork or rear shock, you need a **shock pump**. Get one with a no-leak head if the front or rear shock has standard Schrader valves (Fig. 13.10), and get the adapter you need if your bike's fork requires either a ball needle or a special adapter to insert down inside a sunken Schrader valve.

i-2

LEVEL 2 TOOL KIT

⚙️ ⚙️ LEVEL 2

Level 2 repairs are a bit more complex, and I recommend that you create a well-organized workspace with a shop bench. Keeping your workspace organized is probably the best way to make maintenance and repair easy and quick. You will need the entire Level 1 Tool Kit (Fig. 1.1A) plus the following tools (Fig. 1.2):

- **Portable bike stand**. Be sure that the stand is sturdy enough to remain stable when you're really cranking on the wrenches. If for some reason you can't clamp your bike's seatpost, you will need a bike stand that holds the bike by the bottom bracket and the front or rear end with one wheel out; see the one in Figure 1.4.

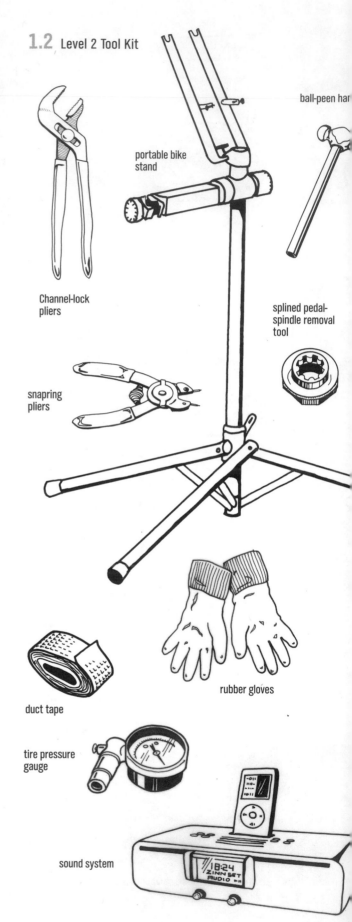

1.2 Level 2 Tool Kit

ball-peen ha[r]

portable bike stand

Channel-lock pliers

splined pedal-spindle removal tool

snapring pliers

duct tape

rubber gloves

tire pressure gauge

sound system

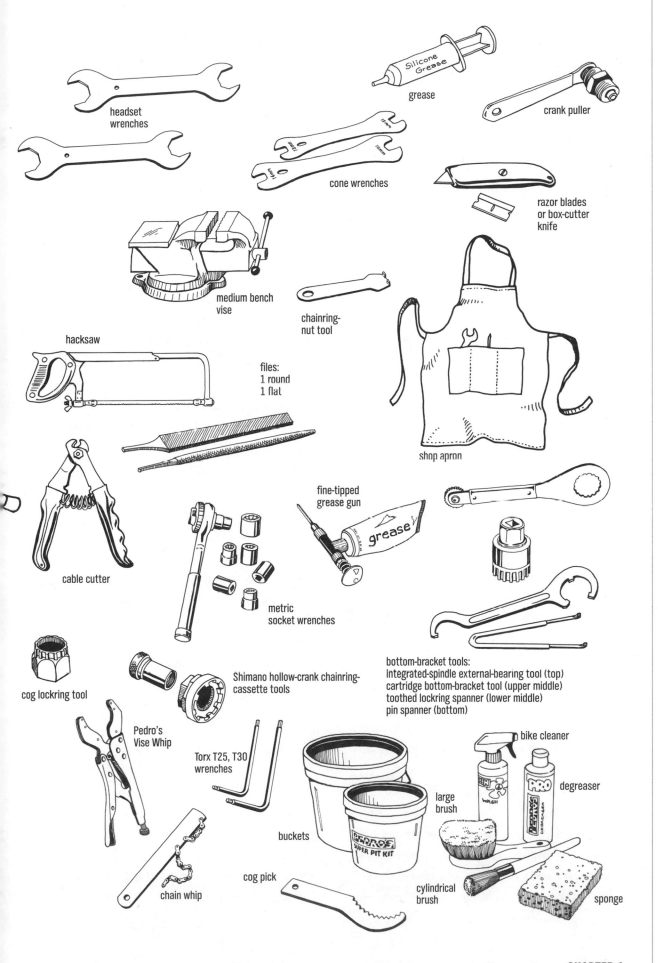

headset wrenches

grease

crank puller

cone wrenches

razor blades or box-cutter knife

medium bench vise

chainring-nut tool

hacksaw

files:
1 round
1 flat

shop apron

fine-tipped grease gun

cable cutter

metric socket wrenches

bottom-bracket tools:
integrated-spindle external-bearing tool (top)
cartridge bottom-bracket tool (upper middle)
toothed lockring spanner (lower middle)
pin spanner (bottom)

cog lockring tool

Shimano hollow-crank chainring-cassette tools

Pedro's Vise Whip

bike cleaner

Torx T25, T30 wrenches

large brush

degreaser

buckets

chain whip

cog pick

cylindrical brush

sponge

- **Shop apron** (this is to keep your nice duds nice).
- **Tire pressure gauge**. It is more accurate than a pump gauge and a must for getting pressure right for technical riding.
- **Hacksaw** with a fine-toothed blade.
- **Box-cutter knife** or **razor blades** (Fig. 6.32).
- **Files**: one round and one flat.
- **Cable cutter** for cutting coaxial shift cable housing without crushing as well as for cutting brake and shifter cables without fraying.
- Set of **metric socket wrenches** that includes 7mm, 8mm, 9mm, 10mm, 13mm, 14mm, and 15mm sizes.
- **Torx wrenches**, which look like hex keys with star-shaped tips. Torx T25 and T30 are common sizes on modern bikes.
- **Crank puller** for removing crankarms (Fig. 8.6). Its push rod is sized for either square-taper spindles (Fig. 8.18) or ISIS or Octalink spindles (Figs. 8.19–20), so get the right one for your bike's crankset.
- **Chainring-nut tool** for holding the nut while you tighten or loosen a chainring bolt (Fig. 8.9).
- **Chainring-cassette removal tools** for Shimano Octalink–style HollowTech I cranks (Fig. 8.12).
- **Bottom-bracket tools**. For external-bearing cranks (Fig. 8.2), you'll need an oversize splined wrench to remove the cups (Fig. 8.14) and, in some cases, a little splined tool to tighten the left crank's adjustment cap. For BB30 cranks (Fig. 8.15), you'll need snapring pliers (Fig. 8.26) and inserts to use with a headset press (Fig. 8.25). For sealed-cartridge bottom brackets (Figs. 8.18–19), you'll need a splined bottom-bracket socket (Fig. 8.27). If your bike has an ISIS or Octalink splined-spindle bottom bracket, you'll need a splined tool with a bore large enough to swallow the fatter spindle (Fig. 8.19). If your bike has a square-taper cartridge bottom bracket (Fig. 8.18), you might as well get the ISIS tool (Fig. 8.19), as it will work on

both types. And for cup-and-cone and adjustable cartridge-bearing bottom brackets (Figs. 8.21–22), you'll need a lockring spanner and a pin spanner to fit the bottom bracket (Fig. 8.30).
- **Snapring pliers** (Fig. 8.26) for BB30 cranks (Fig. 8.15) and other unthreaded bottom brackets with snapring grooves and for use in removing snaprings from suspension forks, pedals, and other parts.
- **Cone wrenches** for loose-bearing hubs (Fig. 6.25). The standard sizes are 13mm, 14mm, 15mm, and 16mm, but check which size you need before buying.
- Medium **ball-peen hammer**.
- Two **headset wrenches**. Be sure to check the size of the headset nuts (Fig. 11.29) before buying these. This purchase is unnecessary if your bike has a threadless headset and you don't plan to work on old bikes. Some suspension forks have crown nuts requiring headset wrenches.
- Medium **bench vise**, bolted securely to the bench.
- **Cog lockring tool** for removing cogs from the rear hub (Figs. 6.38–39).
- **Chain whip** for holding cogs while loosening the cassette lockring (Fig. 6.39) or a **Pedro's Vise Whip**, which holds the cog more firmly (Fig. 6.38) and won't fall off when it rotates.
- **Channel-lock pliers**.
- **Splined pedal-spindle removal tool** (Fig. 9.9).
- Fine-tipped **grease gun**.
- Tube of **silicone-based grease** if you have Grip Shift shifters.
- **Nonlithium grease** for front and rear shocks.
- **Stereo** laden with good tunes.
- You'll also want such stuff as tape, safety glasses, and rubber dish gloves or a box of cheap latex gloves. Buckets, large brushes, sponges, cog picks, degreaser, and dish soap or bike cleaner also will serve you well for cleaning a dirty machine rapidly.

i-3
LEVEL 3 TOOL KIT

⚙️⚙️⚙️ LEVEL 3

If you are an accomplished level 3 mechanic, you can even build a complete bike from a bare frame. That is assuming, of course, that the following tools (Fig. 1.3) are neatly organized in your shop:

- **Parts-washing tank**. Please use an environmentally safe degreaser. Dispose of used solvent responsibly; check with your local environmental safety office.
- Large **bench-mounted vise** to free stuck parts.
- **Headset press**. A simple, inexpensive press can press in any size headset (Fig. 11.43) and can install press-in bottom brackets as well (Fig. 8.25).
- **Fork-crown race punch** (aka "slide hammer") for installing the fork-crown race of the headset (Fig. 11.41).
- **Headset cup remover** (Figs. 11.36–37).
- **Star-nut installation tool** for threadless headsets (Fig. 11.14).
- An extra **Vise Whip** or **chain whip** for disassembling old-style 6- and 7-speed cogsets or freewheels.
- **Freewheel removers** for Shimano, Sachs, and SunTour freewheels.
- Large **ball-peen hammer**.
- **Soft hammer**. Choose a rubber, plastic, or wooden mallet to prevent damage to parts.
- **Torque wrenches** for checking proper bolt tightness. Following manufacturer-specified torque settings prevents parts from stripping, breaking, creaking, or falling off while you are riding. Ideally, you want a small torque wrench for small bolts and a big, long torque wrench for large bolts.
- **Torx** and **metric hex-key bits**.
- Instead of the Torx and metric sockets just mentioned, you can invest in a full selection of Phillips, flat-blade, **Torx, and metric hex-key drive bits** with a tiny Giustaforza torque wrench (in place of a smaller square-drive torque wrench) or a Prestacycle socket wrench, all of which can come in handy for small bolts.
- Set of **metric taps** that includes 5mm by 0.8mm, 6mm by 1mm, and 10mm by 1mm sizes for fixing mangled frame threads.
- **Truing stand** for truing (Figs. 6.20–21) and building wheels (Chapter 12).
- **Dishing tool** for checking that the wheel you just finished building is properly centered (Figs. 12.21–22).
- **Spoke wrenches** of all sizes.
- **Splined** or other **specialty spoke wrench** for wheels with splined or oversized nipples, bladed spokes, and/or internal nipples (see other specialty spoke wrenches in Fig. 1.4).
- **Pin spanner** for adjusting Mavic hubs.
- **Morningstar Freehub Buddy** for flushing and lubricating freehubs (Figs. 6.41, 6.43).
- **Telescoping** or **articulating magnet** for picking up dropped parts or small tools.
- **Valve core removers** for both Schrader and Presta valves. These are used for tire service and shock service.
- **Chain keeper** (attaches to dropout to run chain over for cleaning drivetrain with wheel off).
- **Master link pliers** (Fig. 4.23).
- **Syringe** for bleeding hydraulic brakes—the type varies with brake brand. All hydraulic brakes require some sort of tube and may require only a squeeze bottle of fluid rather than a syringe.
- One healthy dose of **patience** and an equal **willingness to work** and rework jobs until they have been properly finished.

  Other items you might like to have on hand:
- **Spare parts** to save you from last-minute runs to the bike shop, such as several sizes of ball

1.3 Level 3 Tool Kit

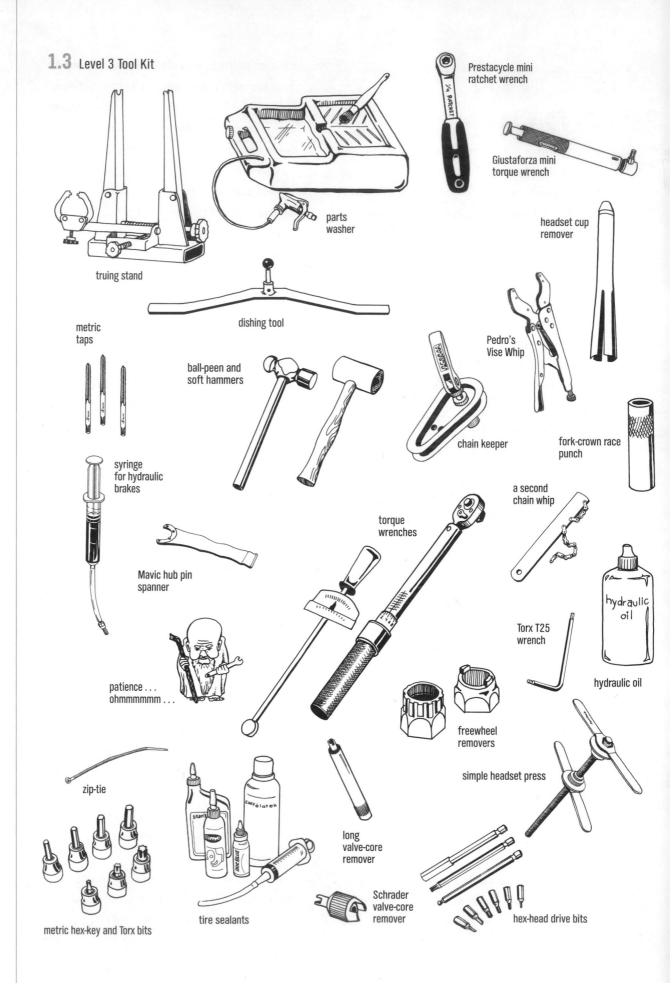

Prestacycle mini ratchet wrench

Giustaforza mini torque wrench

parts washer

truing stand

headset cup remover

dishing tool

metric taps

Pedro's Vise Whip

ball-peen and soft hammers

chain keeper

fork-crown race punch

syringe for hydraulic brakes

a second chain whip

torque wrenches

Mavic hub pin spanner

hydraulic oil

Torx T25 wrench

patience . . . ohmmmmmm . . .

freewheel removers

simple headset press

zip-tie

long valve-core remover

metric hex-key and Torx bits

tire sealants

Schrader valve-core remover

hex-head drive bits

star-nut
installation tool

extra cables,
housings, hoses, and
fittings

master
link pliers

extra tire

splined
spoke
wrench

extra drivetrain
parts

Freehub Buddy

spare master links

10mm
hex key

ticulating magnet

carbon-grip
compound

threadlock
fluid

telescoping
magnet

outboard-motor
gear oil

bearings, zip-ties, spare cables, cable housing, and a lifetime supply of those little cable-end caps. Keep on hand spare tires, tubes, chains, master links, and cogsets. If you expect to be working on suspension forks, rear shocks, and hydraulic brakes, be sure to have spare hoses, seals, and fittings.

- **Carbon-grip compound** for clamping carbon seatposts (Fig. 10.6) and handlebars.
- **Tire sealants** for setting up tubeless tires (Fig. 6.17) or installing into inner tubes for puncture protection.
- **Various fluids**. Special hydraulic brake fluids, hydraulic suspension oils and greases, thread-lock fluid, titanium antiseize compound, out-board-motor gear oil, or specialty freehub lubricants are required for some jobs.

i-4

NOW, IF YOU REALLY WANT A WELL-STOCKED SHOP

The following tools (Fig. 1.4) are not even part of the Level 3 Tool Kit and are not often needed for home bike repairs. That said, they sure do come in handy when you need them.

- Euro-style race team **mechanic's bike stand** that supports the bottom bracket and clamps either the fork ends or the rear dropouts without the wheel on. This is required for bikes with integrated seat masts or seatposts that for some reason cannot be clamped in a bike stand.
- Long **Y-wrench** (aka "three-way spoke wrench") with square-drive, 5mm, and 5.5mm sockets for tightening spoke nipples internal to a deep rim, or a specialty wrench for working a specific type of internal nipple.
- **Antitwist tool** for preventing twisting bladed (aero) spokes during truing.
- **Splined spoke wrench** for adjusting spokes on Mavic tubeless wheels.

1.4 Tools for the well-stocked shop

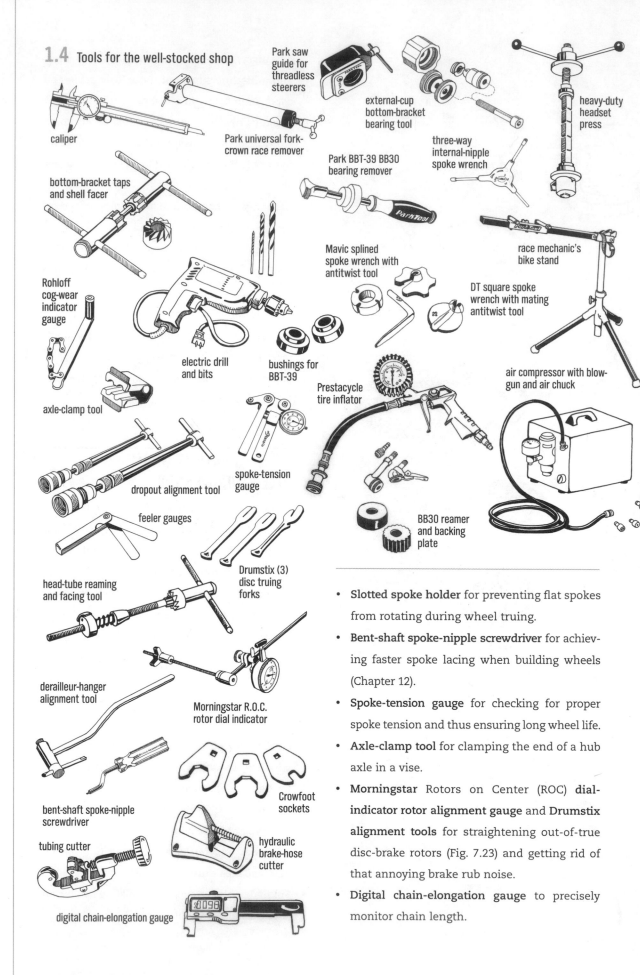

caliper

Park saw guide for threadless steerers

external-cup bottom-bracket bearing tool

heavy-duty headset press

Park universal fork-crown race remover

Park BBT-39 BB30 bearing remover

three-way internal-nipple spoke wrench

bottom-bracket taps and shell facer

Mavic splined spoke wrench with antitwist tool

race mechanic's bike stand

Rohloff cog-wear indicator gauge

DT square spoke wrench with mating antitwist tool

electric drill and bits

bushings for BBT-39

air compressor with blow-gun and air chuck

Prestacycle tire inflator

axle-clamp tool

spoke-tension gauge

dropout alignment tool

feeler gauges

BB30 reamer and backing plate

head-tube reaming and facing tool

Drumstix (3) disc truing forks

derailleur-hanger alignment tool

Morningstar R.O.C. rotor dial indicator

bent-shaft spoke-nipple screwdriver

Crowfoot sockets

tubing cutter

hydraulic brake-hose cutter

digital chain-elongation gauge

- **Slotted spoke holder** for preventing flat spokes from rotating during wheel truing.

- **Bent-shaft spoke-nipple screwdriver** for achieving faster spoke lacing when building wheels (Chapter 12).

- **Spoke-tension gauge** for checking for proper spoke tension and thus ensuring long wheel life.

- **Axle-clamp tool** for clamping the end of a hub axle in a vise.

- **Morningstar** Rotors on Center (ROC) **dial-indicator rotor alignment gauge** and **Drumstix alignment tools** for straightening out-of-true disc-brake rotors (Fig. 7.23) and getting rid of that annoying brake rub noise.

- **Digital chain-elongation gauge** to precisely monitor chain length.

- **Hydraulic brake-hose cutter** for getting an optimal square cut and for reducing the likelihood of fluid leaks.

- Heavy-duty shop-grade **headset press**. Faster and easier to use than the inexpensive one in Figure 1.3, this tool is for pressing in headsets (Fig. 11.43) and bottom brackets into threadless bottom-bracket shells (Fig. 8.25).

- **Park universal fork-crown race remover**. This manly tool allows you to remove headset fork-crown races from any fork without pounding at them with a hammer and screwdriver and marring the fork crown.

- **Saw guide** for cutting threadless steering tubes off straight.

- **Tubing cutter** for cutting handlebars off straight without getting out the hacksaw. Forget about it for cutting off carbon handlebars, though.

- **Caliper** with vernier, dial, or digital measurement for measuring parts in order to optimize function.

- **Head-tube reamer and facer** for keeping both ends of the head tube perfectly parallel and of the proper inside diameter for the headset cups.

- **BB30 reamer and backing plate** for perfecting the fit of bearings in BB30 shell. Use with head-tube reamer and facer handle.

- English-threaded **bottom-bracket tap set** for cutting threads in both ends of the bottom-bracket shell while keeping the threads in proper alignment.

- **Bottom-bracket shell facer**. Like a bottom-bracket tap, this tool cuts the faces of the bottom-bracket shell so they are parallel to each other.

- **Park BBT-39 bearing remover** for BB30. Various supplied bushings also allow pressing in BB30, BB86, BB90, BB92, and BB95 bearings with a headset press or vise (Fig. 8.25).

- **Electric drill** with drill bit set.

- **Crowfoot sockets** for using a torque wrench on a bolt you can access only from the side.

- **Dropout-alignment tools** (aka "tip adjusters"). You need two: one for each dropout or fork end (Figs. 13.31–33, 14.17).

- **Derailleur-hanger alignment tool** for straightening the hanger after you shift it into the spokes or crash on it (Fig. 14.4).

- **Cog-wear indicator gauge** for determining if cogs are worn out.

- **Feeler gauges** for precisely adjusting postmount disc brakes.

- **Air compressor** with blowgun and air chuck. It is useful for lots of things, including overhauling disc brakes and seating tubeless tires.

- **Prestacycle air chuck** with gauge for Presta valves. If you are using an air compressor, this chuck delivers the fastest and most accurate inflation.

i-5
SETTING UP YOUR HOME SHOP

I recommend keeping this area clean and very well organized. Lame as this sounds, remember that "a clean shop is a happy shop"! Make it comfortable to work in and easy to find the tools you need. Hanging tools on pegboard or slatboard or placing them in bins or trays is an effective way to maintain an organized work area. Being able to find the tools you need will increase immensely the enjoyment of working on a bike. It is harder to do a job with love if you're frustrated about not being able to find the cable cutter. Placing small parts in one of those benchtop organizers with several rows of little drawers is another good way to keep chaos from taking over.

i-6
TOOLS TO CARRY WITH YOU WHILE RIDING
a. For most riding

Keep all of the following stuff (see Fig. 1.5) in a bag under your seat or in a hydration pack or

1.5 Tools to take on all rides

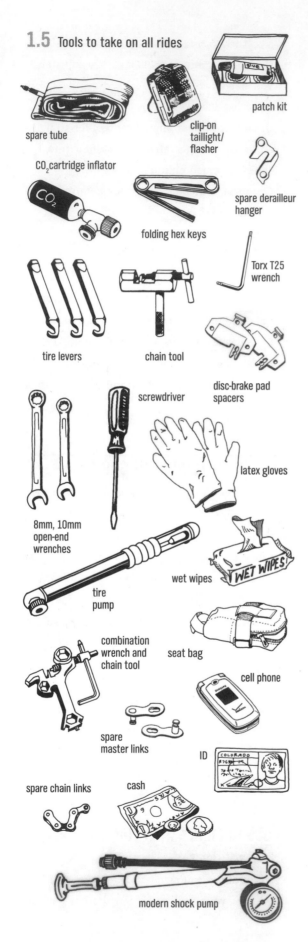

patch kit

spare tube

clip-on taillight/flasher

CO₂ cartridge inflator

spare derailleur hanger

folding hex keys

Torx T25 wrench

tire levers

chain tool

disc-brake pad spacers

screwdriver

latex gloves

8mm, 10mm open-end wrenches

wet wipes

tire pump

combination wrench and chain tool

seat bag

cell phone

spare master links

ID

spare chain links

cash

modern shock pump

fanny pack. The operative words here are "light" and "serviceable." Many of these tools are combined in multitools. Make sure you try all tools at home before depending on them on the trail.

- **Chain tool** that works (try it before an emergency occurs).
- Small **screwdriver** for adjusting derailleurs and other parts.
- Compact set of **hex keys** (also called "hex wrenches" or "Allen keys") that includes 2.5mm, 3mm, 4mm, 5mm, and 6mm sizes. (An 8mm key might be necessary for some bikes; check the fasteners on yours to see which hex keys you may need to carry.)
- **Torx T25 wrench** for disc-brake rotors with Torx screws.
- 8mm and 10mm **open-end wrenches** if your bike has any hex-head bolts on it.
- A good **multitool** to replace with less weight and bulk some or all of the preceding items.
- **Tire pump** and/or **CO₂ cartridge inflator** with a spare cartridge. Larger pumps are faster than itty-bitty minipumps. Make sure the pump or cartridge is set up for your type of valves.
- **Patch kit**. You'll need something after you've used your spare tube. Check at least every year and a half to make sure the patch kit glue has not dried up. Bring glueless patches or foam insulating tape as well.
- At least two plastic **tire levers**, but preferably three.
- **Shock pump** for the front and/or rear shock. If the fork requires a pump adapter, make sure that you carry one.
- Two plastic **pad spacers** if your bike has hydraulic disc brakes (in case you get rescued and have to throw your bike in a vehicle with the wheels off; spacers prevent the pistons from coming out too far if a brake lever is inadvertently squeezed).
- **Spare tube**. This is a no-brainer. Make sure

the valve matches the ones on your bike and pump, and check that the Presta valve collar nuts on the wheels are loose enough to unscrew by hand out on the trail. Keep the tube in a plastic bag to prevent deterioration and to protect it from the sharp tools in your bag.

- **Spare derailleur hanger** that fits your frame in case you crash and bend the derailleur or shift it into the rear wheel spokes.
- **Spare chain links** and two **spare master links** that match the chain width you're using (i.e., 8-, 9-, or 10-speed). If you're using a Shimano chain, you can instead carry at least two "subpin" rivets; master links are preferable for on-trail repairs, though.
- **Identification**.
- **Cash**, for obvious reasons, and as a temporary patch for sidewall cuts in tires.
- **Taillight** that you can clip on or, better yet, leave mounted on your bike in case you stay out after dark.
- **Wet wipes** or **latex gloves** to keep your hands clean.

b. For long or multiday trips

The items in Figure 1.6 are, of course, in addition to proper amounts of food, water, and extra clothes, as well as in addition to the tools shown in Figure 1.5.

- **Spoke wrench** sized to your bike's spokes.
- **Spare spokes**. Innovations in Cycling sells a really cool folding spoke made from Kevlar. It's worth getting one or two for emergency repairs on a long ride.
- Another **spare tube**.
- **Sealant-filled quick aerosol inflator** to rehabilitate a tube or tubeless tire with a slow leak.
- Small plastic bottle of **chain lube**.
- Small tube of **grease**.
- Compact 15mm **pedal wrench** unless the pedals don't have wrench flats. One with

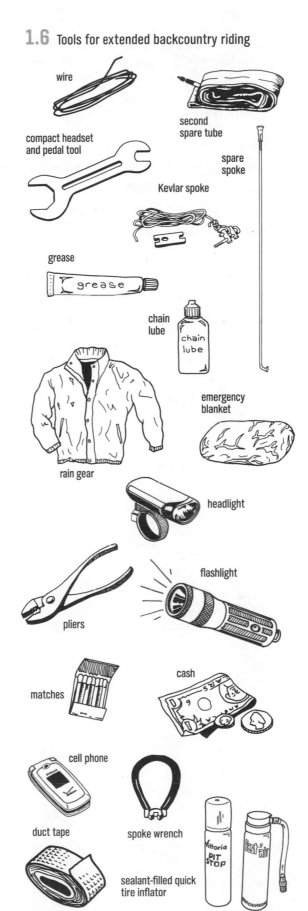

wire

compact headset and pedal tool

second spare tube

spare spoke

Kevlar spoke

grease

chain lube

rain gear

emergency blanket

headlight

flashlight

pliers

matches

cash

cell phone

duct tape

spoke wrench

sealant-filled quick tire inflator

a headset wrench on the other end can be particularly handy if you or your buddy has a threaded headset.

- **Pliers**, useful for innumerable purposes.
- **Wire** and/or a small **bungee cord**, which can be very handy for all kinds of things.
- **Duct tape**. It's like The Force. It has a light side and a dark side, and it holds the universe (and sometimes your bike or your shoes) together.
- **Money**, or its **plastic equivalent**, which can get you out of lots of scrapes.
- **Matches**, because you never know when you might be stranded overnight.
- A lightweight, aluminized, folding **emergency blanket**.

- **Rain gear**.
- **Cell phone**.
- **Headlight**. This can be a lightweight unit that clips onto the handlebar or a headlamp with a strap that fits over your helmet. An extra battery for it is a good idea too.
- Small **flashlight**. This can be a little LED type—just something to help find things in the dark if your headlight dies.

NOTE: *Read Chapter 3, which covers emergency repairs, before embarking on a lengthy trip. And if you are planning a bike-centered vacation, be sure to bring along a Level 1 Tool Kit in the car, some headset wrenches, and various incidentals such as duct tape and sandpaper.*

BASIC STUFF

PRERIDE INSPECTION, WHEEL REMOVAL, AND GENERAL CLEANING

Everything should be made as simple as possible, but not simpler.

—Albert Einstein

TOOLS

chain lubricant

rags

OPTIONAL

solvent (citrus based)

chain-cleaning tool

old water bottle

bucket(s)

large sponge

large and small brushes

dish soap

chain keeper

LEVEL 1

Making sure your bike is safe is essential. It's a good idea to get into the habit of checking your bike before heading out on a ride. Performing a preride inspection regularly could help you avoid delays due to parts failure. I won't even mention the injury risks you face by riding a poorly maintained bike.

After that, unless you always have a mechanic with you, you need to know how to take the wheels off and put them back on, or you won't be able to effectively deal with minor annoyances such as flat tires or jammed chains. And if you do absolutely nothing else to your bike, keeping your chain and a few other parts clean will enhance enjoyment of the ride. This chapter's three cleaning and maintenance procedures are easy to perform and fundamental to keeping your bike running smoothly.

All home mechanics in particular should read "Performing Mechanical Work" in this chapter.

The work in this chapter requires no special tools beyond level 1. If you have never maintained your own bike before, you may find the procedures a bit challenging at first. But with repetition, your confidence will grow and you'll soon find yourself tackling more advanced repairs. So have at it, and enjoy your bike's improved performance!

ii-1
DOING THE PRERIDE INSPECTION

1. **Check to be sure that the quick-release (QR) levers or axle nuts are tight.** They secure the front and rear hub axles to the dropouts.

2. **Check the brake pads for excessive or uneven wear.**

3. **Grab and twist the brake pads and brake arms.** Make sure all bolts are tight.

4. **Squeeze the brake levers.** This should bring the pads flat against the rims (or slightly toed-in) without hitting the tires, or in the case of disc brakes, this should bring the pads against the rotor. Make certain that you cannot squeeze the levers all the way to the handlebar (see §vii-3 and §vii-4 for brake-cable tension adjustment or §vii-15 for hydraulic disc-brake bleeding, after first making sure that the disc-brake pads are in place and in good condition).

15

5. **Spin the wheels.** Check for wobbles while sighting on the rims, not the tires. (If a tire wobbles excessively on a straight rim, it may not be fully seated in the rim; check it all the way around on both sides.) Make sure that the rims do not rub on the brake pads.

6. **Check the tire pressure.** On most mountain bike tires the proper pressure is between 30 and 60 pounds per square inch (psi). Look to see that there are no foreign objects sticking in the tire. If there are, you may have to pull the tube out and repair or replace it. If you are getting flat tires frequently, it might be worth a look at the section on tire sealants (i.e., the goop inside the tube that fills small holes), §vi-10.

7. **Check the tires for excessive wear, cracking, or gashes.**

8. **Be certain that the handlebar and stem are tight.** Check that the stem is lined up with the front tire.

9. **Check that the gears shift smoothly.** The chain should not skip or shift by itself. Make sure that indexed (or "click") shifting moves the chain one cog, starting with the first click. Make sure that the chain does not overshift the smallest or biggest rear cog or the smallest or biggest front chainring.

10. **Check the chain for rust, dirt, stiff links, or noticeable signs of wear.** The chain should be clean and lubricated. (Be cautious about overdoing it with the lube, though. Gooey chains pick up lots of dirt, particularly in dry climates.) The chain should be replaced on a mountain bike about every 500 to 1,000 miles of off-road riding or every 2,000 miles of paved riding.

11. **Apply the front brake, and push the bike forward and backward.** The headset (Fig. 11.1) should be tight and not make clunking noises or allow the fork any fore-and-aft play.

If all these things check out, go ride your bike! If not, check the table of contents or Appendix A, go to the appropriate chapter, and fix the problems before you go out and ride.

ii-2
REMOVING THE FRONT WHEEL

You can't transport your mountain bike easily if you can't remove the front wheel, because removing the front wheel is required for mounting your bike on most roof racks and for jamming a mountain bike inside your car. As outlined in the following sections, wheel removal involves releasing the brake and opening the hub quick-release, the bolt-on skewer, the through-axle mechanism, or the axle nuts on the low-end models.

If your bike has a single-leg fork (i.e., a Cannondale Lefty) or a 20mm through-axle front hub, wheel removal is different. See the note at the end of §ii-5 for a Cannondale Lefty and §ii-10 for a through-axle.

ii-3
RELEASING THE BRAKE
a. Rim brakes

Most rim brakes have a mechanism to release the brake arms so that they spring away from the rim (Figs. 2.1–2), allowing the tire to pass between the pads. If yours does not, you will have to deflate the tire. V-brakes (aka "sidepull cantilevers"—Fig. 2.1) are released by pulling the end of the curved cable-guide tube (aka the "noodle") out of the horizontal link atop one of the brake arms while either holding the link or squeezing the pads against the rim with the other hand (Fig. 2.1). Most cantilever brakes (Fig. 2.2) and U-brakes (Fig. 7.52) are released by pulling the enlarged head of the straddle cable out of a notch in the top of the brake arm while holding the pads against the rim with the other hand (Fig. 2.2).

2.1 Releasing the noodle from the link on a V-brake

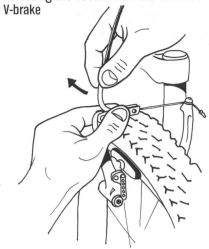

2.2 Releasing a cantilever brake

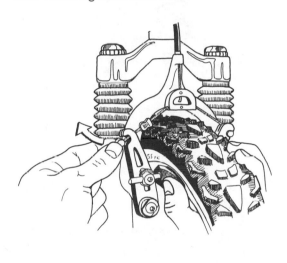

2.3 Opening a quick-release skewer

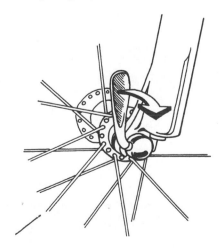

b. Disc brakes

Most disc brakes (Figs. 7.19–20) allow the disc to fall away without the pads being released, as the caliper is bolted to the fork and the disc slips in and out of it easily. However, models manufactured before the advent of disc-brake mounting tabs on the forks make wheel removal much harder. Releasing the old (mid-1990s) Dia-Compe cable-actuated hydraulic disc brakes requires opening a latch (under the caliper) that secures the caliper to the fork. The entire caliper can then be swung up and forward, allowing the wheel to come out.

IMPORTANT: *Do not squeeze the lever of a hydraulic disc brake when there is neither a disc nor a travel spacer between the pads; otherwise, the pistons can pop out too far, and you won't be able to get the rotor back in between the pads without some extra work to push the pistons back. (Travel spacers are flat plastic pieces that usually come with the brakes, but not necessarily with a new bike; you can cut your own spacer from a piece of corrugated cardboard.)*

c. Rare rim-brake types

Roller-cam brakes (Fig. 7.53) are released by pulling the cam down and out from between the two rollers while holding the pads against the rim. Many linkage brakes (Fig. 7.51) are released in the same way as V-brakes or cantilever brakes. Releasing hydraulic rim brakes (Fig. 7.46) usually requires detaching the U-shaped brake booster connecting the piston cylinders together, if installed, followed by unscrewing or quick-releasing one wheel cylinder.

ii-4
DETACHING THE WHEEL WITH A QUICK-RELEASE SKEWER

This is easy, and you don't need a tool.

1. **Pull outward on the quick-release lever to open it** (Fig. 2.3).

BASIC STUFF

2.4 Bolt-on skewer

2. **Unscrew the nut on the opposite end of the skewer's shaft.** Loosen until both the nut and the head of the skewer clear the fork's wheel-retention tabs. Most mountain bike forks have a wheel-retention system consisting of nubs or bent tabs on the fork ends (also known as "dropouts") or an axle washer with a bent tooth hooked into a hole in the fork end. These systems prevent the wheel from falling out if the quick-release loosens.

3. **Pull the wheel off.**

NOTE: *Some bikes have non-quick-release bolt-on skewers (Fig. 2.4). The wheel is removed by unscrewing the skewer with a 5mm hex key until the head and the nut clear the wheel-retention tabs on the fork ends.*

ii-5
DETACHING THE WHEEL WITH AXLE NUTS

1. **Unscrew the nuts on the axle ends** (usually with a 15mm wrench—Fig. 2.5). The nuts unscrew counterclockwise ("lefty loosey, righty tighty").

2. **Loosen the nuts enough to clear the retention tabs on the fork ends.** Most mountain bikes have some type of wheel-retention system consisting of nubs or bent tabs on the fork ends (also known as "dropouts") or an axle washer with a bent tooth hooked into a hole in the fork end. These systems prevent the wheel from falling out if the axle nuts loosen.

3. **Pull the wheel out.**

NOTE: *For Cannondale Lefty forks, first remove the disc brake caliper with a 5mm hex key, and then unscrew the axle bolt (usually with a 5mm hex key as well).*

2.5 Loosening an axle nut

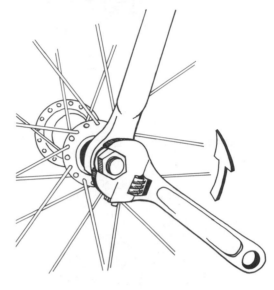

This procedure pulls the wheel right off without any further encouragement from you. On reinstallation, grease the bearing seats on the axle (the thing sticking out from the fork). Slide the hub back on, line it up, and tighten the bolt. Mount the brake again, ensuring that you keep the same spacers between it and the mounting tabs on the fork.

ii-6
INSTALLING THE FRONT WHEEL

With rim brakes, leave the brake open and lower the fork onto the wheel so that the bike's weight pushes the dropouts down onto the hub axle. This action will seat the axle fully into the fork and center the rim in the fork.

With a disc brake, drop the slot in the caliper (the part attached to the fork) over the rotor (the big disc attached to the wheel). Make sure that the rotor does not dislodge either pad. Allow the bike's weight to sit on the hub, ensuring that the axle ends are fully seated in the fork ends.

Continue with the appropriate hub-securing step.

TIGHTENING THE QUICK-RELEASE SKEWER

The quick-release skewer is not a glorified wing nut and should not be treated as such.

1. **Hold the quick-release lever in the "open" position.**

2. **Finger-tighten the opposite-end nut.** Snug it up against the face of the dropout.

3. **Push the lever over** (Fig. 2.6) **to the "closed" position.** It should now be at a 90-degree angle to the axle. If done right, you should have needed a good amount of hand pressure to close the quick-release lever properly; the lever should have left its imprint on your palm for a few seconds.

4. **If the lever does not close tightly enough, open the lever again, tighten the end nut one-quarter turn, and close the lever again.** Repeat until tight.

5. **If the lever cannot be pushed down per–pendicular to the axle and the nut is therefore too tight, open the quick-release lever, unscrew the end nut one-quarter turn or so, and try closing the lever again.** Repeat this procedure until the quick-release lever is fully closed and snug. When you are done, the lever should be pointing straight up or toward the back of the bike so that it cannot hook on obstacles and be accidentally opened.

6. **Double-check that the axle is tight.** Try to knock the wheel out by banging on top of the tire with your hand.

2.6 Tightening the quick-release

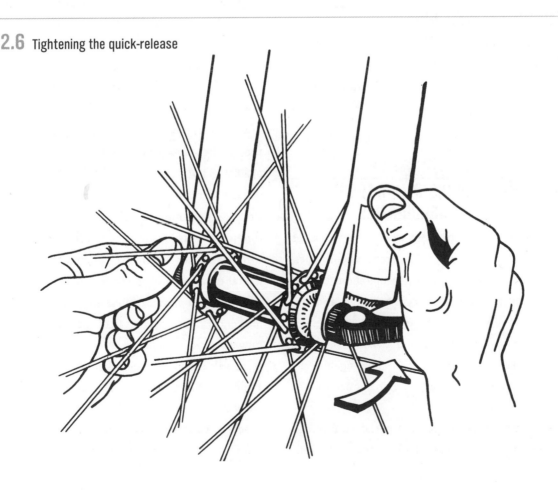

ii-8
TIGHTENING BOLT-ON SKEWERS

Hold the end nut with one hand, and tighten the skewer with a 5mm hex key. If you have a torque specification for the skewer and a torque wrench, use them. If you have a torque wrench and no spec, Control Tech, a company that used to make lots of these skewers, recommends 65 inch-pounds (in-lbs) of tightening torque for steel bolt-on skewers and 85 in-lbs for titanium versions; I recommend following those guidelines. If you do not have a torque wrench, you can approximate the right amount of torque by using a short hex key and tightening as tightly as you can with your fingers. You want the wheel secure, but you also don't want to snap the skewer by overtightening it as a result of leaning on a long hex key with all your might.

ii-9
TIGHTENING AXLE NUTS
(MASS-MERCHANT BIKES)

Snug up the nuts clockwise (opposite direction of Fig. 2.5) with a wrench (usually 15mm). Use the wrench a little on each side until the nuts are quite tight.

ii-10
REMOVING AND INSTALLING FRONT WHEELS WITH THROUGH-AXLES

In the context of the front wheel, through-axles are extra-long, removable front-wheel axles, generally 20mm or 15mm in diameter, that fit through the hub cartridge bearings and are clamped directly into the fork ends. They stiffen the fork against lateral and twisting flex, and they offer a higher degree of safety against the wheel falling out of the fork than a quick-release skewer does.

Any mountain bike, but especially one with a long-travel fork used under extreme conditions, such as a bike used for jumping or free-riding (extreme, fast, and rough, generally downhill riding), will offer improved tracking and steering as well as smoother up-and-down action with a through-axle. They're a necessity on "upside-down" forks, in which the lower legs are the fork's inner legs, motorcycle style, rather than the outer legs. Because the wheel moves up and down with the inner legs, which slide up and down in the fixed upper outer legs, it is not possible to equip them with a brace (which adds considerable lateral and torsional stiffness to a standard telescoping suspension fork) between the lower legs. The through-axle provides the added stiffness.

There are a number of different through-axle systems, both bolt-on and quick-release, but they share some common traits. The axle is part of the fork, not part of the wheel, so it varies according to the fork, not the wheel. All 20mm through-axle hubs have the same (20mm) inside diameter (ID) for the bearings, the same overall width for the hub, and the same position of the disc-brake rotor. Ditto for 15mm or 24mm hubs.

Traditional through-axles (Fig. 2.7) generally resemble a long bolt with a head on the bike's drive side. The head is too large to pass through the hub bearings and the dropouts; it snugs up against the drive-side fork dropout. The ends are usually round, but they may also be hex-shaped. On the other end (the disc-brake-rotor end), the through-axle usually has some sort of bolt system to draw the ends toward each other to remove any lateral movement of the front wheel, and pinch bolts (or a pair of quick-release levers) tighten the fork ends around the ends of the axle once it's fully installed.

Quick-release through-axles (Fig. 2.8), either 15mm or 20mm, have a lever that you flip open, allowing you to use it as a handle to either unscrew or screw the axle out of or into the opposite fork end. When you flip the lever closed, it

2.7 Tightening and loosening a traditional 20mm through-axle

2.8 Tightening and loosening a RockShox Maxle

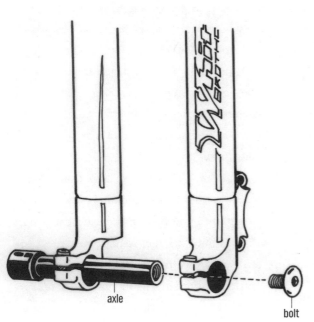

axle

bolt

tighten

loosen

either expands the axle inside its through-hole in the fork end to secure it, or squeezes the fork ends against the hub axle ends. A quick-release through-axle can actually be quicker to install and remove than a standard hub with a quick-release, when you include tightening and loosening the skewer enough to clear the fork-end "lawyer tabs" (i.e., wheel-retention devices), although a quick-release through-axle does complicate mounting the fork on a carrying rack's fork mounts.

To remove most traditional through-axles, loosen whatever clamp bolts or levers are securing the drive-side end of the axle onto the fork legs. Next, loosen the draw bolt in the axle end on the rotor side (Fig. 2.7) to free the opposite shoulder from the fork leg, loosen the pinch bolts on the rotor-side fork end, and pull the axle out to the drive side.

To remove a quick-release through-axle, flip open the lever and unscrew the entire axle from the opposite leg of the fork (Fig. 2.8). On a RockShox Maxle (Fig. 2.8), engage the backside of the lever

into the notch in the protruding end of the axle so that the lever unscrews the axle, rather than spinning freely. Rotate the lever counterclockwise to unscrew the axle, and pull the axle out.

To install a through-axle, stick the wheel into the fork (sans axle) with the rotor between the pads of the disc-brake caliper. If the fork ends have little inboard flanges that sit on the hub ends, everything will be lined up to insert the axle; if not, you'll have to carefully hold the bike up as you line up the hub and fork ends to install the axle. Push the axle through from the side with the bigger hole in the fork end.

On most traditional through-axles, tighten the draw bolt in the axle end on the rotor side (Fig. 2.7) to remove the lateral slop in the wheel and seat the axle head into the drive-side fork end. You may need to snug up the clamping bolts on one fork end a bit so that the axle does not spin when you tighten the draw bolt. Once the axle is seated, tighten whatever clamping bolts are on the fork ends.

BASIC STUFF

On a QR type, tighten the axle into the opposite fork leg (Fig. 2.8) using the quick-release lever as a handle, then flip the quick-release lever over, and you are done! There are no pinch bolts on either fork end. Again, a RockShox Maxle requires opening the lever fully and engaging its backside into the notch in the axle end face so that it turns the entire unit and screws it into the fork end when you twist the lever.

Automobile roof racks and truck-bed carrying racks present a challenge for a through-axle fork. If the rack clamps the fork ends, you must first install a through-axle adapter such as the Hurricane Components Fork Up, which is a tube welded to two slotted plates. The slotted plates clamp onto the fork mount like standard slotted fork ends, and you push the axle through the 20mm or 15mm ID tube once you set the fork over it.

ii-11
CLOSING THE BRAKES

The steps required to close the brakes are the reverse of what you did to release them.

1. **Hook up the brake cable.** With a V-brake (sidepull cantilever), hold the link in one hand, pull the noodle back, push the cable coming out of the noodle into the slot in the end of the link, and pop the end of the noodle back into the slotted hole (Fig. 2.1 in reverse).

   With a cantilever or U-brake, hold the brake pads against the rim with one hand, and hook the enlarged end of the straddle cable back into the end of the brake arm with your other hand (Fig. 2.2 in reverse).

   With most disc brakes, the brake is ready to apply as soon as the wheel is installed.

   Do the reverse of §ii-3 to reconnect the more rare types of brakes, or find the brake type at the beginning of Chapter 7 and read up on it.

2. **Check the brakes.** Squeeze the lever and make sure the cable doesn't slip. Lift the front end of the bike and spin the front wheel, gently applying the brakes several times. Check that the pads are not dragging, and recenter the wheel (or adjust the brakes as described in Chapter 7 for your type of brake).

   If the spring balance in the brakes is off, one pad may rub the rim when the rim is centered in the fork; in that case, skip to §vii-17d (V-brake) or §vii-23 (cantilever) for adjustment procedure.

   A pad may also rub because the fork or wheel is misaligned and there is nothing wrong with the brakes; they are centered. To eliminate the rub, either you'll need to off-center the brakes by adjusting spring tension in the arms as in §vii-17d (V-brake) or §vii-23 (cantilever), or you'll need to hold the rim centered between the brake pads when securing the hub. These should be only temporary fixes; if it's the wheel that's off, get the wheel trued or, better yet, true it yourself (§vi-11). You will know whether the wheel is off if it sits off-center one way when you tighten it in and then, if you flip it around and tighten it in again, it sits off-center to the other side. If the wheel sits off-center both ways, the fork could be off. You can check fork alignment; that procedure is in §xiii-17.

   If everything is reconnected and centered properly and the brakes don't rub, you're done.

ii-12
REMOVING THE REAR WHEEL

Removing the rear wheel is done in the same way as removing the front (§ii-2 to §ii-5), with the added complication of the chain and cogs.

1. **Shift the chain onto the smallest cog.** Lift the rear wheel off the ground, and shift while turning the cranks.

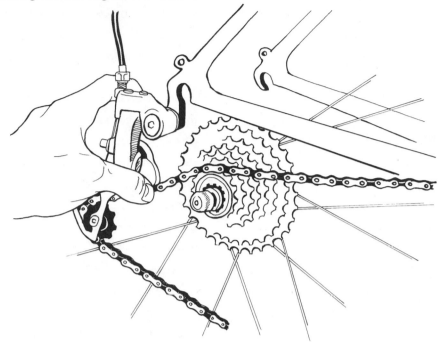

2. **Release the rear brake.** Follow the same procedure as with the front wheel.

3. **Push the wheel out of the rear dropouts.** You'll first need to move the chain out of the way. This is usually a matter of grabbing the rear derailleur and pulling it back so that the jockey wheels (pulley wheels) move out of the way, while pushing forward on the quick-release or axle nuts with your thumbs and letting the wheel fall as you hold the bike up (Fig. 2.9). If the bottom half of the chain catches the wheel as it falls, jiggle the wheel while lifting it to free the cogs from the chain.

ii-13
INSTALLING THE REAR WHEEL

1. **Shift the rear derailleur to high gear.** It will be in its outermost position, under the smallest cog (Fig. 5.4).

2. **Slip the wheel in between the seatstays and chainstays (aka the "swingarm" on a full-suspension bike).** Maneuver the upper section of chain onto the smallest cog (Fig. 2.9). If

the bike has a rear through-axle, you'll need to pull that out first.

3. **Set the bike down on the rear axle.** As you let the bike drop down, guide the disc-brake rotor up between the pads in the caliper or guide the tire up between the rim-brake pads. Pull the rear derailleur back with your right hand, and pull the axle ends back into the dropouts with your index fingers. Your thumbs push forward on the rear dropouts, which should now slide over the axle ends. (If the axle does not slip into the dropouts, you may need to unscrew the quick-release skewer nut further or spread the dropouts apart or squeeze them toward each other to get them to fall between the quick-release ends and the axle ends.)

4. **Check that the axle is fully seated in the dropouts.** This should center the wheel between the brake pads. If the rim rubs on one brake pad, hold the rim in a centered position as you secure the axle.

5. **Secure the axle.** Tighten the quick-release skewer, bolt-on skewer, axle nuts, or through-axle

in the same way as explained for the front wheel.

6. **Reconnect the rear brake.** Follow the same procedure as you did on the front wheel. You're done. Go ride your bike.

ii-14
CLEANING THE BICYCLE

Most cleaning can be done with soap, water, sponges, and brushes. Soap and water are easier on you and on the earth than stronger solvents, which are generally needed only for the drivetrain, if at all.

Avoid using the high-pressure sprayers you find at pay car washes to clean your bike. The soaps can be corrosive, and the high pressure forces water into bearings, pivots, and frame tubes, causing extensive damage over time. If you do use a pressure washer (these are often set up for participants to use at races and bike festivals), never point it at the bike from the side, as it can blow the bearing seals inward; instead, point the washer in the plane of the bike from the top, bottom, front, and back.

If the bike is really dirty, you can start by washing it with a hose while the wheels are on or off. A car-washing brush that you screw onto the end of the hose works well for this. If the weather is cold, wear appropriate clothing.

Scrubbing the bike is easier if you use a bike stand. In the absence of a bike stand, the bike can be hung from a garage ceiling with rope, stood upside down on the saddle and handlebar, or stood vertically and balanced on the front of the fork and the handlebar with the front wheel removed.

1. **Remove the wheels.**
2. **Secure the chain (optional).** If the bike has a chain hanger (a little nub attached to the inner side of the right seatstay, a few centimeters above the dropout), hook the chain over it. If not, pull the chain back over a dowel stick (Fig. 2.10), an old rear hub secured into the dropouts, or a chain keeper (Fig. 1.3).
3. **Fill a bucket with hot water and dish soap.**
4. **Scrub the entire bike and wheels.** Use a stiff nylon-bristle brush for tough dirt and hard-to-reach places and a big sponge for gentler cleaning on accessible areas. Leave the chain, cogs, chainrings, and derailleurs for last.
5. **Rinse the bike.** Hose it off or wipe it with a wet rag.
6. **Check for remaining grime.** ProGold Bike Wash, Pedro's Green Fizz, or equivalent cleaners can remove stuff stuck to the frame and get it sparkling.

Avoid getting water in the bearings of the bottom bracket, headset, pedals, and hubs. Also avoid getting water into the lip seals of suspension forks, as well as any pivots or shock seals on rear-suspension systems. In addition, most metal frames and forks have vent holes in the tubes to allow hot gases to escape during welding. The holes are often open to the outside on the seatstays, fork legs, chainstays, and seatstay and chainstay bridges. Avoid getting water in these holes, especially if you have to use a high-pressure wash (at a race, for example). Taping over the vent holes is a good idea, and you can leave that tape in place permanently to protect the frame on rainy or muddy rides.

ii-15
CLEANING THE DRIVETRAIN

The drivetrain consists of an oil-covered chain running over the gears and derailleurs. Because the drivetrain is totally exposed to the elements, it picks up lots of dirt.

The drivetrain is also what transfers your energy into the bike's forward motion, which means that it should be kept fastidiously clean so that it can move freely. Frequent cleaning and

2.10 Wiping the chain

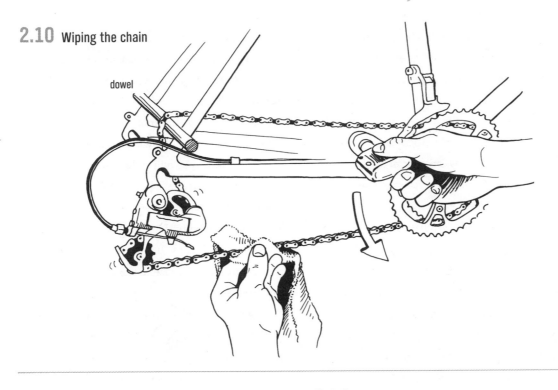

dowel

2.11 Cleaning jockey wheels

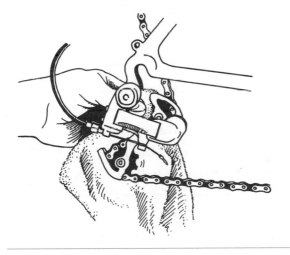

2.12 Cleaning the cogset

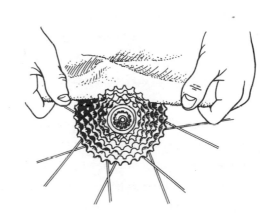

lubrication are required to keep the drivetrain rolling well and to extend the life of your bike.

The drivetrain can often be cleaned sufficiently by using a rag and wiping down the chain, derailleur jockey wheels, and chainrings. You might want to wear rubber gloves for this. If you keep the gloves, rag, and lube near where you store your bike, you will tend to clean it before or after almost every ride and be able to

do so without dirtying your hands. It's a good habit to develop, because the drivetrain will last much longer and perform better with regular attention.

Lubricating the chain regularly is also important; see §iv-1.

1. **Wipe the chain.** Turn the cranks while holding a rag in your hand and grabbing the chain (Fig. 2.10).

BASIC STUFF

2. **Wipe the jockey wheels.** Holding a rag, squeeze the teeth of the jockey wheels between your index finger and thumb as you turn the cranks (Fig. 2.11).

3. **Floss the cogs.** Slip a rag (or, better yet, a piece of Gear Floss absorbent string, available at bike shops) between cogs of the freewheel, and work it back and forth to clean each cog (Fig. 2.12).

4. **Wipe down the derailleurs and the front chainrings with the rag.**

The chain will last much longer if you perform this sort of quick cleaning regularly, followed by dripping chain lube on the chain (see §iv-1) and then doing another light wipe-down. You'll also be able to skip those heavy-duty solvent cleanings that are necessary when a chain gets really grungy. You can get it just as clean as with a solvent if you wipe the chain down thoroughly after lubricating it and clean in between all of the outer link plates with cotton swabs (they won't fit in between the inner link plates, but the roller will spin with them, and they will get clean that way).

You can also remove mud packed into derailleurs and cogs with soapy water and a scrub brush. The soap will not dissolve the dirty lubricant all over the drivetrain, but the brush will smear the lubricant all over the bike if you're not careful. Use a different brush from the one you use for cleaning the frame, because the bristles of this brush will become black and oily. Follow the brushing with a cloth wipe-down of the frame.

ii-16
CLEANING THE CHAIN WITH SOLVENT

 **LEVEL 1**

If you frequently wipe off the chain and lubricate it (Fig. 4.1)—before or after every ride is ideal—you can minimize the need for solvent cleaning, with its associated disposal and toxicity

problems. If you determine that using a solvent is necessary, work in a well-ventilated area, use as little solvent as necessary, and pick an environmentally friendly one. Using one of the many citrus solvents on the market will minimize the danger if you breathe the stuff, or get it onto and into your skin, and will reduce a major disposal problem. If you are using a lot of solvents, organic ones such as diesel fuel can be recycled and therefore may be preferable to citrus solvents, as long as you protect yourself from the fumes with a respirator and dispose of the solvent properly if you are not recycling it.

Because all solvents suck the oils out of your skin, I recommend using rubber gloves, even with "green" solvents. You might also want to rub some skin lotion into your hands before starting, which will help keep your skin from absorbing solvent and will also make your hands easier to clean afterward.

A self-contained chain cleaner with internal brushes and a solvent bath is a quick and convenient way to clean a chain (Fig. 2.13), and this type of cleaning can be done without risk of later chain breakage caused by opening and closing the chain. A nylon brush or an old toothbrush dipped in a solvent is good for cleaning cogs, pulleys, and chainrings, and it can be used for a quick cleaning of the chain as well.

One way to thoroughly clean the chain is to remove it and put it in a solvent bath, but I do not recommend this unless you have a chain with a master link. Opening a standard chain by pushing rivets in and out with a chain tool is hard on the chain and can lead to breakage while riding. Because a 9-speed or 10-speed chain must be narrow to fit in the tight space between cogs, only a very small length of each rivet protrudes from the chain plates. With a Shimano chain, even if you use one of Shimano's special link pins every time you reassemble the chain, you are still weaken-

2.13 Using a solvent-bath chain cleaner

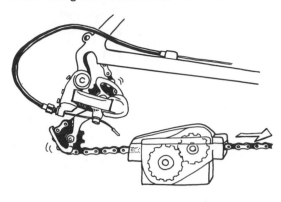

2.14 Dripping chain lube along the top edges of the chain to get it between the plates at each rivet

ing the chain and can bring on breakage under shifting load.

If it is absolutely necessary to remove the chain to clean it, here is the procedure:

1. **Remove the chain.** Follow the directions in §iv-7 or, ideally, those in §iv-11 for using a master link.

2. **Put the chain in an old water bottle that is about one-fourth full of solvent.**

3. **Shake the bottle vigorously to clean the chain.** Do this close to the ground in case the water bottle leaks.

4. **Hang the chain to dry.**

5. **Install the chain on the bike.** Follow the directions in §iv-8 to §iv-10, or, better yet, get a master link and use it to put the chain together (§iv-11).

6. **Lube the chain.** Drip chain lubricant into each of the chain's links and rollers as you turn the cranks to move the chain past the drip bottle. Drip lube on the moving chain by gently squeezing the bottle with the tip on each top edge of the chain (Fig. 2.14) for a couple of turns of the crank on each edge. See §iv-1 for more information.

7. **Lightly wipe down the chain with a rag.**

8. **Deal with the solvent.** You can reuse much of the solvent by allowing it to settle in a clear container over a period of days or weeks. Decant and save the clear stuff, and dispose of the sludge.

To avoid another such visit to solvent city, after every ride or two from now on, wipe with a rag the jockey wheels (Fig. 2.11), chainrings, front derailleur, and chain (turn the crank to pull it through a rag you clasp around it, as in Figure 2.10; there's no need to remove the wheel), and then lubricate the chain (Fig. 2.14). Keep dish gloves and a rag near your bike so that you can clean the drivetrain quickly on your return from a ride without having to scrub dirty oil off your hands afterward.

A clean bike invites you to jump on it and will feel faster. Corrosion problems are minimized, and you can see other problems as they arise. A clean bike is a happy bike.

ii-17
PERFORMING MECHANICAL WORK: A GENERAL GUIDE
a. Threaded parts

All threads must be prepped before tightening. Depending on the bolt in question, prep with lubricant, threadlock compound, or an antiseize compound. Clean off excess thread-prepping compound to minimize dirt attraction.

1. **Lubricated threads:** Most threads should be lubricated with grease or oil. If a bolt is already installed, you can back it out and drip

a little chain lube on it and then tighten it back down. Lube items such as crank bolts, pedal axles, cleat bolts on shoes, derailleur- and brake-cable anchor bolts, and control- lever mounting bolts.

2. **Locked threads:** Some threads need to be locked to prevent the bolts they are on from vibrating loose. These are bolts that need to stay in place but are not supposed to be tightened down fully for some reason or other, usually to avoid seizing a moving part, throwing a part out of adjustment, or strip- ping threads in a soft material. Examples of bolts of this type are derailleur limit screws, jockey-wheel center bolts, brake- mounting bolts (for rim brakes), and spokes. Use Loctite, Finish Line Threadlock, or an equivalent; use Wheelsmith Spoke-Prep or an equivalent on spokes. If the wheel has extremely high spoke tension on both sides, the spokes will stay in adjustment when you use grease on the threads instead of Spoke- Prep or an equivalent. Some spoke nipples made by DT Swiss come with threadlock compound already inside them.

3. **Antiseize threads:** Some threads have a tendency to bind up and gall, making full tightening as well as extraction problematic. They need an antiseize compound on them to prevent galling. Examples of this kind of thread are any steel or aluminum bolt threaded into a titanium part—including any parts mounted to titanium frames, such as bottom-bracket cups—and any titanium bolt threaded into a steel or aluminum part. Use Finish Line Ti-Prep or an equivalent antiseize formulation.

IMPORTANT: *Never thread a titanium bolt into a titanium part. Even with an antiseize compound, a titanium bolt will almost certainly gall and rip the titanium part when you try to remove the bolt.*

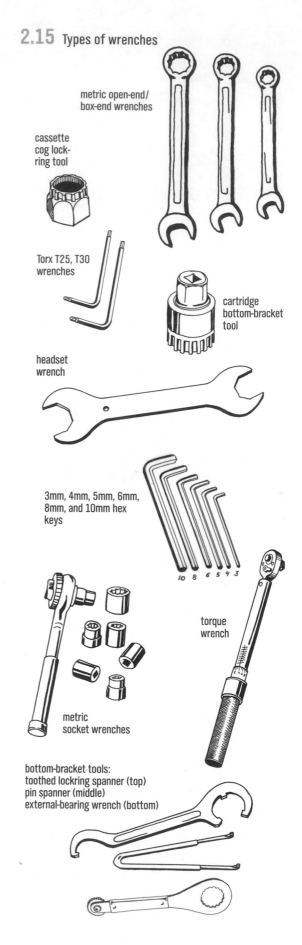

2.15 Types of wrenches

metric open-end/ box-end wrenches

cassette cog lock- ring tool

Torx T25, T30 wrenches

cartridge bottom-bracket tool

headset wrench

3mm, 4mm, 5mm, 6mm, 8mm, and 10mm hex keys

10 8 6 5 4 3

torque wrench

metric socket wrenches

bottom-bracket tools: toothed lockring spanner (top) pin spanner (middle) external-bearing wrench (bottom)

Wrenches (Fig. 2.15) must be fully engaged before tightening or loosening.

1. **Hex keys** (also called "Allen wrenches" or "hex wrenches") and **Torx wrenches** must be fully inserted into the bolt head, or the wrench and/or the bolt hole will round off. A good example is a shoe-cleat bolt; clean dirt and rocks out of shoe-cleat bolts before tapping the hex key in fully with a hammer so that it engages maximally.

2. **Open-end, box-end, and socket wrenches** must be properly seated around a hex bolt, or the bolt head will round off. A good example is an aluminum headset nut.

3. **Splined wrenches** (Torx, cog lockring, and bottom-bracket cup tools) must be fully engaged. If they are not, the splines will be damaged or the tool will snap. If you strip the splines in a cassette lockring, you will not be able to get it off.

4. **Toothed-lockring spanners** need to stay lined up on the lockring. If they slide off, they will not only tear up the lockring; they will also damage the frame paint. Such a lockring can be found on a bottom-bracket adjustable cup.

5. **Pin spanners** need to be fully seated in the pinholes in the part being turned in order to prevent the holes in the part from slipping out and being damaged. You can find pinholes in some bottom-bracket adjustable cups, crank-bolt collars, and cartridge-bearing hubs. Make certain that the pinholes are clean and that the spanner pins are fully engaged before exerting any force on the wrench.

b. Tightening torque

A full list of specific tightening torques can be found in Appendix D. To best understand them, it helps to know a little about metric bolt sizes, particularly as they are used on bikes.

The designation "M" in front of the bolt size number means millimeters and refers to the bolt shaft, not to the hex key that turns it: An M5 bolt is 5mm in diameter, an M6 is 6mm, and so on, but the designation may not have any relationship to the wrench size. For instance, an M5 bolt usually takes a 4mm hex key (or in the case of a hex-head style, an 8mm box-end or socket wrench). However, M5 bolts on bicycles often accept different wrench sizes than are normally found on M5 bolts. Bolts that attach bottle cages to the frame are M5, and although some accept the normal 4mm hex key, many have a rounded "cap" head and take a 3mm hex key. The bolts that clamp a front derailleur around the seat tube, or that anchor the cable on a front or rear derailleur, are also M5, but they instead take a bigger than standard hex key size, namely, 5mm. The big single bolts found on old stems and some seatposts take lots of different bolt sizes (M6, M7, and even M8), but usually only one wrench size (6mm hex key).

Generally, tightness can be classified into four levels:

1. **Snug** (10–30 in-lbs or 1–3 N-m [Newton-meters in SI units]): Small setscrews (such as Grip Shift mounting screw), bearing-preload bolts (as on threadless-headset top caps), and screws going into plastic parts need to be merely snug.

2. **Firmly tightened** (30–80 in-lbs or 3–9 N-m): Small bolts—often M5 size—such as shoe-cleat bolts, cable anchor bolts on brakes and derailleurs, small stem bolts, brake-lever-clamp bolts, and some disc-brake-caliper mounting bolts need to be firmly tightened.

3. **Tight** (80–240 in-lbs or 9–27 N-m): Wheel axles, old-style single-bolt stem bolts (M6, M7, or M8), most M6 disc-brake-caliper mounting bolts, seatpost binder bolts, and seatpost saddle-clamp bolts need to be tight.

4. **Really tight** (280–600 in-lbs or 31–68 N-m): Crankarm bolts, pedal axles, cassette lock-ring bolts, and bottom-bracket cups are large parts that need to be really tight.

c. Cleanliness

1. Do not expect parts to work simply because you've squirted or slathered lubricant on them (meanwhile patting yourself on the back for maintaining your bike). The lube will pick up lots of dirt and get very gunky.

2. Do not expect parts to work if you just wash them but don't lubricate them. They will get dry and squeaky.

d. Test-riding

Always test-ride the bike after adjusting it in the bike stand. Parts behave differently under load.

ii-18
LUBRICATING AND SCHEDULING

After washing the bike or even after riding, many people wonder which parts to lubricate and how to do so without making things worse. Recommended time intervals are based on the assumption that you ride your bike on trails around four hours per week for six months out of the year. If you ride more often or in exceptionally wet and muddy or sandy conditions, more maintenance and lubrication are required, and the converse is obviously true as well.

After dripping oil on a moving part, wipe the area to remove excess oil, and then wipe it again after you ride and dust has stuck to it. Lubing is always better than not lubing, even if you leave excess around.

Although these rules are by no means carved in stone, here are some guidelines about what, how, and when to lubricate your bicycle's parts to keep the bicycle in optimal condition.

Chain (Chapter 4)

Wipe and lube the chain every time you wash your bike. I also recommend lubing the chain after every ride or two, after every ride in wet conditions, and after every ride with a stream crossing.

Check the chain's wear as in Chapter 4, and replace the chain when indicated.

Cables and housings (Chapters 5 and 7)

A half dozen times per season, and more if you ride in wet conditions and/or wash your bike frequently, pop the housings out of their cable stops, slide them up the cable, lube the cable with light oil (Pedro's Syn Lube is a good choice), and slide the housings back in place.

Once every season or two, replace the cables and housings.

Derailleurs and shifters (Chapter 5)

Every time you wash the bike, drip light oil on the derailleur pivots and spring ends.

A couple of times per season, overhaul the derailleur jockey wheels if they are the standard bushing type. With cartridge-bearing jockey wheels, peel off the dust covers and add grease once per season (or more often if the wheels become noticeably harder to turn).

Squirt spray lube inside trigger shifters a couple of times per season. Overhaul twist shifters whenever they get sticky.

Wheels (Chapter 6)

Lubricate the freewheel mechanism a couple of times per season (more in wet conditions).

Overhaul loose-bearing hubs once a year (more in wet conditions).

Lubricate or replace hub cartridge bearings every couple of seasons or when they make noise or become harder to turn.

Brakes (Chapter 7)

Pull cantilever and V-brakes off their pivot bosses, and regrease them every year or two and whenever they get sticky. Make sure you do not get any grease on the brake pads.

Drip light oil on lever pivots and the arm pivot on mechanical disc-brake calipers after every time or two that you wash the bike.

On hydraulic disc brakes, clean and lubricate (with the correct brake fluid for the brake; see Chapter 7) the outside of the hydraulic disc pistons in the caliper whenever they get shoved out too far and you have to push them back in to get them to clear the rotor.

Bleed hydraulic brakes whenever they become mushy and require pumping the lever due to air inside; otherwise bleed them every season or two or more often if brake performance drops off or if the fluid in the reservoir looks dirty or dark.

Cranksets (Chapter 8)

Peel off the bearing covers on integrated-spindle cranks and other bottom brackets with cartridge bearings you can get at, and add grease once per season (more in wet conditions). Overhaul loose-bearing bottom brackets a couple of times per season (more in wet conditions). Replace closed-cartridge bottom brackets as indicated by turning resistance or noise.

Pedals (Chapter 9)

Drip light oil on the springs after every bike washing. Also after every washing, drip wax-based (dry) lube (i.e., White Lightning or Pedro's Ice) on the cleat-contact areas.

With Shimano and other loose-bearing pedals, pull out the axles and overhaul them once per season or more under wet conditions. Do the same with other pedals with bushings inside. Lubricate the inboard bearing on pedals with cartridge bearings and no bushings inside perhaps once every couple of years, unless you pedal through water crossings, in which case do this every season or more.

Saddles (Chapter 10)

Lube the edge of the saddle where it contacts the rail or seatpost clamp whenever it squeaks.

Seatposts (Chapter 10)

Pull the seatpost out and regrease it monthly. Turn the bike upside down overnight, and let the seat tube drain with the seatpost out after every wet ride or washing.

Forks (Chapter 13)

Wipe clean suspension-fork stanchions and dust wipers with a rag after every ride. Drain and replace the oil bath and replace the seals and wipers every season or two or whenever the fork pushes down in a sticky stair-step fashion rather than smoothly. Do so more frequently if the stanchions are scratched or if excessive oil comes out of the fork on every ride.

Frames (Chapter 14)

Wipe clean the rear shock body and dust wiper with a rag after every ride. Overhaul the air can twice per season.

Using a grease gun, lubricate pivots that have Zerk fittings after every few rides. Drip oil on bushing pivots monthly and after each bike washing. Peel pivot cartridge-bearing covers and grease the bearings every season or two and whenever they get noisy or loose.

EMERGENCY REPAIRS

HOW TO GET HOME WHEN SOMETHING BIG BREAKS OR YOU GET LOST OR HURT

Always carry a flagon of whiskey in case of a snake-bite, and furthermore, always carry a small snake.
—W. C. Fields

I've included this chapter so that you do not face disaster if you have a mechanical problem on the trail. If you ride your bike out in the boonies, sooner or later you will encounter a mechanical problem that has the potential to turn into an emergency. The best way to avoid such an emergency is to plan ahead and be prepared before it happens. Proper planning involves steps as simple as bringing along a few tools, spare tubes, and a little knowledge.

If something breaks while you are on the trail, the procedures in this chapter will help you to deal with it, whether or not you have all of the necessary tools. You always have the option of walking, but this chapter is designed to get you home pedaling.

Finally, you may find yourself with a perfectly functioning bicycle and still be in dire straits because you're lost, you've bonked (i.e., your body has run out of fuel), or you've become injured on the trail. Carefully read the final part of this chapter for pointers on how to avoid getting lost or injured and what to do if the worst does happen.

If this chapter does nothing other than alert you to some of the dangers facing you out in the backcountry, then perhaps you'll prepare for them and this chapter will have accomplished its purpose.

iii-1
RECOMMENDED TOOLS TO TAKE ON RIDES

The take-along tool kit for your hydration pack or seat bag is described in §i-6 (Fig. 1.5). If you're going to be a long way from civilization, take along the extra tools recommended for longer trips (Fig. 1.6).

NOTE: *As you will see in this chapter, a chain tool is one of the handiest items you can take along. As the ad says, "Don't leave home without it." A master link is very good to have with you as well.*

iii-2
PREVENTING FLAT TIRES

Your first line of defense to avoid flats is to always have good tires on your bike. Check them regularly for wear, cracking, and tread cuts. Coat tires you don't ride often with 303 Aerospace Protectant or Armor All to prevent ozone cracking.

Using tire sealant inside can greatly reduce the potential for flat tires, as can installing tubeless tires. Using them together—sealant with tubeless tires—almost makes punctures a thing of the past.

Modern sealants are generally thin, liquid latex solutions that coagulate at a puncture, and "Slime" is one of a class of more traditional viscous liquid sealants with chopped fibers in solution that plug holes. Sealant can be injected into an existing tube that has a Schrader valve, and liquid latex can be injected into Presta valves. Installing sealants is covered in §vi-10, and tubeless tires are discussed in §vi-2 and §vi-7. You also can purchase inner tubes with a sealant already inside.

If there is sealant in the tube or tubeless tire and the tire still gets low owing to a small hole through the tread (this is most likely to happen when you stop riding for a while), put more air in and spin the wheel or ride for a couple of miles to get the sealant to flow out to the hole. A large hole will not be filled, although amazingly big holes can be plugged enough to get you home if you locate where the sealant is squirting out through the tire. Rotate the wheel so that the puncture is at the bottom and wait. The sealant may pool enough there to plug the hole. Add more air and continue riding. Note that if the hole is on the rim side (from a "snakebite" puncture or a protruding spoke end, for example; see §iii-3), the sealant will not flow to it.

I do not recommend the old technology of plastic tire liners placed between the tire and tube. They are so stiff that they decrease traction and cornering ability, and they can slip sideways and cut into the tube. There are, however, lighter and less stiff tire liners made of tightly woven Kevlar and other fibers (SpinSkins is one brand). They are fairly expensive, though.

FIXING FLAT TIRES

 **LEVEL 1**

a. With a spare or a patch kit

Simple flat tires are easy to deal with. The first flat you get on a ride, whether in a standard inner tube and tire or in a tubeless tire, is most easily fixed by installing your spare tube (§vi-6 describes how to do it). If you have tubeless tires, simply remove the tire, remove the valve stem from the rim, install a new inner tube, and reinstall the tire. If you can't manage to remove the tire bead from the rim with your fingers alone and don't have any tire levers, you can use the wheel quick-release skewers as levers.

Check your spare tube before leaving home to make sure that it holds air and that you can loosen the valve nut by hand out on the trail (assuming it has a Presta valve; see Fig. 1.1B or Figs. 6.2–3). If your bike has tubeless tires, take the additional step of making sure that the knurled retainer nut that holds the valve stem to the rim can also be loosened by hand out on the trail, in case you have to install a spare tube.

Before installing the new tube, make sure you remove all thorns or glass from the tire and feel around the inside of the tire for any other sharp objects and remove them as well. You will almost always find something sticking through the tire that has caused the flat, although it may be hard to find. If you don't find it and remove it, it will cause a new flat when you reinflate the tire.

Some flats happen without foreign objects sticking through the tire. Sometimes inner tubes just fail, particularly near the valve on the rim side and particularly if you have rim brakes and do a steep descent on a hot day. And a pinch flat will be apparent if you find two adjacent holes on the top and bottom of the tube (aka a "snakebite").

3.1 Tying a knot in a punctured inner tube to seal off the hole

Pinch flats are caused by the tire hitting a hard, sharp edge with insufficient air pressure in the tire to prevent the inner tube from being pinched between the tire and the rim.

Check the rim to see that your flat wasn't caused by a protruding spoke or nipple, a metal shard from the rim, or the edge of a spoke hole protruding through a worn rim strip. The rim strip is the piece of plastic or rubber that covers the spoke holes in the well of the rim (Fig. 6.13), and it prevents punctures to the underside of the tube. Many rim strips are totally inadequate, being either too narrow or prone to cracking or tearing. Also, metal hunks left from the drilling of rims during manufacture can work their way out into the tube. Endeavor to eliminate these problems before leaving on a backcountry ride by shaking out any metal fragments and using good rim strips or a couple of layers of fiberglass-reinforced packing tape (with lengthwise superstrong fibers) as rim strips. If the hole in the tube is on the rim side, tire sealant will not fill the hole because the liquid will be thrown to the outside toward the tread when the wheel turns.

After you run out of spare tubes, use your patch kit to patch additional punctures (find the details in §vi-3 to §vi-5).

In the absence of patches, you can patch punctures with insulating tape (the type used around doors). It's not a bad idea to stick some insulating tape to a frame tube for this kind of occurrence.

b. Without spare tubes or patches

If you're out of spare tubes and patches, you can tie a knot in the inner tube, pump it back up, and ride it home. You'd be amazed how well this works, and it's quick. Simply fold the tube at the puncture and tie an overhand knot with the folded end (Fig. 3.1). To maximize the length of inflatable inner tube, minimize the length of the folded end sticking out of the knot.

Knotting the tube works fine—and you can ride the bike as if nothing had happened—so long as there is only a single puncture in the tube, a snakebite (pinch flat), or multiple punctures all within a few inches of each other that you can seal off with a single knot. Obviously, if you have widely spaced punctures, multiple knots will seal off sections of the tube from air, leaving them flat.

If tying off the tube won't work because the hole is at the valve, or because the tube has more than one hole in it, continue to the next section.

c. Without any way to inflate the tube or a section of a knotted tube

If you are without a pump or air inflation cartridges, if there are multiple knots in the tube or a hole at the valve and no patches, or if the valve is broken, you are going to have to ride home without air in the tube or in a section of it. But riding a flat for a long way will destroy the tire and will probably damage the rim, too. You can minimize that damage, though, by filling the space in the tire with grass, leaves, or similar materials. Pack the stuff in tightly, and then remount the tire on the rim. This fix should make the ride a little less dangerous by minimizing the flat tire's tendency to roll out from under the bike in a turn.

d. When a sidewall is torn

Rocks and glass can cut tire sidewalls. The likelihood of sidewall problems is reduced if you do not venture into the backcountry on old tires with rotten and weakened sidewall cords. If the tire's sidewall is torn or cut, the tube will stick out, and on a tubeless tire, no amount of sealant will close the leak. Patching the tube or installing a new one isn't going to solve the problem, either. Without reinforcement, the tube will soon blow out through the sidewall gash.

Begin by looking for something to reinforce the sidewall (Fig. 3.2). Dollar bills work surprisingly well as tire boots (i.e., temporary internal casing reinforcements). The paper is pretty tough and should hold for the rest of the ride if you are careful. (I told you that cash would get you out of bad situations. Just don't try putting a credit card in there; tire cuts don't take American Express or Visa!) Business cards are a bit small but are better than nothing. You might even try an energy bar wrapper. A small piece of an old tire sidewall or of lawn-chair webbing cut into an oval, or duct tape, might be a good addition to your patch kit for this purpose. You get the idea.

1. **Lay out some cash.** Place the bills or other reinforcement inside the tire over the gash (Fig. 3.2), or wrap it around the tube at that spot. Place several layers between the tire and tube to support the tube and prevent it from bulging out through the hole in the sidewall.

2. **Put a little air in the tube.** This holds the makeshift reinforcement in place.

3. **Mount the tire on the rim.** The procedure is in §vi-6 (starting with step 3) and in Figs. 6.14–15. Make sure that the tire is seated and the boot is still in place.

3.2 Temporary fix for a torn tire casing

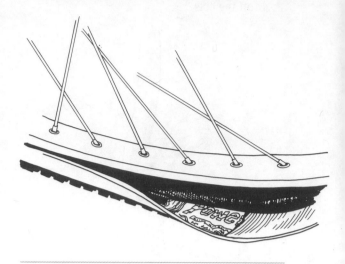

4. **Inflate the tube to about 40 psi.** Much lower than 40 psi will allow the boot to move around and may also lead to a pinch flat if you're riding on rocky terrain. In any case, this type of fix is not a perfect solution, so you will need to check the boot periodically to make certain that the tube is not bulging out again.

iii-4
FREEING A JAMMED CHAIN AND A TWISTED LINK

If the chain gets jammed between the chainring and the chainstay, it may be hard to get it out if the clearance is tight. You may find that you tug and tug on the chain, and it won't come out. Well, chainrings flex, and if you apply some mechanical advantage, the chain will come free quite easily. Just insert a screwdriver or similar thin lever between the chainring and the chainstay, and pry the space open while pulling the chain out (Fig. 3.3). You will probably be amazed at how easy this is, especially in light of how much hard tugging would not free the chain.

If you still cannot free the chain, disassemble it. Open the chain with a chain tool (§iv-7 or §iv-11), pull it out, and put it back together as in Figure 3.4 (§iv-9 to §iv-11). You can push out a pin on a

3.3 Freeing a jammed chain

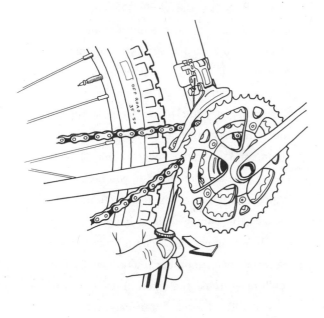

3.4 Fixing a broken chain

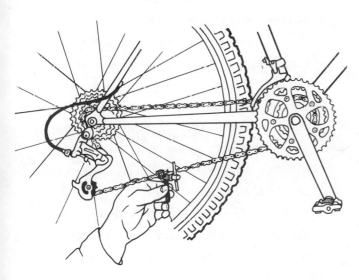

9- or 10-speed chain, push it back in, and get home. But do not ride it very long, because that link will be very weak; the plate will be prone to pry off the end of the rivet upon shifting.

If you have nine or more cogs on the rear wheel, you really need to install a master link (§iv-11) to be able to disassemble and reassemble the thin chain on your bike and expect to use it without worry for a prolonged period. If you already have a master link (Fig. 3.5) in the chain, it will make unjamming it easy; otherwise, carry one that is the proper width for your chain. Wippermann (Fig. 4.24) makes master links for all chain widths.

Once you get rolling again, you may find that if you continued to pedal a split second too long after the chain started to jam, you will have a twisted chain link (Fig. 3.6). A twisted link will continually pop off the cogs and chainrings and won't stay in gear. Once you find the twisted link, it will be obvious why it was popping out of gear—the chain will be running along nicely with the sides of the links vertical, and all of a sudden you will see some links leaning off to the side.

Untwisting such a link is easy if you have two pairs of pliers, two adjustable wrenches, or one of each. With the tools, just grab the links on either side of the twisted one at the rivet pins, and twist them to straighten the link.

Without pliers or wrenches, you can still untwist the link without having to bail on your ride. Shift to the smallest rear cog, and flip the chain off the innermost chainring so it drops

3.5 SRAM PowerLink master link

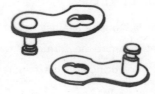

3.6 Twisted chain link

EMERGENCY REPAIRS

3.7 Untwisting a twisted chain link without tools

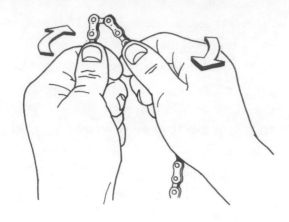

around the bottom-bracket shell and has no tension on it. Fold the chain at the twisted link so that link alone is at the top, horizontal. Grasp the vertical sections of chain running up to it on either side, and pull one hand toward you and push the other hand away from you to untwist the link (Fig. 3.7). Repeat until the twist is gone.

iii-5
FIXING A BROKEN CHAIN

⚙ LEVEL 1

Chains can break when you are mountain bike riding, usually while shifting the front derailleur under load. The side force of the derailleur cage plate pushing laterally against the chain, coupled with the high tension, can pop a chain plate off the end of a rivet. As the chain rips apart, it can cause collateral damage to other parts. The open chain plate can snag the front-derailleur cage, bending it or tearing it off, or it can jam into the rear dropout. When a chain breaks, the end link is certainly shot, and some others in the area may be as well.

1. **Remove the damaged links with the chain tool.** (You or your riding partner did remember to bring a chain tool, right?) Again, the

procedures for removing the damaged links and reinstalling the chain are covered in §iv-7 to §iv-11. If only the outer chain plates of a single link are damaged, you can install a master link (Fig. 3.5), producing a permanent fix that doesn't shorten the chain. Remove the damaged outer plates by pushing out the remaining rivet attaching them to the chain, and install a master link (§iv-11), noting proper orientation if you're using a Wippermann master link (Fig. 4.24).

2. **Replace the damaged links if you can.** Did you bring along extra chain links? If so, replace the same number you removed. If not, you'll need to use the chain in its shortened state. It will still work, but be careful to avoid shifting into the big chainring–largest cog combination. Otherwise, you can rip up the rear derailleur if the chain is not long enough to encompass this span with a little slack.

3. **Join the ends and connect the chain** (Fig. 3.4). The procedure is in §iv-9 and §iv-10 (§iv-11 with a master link). Some lightweight chain tools and multitools are more difficult to use than a shop chain tool. Some flex so much that it is hard to keep the push rod lined up with the rivet. Others pinch the plates so tightly that the chain link binds up. It's a good idea to find these things out before you need to perform repairs on the trail. Try out the tool at home or at your local bike shop. This way you'll know what you're getting into before you reach the trailhead.

iii-6
STRAIGHTENING A BENT WHEEL

⚙ ⚙ LEVEL 2

If the rim is banging against the brake pads or, worse yet, against the frame or fork, pedaling becomes very difficult. This can result from a

3.8 Tightening and loosening spokes

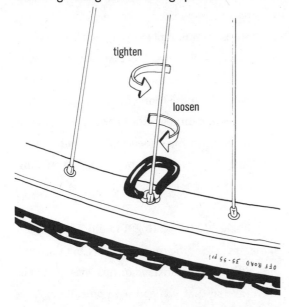

tighten

loosen

3.9 Wrapping a broken spoke

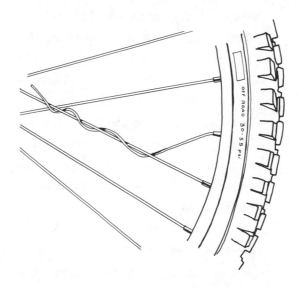

loose or broken spoke or a badly bent, or even broken, rim. The following sections detail four ways to deal with this problem.

a. Tightening loose spokes

If the wheel has a loose spoke or two, the rim will wobble all over the place, and if the tire is hitting the frame, or the rim is hitting the brake pads so hard that you can't ride home on it, you'll want to straighten the wheel before continuing.

1. **Find the loose spoke (or spokes) by feeling all of them.** The really loose ones, which would cause a wobble of large magnitude, will be obvious. If you find a broken spoke, skip to the next section (b). If you discover no loose or broken spokes, skip ahead to d.

2. **Get out the spoke wrench that you carry for such an eventuality.** (If you don't have one, skip to c.)

3. **Mark the loose spokes.** Tie blades of grass, sandwich bag twist-ties, tape, or the like around them so that you can still find the ones that originally caused the problem as the wheel becomes more true.

4. **Tighten the loose spokes** (Fig. 3.8). True the wheel, following the procedures in §vi-11.

b. Fixing and replacing broken spokes

If you break a spoke, the wheel will wobble wildly and the tire will hit the chainstay, preventing you from riding farther unless you want to wear out the tire and wear into the chainstay.

1. **Locate the broken spoke.**

2. **Remove the remainder of the spoke.** Remove both the piece going through the hub and the piece threaded into the nipple. If the broken spoke is on the drive side of the rear wheel, you may not be able to remove it from the hub, because it will be behind the cogs. If so, wrap it around a neighboring spoke (Fig. 3.9), thus preventing it from slapping around, and skip down to step 6.

3. **Get out your spoke wrench.** (If you have no spoke wrench, skip to c.)

4. **Replace the spoke if you can.** If you brought a spare spoke of the right length or a Kevlar replacement spoke (mentioned in §i-6b), you're in business; if not, skip to step 6. Put

the new spoke through the hub hole, weave it through the other spokes the same way the old one was, and thread it into the spoke nipple that is still sticking out of the rim. If the new spoke looks just like the other spokes, mark it with a pen or tie blades of grass, sandwich bag twist-ties, tape, or the like around it to keep track of it as the wheel becomes more true. If you are using a Kevlar replacement spoke, thread it through the hub hole, attach the ends to its included spoke stub, adjust the ends to length, tie them off, and tighten the spoke nipple.

5. **Tighten the nipple on the new spoke.** Use the spoke wrench (Fig. 3.8), checking the rim clearance with the brake pad as you go. Stop when the rim is centered between the pads at that point, and finish your ride. Skip to step 7.

6. **If you don't have a spare spoke but you do have a spoke wrench, bring the wheel into rideable trueness by loosening the spoke on either side of the broken one.** These two spokes come from the opposite side of the hub and will let the rim move toward the side with the broken spoke as they are loosened. A spoke nipple loosens counterclockwise when viewed from its top (i.e., from the tire side—see Fig. 3.8). Ride home conservatively, as

this wheel will rapidly get worse as the loose spokes loosen up even more.

7. **Once at home, replace the spoke.** Follow the procedure in §vi-12, or take the spoke to a bike shop for repair. After you have had a broken spoke more than once on a wheel, all of the spokes on the wheel should be replaced, and the rim may need replacement as well (Chapter 12 will lead you through rebuilding the wheel).

c. Opening the brake to get home

If the rim is banging the brake pads, but the tire is not hitting the chainstays or fork legs, just open the brake so that you can get home. If you have disc brakes, you won't need to do anything with a wobbly wheel that's not hitting the frame other than ride back carefully.

1. **Loosen the brake cable.** Decrease its tension by screwing in (clockwise) the barrel adjuster on the brake lever (Fig. 3.10). Remember that braking on that wheel is greatly reduced or nonexistent, so ride slowly and carefully.

2. **If the rim is still banging the brake pads, loosen the brake cable at the clamp on the brake (usually using a 5mm hex) and then clamp the cable back down.** You can also unhook the cable as you would when removing

3.10 Brake-lever adjusting barrel

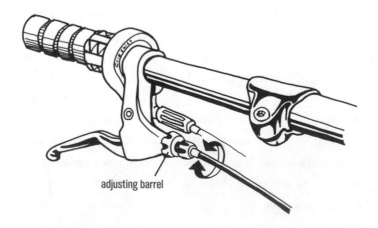

adjusting barrel

the wheel (§ii-3, Figs. 2.1–2), but the brake arm on some cantilever brakes can flip around into the spokes as you ride, so I don't recommend it. You now have no brake on this wheel; ride carefully and walk the bike through difficult sections.

3. **If the bent wheel still won't turn, remove both brake arms from the cantilever posts, put them in your pocket, and pedal home slowly.** You will usually need a 5mm hex key for this. Do not attempt to ride a bike with brakes still attached to the frame or fork but disconnected from the cable. The brake arms will flap around as you ride and may get caught in the spokes, which could crack the seatstay or fork, not to mention your head, in a heartbeat.

If you want to straighten the wheel without using a spoke wrench, follow the procedures for dealing with a bent rim in d. Recognize that if you bend the rim by smacking it on the ground to correct for a loose or broken spoke, you will permanently deform the rim. Try to get home without resorting to this maneuver, because then you will have to replace the rim.

d. Fixing a bent rim

If the rim is only mildly out of true and you brought a spoke wrench, you can fix the rim. The procedure for truing a wheel is explained in §vi-11.

If the wheel is really whacked out, spoke truing won't do much. To get the rim to clear the brakes so that you can pedal home, follow the steps in c above.

If the wheel is bent to the point that it won't turn even when the brake is removed, beat it straight as long as the rim is not broken.

1. **Find the area that is bent outward the most.** Mark it on the outward side.

2. **Hold the wheel by its sides.** Have the bent

part at the top with the mark facing away from you. Make sure to leave the tire on and inflated.

3. **Smack the bent section of the rim against flat ground** (Fig. 3.11).

4. **Put the wheel back in the frame or fork.** See if anything has changed.

5. **Repeat the process until the wheel is rideable.** You may be surprised how straight you can get a wheel this way. Of course, you can also make it a lot worse if you hit it too hard or at the wrong spot.

iii-7
STRAIGHTENING A BENT BRAKE ROTOR

LEVEL 1

You can snag a disc-brake rotor on a rock, root, branch, or another bike's rotor (in the vehicle on the drive to the trailhead) and bend it. Generally, you can bend a rotor easily enough with your hands (leave it attached to the wheel) and get it to pass through the brake caliper well enough to get back to your car or home. It will rub and make noise, but you can ride safely to where you need to go.

If the rotor is bent so badly that you cannot straighten it enough to get it to pass through the caliper, you can remove either the caliper or the rotor for your (slow and careful) ride back to the trailhead. For the caliper, you'll need a 5mm hex key. For the rotor, you'll usually need a Torx T25 wrench, but you always carry one with you in your hydration pack or seat bag (Fig. 1.5), right?

If you remove either the rotor or the caliper and you have hydraulic brakes, I recommend that you wedge something between the brake pads, such as a piece of corrugated cardboard (or, ideally, a disc-brake pad spacer; it's wise to carry one). That way, if you accidentally pull that brake lever, you won't push the pistons out too far, at which point you would be stuck with the tough job of pressing them back in before you could fit a rotor between them again (§vii-12).

If you do remove the caliper, make sure that it cannot get caught in your wheel as you ride. On a cable-actuated disc brake, you can disconnect the cable, stuff the caliper in your pocket or pack, and pull out or tie up the cable. On a hydraulic brake, tie or tape the caliper to your frame.

Once home, flip to §vii-16 on truing rotors to come up with a more lasting fix.

iii-8
REPAIRING A DAMAGED FRONT DERAILLEUR

If the front derailleur is mildly bent, straighten it with your hands or leave it until you get home. If it has simply rotated around the seat tube (the chain, your foot, or a pants leg can catch it and turn it), reposition the front derailleur so that the cage is just above and parallel to the chainrings, and then tighten the derailleur in place with a 5mm hex key. If the derailleur is broken or so bent that you can't ride, you will need to remove it or route the chain around it as described in the following discussions.

3.12 Opening the front-derailleur cage

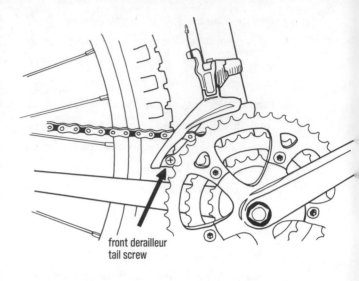

front derailleur
tail screw

a. With only a screwdriver

1. **Get the chain out of the derailleur cage.** To do this, open the derailleur cage by removing the screw at its tail (Fig. 3.12). If for some reason the derailleur cage can't be opened this way, open the chain with a chain tool or by hand at a master link (§iv-7 or §iv-11).

2. **Bypass the derailleur.** Put the chain on a chainring that does not interfere with it (either shift the derailleur to the inside and put the chain on the big chainring, or vice versa).

b. With hex keys and a screwdriver (or a chain tool or master link)

1. **Detach the derailleur from the seat tube.** This usually takes a 5mm hex key.

2. **Remove the screw at the tail of the derailleur cage** (Fig. 3.12).

3. **Separate the derailleur from the chain.** Pry open the cage to do it. You could also disassemble the chain, pull it out of the derailleur, and reconnect it (§iv-7 to §iv-11), but you will shorten the chain's life in the process unless you do it at a master link.

4. **Manually put the chain on.** Choose whichever chainring is best for the ride home. If in doubt, put the chain on the middle one.

5. **Tie the cable up.** You don't want it to catch in your wheel.

6. **Stuff the derailleur in your pocket.**

Now you can ride home.

iii-9
REPAIRING A DAMAGED REAR DERAILLEUR

 **LEVEL 1**

If the rear derailleur gets bent just a bit, you can probably straighten it by hand enough to get home. If it's damaged more than this and you need only to descend back to your home or car, it's your lucky day. Remove the chain with a chain tool (§iv-7) or by hand if the chain has a master link (§iv-11), and coast back down.

If a jockey wheel fell out, you may be able to fix it as described in §iii-10. Or if the return spring breaks and the chain hangs slack, you can try the fix in §iii-11.

The most common rear-derailleur damage occurs when the derailleur gets caught in the spokes. If that happens, you almost invariably bend the derailleur as well as the rear-derailleur hanger—the part that hangs down from the dropout to which the derailleur attaches (Fig. 5.2). For this reason, always carry a spare derailleur hanger with you (Fig. 1.5) when riding a mountain bike (old steel and titanium frames don't have replaceable hangers, but almost all aluminum and carbon and any current frames do; make sure you get the correct one that fits your bike). If you can bend the derailleur and the hanger back enough to ride home, great. If not, or if you break the hanger by bending it back, you'll need to replace the hanger; remove the rear wheel and derailleur to do it.

Once the new hanger is on, check to see that the derailleur jockey wheels line up vertically under the cogs. More often than not, the jockey-wheel cage will be bent in toward the spokes, making it shift poorly and making it likely to go into the spokes again. Often in these cases, the derailleur jockey-wheel cage has gotten bent inward, and as the wheel's spokes have dragged the cage hard around with them, the cage or upper knuckle has rotated beyond its stop. To get the derailleur working again, bend the cage straight and then wind the cage or knuckle back into position past its stop. If it's the stop on the cage and it is removable with a screwdriver, this is easy. If not, flex or bend the tab stop on the upper knuckle plate or cage until it allows the cage or entire derailleur to rotate back; a pair of pliers, screwdriver, or small hammer may do the trick. Often, you break the (already bent and weakened) tab off doing it, but the derailleur will still work. Once the derailleur has been twisted back into position with the chain routed properly, you may have to stick something like a screwdriver or spanner hook into the derailleur jockey-wheel cage to give you the leverage you need to straighten it in all three dimensions.

If the rear derailleur has been bent beyond fixing or is broken, then you will not be able to continue pedaling with the chain routed through it. To pedal home, route the chain around the derailleur, effectively turning your bike into a single-speed for the duration of your ride (Fig. 3.13). Watch out if you don't have a hardtail, though, because the only rear-suspension bikes that can be set up as a single-speed bike are "unified-rear-triangle" bikes, where the dropouts are attached directly to the bottom-bracket shell via rigid chainstays, or "concentric pivot" bikes whose main pivot is centered on the bottom bracket. Other rear-suspension systems will alternately yank on and slacken the chain as they move. Taking the derailleur out

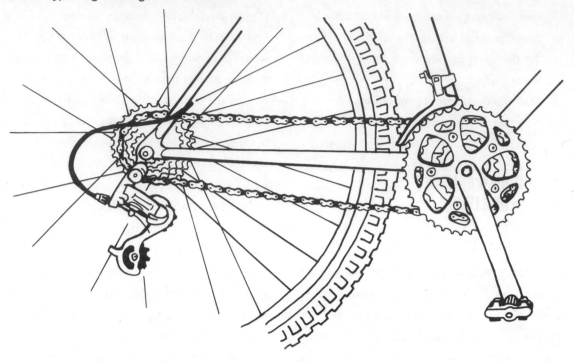

of the equation means that there is nothing to take in or let out the slack. If you have a lockout on the rear shock, you can use that and continue with the following instructions. Otherwise, you must try another way to repair the derailleur, or you will be walking home.

1. **Open the chain and pull it out of the derailleur.** Use a chain tool (§iv-7), or do it by hand if the chain has a master link (§iv-11).

2. **Shift the front derailleur to a selected chainring.** Pick the gear combination in which you think you can make it home most effectively. Be aware that the chain line must be tight and aligned straight (i.e., the chain must parallel the frame), or the chain will fall off the cog and the chainring and frustrate any attempts to pedal.

3. **Choose a rear cog and wrap the chain around it.** Bypass the rear derailleur entirely.

4. **Remove any overlapping chain.** Make the chain as short as you can, where you can still get the ends together. Then, if the bike has

horizontal dropouts, push the wheel forward in the dropouts to get a bit more slack.

5. **Connect the chain.** Use a chain tool as described in §iv-9. Pull the wheel back in the dropouts as far as you can to tension the chain. Now ride home.

iii-10
COMPENSATING FOR A LOST REAR-DERAILLEUR JOCKEY WHEEL

If you can find the jockey wheel and the bolt, just reassemble the parts onto the derailleur (see §v-33).

If you find the jockey wheel but not the bolt, you can reattach the wheel with one of the bolts holding a water-bottle cage on (provided you did not try to save weight by using short bottle-boss bolts!). The thread may be the same, although if the bolt is too long, you will need to be careful that you don't shift the derailleur inward far enough to catch it on the spokes as you ride. Otherwise, try wire or a zip-tie.

If you cannot find the jockey wheel, you can still rig up the derailleur to work or at least to pedal without shifting. If you lost the upper jockey wheel and the derailleur is a type with the same bolts top and bottom, then put the lower wheel on top first. Now, if you found the bolt for the lost wheel, just tighten the bolt back in where it was, making sure the chain is routed over it in the normal fashion as if the jockey wheel were still in place on the derailleur. If the bolt is also missing, you can still rig up a fix. Collect three threaded collars from the Presta valves on both of your wheels and from your spare tube. String them up between the cage plates with a twist-tie, wire, or zip-tie.

iii-11
WORKING WITH A BROKEN REAR-DERAILLEUR RETURN KNUCKLE SPRING

If the spring in the rear derailleur's lower knuckle breaks or gets dislodged, it will not twist the jockey-wheel cage and pull tension on the chain. If you have a bungee cord, hook it to the derailleur's jockey-wheel cage and loop it around the end of the quick-release skewer. Reverse the skewer so that the lever is on the drive side pointed back. Hook the other end of the bungee to wherever you can to maintain good tension, such as a water-bottle cage or the seat tube.

iii-12
RIDING WITH A BROKEN FRONT-DERAILLEUR CABLE

The chain will be on the inner chainring, and you will still be able to use all of the rear cogs. Depending on which chainring you want for your return ride, pick one of these three options:

1. Leave it on the inner ring and ride home.
2. Tighten the inner derailleur limit screw until, with luck, the derailleur sits over the middle chainring (Fig. 3.14). Leave the chain on the middle ring and ride home.

3.14 Tightening the inner front-derailleur limit screw

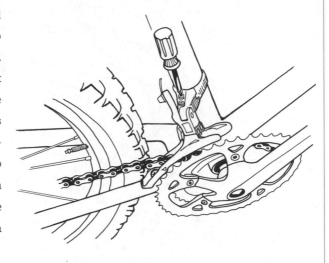

3. Bypass the front derailleur by removing the chain from the derailleur and putting it on the big chainring. You can do this either by opening the derailleur cage with a screwdriver (Fig. 3.12) or by disconnecting and reconnecting the chain with a chain tool or at a master link (§iv-7 and iv-9 to §iv-11 or §iv-12).

iii-13
RIDING WITH A BROKEN REAR-DERAILLEUR CABLE

The chain will be on the smallest or largest rear cog, depending on the type of derailleur, and you will still be able to use all three front chainrings. Most derailleurs use spring tension to move the chain to the small cog, so that is where the chain most likely will be. Conversely, Shimano Low Normal (current) or Rapid Rise (late 1990s) rear derailleurs use spring tension to move the chain to the largest cog, so a broken cable will leave it stuck there. You have three options:

1. Leave the chain on the cog it's on and ride home.
2. With a standard rear derailleur, move the chain to a larger cog, push inward on the

3.15 Broken rear-derailleur cable—option 2

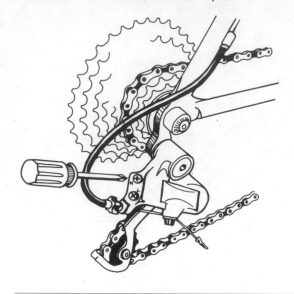

3.16 Broken rear-derailleur cable—option 3

derailleur with your hand, and tighten the high-gear limit screw on the rear derailleur (usually the upper of the two screws) until it lines up with a larger cog (Fig. 3.15). Move the chain to that cog and ride home. With a Shimano Low Normal or Rapid Rise rear derailleur, move the chain to a smaller cog, push outward on the derailleur with your hand, and tighten the low-gear limit screw on the rear derailleur (usually the lower of the two screws) until it lines up with a smaller cog. Move the chain to that cog and ride home. You may have to fine-tune the adjustment of the derailleur limit screw to get it to run quietly without skipping.

3. **If you do not have a screwdriver, you can push inward on a standard rear derailleur while turning the crank with the rear wheel off the ground to shift to a larger cog.** Jam a stick in between the derailleur-cage plates to prevent the derailleur from moving back down to the small cog (Fig. 3.16). Don't try this with a Shimano Low Normal or Rapid Rise rear derailleur, because the stick will be too close to the spokes for comfort.

iii-14
GETTING HOME WITH A BROKEN BRAKE CABLE OR A BLOWN HYDRAULIC BRAKE HOSE

Walk home or ride slowly and carefully home if the trail is not dangerous.

iii-15
RIDING WITH A FLAT SUSPENSION FORK

If you have a blown or leaking air-spring fork and can't pump it, there's not much you can do. You will just have to ride back with it that way. If the fork has a lockout lever or compression-damping adjustment, tighten it down to minimize bottoming out. Go slowly and keep your weight back.

iii-16
RIGGING BROKEN SEAT RAILS OR A SEATPOST CLAMP

If you can't tape or tie the saddle back on, try wrapping your gloves or some clothing over the top of the seatpost to pad it. Sticking an inverted water bottle over the top of the post also might make it rideable. Otherwise, remove the seatpost and ride home without it.

iii-17
RIDING WITH A BROKEN SEATPOST

If the seatpost shaft breaks, you can splint it internally with a stick, tape it up, and ride very carefully. A better solution is to ride home standing up.

iii-18
RIDING WITH A BROKEN HANDLEBAR

It's probably best to walk home. You could splint the broken handlebar by jamming a stick inside and wrapping it with duct tape. If the break is right next to the stem clamp, you could also loosen the clamp, move the handlebar over so that the break is inside the clamp, and retighten it. In either case, you must ride very carefully. The stick could easily break or the clamp could let go of the broken handlebar, leaving you with no way to control the bike. A sudden collision of your face with the ground would follow. From what I've heard, that can be a painful experience. In fact, now that I think of it, you might want to just walk your bike home.

iii-19
FIXING A BROKEN LINKAGE BOLT ON REAR SUSPENSION

Try sticking a hex key in where the bolt was and tape it in place.

iii-20
DEALING WITH A SEIZED FREEHUB OR FREEWHEEL

If the rear cogs will not freewheel, you cannot coast. If you do stop pedaling, the forward-turning cogs will pull the slack chain around and rip up the rear derailleur. Try squirting some chain lube into the front and back of the freewheel mechanism. If you have no chain lube and the temperature is above freezing, try squirting water in to restore the freewheeling action. If the temperature is below freezing, you can sometimes free a frozen freehub by peeing on it. Hey, don't laugh. It's warm!

No matter what liquid you use for lubrication, you may need to hit the freehub with a stick to get it to turn.

iii-21
AVOIDING GETTING LOST OR HURT AND DEALING WITH IT IF YOU DO

Mountain biking in the backcountry can be dangerous. You need to prepare properly and take personal responsibility for your own and others' safety when riding in deserted country. Two deaths near Moab, Utah, in the summer of 1995 highlight the risks facing anyone who rides off into the backcountry.

The two who died in Moab were riding the popular Porcupine Rim Trail. They got lost on the descent off Porcupine Rim, missed the turn into Jackass Canyon, and then headed into Negro Bill Canyon—which divides the Porcupine Rim Trail from Moab's most famous ride, the Slickrock Trail. It may come as a surprise that people could die and go undiscovered for 17 days so close to a main highway into town (which was right below them) and to two heavily traveled trails. But since they hadn't told anyone of their plans, no one in town noticed when they did not return.

Their parents, not hearing from them for a few days, called the sheriff, and a search was mounted.

Once the riders got lost, they abandoned their bikes and tried to walk down to the road, instead of riding back the way they had come. That road and the Colorado River are very close as the crow flies and are visible at a number of points but, owing to the numerous cliffs, are quite difficult to reach. The two climbed, fell, or slid down to a ledge from which they apparently were unable to climb either up or down, and there they slowly perished from exposure.

They died on this ledge in such a way that they were very difficult to spot from the air. They had placed no items to indicate their positions to airborne spotters. Had searchers found their bikes, they could have concentrated the search on a small area. Regrettably, thieves took their bikes and helmets and did not alert the authorities.

Eventually, a helicopter searcher saw the bodies on the ledge, and a Forest Service ranger rappelled 160 feet down to them. He was able to then walk out unaided, indicating that perhaps the riders were so injured, exhausted, delirious, or hypothermic that they had been unable to take the same route out.

Cliffs, steep hills, and an array of other natural features can also pose a risk. In the fall of 1995, another Moab rider barely managed to jump off his bike before it went hurtling over the edge of a cliff and dropped some 400 feet. Anyone who has ridden much in the canyon country of the Southwest can tell you that there are countless other trails near cliff edges that present a similar threat.

Even in seemingly safe areas, the risks can be high. Pro rider Paul Willerton came close to meeting his end on a relatively standard, cliff-free, but isolated trail near Winter Park, Colorado. Unable to walk after crashing and breaking his leg, Willerton had to drag himself many miles using only his arms.

We all tend to think that nothing like this will ever happen to us. But it can happen, and far too easily. That shouldn't discourage you from riding in the backcountry, but it should encourage you to think and utilize the following 12 basic backcountry survival skills. They could make the difference between life and death.

1. **Always take plenty of water.** You can survive a long time without food but not without water.

2. **Tell someone where you are going and when you expect to return.** If you know of someone who is missing, call the police or sheriff.

3. **If you find personal effects on the ground, assume that someone could be lost or in trouble.** Report the find and mark the location.

4. **If you get lost, backtrack.** Even if going back is longer, it is better than getting stranded.

5. **Don't go down something you can't get back up or go up something you can't get back down.**

6. **Bring matches, extra clothing and food, a flashlight, and perhaps an aluminized emergency blanket in case you have to spend the night out or need to signal searchers.**

7. **If the area is new to you, go with someone who is familiar with it or take a map and compass—and know how to use them.**

8. **Wear a helmet.** It's hard to ride home with a cracked skull.

9. **Bring basic first aid stuff and bike tools, and know how to use them well enough to keep yourself and your bike going.**

10. **Walk your bike when it's appropriate.** Falling off a cliff is a poor alternative to taking a few extra seconds or displaying less bravado. Try riding on difficult sections of trail to improve your bike handling, but if the risk of falling off a cliff is great or a mistake could leave you injured a long way from help, find another place to practice those moves.

11. **Don't ride beyond your limits if you are a long way out.** Take a break. Get out of the hot sun. Avoid dehydration and bonking by drinking and eating enough.

12. **Teach your friends all these things.**

These rules are in addition to the following International Mountain Bike Association Rules of the Trail, which we would all do well to adhere to:

1. **Plan ahead.**

2. Always yield trail.
3. Never scare animals.
4. Ride on open trails only.
5. Control your bicycle.
6. Leave no trace.

Keep in mind that your decisions affect yourself and could affect your riding partners, your families, and countless others. Recognize that endangering yourself can also endanger the person trying to rescue you. Search-and-rescue parties are usually made up of helpful people who will gladly try to save you, but no one appreciates being put in harm's way unnecessarily.

In summary, make appropriate decisions when cycling the backcountry. Learn survival skills and prepare well. Understand that even though you have a $4,000 bike and are riding on popular trails, you are not immune to danger. When ignorance makes us oblivious to danger, it sadly becomes the danger itself.

CHAINS

A chain is only as strong as its weakest link.
—Anonymous

A sausage is only as good as its last link.
—Bluto

TOOLS

chain lubricant

12-inch ruler

chain tool

lots of rags

rubber gloves

OPTIONAL

chain-elongation
   indicator

master link pliers

solvent (citrus
   based)

self-contained chain
   cleaner

old water bottle

caliper

pliers

solvent tank

Rohloff cog-wear
   indicator

A bike chain is a simple series of links connected by rivets. Rollers surround each rivet between the link plates and engage the teeth of the cogs and chainrings. It is an extremely efficient method of transmitting mechanical energy from the pedals to the rear wheel. In terms of weight, cost, and efficiency, the bicycle chain has no equal, and—believe me—people have tried without success to improve on it for years.

To keep your bike running smoothly, you have to take care of the chain. It needs to be kept clean and well lubricated in order to transmit your energy efficiently and shift smoothly. Chains need to be replaced frequently to prolong the working life of other, more expensive, drivetrain components because a chain gets longer as its internal parts wear, thus contacting the gear teeth differently than intended.

CHAIN SERVICE AND ASSEMBLY

iv-1
LUBRICATING THE CHAIN

When lubricating the chain, use a lubricant intended for bicycle chains. If you want to get fancy about it, you can assess the type of conditions in which you ride and choose a lubricant intended for those conditions. Some lubricants are dry and pick up less dirt in dry conditions. Some are sticky and therefore less likely to wash off in wet conditions. Still others claim to be "metal conditioners" that actually penetrate and alter the surface of the metal. One of these, ProGold's ProLink, gives me longer chain life in all riding conditions, with daily use, than anything else I have tried, so that's what I use. I'm not saying that there aren't other equally good products, but by recommending one that I know is good, I can cut down on the e-mails asking me what chain lube I suggest.

Chain lubes generally come in spray cans and in squeeze bottles. Sprays should be avoided for regular maintenance chores because they tend to spew too much oil over everything, including in the air where you can inhale the lube. The chain needs oil only between contacting parts. On the outside, a thin film is sufficient to keep corrosion at bay; more than that will only attract dirt and gunk without improving the function of the chain.

51

4.1 Lubing the chain

1. **Drip a small amount of lubricant across each roller** (Fig. 4.1). Periodically move the chain so that you can easily access the links you are working on. To speed the process, turn the crank slowly while dripping lubricant onto the chain as it goes by. Yes, this method will cause you to apply excess lubricant, which will pick up more dirt. But overlubricating is far preferable to not lubricating, and if you wipe and lube the chain after each ride or two, it won't build up excessive grime.

2. **Wipe the chain off lightly with a rag.** In wet conditions, expect to use more lubricant (after every ride or even during a long, rainy ride).

iv-2
CLEANING THE CHAIN BY FREQUENT WIPING AND LUBRICATION

Cleaning the chain can be accomplished in a number of ways. The simplest method to maintain a chain is to wipe it down frequently, lubricate it, and then wipe off the excess lube. If you do this procedure before every ride, you will never need to clean the chain with a solvent. The lubricant softens the old sludge buildup, which is driven out of the chain when you ride. Of course, the lubricant also picks up new dirt and grime, but if you wipe them off before they're driven deep into the chain and relubricate the chain frequently, it will stay clean and supple. Chain cleaning can be performed as follows with the bike standing on the ground or in a bike stand:

4.2 Wiping the chain with a rag

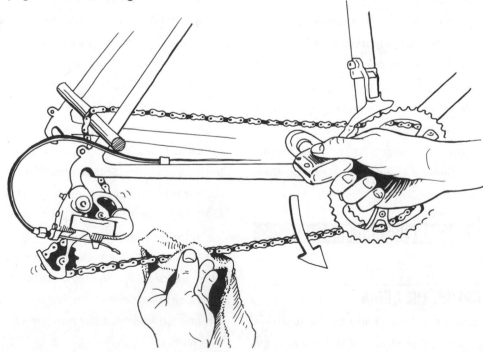

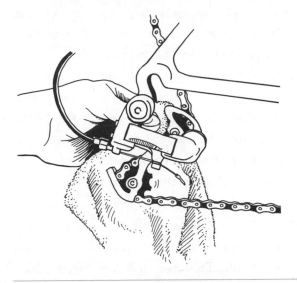

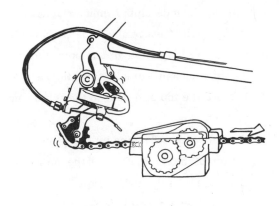

1. **Grab the chain with a rag.** Grasp the lower length of the chain (between the bottom of the chainring and the rear-derailleur lower jockey wheel).

2. **Turn the crank backward a number of revolutions.** Pull the chain through the rag (Fig. 4.2). Periodically rotate the rag to present a cleaner section of it to the chain.

3. **Lubricate the chain as in §iv-1.**

To encourage regular care, leave a pair of rubber gloves, a rag, and some chain lube next to your bike. Then, whenever you return from a ride, put on the gloves, wipe and lube the chain, and put your bike away. It takes maybe a minute, your hands stay clean, and your bike is ready for the next ride. If you can find time to take a shower after you ride, you can find time for this. Wipe the chainrings, cogs, front derailleur, and jockey wheels (Fig. 4.3) while you're at it, and the entire drivetrain will always work ideally.

iv-3
USING CHAIN-CLEANING UNITS

Several companies make chain-cleaning units that scrub the chain with a solvent while it is on the bike. These chain cleaners are generally made of clear plastic and have two or three rotating brushes that scrub the chain as it moves through the solvent bath (Fig. 4.4). The units offer the advantage of letting you clean the chain without removing it from the bike. Regularly removing the chain shortens any chain's life; moreover, with 9- or 10-speed chains unless you use a master link, you may find that the chain breaks under high load, thereby driving your foot, and perhaps your entire body, into the ground.

Most chain-cleaning units come with a non-toxic, citrus-based solvent. For your safety, and other environmental reasons, I strongly recommend that you purchase nontoxic citrus solvents for the chain-cleaning unit, even if it already comes with a petroleum-based solvent. If you recycle used diesel fuel, then go ahead and use it. In any case, wear gloves and glasses when using any solvent.

Citrus chain solvents often contain some lubricants, so they won't dry the chain out. The combination of lubricant and solvent is why diesel fuel has had such a following as a chain cleaner. A really strong solvent without lubricant (acetone, for example) will displace the oil from inside the rollers. The solvent will later evaporate, leaving a dry, squeaking chain that is hard to rehabilitate. The same can happen with a citrus-based solvent that does not include a lubricant if no lubricant is separately applied, especially if the chain is not allowed to dry long enough. The procedure for using a chain-cleaning unit is straightforward:

1. **Remove the top and pour in the solvent up to the fill line.**
2. **Place the chain-cleaning unit up against the bottom of the chain.** Reinstall the top so that the chain runs through it (Fig. 4.4).
3. **Turn the bike's crank backward.** Run the chain through the unit's brushes until it is clean.
4. **Remove the unit from the chain.**
5. **Lubricate the chain as in §iv-1.**
6. **Let the solvent settle, decant the clear portion, and discard the sludge.**

iv-4
REMOVING AND CLEANING THE CHAIN

 **LEVEL 1**

You can also clean the chain by removing it from the bicycle and cleaning it in a solvent. I do not recommend this procedure unless the chain has a master link, because repeatedly disassembling the chain by pushing rivets in and out weakens it.

Mountain bike chains are prone to breakage because of the conditions in which they are used, but chain breakage is even more of an issue because of the narrow width of 9- and 10-speed chains. A chain that breaks during riding generally does so when you shift the front derailleur while pedaling hard. This technique can pry a link plate open so that the head of a rivet pops out of the plate, tearing the chain apart. Chain disassembly and reassembly expand the size of the rivet hole where you put the chain together, allowing the rivet to pop out more easily. Shimano

supplies special "subpins" for reassembly of its chains that are meant to prevent this problem, but the chain is still not as strong there as if you had left the original pin in place.

A hand-opened master link can avoid the problem of repeatedly opening and reassembling the chain. Master links are standard on SRAM, Wippermann, Taya, and KMC chains. An aftermarket master link, like Lickton's SuperLink, can also be installed into any chain so long as you make sure that the master link is the right width.

If you do disassemble the chain (see §iv-7 or §iv-11 for instructions), you can clean it well, even without a solvent tank. Just drop the chain into an old jar or water bottle half filled with solvent. Using an old water bottle or jar allows you to clean the chain without touching or breathing the solvent—something to be avoided even when you are using citrus solvents.

The procedure for cleaning the chain without using a chain-cleaning unit could not be simpler:

1. **Remove the chain from the bike** (§iv-7 or §iv-11).
2. **Drop it in a water bottle or jar.**
3. **Pour in enough solvent to cover the chain.**
4. **Shake the bottle vigorously.** Keep it low to the ground in case the top pops off or the jar breaks.
5. **Hang the chain to air-dry.**
6. **Reassemble it on the bike** (see §iv-8 to §iv-11).
7. **Lubricate it as in §iv-1.**

Whatever you do, don't leave the chain to soak for extended periods in citrus-based solvents, because these are water based and will cause the chain to oxidize (rust), making it move with more friction and be more prone to breakage. (Some people believe in having two chains they rotate on and off the bike, leaving one soaking in solvent while the other one is on the bike.

Although this would work with diesel fuel as the solvent, it won't work with water-based solvents. In any case, you gain nothing by soaking the chain for extended periods, so just don't do it.)

After removing the chain, allow the solvent in the bottle or jar to settle for a few days so that you can decant the clear stuff and use it again. I'll say this throughout the book: Use a citrus-based solvent. It is not only safer for the environment; it is also gentler on your skin and less harmful to breathe. Wear rubber gloves when working with any solvent, and use a respirator meant for volatile organic compounds if you are not using a citrus-based solvent. There is no sense in fixing your bike to go faster if you end up becoming a slow, sickly bike rider.

iv-5
REPLACING THE CHAIN

 LEVEL 1

As the rollers, pins, and plates wear out, the chain lengthens. That, in turn, hastens the wear and tear on other drivetrain parts. An elongated chain concentrates the load on each individual gear tooth, rather than distributing it over all of the teeth that the chain is wrapped around, and as a result the gear teeth become hook-shaped and the tooth valleys become wider. If such wear has already occurred, a new chain will not solve the problem. A new chain will not mesh properly with deformed teeth, and it is likely to skip whenever you pedal hard. So before all of that extra wear and tear hits your pocketbook, get in the habit of checking the chain on a regular basis (§iv-6) and replacing it as needed.

How long it takes for the chain to wear out will vary, depending on chain type, maintenance, riding conditions, and strength and weight of the rider. Figure on replacing the chain every 500 to 1,000 miles, especially for bikes ridden in dirty conditions by a large rider. Lighter riders riding mostly on paved roads can often extend replacement time to more than 2,000 miles.

iv-6
CHECKING FOR CHAIN ELONGATION

 **LEVEL 1**

a. Chain-elongation gauges

The simplest accurate method for checking chain elongation is to use a gauge. Make sure you check a number of spots on the chain; you'll find variation.

The Rohloff gauge (Fig. 4.5) is simple, quick, and reliable. It's a go/no-go gauge. Brace the hook end against a chain roller, and if the opposing curved tooth falls completely into the chain so that the length of the tool's body contacts it, the chain is shot. If the chain is still in good shape, the curved tooth will not go all of the way in. The tooth marked "S" is for checking a chain running strictly on steel rear cogs, and the tooth marked "A" is for checking aluminum and titanium cogs, but I use just the A side. I find that if the A edge comes down to the chain and I replace it right then, I get almost infinite life out of my chainrings and cogs, even titanium ones. That's worth it to me.

The ProGold chain gauge (Fig. 4.6) is also quick and accurate. Brace the hooked end against a chain roller, and let the long tooth drop into the

---

4.5 Checking chain wear with the Rohloff gauge. If the curved tooth with the S (steel cogs) falls completely into the chain, replace the chain (A is for aluminum cogs).

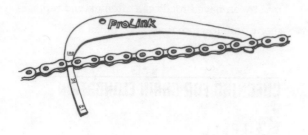

chain. If it drops in close to the 90 percent mark, that is equivalent to the A side of the Rohloff dropping down flush with the chain.

Park, Wippermann, and others offer chain-elongation gauges as well, and Feedback Sports even makes a digital one, shown in Figure 1.4. Some gauges are definitely less convenient to use than the Rohloff and ProGold units, both of which I can recommend without reservation.

b. Ruler method

Another way to measure chain wear is with an accurate ruler. Chains are measured on an inch standard and should measure ½ inch between adjacent rivets (and nominally have ³/₃₂-inch-wide rollers on derailleur chains and often ⅛-inch-wide rollers on single-cog bicycles). There should be exactly an integral number of links in 1 foot—12 links, to be exact, where each complete link consists of an inner and an outer pair of plates (Fig. 4.7).

1. **Set one end of the ruler on a rivet edge.**
2. **Measure to the rivet edge at the other end of the ruler, 12 links away.** The distance between these rivets should be 12 inches exactly. If it is 12⅛ inches or greater, replace the chain; if it is 12¹/₁₆ inches or greater, replacing it is a good idea (and a necessity if you have any titanium or alloy cogs or an 11-tooth small cog). Some chain manufacturers recommend replacement if elongation is

1 percent, or ½ inch in 50 complete link pairs (50 inches), which is a little less than ⅛ inch over 12 link pairs (1 foot). If the chain is off the bike, you can hang it next to a new chain for comparison; if the used one is more than a third of a link longer for the same number of links, I recommend replacing it.

If you always replace the chain as soon as it becomes elongated beyond the spec I've indicated on these chain-elongation gauges, you will replace at least three chains before needing to change the cogs.

iv-7
REMOVING THE CHAIN

 **LEVEL 1**

The following procedure applies to all standard derailleur chains except those with a master link. Master-link-equipped chains include all SRAM, Wippermann, KMC, and Taya chains. All of these chains snap open by hand at the master link (see §iv-11), although if need be, they can also be opened at any other link with the use of a chain tool as described here.

1. **Place any link over the back teeth on a chain tool** (Fig. 4.8).
2. **Tighten the chain-tool handle clockwise.** Push the link rivet out unless you don't have a master link or a Shimano chain and a new subpin for it. In that case, leave 1mm or so of rivet protruding inward from the chain plate to hook the chain back together when reassembling.
3. **Separate the chain.** Flex it away from the pushed-out pin if you left the stub in. If you

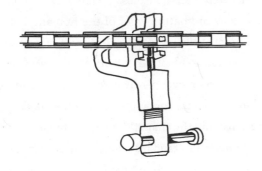

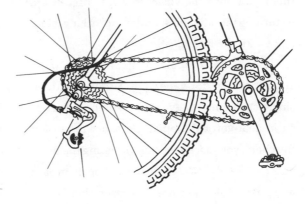

pushed the pin all the way out, the two ends will just pull apart, but you won't be able to reconnect them without a subpin or a master link.

iv-8
DETERMINING CHAIN LENGTH AND ROUTING

a. Chain length with a derailleur

Installing a new chain is a fairly easy process:

1. **Determine the chain length.** If you are putting on a new chain, determine how many links you'll need in one of two ways: (a) Under the assumption that your old chain was the correct length, compare it with the new one, and use the same number of links. (b) If you have a standard long-cage mountain bike rear derailleur on your bike, wrap the chain around the big chainring and the biggest cog without going through either derailleur. Bring the two ends together until the ends overlap; one full link (Fig. 4.7—a complete link pair) should be the amount of overlap (Fig. 4.9). Remove the remaining links and save them in your spare-tire bag so that you have spares in case of chain breakage on the trail.

2. **Route the chain properly.** Shift the derailleurs so that the chain will rest on the smallest cog in the rear and on the smallest chainring up front. Starting with the rear-derailleur pulley that is farthest from the derailleur body (this will be the bottom pulley once the chain is taut), guide the chain up through the rear derailleur, going around the two jockey pulleys. Make sure the chain passes inside of the prongs on the rear-derailleur cage. Guide the chain over the smallest rear cog. Guide the chain through the front-derailleur cage. Wrap the chain around the smallest front chainring. Bring the chain ends together so that they meet.

3. **Connect the chain.** Use a master link, a Shimano subpin, or the existing pin you pushed out, and follow the instructions in §iv-9, §iv-10, or §iv-11 for the appropriate connector.

b. Chain length with a single-speed or internal-gear rear hub

Bikes made for single-speed or Rohloff and other internal-gear hubs have a system to vary the distance from the crank to the rear hub. Bikes not made for these hubs can be fitted with adapters to tension the chain.

The simplest made-for-single-speed system is rear dropouts with long, horizontal slots in which you can pull the wheel back and forth and clamp it in place where you choose. Some of these systems have adjuster screws with locknuts on them; you push the wheel forward or backward by turning the adjuster screw(s) and locking it into place with the locknut(s).

Sliding rear dropouts (Fig. 14.3) are a more elegant system for varying drivetrain length on single-speed/internal-gear frames. The axle ends sit in near-vertical dropout slots, but to tension the chain, you loosen the bolts securing the dropouts to the ends of the chainstays. Slide them back and forth while the wheel is already clamped in, and lock it in place by tightening the bolts securing the sliding dropouts to the frame.

Another method is an eccentric bottom bracket; the bottom-bracket shell is oversized, and the bottom-bracket bearing and axle assembly mounts into a tunnel bored off-center in an aluminum cylinder (I'll call this the eccentric cylinder). The eccentric cylinder clamps into the oversized bottom-bracket shell, either by means of a slot in the shell closed by pinch bolts, setscrews on the shell driven into the eccentric cylinder, or a sliding wedge piece in the eccentric cylinder. You tension the chain by loosening the pinch bolts, setscrews, or wedge bolts and rotating the eccentric cylinder (usually with a pin tool in a pair of holes in the face of the eccentric cylinder) to move the crank toward or away from the rear hub.

With any of these types, first set the distance from the wheel to the crank at its minimum by sliding the wheel or the sliding dropouts all of the way forward or by rotating the eccentric bottom bracket so that the bottom-bracket spindle is as close to the back of the bottom-bracket shell as possible. Wrap the chain around the cog and chainring, and make it the minimum length that still allows you to connect the ends. Once the chain is connected, tighten the chain by sliding the wheel back or by moving the bottom bracket forward, depending on the system you have. You

want the chain not to be taut like a drumhead, as this would create excess pedaling resistance as well as premature wear of the hub and bottom-bracket bearings. You also don't want the chain so loose that it can fall off. A good test is to push the chain over gently with your thumb just behind the chainring while turning the crank. If you can derail the chain this way, tighten it more.

To adapt a standard frame to use a single-speed or internal-gear hub, you can install a chain tensioner to pull a slack chain taut. Often called a "singleator," after the Surly model of that name, it is usually a spring-loaded arm with a single jockey wheel or roller that bolts into the rear-derailleur hanger on the dropout. The jockey wheel or roller pushes up or down on the chain coming to the bottom of the rear cog to keep it tight (two springs are often supplied so that you can choose if you want the roller to push up or down on the chain). The jockey-wheel shaft is often free to move laterally in order to center the roller or jockey wheel on the chain.

Another type is a U-shaped clamp with a roller bolted through the ends of the U. The unit clamps around the chainstay and can be slid back and forth to vary the pressure of the roller on the chain; one of these is pictured at the center of the chainstay in Figure 5.45.

For single-speed adapters with a single roller, make the chain just long enough to give the minimum amount of slack when wrapped around the chainring and cog without the roller in place. The chain tensioner will do the rest.

A twin-jockey-wheel type (the Paul Melvin, Rohloff Twin Pulley, or Shimano Alfine), which cannot be used with a fixed gear or a coaster brake, also bolts to the rear-derailleur hanger and has a pair of jockey wheels in a spring-loaded cage that force a Z-bend in the chain to keep it tight. It is set up like a fixed-position rear derailleur and consequently requires more chain length than a single-roller tensioner. You want enough chain length that the jockey wheels are not stretched out in a straight line but not so much that they cannot take up all the slack. There is a lot of latitude here.

iv-9
CONNECTING A 5-, 6-, 7-, OR 8-SPEED CHAIN (WITHOUT A MASTER LINK OR A SPECIAL CONNECTING PIN)

A "standard" chain—that is, a non-Shimano chain without a master link—is a disappearing breed, as newer mountain bikes have more rear cogs and correspondingly narrow chains.

NOTE: *If you have a Shimano chain or a chain with a master link, go to §iv-10 or §iv-11 as appropriate. Don't connect it as described here using the original rivet; otherwise, you could be injured if the chain breaks.*

ANOTHER NOTE: *This section applies only to wider chains, such as 5-, 6-, 7-, and 8-speed chains. Never use the same pin (except in an emergency out on the trail) on a 9- or 10-speed chain or on any master-link-equipped chain or Shimano chain.*

Connecting a chain without a master link or a Shimano subpin is much easier if the link rivet that was partially removed when the chain was taken apart is sticking out toward you. Positioning the link rivet this way allows you to use the chain tool in a much more comfortable manner (driving the rivet toward the bike as in Fig. 4.10, instead of from the wheel side).

1. **Push the ends of the chain together.** Snap the end link over the little stub of pin you left sticking out to the inside between the opposite end plates. You will need to flex those end plates apart as you push the same link in to get the pin to snap into the hole.

2. **Push the rivet through with the chain tool** (Fig. 4.11). Make the same amount protrude on either side.

3. **Fold the link.** The link will likely be stiff because of the outer plates' being pushed closer together than they were meant to be.

4.10 Chain assembly

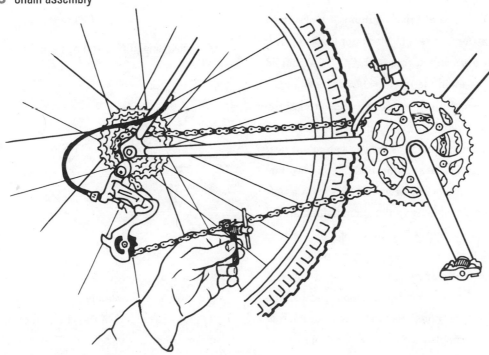

If this link does not fold as easily as the surrounding links (Fig. 4.12), continue on with step 4. If it folds freely, you're done.

4. **Put the link over the set of teeth on the tool closest to the screw handle** (Fig. 4.13). If your chain tool has only one set of teeth, free the stiff link by flexing it laterally with your fingers (Fig. 4.14) instead.

5. **Push the pin a fraction of a turn to spread the plates apart.**

iv-10

CONNECTING A SHIMANO CHAIN

Shimano chains have a special connecting pin ("subpin" in Shimano-speak) to ensure a strong chain connection. Insert the subpin in the same direction that you pushed out the old rivet.

Post-2010 10-speed Shimano chains (Shimano introduced 10-speed mountain bike drivetrains and chains for the 2011 model year) are asymmetrical due to the different shifting requirements on each side of the chain for climbing up the cogs versus climbing up the chainrings. Make sure the Shimano logo is to the outside; that is how you know it is oriented properly.

1. **Get out your Shimano subpin.** It looks like a silver (for 9-speed) or black (for 8-speed) rivet with a second segment ending in a pointed tip; the main identifying characteristic of the 10-speed pin is a set of two lines around the circumference of the leading edge of the pin. The subpin is twice as long as a standard rivet and has a breakage groove at the middle of its length. One or two subpins come with a new Shimano chain. If you are reinstalling an old Shimano chain, get a new subpin at a bike shop. If you don't have a subpin and are going to connect it anyway, follow the procedure in §iv-9, but get a new chain soon, because the chain is far more likely to break than if it had been assembled with the proper subpin.

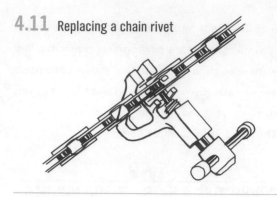

4.11 Replacing a chain rivet

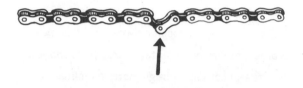

4.12 Stiff link

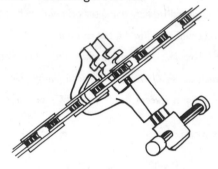

4.13 Loosening a stiff link

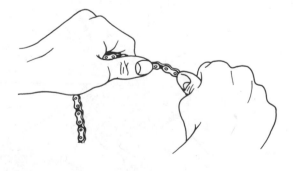

4.14 Loosening stiff link(s) by hand

2. **Remove any extra links.** Push the appropriate rivet completely out. Remove extra lengths at the end of the chain ending in an inner link (i.e., the right-hand end in Fig. 4.9

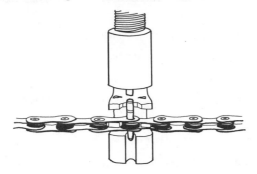

ends in an inner link rather than in an outer link, which has open outer plates like the left-hand end in Fig. 4.9).

3. **Line up the chain ends.** The holes must overlap.

4. **Push the subpin in with your fingers, pointed end first.** It will go in about halfway.

5. **With the chain tool, push the subpin into place (Fig. 4.15).** Push until there is only as much left protruding at the tail end as the other rivets in the chain.

6. **Break off the leading half of the subpin.** Use the hole in the end of a Shimano chain tool or a pair of pliers (Fig. 4.16).

7. **Check the link's freedom of movement.** If the chain kinks at the link you just assembled (Fig. 4.12), push the link rivet in a little deeper (Fig. 4.11) if it isn't sticking out as much on the backside. Or, if you pushed the link rivet in too far, push it back a hair from the other side with the chain on the teeth closer to the screw (Fig. 4.13 if you're using a chain tool with two sets of teeth). Note that Shimano chain tools (Figs. 4.17–18) do not have two sets of teeth because it is usually hard to push a Shimano subpin in too far; it will usually be easy, hard, easy, hard, and then very hard to push in as you turn the chain-tool handle, and you will tend to stop before pushing it too far. Otherwise, carefully flex the chain back and forth with your thumbs at the stiff rivet (Fig. 4.14).

NOTE: *If you have a 9-speed chain and an older chain tool, you may find that the prongs in the tool to hold the chain are too far from the backing plate of the tool and will get bent. Shimano tools TL-CN23 (Fig. 4.17) and TL-CN32 (Fig. 4.18) work on all Shimano chains. Many other brands also work; see the Pro Tip on chain tools.*

iv-11
CONNECTING AND DISCONNECTING A MASTER LINK

a. SRAM (Sachs) PowerLink, SuperLink, and KMC Missing Link

These links all work the same. SRAM (which purchased Sachs) licensed Lickton's SuperLink design (Fig. 4.22), and the Missing Link works the same way. (The SRAM 10-speed PowerLock link and the discontinued KMC Missing Link II are not supposed to be openable; SRAM PowerLock master links with an "M" or "N" stamped on them were recalled in late 2009.) The master link is made up of two symmetrical link halves, each of which has a single pin sticking out of it. There is a round keyhole in the center of each plate that tapers into a slot on the end opposite the pin.

Connecting

1. **Put the pin of each half of the link through the hole in each end of the chain.** One pin will go down and one up (Fig. 4.22).

Proper chain tools

If you ride a lot, you will change the chain frequently. It then becomes worthwhile to have a good chain tool (i.e., chain-breaker tool). If you currently have just a cheap little chain tool, you will be glad you made the investment to upgrade.

Shimano's $35 TL-CN23 or $120 TL-CN32 tool will work on all 7-, 8-, 9-, and 10-speed Shimano chains. The TL-CN23 is a small tool (Fig. 4.17), and the TL-CN32 (as well as its predecessors, the TL-CN31 and TL-CN30) is a professional tool with wooden handles (Fig. 4.18) that even has spare driver pins hidden in the base. Most important about the TL-CN32 (and the TL-CN31 and TL-CN30) is that it has four locating teeth in a row to hold the chain, rather than just the two that most chain tools have (Pedro's $45 Pro chain tool [Fig. 4.19] also has four teeth). These extra two teeth, one extending out on either side of the tool, hold the chain much better than does a tool with only two teeth.

The $100 Pedro's Tutto (meaning "all" in Italian) chain tool introduced in 2010 works on all $3/32$-inch chains from 5-speed through 11-speed.

The $200 Rohloff Revolver chain tool (Fig. 4.20), which has been around for well over a decade and continues to work on modern chains as well as twenty-year-old ones, has a thumbscrew that tightens down against the chain and secures it. The tool also has a revolving plate with different patterns on it to repeen the end of the rivet in whatever style you choose.

Park's $35 CT-3 (Fig. 4.21) is a standard shop chain tool, with both a front set of teeth and a back set of teeth, for prying a link apart a bit to free a stiff link, as in Figure 4.13.

I have successfully used a Shimano TL-CN31 (9-speed tool) and the Pedro's tool for years on every kind of chain from Shimano, Wippermann, and SRAM for 7-, 8-, 9-, and 10-speeds. As the chains became narrower on the outside, the supporting center section on newer Shimano chain tools was moved closer to the chain-locating teeth to fully support the rear outer link plate while driving the pin in. If you use an older-generation chain tool (for wider chains) with a one-generation newer (narrower) chain, eventually you will damage the tool, as this usage puts too much lateral load on the chain-locating teeth. A two-generation older chain tool will not seat the chain connector pins, so don't use it. Ideally, it is best to get the latest tool to do the best job with the latest chains, and it will also be compatible with all of the older (wider) chains.

I think that if you are careful, you need only one good tool that is at most one generation back (i.e., it is meant for at least 9-speed chains), and you can use it on any chain up through 10-speeds. By "careful," I mean that you must make sure that the connecting pin and the holes are all lined up perfectly (which the Rohloff, Shimano, and Pedro's Pro tools definitely help guarantee). I also mean that you must make sure that you stop at the right point and do not go too far or not far enough. For this, you need a feel for the loose-tight-loose-tight pressure changes as you push a Shimano connecting pin into place, as well as an eye for when the pin is protruding (or recessed) the same amount on both faces of the chain.

4.17 Shimano TL-CN23 tool

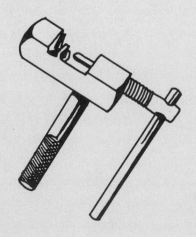

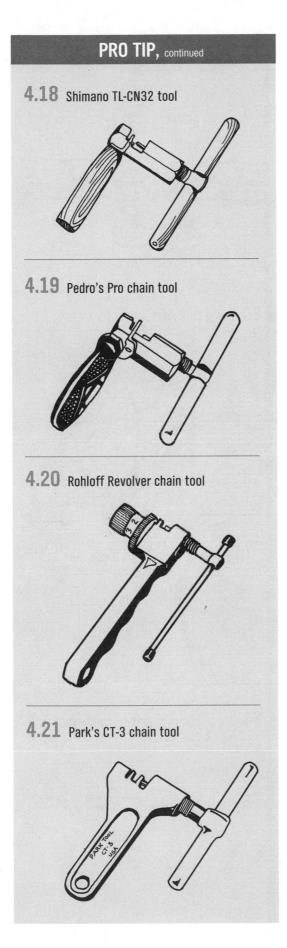

4.18 Shimano TL-CN32 tool

4.19 Pedro's Pro chain tool

4.20 Rohloff Revolver chain tool

4.21 Park's CT-3 chain tool

2. **Pull the links close together, and insert each pin into the keyhole in the opposite plate.**

3. **Tug on the chain.** This slides the groove at the top of each pin to the end of the slot in each plate.

Disconnecting

1. **Squeeze the master-link plates toward each other.** This will free the plate from the grooves in the pins.

2. **Push the chain ends toward each other.** This brings the pins to the center hole in each plate. If you have a pair of master-link pliers, which makes this job far easier, use them to grab the two rollers through which each pin of the master link is inserted (Fig. 4.23). Squeeze the pliers at the same time you squeeze the link plates toward each other with your fingers. The link will come right apart. Master-link pliers are one of the slickest tools in existence; with them you can easily open SRAM 10-speed PowerLock master links, which are supposed to be unopenable.

NOTE: *Without master-link pliers, it is often hard to open an old, dirty master link. The problem may seem to be that you don't have enough hands. Try squeezing the link plates toward each other with a clothespin or a pair of Vise-Grip pliers set on very low pressure to disengage the link plates from the pin grooves while you push the ends toward each other. In desperation, you may have to just open the chain somewhere else, reassembling it using a second master link or, in an emergency, as in §iv-9.*

3. **Pull the two halves of the master link apart.**

b. Wippermann ConneX link

The Wippermann link works much the same way as the SRAM PowerLink, but unlike other master links, the edges of the link plates are not symmetrical. This means that there is a definite orientation for the link, so make sure that you don't install it upside down.

Orient the ConneX master link so that its taller convex edge is away from the chainring or cog (Fig. 4.24). The link plate is bowl-shaped, and if you have the convex bottom of the bowl toward the cog or chainring, then when it is on an 11- or 12- or maybe even a 13-tooth cog, the convex edge will ride up on the spacer between cogs, lifting the rollers out of the tooth valleys and causing the chain to skip under load. Another way to think about this orientation is to notice that the pair of connected holes on each plate (into which you push the pin) forms a heart shape. When the chain is on the top of the cog or chainring, make sure that the heart is right side up as in Figure 4.24.

Remove and install the ConneX link the same way as the SRAM PowerLink in §iv-11a. In addition, make sure that the convex link edge is facing outward from the chain loop (Fig. 4.24) as described in the previous paragraph, so that the long concave edge can run over the cog spacers on the smallest cogs without lifting the chain.

c. Taya master link

Connecting

1. **Connect the chain ends with the plate that has two rivets sticking out of it** (Fig. 4.25).
2. **Snap the outer master-link plate over the rivets and into their grooves.** To facilitate hooking each keyhole-shaped hole over its corresponding rivet, flex the plate with the protruding rivets so that the ends of the rivets are closer together.

Disconnecting

1. **Flex the master link so that the pins come closer together.**
2. **Pull the plate with the oval holes off the rivets.**

4.22 SRAM PowerLink (also Sachs PowerLink and Lickton's SuperLink)

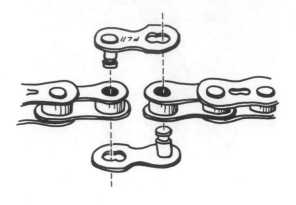

4.23 Using Park master-link pliers

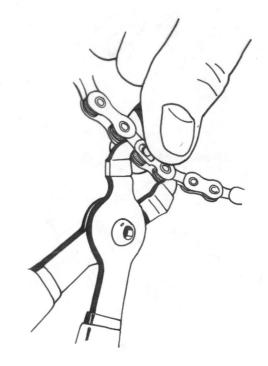

4.24 Wippermann ConneX link (note that high bump faces away from the chainring)

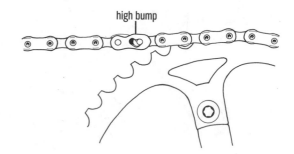

high bump

4.25 Taya chain master link

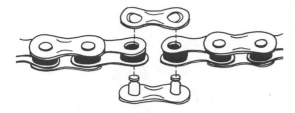

iv-12
INSTALLING A BELT DRIVE

The Gates Carbon Drive toothed belt (Fig. 4.26) works only on single-speed bikes and bikes with internal-gear rear hubs. The belt is a continuous loop that cannot be opened, so installing it requires a frame whose right dropout, chainstay, or seatstay will come apart. The bike must also have a means to tension the belt by adjusting the distance between the rear hub and the crank, such as the systems described in §iv-8b. Like any single-speed system, the Gates belt will work only on hardtail frames or full-suspension frames in which the distance from the bottom bracket to the rear hub does not change as it absorbs bumps. The only suspension systems like this are concentric-pivot systems (where the rear swingarm pivots around the bottom bracket), unified-rear-triangle systems (where the bottom bracket and dropouts are rigidly attached to each other), and softtails (where the suspension movement works by means of flex in the chainstays).

The belts come in only certain lengths denoted by the number of teeth on the belt. You cannot adjust the belt length; you have to get the right length belt for your frame and front and rear belt sprockets. Gates has online charts for determining length at carbondrivesystems.com. Keep in mind that the number of teeth on the sprockets does not equate to standard chainring and cog sizes, because there are more belt sprocket teeth per inch than chainring teeth. As with a chain drive, the gear ratio is proportional to the ratio of front sprocket size to rear sprocket size.

The belt comes coiled in a thin box. Taking it out of the box requires some finesse because if you inadvertently put a sharp bend in the belt while trying to uncoil it, you will break the carbon fibers that give the belt its tensile strength. Pull the belt open slowly, and then give it a little flip. If this is not enough to uncoil the belt without putting a sharp bend in it, look at the carbondrivesystems.com

4.26 Gates Carbon Drive belt system

support page for links to video and photographic sequences of the uncoiling method.

As in §iv-8b, first set the distance from the wheel to the crank at its minimum by sliding the wheel or the sliding dropouts all the way forward or by rotating the eccentric bottom bracket so that the bottom-bracket spindle is as close to the back of the oversized bottom-bracket shell as possible. Slip the belt around the front and rear sprockets from the side. Tighten the belt by sliding the wheel back or by moving the bottom bracket forward, depending on the frame you have.

The best way to determine proper belt tension is to use a Carbon Drive tension gauge. Without the gauge, push down on the belt halfway between the front and rear sprockets. The belt should deflect approximately ½ inch with 5–10 pounds of force.

TROUBLESHOOTING CHAINS

iv-13

CHAIN SUCK

Chain suck occurs when the chain does not release from the bottom of the chainring and pulls up rather than running straight to the lower rear-derailleur jockey wheel. The chain will come around and get "sucked" up by the inner or middle chainring until it hits the chainstay (Fig. 4.27). Sometimes the chain becomes wedged between the chainstay and the chainring.

A number of things can cause chain suck. To eliminate chain suck, try the simplest methods first and move down this list if it persists:

1. **Clean and lube the chain, and clean the chainrings.** See whether the chain now runs properly. A rusty chain will take longer to slide off the chainring than will a clean, well-lubed chain.

2. **Check for tight (or stiff) links** (Fig. 4.12). Slowly turn the crank backward, and watch the chain

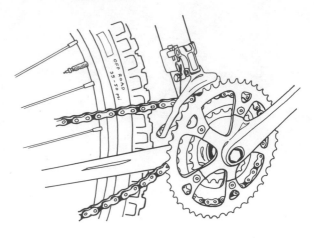

4.27 Chain suck

move through the derailleur jockey wheels. A stiff link will cause the lower jockey wheel to jump forward. Loosen stiff links by flexing them side to side with your thumbs and fingers (Fig. 4.14) or by using the back teeth on a chain tool that has them (Fig. 4.21). Set the stiff link over the back teeth closest to the screw handle (Fig. 4.13), and push the pin a fraction of a turn to spread the link.

3. **Check that there are no bent or torn teeth on the chainring.** Replace the chainring, or try straightening any broken or torn teeth you find by using pliers or by filing away rough, bent-over edges.

4. **Try another chain with wider spacing between link plates.** If the chain is too narrow, it can pinch the chainring. You can use a caliper to compare link spacing of various chains (Fig. 1.4). If you choose a chain that is too wide, however, it may work better on the front chainrings but could get stuck between the rear cogs.

5. **Replace the inner chainring with a thin chromed or stainless steel one.** The thin, slick teeth will release the chain more easily.

6. **Increase the rear derailleur's pivot-spring (p-spring) tension** (see §v-2g). This will increase

the tension on the lower run of the chain as it comes off the bottom of the chainring.

7. **Get an anti–chain suck device that attaches under the chainstays.** Ask your bike shop about what is available.

iv-14
SQUEAKING CHAIN

Squeaking is caused by dry or rusted surfaces inside the chain rubbing on each other.

1. **Wipe down the chain** (Fig. 4.2), **lubricate it** (Fig. 4.1), **and go for a test ride.** Try ProGold ProLink lube (it can penetrate and clean up the surfaces enough to rehabilitate a squeaky chain). Ride for a half hour or more, and then wipe and lubricate the chain with ProLink again and ride another half hour or more. Remember not to use a wax-based lubricant; using one might have even brought on the chain chirp in the first place.

2. **If the squeak is not gone, replace the chain.** If the initial remedy does not work, the chain is probably too dry and rusted deep inside. Chains often don't heal from this condition. Life is too short, and bike riding is too joyful to put up with the sound of a squeaking chain.

iv-15
SKIPPING CHAIN

There can be a number of causes for a chain to skip and jump as you pedal.

a. Stiff links

1. **Turn the crank backward slowly to see if a chain link is stiff** (Fig. 4.12). A stiff link will be visible because it will be unable to bend properly while going through the rear-derailleur jockey wheels. The link will deflect the jockey wheels when passing through.

2. **Loosen stiff links by flexing them from side to side between the index finger and thumb of** both hands (Fig. 4.14) **or by using the second set of teeth on a chain tool that has back teeth** (Fig. 4.21). Set the stiff link over the teeth closest to the screw handle, and push the pin a fraction of a turn to spread the link (Fig. 4.13).

3. **Wipe down and lubricate the chain.**

b. Rusted chain

A rusted chain will often squeak as well as skip. If you watch it move through the rear derailleur, many links will appear tight; they will not bend easily and will cause the jockey wheels to jump back and forth.

4. **Lubricate the chain with ProLink** (Fig. 4.1). Ride a few miles, and see if the chain action improves.

1. **If the chain doesn't improve, replace it.**

c. Worn-out chain

If the chain is worn-out, it will be elongated and will skip because it does not mesh well with the cogs. A new chain will fix the problem unless the worn chain was used long enough to ruin some cogs.

1. **Check for chain elongation as described in §iv-6.**

2. **If the chain is elongated beyond the specifications discussed in §iv-6, replace it.**

3. **If replacing the chain does not help or makes matters worse, see the next section.**

d. Worn cogs

If you just replaced the chain and it is now skipping (despite the rear derailleur being in adjustment; see §v-2), at least one of the cogs is probably worn out. If this is the case, the chain will probably skip on the cogs you use most frequently and not on others. However, if the chain skips only on the smallest cog or two and you have a Wippermann chain, check that you have not installed the ConneX link upside down (see §iv-11b).

1. **Check each cog visually for wear.** If its teeth are hook-shaped, the cog is shot and should be replaced. Rohloff makes a simple "HG-IG-Check" tool (pictured in Fig. 1.4) that checks for cog wear by putting tension on a length of chain wrapped around the cog. If the last chain roller on the tool hooks on the tooth and resists you flipping it in and out of the tooth pocket while the tool handle is under pressure, or, worse, if the entire measurement chain except the first roller slides easily away from the cog teeth while the handle is under pressure, the cog is worn-out. The tool works only on cogs smaller than 21 teeth.

2. **Replace the worn cogs (or the entire cogset or freewheel).** See "Cog Change" in §vi-20 to §vi-22.

3. **Replace the chain.** An old chain will wear out new cogs rapidly.

e. Misadjusted rear derailleur

If the rear derailleur is poorly adjusted or bent, it can cause the chain to skip by lining up the chain between gears.

1. **Shift back and forth and pedal backward.** The rear derailleur should shift equally well in both directions. The chain should pedal backward without catching.

2. **Adjust the rear derailleur.** Follow the procedure described in §v-2.

f. Sticky shift cable

If the shift cable does not move freely enough to let the derailleur's spring return the chain to be lined up under the cog, it will jump off under load. Frayed, rough, rusted, or worn cables or housings will cause the problem, as will overly thick cables or kinked or sharply bent housings. Replacing the shift cables and housings (§v-2) should eliminate the problem.

g. Loose rear-derailleur jockey wheel(s)

A loose jockey wheel on the rear derailleur can cause the chain to skip by letting it move too far laterally.

1. **Check that the bolts holding the jockey wheel to the cage are tight.** Use the appropriate hex key (usually 3mm).

2. **Tighten the jockey-wheel bolts if necessary.** Hold the hex key close to its bend so that you don't have enough leverage to overtighten the bolts. If the jockey-wheel bolts loosen regularly, put Loctite on their threads.

h. Bent rear derailleur or rear-derailleur hanger

If the derailleur or derailleur hanger is bent, adjustments won't work. You will probably know when it happened, too. The bending occurred either when you shifted your derailleur into your spokes, when you crashed onto the derailleur, or when you pedaled a stick or a tumbleweed through the derailleur.

Unless you have a derailleur-hanger alignment tool and know how to use it (Fig. 14.4), take the bike to a shop and have it checked, and have the dropout-hanger alignment corrected. Some bikes, especially those made out of carbon, aluminum, or magnesium, have a replaceable (bolt-on) right rear dropout and derailleur hanger, which you can purchase and bolt on yourself.

If a straight derailleur hanger does not correct the misalignment, the rear derailleur is bent. This is generally cause for replacement of the entire derailleur (see §v-1). With some derailleurs, you can just replace the jockey-wheel cage, which is usually what is bent. If you know what you are doing and are careful, you can sometimes unbend a bent derailleur cage back with your hands. This seldom works well, but it's worth a try if your only other alternative is to replace the entire rear derailleur. Just make sure you don't bend the derailleur hanger in the process.

i. Worn derailleur pivots

If the derailleur pivots are worn, the derailleur will be loose and will move around under the cogs, causing the chain to skip. The solution is to replace the derailleur.

j. Bent rear-derailleur mounting bolt

If the mounting bolt is bent, the derailleur will not line up straight. To fix the derailleur, get a new bolt and install it following the instructions in §v-1. Be sure to observe how the spring-loaded assembly goes together during disassembly to ease reassembly.

k. Missing or worn chain rollers

A chain that passes the elongation tests mentioned in §iv-6 can still skip because here and there one of the cylindrical rollers has broken and fallen off its rivet or is so worn that it is spool-shaped. If you don't happen to check that particular link with the chain-elongation gauge, you'll likely miss broken rollers. The width of the gauge is the same as between the inner plates, so the gauge won't catch worn-out, spool-shaped rollers either, because it will ride up on the edges of the rollers and not fall down into the center of the narrower waist of the worn roller. You might never know the chain is shot without inspecting every link.

l. Inverted ConneX link

If you have a Wippermann chain and have the ConneX master link upside down (described in §iv-11b), the taller link edge will ride up on the spacers between the smallest cogs, lift the rollers off the cog, and cause the chain to skip. Remove, invert, and reinstall the ConneX master link as described in §iv-11b.

TRANSMISSION

FRONT AND REAR DERAILLEURS, CABLES, AND SHIFTERS

Most Americans want to be somewhere else, but when they get there, they want to go home.

—Henry Ford

TOOLS

2mm, 3mm, 4mm, 5mm, and 6mm hex keys

Torx T25 key

flat-head and Phillips screwdrivers, small and medium

pliers

indexed-housing cutter

cable cutter

grease

chain lubricant

rubbing alcohol

There is nothing like having the derailleurs working smoothly, predictably, and quietly under all conditions. Knowing that you can shift whenever you need to inspires confidence when riding on difficult single-track sections of trail. It is also a lot more pleasant to ride through beautiful terrain without the grinding and clunking noises of an out-of-whack derailleur.

Improperly adjusted rear derailleurs are a common problem, which is surprising because derailleur adjustments are easy provided the equipment is clean and in good working order. With a few simple tweaks of the limit screws and the cable tension, you're on your way. Once you see how easy it is to keep the derailleurs in tune, you will be able to keep yours in adjustment all the time.

THE REAR DERAILLEUR

The rear derailleur is one of the more complex parts on a bike (Fig. 5.1). It moves the chain from one rear cog to another, and it also takes up chain slack when the bike bounces or the front derailleur is shifted.

The rear derailleur bolts to a hanger on the rear dropout (Fig. 5.2). Two jockey wheels (pulley wheels) hold the chain tight and help guide the chain as the derailleur shifts. Depending on the model, a rear derailleur has one or two springs in the lower, or both upper and lower, knuckles that pull the jockey wheels tightly against the chain, creating a desirable amount of chain tension.

Except on Shimano's reverse-action Low Normal or (older) Rapid Rise derailleurs, increasing the tension on the rear-derailleur cable moves the derailleur inward toward the larger cogs. When the cable tension is released, a return spring between the derailleur's two parallelogram plates pulls the chain back toward the smallest cogs. By connecting the return spring to the other pair of corners of the rear derailleur's parallelogram linkage, Low Normal and Rapid Rise derailleurs work in exactly the opposite fashion. In fact, Low Normal refers to exactly this phenomenon—that

5.1 Rear derailleur, exploded view

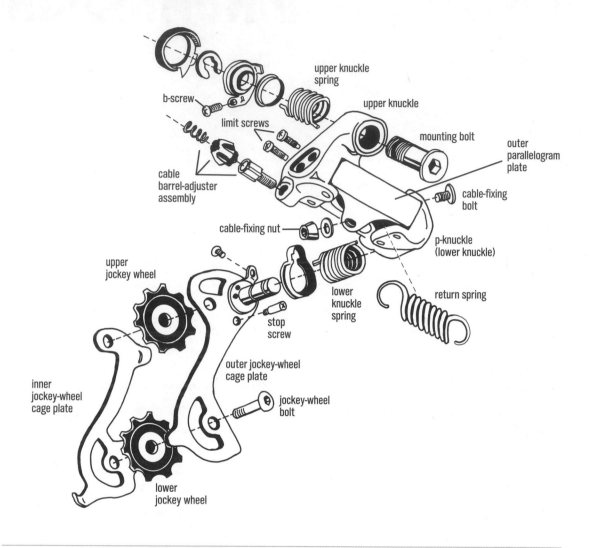

is, the derailleur's "normal" position, when the cable tension is removed, is in the low-gear position (large cog) rather than in the high-gear position found in traditional rear derailleurs. (Just to clarify some Shimano terminology, "Top Normal" refers to a standard rear derailleur that moves to the smallest cog [top gear] when there is no cable tension. As I said, "Low Normal" refers to a rear derailleur that moves to the largest cog [low gear] when there is no cable tension. And "Shadow" refers to a Shimano low-profile rear derailleur whose mounting bolt is very short so that the

5.2 Right rear dropout details

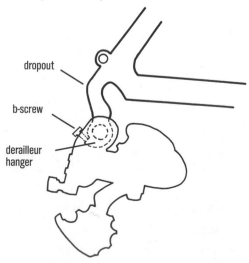

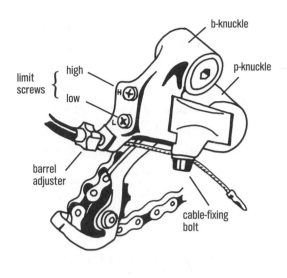

limit screws — high — low

b-knuckle

p-knuckle

barrel adjuster

cable-fixing bolt

derailleur doesn't stick out very far from the bike where it can catch on rocks and branches.)

The chain length, the balance between the springs in the upper and lower knuckle pivots, and the b-screw (Fig. 5.2) adjustment determine how closely the derailleur tracks the cogs during its lateral movement and how well it keeps the chain from bouncing off the front chainrings when the bike hits bumps. The two limit screws on the rear derailleur (Fig. 5.3) prevent the derailleur from moving the chain too far to the inside (into the spokes) or to the outside (into the dropout). In addition to limit screws, most rear derailleurs have a cable-tensioning barrel adjuster located at the back of the derailleur, where the cable enters it (Fig. 5.3). This barrel adjuster can be used to fine-tune the shifting adjustment to land the chain precisely on each cog with each click of the shifter. Rear derailleurs also often have a tensioning screw (the b-screw) at the back of the derailleur (Fig. 5.2) that rotates it around its mounting point to control the space between the bottom of the cogs and the upper jockey wheel.

INSTALLING THE REAR DERAILLEUR

 LEVEL 1

1. **Grease the derailleur's mounting bolt threads.**
2. **Line up the derailleur for mounting.** Rotate the derailleur back (counterclockwise) so that the b-screw (shown in Fig. 5.1) on the upper knuckle ends up behind the flat on the back of the derailleur hanger on the right rear dropout (Fig. 5.2). Some inexpensive derailleurs do not have a b-screw; instead, they just have a nonadjustable tab extending inward where the b-screw would be. Make sure this tab is behind the flat on the derailleur hanger.
3. **Tighten the mounting bolt until the derailleur is snug against the hanger.** Torque is 8–10 N-m.

NOTE: *Shimano Saint rear derailleurs do not mount to the dropout derailleur hanger. Rather, they mount onto the axle of the rear hub. To install one, install the rear wheel into the dropouts and push the axle through it from the nondrive side. Making sure the axle is seated fully into the dropouts, install the rear derailleur onto the greased, threaded, drive-side end of the axle; there is a hub-axle fixing nut built into its upper knuckle. Make sure that the derailleur's end stopper is in the dropout slot adjacent to the hub axle and that the b-screw is behind the dropout-hanger tab (same as shown in Fig. 5.2). Tighten the hub axle with a 6mm hex key from the nondrive side.*

There is one additional adjustment for a Shimano Saint derailleur. After performing all of the standard rear-derailleur adjustments described in steps 4 through 7, come back to this section. With a 2mm hex key, turn the bump stopper screw on the front of the upper knuckle (it is on the opposite side of the knuckle from the b-screw) to stop the derailleur so that the lower pivot cannot hit the chainstay. Pull up on the lower jockey wheel to swing the derailleur up as high as it will go, and turn the bump stopper screw to stop it when the lower derailleur-pivot body is 5–10mm below the chainstay.

4. **Route the chain through the jockey wheels and connect it.** Make sure that it is the correct length (see §iv-8 to §iv-11).

5. **Install the cables and housings** (see §v-7 to §v-15).

6. **Pull the cable tight with a pair of pliers, and tighten the cable anchor bolt.** This will require either a 5mm hex key, a Torx T25, or an 8mm box wrench.

7. **Follow the adjustment procedure described in the next section.**

v-2
ADJUSTING THE REAR DERAILLEUR AND RIGHT-HAND SHIFTER

Perform all of the following derailleur adjustments with the bike held in a stand or hung from the ceiling. That way, you can turn the crank and shift gears while you put the derailleur through its paces. After adjusting the derailleur off the ground, test the shifting while riding. Derailleurs often perform differently under load than in a bike stand.

Before starting, lubricate or replace the chain (see Chapter 4) so that the whole drivetrain runs smoothly.

a. Limit-screw adjustments

The first, and most important, rear-derailleur adjustment is setting the limit screws. Properly set, these screws (Fig. 5.3) should make certain that you will not ruin the frame, rear wheel, or derailleur by shifting into the spokes or by jamming the chain between the dropout and the smallest cog. It is never pleasant to see your expensive equipment turned into shredded metal. All it takes to turn these limit screws is a small screwdriver. Remember, it's "lefty loosey, righty tighty" for turning these screws.

b. High-gear limit-screw adjustment

This screw limits the outward movement of the rear derailleur. You will tighten or loosen this screw until the derailleur shifts the chain to the smallest cog quickly but does not overshift.

How do you determine which limit screw works on the high gear? Often, it will be labeled "H," and it is usually the upper of the two screws (Fig. 5.3). If you are not certain, just try both screws. Whichever screw, when tightened, moves the derailleur inward when the chain is on the smallest cog is the one you are looking for. On most derailleurs, you can also see which screw to adjust by looking in between the derailleur's parallelogram side plates. You will see one tab on the back end of each plate. Each tab is designed to hit a limit screw at one end of the movement. Shift into the highest gear and notice which screw is touching one of the tabs; that is the high-gear limit screw. The procedure for the limit-screw adjustment is as follows:

1. **Shift the chain to the large front chainring.**
2. **Shift to the smallest rear cog** (Fig. 5.4). Do this gently in case it overshifts into the dropout.
3. **If there is hesitation dropping to the small cog, adjust the cable tension.** Don't touch the limit screws yet.

(a) With a traditional rear derailleur, loosen the cable a little to see if it is stopping the derailleur from moving out far enough. Do this by turning the barrel adjuster on the derailleur or shift lever clockwise (when viewed from the end of the barrel adjuster, as if it were a screw viewed from the top) or by loosening the cable anchor bolt, letting out some slack in the cable, and retightening the bolt.

(b) With a Low Normal or Rapid Rise rear derailleur, you are pulling cable (rather than releasing cable), and because you can keep

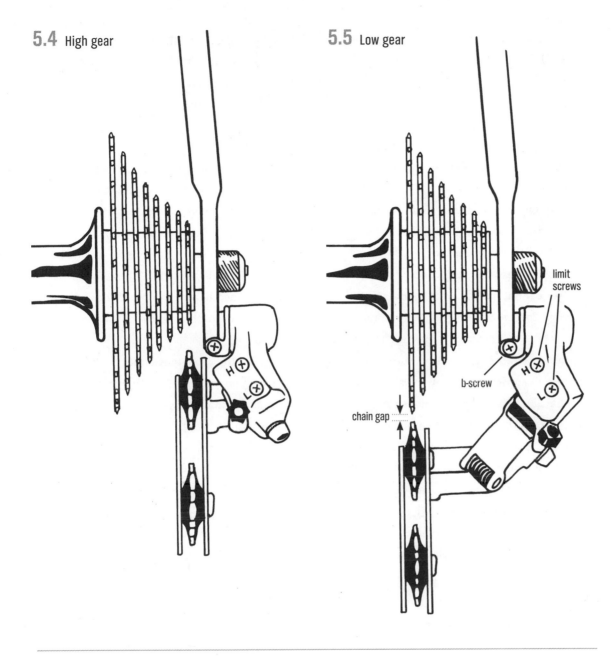

pulling more, if the chain won't drop to the small cog, the limit screw is stopping it, so go to step 4.

4. **If the chain still won't drop without hesitation to the smallest cog, loosen the high-gear limit screw.** Loosen it one-quarter turn at a time, continuously repeating the shift, until the chain reliably drops quickly and easily.

5. **If the derailleur goes past the smallest cog, tighten the high-gear limit screw.** Tighten it one-quarter turn and redo the shift. Repeat

until the derailleur shifts the chain quickly and easily into the highest gear without throwing the chain into the dropout.

c. Low-gear limit-screw adjustment

This screw stops the inward movement of the rear derailleur, preventing it from going into the spokes. This screw is usually labeled "L," and it is usually the bottom screw (Fig. 5.3). You can check which one it is by shifting to the largest cog, maintaining pressure on the shifter, and turning the screw to see if it changes the position of the derailleur.

1. **Shift the chain to the inner chainring on the front.**

2. **Shift the rear derailleur to the largest cog** (Fig. 5.5). Do it gently in case the limit screw does not stop the derailleur from going into the spokes.

3. **Tighten the low-gear limit screw if the derailleur touches the spokes or shoves the chain over the largest cog.**

4. **Loosen the low-gear limit screw if the derailleur cannot push the chain onto the largest cog.** Loosen it one-quarter turn until the chain shifts easily up to the cog but does not brush the spokes. On a Low Normal or Rapid Rise rear derailleur, you must first check that the cable tension is not so high that it prevents the chain from getting to the large cog. Loosen the cable by turning the barrel adjuster on the derailleur or shift lever clockwise (when viewed from the end of the barrel adjuster, as if it were a screw viewed from the top), or by loosening the cable anchor bolt, letting out some slack in the cable, and retightening the bolt.

d. Cable-tension adjustment: Indexed rear shifters

With an indexed shifting system (one that "clicks" into each gear), the cable tension determines whether the derailleur moves to the proper gear with each click.

1. **With the chain on the large chainring in the front, shift the rear derailleur to the smallest rear cog.** Keep clicking the shifter until you are sure it will not let any more cable out (or it will not pull any more cable if you have a Low Normal or Rapid Rise rear derailleur).

2. **Shift one click in the other direction.** This should move the chain smoothly to the second cog.

3. **Adjust the cable tension if the chain climbs slowly or not at all to the second cog.** On a traditional rear derailleur, increase the tension in the cable by turning either the derailleur-cable barrel adjuster (Fig. 5.3) or the shifter barrel adjuster (Fig. 5.6) counterclockwise (when viewed from the end of the barrel adjuster, where the cable housing inserts into it, as if it were a screw viewed from the top). Turn the opposite way for a Low Normal or Rapid Rise derailleur.

5.6 Shifter barrel adjuster for cable tension

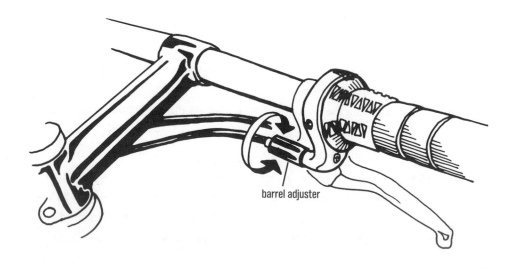

barrel adjuster

If you run out of barrel-adjustment range and the cable is still not tight enough, retighten both adjusters clockwise, to one turn from where they stop, loosen the cable anchor bolt, and pull some of the slack out of the cable. Tighten the anchor bolt and repeat the adjustment. If the derailleur has no barrel adjuster, use the barrel adjuster on the shifter.

4. **Adjust the cable tension if the chain overshifts the second cog.** On standard derailleurs, decrease the cable tension by turning one of the barrel adjusters clockwise. With a Low Normal or Rapid Rise derailleur, increase the tension by turning one of the barrel adjusters counterclockwise. Again, always determine clockwise and counterclockwise from the position of the end of the barrel adjuster where the cable housing inserts into it.

5. **With the chain on the middle chainring in the front (or on either chainring of a double crank), shift the rear derailleur to one of the middle rear cogs.**

6. **Shift the rear derailleur back and forth a few cogs.** Check for precise and quick movement of the chain from cog to cog. Fine-tune the shifting by making small adjustments to the cable-tensioning barrel adjuster on the shifter or rear derailleur.

7. **With the chain on the large chainring in the front, shift the rear derailleur to the largest rear cog.** Shift up and down one click in the rear, again checking for symmetry and precision of chain movement in either direction between the two largest cogs. Fine-tune the barrel adjuster until you get it just right.

8. **Go back through the gears.** On a bike with a triple crank and the chain in the middle chainring in front, the rear derailleur should shift smoothly back and forth across all the cogs. With the chain on the big chainring of either a triple or a double crank, the rear derailleur should shift easily on all but perhaps the largest one or two cogs in the rear. With the chain on the inner chainring, the rear derailleur should shift easily on all but perhaps the two smallest cogs.

9. **Skip to step f.**

NOTE: *If the shifter barrel adjuster does not hold its adjustment, derailleur performance will steadily worsen as you ride. This problem has occurred in early XTR shifters, which have no springs or notches to hold the adjuster in place, as most barrel adjusters have. If you have this problem, there are a couple of things you can do besides getting a new shifter. One is to put Finish Line Ti-Prep on the threads to create a bit more friction; I have found this to be a temporary fix only. Applying Loctite or scoring the threads crosswise may also help, although I have not tried either method. One foolproof solution, though a bit of a hassle, is to keep the shifter barrel adjuster turned all the way in and make all cable-tension adjustments with the barrel adjuster on the rear derailleur. This fix will not work with barrel-adjuster-free rear derailleurs, though.*

ANOTHER NOTE: *If the cable tension is okay in the midsized cogs, too high in the large cogs, and too low in the small cogs (or the opposite with a Low Normal or Rapid Rise rear derailleur), then the rear derailleur is moving more than one cog spacing with each click of the shifter. The problem could be that you are using an 8-speed shifter with a 9-speed cogset or another mismatched combination.*

If the shifter and cogs are both for the same number of gears, the problem could be that some of the spacers between cogs are too thin, making the entire stack of cogs narrower than it should be. This is a rare, albeit not unprecedented, situation when you are using components from a single manufacturer that have all been designed to work together, but it is not uncommon when you are mixing components from different manufacturers.

You can remedy this spacing problem without going out and buying a new cogset, however. Remove the cassette lockring (see §vi-20), and pull apart those cogs that are separable from each other. Trace around one of the spacers on a piece of aluminum you have cut from a beer or pop can. Follow the tracing with a box-cutter knife or similar implement in order to cut out a spacer shim. Fine-tune its shape until the shim will slip over the freehub body. Reassemble the cogset onto the freehub, placing the shim between a spacer and a cog where it seems that the shifting starts to get thrown off. If this improves shifting but does not completely fix the problem, try adding another beer-can shim. A beer-can shim is approximately 0.1mm thick, and I have seen 0.3mm variation between the total stack height of an SRAM and a Shimano 11–34 9-speed cogset, for example. Experiment with various positions for the shim(s) within the cogset until you have optimized your shifting performance.

e. Cable-tension adjustment: Nonindexed rear shifters

If your bike does not have indexed shifting, adjustment is complete after you remove the slack in the cable. With proper cable tension, when the chain is on the smallest cog, the derailleur should move as soon as the shift lever does. If there is free play in the lever, tighten the cable by turning the cable barrel adjuster on the derailleur or shifter counterclockwise. If the rear derailleur and shifter don't have barrel adjusters, loosen the cable anchor bolt, pull some slack out of the cable with pliers, and retighten the clamp bolt.

In most cases, you can stop after adjusting the limit screws and cable tension, but there is more you can do if you are a stickler for optimum performance. If you are still having shifting trouble, proceed to at least step f, and maybe to step g and its following note as well. And if you have a problem with the chain bouncing off, attend to step g.

f. Chain gap: The b-screw adjustment

You can get a bit more shifting precision by adjusting the small screw (b-screw—see Fig. 5.2) that changes the derailleur's position against the derailleur-hanger tab on the right rear dropout. Viewing from behind with the chain on the inner chainring and largest cog (Fig. 5.5), adjust the screw so that the upper jockey wheel is close to the cog but not pinching the chain against the cog. Repeat on the smallest cog (Fig. 5.4). You'll know that you've moved the jockey wheel in too closely when it starts making noise.

SRAM (maker of Grip Shift) suggests setting the b-screw on its early ESP derailleurs with the chain on the middle chainring and largest cog. Viewing from the drive side, turn the screw so that the length of chain across the "chain gap" (from where the chain leaves the bottom of the cog to its first contact at the top of the upper jockey wheel) is 1 to 1¼ links (Fig. 5.7), where one link is a complete male-female link pair (Fig. 4.7). SRAM derailleurs from 2000 and later specify a 6mm vertical distance from the top of the upper jockey wheel to the bottom of the large cog (the chain

5.7 Chain-gap adjustment of an early SRAM derailleur

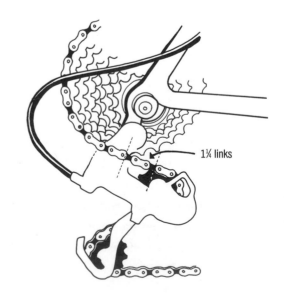

1¼ links

gap depicted in Fig. 5.5), when in the small chainring–large cog combination.

g. Lower-knuckle pivot-spring tension adjustment

The lower pivot spring twists the derailleur forward and puts pressure on the chain through the jockey wheels. By increasing the lower-knuckle p-spring tension, you can bring the upper jockey wheel closer to the cogs and increase tension in the lower run of the chain. This procedure will keep the chain from bouncing as much over rough terrain. It does put more drag (i.e., friction) on the chain, so I wouldn't do it on a cross-country bike unless I had to. But increasing the p-spring tension can be well worth doing for downhill racing and other gravity-driven riding.

This is definitely a complex adjustment requiring disassembly of the derailleur pivot, so be sure it is justified. Also, if you were thinking about replacing the steel pivot bolt with a lightweight aluminum one, now is the time to do it.

On post-1997 Shimano XT, LX, and STX rear derailleurs, and a year or two later with other models, there is a setscrew on the side of the lower pivot (Fig. 5.8) that makes it possible to disassemble the pivot without disconnecting the derailleur from the cable and the chain. Nevertheless, I recommend removing the derailleur first. You would have to unscrew the mounting bolt anyway, and the derailleur will get so twisted around that it will be hard to tell which way is up with the cable and chain connected. You could end up turning the jockey cage in the wrong direction and deforming the spring so that it would not fit back in the knuckle.

The setscrew on the lower pivot engages a groove in the pivot shaft to keep it from pulling apart. Remove the screw with a 2mm hex key (Fig. 5.8), and pull the jockey cage away from the spring. Put the spring in the next spring hole to increase its tension (Fig. 5.9), push the pivot assembly back together, and replace the setscrew. Shimano derailleurs come with the p-spring in the low-tension hole.

Increasing p-spring tension on older Shimano derailleurs is more complicated because there is no setscrew on the lower-knuckle housing. After

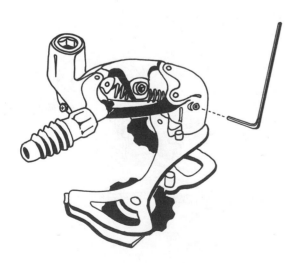

5.8 Removing the p-knuckle screw with a 2mm hex key

5.9 Increasing the p-spring tension by putting the spring end in a different hole

TRANSMISSION

5.10 Removing the stopscrew that prevents the jockey cage from twisting all the way around

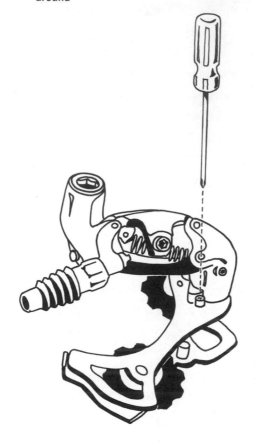

5.11 Unscrewing the pivot bolt with a 5mm hex key to pull the derailleur cage off the p-spring

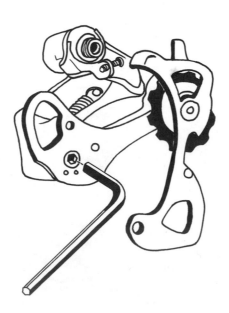

removing the derailleur from the bike, remove the tall stopscrew that prevents the jockey cage from twisting all the way around (Fig. 5.10). Remove the upper jockey wheel, and unscrew the pivot bolt from the back with a 5mm hex key (Fig. 5.11). Pull the derailleur cage off the end of the spring, and move the end of the spring into the other spring hole. Wind the jockey-wheel cage back around, screw it all back together with the pivot bolt, and replace the stopscrew.

NOTE: *If you cannot get the rear derailleur to shift well, if it makes noise in even mild cross-gears no matter what you do, or if it throws the chain off despite your best efforts, refer to the chainline discussion in the troubleshooting section at the end of this chapter after ensuring that neither the derailleur nor the derailleur hanger on the frame dropout is bent.*

THE FRONT DERAILLEUR

The front derailleur moves the chain between the chainrings. The working parts consist of a cage to enclose the chain, a linkage, and an arm attached to the shifter cable. The front derailleur is attached to the frame, usually by a clamp surrounding the seat tube (Fig. 5.12). Some frames do not have room for a front-derailleur band

5.12 Down-swing front derailleur

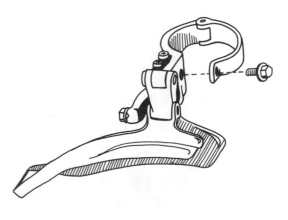

clamp, either because there are rear suspension parts in the way, the seat tube is nonstandard in shape or angle, or the chainstays attach where the front derailleur clamp would need to be. Front derailleur models for bikes like this bolt directly into threaded holes in the side of the swingarm (rear-suspension member) or the seat tube (Figs. 5.13–14), or they attach to the face of the bottom-bracket shell. Bike manufacturers may also select bottom-bracket-mounted front derailleurs for standard-design bikes because the assembly and adjustment of them on the bikes in the factory assembly line are faster. Shimano bottom-bracket-mounted front derailleurs are called "E-type," and some mount both to the face of the bottom bracket and to a braze-on boss (or band clamp adapter) on the seat tube (Fig. 5.15).

Standard seat-tube band clamps also vary. Besides needing to be the correct diameter for the seat tube (or to be supplied with shims to make them fit smaller seat tubes), these band clamps can also have a high clamp or a low clamp relative to the derailleur mechanism.

Front derailleurs vary in pivot geometry as well. A "top-swing" front derailleur has a band clamp or bolt-on plate that is lower than the height of the top of the front derailleur's cage, and the derailleur's activation linkage and pivots are behind the cage. Figure 5.15 shows a bolt-on E-type top-swing front derailleur, whereas Figures 5.33A–B depict a top-swing clamp-type derailleur from the back. A traditional or "down-swing" front derailleur has a band clamp or bolt-on mounting plate well above the cage, and the large outer linkage plate and cage pivot are above the cage (Figs. 5.12 and 5.17–18). Which style to choose depends largely on the bike's frame design, as often a pivot or shock mount on the frame will preclude the use of one clamp style or another.

5.13 SRAM direct-mount top-pull top-swing front derailleur

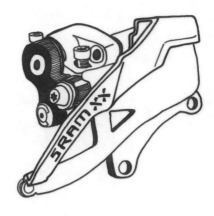

5.14 Shimano direct-mount down-swing front derailleur

5.15 XTR bottom-bracket-mount (E-type) top-swing front derailleur and band-clamp adapter (bottom left)

TRANSMISSION

The direction that the cable pulls also distinguishes front derailleurs from each other. A "bottom-pull" front derailleur requires the cable to come from below, generally by wrapping underneath the bottom-bracket shell. A "top-pull" front derailleur is activated by a cable pulling on it from above, generally after it runs along the top tube and the cable housing terminates at a cable stop on the back of the seat tube. Many modern front derailleurs have a dual cable-pull option; the cable can come from below or above—either straight to the cable anchor bolt from above or over the top of a rocker-arm assembly, wrapping down again to attach at the bolt (see Figs. 5.33A–B).

v-3
INSTALLING THE FRONT DERAILLEUR: BAND TYPE

⚙ LEVEL 1

1. **Clamp the front derailleur around the seat tube.** Make sure that you have either the right-size band clamp for your seat tube or the correct shims in place under it to make it fit the seat tube. Some front derailleurs have a size-specific band-clamp diameter matching that of the seat tube, but modern Shimano and older SRAM front derailleurs work on more than one seat-tube diameter. They have a band clamp for a 35mm (1⅜-inch) diameter seat tube, but they come with shims for either 31.8mm (1¼-inch) or 28.6mm (1⅛-inch) seat tubes. In the case of Shimano front derailleurs, C-shaped aluminum shims are held in place by C-shaped plastic brackets that clip within the circle of the front-derailleur band clamp.

2. **Adjust the height and rotation as described in §v-5a.**

3. **Tighten the clamp bolt** (Fig. 5.12).

v-4
INSTALLING THE FRONT DERAILLEUR: DIRECT MOUNT AND BOTTOM-BRACKET MOUNT

⚙ ⚙ LEVEL 2

a. Direct mount

Full-suspension bikes often need special front-derailleur mounting, because a clamp-on front derailleur might interfere with the rear swingarm as it moves through its travel or because the seat tube is not round. One solution is to bolt the front derailleur directly to either the seat tube or the swingarm (Figs. 5.13–14); a mounting bracket with a couple of bolt holes or a tongue-and-groove arrangement and a single bolt will be welded onto or machined into the seat tube or the front of the swingarm (the moving chainstay on a rear-suspension bike). In the case of the swingarm mount, the front derailleur will move forward and back over the chainring as the suspension moves.

Direct-mount front derailleurs that bolt straight to the frame are pretty simple to mount (just bolt them on!), but they are generally chainring-size-specific as well as frame-specific. For instance, SRAM XX direct-mount front derailleurs are marked "39" or "42," depending on whether they are for the 26–39 or 28–42 chainring set, but they also come in S1, S2, and S3 configurations depending on the mounting system on the frame, and there is a top-pull and a bottom-pull model in each configuration as well. The derailleur for a Specialized Epic with a 28–42 crankset, for example, will be stamped "S1 42" between the mounting holes on the derailleur back plate, and it will be bottom-pull.

b. Bottom-bracket mount

Shimano E-type (i.e., bottom-bracket face-mounting type) front derailleurs (Fig. 5.15) are direct-mount front derailleurs that mount to a plate that fits between the bottom-bracket cup and the bottom-bracket shell. They are more complicated to mount than simply bolting the derailleur to threaded holes in the frame. To install one, do the following:

1. **Remove the bottom bracket** (see §viii-12 and §viii-14).

2. **Slip the (E-type) derailleur bracket over the right-hand bottom-bracket cup.** Start the cup into the bottom-bracket shell a few threads.

3. **Attach the bracket to the seat tube.** With less expensive models, place the bracket's C-shaped stabilizer around the seat tube. This fixes the rotational adjustment. With a high-end E-type front derailleur (Fig. 5.15), loosely screw the mounting bolt into the frame's special braze-on boss designed for it. If the frame does not have the braze-on boss, a separate seat-tube band clamp with a threaded hole in the side is used (see Fig. 5.15). The circular band will need to be bent to fit if the frame has an oval-shaped seat tube.

4. **Tighten the right-hand bottom-bracket cup against the bottom-bracket face.**

5. **If applicable, tighten the mounting bolt into the braze-on boss (or band-clamp hole).**

6. **Complete the bottom-bracket installation** (see §viii-7 to §viii-11).

NOTE: *There are no (or limited) height and rotational adjustments on these derailleurs, and they must be used with the chainring size for which they were intended. They can be turned only slightly to line up better with the chain.*

Some E-type front derailleurs have two mounting-bolt holes to allow for two possible outer chainring sizes. The derailleur's rotational adjustment can be fine-tuned without the braze-on boss, because the band clamp can be twisted around the seat tube a few degrees.

ADJUSTING THE FRONT DERAILLEUR AND LEFT-HAND SHIFTER

a. Position adjustments

With a seat-tube-clamp front derailleur, the position is adjusted with a 5mm hex key, a Torx T25, or an 8mm box wrench on the band-clamp bolt. Direct-mount and Shimano E-type front derailleurs have little or no vertical or rotational (twist about the seat tube) adjustments.

1. **Position the height of the front derailleur.** Set the outer cage about 1–2mm (1/16–1/8 inch) above the highest point of the outer chainring (Fig. 5.16). Out of the box, new Shimano front derailleurs have a piece of clear tape on the cage illustrating the proper gap, with teeth drawn onto it to line up with the chainring teeth. They also have a plastic block called a "Pro-set alignment block" installed that forces the derailleur out to the high-gear

5.16 Proper clearance

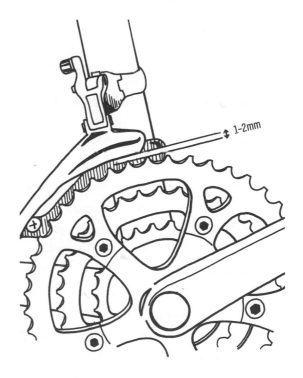

1–2mm

5.17–5.18 Proper cage alignment

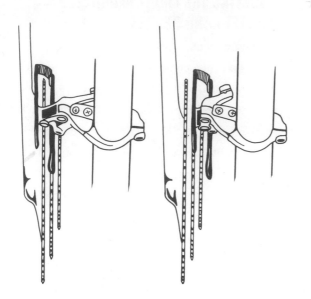

5.19 Limit screws

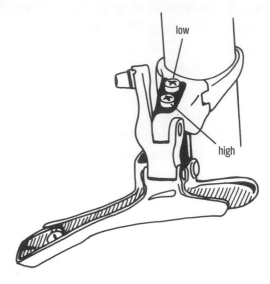

position. Leave that block in place for this step, and remove it for the second part of step 2 (and from then on!).

2. **Position the rotation of the front derailleur about the seat tube.** The outer plate of the derailleur cage should be parallel to the chainrings (or to the chain in the lowest and highest gears) when viewed from above. Check this by shifting to the big chainring and smallest cog and sighting from the top (Fig. 5.17). Most derailleurs need the outer face of the cage to be exactly parallel to the chainring; check this by measuring the space between the cage and the inner side of the crankarm as it passes by. The cage of some derailleurs flares wider at the tail, and the cage should be parallel to the chain in the lowest and highest gears. The outer tail of the derailleur cage on these models needs to be out a bit from parallel to the plane of the frame in order to parallel the chain. Similarly, when on the inner chainring (Fig. 5.18) and largest cog, the inner-cage plate should par-

allel the chain, making the tail a bit in from parallel with the plane of the frame.

b. Limit-screw adjustments

The front derailleur has two limit screws that stop the derailleur from throwing the chain to the inside or outside of the chainrings. These are usually labeled "L" for low gear (small chainring) and "H" for high gear (large chainring) (Fig. 5.19). On most derailleurs, the low-gear screw is closer to the frame; however, Shimano XTR differential-plate derailleurs, among others, have the limit-screw positions reversed, but their adjustment is the same.

If in doubt, you can determine which limit screw controls which function by the same trial-and-error method outlined for the rear derailleur. Shift the chain to the inner ring, and then tighten one of the limit screws. If tightening that screw moves the front derailleur outward, then it is the low-gear limit screw. If turning that screw does not move the front derailleur, then the other screw is the low-gear limit screw.

c. Low-gear limit-screw adjustment

1. **Shift back and forth between the middle and inner chainrings.**

2. **Tighten the low-gear limit screw if the chain drops off the little ring to the inside.** Tighten it (clockwise) one-quarter turn and try shifting again.

3. **If the chain does not drop easily onto the inner chainring, loosen the low-gear limit screw.** Loosen it (counterclockwise) one-quarter turn and repeat the shift. Make sure that overly high cable tension is not preventing the derailleur from reaching the inner limit screw; if it is, back off on the cable tension by turning the shifter barrel adjuster clockwise.

d. High-gear limit-screw adjustment

1. **Shift the chain back and forth between the middle and outer chainring.**

2. **Tighten the high-gear limit screw if the chain jumps over the big chainring.** Tighten it (clockwise) one-quarter turn and repeat the shift.

3. **If the chain is sluggish going up to the big chainring or does not go up at all, loosen the high-gear limit screw.** Loosen it (counterclockwise) one-quarter turn and try the shift again.

e. Cable-tension adjustment

1. **With the chain on the inner chainring, remove any excess cable slack.** Turn the barrel adjuster on the shifter (as shown in Fig. 5.6, except on the left shifter) counterclockwise (again, determine rotation direction by looking at the adjuster from the end from which the cable housing emerges, as if you were looking at the top of a bolt). (Or tighten the cable without the barrel adjuster: Loosen the cable anchor bolt, pull the cable tight with pliers, and tighten the bolt.)

2. **Check that the cable is loose enough.** It should allow the chain to shift smoothly and repeatedly from the middle to the inner chainring.

3. **Check that the cable is tight enough.** The derailleur should start to move as soon as you move the shifter.

NOTE: *This tension adjustment should work for indexed as well as friction shifters. With indexed front shifting, you may want to fine-tune the barrel adjuster to avoid noise from the chain dragging on the derailleur in some cross-gears or to get more precise shifting.*

ANOTHER NOTE: *Some front derailleurs have a cam screw at the end of the spring to adjust spring tension. For quicker shifting to the smaller rings, increase the spring tension by turning the screw clockwise.*

NOTE ON SHIFTING TROUBLE: *If you cannot get the front derailleur to shift well, it rubs in cross-gears no matter what you do, or it throws the chain off despite your best efforts, refer to the chainline discussion in the troubleshooting section at the end of this chapter.*

v-6
REPLACING AND LUBRICATING SHIFT CABLES AND HOUSINGS

 LEVEL 2

For derailleurs to function properly, they must be connected to clean, smooth-running cables (also called "inner wires"). Because of all the muck that you encounter while riding a mountain bike, you need to regularly replace those cables. As with replacing a chain, replacing cables is a maintenance operation, not a repair operation. Do not wait until cables break to replace them. Replace any cables that have broken strands, kinks, or fraying between the shifter and the derailleur. Also replace housings (also called "outer wires") if they are bent, mashed, or just plain gritty, or if the color clashes with your bike (this is really important).

v-7
BUYING CABLES

1. **Buy new cables and housing with at least as much length as the ones you are replacing.**

2. **Make sure that the cables and housing are for indexed systems.** These cables will stretch minimally, and the housings will not compress in length. Under an external plastic sheath, indexed housing is not made of steel coil as brake housings are; it is made of parallel (coaxial) steel strands of thin wire. If you look at the end, you will see numerous wire ends sticking out surrounding a central Teflon tube (make sure it has this Teflon liner, too) (Fig. 5.20). Gore-Tex cable is discussed in §v-17.

3. **Buy cable crimp caps and tubular cable-housing end ferrules** (Fig. 5.20). Caps prevent cable fraying and ferrules prevent housing from kinking at the cable stops, shifters, and rear derailleur. You might also consider getting ferrules that have a long nose that sticks out through the slot in a cable stop on the frame. A tubular rubber dust shield comes with them and slips onto the long nose from the opposite side of the cable stop to prevent entry of dirt and water into the housing. While you're at it, buying rubber cable donuts (Fig. 5.35) or, better yet, sheathing for bare-cable runs may be worthwhile for protecting your bike's paint job.

v-8
CUTTING THE HOUSING TO LENGTH

1. **Use a special cable-housing cutter.** Park, Shimano, Pedro's, and Wrench Force (see §i-2) make these cutters. Standard side cutters for cutting wire will not cut index-shift housing, and they won't do a good job on cables, either.

5.20 Cable-housing types and end caps

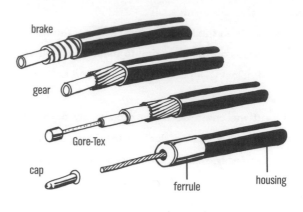

brake
gear
Gore-Tex
cap
ferrule
housing

5.21–5.22 Correct housing length

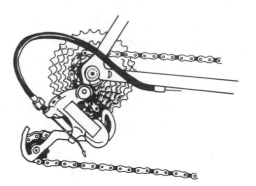

2. **Cut the housing to length.** Cut to the same lengths as your old ones if you liked their function; otherwise, cut housing so that the housing sections curve smoothly from cable stop to cable stop and so that turning the

handlebar does not pull or kink them. Allow for enough length at the rear derailleur so that the derailleur can freely swing back (Fig. 5.21) and forth (Fig. 5.22 for chainstay cable; Fig. 5.31 for seatstay cable). Current SRAM and old Sachs DiRT rear derailleurs (SRAM now owns Sachs) use a short housing section without a cable loop (the bare cable runs over a pulley), and they are particularly sensitive to housing length. The housing should curve gently into its receptacle without being so short that it limits derailleur movement or so long that it has a sharp bend; the latter is particularly important to watch for with a seatstay cable as the derailleur swings backward. Make sure your cut is square.

3. With a sharp tool such as an awl, open each Teflon sleeve end that has been smashed shut by the cutter.

4. Place a ferrule (Fig. 5.20) over each housing end.

v-9
REPLACING CABLE IN SRAM TRIGGER LEVERS, OLDER SHIMANO RAPIDFIRE LEVERS, OR THUMB SHIFTERS

1. Disconnect the cable at the derailleur, and clip off the end cap.

2. Shift to the lever setting that lets the most cable out. On most systems, this will be the highest-gear position for the rear shift lever (small cog) and the lowest for the front (small chainring). On Low Normal or Rapid Rise systems, however, this will be the low-gear position front and rear.

3. Push out the old cable and recycle it. You may need to uncover the cable head first. On some SRAM trigger levers, open the rubber cable-change flap. On many recent SRAM trigger levers, you must remove the cover

5.23 Prying the cable head from its pocket on a SRAM XX trigger lever

5.24 Rapidfire shifter

5.25 Thumb shifter

over the cable-release lever (upper lever); this may require a Torx wrench. Once the cover is off, push on the cable as you pry the cable head outward with a pick or knife tip from its pocket under the flat spring coil (Fig. 5.23). On many Shimano Rapidfire levers, unscrew the large plastic plug that covers the cable-access hole if one is present.

4. **Slide in the new cable.** Push the cable into the recessed hole in which the cable head seats and out through the barrel adjuster (Figs. 5.23–25). Replace the lever cover if you removed it.

5. **Guide the cable through each housing segment and cable stop.** Slotted cable stops on a frame allow you to slip the cable and housing in and out from the side. If present, replace the plastic plug or rubber flap over the cable-access hole in the shifter.

---
v-10
REPLACING SHIFT CABLE IN SHIMANO "DUAL CONTROL" INTEGRATED SHIFTER/ HYDRAULIC DISC-BRAKE LEVERS

These models are 2003 (and later) XTR, 2004 (and later) XT, and 2005 (and later) LX, and any one may be used with the Saint group. Note that cable change is different (and more complicated) for the front shifter than for the rear one.

When moved laterally downward with the palm side of the fingertips, the brake lever on these units (Fig. 5.26) pulls shift cable. When the brake lever is moved laterally upward with the back (fingernail) side of the fingertips, it releases shift cable. (Of course, when the brake lever is pulled straight back toward the handlebar, it pushes on the hydraulic fluid to apply the disc brakes.)

a. Either lever

1. **Disconnect the cable at the derailleur, and clip off the end cap.**

2. **Shift to release the maximum amount of cable.** Flip the underside of the brake lever or the auxiliary thumb-release lever repeatedly until the indicator needle reaches the "L" position on the gear-indicator window.

b. Rear (right) lever

1. **Remove the large plastic Phillips screw plug.** It's on the opposite side of the lever body from the barrel adjuster.

2. **Push the cable out.** The end should pop right out of the hole the screw plug was in. You may need to coax it a bit with a paper clip or thin knife to guide it out of the hole while you push the cable.

3. **Slide the new cable straight in.** Go through the unplugged hole in the cover and straight out through the barrel adjuster.

5.26 Replacing the cable in a left Shimano XT Dual Control shifter/hydraulic brake lever

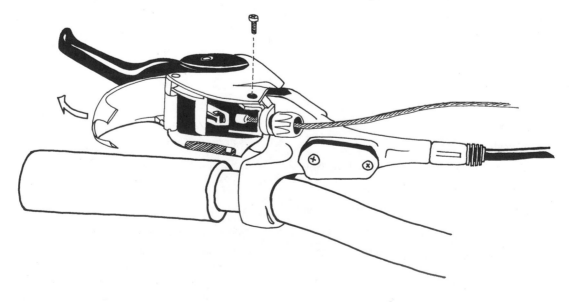

4. **Guide the cable through each housing segment and cable stop.** Slotted cable stops on the frame allow you to slip the cable and housing in and out from the side.

5. **Replace the plastic plug in the shifter's cable-access hole.**

c. Front (left) lever

1. **Open the cover concealing the cable hook.** This is quite ingeniously designed and consequently simple to perform. On pre-2008 models, remove the Phillips screw on the cover adjacent to the barrel adjuster (Fig. 5.26); it is on the opposite side of the shifter housing from the gear-indicator window. Do not remove the other two, smaller Phillips screws also on the same plastic cover piece. Flip open the shifter-housing cover; it has the Shimano logo on it and hinges from its end opposite the barrel adjuster. More recent dual-control levers with the drum-shaped body have a simple flip-open cable-access cover held down by a plastic screw plug.

2. **Push the cable out.** While jiggling the cable to free it from the cable hook, pry up on the cable where it exits the cable hook to flip the cable head out of the hook (Fig. 5.26). Pull the old cable out.

3. **Engage the head of the new cable.** Snap the head of the new cable into the cable hook.

4. **Shift the lever to its maximum cable pull position.** With the palm side of the fingers, shift the brake lever laterally repeatedly through all of its clicks.

5. **Push the cable out through the barrel adjuster.**

6. **Close the cover and tighten the screw (gently!).**

7. **Guide the cable through each housing segment and cable stop.** Slotted cable stops on the frame allow you to slip the cable and housing in and out from the side.

v-11
REPLACING 1996–2000 SHIMANO XTR RAPIDFIRE CABLE

The 1996–2000 Shimano XTR shifters have a plastic cover over the wire-end hook (Fig. 5.27) and also have a slotted barrel adjuster and shifter body.

1. **Shift the smaller (upper and forward) finger-operated lever until it lets all the cable out.**

5.27 Replacing the cable in a 1996–2000 Shimano XTR Rapidfire SL shifter

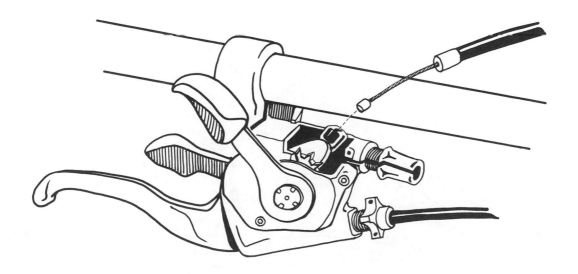

2. **Turn the shifter barrel adjuster so that its cable slot is lined up with the slot in the shifter body** (Fig. 5.27). The slot is on the opposite side from the gear indicator. Barrel adjusters for 1999–2000 XTR are in a plastic housing that pulls out of the lever body; with this type, pull the entire barrel adjuster straight out.

3. **Unscrew the Phillips-head screw on the plastic cover.** It will not come completely out (so that you could lose it), being retained in the cover by a plastic ring. Open the cover.

4. **Pull the cable out.** Pull it down out of the slot, and then pull its head out of the hook.

5. **Install the new cable.** Slip the cable head into the cable hook (Fig. 5.27), and pull the cable into the slot. Turn the barrel adjuster so that the slots no longer line up. Or with 1999–2000 XTR, push the barrel adjuster back in.

6. **Close the cover and tighten the screw (gently!).**

7. **Guide the cable through each housing segment and cable stop.** Slotted cable stops on the frame allow you to slip the cable and housing in and out from the side.

NOTE: *Replacing the thin cables connected to the XTR "Rapidfire Remote" bar-end-mounted shifters (which were manufactured for only a couple of years) requires buying the thin double-headed cables and housings from Shimano. The small heads simply slip through the holes in both sets of shift levers (on the handlebar and on the bar end) from the backside. Install the remote shifter's little plastic caps onto the metal cable heads to keep them from pulling back through. That's it.*

v-12
REPLACING CABLE IN SRAM (GRIP SHIFT) AND SACHS TWIST SHIFTERS FROM 1998 AND LATER

Changing cables is easy on current Grip Shift and Half Pipe shifters via the cable-hole cover. The high-end twist-shifter models got this feature in 1998, and by 2000 all SRAM shifters had the quick-cable-change system.

1. **Disconnect the cable at the derailleur, and cut off the end cap.**

2. **Twist the shifter to let out the maximum amount of cable.** Shift to the highest number on the rear shifter and to "1" on the front.

3. **Get at the end of the cable.** This differs by model. Some have a rectangular rubber hatch that you pull open (Fig. 5.28). While pushing

5.28 SRAM Half Pipe twist shifter

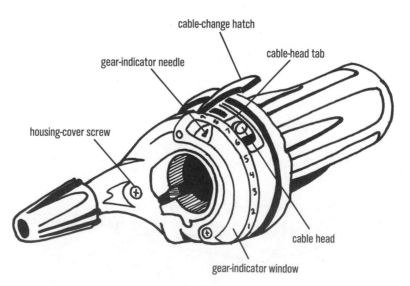

cable-change hatch

gear-indicator needle

cable-head tab

housing-cover screw

cable head

gear-indicator window

back on the cable, you then pry up the plastic tab that obscures half of the cable head. Use a small screwdriver. The cable should pop out from under the hook on the tab. Other high-end SRAM shifters have a plastic hatch that you slide off to the side. Once the hatch is off, you will see the cable head on the front shifter and a small setscrew on the rear shifter that you remove with a 2.5mm hex key to reveal the cable head. On inexpensive shifters, peel back the corner of the rubber grip cover and you will see the cable head.

4. **Push out the old cable.**

5. **Slide in the new cable and pull it snug.** Replace the setscrew, if present, and care-

fully screw it in until it contacts the cable head. If the screw feels as though it has stripped the threads, it hasn't—it just has gone in beyond the threads and is turning freely. No worries.

6. **Push the cover that conceals the cable head back into place.**

v-13
REPLACING CABLE IN (AND OVERHAULING) PRE-1998 GRIP SHIFT

Prior to 1998, all Grip Shifts had to be disassembled to replace the cable; 1998–2000 inexpensive shifters still require disassembly for cable changing.

5.29 Pre-1998 Grip Shift right shifter

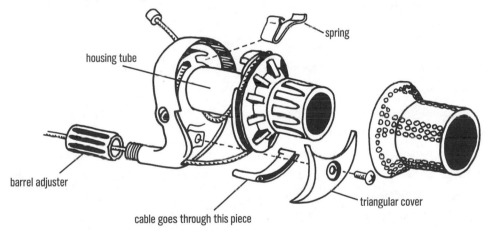

housing tube

spring

barrel adjuster

cable goes through this piece

triangular cover

5.30 Pre-1998 Grip Shift left shifter

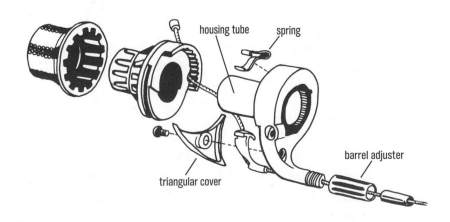

housing tube

spring

triangular cover

barrel adjuster

1. Disconnect the derailleur cable.

2. **Move the brake lever inboard to make room for pulling the grip apart.** If a bend in the handlebar or other obstruction prevents this, you must roll or slide the handlebar grip away from the Grip Shift to allow room for the shifter to slide apart.

3. **Remove the triangular plastic cover holding the two main sections together** (Figs. 5.29–30). Use a Phillips screwdriver.

4. **Pull the outer shifter section away from the main body to separate it from the inner housing.** Watch for the spring (Figs. 5.29–30) to ensure that it does not fall out. The spring can be nudged back into place if it does.

5. **Pull the old cable out and recycle it.**

6. **Clean and dry the two parts.** A rag and a cotton swab are usually sufficient. Finish Line offers a cleaning and grease kit specifically designed for Grip Shift shifters. A really gummed-up shifter may require a solvent and compressed air to clean and dry it.

7. **Lubricate the inner housing tube and spring cavity, all cable grooves, and the indexing notches in the twister.** Use a nonlithium grease such as SRAM Jonnisnot or Finish Line's silicone-based Teflon grease.

8. **Thread the cable through the hole, seating the cable end in its little pocket.**

9. **Route the cable through the shifter.** For the rear shifter, loop the cable once around the housing tube, and exit it through the barrel adjuster (Fig. 5.29). For the front shifter, the cable routes directly into its guide (Fig. 5.30).

10. **Make sure the spring is in its cavity in the housing.** Hold the spring in with a small amount of grease if need be.

11. **Slide the outer (twister) body over the inner tube.** Be sure that the shifter is in the position that lets the most cable out (on models with numbers, line up the highest number with the indicator mark on rear shifters, lowest number on front shifters).

12. **Lift the cable loop into the groove in the twister** (Fig. 5.29). Push straight inward on the twister as you pull tension on the cable exiting the shifter. The twister should slide in until flush under the housing edge; you may have to jiggle it back and forth slightly while pushing in to get it properly seated.

13. **Replace the cover and screw.**

14. **Check that the shifter clicks properly.**

15. **Slide the grip back into place.**

16. **Guide the cable through each housing segment and cable stop.** Slotted cable stops on the frame allow you to slip the cable and housing in and out from the side—use them that way to save yourself some effort.

v-14
ATTACHING CABLE TO THE REAR DERAILLEUR

1. **Put the chain on the cog that is aligned with where the derailleur spring pulls it to rest.** Except with Low Normal or Rapid Rise derailleurs, put the chain on the smallest cog so that the rear derailleur moves to the outside. With Low Normal or Rapid Rise derailleurs, start with the chain on the largest cog.

2. **Route the cable.** Run the cable through the barrel adjuster, and route it through each of the housing segments until you reach the cable anchor bolt on the derailleur. Make sure that the rear shifter is on the setting that releases the most cable.

3. **Tighten the barrel adjusters in all the way, and then back them out one turn.** The shifter has a barrel adjuster, and the rear derailleur likely has one as well.

4. **Pull the cable taut and into its groove under the cable anchor bolt** (Fig. 5.30).

5. **Tighten the bolt.** On most derailleurs this

5.31 Attaching a rear-derailleur cable

takes a 5mm hex key, but many take a Torx T25 or an 8mm box wrench.

v-15

ATTACHING CABLE TO THE FRONT DERAILLEUR

1. **Shift the chain to the inner chainring so that the derailleur moves farthest to the inside.** This ensures that the maximum amount of cable is available to the derailleur.

2. **Tighten the shifter barrel adjuster in all the way, and then back it out one turn.**

3. **Hook up the cable.** Place the cable into its groove under the anchor bolt on the derailleur arm while pulling the cable taut with pliers (Fig. 5.32), and tighten the bolt with a 5mm hex key, a Torx T25, or an 8mm box wrench, as required. Make sure you do not hook up a top-pull-style front derailleur from the bottom, or vice versa.

Many front derailleurs now work both top-pull and bottom-pull style. They are actually top-pull front derailleurs, because you hook up directly to the cable anchor bolt when the cable comes from the top (Fig. 5.33A). But if the frame routes the cable to the front derailleur from the bottom, it is no problem; you simply run the cable

5.32 Pull the cable tight before tightening the clamp bolt with a hex key

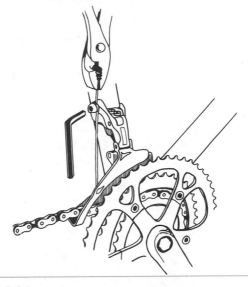

5.33A Over-the-top-tube (i.e., top-pull) cable routing to a Shimano low-clamp top-swing front derailleur

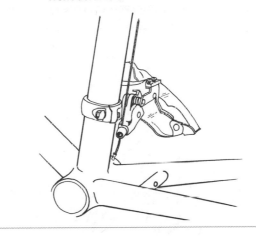

5.33B Under-the-bottom-bracket (i.e., bottom-pull) cable routing to a Shimano top-swing front derailleur

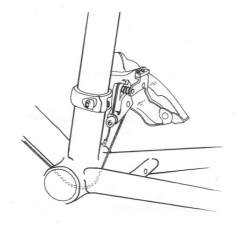

TRANSMISSION

up, over, and around a pivoting rocker arm to the cable anchor bolt located on its outboard end (Fig. 5.33B). Note that some derailleur models require housing to run the full length of the cable to the front derailleur, terminating at a housing stop forged into the derailleur body.

v-16
ADDING FINAL CABLE TOUCHES

A high-quality cable assembly includes the cable-housing end ferrules throughout, ideally ones with rubber seals on them to keep contamination out of the housings, and crimped cable caps. Clip cables about 1–2cm past the cable-clamp bolts before crimping the cable caps on (Fig. 5.34). Also, little rubber cable O-rings, commonly called "donuts" (Fig. 5.35), or pieces of thin cable sheathing can be installed to keep the bare cables from scratching the frame's finish. The drawback to

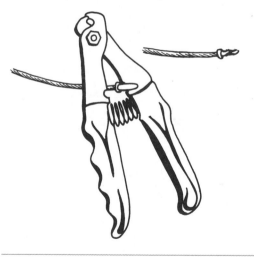

5.34 Crimp the cable end caps

the donuts is that they stay in place only briefly. They wear quickly to the point that they slip back and end up piled up at the rear cable stop on the top of the top tube.

v-17
USING GORE-TEX CABLES

If you are using Gore-Tex cables, follow the instructions on the package, as these cables require very special treatment in order to work properly. The Gore-Tex needs to be removed from the cable at the last inch or so before the cable anchor bolt, as well as from all the cable that is inside the shift lever or Grip Shift. A plastic tube covers the cable (Fig. 5.20) over its entire length from shifter to derailleur. A little rubber accordion-like seal (called a "Grub") at the anchor bolt covers the end of the cable-cover tube and keeps dirt and water out of it.

v-18
LUBRICATING CABLE

New cables and housings with Teflon liners do not need to be lubricated. Used cables and housings can be lubricated with chain lubricant. Grease sometimes slows cable movement, so various manufacturers recommend (and some even supply) their own molybdenum disulfide grease for cables.

1. **Pull the housing segments out of their slotted cable stops.** There is no reason to disconnect the cable at the derailleur.

5.35 Little rubber donuts (O-rings)

2. Use lubricant to coat the areas of the cable that will be inside of the cable housing segments.

NOTE: *If the bike does not have slotted cable stops, you might as well replace the cables and housings because an old cable will have a frayed end and will be hard to put back through the housing after lubrication. That's another reason to keep extra cables, housing ferrules, and cable ends in your workshop.*

v-19
REDUCING CABLE FRICTION EASILY

Besides replacing your cables and housings with good-quality cables and lined housings, you can take other steps to improve shifting efficiency.

1. **Route the cable so that it makes smooth bends and so that turning the handlebar does not increase the tension on the shift cables.** (This is the most important friction-reducing step.)

2. **Choose cables that offer low friction.** "Die-drawn" cables, which have been mechanically pulled through a small hole in a piece of hard steel called a die, move with lower friction than standard cables. Die-drawing flattens all of the outer strands and smoothes the cable surface. Thinner cables and lined housings with a large inside diameter also reduce friction. Gore-Tex cables are cables coated with Gore-Tex. They offer low friction and are sealed end to end with a plastic sheath (Fig. 5.20).

3. **Increase the size of the derailleur-return spring to quicken shifting when the cable is released (as opposed to pulled).** You can buy a stiffer spring at your bike shop designed specifically for some Shimano derailleurs.

SHIFTERS

Twist shifters (of which Grip Shift by SRAM is the predominant one), Rapidfire levers, thumb shift-

5.36 Grip Shift

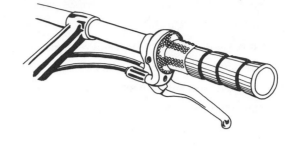

5.37 Rapidfire shifter

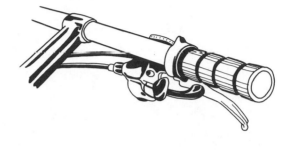

5.38 Thumb shifter

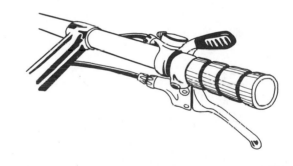

ers (Figs. 5.36–38), SRAM trigger levers (Fig. 5.23), and Shimano's post-2003 Dual Control brake and shift levers (Fig. 5.26) all move the derailleurs, but each goes about it in a very different way.

v-20
REPLACING AND INSTALLING BAR ENDS AND GRIPS

 LEVEL 1

Replacing shifters requires removing at least grips and often bar ends and brake levers as well. Shifters are generally labeled "right" and "left,"

TRANSMISSION

but if you're in doubt, you can tell which is which because the right one has a lot more clicks. This is not true of friction shifters.

1. **If bar ends are installed, remove them.** This usually requires a 5mm hex key.

2. **Remove the grips.** Remove standard grips by rolling them back or lifting them away from the handlebar at either end, squirting water or rubbing alcohol underneath, and twisting back and forth while sliding them off; alternatively, use the compressed-air method mentioned in the next step. If you are not planning to reuse the grips, you can cut them off. If you see clamp bolts at either end of your grips, you have bolt-on grips, which are very easy to remove. Just loosen the bolt(s) and slide the grip off.

3. **Install the new grips.** If you have bolt-on grips, simply slide them on and tighten the clamp bolts. When installing standard grips, squirt rubbing alcohol inside to make them slide on easily; they will slip for a number of days until the alcohol evaporates. You can also lubricate them with spray adhesive, and they will slide right on and not move once the glue sets.

If the grips have closed ends, you can punch a hole in the ends and put the grips on by inflating them with an air compressor. Because of the length of the handlebar, it will take two people to span the reach and install the grips. Cover the opposite end of the handlebar (the palm of your helper's hand works well), and push the grip with the little hole in it onto the handlebar (at your end) an inch or so. Press the compressed-air-gun tip against that hole, and the grip will balloon up and slide right on. Then push the fully closed grip an inch or so onto the opposite end of the handlebar, and again press the air-gun tip against the first grip's hole. This will inflate both grips so that they can easily be pushed

on. Removal can be done the same way, in reverse.

v-21
REPLACING A SHIMANO SHIFTER AND INTEGRATED BRAKE LEVER

If you are replacing the entire brake lever and shifter unit, proceed as follows (Fig. 5.36):

1. **Remove the old brake lever and shifter.**

2. **Slide the new brake lever and shifter onto the bar.** Make sure that you put the right shifter on the right side.

3. **Slide the grip back into position.**

4. **Mount the bar end if you have one.**

5. **Rotate the brake lever to the position you like.**

6. **Tighten the brake-lever fixing bolt.**

v-22
REPLACING THE SHIFTER UNIT ON SHIMANO INTEGRATED BRAKE AND SHIFT LEVERS

These instructions apply to Shimano Rapidfire shifters (Figs. 5.24, 5.27, and 5.37).

1. **Click the shifter to release the maximum amount of cable.**

2. **Unbolt the old shift lever from the brake-lever body.**

3. **Position the new shifter exactly as the old one was.**

4. **Replace the bolt and tighten it.**

5. **Install the cable and tighten it.**

NOTE: *For Rapidfire Remote installation, mount the remote lever onto the tip of the bar end by using a 2mm hex key. Hook up the cables as described in §v-11.*

v-23
REPLACING SRAM GRIP SHIFT, HALF PIPE, AND OTHER TWIST SHIFTERS

See Figure 5.36 for SRAM Grip Shift and Figure 5.39 for Half Pipe.

1. **Remove the old shifter.** Replace the brake lever if you had to remove it to get the old shifter off.

2. **Loosen and slide the brake lever inward.** This allows room for the shifter.

3. **Slide the appropriate (right or left) new shifter on with the cable-exit barrel pointing inward.**

4. **Slide on the plastic washer over the handle-bar that separates the grip from the Grip Shift.** This step is not necessary with Half Pipes or with 2001 (and later) Shorties, as the plastic washer is integrated within the shifter.

5. **Replace the grip (and bar end).**

6. **Butt the Grip Shift up against the plastic washer or the grip.** Rotate the shifter until the cable-exit barrel is oriented so that it will not interfere with the brake lever.

7. **Tighten the mounting bolt to the handlebar with a 2.5mm or 3mm hex key.**

8. **Slide and rotate the brake lever to the position you like, and tighten it down.**

9. **Route the cable to the derailleur and tighten it.** If you need to install the cable into the new shifter, see §v-12 or §v-13.

5.39 Squeeze the two tabs together to release the Half Pipe retaining washer

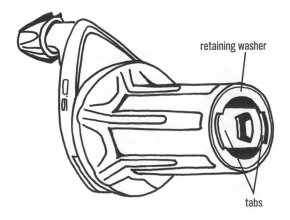

retaining washer

tabs

v-24
REPLACING TOP-MOUNTED THUMB SHIFTERS OR TRIGGER LEVERS NOT INTEGRATED WITH THE BRAKE LEVER

Thumb shifters are shown in Figure 5.38.

1. **Remove the bar end, grip, brake lever, and old shifter.**

2. **Slide on the replacement shifter.**

3. **Slide on the brake lever, grip, and bar end.**

4. **Tighten the bar end and brake lever in the position you want.**

5. **Tighten the shifter in the position that is comfortable for you.** Make sure the position allows easy access to the cable barrel adjuster and free cable travel. Some SRAM trigger levers allow attachment to various "MatchMaker" clamps (Fig. 5.23); more options for positioning the lever to your preference are available with this design.

6. **Install the cable and tighten it.**

SHIFTER MAINTENANCE

v-25
SRAM GRIP SHIFT

A Grip Shift unit (Figs. 5.29, 5.30, 5.36, and 5.39) requires periodic cleaning and lubrication, as described in this section. Clean only with soap and water, and lubricate only with nonlithium (preferably silicone-based Teflon) grease, such as Grip Shift Jonnisnot.

If shifting has become poor on Half Pipes or other Grip Shifts with the quick-cable-change feature, try replacing the cable and housing first before disassembling the shifter for cleaning.

a. Short Grip Shifts

The exploded diagrams in Figures 5.29–30 and the text in §v-13 detail how to take apart, clean, and grease a short-length Grip Shift (except for the 2001 [and later] Shortie, which follows the same disassembly procedure as Half Pipes [Fig. 5.39], described in the next paragraph). With older models and some current inexpensive models, so long as you have the shifter disassembled, you might as well replace the cable (§v-13), because shifter disassembly is required for the task.

b. Long (Half Pipe) Grip Shifts or post-2001 Shortie Grip Shifts

This section also applies to SRAM's Shortie shifters from 2001 and later.

1. **Twist the shifter away from you to let out all the cable.** Turn it to "1" on the front shifter and "9" on the rear.

2. **Remove the cable** (§v-12) **and the fixed grip** (§v-20). Note that, unlike the older Grip Shift models, you do not remove the triangular housing cover to get the twist grip off.

3. **Remove the shifter from the handlebar by using a 3mm hex key on the setscrew.**

4. **Squeeze the tabs on the end of the shifter housing tube together, and remove the plastic retaining washer from the end** (Fig. 5.39). You may have to pry inward with a screwdriver on each tab.

5. **Separate the grip and remove the long coil spring.** Slowly slide the grip outward as you twist the shifter gently away from you in the cable-release direction. If you pull too fast, the long coil spring inside (Fig. 5.40) may pop out.

6. **Remove the two Phillips screws, and pop off the clear plastic window covering the gear-indicator needle** (shown in Fig. 5.28).

7. **Pull straight out on the gear-indicator needle** (shown in Fig. 5.28), **and remove it.**

8. **Pull the small leaf spring** (Fig. 5.40) **up and out using needle-nose pliers or tweezers.** The spring looks like a flat bent piece of steel; note its position before removing it.

9. **Remove the housing-cover screw** (shown in Fig. 5.28). This takes a Phillips screwdriver or a 2.5mm hex key.

10. **Slide the outer parts (the housing cover and cable spool) away from the housing** (Fig. 5.40). Be careful not to break the tab on the housing cover. To get the housing cover to come up, you may need to push up on it with the end of a paper clip through the hole for the housing-cover screw.

11. **Clean all of the parts with soap, water, and clean rags.** Do not use solvents.

12. **Lubricate the large tube extending from the housing, the cable track, and all detents for the springs.** Use a nonlithium grease such as SRAM Jonnisnot or Finish Line's silicone-based Teflon grease.

13. **Slide the housing cover and spool back down onto the housing tube.** First slip the cover's tab into the spool's groove (Fig. 5.41). Replace the housing-cover screw.

14. **Set the leaf spring in place into the spool** (Fig. 5.40). Carefully press down on one end of the

5.40 Half Pipe springs

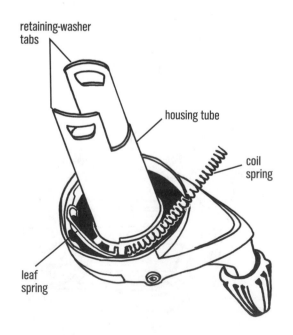

retaining-washer tabs

housing tube

coil spring

leaf spring

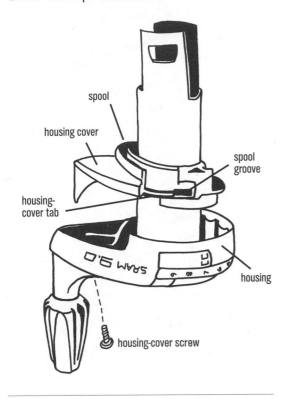

spool

housing cover

spool groove

housing-cover tab

SRAM 9.0

housing

housing-cover screw

spring as you work to seat the other end in place in the same position it was in before.

15. **Install one end of the coil spring onto its tab** (Fig. 5.40). Slide the outer grip onto the tube, angle the other end of the spring up toward the grip, and pop the other end of the spring onto the tab inside the grip.

16. **Rotating the grip slightly away from you to compress the coil spring, slide the grip inward until it engages in the housing.**

17. **Replace the plastic retaining washer over the tabs on the housing tube** (Fig. 5.39).

18. **Rotate the shifter away from you to the position that would let out the most cable.**

19. **Peer into the curved slot that the gear-indicator needle slides in.** If you followed step 18, you should see the receptacle for the needle at one end of the slot. Slip the gear-indicator needle (Fig. 5.28) back into its receptacle, replace the plastic window, and install the two screws that hold it on.

20. **Install the shifter onto the handlebar using a 3mm hex key.** Check that it works.

21. **Install a new cable (§v-12) and connect it to the derailleur.**

Your bike is now ready to ride.

v-26

SHIMANO RAPIDFIRE SL, RAPIDFIRE PLUS, AND DUAL CONTROL LEVERS

Shimano Rapidfire SL (Fig. 5.27), Shimano Rapidfire Plus (Fig. 5.37), and Shimano Dual Control shifters (Fig. 5.26) are not designed to be disassembled by the consumer. Squirting a little chain lube inside every now and then is a good idea, though. If a Rapidfire lever stops working, a new shifter unit is needed. On an integrated Rapidfire unit, the brake lever does not need to be replaced; just bolt the new Rapidfire shifter to it (§v-22). If you manage to break a Shimano Dual Control shifter, you will be replacing the entire (expensive!) hydraulic brake master-cylinder and shifter-lever unit. Maybe it was still under warranty.

Sometimes the gear-indicator unit on a Shimano shifter stops working, and it can even jam the lever and stop it from reaching all the gears. This problem was most common in the 1993 and 1994 models. The indicator can be removed from the shifter with a small screwdriver. The indicator's little link arm needs to be stuck back into the hole it came from. Once the indicator jams, you can expect it to happen again; eventually, you will want to replace the lever or dispense with the indicator.

Once you get used to shifting Shimano Dual Control levers solely with the front and back of your fingers, moving the brake-lever blade laterally in either direction, you can remove the optional auxiliary release lever that allows you to shift with your thumb to let cable out. There is a little screw holding it on that you simply unscrew from the nut and the circlip. If you still have the rubber cap, you can push it over the sharp metal tab that is now exposed.

v-27
AN ORIGINAL SHIMANO RAPIDFIRE

Shimano's first attempt at a two-lever mountain shifter did not work very well. If you are having trouble with yours, I recommend throwing it out and getting a new system. You know you have an original Rapidfire if the thumb operates both the down- and upshift levers. Newer Rapidfire SL and Rapidfire Plus levers (Figs. 5.27 and 5.37) have a thumb-operated cable-pull lever and a finger-operated cable-release lever.

v-28
THUMB SHIFTERS

Indexed (click) thumb shifters (Fig. 5.38) are not to be disassembled beyond removing them from their clamp. Periodic (semiannual or so) lubrication with chain lube is recommended and is best accomplished from the backside once the shifter assembly is removed from its clamp (Fig. 5.42).

Frictional (nonclicking) thumb shifters can be disassembled, cleaned, greased, and reassembled. Put the parts back the way you found them. You can avoid the hassle of disassembly by squirting chain lube in instead.

v-29
CHAIN-RETENTION DEVICES FOR DOWNHILL, FREERIDE, SLALOM, AND JUMP BIKES

Modern chain guides mount on ISCG (International Standard Chain Guide), also known as ICMS (International Chainguide Mounting Standard), integrated onto the exterior of the bottom-bracket shell (Fig. 5.43). These are three mounting tabs with M6X1 threaded holes; they radiate out from the face of the bottom-bracket shell at angles and distances from center proscribed

5.42 Indexed thumb shifter, exploded view

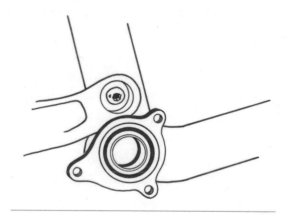

5.43 ISCG mounts on the frame's bottom-bracket shell

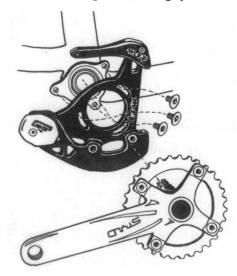

5.44 MRP chain guide/bash ring system

by the international standard. The fixed-position mounts eliminate the twisting and spacing problems that can occur without them.

The frame must also have ISCG mounts if you wish to use a Truvativ HammerSchmidt crankset, which is a crank with an internal two-speed transmission.

Most chain guide systems (Fig. 5.44) consist of a mounting plate that bolts to the ISCG tabs with adjustable-position enclosed rollers that are positioned at about 11 o'clock and 7 o'clock on the top and bottom of a "bash ring." A bash ring looks like a chainring without teeth, and it mounts to the crank spider where the outer chainring would ordinarily be mounted.

Tension arms, rollers, giant front-derailleur cages (of which an early version is illustrated in Fig. 5.45), and other chain-retention systems have become a part of downhill racing, because of the extraordinary demands the sport places on the drive system. Downhill-specific products are outside the scope of this book, but once assembled on the bike, most of these drivetrain items will be completely obvious in their function and maintenance.

v-30
BELT DRIVE

The Gates Carbon Drive belt-drive system (Fig. 4.26) is becoming more popular on single-speed bikes and bikes with internal-gear rear hubs. Keys to making this system work are described in §iv-12.

v-31
ROHLOFF AND OTHER INTERNAL-GEAR HUBS

Internal-gear systems offer the nice advantage of being able to shift when you're not pedaling and not having derailleurs get clogged with mud or caught on things. Bikes using internal-gear rear hubs require a frame with a system like those described in §iv-8b to tension the chain either by adjusting the distance between the rear hub and the crank or by using a chain tensioner with a roller pushing on the chain. And as it says in §iv-8b, the only full-suspension bikes you can use them on without a chain tensioner are those in which the distance from the bottom bracket to the rear hub does not change as it goes over bumps. The only full-suspension bikes that are thus

5.45 This sucka ain't goin' nowhere

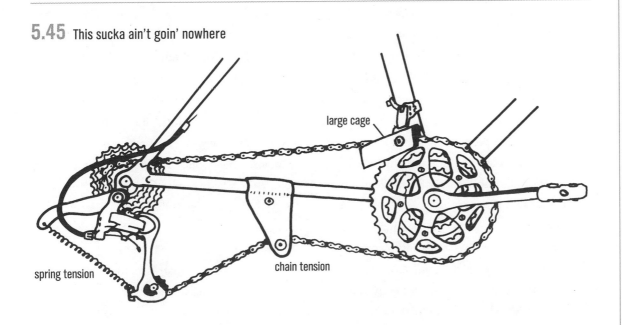

large cage

spring tension

chain tension

5.46 Removing the cog from a Rohloff SpeedHub

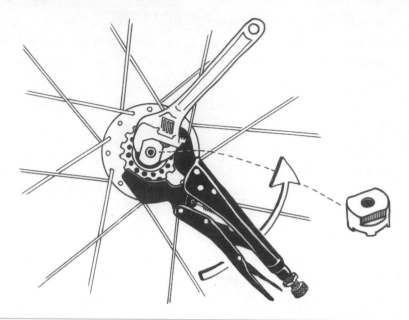

qualified are concentric-pivot systems (where the rear swingarm pivots around the bottom bracket), unified-rear-triangle systems (where the bottom bracket and dropouts are rigidly attached to each other), and softtails (where the suspension movement works by means of flex in the chainstays).

The hub shell of an internal-gear hub rotates at a different speed from its cog in all gears except the one-to-one gear—the gear in which the cog and hub shell are directly linked. In a gear that multiplies the rotation of the hub from that of the cog (a high gear), a torque is generated trying to twist the axle forward. In a gear that reduces the rotation of the hub from that of the cog (a low gear), a torque is generated trying to twist the axle backward. Internal-gear hubs thus require a method to anchor the hub axle to the frame more securely than by simply clamping the axle ends, as on a normal hub. The wider the gear range, the higher this torque is twisting the axle, and the more secure must be the clamping method to resist it. The most basic system to counteract the torque on the axle is a long, flat torque arm made of steel plate that bolts to a clamp wrapped around the left chainstay, similar to what you would see on a bike with a coaster brake or your grandfather's old British three-speed.

The Rohloff SpeedHub is the internal-gear hub of choice for mountain biking because of its wide range as well as its robust construction. This hub, available in myriad variations to anchor its internals, and the plate on the left end of the hub can be interchanged with different torque arms to fit different bikes. The slickest anchoring system for the Rohloff SpeedHub is a round plate with a little rectangular block sticking up from it that is an inch out radially from the axle stub in the center. That little rectangular stub on the plate is the torque arm, and all you need is a left-side dropout with a slot long enough to secure it. (Fig. 14.3) Another system for fitting a Rohloff hub onto a mountain bike with disc-brake mounts is to use a Rohloff "SpeedBone," which is a torque arm that bolts to the disc-brake mounts on the left dropout.

The Rohloff SpeedHub has a dual-cable twist shifter that moves it through all of its 14 speeds. The gear ratios are spaced evenly, approximately 13.5 percent apart, and their range spans approximately the same gear range as a standard 27-speed mountain bike system.

Even though the Rohloff shifter seems to click into each gear, the shift indexing is inside the hub, not in the shifter. There is no wear on the indexing system, nor is there a need to adjust it.

The most common SpeedHub variation used on mountain bikes has a detachable external cable box. The two cables enter the cable box on the left side of the SpeedHub through barrel adjusters. A slew of countersunk holes around the exterior of the hub end plate allow you to rotate the attachment position of the cable box so that the cables enter their barrel adjusters smoothly, whether you are routing to it over the top of the top tube and seatstays or underneath the down tube and chainstays. Using the barrel adjusters, adjust the cable tension so that there is 2mm of rotational play in the shifter between gear clicks.

To most easily remove the wheel and to ensure that the cable box, shifter, and hub internals are in agreement about what gear they are in when you put the wheel back in, always remove and install the wheel with the shifter in gear position 14. Because you can shift the bike while it is stopped, this is not a problem. Unscrew the knurled thumbscrew on the face of the cable box, and pull off the cable box. Now you can remove the wheel as you would a normal rear wheel.

To reinstall the wheel, drop it in with the chain on the cog as you would with a normal single-speed rear wheel. If you forgot to shift to position 14 (all 14 gear positions are numbered on the twist shifter) before removing the wheel, you can get into that gear now. To do so, turn the shifter to position 14 and turn the hexagonal peg on the hub plate that the cable box engages with (it looks like a nut sticking out of the center of a round brass flange) to the last gear position by turning it counterclockwise through all of its clicks with an 8mm box wrench. (If, when you start riding, all 14 gears are not usable, you mounted the cable box somewhere in the middle of the gear range, and

you need to pull off the cable box, twist the shifter to position 14, and turn the hexagonal peg as I just described before reinstalling it.)

Set the cable box in place over the hexagonal peg so that the two locating pegs insert into the two holes in the back of the cable box. Twiddle the shifter back and forth around position 14 until the cable box drops into place over the hexagonal peg. Tighten the knurled thumbscrew to secure the cable box. You're now ready to ride.

The hub needs to be filled with 25 ml of Rohloff oil, which must be changed every 3,000 miles. You also should put a drop of oil on the hexagonal peg and the hole into which it engages in the cable box every few times you remove the wheel. Otherwise, maintenance is generally minimal aside from normal cable maintenance.

DERAILLEUR MAINTENANCE

v-32
MAINTAINING JOCKEY WHEELS

LEVEL 1

The jockey wheels (aka "guide pulleys"—Fig. 5.47) on a derailleur will wear out over time. For best performance, standard jockey wheels should be overhauled every 200–500 miles. That should take care of the gunk that the chain and the trail regularly deliver to them. The mounting bolts on jockey wheels also need to be checked regularly. If a loose jockey-wheel bolt falls off while you are riding, you'll need to follow the procedure for a broken rear derailleur on the trail, described in §iii-9.

Some expensive guide pulleys have cartridge bearings (Fig. 5.47, bottom), whereas standard ones (Fig. 5.47, top and center) have a center bushing sleeve made of either steel or ceramic (SRAM upper jockey wheels have an oversized steel center bushing). A washer with a curved rim facing inward (visible in Fig. 5.47, center) is usually

5.47 Jockey wheels, exploded view

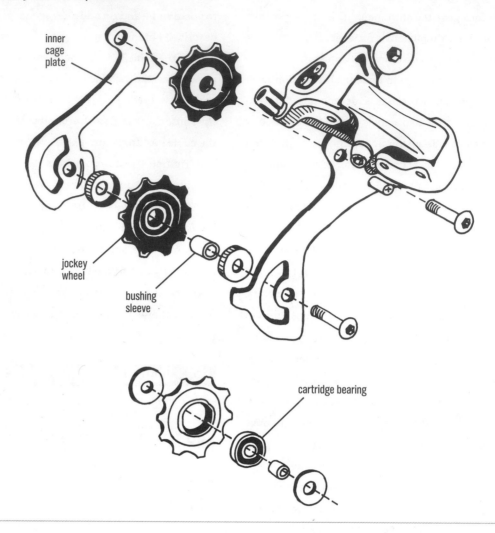

inner
cage
plate

jockey
wheel

bushing
sleeve

cartridge bearing

---

installed on both sides of a standard jockey wheel. Some guide pulleys also have rubber seals around the edges of these washers.

v-33
OVERHAULING STANDARD JOCKEY WHEELS

1. Remove the jockey wheels by undoing the bolts that hold them to the derailleur (Fig. 5.47). This usually takes a 2.5mm or 3mm hex key.

2. Wipe all parts clean with a rag. A solvent is usually not necessary but can be used.

3. If the teeth on the jockey wheels are broken or worn off, replace the wheels.

4. Smear grease over each bolt and sleeve and inside each jockey wheel.

5. Reassemble the jockey wheels on the derailleur. Be sure to properly orient the inner cage plate (the larger part of the cage plate should be at the bottom jockey wheel).

v-34
OVERHAULING CARTRIDGE-BEARING JOCKEY WHEELS

If the cartridge bearings (bottom, Fig. 5.47) in high-end jockey wheels do not turn freely, they can usually be overhauled.

1. Remove the jockey wheels by undoing the bolts that hold them to the derailleur (Fig.

5.47). This usually takes a 2.5mm or 3mm hex key.

2. **Pry the plastic cover off one or, preferably, both sides of the bearing** (Fig. 6.32). Use a single-edge razor blade or box-cutter knife.

3. **With a toothbrush and solvent, clean the bearing.** Use a citrus-based solvent, and wear gloves and glasses to protect skin and eyes.

4. **Blow the solvent out with compressed air or your tire pump, and allow the parts to dry.**

5. **Squeeze new grease into the bearing, and replace the covers.**

6. **Reassemble the jockey wheels on the derailleur.** Be sure to orient the inner cage plate properly (the larger part of the cage plate should be at the bottom jockey wheel).

v-35
OVERHAULING THE REAR DERAILLEUR

Except for the jockey wheels and upper and lower main pivots, most rear derailleurs are not designed to be disassembled. If the pivot springs seem to be operating effectively, all you need to do is overhaul the jockey wheels (§v-34) and clean and lubricate the parallelogram and spring as follows next.

v-36
PERFORMING A MINOR WIPE AND LUBE

1. **Clean the derailleur as well as you can with a rag.** Be sure to get in between the parallelogram plates.

2. **Drip chain lube on both ends of every pivot pin.**

3. **Grease the spring contacts.** If there is a clothespin-type spring in the parallelogram (as opposed to a coil spring running diagonally from one corner of the parallelogram to the other), put a dab of grease where the spring end slides along the underside of the outer parallelogram plate.

v-37
OVERHAULING THE UPPER PIVOT

⚙️ ⚙️ LEVEL 2

CAUTION: *Don't do this job unless you absolutely must in order to rehabilitate a poorly functioning rear derailleur. The strong spring resists your best intentions at reassembly, and you may not be able to get it back together properly, even with a second set of hands.*

1. **Remove the rear derailleur.** This usually takes a 5mm hex key to unscrew it from the frame and to disconnect the cable.

2. **With a screwdriver, pry the circlip** (Fig. 5.48) **off the threaded end of the mounting bolt.** Don't lose the bolt; it will tend to fly when it comes off.

3. **Pull the mounting bolt and the upper pivot spring out of the derailleur.**

4. **Clean and dry the parts with or without the use of a solvent.**

5. **Grease the parts liberally and reassemble them.**

6. **Engage the spring ends into their holes.** If there are several holes, and you don't know

5.48 Rear-derailleur pivots

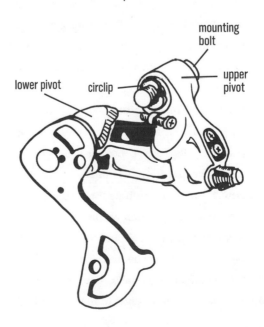

lower pivot   circlip   mounting bolt   upper pivot

TRANSMISSION

which one the spring was in before, try the middle one. (If the derailleur does not keep tension on the chain well enough, you can later try another hole that increases the spring tension.)

7. **Squeeze the parts together, and replace the circlip with pliers.**

v-38
OVERHAULING THE LOWER PIVOT

LEVEL 2

1. **Remove the derailleur from the bike.** This usually takes a 5mm hex key to unscrew it from the frame and to disconnect the cable.

2. **Open the derailleur knuckle.** Shimano derailleurs can be divided into two types: ones that have a setscrew on the side of the lower pivot and ones that do not. If yours has a setscrew (Fig. 5.8), remove it using a 2mm hex key, and pull the jockey cage away from the derailleur.

   If the derailleur has no setscrew, find and unscrew the tall cage stopscrew on the derailleur cage (Fig. 5.10); it is located near the upper jockey wheel. This screw is designed to maintain tension on the lower pivot spring and prevent the cage from springing all the way around. Once the screw is removed, slowly guide the cage around until the spring tension is relieved. Remove the upper jockey wheel, and unscrew the pivot bolt from the back with a 5mm (sometimes 6mm) hex key (Fig. 5.11). Be sure to hold the jockey-wheel cage to keep it from twisting.

3. **Determine in which hole the spring end has been placed, and then remove the spring.**

4. **Clean and dry the bolt and the spring with a rag.** A solvent may be used if necessary.

5. **Grease all parts liberally.**

6. **Replace the spring ends in their holes in the** derailleur body and jockey-wheel cage (Fig. 5.9). Put the spring in the adjacent hole if you want to increase its tension (see §v-2g).

7. **Close the derailleur knuckle.** If the derailleur has a setscrew, push the assembly together, wind the spring, and replace the setscrew. If the derailleur does not take a setscrew, wind the jockey-wheel cage back around, screw it all back together with the pivot bolt, and replace the stopscrew.

v-39
OVERHAULING THE PARALLELOGRAM

LEVEL 2

Very few derailleurs can be completely disassembled. Those that can (Mavic, first-generation SRAM, and 2002 high-end SRAM) have removable pins holding them together. The pins have circlips on the ends that can be popped off with a screwdriver, after which the pins can be pulled out. Disassemble the derailleur carefully in a box so that the circlips do not fly away, and make note of where each part belongs so that you can get all the parts back together again. Clean all parts, grease them, and reassemble.

v-40
REPLACING STOCK BOLTS WITH LIGHTWEIGHT VERSIONS

Lightweight aluminum and titanium derailleur bolts used to be common replacement items for many derailleurs, but as the bolt shapes on modern derailleurs change so rapidly with each model year, this has ceased to be a profitable business for small machine shops. Removing and replacing jockey-wheel bolts is simple, as long as you keep all of the jockey-wheel parts together and put the inner cage plate back on the way it was. Upper and lower pivot bolts are replaced following the instructions in §v-37 and §v-38.

TROUBLESHOOTING REAR-DERAILLEUR AND RIGHT-HAND SHIFTER PROBLEMS

Once you have made the adjustments outlined previously, the drivetrain should be quiet and should stay in gear, even if you turn the crank backward. If you cannot fine-tune the adjustment so that each click with the right shifter results in a clean, quick shift, you need to check some of the following possibilities. For skipping- and jumping-chain problems, see also the troubleshooting section at the end of Chapter 4.

v-41
SHIFTER COMPATIBILITY

Check to see whether the shifter is compatible with the derailleur and cogs. This is especially important if any of these parts are not original equipment on the bike. It should be obvious that a 7-speed shifter will not work on an 8-, 9-, or 10-speed cassette, but components of different brands for the same number of speeds often will not work together either. If the shifter is a different brand from the derailleur, be certain that they are designed to work together. The most common example of this is SRAM's Grip Shift, some models of which are specifically designed to work with a Shimano rear derailleur (SRAM got its start making twist shifters to retrofit onto Shimano-equipped bicycles). Otherwise, only SRAM rear derailleurs work with SRAM shifters.

If the shifter and derailleur are incompatible, you will need to change one of them. Quality being equal, I suggest replacing the less costly item (generally the shifter, except in the case of Shimano Dual Control levers for hydraulic disc brakes).

v-42
STICKY CABLES

Check the derailleur cables to confirm that they run smoothly through the housing. Sticky cable movement will cause sluggish shifting. Lubricate the cable by smearing it with chain lube or a specific lubricant that came with the shifters (§v-18).

If lubricating the cable does not help, replace the cable and housing (see §v-7 to §v-17).

v-43
BENT REAR-DERAILLEUR HANGER

A bent hanger will hold the derailleur crooked and bedevil shifting. Instructions for straightening the hanger are in §xiv-5.

v-44
BENT REAR-DERAILLEUR CAGE

A bent derailleur cage will hold the jockey wheels at an angle to the cogs. Mild bending can be straightened by hand, eyeballing the crank for reference.

v-45
LOOSE PIVOTS (WORN-OUT REAR DERAILLEUR)

A loose and floppy rear derailleur will not shift well. Replace it.

TROUBLESHOOTING FRONT-DERAILLEUR AND LEFT-HAND SHIFTER PROBLEMS

v-46
CHAIN SUCK

For chain suck problems, refer to the troubleshooting section at the end of Chapter 4.

v-47
CHAINLINE

Your bike probably has chainline problems if (1) the chain falls off to the inside no matter how much you adjust the low-gear limit screw, cable tension, and derailleur position; (2) there is chain rub, noise, or auto-shift problems in mild cross-gears that are not corrected with derailleur adjustments; or (3) the front derailleur cannot move the chain onto the large chainring even if the outer limit screw is backed all the way out.

NOTE: *If problem 2 occurs intermittently on a full-suspension bike (for example, when you are sitting but not when you are standing), it could be that as the rear suspension compresses, the chain is no longer running in the groove formed for it in the front-derailleur cage. Instead, the chain is hitting the forward ridge above the groove. You may have to put up with this problem because your alternative is to tighten the suspension (i.e., increase the spring rate) so that it does not move*

5.49 Measuring chainline

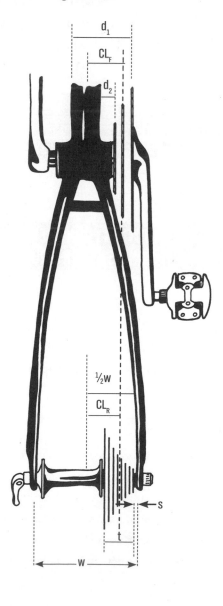

as much or to get a derailleur without the internal cage shaping (which won't shift as fast).

Chainline is the relative alignment of the front chainrings with the rear cogs; it is the imaginary line connecting the center of the middle chainring with the middle of the cogset (Fig. 5.49). In theory, this line should be straight and parallel to the vertical plane of the bicycle. Even owners of new bikes may find poor chainlines, owing to mismatched cranks and bottom brackets.

The chainline is adjusted by moving or replacing the bottom bracket to move the cranks left or right. You can roughly check the chainline by placing a long straightedge against the middle chainring and back to the rear cogs; it ideally would come out in the center of the rear cogs. But the tire-clearance issues of most mountain bikes, particularly on full-suspension models with large tires, make this unreasonable to expect; the chainrings have simply got to be farther out than the cogs or the bike designer cannot fit everything in.

Continue to the next section for a precise chainline-measurement method.

v-48
PRECISE CHAINLINE MEASUREMENT

 LEVEL 2

You will need a caliper (Fig. 1.4). The position of the middle chainring, as measured from the center of the seat tube to the center of the middle chainring, is often called the chainline, although this is only the front end point of the line.

1. **Find the front end point of the chainline** (CL_F in Fig. 5.49) **as follows:**

    (a) Measure from the left side of the down tube to the outside of the large chainring (d_1 in Fig. 5.49). (Do not measure from the seat tube, as it may be oval where it meets the bottom-bracket shell. The frame tubes are labeled in Fig. 14.1.)

(b) Measure the distance from the right side of the down tube to the inside of the inner chainring (d_2 in Fig. 5.49).

(c) Add these two measurements and divide the sum by two:

$$CL_F = (d_1 + d_2) \div 2$$

2. **Find the rear end point of the chainline** (CL_R in Fig. 5.49). This is the distance from the center of the plane of the bicycle to the center of the cogset.

(a) Measure the thickness of the cog stack, end to end (t in Fig. 5.49).

(b) Measure the space between the face of the smallest cog and the inside face of the dropout (s in Fig. 5.49).

(c) Measure the length of the axle from dropout to dropout (w in Fig. 5.49). This dimension is also called the "axle overlock dimension," referring to the distance from locknut face to locknut face on either end. Generally, on any mountain bike since 1989 or so, this will be 135mm.

(d) Subtract one-half of the thickness of the cog stack and the distance from the inside face of the right rear dropout from one-half of the rear-axle length:

$$CL_R = w/2 - t/2 - s$$

3. **See if $CL_F = CL_R$.** If it does, the chainline is perfect. This, however, almost never occurs on a mountain bike, because of considerations about chainstay clearance of the tire and the chainrings, prevention of chain rub on large chainrings in cross-gears, and inward movement range of the front derailleur. Shimano specifies a "chainline" (meaning CL_F, the front end point of the chainline) as 47.5mm for bikes with a 68mm-wide bottom-bracket shell and 50mm for 73mm-wide shells (both of these specified dimensions are plus or minus 1mm). CL_R, the rear end point of the chainline, on the other hand, usually comes out around 44.5mm.

Shimano's specifications, then, are primarily intended to avoid chainring rub on chainstays, not to promote ideal shifting. I recommend having the chainrings in toward the frame as far as you can without rubbing the frame or losing front-derailleur shifting performance because of bottoming out on the seat tube. Your bike will shift best and run quietest if you get the chainline at around 45mm, but you may have some problems getting there, such as the following:

(a) The inner and middle chainrings might rub the chainstay.

(b) The front derailleur may bottom out on the seat tube before moving inward enough to shift to the inner chainring (this is particularly a problem with bikes with oversized seat tubes).

(c) When crossing to the smallest cog from the inner and even the middle chainring, the chain may rub on the next larger chainring (this is not a problem if you simply avoid those cross-gears).

4. **To improve the chainline, move the chainrings.** There is little or nothing you can do with the rear cog position. The chainrings are moved by using a different bottom bracket, by exchanging the bottom-bracket spindle for a longer or shorter one, or by moving the bottom bracket right or left (bottom-bracket installation and overhauling are covered in Chapter 8).

NOTE: *Some brand-new bikes have terrible chainlines that can be corrected only with the installation of a new bottom bracket. This problem usually has to do with a conceptually impaired bean-counting product manager selecting the parts for a given bike model. Product managers know that customers often pay*

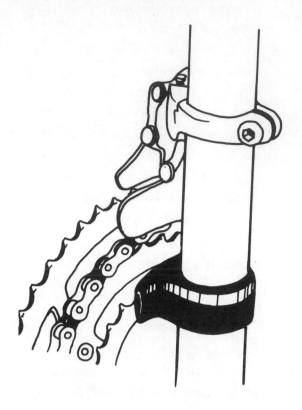

attention to the quality and brand of the cranks on the bike and pay little heed to the quality of the bottom bracket—the unseen part of the mix. With a cheap bottom bracket with an overly long spindle, the cranks may sit way too far out, and the chainline will stink. You will end up having to replace the longer bottom bracket with a shorter one if you want the bike to shift decently. In such a case, good shops will replace the bottom bracket before selling the bike to you.

ANOTHER NOTE: The chainline can also be off if the frame is out of alignment (see §xiv-13). If that's the case, it is probably not something you can fix yourself.

5. **If the chain is still dropping on shifts, or if you don't want to mess with the chainline, install an inner chain stop.** Try a Third Eye Chain Watcher (Fig. 5.50), a Jump Stop, or a Deda Elementi Dog Fang. All three clamp around the seat tube next to the inner chainring. Clamp one on and adjust the position so that it nudges the chain back on when it tries to fall off to the inside.

6

WHEELS

TIRES, RIMS AND SPOKES, HUBS, CASSETTES, AND FREEWHEELS

I'm just sitting here watching the wheels go round and round.

—John Lennon

Early bicycles may have existed without pedals and steering systems, but they always had wheels. After all, without wheels, it ain't a bike!

With the exception of molded composite versions, wheels on mountain bikes are strung together with spokes. The hub is at the center, and its bearings allow the wheel to turn freely around an axle. The rim is supported and aligned by the tension on the spokes. On most bikes, the rim serves as both support for the tire and a braking surface.

On the rear wheel, a freewheel or cassette freehub (rear hub with a built-in freewheel) allows the wheel to spin while coasting and engages when forward force is applied to the pedals (Fig. 6.1).

The tires provide grip and traction for propulsion and steering. The air pressure in the tire is your first line of suspension. On most mountain bikes, inner tubes keep the air inside the tires, but tubeless tires are making huge inroads into this dominance, particularly at the high-cost end.

This chapter addresses how to replace or repair a tire or inner tube, fix a broken spoke or bent rim, overhaul hubs and freehubs, maintain and replace freewheels, and maintain and replace cogs. Have at it.

TIRES AND INNER TUBES

🔧 LEVEL 1

Standard inner tubes and clincher tires as well as tubeless clincher tires are included here. Tubular (i.e., "sew-up") mountain bike tires are much too rare to cover in this book, so please consult *Zinn and the Art of Road Bike Maintenance* for instructions on working with tubular tires.

vi-1
REMOVING A STANDARD TIRE AND TUBE

NOTE: *If you have tubeless tires, skip to §vi-2.*

1. **Remove the wheel** (see §ii-2 and §ii-12). If the wheel is on a Cannondale Lefty one-legged fork, you can skip this step, because you can change the tire while the wheel is on the bike!

TOOLS

spoke wrench

13mm, 14mm, 15mm, 16mm, and 17mm cone wrenches

17mm open-end wrench (or an adjustable wrench)

screwdriver

5mm, 6mm, and 10mm hex keys

grease

oil

chain whip

Pedro's Vise Whip

cassette lockring remover

large adjustable wrench

freewheel remover (if your bike does not have a cassette)

tire pump

tire levers

tube patch kit

continued

OPTIONAL

Morningstar J-tool

soft hammer

fine-tip grease gun

tire sealant

Teflon tape

citrus solvent

Rohloff HG-IG-Check

6.1 The whole thing

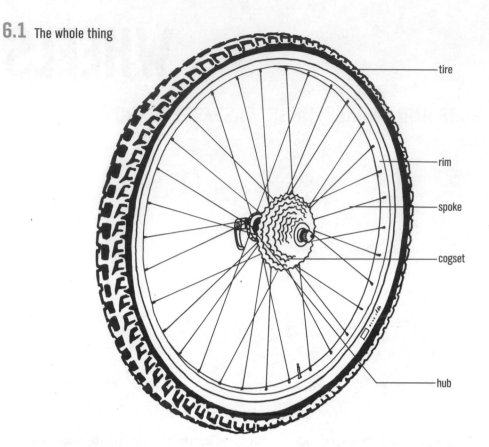

tire

rim

spoke

cogset

hub

6.2 Schrader valve

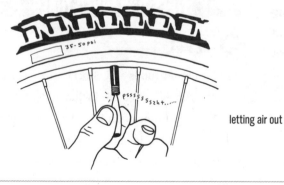

6.3 Presta valve

letting air out

2. If the tire is not already flat, deflate it.

(a) To deflate a Schrader valve (the kind of valve you would find on a car tire), push down on the valve pin with something thin enough to fit in that won't break off, such as a pen cap or a paper clip (Fig. 6.2).

(b) Presta valves are thinner and have a small threaded rod with a tiny nut on the end. To let air out, unscrew the little nut a few turns and push down on the thin rod (Fig. 6.3). To seal, tighten the little nut down again (with your fingers only!); leave it tightened down for riding.

NOTE: *If your bike has deep-section rims (often carbon) that are too tall for a normal valve stem, you will require "valve extenders"—thin, threaded tubes that*

Valve extenders

Valve extenders are made for Presta valves, and they solve the problem of using an inner tube with a standard valve on a deep-section rim that requires a long valve. One type of valve extender is simply a thin tube like a drinking straw with threads inside one end to screw onto the cap threads of the valve (Fig. 6.4A). Unscrew the little nut atop the valve hard enough that it always stays open and does not screw closed on its own. If the valve has some problems—an imperfect seal, a bent rod—it can leak when the nut is not tightened down, making this type of valve extender problematic.

To deflate tires that have simple drinking-straw-type valve extenders, you need to insert a thin rod (a spoke is perfect) down into the valve extender to release the air.

To install drinking-straw-type valve extenders so that they seal properly and allow easy inflation, you need to unscrew the little nut on the Presta valve until it is against the mashed threads at the top of the valve shaft (they are mashed to keep the nut from unscrewing completely). Back the nut firmly into these mashed threads with a pair of pliers so that it stays unscrewed and does not tighten back down against the valve stem from the vibration of riding, thus preventing air from going in when you pump it. Wrap a turn or two of Teflon pipe thread tape around the top threads on the valve stem before screwing on the valve extender; if you do not, air will leak out during pumping and the pressure gauge on your pump will not give an accurate reading of tire pressure. Tighten the valve extender onto the valve with a pair of pliers.

Alternatively, if you can find inner tubes with removable Presta valve cores, you can get valve extenders for them that are threaded at the base with the same thread as on the base of a valve core. They will have threads inside the other end to accept a valve core (Fig. 6.4B). Deflating or inflating the tire with one of these

6.4A Drinking-straw-type valve extender

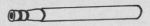

6.4B Removable-core valve extender (showing separate Presta valve core)

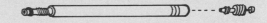

6.4C Topeak/Spinergy valve extender

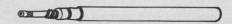

valve extenders is no different from deflating or inflating any tire with a standard Presta valve, making them the valve extender of choice. To install one of these valve extenders, unscrew the valve core (counterclockwise) with a Presta valve-core wrench or adjustable wrench and remove it. Screw the valve extender into the valve body where the core was; tighten it firmly with pliers or a wrench on its wrench flats. Screw the valve core into the valve extender, and tighten it with a Presta valve-core wrench or adjustable wrench.

Some valve extenders (Topeak, Spinergy) have a thin knurled knob on top with a shaft running all the way down to grab the nut atop the valve (Fig. 6.4C). They actually allow you to tighten or loosen the valve nut with the extender in place, thus behaving for all intents and purposes like a standard Presta valve. With this type of extender, unless it has a rubber seal at its base, you should also wrap a turn or two of Teflon pipe thread tape around the top threads on the valve stem before screwing on the valve extender; if you do not, air will leak out during pumping and the pressure gauge on your pump will not give an accurate reading of tire pressure. Tighten the valve extender onto the valve stem with a pair of pliers.

screw onto the Presta valve stems—so that you can inflate and deflate the tire. See the Pro Tip on valve extenders for more information.

3. **Starting adjacent to the valve stem, push up on the sidewall with your thumbs to lift it over the rim wall.** If you can push the tire bead off the rim with your thumbs without using tire levers, by all means do so, for there is less chance of damaging either the tube or the tire.

6.5 Removing the tire with levers

6.6 Pulling out bead with third lever

6.7 Removing the inner tube

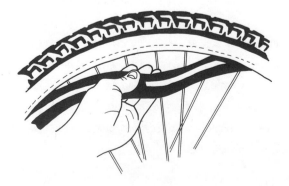

4. **If you can't get the tire off with your hands alone, insert a tire lever, scoop side up, between the rim sidewall and the tire until you catch the edge of the tire bead.** Again, this is most easily done adjacent to the valve stem.

5. **Pry down on the lever until the tire bead is pulled out over the rim** (Fig. 6.5). If the lever has a hook on the other end, hook it onto the nearest spoke. Otherwise, keep holding it down.

6. **Place the next lever a few inches away.** Do the same thing with it (Fig. 6.5).

7. **If needed, place a third lever a few inches farther on.** Pry it out, and continue sliding this lever around the tire, pulling the bead out as you go (Fig. 6.6). Some people slide their fingers around under the bead, but beware of cutting your fingers on sharp tire beads.

NOTE: *There are various "quick" tire levers on the market that require the use of only one lever. But if the tire is really stubborn, the tried-and-true three-lever method outlined here may be the only way to get the tire off.*

PRO TIP

Tire removal

Removal of the tire is most easily accomplished by starting near the valve stem. That way, the beads of the deflated tire can fall into the dropped center of the rim on the opposite side of the wheel, making it effectively a smaller-circumference rim from which you are pushing the tire bead. If, instead, you try to push the tire bead off (or onto) the rim on the side opposite the valve stem, the circumference on which the bead is resting is larger, because the valve stem is forcing the beads to stay up on their seating ledges opposite the side where you are working. (Fig. 6.8 illustrates a tubeless tire, but it does show the tire beads, rim ledges, and valley that I am talking about.)

8. Once the bead is off on one side, pull out the tube (Fig. 6.7). If you are patching or replacing the tube, you do not need to remove the other side of the tire from the rim. If you are replacing the tire, the other bead should come off easily with your fingers. If it does not, use the tire levers as outlined previously.

REMOVING A TUBELESS TIRE

If your wheels have tubeless tires, do all tire removal and installation with your hands only, as tire levers can damage the sealing flap extending beyond the tire bead (Fig. 6.8), and then the tire will not seal. If you are planning to patch the tire, you must find the leak before removing it from the rim (§vi-3).

Because the "UST" tubeless system is the only one in wide use, this section specifically addresses that system.

1. **Remove the wheel** (see §ii-2 and §ii-12). If the wheel is on a Cannondale Lefty one-legged fork, you need not remove the wheel!

6.8 Cross-section of UST tubeless tire and rim

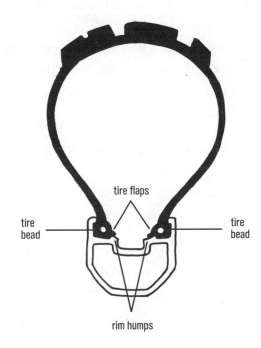

tire flaps

tire bead

tire bead

rim humps

2. **If the tire is not already flat, deflate it at the valve.**

(a) Tubeless tire valves screw into the rim with rubber seals around them. They can be either Schrader valves (the kind of valve you would find on a car tire), Presta valves (Fig. 1.1B), or both. Mavic UST valves are both; unscrew and remove the outer, Schrader-size externally threaded tube to make this valve a Presta valve. To use a Mavic valve as a Schrader valve, screw on the Schrader tube after unscrewing the little nut on the end of the inner Presta valve.

(b) To deflate a Schrader valve, push down on the valve pin with something thin enough to fit in that won't break off, such as a pen cap or a paper clip (Fig. 6.2).

(c) To let air out of a Presta valve, unscrew the little nut a few turns and push down on the thin rod (Fig. 6.3). To seal, tighten the little nut down again (with your fingers only!). Leave it tightened for riding.

3. **Push inward on the tire bead all the way around with your thumbs.** This pops the bead off the "hump" (Fig. 6.8) so that it'll fall into the dropped center of the rim.

4. **Starting adjacent to the valve stem, push the tire off the rim with your thumbs.** The Pro Tip on tire removal in §vi-1 explains why you start at the valve stem.

FINDING LEAKS

Keep in mind that you can patch only small holes. If the hole is bigger than the eraser end of a pencil, a round patch is not likely to work. A slit of up to an inch or so can be repaired with a long oval patch.

1. **If the leak location is not obvious, put some air in the tube.** Inflate it until it is two to three times larger than its deflated size. Be

6.9 Checking for a puncture

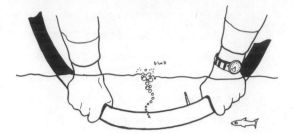

6.10 Smearing the patch glue

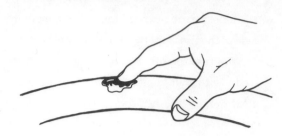

careful. It will explode if you put too much air in; latex and urethane tubes are especially prone to this.

NOTE: *For tubeless tires, leave the tire on the rim and inflate it to 25–50 psi; then continue with steps 2 and 3.*

2. **Listen and/or feel for air coming out.** Mark the leak(s).

3. **If you cannot find the leak by listening and/or feeling, submerge the tube in water.** Look for air bubbling out (Fig. 6.9), and mark the spot(s). With a tubeless tire, submerge it while mounted on the rim.

NOTE: *The following instructions apply to patching a tube, but the procedure is the same for patching a tubeless tire, except that you patch the inside of the tire versus the outside of a tube. Also, you can always stick a tube inside a tubeless tire if you don't want to deal with patching the tire. As for repairing a tubeless tire where there are a lot of cacti or thorns, it is arduous and next to impossible to find and patch all of the holes. Rather than throw the (expensive) tire out, put some tire sealant inside it (§vi-10).*

vi-4
USING STANDARD PATCHES

1. **Dry the tube thoroughly near the hole.**

2. **Rough up and clean the surface within about a 1-inch radius around the hole.** Use a small piece of sandpaper (usually supplied with the patch kit). Do not touch the sanded area, and

don't rough up the tube with one of those little metal "cheese graters" that come with some patch kits. They tend to do to your tube what they do to cheese.

3. **Use a high-quality patch kit for bicycle tires.** It will have thin, usually orange, gummy edges surrounding a black rubber patch in the center.

4. **Apply patch cement over an area centered on the hole** (Fig. 6.10). Apply a thin, smooth layer to an area that is bigger than the patch.

5. **Let the glue dry.** Wait until there are no more shiny, wet spots (5–10 minutes).

6. **Remove the foil backing from the gummy underside of the patch.** Don't remove the cellophane top cover.

7. **Stick the patch over the hole, and push it down in place.** Make sure that all the gummy edges are stuck down. You are done, unless

6.11 Removing the cellophane backing

Tire size

Ideal tire size is related to terrain and riding style. Some of this is obvious: Bumpier surfaces and higher speeds demand bigger tires. Climbing, especially on smooth surfaces, rewards light weight, and smaller tires can be lighter. However, rolling resistance on anything but smooth roads will generally be improved with a larger, softer tire.

Thing is, it's not always simple to figure out what tire size you're actually getting from the dimensions listed on the tire or on the box. The good news is that there is an international standard numbering system for bicycle tires and rims that is straightforward and understandable. Formerly called "E.T.R.T.O." (European Tyre and Rim Technical Organisation), it has become "ISO" (International Organization for Standardization). The first number in the ISO code is the width of the tire or the inner width of the rim between the sidewall hooks ("W" in Fig. 6.12). The second number determines what rim the tire will fit on and is the rim's "bead seat diameter" ("BSD" in Fig. 6.12), which is the diameter of the shelf that the tire bead rests on. So a 700 × 23 tire would be a 23–622, a 29 × 2.35 mountain bike tire would be a 61–622, and a 28 × 1 road tire would be a 25–622. (Yes, 700C, 28-inch road, and 29-inch mountain bike tires all take the same rim diameter.)

The bad news is that, even though tires often have the ISO code molded into them, tires and rims are not listed in catalogs this way.

Originally, the numbers, like 26-inch or 700C, referred to the diameter of the tire in inches or millimeters, but with time, different tire widths for each given rim size came along. These tires consequently had different diameters from the original upon which the number was based, but the 26-inch or 700C designation was carried forward anyway, followed by a second number indicating the tire width in inches, such as 26 × 2.35.

For mountain bikes, you will generally want to buy only tires with a decimal tire width (26 × 2.2, 29 × 2.0, etc.). Avoid tires with the width indicated as a fraction, because equivalent numerical values do not equate to equivalent tire sizes. Even though, for example, 1½ is numerically equivalent to 1.5, the rim size will almost always be different for tires listed this way. For instance, 26 × 1.0 through 26 × 2.5 (with two ignorable exceptions) are tire sizes that fit on 26-inch mountain bike rims, which have a BSD of 559mm (so a 26 × 1.0 is an ISO 25–559). But a 26 × 1 is a 650C (ISO 571) triathlon size, 26 × 1¼ and 26 × 1⅜ are both ISO 597, 26 × 1½ is 650B (ISO 584), and 26 × 1¾ is an ISO 571 Schwinn cruiser size (yes, same BSD as a 26-inch triathlon tire).

6.12 Clincher rim width (W) and bead seat diameter (BSD)

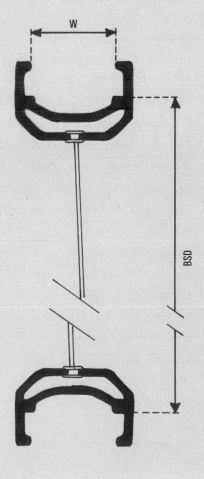

you want to peel off the cellophane cover (optional).

8. **Although there is no need to do so, you may remove the cellophane top covering.** Be careful not to peel off the edges of the patch when removing the cellophane (Fig. 6.11). If the cellophane atop the patch is scored, fold the patch so that the cellophane will split at the scored cuts. Peel outward from the center, and avoid pulling the newly adhered patch away from the tube.

vi-5
USING GLUELESS PATCHES

There are a number of adhesive-backed patches on the market that do not require cement to stick them on. Most often, you simply need to clean the area around the hole with the little alcohol pad supplied with the patch. Let the alcohol dry, peel the backing off, and stick on the patch. The advantage of glueless patches is that they are very fast to use, take little room in a pack, and free you from the experience of opening your patch kit only to discover that the glue tube has dried up.

On the downside, I have not found any glueless patches that stick nearly as well as the standard type. With a standard patch installed on a tube, you can inflate the tube to look for more leaks without having it in the tire. If you do that with a glueless patch, it usually lifts the patch enough to start it leaking. You must install it in the tire and on the rim before putting air in it after patching. And don't expect the glueless patch to be a permanent fix, as you can with a glued-on standard patch.

vi-6
INSTALLING A TUBE AND TIRE

Feel around the inside of the tire to see if there is anything sticking through that can puncture the

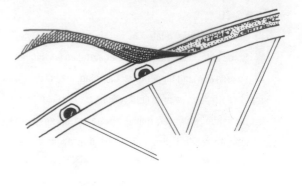

6.13 The rim strip protects the inner tube from the ends of the spokes

tube. This is best done by sliding a rag all the way around the inside of the tire. The rag will catch on anything sharp and saves your fingers from being cut by whatever is stuck in the tire.

1. **Check for tire wear.** Replace any tire that has worn-out or cracked tread or areas (inside or out) where the tread-casing fibers appear to be cut or frayed.

2. **Examine the rim tape.** Check that the rim tape (Fig. 6.13) is in place and that there are no spokes or anything else sticking up that can puncture the tube. Replace the rim tape if necessary. With an asymmetrically drilled rim, make sure the adhesive and/or the fit of the rim tape is very good. If the rim tape slides over even a little bit, it can expose the edge of one of the offset holes and puncture the tube.

3. **By hand, push one side bead of the tire onto the rim.** Ideally, first you want to check the direction of the tire rotation and orient the tire label so that it is next to the valve stem for ease of finding both.

4. **Optional: Smear talcum powder around the inside of the tire.** This prevents the tube and tire from adhering to each other. Don't inhale the stuff.

5. **Put just enough air in the tube to give it shape.** Close the valve if it is a Presta.

6.14 Installing a tire by hand

6.15 Finishing installation at the valve

6. **Push the valve through the valve hole in the rim.**

7. **Push the tube up inside the tire all the way around.**

8. **Starting at the side opposite the valve stem, push the tire bead onto the rim with your thumbs.** See the Pro Tip on tire removal for the reason. Be sure that the tube doesn't get pinched between the tire bead and the rim.

9. **Push the tire onto the rim.** Work around the rim in both directions with your thumbs toward the valve stem (Fig. 6.14). Finish from both sides at the valve (Fig. 6.15). You can usually install a mountain bike tire without tools. If you cannot, first try deflating the tube when you have gotten as far around as you can with your hands. You should now be able to push the tire on the last bit, as deflating the tube will allow the beads on the far side, opposite the valve stem, to drop into the lower center of the rim. If this does not allow you to complete the mounting by hand, use tire levers to pry the tire bead on, but make sure you don't catch any of the tube under the edge of the bead. Finish the same way at the valve.

10. **Push up on the valve stem.** This pulls up any nearby folds of the tube stuck under the tire bead (Fig. 6.16) when you pushed the last

6.16 Seating the tube by pushing up on the valve

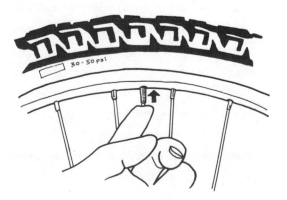

bit of bead onto the rim. You may have to manipulate the tire so that all the tube is tucked under the tire bead.

11. **Inspect for any part of the tube that might be protruding from under the edge of the tire bead.** Go all the way around the rim. If you have a fold of the tube under the edge of the bead, it can blow the tire off the rim either when you inflate it or while you are riding. It will sound like a gun blast and will leave you with an unpatchable tube.

12. **Pump the tire up.** Generally, 35–45 psi is a good amount. Much more, and the ride gets harsh. Much less, and you run the risk of a pinch flat, or "snakebite."

vi-7
INSTALLING A UST TUBELESS TIRE

These instructions apply to the UST tubeless system. To prevent damage to the seal, do not use tire levers for this procedure.

1. **Examine the rim to be sure that the tire will seal to it.** First of all, it must be a UST rim (and tire); only a rim without spoke holes on the inside, and with the "hump" along the edge of each bead ledge, will seal with the tire (Fig. 6.8). Furthermore, the rim edges and the hump must not be dented or gouged, or air will escape at those spots.

2. **Wet the edges of the tire.** Put dish soap in the water to facilitate sealing the tire as well as seeing leaks.

3. **Push one bead of the tire onto the rim with the tire properly oriented.** Determine rotation direction (see the Pro Tip on tire direction), and locate the label at the valve stem. Starting opposite the valve, push one bead of the tire onto the rim with your thumbs and fingers only, finishing at the valve.

4. **Push the other bead onto the rim by hand.** Again, start on the side of the rim oppo-

site the valve stem (see the Pro Tip on tire removal) and finish at the valve stem. If you instead start at the valve stem, you will have to work harder, because the valve holds the tire bead up on the ledge and forces the rim to stretch around a larger circle. I highly recommend adding tire sealant just before you push the last of the bead on to close off any slow leaks and to seal future punctures (see §vi-10 and Fig. 6.17).

5. **Pump the tire up with a floor pump.** Put air in as fast as possible until you hear the tire seat. Just as with a tubeless car tire, seating the bead is a lot more effective with an air compressor (Fig. 1.4), but it can be done with a manual pump. Sometimes, a UST tire can even be seated using a hand pump, but be aware that you must get a lot of air into the tire in a hurry to force the beads to pop up over the humps and then onto the ledges.

6. **Pump up (or deflate) to your desired riding pressure.**

vi-8
INSTALLING A STANDARD TIRE AS A TUBELESS TIRE

With "Stan's NoTubes" tubeless systems, you can make a standard rim and tire become tubeless.

Stan's system includes liquid latex–based sealant, spoke tape, and a rubber rim strip with an integral Presta valve and thick edges to seal the tire beads. The rim strips are available for three different 26-inch rim widths, as well as for 29-inch wheels. You can also forgo the rim strip and simply tape over the rim holes with both strapping tape and electrical tape and use Stan's sealant (this was the original way Stan offered the system).

Do this only on wheels that you use frequently, because standard tires that you don't ride often are difficult to keep sealed with the sealant solution. If the wheel just sits, rather than being constantly stirred up by riding, the latex in the solution tends to pool and harden at the bottom of the tire.

1. **On a standard rim, enlarge the valve hole.** Unless you are using a UST or other tubeless rim (Fig. 6.8), use a drill to enlarge the inside valve hole to ⅜ inch (NOT the hole toward the hub!). Smooth the burred edge with a round file or sandpaper. This allows clearance for the rubber-sealing section at the base of the valve stem. With a UST or other tubeless rim, skip this step and go to the second part of step 3.

2. **Tape the rim.** Wrap two layers of Stan's spoke tape or half-inch-wide fiberglass-reinforced strapping tape around the rim, completely covering the rim holes. Cut through the tape at the valve hole.

3. **Install the Stan's rim strip with integral valve.** Stretch it evenly around the rim, and push the edges under the rim hooks; wetting the strip with soapy water makes this easier. If you are using a UST rim (Fig. 6.8), install the valve without tape or rim strip. (If you are using Stan's old system, i.e., using Stan's sealant without the rim strip, wrap a layer of electrical tape over the strapping tape. This method works better if you first smooth the edges of the rim holes with sandpaper and clean the rim bed with rubbing alcohol before applying the strapping tape in step 2. Then install the valve, first dripping a little sealant solution around the rubber base and rubber washer.) Tighten the valve nut down by hand against the rim. To check if you got the rim strip on correctly, inflate the tire first with soapy water, covering it and the rim edge before adding the sealant.

4. **Determine rotation direction** (see the Pro Tip on tire direction). Locate the label at the valve stem.

5. **Install one bead of the tire on the rim.**

6. **Cover the sidewalls and along the rim beads with soapsuds.** Use a one-to-eight solution of dish soap and water.

7. **Put in sealant.** Shake the sealant bottle well, and turn it upside down when pouring to keep the particles in solution. Put 60g (1.5 scoops—or 2–2.5 scoops for large tires or more sealing protection) of sealant solution into the tire (Fig 6.17). If you have Stan's 2 oz. refill bottle or a sealant syringe, you can install both beads of the tire first, then unscrew the valve core and squirt in the sealant through the valve stem.

8. **Install the other tire bead.** Follow step 3 for installing UST tires.

6.17 Putting tire sealant in a tubeless tire

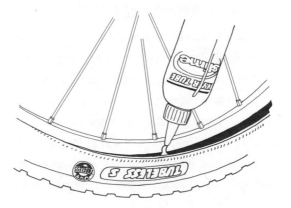

9. **Inflate the tire to a maximum of 40 psi.** Ideally, use an air compressor, which will help seat the beads quickly. Wear safety glasses.

10. **Move sealant to leaks.** Wherever you see soap bubbles indicating escaping air, tip the wheel so that the latex solution flows to the area and fills the holes. Continue doing this, repeatedly reinflating the tire to 40 psi, until the tire seals completely.

When you are riding, the latex splashing around inside will not seal the tire beads or sidewalls if you did not seal them completely before. If you have leaks, redo step 7. If the tire fits too loosely to seal, add thicker rim tape. If it won't seal, slap the tire above the valve while inflating. If it still won't seal, mount it with an inner tube to best shape the tire and remove kinks where it had been folded. Then try again with sealant and without the tube at a later time.

Tire sealants are blurring the lines between "standard" 26-inch mountain bike tires and UST tires. For instance, a TNT (Tube No Tube) tire is essentially a beefed-up standard tire or a superlight UST tire that comes with sealant. If you run a TNT with a tube on a standard rim, it provides better sidewall cut resistance. If you run it on a UST rim with the sealant, you have a superlight and reliable tubeless tire.

vi-9
PATCHING TIRE CASING (SIDEWALL) WITH A STANDARD TIRE AND TUBE

Unless it is an emergency, do not try to patch a sidewall! If the casing is cut, it's best to get a new tire because patching the tire casing is dangerous. No matter what you use as a patch, the tube will find a way to bulge out of the patched hole, and when it does, the tire will go flat immediately. Imagine coming down a steep descent and suddenly your front tire goes completely flat—

you get the picture. In emergency situations, you can put layers of nonstretchable material, such as a dollar bill, an empty energy bar wrapper (or two), or even a short section of the exploded tube (double thickness is better) between the tube and tire (see §iii-3d and Fig. 3.2).

vi-10
USING TIRE SEALANTS

Tire sealants can virtually eliminate flat tires caused by tread punctures, but they do not fix sidewall cuts, pinch flats, or rim-side punctures. A typical tire sealant, Slime, is a glycol-based green goo full of chopped fibers; when poured into an inner tube, it flows to punctures and seals them. There are other brands and colors of glycol-based fibrous tire sealants as well; these instructions generally apply to them all.

Another type of sealant has a liquid latex base and is generally white or light colored. It can come as a liquid in a bottle, such as Stan's, CafféLatex, or Schwalbe Doc Blue sealant (Fig. 6.18), or it can come as an aerosol latex foam, such as Vittoria Pit Stop or Hutchinson Fast'Air (Fig. 6.19).

NOTE: *You can also purchase inner tubes with sealant already inside.*

ALSO NOTE: *The inner tube must be of proper size. If it is too small (for instance, a 26 × 1.325 to 1.5-inch tube inside a 26 × 2.0-inch tire) and stretches when inflated in the tire, any holes will stretch open and won't seal.*

a. Putting tire sealant in a tubeless tire

Simply pop the tire off of one side of the rim (§vi-2), shake the bottle, and squirt 2–4 oz. (¼–½ cup) or so of sealant (Fig. 6.18) into the tire (Fig. 6.17). Push the tire bead back onto the rim (§vi-7) and inflate. This method works with glycol-based and latex-based sealants and can eliminate the aggravating air loss common with many UST tubeless tires.

Some sealants can be injected via a hose on a syringe right through the valve (but Stan's and

6.18 Liquid tire sealants

6.19 Aerosol latex sealants

glycol-based sealants will clog the valve). If you remove the (removable) valve core, you can use this method with all sealants; follow the procedure in step c.

b. Installing aerosol sealant through a valve

This is a great on-trail fix for any tire, tubed or tubeless. It's also useful prophylactically in an inner tube. The tire (and tube, if applicable) should be installed on the rim before sealant is added.

1. **Deflate the tire.**
2. **Screw the end of the aerosol sealant can's nozzle or hose onto the valve** (Fig. 6.19). Open the Presta valve, or remove the Schrader valve cap first.
3. **Deploy the full contents of the can into the tire.** This will inflate the tire as well as filling it with sealant.
4. **If the tire has a leak, rotate the wheel until the hole is at the bottom.** Hold the wheel that way until the sealant has filled the hole and no more air is escaping. Go ride, or spin the wheel for a while to further spread the sealant around in the tube.

Alternatively, the old-school way to seal a slow leak in an inner tube, or to add some puncture resistance to it, is to pour a can of evaporated milk into a pump you don't care about and pump it in through the valve. This works quite well for tiny leaks, but if you get a blowout after the milk has been in there awhile, boy, does it ever stink!

c. Sealing a tubeless tire or inner tube with sealant through a valve without a core

The valve core must be removable. All Schrader cores are removable, but removable Presta cores are rare on inner tubes and common on tubeless (or tubular) valves. You can tell if a Presta valve core is removable because there will be two wrench flats on opposite sides of the small valve-cap threads.

1. **Unscrew the valve core (counterclockwise), and remove it.** Schrader valves require a thin, two-prong core remover (Fig. 1.3), whereas Presta cores can be removed with an adjustable wrench or specific Presta valve-core wrench.
2. **Inject 2–4 fluid ounces of sealant.** With the valve at four o'clock, put the hose or hose adapter of a syringe injector (Fig. 6.18) or squeeze bottle over the valve, or jam the tip of a squeeze bottle of sealant into the valve stem and squeeze.
3. **Screw the valve core back in (clockwise).**

4. **Pump the tire to 40 psi.**

5. **If the tire has a leak, move the sealant to it.** Rotate the wheel until the hole is at the bottom, and hold the wheel that way until the sealant has filled the hole and no more air is escaping. Go ride, or spin the wheel for a while to further spread the sealant around in the tube.

d. Maintaining sealant-filled tires

Inflating or deflating

Always have the stem at four o'clock, and wait a minute for the sealant to drain away; if you don't, sealant will leak out, eventually clogging the valve.

Sealing punctures

1. **If you find that the tire has gone flat, pump it up and ride it a bit to see if it seals.**

2. **If you get numerous punctures, you may need to pump repeatedly and ride before the tube seals up.**

3. **Pinch flats, caused by the tube being pinched between the tire and rim, won't seal because one of the two "snakebite" holes is on the rim side.** Punctures on the rim side of the tube will not seal, because the sealant is thrown to the outside. ·

4. **If you have removed an embedded nail or other foreign object, rotate the wheel to place the hole at the bottom to seal it.**

5. **Patch sidewall gashes in tubes; if the tire sidewall has a gash, replace the tire.**

RIMS AND SPOKES

vi-11

TRUING A WHEEL

 **LEVEL 2**

For more information on truing wheels, see §xii-4 on wheel building.

If your wheel has a wobble in it, you can fix the wobble by adjusting the tension on the spokes. An extreme bend in the rim cannot be fixed by spoke truing alone, because the spoke tension on the two sides of the wheel will be so uneven that the wheel will rapidly fall apart.

Get a spoke wrench of the right size for the spoke nipples—they come in different sizes (as well as shapes), and you will wreck the nipples if you use a spoke wrench that is too large.

1. **Check for broken or loose spokes in the wheel.** Feel for any spokes that are so loose that they flop around. If there is a broken spoke, follow the replacement procedure in §vi-12. If there is a single loose spoke, check to see that the rim is not dented or cracked in that area. I recommend replacing the rim if it is (Chapter 12). If the rim looks okay, mark the loose spoke with a piece of tape, and tighten it up with the spoke wrench until it seems to be at the same tension as adjacent spokes on the same side of the wheel (pluck the spoke and listen to the tone). Then follow the truing procedure here.

2. **Check the hub-bearing adjustment.** Grab the rim while the wheel is on the bike, and flex it side to side. If the bearings are loose, the wheel will clunk side to side. The hub will need to be tightened before you true the wheel, or else the wheel will behave erratically. Follow the hub-adjustment procedure in §vi-15d, steps 1–4.

3. **Put the wheel in a truing stand if you have one.** Otherwise, leave the wheel on the bike, suspend the bike in a bike stand or from the ceiling, or turn it upside down on the handlebar and saddle.

4. **Adjust the truing stand feeler so that it scrapes the rim at the biggest wobble.** If you do not have a stand and are truing the wheel on the bike, push one of the brake pads over to serve as a trueness indicator.

6.20 Lateral truing if rim scrapes on left

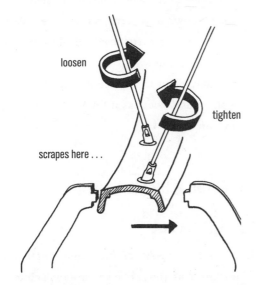

loosen

tighten

scrapes here . . .

6.21 Lateral truing if rim scrapes on right

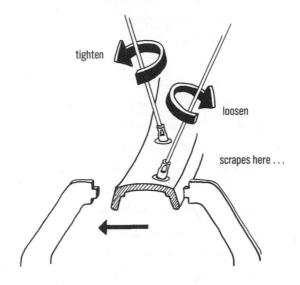

tighten

loosen

scrapes here . . .

5. **Where the rim scrapes, tighten the spoke or spokes that come to the rim from the opposite side of the hub, and loosen the spoke or spokes that come from the same side of the hub as the rim scrapes** (Figs. 6.20–21). This approach will pull the rim away from the feeler or brake pad. When correcting a wheel that is laterally out of true (wobbles side to side), always adjust spokes in pairs: one spoke coming from one side of the wheel, the other from the opposite side.

NOTE ON DIRECTION TO TURN THE NIPPLES: *Tightening spokes is similar to opening a jar upside down. With the jar right side up, turning the lid to the left opens the jar, but this reverses when you turn the jar upside down (try it and see). Spoke nipples are just like the lid on that upside-down jar. In other words, when the nipples are at the bottom of the rim, counterclockwise tightens and clockwise loosens (Figs. 6.20–21). The opposite is true when the nipples you are turning are at the top of the wheel. It may take you a few attempts before you catch on, but you will eventually get this process. If you temporarily make the wheel worse, simply reverse what you have done and start over.*

It is best to tighten and loosen by small amounts (about one-quarter turn at a time), decreasing the amount you turn the spoke nipples as you move away from the spot where the rim scrapes the hardest. If the wobble gets worse, then you are turning the spokes in the wrong direction.

NOTE ON TWISTED SPOKES: *As you turn the nipple on a tight spoke, particularly a thin one or a flat, aero one, the spoke will tend to twist. To avoid this, when you tighten or loosen a spoke, twist it in the correction direction, and then twist back half as far. This will be enough to unwind most spokes. Aero spokes or superlight spokes may still have a twist in them. With aero spokes, it is best to hold the spoke from twisting as you turn the nipple. For flat steel spokes, DT Swiss makes a red plastic spoke wrench with a long, conical groove down the spoke side to fit an L-shaped steel tool to keep the spoke from twisting (§i-4, Fig. 1.4). The long part of the L-shaped tool is slotted for the aero spoke to keep it from twisting as you turn the nipple, and its conical exterior fits in the groove in the spoke wrench. For large, flat, aluminum spokes, you'll need a slotted tool from the wheel manufacturer to hold them. With superlight round spokes, you won't really be able to tell whether the spokes have unwound, other than the wheel may "ping" when you first ride it as the spokes unwind and settle in. You may need to retrue the wheel once they have settled in.*

NOTE ON INTERNAL NIPPLES: *Some deep-section carbon rims require the nipples to be inside the rim; the holes are not big enough for a nipple to fit through. You must remove the tire and rim strip. Then reach down into the spoke holes with the correct-size socket. The simplest tool for this is either a Y-wrench with 5mm and 5.5mm hex sockets and a square-drive socket (for upside-down standard nipples inside of the rim) on the ends of its three long arms (§i-4, Fig. 1.4) or a specialty wrench for the particular brand of internal spoke nipples.*

NOTE ON NIPPLES AT THE HUB: *Some wheels have the spoke nipples at the hub and not at the rim. You need a special spoke wrench (it should come with the wheels) to get at them. You must be particularly careful about the rotation direction to make sure you are tightening or loosening as you intend (see the preceding discussion about jar lids).*

6. **As the rim moves toward center, readjust the truing-stand feeler (or the brake pad).** Again, make it scrape the most out-of-true spot on the wheel.

7. **Check the wobble first on one side of the wheel and then on the other.** Adjust spokes accordingly so that you don't end up pulling the whole wheel off-center by chasing wobbles on only one side. As the wheel gets closer to true, you will need to decrease the amount you turn the spokes to avoid overcorrecting.

8. **Accept a certain amount of wobble, especially if truing in the bike.** The in-the-bike method of wheel truing is not very accurate and is not at all suited for making a wheel absolutely true. If you have access to a wheel-dishing tool, check to make sure that the wheel is centered (§xii-5). And if you notice

wide variations in spoke tension on the same side of the wheel or the wheel hopping up and down as it turns, remove the tire and check the radial trueness (wheel roundness, §xii-4b). If there is a big dent in the rim, you may need to replace it. The wheel will rapidly lose trueness if the spoke tension is uneven.

vi-12
REPLACING A BROKEN SPOKE

LEVEL 2

1. **Get a new spoke of the same length and thickness as the spoke you are replacing.**

NOTE: *The spokes on the front wheel are usually not the same length as the spokes on the rear. Also, the spokes on the drive side of the rear wheel are almost always*

6.22 Weaving in a new spoke

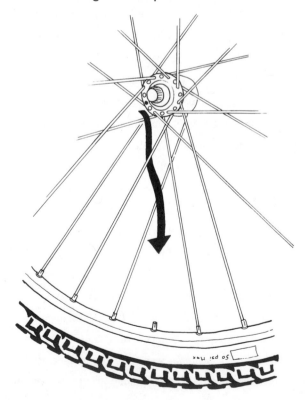

shorter than those on the other side. Same goes for a disc-brake side of a front wheel.

2. **Thread the spoke through the spoke hole in the hub flange.** If the broken spoke is on the drive side of the rear wheel, you will need to remove the cassette cogs or the freewheel to get at the hub flange (§vi-20 and §vi-21). If the spoke is adjacent to the disc-brake rotor, remove the rotor (§vii-13a).

3. **Weave the new spoke in with the other spokes just as it was before** (Fig. 6.22). It may take some bending to get it in place.

4. **If the nipple is in good shape, thread the spoke into the same nipple.** Otherwise, use a new nipple. You'll need to remove the tire, tube, and rim strip to install one.

5. **Mark (with tape) and tighten the new spoke.** Tighten it up about as snugly as the neighboring spokes on that side of the wheel are tightened. If the wheel was true before the spoke broke, tighten just this one spoke until the wheel is true again.

6. **Follow the steps for truing a wheel as outlined in §vi-11.**

vi-13
OVERHAULING HUBS

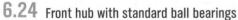 **LEVEL 2**

Hubs should turn smoothly and noiselessly. If they are regularly maintained (and of decent quality to start with), you can expect them still to be running smoothly when you are ready to give up on the rest of your bike.

There are two general types of hubs: the "sealed-bearing" (or "cartridge-bearing") type (Fig. 6.23) and the standard "cup-and-cone" type (Fig. 6.24). All hubs have a "hub shell" that contains the axle and bearings and is connected to the rim with spokes.

Standard cup-and-cone hubs have loose ball bearings that roll along very smooth bearing surfaces called "bearing races," with an axle going through the center of the hub. These hubs also have a pair of conical nuts called "cones" that thread onto the axle (Fig. 6.24). On each side of the hub, a cone presses the bearings gently

6.23 Front hub with cartridge bearing

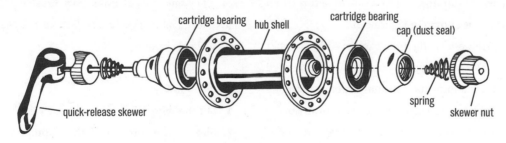

cartridge bearing   hub shell   cartridge bearing   cap (dust seal)

quick-release skewer   spring   skewer nut

6.24 Front hub with standard ball bearings

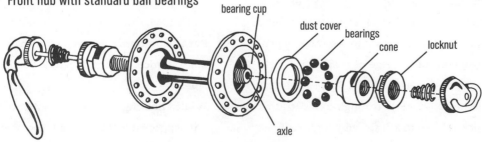

bearing cup   dust cover   bearings   cone   locknut

axle

inside the bearing cup and guides the bearings as they travel along the bearing race. In high-quality hubs, the bearing-race surfaces on the cone and cup have been machined to minimize friction. The operation of the hub depends on the smoothness and lubrication of the cones, ball bearings, and cups. Outboard of the cones are one or more spacers (or washers), followed by threaded locknuts that tighten down against the cones and spacers to keep the hub in proper adjustment. The rear hub will have more spacers on both sides, especially on the drive side (Fig. 6.36).

The term "sealed-bearing hub" is a bit of a misnomer, because many cup-and-cone hubs offer better protection against dirt and water than some sealed-bearing hubs. The term "cartridge-bearing hub" is more accurate, because the distinguishing feature of these hubs is that the bearings, races, and cones are all assembled as a cartridge unit at the factory and then plugged into a hub shell that is machined to accept the cartridge bearing. Cartridge-bearing front hubs have two bearings, one on either end of the hub shell (Fig. 6.23). Rear hubs (Fig. 6.35) have at least two and come with additional bearing cartridges to stabilize the rear freehub body (the part onto which the rear cogs are attached), assuming it is not a hub for a thread-on freewheel as shown in Figure 6.36.

Cartridge-bearing hubs can have any number of axle-assembly types. Some have a threaded axle with locknuts quite similar to a cup-and-cone hub. Much more common on mountain bikes are aluminum axles, often very large in diameter with correspondingly large bearings. Their end caps usually snap on, screw on, or are held on with setscrews or circlips. The large-diameter axles and bearings are meant to prevent independent movement of the legs of suspension forks or rear-suspension assemblies. Some have very large-diameter (20mm) "through-axles" (rather than quick-release axles) for very high stiffness

(see §ii-10). On these, the fork ends—and sometimes the frame's rear dropouts—clamp around the ends of the axle.

vi-14
REMOVING HUB FROM BIKE

1. **Remove the wheel from the bike** (§ii-2 to §ii-5, §ii-10, and §ii-12).
2. **Remove the quick-release skewer or other hardware that holds the wheel onto the bike.**

vi-15
OVERHAULING STANDARD CUP-AND-CONE HUB, FRONT OR REAR

Take some time to evaluate the hub's condition before disassembling it. That will help you to isolate problems. Spin the hub while holding the axle, and turn the axle while holding the hub. Does it turn roughly? Is the axle bent or broken? Wobble the axle side to side. Is the bearing adjustment loose?

NOTE: *Some hubs have large rubber seals covering the axle nuts that can squeal hideously, even though the inside workings of the hub are in good shape. The squeal can be caused by dust in the seal or by the seal not being seated properly against the hub face. Pull the seal off by squeezing and yanking it. Brush it off, put it back into its mating grooves on the hub, and the noise will probably be gone.*

a. Disassembly

1. **Set the wheel flat on a table or workbench.**
2. **Slip a cone wrench of the appropriate size onto the wrench flats on one of the cones.** Size is usually 13mm, 14mm, or 15mm. On a rear wheel, work on the nondrive side.
3. **Put an appropriately sized wrench or adjustable wrench on the locknut on the same side.**
4. **While holding the cone with the cone wrench, loosen the locknut** (Fig. 6.25). This

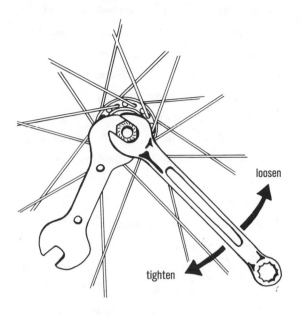

loosen

tighten

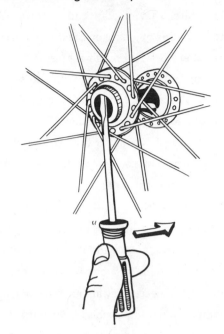

procedure may take considerable force, as these are often fastened together very tightly to maintain the hub's adjustment. Make sure that you are unscrewing the locknut counterclockwise ("lefty loosey, righty tighty," as shown in Fig. 6.25).

5. **As soon as the locknut loosens, move the cone wrench from the cone on top to the cone on the opposite end of the axle.** This holds the axle in place as you unscrew the locknut. The locknut will generally unscrew with your fingers; use a wrench on it if necessary to get past any damaged threads.

6. **Slide any spacers off.** If they will not slide off, the cone will push them off when you unscrew it. Note that some spacers have a small tooth or "key" that corresponds to a groove along the axle; make sure it's lined up before you unscrew the cone, or you'll damage the threads.

7. **Unscrew the cone from the axle.** Again, you may need to hold the opposite cone with a wrench and use a wrench on this cone. If the cone is a split type with a pinch bolt to clamp it onto the axle, loosen the pinch bolt.

8. **Keep track of the various parts.** Line up nuts, spacers, and cones on your workbench in the order in which they were removed (Fig. 6.24). Or slide a twist-tie through all the parts in the correct order and orientation. Either method serves as an easy guide when reassembling the hub.

9. **Flip the wheel over.** To catch any bearings that might fall out, put your hand over the end of the hub from which you removed the nuts and spacers, and place a rag underneath the wheel.

10. **Pull the axle up and out.** Be careful not to lose any bearings that might fall out of the hub or that might stick to the axle. Leave the cone, spacers, and locknut all tightened together on the opposite end of the axle from the one you disassembled. If you are replacing a bent or broken axle, measure the amount of axle sticking out beyond the locknut, and put the cone, spacers, and locknut on the new axle identically.

11. **Remove all the ball bearings from both sides of the hub.** They may stick to a screwdriver with a coating of grease on the tip, or you can push them down through the center of the hub and out the other side with the screwdriver. Tweezers or a small magnet might also be useful for removing bearings. Put the bearings in a cup, a jar lid, or the like. Count the bearings, and make sure you have the same number from each side.

12. **With a screwdriver, gently pop off the seals that are pressed into either end of the hub shell** (Fig. 6.26). Be careful not to deform them; leave them in if you can't pop them out without damage. If they are not removed, it is tedious, but not impossible, to clean the dirty grease out of their concave interiors with a rag and a thin screwdriver.

b. Cleaning

1. **Wipe the hub shell out with a rag.** Remove all dirt and grease from the bearing surfaces. Using a screwdriver, push a rag through the axle hole in the hub and spin the wheel around it to clean out any grease or dirt. Wipe off the outer faces of the shell. Finish with a very clean rag on the bearing surfaces. They should shine and be completely free of dirt or grease. If you let your hub go too long between overhauls, the grease may have solidified and glazed over so completely that you will need a solvent to remove it. If you are working on a rear cassette hub, take this opportunity to lubricate the cassette (see §vi-23.)

2. **Wipe the axle, nuts, and cones with a rag.** Clean the cones particularly well with a clean rag. Again, a solvent may be required if the grease has solidified. Get any dirt out of the threads on the disassembled axle end; if you do not, the cone will push any dirt that remains into the hub upon reassembly.

3. **Wipe the grease and dirt off the seals.** A rag over the end of a screwdriver is sometimes useful for getting inside. Again, glaze-hard grease may have to be removed with a solvent. Keep the solvent out of the freehub body.

4. **Wipe off the bearings.** Rub all of them together between two rags. This may be sufficient to clean them completely, but small specks of dirt can still adhere to them, so I prefer to take the next step as well.

5. **Superclean and polish the bearings.** (If you are overhauling low-quality hubs, skip to step 6.) I prefer to wash the ball bearings in a plugged sink with an abrasive soap such as Lava, rubbing them between my hands as if I were washing my palms. This really gets them shining, unless they are caked with glaze-hard grease. Make sure you have plugged the sink drain! This method has the added advantage of cleaning my hands for the assembly step. It is silly to contaminate your superclean parts with dirty hands. If there is hardened glaze on the bearings, soak them in a solvent. If that does not remove the glaze, buy new bearings at the bike shop. Take a few of the old bearings along so that you are sure to buy the right size.

6. **Dry all bearings and any other wet parts.** Inspect the bearings and bearing surfaces carefully. If any of the bearings have pits or gouges, replace all of the bearings. The same goes for the cones. A lack of sheen or a patina on either balls or cones indicates wear and is cause for replacement. Most bike shops stock replacement cones. If the bearing cups in the hub shell are pitted, the only thing you can do is buy a new hub. Regular maintenance and proper adjustment can prevent pitted bearing races in the hubs.

NOTE: *Using new ball bearings when overhauling standard cup-and-cone hubs ensures round, smooth* bearings. However, do not avoid performing an overhaul just because you don't have any new ball bearings. Inspect the ball bearings carefully. If there is even the slightest hint of uneven wear or pitting on the balls, cups, or cones, throw the bearings out and complete the overhaul with new bearings. Err on the side of caution.

c. Assembly and lubrication

1. **Press in the seals or dust covers on both ends of the hub shell.**

2. **Smear grease with your clean finger into the bearing race on one end of the hub shell.** I like using light-colored or clear grease so that I can see if it gets dirty, but any bike grease will do. Grease not only lubricates the bearings; it also forms a barrier to dirt and water. Use enough grease to cover the balls halfway. Too much grease will slow the hub by packing around the axle.

3. **Stick half of the ball bearings into the grease.** Make sure you put in the same number of bearings that came out. Distribute them uniformly around in the bearing race.

4. **Smear grease on the cone that is still attached to the axle, and slide the axle into the hub shell.** Lift the wheel up a bit (30-degree angle), so that you can push the axle in until the cone slides into position and keeps all the bearings in place. On rear hubs it is important to replace the axle and cone assembly into the same side of the hub from which it was removed because of the spacing for cogs.

5. **Turn the wheel over.** Hold the axle pushed inward with one hand to secure the bearings (Fig. 6.27).

6. **Smear grease into the bearing race that is now facing up.** Lift the wheel and allow the axle to slide down just enough so that it is not sticking up past the bearing race. Make sure no bearings fall out of the bottom. If the

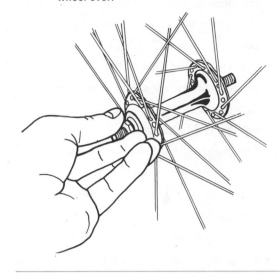

6.27 Push inward on the axle and flip the wheel over.

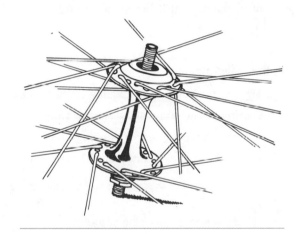

6.28 Set the axle on the floor to keep the cone in contact with the bearings.

race and bearings are properly greased and the axle remains in the hub shell, they are not likely to fall out.

7. **Place the remaining bearings uniformly around in the grease.** The top end of the axle should still be below the bearing race. Make sure you have inserted the correct number of bearings.

8. **Slide the axle back up into place.** Set the wheel down on the table so that the wheel rests on the lower axle end, seating the cone against the bearings (Fig. 6.28).

9. **Apply a film of grease to the top cone-bearing surface.** With your fingers, screw the top cone down into place. Seat it snugly onto the bearings.

10. **In correct order, slide on the washer and any spacers.** Watch for those washers with the little tooth or "key" that fits into the lengthwise groove in the axle.

11. **Use your fingers to screw on the locknut.** Note that the two sides of the locknut are not the same. If you are unsure about which way the locknut goes back on, check the orientation of the locknut that is on the opposite end of the axle (this locknut was not removed during this overhaul and should therefore be in the correct orientation). As a general rule, the rough surface of the locknut faces out so that it can get a better bite into the dropout.

d. Hub adjustment

1. **Tighten the cone until it lightly contacts the bearings.** The axle should turn smoothly without any roughness or grinding, and there should be a small amount of lateral play.

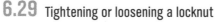

6.29 Tightening or loosening a locknut

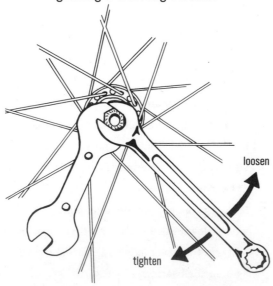

loosen

tighten

Tighten the locknut until it is snug against the cone. The slight looseness in the hub (called axle-end play) will be taken out when the quick-release skewer is tightened down with the wheel in the frame. If the hub is a bolt-on type without a quick-release skewer, you want to adjust it without any play in it.

2. **Place the cone wrench into the flats of the hub cone.** Tighten the locknut with another wrench (Fig. 6.29). To hold the adjustment, tighten the locknut as much as you can against the cone and spacers. Be aware that you can ruin the hub if you accidentally tighten the cone down against the bearings instead of against the locknut. If the cone is a split type with a pinch bolt to clamp it onto the axle, tighten the pinch bolt.

3. **If the adjustment is off, loosen the locknut while holding the cone with the cone wrench.** If the hub is too tight, unscrew the cone a bit. If the hub is too loose, screw the cone in a bit.

4. **Repeat steps 1–3 until the hub adjustment feels right.** It should have a slight amount of end play so that the pressure of the quick-release skewer will compress it to a perfect adjustment. Tighten the locknut firmly against the cone to hold the adjustment.

NOTE: *You may find that tightening the locknut against the cone suddenly turns your "Mona Lisa" perfect hub adjustment into something less beautiful. If it is too tight, back off both cones (by using a cone wrench on either side of the hub, each on one cone) a fraction of a turn. If too loose, tighten both locknuts a bit. If still off, you might have to loosen one side and go back to step 1. It's rare that I get a hub adjustment perfectly "dialed in" on the first try, so expect to tinker with the adjustment a bit before it's right.*

5. **Put the skewer back into the hub.** Make sure that the conical springs have their narrow ends to the inside (see Fig. 6.24).

6. **Install the wheel in the bike, tightening the skewer.** Check that the wheel spins well without any side play at the rim. If it needs readjustment (too tight or too loose), go back to step 3.

Congratulate yourself on a job well done! Hub overhaul is a delicate job, and it makes a significant difference in the longevity and performance of your bike.

vi-16
OVERHAULING CARTRIDGE-BEARING HUBS

Compared to hubs with cup-and-cone bearings, cartridge-bearing hubs (Figs. 6.23 and 6.35) generally do not need much maintenance. However, if you ride through water above the hubs or direct a high-pressure sprayer into them, you can expect water and dirt to get through the seal no matter how good it may be. If the ball bearings inside the cartridges get wet or start making noise, they should be overhauled or replaced.

There are many types of cartridge-bearing hubs, and it is outside the scope of this book to explain how to disassemble every one of them, but I'll cover the main ones in this section (and rear Mavic hub overhaul in §vi-23d). It is usually not too hard to figure out how to take apart any hub. Some cartridge-bearing hubs have externally threaded axles with locknuts that you simply unscrew. After that, they may still require insertion of hex keys in the ends to unscrew parts from internal axle threads. On those devoid of external locknuts, though, there will generally be end caps (Fig. 6.23) that can be removed by one of the following approaches:

- Pulling or prying them off.
- Sliding them off after loosening a setscrew on each cap.
- Unscrewing the caps with 5mm hex keys inserted into the 5mm hex holes in either axle end.

- On Mavic, unscrewing the axle with a 5mm hex key while holding the other end with either a pin tool in the adjuster ring (front) or a 5mm hex key (front) or 10mm hex key (rear) in the bore of the axle, often after pulling off the end cap on the adjuster end.
- Yanking the rear cassette cogset straight off the hub by hand (DT Swiss).

If you see hex flats inside the axle end, you will be sticking a hex key in there. If both axle ends have them, put a 5mm hex key in each end and unscrew the end caps. If only one end has them, the other end must first pull off before you can use the hex key.

If you see no hex hole in the end, then usually at least one end of the axle will pull off. It is usually held on by a rubber O-ring engaging grooves at the end of the axle and inside the end cap, so a good yank will get it off. In practice, however, this often requires more than just your fingers. If you have an axle-clamp tool (§i-4, Fig. 1.4), put it in a vise and grab the end of the axle with it to pull the cap off. Without that, you can just grab the outside of the cap with a vise and yank up on the wheel. If both ends are like this, yank both ends off (DT Swiss is a good example).

On a DT Swiss or Hügi rear hub, you can often get the drive-side end cap off simply by yanking up on the cogs; the entire freehub body and end cap will come off.

On Mavic rear hubs, pull the left end cap off, stick a 10mm hex key inside to engage the axle, stick a 5mm hex key in the other end, and unscrew.

On a DT Swiss or Mavic rear hub, once the axle or drive-side axle end cap is out, you can (carefully) pull off the freehub body while turning it counterclockwise. Be ready to catch pawls and tiny springs (Mavic) or ratchet rings and large springs (DT Swiss). Slide the freehub up a bit, see where the pawls are, and hold them in place with your fingers; then pull the freehub up and off.

6.30 Tapping out a cartridge bearing

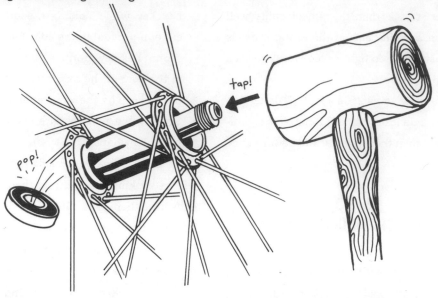

If you were able to pull the axle all the way out, you can now drive the bearings out of the hub with as big a rod or hex key as you can fit and cock at an angle to hit the backside of the opposite bearing. Smack it with a hammer until the bearing pops out (Fig. 6.31). You should not plan to reuse this bearing.

Some axles have a shoulder on each end against the bearing (DT Swiss is a good example). In this case, smack the end of the axle to drive the bearing out using a soft hammer (Fig. 6.30), a table against the axle, or a socket of the right size placed against the end of the axle to protect it from a hard hammer. Smack the end of the axle the other way to knock out the other bearing. On a DT Swiss rear hub, you can get the nondrive bearing out this way, but you cannot remove the drive-side bearing without first unscrewing from the hub the radial teeth that engage the freehub star ratchets. This requires a special DT Swiss tool held in a very solid vise.

Once the freehub body has been removed from the hub, driving the bearing(s) out can often be done easily with a hex key of appropriate diameter. If the bearings don't come out of the freehub

6.31 Tap bearing out with a long hex key.

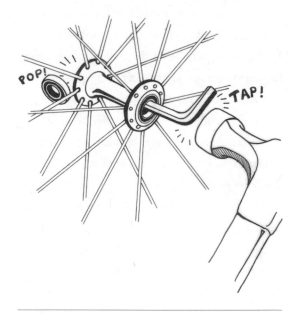

6.32 Removing a seal from a cartridge bearing

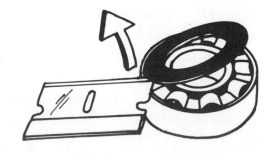

body without undue force, you may be able to leave them in the hub shell and pop off the outer bearing seal on each with the tip of a razor blade (Fig. 6.32). If the grease inside is pretty clean, you can just wipe it out and pack new grease in from the outside. That may be all that is necessary.

Cartridge bearings are vulnerable to lateral stress; if you have to use a lot of force to pound them out, they will need to be replaced. Once the cartridge bearings are out, you can sometimes overhaul them (if not, you'll need to buy new ones).

1. **Gently pop off the bearing covers with a single-edge razor blade** (Fig. 6.32).

2. **Squirt a citrus-based solvent into the bearing under pressure.** Wear rubber gloves and protective glasses. Wash out grease, water, and dirt. Scrub with a clean toothbrush. Don't brush your teeth anymore with this toothbrush.

3. **Blow out the bearing with compressed air to dry it.**

4. **Pack it with grease, and snap the bearing covers back on.** Replace the bearing if it doesn't turn smoothly.

5. **Install the bearings.** The closest thing the average home mechanic will have to a proper tool for pressing in a cartridge bearing is a quick-release skewer and a socket wrench (or the old bearing). Place the new bearing in proper alignment where it will go in. Place a socket whose outside diameter (OD) is just slightly smaller than the bearing's OD against the new bearing, or do the same with the old bearing (but if the bearing seat is deeper than the bearing, the old bearing can get stuck, so be cautious). Using washers or something of the sort to protect the bearing seat on the opposite end, install the skewer (without the springs on it), and spin it to tighten it until the bearing is fully pressed in place (Fig. 6.33). If possible, do the same with the outer bear-

6.33 Pressing in the bearing with a skewer and a socket

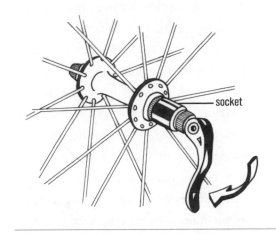

socket

6.34 Pressing a bearing into a freehub

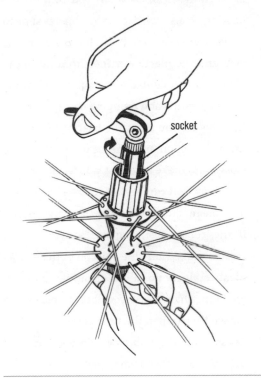

socket

ing in the freehub body once it is in place on the hub (Fig. 6.34).

If you are installing ceramic cartridge bearings, it is worth thinking ahead of time about maintenance when you are determining the orientation of the bearings. The ceramic bearings you have in your hand most likely will be hybrid ceramic bearings (see §vi-17), which means that the balls are ceramic but the races are made of steel. Even though the ceramic balls cannot rust and are more than twice as hard as steel balls, the steel races can rust. As you don't want to be making this investment frequently, take a moment to investigate the easiest way to maintain them in the future.

Ceramic cartridge bearings, like most steel cartridge bearings, have bearing retainers that separate the balls from each other. The retainers reduce friction by preventing neighboring balls, whose adjacent sides are turning in opposite directions, from rubbing against each other. The bearing retainer may be asymmetrical, so when you remove the bearing seals (with a razor blade slipped under the edge), you'll see the balls on one side and the plastic retainer from the other side. Proper maintenance requires cleaning out the bearing and pumping new grease into it, so before you press the bearings in, determine on which side the bearing retainer is closed and make sure that side faces inboard. That way, you can pry off the bearing covers and clean and grease the bearings easily. If the ceramic bearing has a symmetrical retainer concealing the balls on both sides as most retainers do in steel bearings, so be it; you'll just have to do your best to clean and grease them when the time comes.

6. **Reassemble the hub axle and end caps the opposite way they came apart.**

7. **Tap on either end of the axle with a soft hammer.** Sometimes the bearings will be slightly out of alignment after installation, making the hub noticeably hard to turn, and this tap will free the bearings. With Mavic hubs, once the wheel is mounted in the frame or fork with the skewer tightened, turn the threaded ring on one face of the hub (the side opposite the cogs on the rear) with the Mavic pin tool. Screw it in to remove side play; unscrew it to eliminate hub binding. If the ring doesn't hold its adjustment, apply a little Loctite to the adjuster threads.

vi-17
UPGRADING BEARINGS

Following the instructions in §vi-15 or §vi-16 (depending on whether the hub is loose bearing or cartridge bearing), you can replace old bearings with supersmooth ceramic bearings, higher-grade steel bearings, or new bearings of the same type. Ball bearings are higher-grade if the balls are smoother, harder, rounder, and more uniform in size. Cartridge bearings are higher-grade if both the balls and races are smoother, harder, and more uniform. Ceramic bearings are generally higher-grade than even the best steel ones, because the ceramic balls are harder, smoother, rounder, and more uniform in size than steel balls. Expect to pay a lot for ceramic bearings (and even for high-grade steel bearings). Ceramic balls should run smoother and last longer, because, besides being smoother and harder, they cannot rust and are less sensitive to lubrication.

Hybrid ceramic bearings have ceramic balls and steel races; full-ceramic bearings have ceramic races as well as ceramic balls and are the most expensive. Full-ceramic bearings should be factory installed, because the ceramic race cannot be pressed in (it has no flexibility and may crack). Instead, the seat in the part into which it fits must be larger so that the bearing fits in without pressure, and then it must be glued in.

vi-18
WORKING WITH GREASE GUARD HUBS

Wilderness Trail Bikes, SunTour, and others have made high-end hubs, some labeled "Grease Guard," that have small grease ports that accept a small-tipped grease gun. The tip in this type of grease gun is about the size of the tip of a pencil. Injecting grease into these grease ports forces grease through the bearings from the inside out, squeezing the old grease out of the outer end. Grease-injection systems do not eliminate the need for overhauling the hubs. Grease injection merely extends the amount of time between overhauls. Furthermore, these systems are only as good as you are about using them.

FREEHUBS, FREEWHEELS, AND COGS

Freehubs and freewheels are freewheeling mechanisms, meaning that they allow the rear wheel to turn forward freely while the pedals are not turning.

A freehub is an integral part of the rear hub. The cogs slide onto the freehub body, engaging longitudinal grooves, or "splines" (Fig. 6.35). A freehub can also be called a "cassette hub," the group of cogs being the "cassette."

A freewheel is a separate unit with the cogs attached to it. The entire freewheel threads onto the drive side of the rear hub (Fig. 6.36). Interchanging cogs on a freewheel is more difficult than on a freehub, and a freewheel does not support the drive side of the hub axle, two reasons why thread-on freewheels have fallen out of fashion. Freewheels can be removed by using a tool made to fit the specific freewheel. Entire freewheels with different gear combinations can be changed in this way.

6.35 Rear freehub with cartridge bearings and a cassette cogset

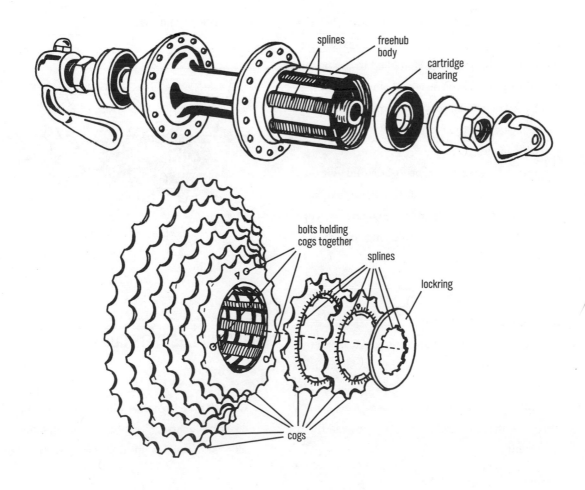

splines

freehub body

cartridge bearing

bolts holding cogs together

splines

lockring

cogs

6.36 Threaded rear hub with standard ball bearings and a freewheel

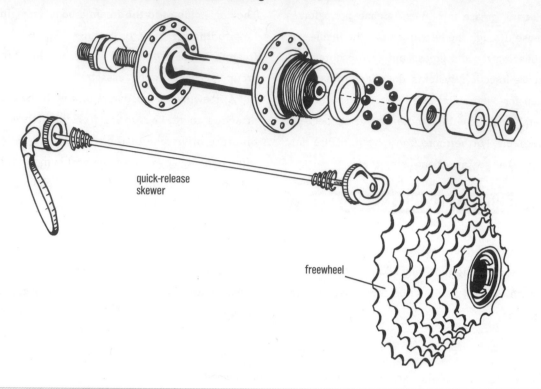

quick-release
skewer

freewheel

Freehubs and freewheels usually rely on a series of spring-loaded pawls that engage internal teeth when pressure is applied to the pedals but allow the bike to freewheel when the rider is coasting. The pawls riding over the teeth as they rotate past make the familiar clicking noise when you are coasting.

Many freehubs can be lubricated without removing them from the hub. Changing gear combinations is accomplished by removing the cogs from the freehub body and putting on different ones.

vi-19
CLEANING REAR COGS

The quickest, albeit perfunctory, way to clean the rear cogs is to slide a rag or Gear Floss string back and forth between each pair of cogs (Fig. 6.37). The other way is to remove them (see §vi-20) and wipe them off with a rag or immerse them in solvent.

6.37 Cleaning the cogs

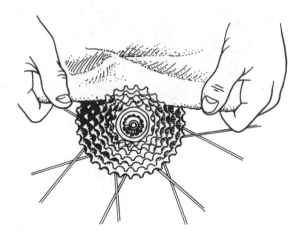

vi-20
CHANGING CASSETTE COGS

⚙️ ⚙️ LEVEL 2

1. Get out a Pedro's Vise Whip or chain whip, a cassette-lockring remover, a wrench (adjustable or open) to fit the remover, and the

6.38 Removing a cogset with a Pedro's Vise Whip

loosen

6.39 Removing a cogset with a chain whip

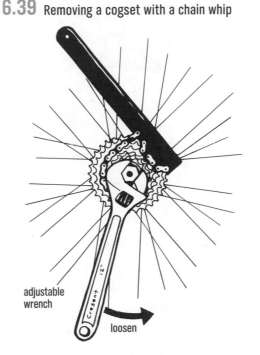

adjustable wrench

loosen

cog(s) you want to install. Note that some very old cassettes from the early 1980s have a threaded smallest cog instead of a lockring. These require two chain whips and no lockring remover.

2. **Remove the quick-release skewer from the hub axle.**

3. **Clamp the Vise Whip** (Fig. 6.38) **or wrap the chain whip** (Fig. 6.39) **around a cog at least two up from the smallest cog.** Wrap a chain whip in the drive direction (Fig. 6.39). In place of the Vise Whip or chain whip, you can substitute a Pedro's tool that has two pins to hold the first cog; it will be labeled "11T" on one side and "12T" on the other side, because the pins will be located differently depending on the size of the first cog (11- or 12-tooth).

4. **Insert the splined lockring remover into the lockring.** The lockring is the threaded disc with a splined hole holding the smallest cog in place. Unscrew the lockring in a counterclockwise direction while holding the Vise Whip or chain whip to keep the cassette

from turning (Figs. 6.38–39). If the lockring is so tight that the tool pops out and damages it, put the quick-release skewer without its springs through the hub and tool and tighten the lockring. Loosen the lockring a fraction of a turn, remove the skewer, and unscrew the lockring the rest of the way.

5. **Pull the cogs straight off.** Some cassette cogsets are all single cogs separated by loose spacers, some cogsets are bolted together, and some cogsets are a combination of both.

6. **Clean the cogs with a rag or a toothbrush.** Use a solvent if necessary, and don't put the toothbrush back by the bathroom sink!

7. **Inspect the cogs for wear.** If the teeth are hook-shaped or the chain can be lifted off them when it is wrapped around the cog under tension, they may be ripe for replacement. If you have access to Rohloff's HG-IG-Check cog-wear indicator gauge (Fig. 1.4), wrap its measurement chain around the cog (while the cogset is on the freehub) and pull on the handle. If the last chain roller on the

6.40 Large spline vs. large spleen

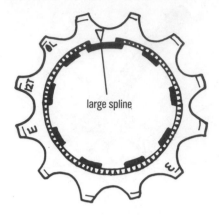

large spline

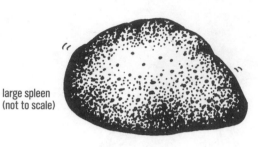

large spleen
(not to scale)

tool hooks on the tooth and resists your flipping it in and out of the tooth pocket while the tool handle is under pressure, or worse, if the entire measurement chain except the first roller slides easily away from the cog teeth while the handle is under pressure, the cog is worn-out. The tool works only on cogs up to 21 teeth.

8. **Replace the cogs.**

(a) If you are replacing the entire cogset, just slide the new one on. Usually, one spline is wider than the others to ensure proper alignment (Fig. 6.40).

(b) If you are installing a 9-speed cassette, see the notes under step 9.

(c) If you are replacing some individual cogs within the cogset, be certain that they are of the same type and model. For example, not all 16-tooth Shimano cogs are alike. Most cogs have shifting ramps, differentially shaped teeth, and other asymmetries. They differ with model as well as with sizes of the adjacent cogs, so you need to buy one for the exact location and model. Install them in decreasing numerical sequence with the numbers facing out.

NOTE: *Some bolt-together cogsets are held together by three long bolts (Fig. 6.35) and can be disassembled for cleaning and then reinstalled onto the freehub as* individual cogs to facilitate future cog changes and cleaning (the bolts are used to make assembly quicker at the bike factory and serve no structural purpose). But high-end cogsets usually have lightweight splined aluminum carriers onto which the cogs are mounted. These cannot be disassembled, and you must replace the entire carrier with cogs assembled onto it.

9. **When all the cogs are on, tighten the lockring with the lockring remover and wrench.** (If you have the old freehub type with the thread-on first cog, tighten that instead with a chain whip.) Make sure that all of the cogs are seated and can't wobble side to side, which would indicate that the first or second cog is sitting against the ends of the splines. If the cogs are loose after you've tightened the lockring, loosen the lockring, line up the first and second cog until they fall in place, and tighten the lockring again. Make sure that the lockring is compatible with both the freehub and the cogset; these can vary depending on manufacturer and size of the first cog.

NOTE ON COMPATIBILITY: *These instructions for removing and replacing cogs apply to 10-, 9-, 8-, 7-, and 6-speed cogsets. But the freehub bodies vary, so make sure you use, for example, only an 8-speed cogset on a freehub body designed for eight cogs.*

NOTE ON 11-TOOTH COGS: *Some 8- and 9-speed freehub bodies will not accept 11-tooth cogs (for example,*

1992–1994 XTR freehub bodies will not accept 11–28 or 11–30 cogsets). To accept the small 11-tooth cog, the splines of current freehub bodies stop about 2mm before the outer end of the freehub body. If you are motivated to do so, you can grind the last 2mm of splines off an old-style 8-speed freehub so that it will accept an 11-tooth cog. But be aware that the steel is very hard, and you may need a rotary grindstone to do the job!

vi-21
CHANGING FREEWHEELS

⚙️ ⚙️ ⚙️ LEVEL 3

If you have a freewheel (Fig. 6.36) and want to switch it with another one, follow this procedure. Replacing individual cogs on an existing freewheel is beyond the scope of this book and is rarely done these days because of the unavailability of spare parts.

1. Get out the appropriate freewheel remover for your freewheel, a big adjustable wrench to fit it, and the freewheel you are replacing it with.

2. Remove the quick-release skewer, and take the springs off it.

3. **Place the freewheel remover into the end of the freewheel so that the notches or splines engage.** Slide the skewer back in from the nondrive side, and thread the skewer nut back on, tightening it against the freewheel remover to keep it from popping out of its notches.

4. **Loosen the freewheel counterclockwise.** Put the big adjustable wrench onto the flats of the freewheel remover. It may take considerable force to free the freewheel, and you may even need to put a large pipe on the end of the wrench for more leverage. Have the tire on the ground for traction as you apply pressure to the wrench. Once the freewheel pops loose, stop and loosen the skewer nut before

continuing to unscrew the freewheel; otherwise, you could snap the skewer in two.

5. **Loosen the skewer nut a bit, and unscrew the freewheel a bit more.** Repeat until the freewheel is loose enough that there is no longer any danger of having the freewheel remover pop out of the notches it engages.

6. **Remove the skewer and spin off the freewheel.**

7. **Grease the threads on the hub and on the new freewheel.**

8. **Thread on the new freewheel by hand.** Tighten it using a chain whip or the freewheel remover and a wrench or by putting the freewheel on the bike and pedaling.

9. **Replace the skewer with the narrow ends of its conical springs facing inward.**

vi-22
REPLACING/FLIPPING ROHLOFF SPEEDHUB COG

⚙️ ⚙️ ⚙️ LEVEL 3

To remove a cog from a Rohloff SpeedHub, you will need the special Rohloff driver (sprocket remover tool). If the cog is worn and you're replacing the chain, you can simply flip it over and double its life, because it is symmetrical.

1. **Remove the quick-release skewer, and take the springs off it.**

2. **Place the Rohloff driver into the center of the cog so that its four prongs engage the two notches in the end of the hub.** Slide the skewer back in from the nondrive side, and thread the skewer nut back on, tightening it against the freewheel remover to prevent the remover from popping out of its notches.

3. **Clamp the cog with a vise whip (Fig. 6.38), or wrap a chain whip around it in the direction opposite the pedaling direction** (the reverse direction of Fig. 6.39).

4. **Holding the cog remover (driver) with a 24mm wrench or an adjustable wrench, unscrew the cog counterclockwise with the Vise Whip or chain whip.**

5. **Pull the cog off, leaving the driver in place.**

6. **Using the driver to line up the cog with the threads, screw on the flipped-over or new cog.** Tighten it (clockwise) with the Vise Whip or chain whip. Now you can remove the driver and replace the quick-release skewer, along with its springs.

7. **Check that the cog flanges are pristine.** If the flange of the cog that recesses into the hub shell is damaged, it could in turn damage the rubber seal on the end of the hub, causing oil to leak out of the hub.

vi-23
LUBRICATING FREEHUB MECHANISMS

Most people ignore their freehubs, even while maintaining the rest of their bicycle very well. In addition, the simple method employed in some bike shops of dunking freehubs in a tub of solvent has the net negative effect of pulling contaminants deep within the freehub, which then lets solvent seep out during riding, thereby contaminating lubricants in the freehub and wheel bearings. This could explain why freehubs are one of the most often purchased replacement parts in bike shops. But a little simple lubrication on a regular basis can prevent the demise of these parts.

Many freehubs can be adequately cleaned and lubricated simply by dripping chain lube into them once the axle assembly is out (step a explains how). But you can drip in only a thin lubricant this way, which will not protect or hold up as long as a thicker formulation will. Also, a thin lubricant will get into the wheel bearings, contaminating and thinning the grease on them. See section b for instructions for injecting cleaning solvents as well as thicker, more protective lubricants into a Shimano freehub.

Some high-end freehubs have grease-injection holes on the freehub body that accept a fine-tip grease gun. With these, you remove the cogs to get at the hole, and you want that hole clean before inserting the grease gun tip, or you will push a plug of dirt right into the freehub mechanism. Rather than using bearing grease in the grease gun, inject a thinner lube into it, such as outboard-motor gear oil, or a special freehub formulation such as Morningstar's Freehub Soup. Using one of these will keep grease from thickening up inside and sticking the pawls in cold temperatures, preventing engagement of the freehub. In most freehubs (but not DT Swiss freehubs and the like), the springs are very light, and it does not take much in the way of sticky or cold-thickened lube to stop them from pushing the pawls radially outward. Believe me, it's a good way to end up on your nose when you apply power to the pedal and the freehub slips.

If the freehub has teeth on the faces of the hub shell and freehub (DT Swiss/Hügi or old Mavic freehubs have these radial teeth), you can just drip oil into the crease between the freehub and the hub shell as you turn the freehub counterclockwise. DT Swiss/Hügi hubs pull apart easily for lubrication; follow the instructions in section d.

a. Standard freehub oiling

🛠 LEVEL 1

1. **Disassemble the hub-axle assembly (see §vi-13 to §vi-16).** "Standard" freehubs are Shimano or similar, and the best method for lubricating them, described in the next section, uses a Freehub Buddy tool. But if you do not have the tool, some lubrication is way better than nothing, so at least do it this way.

2. **Wipe clean the inside of the drive-side bearing surface.** Inspect it for discoloration of the bearing race.

3. **Drip in chain lube between the bearing surface and the freehub body as you spin the freehub counterclockwise.** Have the wheel lying flat and the freehub pointed up toward you. You will hear the clicking noise of the freehub pawls smoothing out as lubricant reaches them. Keep it flowing until old black oil flows out of the other end of the freehub.

4. **Wipe off the excess lube, and continue with the hub overhaul.**

b. Thorough Shimano freehub lubrication without disassembly

 **LEVEL 3**

The best way to lubricate a Shimano freehub is to inject lubricant under pressure using a Morningstar Freehub Buddy tool (Fig. 6.41). Once the hub is apart, most of the work is done. This tool is easy to use, but first you may want to order a reusable dust cap from Morningstar (see the note under step 5).

1. **Disassemble the hub-axle assembly as described in §vi-15.**

2. **Pry out the freehub dust cover.** Use a screwdriver and work your way around (Fig. 6.42). This exposes the hub bearing race.

3. **Push the Freehub Buddy into the bearing race** (Fig. 6.43).

4. **If the freehub has a crunchy feel to it, flush it with solvent.** You might consider removing the freehub and flushing it as in section c. With the Freehub Buddy, force-thread the tip of a turkey baster filled with citrus degreaser or diesel fuel into the threaded hole in the center of the Freehub Buddy, and squirt it in as you slowly turn the freehub. Tilt the wheel with a bucket below to catch the dirty solvent.

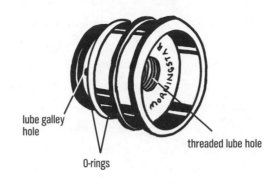

6.41 Morningstar Freehub Buddy

lube galley hole

O-rings

threaded lube hole

6.42 Prying out a Shimano freehub dust cover with a screwdriver

POP!

6.43 Freehub Buddy tool installed in the end of a Shimano freehub body

BUDDY

5. **Inject lubricant.** Force-thread the tip of a tube of outboard-motor gear oil or Morningstar's Freehub Soup syringe into the Freehub Buddy's threaded hole (Fig. 6.41), and squeeze the lube in. Either one is the perfect weight for a freehub; the Soup is specially formulated for longer freehub life. The gear oil

comes in a huge tube whose end fits nicely into the center hole of the tool, whereas the Soup is already packaged in a syringe designed to fit the tool. In a pinch, chain lube can be squirted into the Freehub Buddy. Lubricant will exit through the lube galley hole in the side of the tool between the two rubber O-rings (Fig. 6.41). The smaller O-ring at the closed end of the Freehub Buddy seals off the center of the hub to prevent lubricant from going in there, and the larger O-ring prevents lube from squirting back out the front of the freehub.

Whichever lubricant you use, squeeze it into the Freehub Buddy until all the old dirty lubricant squeezes through the freehub and out the back end of it. Keep going until clean lube oozes out.

Other than by disassembling the entire freehub, you can get a lubricant thicker than thin chain lube into the freehub only with the Freehub Buddy, and a thicker lubricant protects better. Be certain that it's not too thick, however. Filling a freehub with thick grease in cold weather may cause the pawls to stick and not spring back into the freehub teeth to lock up when you want to pedal forward. You could end up freewheeling in both directions! Always spin the freehub by hand, and if it does not engage well, purge again with lighter oil that is compatible with the grease you put inside.

NOTE: *Many freehub dust caps are made of stamped sheet metal, and they may be ruined upon removal. Shimano does not sell them separately, which complicates freehub service considerably. Morningstar sells machined, removable dust caps with an O-ring seal as well as freehub tools and lubricants.*

6. **Overhaul the hub and replace the axle assembly.**

c. Alternative method of thorough Shimano freehub lubrication without complete disassembly

⚙ LEVEL 1

1. **Disassemble the hub-axle assembly as described in §vi-15 and §vi-16.**
2. **Remove the freehub body with a 10mm hex key inserted into the internal freehub-fixing bolt.**
3. **Completely flush out the freehub.** With a rubber stopper from a hardware store, close off the bottom of the freehub body. Pour solvent into the outer opening, spinning the mechanism and thereby letting contaminants run out. If there is a rubber seal, remove it. Repeat until clean. Don't dunk the freehub in a solvent tank; this will pull dirt into it.

Squirt in a quantity of outboard gear lube, and then park the body on paper towels and let the excess drain off. With this method, you do not need to remove the freehub body dust seal.

NOTE: *You can also disassemble a Shimano freehub by unscrewing (clockwise—it's left-hand threaded) the hub-bearing cup. Morningstar sells a tool that fits into the cup's two notches. I won't go into the details here, but I do illustrate it in my Mountain Bike Performance Handbook.*

d. Mavic freehub lubrication

⚙ LEVEL 1

1. **Remove the axle end cap(s).** Depending on model, this usually involves pulling the non-drive-side dust cap straight off.
2. **Remove the axle.** Using two hex keys, one in either end, loosen counterclockwise, unscrew, and remove (Fig. 6.44). Depending on the model, this takes two 5mm hex

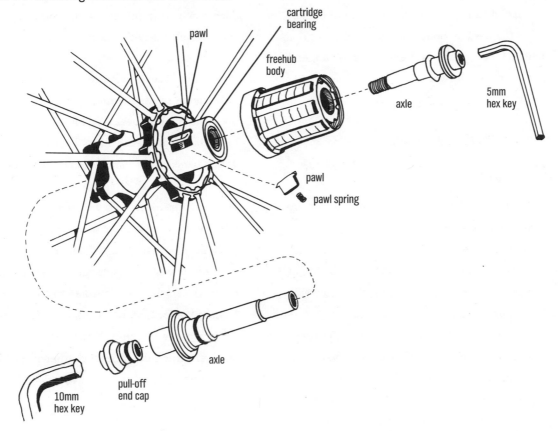

keys or one 10mm and one 5mm, or it can require unscrewing external locknuts from external threads on a steel axle with cone wrenches.

3. **Turn the wheel on its side, freehub up.** Place the wheel on a clear surface where you can catch—or at least see—any pawls or pawl springs that might fly away.

4. **Rotate the freehub body slowly counterclockwise as you pull up on it, and remove it** (Fig. 6.44). Slide the freehub up a little, find where the pawls are, and hold them with your fingers before pulling the freehub completely off.

5. **Pull the outer rubber seal off.**

6. **Clean the pawls, springs, seal, and hub shell.**

7. **Replace the seal, square side in.** Do not grease the seal; it's outside the freehub body, and grease will only attract dirt.

8. **Replace the springs and pawls.**

9. **Lubricate the freehub.** Put 10 or so drops of 10-weight mineral oil (Mavic recommends its M40122 mineral oil or Phil Wood Tenacious Oil) on the plastic bushing and the ratchet teeth in the freehub.

10. **Reinstall the freehub body.** Turn it counterclockwise while holding the pawls down with your fingers.

11. **Replace the axle.** Simple.

🔧 LEVEL 1

DT Swiss and DT-Hügi high-end star-ratchet freehubs pull apart easily for cleaning and lubrication.

1. **Remove the quick-release skewer.**

2. **Lay the wheel on its side, cogs up; grasp the cogset; and pull up.** The freehub body will come off, bringing the axle end cap with it.

3. Clean and grease the spring, both star-shaped ratchets, and the teeth that engage on the freehub body and hub shell.

4. Push the freehub and end cap back on, and replace the skewer.

That's it!

e. Fulcrum freehub lubrication

LEVEL 1

1. On high-end Fulcrum rear hubs, begin by removing the skewer.

2. **Unscrew the locknut.** Insert a 5mm hex key into the drive-side axle, and put a 17mm open-end or box wrench on the drive-side locknut. While holding the 5mm hex key, unscrew the locknut clockwise (in other words, it's left-hand threaded, and you need to unscrew it in the opposite direction from what you would expect). Older Fulcrum models have a little setscrew on the 17mm locknut that you loosen with a 2mm hex key in order to unscrew the locknut.

3. **Pull the freehub straight off.** Older models have individual coil springs under each of the three pawls. These can go flying, and they are hard to clean and to insert back into the hub shell. When removing the freehub body, wrap a twist-tie around the three pawls as they expose themselves from the hub shell as you pull; if you don't do this, the three pawls and the three springs will fly away. Newer Fulcrum models have a single circular, wire spring wrapped around all three pawls (it fits in a groove in the freehub body as well as one cut across the flanks of each pawl). With the new style, you can pull the freehub off with abandon, and nothing will go flying.

4. **Clean and grease the three pawls and the radial teeth inside the hub shell.**

5. **Slide the freehub back in while slowly turning it backward.** Push inward on each pawl with a pencil tip as you do this until all three are engaged and the freehub body drops into place. Again, older Fulcrum models require the use of a twist-tie to hold the pawls in place as you push it in. Pull the twist-tie off after the pawls are inside the hub shell and before the freehub is pushed all the way in.

6. **Tighten the locknut.** While holding the drive-side end of the axle with a 5mm hex key inside its bore, tighten the locknut counterclockwise —remember, it's left-hand threaded!—with a 17mm hex key.

vi-24
LUBRICATING FREEWHEELS

1. **Wipe dirt off the face of the fixed part of the freewheel surrounding the axle.**

2. **Drip lubricant into the crease between the fixed and moving parts of the freewheel as you spin the cogs in a counterclockwise direction.** Have the wheel lying flat with the cogs facing up toward you. You will hear the clicking noise inside become smoother as you get lubricant in there. Be sure to keep the lubricant going in until the old, dirty oil flows out the backside around the hub flange.

3. **Wipe off the excess oil.**

7

BRAKES

CABLES, LEVERS, AND CALIPERS

Well, I predict that if you think about it long enough you will find yourself going round and round and round and round until you finally reach only one possible, rational, intelligent conclusion. The law of gravity and gravity itself did not exist before Isaac Newton. No other conclusion makes sense.

—Robert M. Pirsig,
Zen and the Art of Motorcycle Maintenance

Oh, well. We came after Newton, so we'd better have a good set of brakes.

—Lennard Zinn

TOOLS

2.5mm, 3mm, 4mm, 5mm, and 6mm hex keys

9mm and 10mm open-end wrenches

small adjustable wrench

pliers

grease

screwdrivers, flat-head and Phillips

Torx T10 and T25 wrenches

cable-housing cutter

sharp knife

isopropyl alcohol

OPTIONAL

Morningstar Roc-Tech tool

bleed kit for your hydraulic brake

hydraulic fluid specific to your brake

continued

Not that long ago (1996, when we published the first edition of this book), by far the most common brake for mountain bikes was the cable-actuated center-pull cantilever (Figs. 7.29–45). But "sidepull-cantilever" brakes, otherwise known as "V-brakes" (Fig. 7.24), almost completely eliminated standard cantilevers except on bikes using road bike brake levers, such as for cyclocross. And now, disc brakes (Figs. 7.16–17) have replaced V-brakes as the standard on mountain bikes.

V-brakes offer more flexibility than cantilevers: They can be used on rear-suspension frames without added complexity because they do not require a cable hanger, and parallel-push V-brake designs allow swaps among wheels with different rims without pad readjustment. V-brakes are also more powerful than cantilevers because their arms are longer, and the direct cable pull from one arm to the other is more efficient than yanking up on a straddle cable tying the two arms together, the way that cantilevers operate. Adjusting

V-brakes is also much quicker and simpler than adjusting cantilevers.

Disc brakes, which squeeze the pads against a hub-mounted disc (or "rotor"), stay much cleaner than rim brakes, as mud and water are thrown away from them by the tires, rather than into them, resulting in little drop-off in performance in wet conditions. Additionally, the rim does not heat up during braking with disc brakes, so they can offer consistent performance over a wide range of conditions. However, rim brakes can fade from heating up on a long, steep descent, and that heat can even burst the tire. Like car brakes, disc brakes can also have both high stopping power and good modulation of that power. Like a V-brake, a disc brake does not get in the way of movement of a suspension frame, and removal and installation of the wheel require no fiddling with releasing the cable.

Still, there are a lot of old-style center-pull cantilever brakes out there; hence, working on

continued

OPTIONAL

piston-bore-plug
removal tool
specific to your
one-piece hydraulic
disc caliper

full set of Torx
wrenches up to T30

them is thoroughly covered in this chapter. They're light and simple, they offer good mud clearance, and, above all, they stop your bike. Like V-brakes, cantilevers pivot on bosses attached to the frame and fork.

There are several other mountain bike brake options as well, most of which are only found on bikes from the last century. Linkage brakes that mount on the cantilever bosses offer the same advantage of operating without a cable stop as V-brakes and disc brakes. Hydraulic rim brakes (Fig. 7.46) that mount on cantilever bosses have long been the choice of observed trials riders because of their high stopping power and ability to lock up the wheel. Roller-cam brakes (Fig. 7.53) and U-brakes (Fig. 7.52) also mount on pivot posts attached to the frame and fork, but the posts for these brakes are positioned farther from the hub than those used for standard cantilevers and V-brakes.

vii-1
RELEASING BRAKES TO REMOVE A WHEEL

- **Disc brakes** (Figs. 7.16–17): Just drop the wheel right out. The disc falls straight out of the caliper (other than in a couple of old designs for frames and forks without built-in disc-brake mounts).
- **V-brakes** (Fig. 7.24): Hold the brake-arm link while pulling back and up on the cable "noodle" until it comes out of the slotted hole in the link (see Fig. 2.1). You can also hold the pads against the rim and pull the cable noodle back and up to release it from the link, but this approach requires more force.
- **Cantilevers** (Fig. 7.35) **and U-brakes** (Fig. 7.52): Hold the pads against the rim, and pull the head of the straddle cable out of the hook at the end of one brake arm (see Fig. 2.2).
- **Magura hydraulic rim brakes** (Fig. 7.46): If the brake has a stiffening arch over the wheel (Fig. 7.46), pull its left end off the bolt head it slips

over. If the brake has a quick-release lever on one side, open it and pull the brake bracket off the brake boss (Fig. 7.47). If there is no quick-release, unscrew the mounting bolt on one side to pull the brake bracket off.

- **Other types:** See the section on your particular brake.

CABLES AND HOUSINGS

Cables transfer braking force from the levers to the wheel on nonhydraulic brakes, and proper installation and maintenance of the cables are critical to good brake performance. If there is excess friction in the cable system, the brakes will not work properly, no matter how well the brakes, calipers, and levers are adjusted. Each cable should move freely; replace any cable that has any broken strands.

vii-2
ADJUSTING CABLE TENSION

LEVEL 1

As brake pads wear and cables stretch, the cable needs to be shortened. The barrel adjuster on the brake lever (Fig. 7.1), through which the cable passes, offers adjustment to mitigate these kinds of changes. The cable should be tight enough that

7.1 Adjusting cable tension

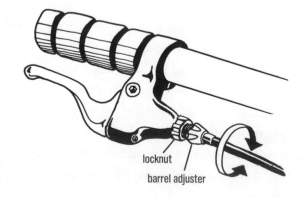

locknut

barrel adjuster

the lever cannot be pulled all the way to the grip, yet loose enough that the brake pads (assuming they are centered and the wheels or rotors are true) are not dragging.

vii-3
INCREASING CABLE TENSION

1. **Back out the barrel adjuster by turning it counterclockwise** (Fig. 7.1) **after loosening the locknut.** (Determine clockwise versus counterclockwise rotation direction of the barrel adjuster from the perspective of the end where the cable housing enters.) Some barrel adjusters have no locknut (Fig. 7.11); just turn them and they will hold their adjustment by friction.

2. **Adjust the cable tension so that the brake lever does not hit the grip when the brake is applied fully.**

1. **Lock in the tension by tightening the locknut down against the lever body while holding the barrel adjuster.** Again, some levers do not have a locknut on the barrel adjuster and stay in place without it (Fig. 7.11).

2. **If you need to take up more slack than the barrel adjuster allows, tighten the cable at the brake.** Screw the barrel adjuster most of the way in so as to leave some adjustment in the system for brake setup and cable stretch over time. Loosen the bolt clamping the cable at the brake. Check the cable for wear. If there are any frayed strands, replace them (see §vii-6). Otherwise, pull the cable tight and retighten the clamping bolt. Tension the cable as needed with the lever barrel adjuster.

vii-4
REDUCING CABLE TENSION

1. **Back out the locknut on the barrel adjuster** (Fig. 7.1) a few turns (counterclockwise).

(Determine clockwise versus counterclockwise rotation direction of the barrel adjuster from the perspective of the end where the cable housing enters.)

1. **Turn the barrel adjuster clockwise** (Fig. 7.1) **until the brake pads are properly spaced from the rim.**

1. **Tighten the locknut clockwise against the lever body to lock in the adjustment** (Fig. 7.1).

1. **Double-check that the cable is tight enough that the lever cannot be squeezed all the way to the grip.** Check pad alignment with the braking surface and adjust as needed (see §vii-17b and §vii-23 for V-brakes and cantilevers, respectively).

vii-5
MAINTAINING CABLES

🔧 LEVEL 1

1. **If the cable is frayed or kinked or has any broken strands, replace the cable** (see §vii-6).

2. **If the cable is not sliding well, lubricate it.** Use molybdenum disulfide grease if you have it on hand; otherwise, try a chain lubricant. White lithium-based greases can eventually gum up cables and restrict movement.

3. **To lubricate, open the brake** (via the cable quick-release as you do when you remove a wheel; see §vii-1).

4. **Pull each section of cable housing out of each slotted cable stop.** If your bike does not have slotted cable stops, you will have to detach the cable at the caliper and pull it completely out.

5. **Slide the housing up the cable, rub lubricant with your fingers on the cable section that was inside the housing, and slide the housing back into place.**

6. **If the cable still sticks, replace it.**

vii-6

INSTALLING CABLES

 LEVEL 2

As with chains and derailleur cables, brake-cable replacement is a maintenance operation, not a repair operation; don't wait until a cable breaks or seizes to replace it. Try using die-drawn cables; they have been pulled through a constricting die and will operate with less friction, because the exterior strands have been flattened. Purchase good-quality cables with lined housings. Most brake-cable housing is spiral-wrapped to prevent splitting under braking pressure (see Fig. 5.20). Teflon-lined housing reduces friction and is a must on a mountain bike unless you're using a cable-housing system with separate cable sheaths, such as Nokon (you assemble the housing onto the sheath out of separate snap-together segments) or Gore-Tex RideOn. The Gore-Tex must be peeled off the RideOn cable at the last couple of inches on both ends where it enters the brake lever and clamps to the brake; if this is not done, the Gore-Tex coating can get completely wadded up and prevent cable movement. A thin plastic tube runs through all of the housing segments and sheaths the cable end to end against crud. A rubber accordionlike seal (called the "Grub") covers the end of the plastic tube at each brake and prevents the access of dirt at its one possible entry point.

NOTE: *When you are installing a new cable, it is a good idea to replace the housings as well, even if you don't think they need to be replaced. Daily riding in particularly dirty conditions may demand the replacement of cables and housings every couple of months.*

Except in cases in which manufacturers supply lubricants with their cables and housings to be applied during their installation, in my opinion it is usually best not to use a lubricant on new cables and lined housing. Lubricant can attract dirt and even gum up inside the housing.

1. **Remove the old cable.**

2. **Cut the housing sections long enough to reach the brakes, and route them so that they do not make any sharp bends.** If you are replacing existing housings, look at where they bend before removing them. If the bends are smooth and do not bind when the wheel is turned or the suspension moves, cut the new housings to the same lengths. If you see that binding has been occurring, cut each new segment longer than you think necessary and keep trimming it back until it gives the smoothest path possible for the cable, without the cable tension being affected by turning the handlebar or by movement of the rear swingarm on a full-suspension bike.

7.2 Cable installation at the brake lever (note that slots are lined up in lever body, barrel adjuster, and locknut)

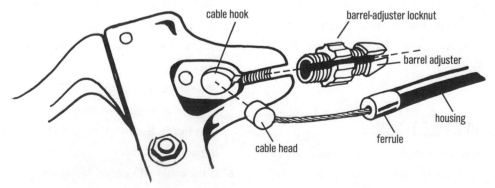

cable hook

barrel-adjuster locknut

barrel adjuster

housing

ferrule

cable head

7.3 Slotted cable stop

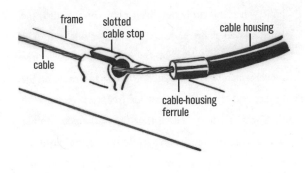

frame

slotted
cable stop

cable housing

cable

cable-housing
ferrule

7.4 Suspension-fork cable hanger

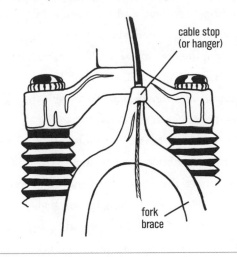

cable stop
(or hanger)

fork
brace

7.5 Stem-clamp cable hanger

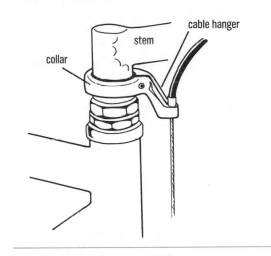

cable hanger

stem

collar

7.6 Headset cable hanger

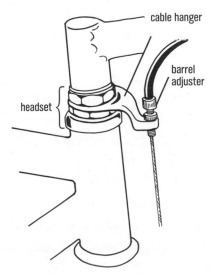

cable hanger

barrel
adjuster

headset

Use a cutter specifically designed for cutting housings, or a sharp side-cutter.

3. **After cutting, make sure the end faces of the housing are open and cut off straight.** If not, flatten the cut straight with a file or a clipper.

4. **If the end of the Teflon housing liner is mashed shut after cutting, open it up with a sharp object.** Use a nail or a toothpick, or push a length of cable through from the opposite end to open up the closed-off liner end.

5. **Slip a ferrule over each housing end for support** (see Fig. 5.20).

6. **Decide which hand you want to control which brake.** USA standard is that the right hand controls the rear brake.

7. **Tighten the adjusting barrel to within one turn of being screwed all the way in.**

8. **Rotate the barrel adjuster and locknut so that their slots line up with those on the lever and lever body** (Fig. 7.2).

9. **Insert the round head of the cable into the lever's cable hook** (Figs. 7.2, 7.9, and 7.11).

10. **Pull the cable into the lined-up slots on the barrel and nut.**

11. **Turn the barrel so that the slots are offset to prevent the cable from slipping back out.** If you have an old-style lever that is not slotted, you will have to feed the entire length of the cable from the cable hook out through the hole in the lever body.

12. Slide the rear-wheel brake cable through the housing sections, and then route the cable and housing from the brake lever to the brake, sliding the housing and cable into the slot in each stop (Fig. 7.3). If you don't have slotted stops, you will have to feed the cable through the hole in each cable stop.

13. **For the front brake, continue with step 14. For the rear brake, skip to step 15.**

14. **Terminate the housing for the front brake.** With a V-brake, terminate the housing in the top of the "noodle" guide tube (Fig. 7.24 or 7.25). On a cable-actuated disc brake (Fig. 7.17), the housing usually terminates at a stop on the brake caliper. With a cantilever brake and a suspension fork, terminate the front-brake housing at the stop on the fork brace (Fig. 7.4). For cantilevers without suspension, you may have a cable stop that is integral to the stem or on a hanger above the headset (Figs. 7.5–6); if the brake cable passes through either a cable stop hanging from the stem or a stem through-hole, I recommend bypassing it, as either requires readjustment of the front brake with any change in stem height. Instead, use a cable hanger with a collar that slips around the stem or steering tube above the headset (Fig. 7.5) or one that slips into the headset stack between locknuts (Fig. 7.6).

15. **Attach the cable to the brake.** Pull the cable taut and tighten the cable-clamping bolt (see the section on your type of brake). Pull the lever as hard as you can, and squeeze it repeatedly for about a minute to stretch the new cable.

16. **Adjust cable tension with the lever barrel adjuster** (as described in §vii-2 to §vii-4).

17. **Cut off cable ends about 2½ inches (65mm) past the cable anchor bolts.**

18. **Crimp end caps on all exposed cable ends to prevent fraying** (Fig. 5.34), **and bend the extra to the side.**

19. Follow the adjustment procedure for your brake, if need be.

NOTE: *Once the cable has been properly installed, the lever should snap back quickly when released. If it does not, recheck the cables and housings for free movement and sharp bends. Release the cable at the brake, and check the levers for free movement. With the cable still loose, check that the brake pads do not drag on the tire as they return to the neutral position, make sure the brake arms rotate freely on their pivot bosses, and check that the brake-arm return springs pull the pads away from the rims.*

BRAKE LEVERS

The levers must operate smoothly and be set up so that you can easily reach them while riding.

vii-7
LUBRICATING AND SERVICING LEVERS

1. **Lubricate all pivot points in the lever with grease or oil.**

2. **Check return-spring function for levers that have them.**

3. **Make sure that the lever or lever body is not bent in a way that hinders movement.**

4. **Check for stress cracks, and if you find any, replace the lever.**

For more on hydraulic brake levers, see §vii-15c.

vii-8
REMOVING, INSTALLING, AND POSITIONING LEVERS

 **LEVEL 1**

Brake levers mount on the handlebar inboard of the grip and bar end. They are also mounted inboard of twist shifters and usually outboard of thumb shifters (Fig. 7.7). Dual-lever trigger shifters on separate band clamps usually mount

7.7 Brake lever position relative to shifter

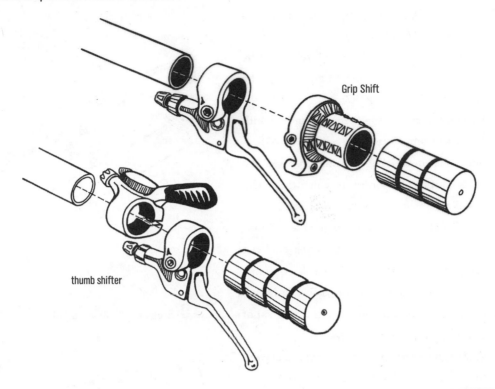

Grip Shift

thumb shifter

inboard of the brake lever but can be reversed. Integrated systems include both brake lever and shifter in a single unit (Fig. 7.11).

Split-clamp levers (Fig. 7.8) mount with two bolts and a separate semicircular band; these can come off and on the handlebar without your having to remove bar ends, grips, and shifters, so skip to step 6. Unfortunately, most brake levers have a wrap-around clamp with a single bolt (Fig. 7.7) so that grips, bar ends, and twist shifters cannot be on the handlebar when you are removing and installing them.

1. **If the bar end is installed, remove it by loosening the mounting bolt and sliding the bar end off the bar.**

2. **Remove the handlebar grip.** Lift the edges on both ends, squirt rubbing alcohol or water underneath, and twist the grip until it becomes free and slides off. Alternatively, if you have closed-end grips and an air compressor, you can blow them off by punctur-

7.8 Split-clamp hydraulic brake lever

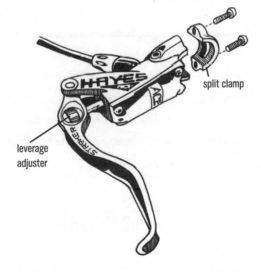

split clamp

leverage adjuster

ing the end of one grip and blasting air into it with the end of the air blowgun pressed against the hole. Seal the end of the other grip if it also has a hole, and cover the end of the handlebar with your hand once the opposite grip has blown off in order to blow the one with the blowgun off toward you. For bolt-on grips, simply loosen the pinch bolts and slide them off.

3. **If the twist shifter is installed, remove it by loosening the mounting bolt and sliding the shifter off the bar** (Fig. 7.7).

4. **Loosen the brake lever's mounting bolt with a hex key, and slide the lever off** (Fig. 7.7).

5. **Slide the new lever on, and replace the other parts in the order in which they were installed.** If necessary, slide on grips using rubbing alcohol (it dries quickly) as a lubricant; water works, too, but the grips will twist for a lot more rides. With closed-end grips and an air compressor, you also can inflate each grip so that it slides on in a reversal of the removal procedure in step 2.

6. **Make certain the levers do not extend beyond the ends of the handlebar.** Rotate them and slide them inward to your preferred location. Also see the Pro Tip on optimizing V-brake performance.

7. **Tighten all mounting bolts on levers, shifters, and bar ends.**

NOTE: *If your bike has a carbon-fiber handlebar, you may need to use lower than normal torque on the mounting bolts to prevent damage to the handlebar. Consult the handlebar or bicycle manufacturer regarding this detail.*

vii-9
ADJUSTING REACH AND LEVERAGE

Some levers have a reach-adjustment setscrew; it may be on the lever body near the barrel adjuster (Figs. 7.9–10) or on top of (Fig. 7.8) or under the lever. If you have small hands, you may want to tighten the reach-adjustment setscrews so that you can reach the levers more easily.

Some cable brakes also have a leverage adjustment (Figs. 7.9 and 7.11), which moves the cable end in or out relative to the lever pivot. The closer

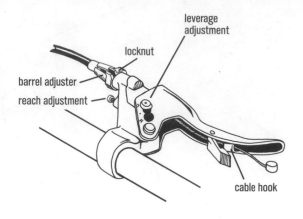

7.9 Shimano brake lever for simple V-brakes

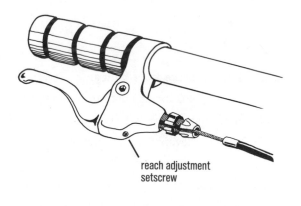

7.10 Brake reach adjustment

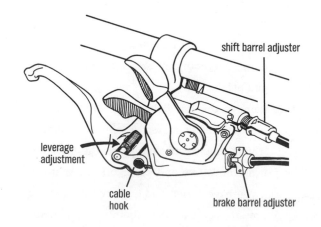

7.11 Rapidfire integrated shift/brake levers (XTR shown)

the cable passes by the pivot, the higher is the leverage but the less cable the lever pulls, and vice versa. To start with, set the leverage adjustment at the position that offers the weakest leverage (sometimes demarcated with an "L" on the lever), where the cable head or cable path is farthest from the pivot. Only increase the leverage if you become very confident in using the brakes.

On higher-end brake levers, a long screw performs the leverage adjustment (Fig. 7.11). On some Shimano and SRAM levers, leverage is adjusted by installing, relocating, or removing a series of inserts. On Shimano LX, DX, and M600, adjust leverage by loosening a small bolt on the upper face of the lever arm with a 3mm hex key, sliding the leverage adjuster up and down, and retightening the bolt (Fig. 7.9). The ends of the adjustment range are generally clearly marked with an "L" for lowest leverage (cable path farthest from the lever pivot) and an "H" for highest leverage (cable path closest to the lever pivot). These Shimano (LX, DX, and M600) and SRAM levers have a hook to hold the cable end far out along the lever (Fig. 7.9); the cable passes over a trough whose position away from the pivot determines the leverage. On other levers, a rotating notched eccentric disc adjusts the cable-head position relative to the pivot. Again, analogous to sitting on a teeter-totter, leverage is increased (and amount of cable pulled is reduced) if the cable head or cable path is closer to the lever pivot, and vice versa.

NOTE: *The levers for V-brakes are initially set up with intentionally low leverage (and correspondingly high cable pull), because of the high leverage of the long brake arms. If you use a lever from a cantilever brake with a V-brake, you have more leverage and can end up on your nose. Always start with V-brake levers adjusted to the lowest leverage (cable passing farthest from the lever pivot), and increase from that setting if you wish.*

Disc brakes can offer great stopping and modulation, but installing them correctly is a must. Once properly installed, discs require less maintenance than do rim brakes, because the tire is not dragging mud into them. There is no need to be intimidated by disc brakes; although they are small and enclosed and therefore somewhat mysterious, these brakes are really quite simple.

vii-10
CHECKING AND REPLACING DISC-BRAKE PADS

 **LEVEL 1**

Disc-brake pads are less easy to see than rim-brake pads, so you should be even more diligent about checking them for wear. The friction material needs to be at least the thickness of a dime (about 1.2mm); with most pads this means that the entire pad and backing plate together should be greater than 2.5mm. Some brakes supply a pad-wear gauge; Magura, for instance, has a 4.1mm-thick "finger" sticking off the plastic pad spacer that comes with the brakes. Apply the brakes against the rotor by squeezing the lever, and the "finger" should fit between the steel ears of the pads. If it doesn't, the distance between the pad backing plates is too small, indicating that too much pad material has worn off.

The wheel must be off for disc-brake pads to be removed. On cable-actuated disc brakes, unscrew the inboard pad-adjuster knob or bolt until it stops (to spread the pads as far apart as possible).

On cotterless types of pads, grab a tab on the pad with your fingers or needle-nose pliers and pull it toward the center of the caliper slot and out (Fig. 7.12). You have to do this from underneath the caliper, so it's often not easy to get to.

7.12 Changing Hayes brake pads (the caliper is shown apart only for the purpose of illustration; the pads clip in and out without dismantling the caliper)

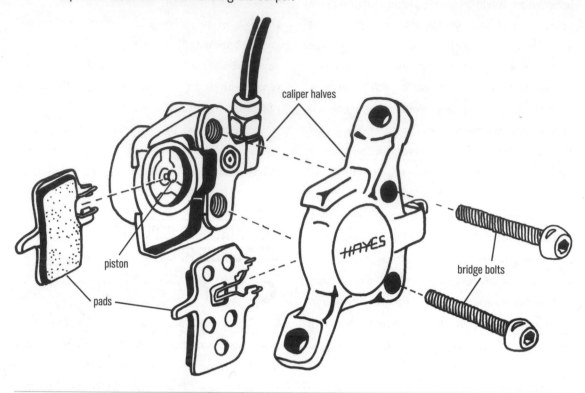

caliper halves

piston

pads

HAYES

bridge bolts

The pads need space to pull inward and out, one at a time, so you may need to first slip a plastic pad spacer, tire lever, or flat-head screwdriver between the pads and carefully rock it back and forth to separate them without damaging them.

Cottered pads require that you remove a cotter pin or bolt and then pull the pads out (Fig. 7.19), but they're usually easy to get out because they come out of the top of the brake. The cotter pin may be a threaded bolt, a pin with a retaining clip holding it in, or both (Fig. 7.19). Catch the spreader spring too if there is one.

Clean the pads with isopropyl alcohol or a dry, oil-free rag, or rub the pads against each other. Check for pad wear, scoring, or glazing—anything that could damage the rotor or endanger braking effectiveness. Brakes fade when the pads and rotors get too hot, after which blue discoloration of the rotor and glazing of the pads occur, indicating that resins holding the pad

material have broken down and recrystallized on the surface. Glazed pads must be discarded.

Although it's not mandatory, you'll reduce the potential for introducing dirt into a hydraulic caliper if, before replacing the pads, you clean around the pistons with a Q-tip soaked in brake fluid for that brake.

Replace the new pads the way the old ones came out, noting that the left and right pads may differ; it should be obvious if you try to put a pad in the wrong side.

Cotterless pads usually snap back in—either onto a nub on the piston with a wire catch (as on Hayes, Fig. 7.12) or magnetically. If the pads are not symmetrical and you reverse them, they may not snap back into place because the piston is often offset from the center of the cutaway for the pad. If there is a spring-steel pad spreader clip between cotterless pads, it may go in after the pads are inserted, or it may go in like a sandwich with the pads.

On cottered pads, the ears on the pads may not line up with the cotter hole if reversed (Fig. 7.19). On cottered pads that have a little butterfly-shaped spring-steel piece that pushes the pads apart (Fig. 7.19), make a sandwich of the new pads and the butterfly spring and push them back in together. Then push in or screw in the cotter pin and replace its circlip if it has one.

vii-11
SELECTING AND BURNING IN DISC-BRAKE PADS

Make sure you buy pads meant for the exact make and model of the brake; there are myriad shapes of disc-brake pads, and they're not interchangeable.

When buying pads, you may have a choice of pad compounds, and your choice should be based on the type of riding you do. Metallic pads deal with heat better, whereas resin pads give better modulation, and hence control, of wheel speed. Resin pads also wear out faster than metallic pads, especially in wet conditions.

New pads need to be burnished (or "burned in" or "bedded in") with repeated braking before they reach full braking power. If you instead just slam on the brakes when the pads are new, you can damage them so that they won't reach full power, and they may squeal mercilessly to remind you on every ride.

Burn in the pads by braking firmly and evenly without letting the brake get too hot. It's best to do this with one brake at a time, rather than with both brakes. Every manufacturer has a different procedure, but all say that it takes somewhere in the range of 20 to 40 stops to bed in the pad. I recommend that you start by applying the brake 10 times to bring the speed down from about 10–12 mph to walking speed. Then increase the speed to 15–18 mph and brake to walking speed 10 more times. This works the heat cycle evenly

over the rotor and reduces the potential for squeal problems.

vii-12
PUSHING DISC-BRAKE PISTONS BACK IN WHEN PADS RUB

Sometimes pistons get pushed so far out that they drag on the rotor or won't even let the rotor back in when the wheel is out. This can easily happen if the lever is applied without a rotor or spacer between the pads. You will have to push the pistons back in, and on some brakes this is best done with the pads out, whereas on others it is best done with the pads in.

If the wheel is out and the rotor will not go in, you will first have to push the pads and pistons back by jamming in the plastic pad spacer (which you should have had in when you pulled the lever when the wheel was out; it would have prevented this from happening). Once you have some space between the pads, you might as well try pushing the pistons back with the pads in. Using a plastic tire lever or a flat-head screwdriver, carefully (so that you don't gouge the pads) twist the tire lever or screwdriver back and forth until there is enough space between the pads that the rotor can turn without rubbing.

On Hayes and Stroker brakes, to get the pistons fully back in place, remove the pads (§vii-10; Fig. 7.12) first. Carefully push the pistons back in with the box end of a wrench, with the size depending on brake model (8mm for Stroker, 9mm for El Camino, and 10mm for HFX). Avoid pressing on and damaging the pin sticking out of the piston (Fig. 7.12); this engages the wire catch on the back of the pad and holds it in. Replace the pads.

Sometimes, the brake in normal usage doesn't retract the pads fully and they rub. This indicates contamination, and you'll have to clean around the piston to get this to stop.

7.13A Piston and square seal

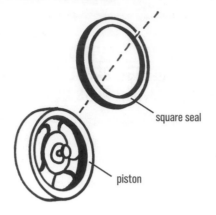

square seal

piston

7.13B Caliper cylinder cutaway view

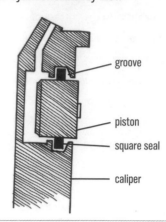

groove

piston

square seal

caliper

On most hydraulic disc brakes, each piston is pulled back in by a square cross-section O-ring seal surrounding the waist of the piston (Fig. 7.13A). This "square seal" sits in a groove running around the bore of the piston cylinder; you can see it in cross-section in Figure 7.13B. When fluid is forced in behind the piston when the lever is squeezed, the piston moves outward, and the square seal will start to twist out into the tapered section of the groove shown in Figure 7.13B. When the hydraulic pressure is relieved when the lever is released, the square seal will untwist back to its original configuration, bringing the piston back with it, as long as the seal is not damaged and is not broken by contamination.

If dirt is present, it can inhibit piston retraction, either by breaking the seal or by creating more friction around the sides of the piston than the square seal can overcome. In this case, simply forcing the pistons back into their bores exacerbates the problem by pushing even more dirt under or against the square seal. So clean around the piston and lubricate it.

If you have this problem of pad spacing from the rotor being reduced to almost nothing while riding, remove the pads (§vii-10). While holding one piston in place with a plastic tire lever or a box-end wrench, carefully squeeze the lever to push the

other piston out a bit more to expose more of it for lubrication. Using a cotton swab soaked in hydraulic fluid of the type that's in your brake, wipe off any grime from around the piston and lubricate it the same way with clean hydraulic fluid.

Carefully prying against the opposite side of the caliper, push the piston back into its bore with the plastic tire lever or box-end wrench. Repeat the procedure to clean and lube the other piston, push it back in as well, and replace the pads.

If you use the wrong implement to push directly on the piston, you can crack it.

Also, if the piston comes out too far and you cannot push it back in far enough against fluid pressure, open the bleed screw slightly while pushing the piston back, and close the bleed screw immediately to prevent the entry of air.

vii-13
INSTALLING AND ADJUSTING DISC BRAKES

 LEVEL 2

Once you are used to the procedure, you will find that you can install and adjust many disc brakes more quickly than V-brakes or cantilevers! Simply bolt the rotor to the hub, tighten the lever onto the handlebar (see §vii-8 for instructions on this), bolt the caliper to the mounts on the frame or fork, and tie down the hose or cable. But the space between the pads and rotor is small, and the speed of accurate mounting depends on you, the brake, and the type of mount the brake accepts.

The two types of mounts built into frames and forks are International Standard (IS) mounts (Fig. 7.16) and postmounts (Fig. 7.17). IS mounts are drilled transversely (toward the wheel) and are not threaded, whereas postmounts are threaded directly into the frame or fork. IS mounts, front or rear, are 51mm apart. Since the 2000 model year, the postmount standard for frames and forks is 74mm. Older postmounts are less standardized, so be aware of this if you intend to put an old brake on a new frame, or vice versa. Original Hayes and Manitou fork postmounts were 68.8mm apart. For a brief time, Hayes and Manitou adopted 70mm front postmount caliper spacing but abandoned it within a season. Rear chainstay postmounts and early seatstay postmounts were 21.5mm apart. (Confused yet?)

CAUTION: *Unless you want to do a lot of fiddling and chasing of obsolete parts, do not buy pre-2000 disc brakes on eBay or from anywhere else, because chances are they will not work with current forks and hubs. In 1997 or thereabouts, many disc-brake and suspension-fork makers agreed on the IS mount of 51mm front and rear, but the agreement did not cover rotor mounting, and manufacturers were all over the map with rotor-mounting systems. So rotors made prior to 2000 other than Hayes will generally not fit on current disc-brake hubs.*

In 2000, fork and disc-brake makers adopted the IS 2000 standard, which also incorporated the six-bolt rotor-mounting pattern (Fig. 7.14) that Hayes had established. And although old Hayes rotors will work on current wheels, Hayes's postmount caliper dimensions, as you saw previously, were all over the place until 2000, so you would at minimum need an obsolete

adapter to put a pre-2000 Hayes brake on a fork with IS mounts, and it would not work at all with a current postmount fork. Also, the Hayes rear chainstay postmount dimensions have been abandoned.

The good news is that since 2000, the forks, frames, brakes, and rotors of the major manufacturers, with the inclusion of a second rotor-mounting standard, Shimano's "Center Lock" rotor mount (Fig. 7.15), are completely cross-compatible.

After installation, follow the pad bed-in procedure in §vii-11 to get full brake performance.

Avoid touching the rotor's braking surface and getting grease or oil on it. If brake performance ever drops off, clean the rotor and pads with alcohol. And for obvious reasons, never touch a rotor that's hot after heavy braking.

Never squeeze the lever without a disc or another spacer between the pads, as you can push a piston all the way out. For bike travel with the wheel out, insert a spacer between the pads—either one that came with the brake or a chunk of corrugated cardboard you cut for the purpose.

a. Rotor installation and removal

Installation

Until model year 2000, rotor bolt patterns varied. Starting in 2000, Hayes's six-bolt pattern (Fig. 7.14) became the standard. However, beginning in 2003, Shimano's brake rotors had a splined hub attachment, called Center Lock (Fig. 7.15). The splined aluminum adapter riveted to the steel rotor slips onto the splines of the hub, and a single lockring holds it in place. Other manufacturers offer hubs compatible with these rotors. (Incidentally, the rotor should still be positioned in the same place relative to the axle end in either case, so a wheel with a Center Lock rotor should work fine in a brake set up for a bolt-on rotor of the same diameter.)

Multiple-bolt rotor

1. Loosely bolt the rotor to the hub flange (Fig. 7.14). The logo on the rotor should face outward so that the rotor turns in the proper direction.

2. Gradually snug the bolts, alternately tightening opposing bolts rather than adjacent bolts. A T25 Torx wrench (like a hex key but with a star-shaped end) is usually required for this. Torque for rotor bolts ranges from 18 in-lbs (2 N-m) for some manufacturers to 55 in-lbs (6 N-m) for others.

Shimano Center Lock splined rotor

1. Slip the rotor splines over the hub splines (Fig. 7.15) with the logo on the rotor facing you.

2. Thread on the rotor-securing lockring, and tighten it with the same splined lockring-remover tool used for rear gear cassettes. If you have a torque wrench that fits the lockring tool, tighten it to 40 N-m (350 in-lbs).

7.14 Bolting rotor onto hub

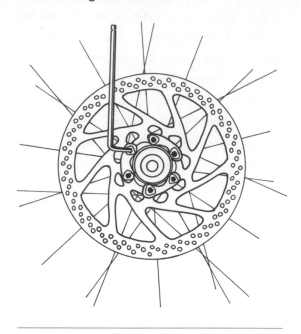

Removal

Multiple-bolt rotor

. When removing a bolt-on disc rotor, you must loosen all the screws a fraction of a turn before

7.15 Installing Shimano Center Lock splined rotor onto the splines of a Center Lock hub with a cassette lockring tool

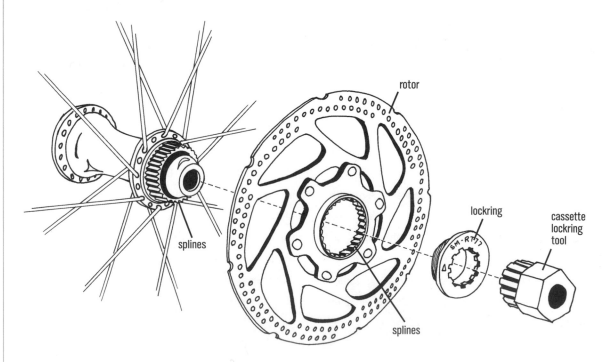

unscrewing any of them. On braking, the rotor may rotate relative to the hub a bit and lean against one side of each screw. If you remove one screw while the others are still tight, the rotor hole's wall will still be pressed against the side of the screw, and the threads on the screw will be damaged. Then you will wreck the threads in your hub when you put the damaged screw back in.

If you have an old Shimano 6-bolt rotor with the plates bent up around the triangular bolt heads (Fig. 7.14), bend the plate edges back down before unscrewing the bolts.

NOTE ON HUBS WITH ADAPTERS: *Adapters are available to convert Center Lock hubs to accept 6-bolt rotors. Also, some older disc-brake hubs do not accept a rotor without an adapter. The adapter is attached to the hub, and the rotor is bolted to the adapter.*

Shimano Center Lock splined rotor

Unscrew the lockring with the splined lockring-removal tool (Fig. 7.15), and pull the rotor off.

b. IS disc-brake caliper installation onto IS mounts

IS brake calipers have two transverse-drilled threaded bolt holes and attach directly to IS mounts (Fig. 7.16).

NOTE: *If you are using a caliper adapter bracket to mount a postmount brake caliper to an IS fork or frame, first bolt the adapter to the frame or fork mounts, and then follow the directions in section c for installing a caliper onto postmounts. If you are using a rotor that is a different size from the rotor that the brake came with, you will need an adapter anyway.*

ANOTHER NOTE: *If you are installing a caliper that is not connected to its lever, skip to section e to cut the hose to length, then skip to §vii-14a to fill it with fluid and bleed it, and then come back here and begin with step 1.*

1. **Install the wheel on the bike.**
2. **Slip the caliper over the rotor and up against the frame or fork mounts.**
3. **Loosely install the mounting bolts** (Fig. 7.16).

7.16 Mounting a hydraulic IS brake caliper on IS mounts

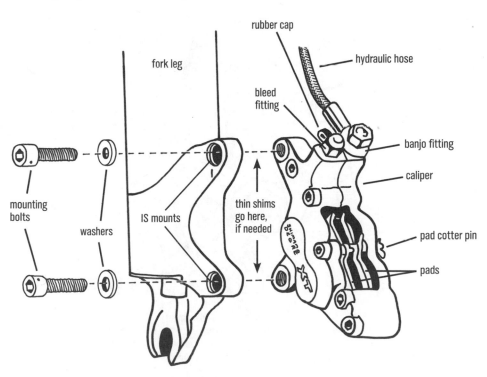

rubber cap

hydraulic hose

fork leg

bleed fitting

banjo fitting

caliper

mounting bolts

IS mounts

thin shims go here, if needed

pad cotter pin

washers

pads

4. **Pull the brake lever to squeeze the pads** against the rotor.

5. **Measure the gap between the caliper and the** mounting tab at each bolt while squeezing the brake lever.

6. **Make a stack of shim washers adding up to** that measurement.

7. **Unscrew the mounting bolts, and slide each** stack of shim washers on its bolt between the caliper and mount tab as indicated in Figure 7.16.

8. **Tighten the bolts.** It's best to apply a counterclockwise torque on the caliper with your hand while tightening the bolts. This will take out the play so that the rotor won't twist the caliper on its mounts on the first hard brake application. Bolt-tightening torque varies from 53 to 110 in-lbs, depending on brand.

9. **Spin the wheel.** The pads should not rub. If they do, add or remove shims until the rubbing has been eliminated.

10. **If the rotor is wobbly, straighten it.** See §vii-16 for instructions.

NOTE: *Some IS brake calipers have only one moving pad; they flex the rotor toward the stationary inboard pad. The stationary inboard pad is adjusted independently with a 5mm hex key or with a thumbscrew so that it just clears the rotor without rubbing.*

Some IS brakes use a "floating caliper" in which the entire caliper moves as the pad (or pads) on the outboard side push(es) against the rotor and pull(s) the stationary pad (or pads) over to the rotor. It is almost impossible to eliminate pad rub with these brakes. The same is true with a "floating rotor": The caliper is fixed, but the rotor slides laterally on plastic bushings.

c. Disc-brake caliper installation onto postmounts

Mounting postmount brakes onto an adapter bracket on IS mounts—front or rear—follows this same procedure: Just bolt the bracket first to the IS mounts, making it essentially a postmount.

7.17 Mounting a cable-actuated postmount brake caliper on fork postmounts

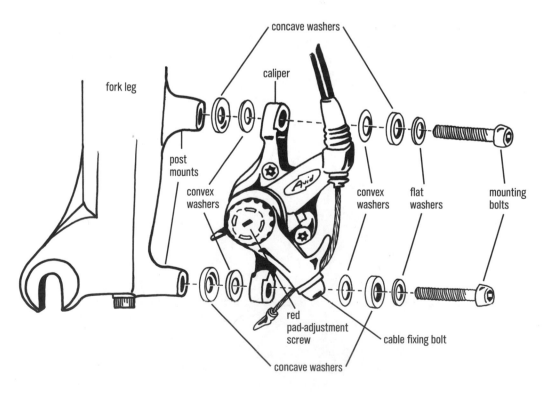

Mounting any IS brake to postmounts is possible with yet a different adapter. If you are using a rotor of a different size than the brake came with, you will need an adapter anyway.

The beauty of postmounts (Fig. 7.17) is that the brake can be moved laterally without the necessity of installing shims (thin washers) between the caliper and the mounts (as must be done with IS mounts; see section b above). This advantage applies even if you are mounting an IS brake via an adapter to a postmount frame or fork, or vice versa.

1a. If you are using an IS caliper on a postmount frame or fork, tighten the correct adapter bracket to the caliper first. Torque is usually 6–8 N-m.

1b. If you are using a postmount caliper on an IS frame or fork, tighten the correct adapter bracket to the IS mounts first. Torque is usually 6–8 N-m.

2. Loosely bolt the postmount caliper to the postmounts on the fork (Fig. 7.17), frame, or adapter bracket. If the brake has concave and convex washers, keep them in the same order as in Figure 7.17.

NOTE: *If you are installing a caliper that is not connected to its lever, skip to section e to cut the hose to length, then skip to §vii-14a to fill it with fluid and bleed it, and then come back here and begin with step 3.*

3. Install the wheel. The caliper slot will be over the rotor, and the caliper will have some lateral freedom of movement.

4. While squeezing the brake lever, shake the caliper to get it to find its natural position over the rotor, and tighten the mounting bolts.

5. Spin the wheel to check for brake rub. If you hear rub, peer through the gap between the rotor and the pads, and with a white background for contrast, note which pad (or worse, which side of the caliper slot) is rub-

bing. Loosen the bolts again, and slip a business card or two between the rubbing pad and the rotor.

6. Repeat steps 4 and 5 until the rotor spins without rub. If you're desperate, just loosen the bolts, eyeball the gap, push the caliper as you see fit, and tighten while holding the caliper; expect some frustration.

7. If the rotor is bent, straighten it. See §vii-16 on rotor truing.

Shimano supplies little plastic clips to snap on over the bolts around the knurled part of their head to prevent the bolts from unscrewing; it's a good idea to install these if you have them.

NOTE: *Some disc brakes work by flexing the rotor toward a fixed pad. The foregoing procedure will work for installing them provided you first tighten the fixed-pad adjuster screw a bit—perhaps a half turn. Once the caliper is bolted down, back out the fixed-pad adjuster screw so that the pad just barely clears the rotor.*

Alternatively, on Avid cable-actuated disc calipers (Fig. 7.17), turn the large red screw on the wheel side until the fixed pad centers the rotor in the caliper slot. Then turn the red screw on the cable side until the rotor is pinched between the pads and is centered in the slot. Loosen and then tighten the mounting bolts and back off the fixed-pad (wheel-side) screw until the rotor spins freely. Now tighten the cable (see §vii-13d), and back off on the red screws on either side a few clicks each to get the desired pad-to-rotor spacing.

A bent rotor will rub or at least reduce pad adjustment range. See §vii-16 on rotor truing.

d. Hookup of cable-actuated disc brakes

Route the cable housing to the brake following the procedures in §vii-6 for cable installation. Tie the housing down with zip-ties where there are no cable stops. Push the cable through the housing stop on the caliper, and tighten it under the cable anchor bolt.

e. Cutting hydraulic disc-brake hoses to length

When you route the hose to the brake, make it curve smoothly without kinks and without large loops that can catch on things, and make sure the hose is not so short that it is tight across spans where it is vulnerable. If the frame has disc-brake hose guides, use those. Otherwise, tie the hose down to the frame or fork with zip-ties, tape, guides that clip or screw into cable guides, or adhesive-backed hose guides.

Don't expect aftermarket brake hoses to be the right length for your bike; you may need to cut them. If one end of the hose has a permanent crimped end on it, don't cut that end. Generally, on the end you can cut, there will be a brass, olive-shaped ring around the end of the hose crushed by a sleeve nut to seal against leaks (Fig. 7.18 or 7.49). This brass "olive" will need to be replaced after you cut the hose. Hydraulic hoses sheathed in braided stainless-steel wire cannot be cut.

1. **Remove the wheel and the brake pads** (§vii-10). You don't want to get brake fluid on either the rotor or the pads.

2. **Disconnect the hose from the fittings.** This can be done at either the lever or the caliper, but it can't be done at an end that has a permanent crimped fitting (Fig. 7.19). Unscrew the sleeve nut holding the hose (Figs. 7.18, 7.49). The sleeve nut is often covered by a plastic or rubber cover; slide it up the hose for access. Alternatively, a screw with a fluid port in it passing through a "banjo" fitting (Fig. 7.21) may attach the hose; remove the banjo bolt, keeping track of the O-rings that go on either side of the banjo.

3. **If possible, gently pull the hose straight off.** Be very careful, because on some brakes you may break a thin, barbed nipple that runs up into the tube. As part of the sealing system, many brakes have a thin barbed fit-

ting extending up inside the hose under the brass olive ring, and the olive, compressed by the sleeve nut, tightens the hose around the barbs. Whereas this barbed fitting is generally a separate piece that slides up inside the hose as in Figure 7.18, on some brakes this barbed fitting is part of the lever, and if you bend the hose sideways while you pull on it, you can break off the barbed fitting.

4. **If the hose did not pull off easily, carefully cut the brass olive open with a hacksaw and peel it away from the hose.**

5. **Pull the hose off, and slide the sleeve nut and rubber cover up the hose beyond where you plan to cut.**

6. **Cut the hose to length with a sharp knife, making a clean, perpendicular cut.** Many brakes come with a pair of grooved plastic blocks with which you can clamp the hose in a vise while cutting.

7. **Install the barbed fitting.** If the brake has a separate barbed fitting, tap it into the hose while it is still held between the plastic grooved blocks. Or, if it is threaded externally and has a Torx hole in the end, screw it into the hose with a Torx key. First slip the new brass olive over the end of the hose after the hose nut and rubber nut cover (Fig. 7.18).

8. **Tighten the sleeve nut (maximum torque: 40 in-lbs).** Slide the plastic or rubber nut cover back into place over the nut.

9. **Confirm that the hose routing works.** Make sure that the hose does not get yanked when you turn the handlebars. Some brakes allow adjustment of the angle of the banjo at the caliper (through loosening of the banjo bolt) to smooth the hose routing.

10. **Skip to §vii-14.** However, if the brake was previously connected, and you think you might have prevented the entry of air into the system, then install the pads and wheel

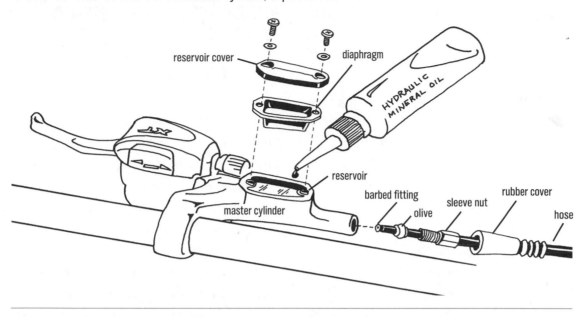

reservoir cover
diaphragm
HYDRAULIC MINERAL OIL
reservoir
master cylinder
barbed fitting
olive
sleeve nut
rubber cover
hose

7.19 Shimano XT two-piston disc-brake caliper with spacer block and bleeding apparatus, exploded view

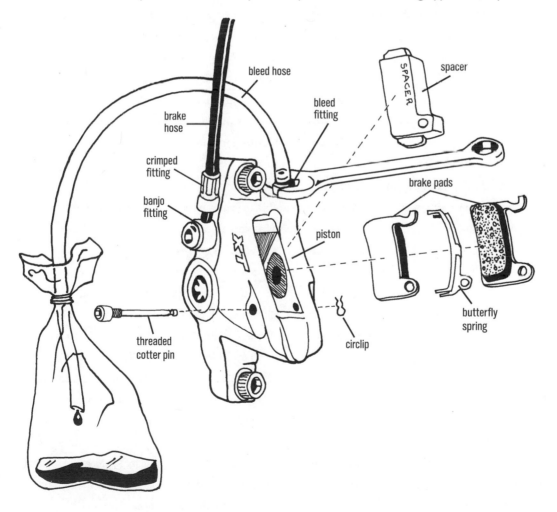

bleed hose
spacer
brake hose
bleed fitting
crimped fitting
brake pads
banjo fitting
piston
threaded cotter pin
circlip
butterfly spring

again and squeeze the lever. If the lever feels firm, you're done. If it doesn't, there is air in the line, and you must bleed the air from the system (see §vii-14).

f. Lever reach, lever pull, and pad spacing

The reach adjustment can be a small setscrew under or on the front of the lever blade, perhaps under a dust cover, or it may be a knob on the lever blade. This may or may not be independent of any lever pull and pad spacing adjustments.

Lever pull and pad spacing are closely related, as the closer the pads are to the rotor, the less pull it takes to stop. But the pads will rub if too close. Adjustments exist on some brakes but not on others.

Lever pull and reach with cable-actuated brakes can be adjusted by the cable barrel adjuster and reach adjustment screw on the lever (see §vii-9 for details). Pad spacing, and hence lever pull, on cable-actuated disc brakes can be adjusted with a knob or screw on the wheel side of the caliper. Same goes with hydraulic brakes with only one moving piston.

Some hydraulic brakes have an adjuster screw or knob on the lever that pushes the master-cylinder piston, thereby changing the amount of lever travel required. Some have a knob on the lever or reservoir to adjust the pad contact point in the lever's travel while riding. Some brakes have a knob to adjust leverage that actually moves the lever pivot in and out via a cam mechanism; changing leverage changes lever pull.

On brakes with both a reach adjustment and a pad position/application adjustment, don't adjust the reach to the closest position as well as the pad position to its maximum firmness. This could result in insufficient lever movement to achieve the necessary brake power to safely control your bike.

vii-14
BLEEDING (OR FILLING) HYDRAULIC DISC BRAKES

⚙ ⚙ LEVEL 2

Brakes must be bled whenever they have air in the system. The symptom is a lever that is not firm when pulled and/or that becomes more firm with repeated pumping. Separately, given enough usage in dirty conditions, dirt can get past the seals and contaminate the fluid, so flushing the old fluid out with new fluid will improve performance.

The procedure for filling an empty brake system is the same as for bleeding one. In general, you move fluid down through the system by filling the reservoir at the top and forcing fluid down with the lever or by sucking from a syringe at the caliper, or you force fluid up from a syringe or squeeze bottle through the caliper to the lever reservoir, or you do a combination of both. Air bubbles float up to the top of the fluid to the reservoir.

It is unrealistic to include complete bleeding instructions here for every brake. With one of the three following methods, you should be able to bleed almost any brake, but it is, of course, preferable to follow specific instructions that come with a brake's bleed kit.

With all brakes:

1. **Remove the wheel.**
2. **Remove the brake pads** (§vii-10).
3. **Install a spacer block between the pistons** (Fig. 7.19). The spacer allows you to apply hydraulic pressure while keeping the pistons pushed back in their bores. Many brakes come with a bleed spacer. Do not install a spacer between Hayes/Stroker pistons.

IMPORTANT—PAD PROTECTION: *Avoid getting fluid on the pads, which will ruin them. Replace pads contaminated by brake fluid, and clean rotors contaminated by brake fluid with rubbing alcohol.*

IMPORTANT—FLUID TYPE: *Use the recommended brake fluid for your brake. Some systems use mineral oil, and some use DOT (automotive) brake fluid (DOT stands for Department of Transportation). Do not interchange mineral oil and DOT fluid in a brake; doing so will ruin the seals inside.*

Not all mineral oil is the same (viscosity, purity, boiling point, etc. vary), nor is all DOT fluid the same. DOT has a standardized numbering system. The higher the DOT number, the higher the boiling point, and your brake was designed to operate in a certain temperature range with a DOT fluid for that range. If you were to use DOT 3 or DOT 4 fluid, for instance, in a brake designed for DOT 5.1, you might be without brakes when you need them the most—when they get really hot under heavy braking (see following warning).

WARNING—BOILING FLUID: *With brakes using DOT fluid, add fluid only from a container that has never been opened before. DOT fluid absorbs water, and the more water it has absorbed, the lower its boiling point. Opening the container for a short time can be enough to bring the boiling point down significantly (if you leave a glass of DOT fluid out overnight in a humid area, it will overflow the glass by morning!).*

Why is the boiling point of the fluid important? A hydraulic brake works because liquids are essentially noncompressible, so pushing on a piston at one end of a column of liquid (at the lever, aka the master cylinder) can push a piston just as forcefully at the other end of the column of liquid (at the caliper). Gases, in contrast, are compressible; that's why you have compressed air in your tires and front and rear shocks. But if hydraulic fluid boils, gas bubbles form in the hydraulic lines, and pulling the lever will only compress the gas; it won't forcefully push the caliper pistons.

"Vapor lock" occurs when the caliper gets so hot that the fluid inside boils. Your only hope is to pump the lever rapidly to compress the bubbles enough to partially function. Once vapor lock happens, you need to replace the fluid in a DOT-fluid brake with new DOT fluid. With mineral oil, you need only let the brake cool down, because oil doesn't absorb water.

IMPORTANT: *DOT fluid can dissolve paint, so wipe it off wherever it dripped on the bike, and rinse with isopropyl alcohol quickly.*

a. Bleeding brakes that have a screw-on reservoir cover

One way to bleed brakes is to add extra fluid to the reservoir at the master cylinder (the lever) and squeeze old fluid and air out at the caliper as well as allow bubbles to come up to and out of the fluid in the reservoir. This works for Shimano brakes and will work for others with a lever reservoir with a cover that can be opened.

1. **Turn the handlebar and the lever so that the reservoir is level, and ensure that the hose is trending downward the entire way to the caliper.** You can unbolt the caliper so that it hangs by the hose.

2. **Remove the reservoir cover and diaphragm** (Fig. 7.18). Tiny screws secure it; make sure your screwdriver or wrench is completely engaged in each one.

IMPORTANT: *Make sure you remove the rubber diaphragm under the cover! You would not be the first one to think you were looking at the inside of the reservoir and not the top of the diaphragm, wondering why the fluid you keep adding does not disappear and why the brakes don't tighten up!*

3. **Add fluid at the lever reservoir** (Fig. 7.18). Use fluid specified by the brake manufacturer.

4. **Completely remove the rubber cover from the fitting's nipple** (Fig. 7.16).

5. **Put a box-end wrench on the bleed fitting.** Size will vary with application. If you don't have a box-end wrench, a standard open-end wrench will do, but be mindful not to round off the nipple hex as you work.

6. **Put a clear tube on the caliper bleed-fitting nipple** (Fig. 7.19) **leading into a bottle or a plastic bag.** It is preferable to put a box-end wrench on the bleed fitting before pushing the hose onto the nipple—the wrench then stays in place as you open and close the fitting.

7. **Unscrew the bleed fitting one-eighth turn.**

8. **Squeeze the lever repeatedly.** Make sure you have a spacer (you can make one out of a chunk of wood) between the pistons (Fig. 7.19) before squeezing the lever! Tighten the bleed fitting before releasing the lever each time. This pushes fluid in and air out. Push until fluid flows out into the bleed tube you attached at the caliper.

9. **Use both of these techniques to be sure that you remove all the air:**

    (a) Push air bubbles out of the caliper: Squeeze the lever with the bleed nipple open, tighten the nipple, release the lever, open the bleed nipple, squeeze the lever, tighten the nipple, release the lever, and repeat, keeping the reservoir topped up, until no more bubbles appear in the bleed tube.

    (b) Repeatedly squeeze the brake lever with the bleed nipple closed, making sure that you keep the fluid level in the reservoir topped up. While you are squeezing, air bubbles should rise through the port into the reservoir.

10. **While squeezing the brake lever, open and close the bleed nipple in rapid succession for about a half second each time.** This optional procedure can release trapped air bubbles from the caliper. Repeat two or three times (refilling as needed at the reservoir), and finish by tightening the bleed nipple.

11. **Squeeze the lever fully.**

    (a) If the lever feels solid, as it should—meaning that it comes inward perhaps a third of the way toward the handlebar grip at most—then skip to step 12.

    (b) If the lever still does not feel solid, squeeze and hold it while you shake the hose and the caliper, and tap on the hose and the caliper with the plastic head of a screwdriver to free any stuck air bubbles. When they have all been removed, the lever should feel firm, and the lever should sink back to the grip. Continue with step 12.

12. **Refill the reservoir to the top** (Fig. 7.18).

13. **Replace the diaphragm, cover, and cover screws** (Fig. 7.18).

14. **Install the pads and wheel, and check the brake function.**

15. **Retighten the brake lever to the handlebar in its normal riding position.**

16. **Zip-tie the lever around the handlebar overnight to check for fluid leaks.** If the zip-tie is still tight around the lever and the handlebar grip the next morning, there are no leaks.

b. Bleeding Hayes and Stroker brakes

The reservoir in Hayes and Stroker (same company, temporarily different brand—long story) hydraulic brakes is an expandable bladder inside the lever, like the plastic sack in a baby bottle.

7.20 Catching fluid being bled from a Hayes HFX Mag brake

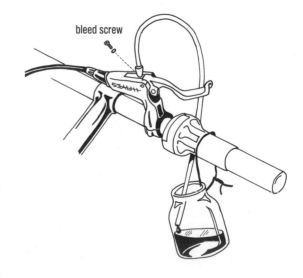

bleed screw

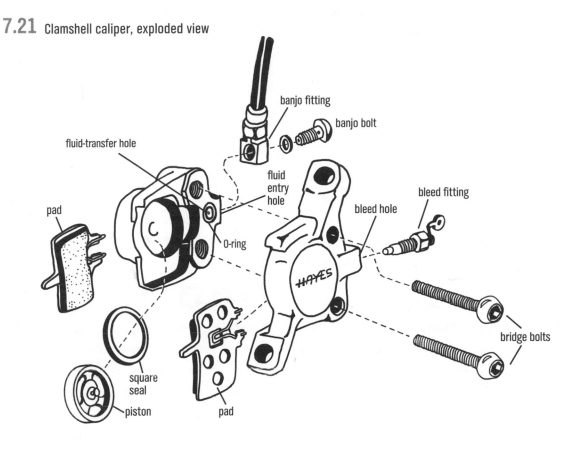

7.21 Clamshell caliper, exploded view

labels: banjo fitting, banjo bolt, fluid-transfer hole, fluid entry hole, bleed fitting, bleed hole, pad, O-ring, HAYES, bridge bolts, square seal, piston, pad

Because air bubbles can't just come up out of the system to the top of a rigid reservoir and then stay out of the system (as long as the bike stays upright), you must bleed them from the bottom (the caliper) to the top (the lever).

1. **Orient the lever so that the bleed screw is at the top.** Mount the bike in a stand, turn the handlebar, and rotate the lever on the handlebar such that the lever is the highest point in the system. Turn the lever until the bleed screw—at the base (both sides) of El Caminos and Stokers and at the front of the lever on HFX—points straight up (Fig. 7.20).

2. **Push the pistons fully back into their cylinders.** Carefully push the pistons back in with the box end of a wrench (use an 8mm for Stroker, 9mm for El Camino, and 10mm for HFX). Avoid damaging the pin sticking out of the piston (Fig. 7.12).

3. **Completely remove the rubber cover from the caliper bleed fitting.**

4. **Push a short section of clear tube onto the tip of the squeeze bottle that comes with a Hayes bleed kit.** Push the tube past the ridge on the tapered tip so that it stays on.

5. **Fill the squeeze bottle with brake fluid.** Use DOT 3 or DOT 4 brake fluid from a previously unopened container (see previous warning about boiled fluid).

6. **Push the other end of the squeeze bottle tube over the caliper bleed fitting.** See the bleed fitting in Figure 7.21.

7. **Connect the longer bleed tube to the lever bleed hole.** The bleed kit should have come with a longer clear tube with a selection of plastic and metal fittings for various Hayes and Stroker models. Plug the proper fitting into the tube. Remove the screw or plug from

the lever bleed hole, and stick the fitting into it (Fig. 7.20).

8. **Hang a container from the handlebar with wire or a zip-tie, and direct the other end of the tube into it** (Fig. 7.20).

9. **With the caliper bleed fitting closed, squeeze the fluid bottle repeatedly until any air bubbles in the tube come back into the bottle.** The bottle should be pointed straight down; keep it that way throughout the following steps.

10. **Loosen the bleed fitting on the caliper one-fourth turn, and squeeze new fluid in for a count of five.** If the tube is popping off the caliper bleed nipple, put an "olive"—the barrel-shaped brass ring seal (Fig. 7.18)—on the bottle's bleed tube before you stick it on the nipple. Push the olive down over the tube and nipple so that the tube won't pull off.

11. **Let off for about three counts (until the squeeze bottle returns to its natural shape).** This draws air out of the caliper and up into the squeeze bottle.

12. **Squeeze for five counts, let off for three, and repeat until no more bubbles come out of the caliper.**

13. **Squeeze firmly on the bottle until clean fluid without bubbles comes out of the tube at the lever.**

14. **While still squeezing the bottle, quickly pull the lever to the grip and release.** Look for air coming out of the bleed tube at the lever. Repeat until no more air emerges.

15. **While still squeezing, close the caliper bleed fitting.** Don't overtighten the fitting—it is small, and you need to tighten it only enough to create a seal.

16. **Remove the tubes from the caliper and lever.**

17. **Replace the lever bleed screw or plug.**

18. **Replace the rubber cover on the caliper bleed fitting.**

19. **Install the pads (§vii-10) and wheel, and pump the lever.** The lever should feel firm, and it should not come back to the grip. Repeat the bleed if the lever feels spongy.

20. **Check for fluid leaks by putting a zip-tie around the lever overnight.** If the zip-tie is still tight around the lever and the handlebar grip the next day, the system is completely sealed.

c. Vacuum-bleeding Avid and post-2010 SRAM brakes

⚙️ ⚙️ ⚙️ LEVEL 3

There is some air trapped in any DOT fluid, and pulling a vacuum over the fluid can draw some of that air out. You can bleed Avid (and new SRAM—Avid is a SRAM subsidiary) brakes as in section a, but the vacuum bleed method will remove more air from the system. The Avid/SRAM bleed kit has a pair of syringes with screw-on fittings designed to pull a vacuum to draw bubbles out of new fluid you add to the system. You must have this bleed kit to perform this operation.

1. **De-gas the fluid in one syringe.** Lightly pull on the plunger of a syringe filled halfway with DOT fluid from a previously unopened container (see previous warning on boiled fluid). The tip must be sealed off by closing the clamp on the hose, and the syringe must be pointed down.

2. **If the brake lever has a pad contact knob, turn it all the way to the "out" position.**

3. **Screw the syringes onto the bleed ports.** The one filled with de-gassed fluid goes on the caliper; the empty one goes on the lever. The lever should be rotated vertically down so that the bleed hole is at the top of the reservoir. The clamps on the hoses of both syringes should be open.

4. **Rubber-band the lever to the grip.** This closes the hole between the hose and reservoir.

5. **Suck the air out of the caliper.** Lightly pull a vacuum on the syringe plunger with the syringe pointed down, drawing air bubbles up through the fluid in the syringe. Close the clamp on the syringe hose.

6. **Remove the rubber band from the lever.**

7. **Push the air out of the hose.** Push the caliper syringe plunger to force half of its contents up to the lever syringe.

8. **Close both syringe clamps.** Close the clamp on the lever syringe first.

9. **Remove the caliper syringe, and replace the caliper bleed screw.**

10. **Gently pull on the lever syringe plunger.** This sucks air out of the lever. Make sure the syringe is pointed down. Release the plunger to let fluid replace the air you pulled out. Repeat this while tapping on the lever with a screwdriver handle and pulling and releasing the lever to free stuck bubbles.

11. **Close the syringe clamp.**

12. **Rotate the lever to horizontal.** The bleed hole needs to be pointed straight up.

13. **Remove the syringe.**

14. **Replace the bleed screw.** Put a drop of DOT fluid on the open bleed hole before putting in the screw.

15. **Clean DOT fluid off the lever and bike.** Wipe the surfaces first, then spray them with isopropyl alcohol and wipe again.

vii-15
OVERHAULING DISC BRAKES

⚙️ ⚙️ ⚙️ LEVEL 3

Regular bleeding and fluid replenishment clean dirt out of the system and lengthen the time between overhauls of hydraulic brakes. On many disc brakes, overhaul is relatively simple, but you will need an air compressor to get the pistons out of the caliper. There are two kinds of hydraulic calipers: clamshell models whose two pieces bolt together and single-piece calipers. Buy new seals for the part of the brake you are overhauling before you start. A speck of dirt or hair in a hydraulic disc brake can cause a leak, so work in a clean area with clean methods.

a. Overhauling a clamshell hydraulic caliper

1. **Remove the caliper from the bike.** See Figures 7.16–17.

2. **Remove the brake pads** (§vii-10).

3. **Disconnect the hose.** If there is nothing wrong with the hose or its fittings, you want to save yourself the effort of replacing the brass olive ring seal on the hose (see §vii-13e and Fig. 7.18 or 7.49). Some brakes have a fitting screwed into the caliper with a hollow bolt to which the hose nut is attached, called a banjo fitting (Figs. 7.16, 7.19, and 7.21), because the head of it looks like a . . . you guessed it. If yours has a banjo, unscrew the hollow banjo bolt holding it on, but don't disconnect the hose from the banjo.

4. **Remove the bridge bolts** (Fig. 7.21) **holding the caliper clamshell halves together.**

5. **Remove the piston(s).** This is best done by blowing compressed air into the fluid-transfer hole while plugging either the bleed hole or the fluid-entry hole with your finger (Fig. 7.21), depending on which piston you are removing. Be careful not to get hit with fluid or parts. Wear safety glasses, and cover the piston with your hand so that no springs or other parts fly away.

6. **Dig the piston seals out of their grooves in the cylinder bores.** Use a fingernail or a toothpick to avoid scratching the bores. You'll

find there are relatively few parts inside the caliper—an object that you might assume is much more complicated—usually just a couple of pistons and a few seals (Fig. 7.21).

7. **Clean all parts carefully with isopropyl alcohol.** Inspect. Replace any cracked or scratched parts.

8. **With compressed air, blow out the caliper-seal grooves and the bleeder hole.** Wear safety glasses. Check that the seal grooves are completely clean.

9. **Let the parts dry.** Compressed air is humid, which contaminates DOT fluid.

10. **Lubricate the pistons and new seals with brake fluid.**

11. **Put all of the parts back together in the way that you found them.**

12. **Bolt the caliper together to the recommended torque.** Check Appendix D or the brake manual for torque specs.

13. **Reinstall the hose.**

14. **Install and center the caliper** (§vii-13b or §vii-13c).

15. **Bleed the system** (§vii-14).

b. Overhauling a one-piece hydraulic caliper

1. **Remove the caliper from the bike.** See Figures 7.16–17.

2. **Remove the brake pads** (§vii-10).

3. **Disconnect the hose.** If it has a banjo fitting (Figs. 7.16, 7.19, and 7.21), unscrew the hollow banjo bolt holding it on, but don't disconnect the hose from the banjo. Save the two O-rings if you did not get new ones.

4. **Remove the bore plugs** (Fig. 7.22). You will need a tool specific to the brake caliper for this.

5. **Push the outer piston out.** Reach in with your finger through the open bore to push the piston into the rotor gap so that it will fall out.

7.22 One-piece hydraulic caliper, exploded view

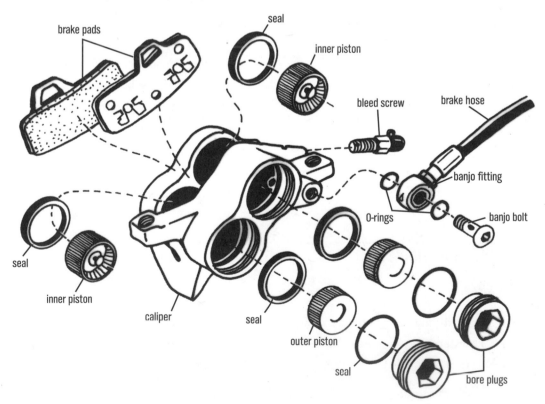

6. **Blow the inner piston out.** Blow with compressed air through the fluid-entry (banjo) hole to push the piston into the rotor gap so that it will fall out.

7. **Clean all parts carefully with isopropyl alcohol.** Inspect. Replace any cracked or scratched parts.

8. **With compressed air, blow out the caliper-seal grooves and the bleeder hole.** Wear safety glasses. Check that the seal grooves are completely clean.

9. **Let the parts dry.** Compressed air is humid, which contaminates DOT fluid.

10. **Lubricate the pistons and new seals with brake fluid.**

11. **Install the square seals in the cylinder grooves.**

12. **Install the inner piston.** Slide the piston up into the rotor gap and push it in place with your finger through the open bore.

13. **Install the outer piston.**

14. **Install new bore plug seals** (Fig. 7.22).

15. **Tighten in the bore plugs.**

16. **Reinstall the hose.**

17. **Install and center the caliper** (§vii-13b or §vii-13c).

18. **Bleed the system** (§vii-14).

c. Overhauling the lever ("master cylinder")

Levers rarely need to be overhauled if you bleed the brakes regularly and don't break any fittings on the lever in the process. They are high above the dirt and grime, so any dirt getting into the piston has to travel up from the caliper, which ain't easy.

Generally, you need to remove the lever unit from the handlebar, disconnect the hose (Fig. 7.18), and remove the lever blade from the housing. Carefully keep unscrewing things or removing circlips and pins until the lever comes apart, noting the order of the parts as you progress. Don't try to remove the rubber seals from the piston. On some brakes (Hayes HFX, for instance; Fig. 7.20), the cylinder is separate from the lever body rather than being machined into it. Remove the cylinder assembly. It is a cartridge that you replace as a unit; do not take out the little piston and seals.

Clean all of the parts with isopropyl alcohol and inspect them, replace any worn ones, lubricate the parts with brake fluid, and put them back together. Install the lever blade, mount the unit onto the handlebar, connect the hose, and bleed the system (§vii-14).

d. Overhauling mechanical disc-brake calipers

Mechanical disc brakes (Fig. 7.17) usually push the pistons by means of a number of ball bearings rolling in a nautilus-shaped track. Methods to disassemble them vary, and the how-to is usually not in the accompanying instruction manual. But as long as you are careful, keep the parts in order, and don't lose any, it is not particularly complicated to take mechanical disc brakes apart and put them back together.

Remove the pads, after which the pistons will usually come out one at a time through the rotor slot. If you can do it this way, you will avoid taking the entire brake apart, which is fine, as the pistons are probably all you need to clean anyway. For example, on Avid, to get out either piston, turn its red plastic screw (Fig. 7.17) clockwise until it pops out. The wheel-side piston is threaded on the outside and has a flat rectangular bar sticking out from the back to engage the plastic knurled disc. Once this piston is out, snap out the red knob—it just pops out with little prongs to hold it in when you replace it. After cleaning the inboard piston and its threaded receptacle, grease the threads and replace that piston and the red knob (don't grease the knob). The outboard piston has a rod sticking straight out from the back. A ring of spring steel around the piston holds it in a hole in the drive mechanism. Don't grease any part of this piston; it doesn't need grease, and grease will only attract dirt. The pistons are magnetic, so expect a bit of a hassle getting them lined up and back in; they will be attracted to each other. Drive in the outboard piston with the inboard piston (turn the red knob). Installing the pads and a spacer in between may help.

If you want to get at the ball-bearing mechanism, start by unbolting the arm. Simply clean and grease everything, and put it back in the way you found it. Be careful, but don't be intimidated.

vii-16
TRUING DISC-BRAKE ROTORS

 LEVEL 2

Even when you get a caliper perfectly centered over a rotor (disc), the brake will squeal and howl if the rotor gets bent. The spacing between brake pads and rotor is so tight on a bicycle disc brake—around 0.015 inch (0.4mm)—that there is almost no room for any rotor wobble whatsoever. And unlike car brake discs, bicycle rotors are thin and relatively unprotected; they can be bent by rocks thrown up while you are riding, when you are in a crash, or when you are packing your wheel in a car or a bike bag. They can also warp from heat buildup on a long, steep descent on a hot day. One way or another, the rotors will likely get bent eventually, so you need to be able to straighten them.

If a rotor is really "potato-chipped," you will first need to remove it from the hub and pound it as flat as you can with a hammer on an anvil. Then you can proceed with any of the methods detailed here.

a. Eyeballing the rotor in the caliper

By eyeballing, you can often do an adequate job to at least minimize brake-pad rub, but be forewarned that this approach requires patience,

because it can be hard to tell on which pad the rotor is rubbing as the gap is so small. Place a piece of white paper on the floor or the wall, below or level with the caliper, so that you can see the space between the rotor and the pads. Slowly turn the wheel, marking with a felt-tip pen where the disc rubs on each pad. Carefully bend the disc into alignment with your fingers, rechecking it constantly by spinning it again through the brake. A rotor bends easily by hand.

b. Rigging up a pointer

A more accurate way that's almost as cheap as eyeballing, but requires as much patience, is to attach a pointer to the frame or fork in such a way that you can adjust it to graze the rotor as you would a feeler on a truing stand. This pointer may be made of wire bent around the caliper. You can also remove the caliper and screw a piece of metal with a hole in it onto one of the caliper-mounting tabs. Bend the rotor away from the pointer where it touches as you rotate the wheel. The pointer must be mounted securely for this method to work; otherwise, you can make mistakes, thinking the disc is bent one way when it is actually bent the other.

c. Truing a rotor with a Morningstar ROC tool

If you straighten rotors a lot, eyeballing the rotor or using a rigged-up pointer will soon drive you mad. Happily, the Morningstar Rotors on Center dial indicator tool (Fig. 7.23) shows the lateral position of the rotor within 0.001 inch (0.025mm), so you can get the rotor as straight as it was when it was brand new. The ROC indicator includes a base that clamps through the center of the hub in place of the skewer when it is on the bike or in a truing stand. The tool costs less than $100—a good deal if you align rotors frequently.

Tighten the ROC tool's long mounting screw through the axle, and set the dial indicator foot

7.23 Truing a bent rotor with a Morningstar ROC dial indicator and Drumstix tools

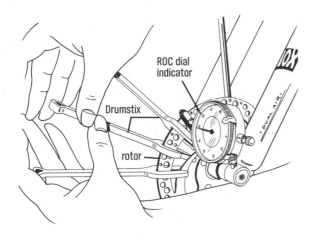

7.24 Shimano parallel-push V-brake

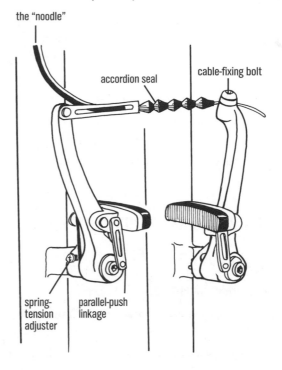

7.25 Simple V-brake (aka "sidepull cantilever brake")

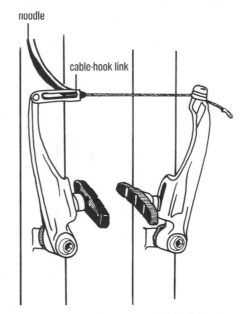

against the rotor. Rotate the indicator face cover so that the needle is on zero; wherever the needle indicates the greatest deflection in either direction, bend the rotor back, continually rechecking it with the dial indicator.

You can bend the rotor back with your thumbs—I have aligned a lot of very badly bent rotors to near perfection this way. Better yet, Morningstar's "rotor tuning forks," dubbed "Drumstix" (Fig. 7.23), slip onto the rotor and provide leverage to precisely bend the rotor. Stabilize the rotor in position with the two symmetrical Drumstix, one on either side of the bent spot, and with the third Drumstix, which has an angled slot for the rotor, bend the rotor to eliminate the warped spot.

V-BRAKES

As you can see in Figures 7.24–25, V-brakes (aka "sidepull cantilevers") have tall, cantileverlike arms, a horizontal cable-hook link on top of one arm, and a cable clamp on top of the other. A curved aluminum guide pipe (noodle) hooks into the horizontal link, taking the cable from the end of the housing out through the link, and directing

it toward the cable clamp on the opposite arm. V-brakes usually have long, thin brake pads with threaded posts. Some V-brakes have "parallel-push" linkages (Fig. 7.24), which move the brake pads horizontally rather than in an arc around the brake boss the way a cantilever moves. Simple V-brake designs mount the pad directly to the arm so that it moves in a cantileverlike arc (Fig. 7.25).

Because of their long arms, V-brakes are extremely powerful and can be very grabby if used with a center-pull cantilever brake lever; it is important that you use the levers that were designed for use with V-brakes if those brakes are the type you have (see §vii-9 regarding leverage).

vii-17
INSTALLING AND ADJUSTING V-BRAKES

 LEVEL 1

a. V-brake mounting

1. **Grease the brake bosses on the frame or fork.**
2. **With most V-brakes, slide each brake arm on, inserting the spring pin into the center hole of the boss.** You may need to pull outward on the return spring (the tall vertical wire—see Fig. 7.26) to get the pin to line up with the center hole. Tighten the brake bolt with its

7.26 Finalizing pad-to-rim adjustment

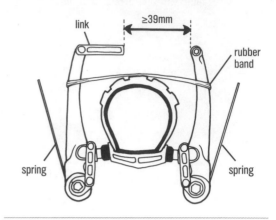

washer into the boss. You want this bolt to be snug, but if you overtighten it, you may mushroom the end of the brake boss so that the brake arm does not pivot freely. See the torque table in Appendix D.

b. V-brake pad adjustment

These instructions apply to brake pads with threaded posts. For V-brakes with unthreaded pad posts, follow the pad-adjustment procedure

7.27 V-brake pad-holder assembly

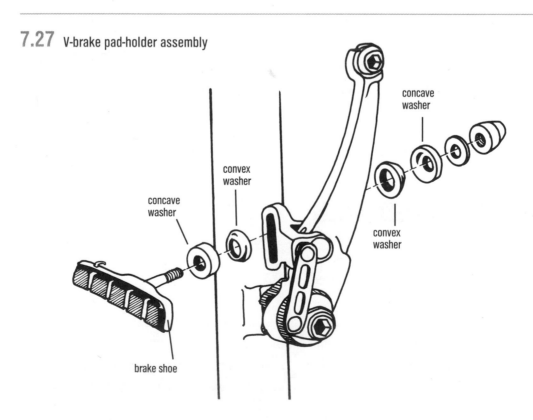

Optimizing V-brakes

To get maximum performance from V-brakes with a minimum of application effort, you can increase the leverage at the brake lever. But if you do so, you must also position the lever so that you can reach it only with your forefinger; otherwise you may grab too much brake and do an endo (i.e., go arse over teakettle).

Even though a lot of people want a hard feel to the brakes, the harder the brakes feel, the less power there is. The hard feel indicates less mechanical advantage; it feels hard because you are doing all of the work! A softer feel indicates that you have more leverage. You will do less work and stop the bike more easily.

If you set up the brake levers for high leverage, you may lose some pad travel. You will be moving the cable hook (or the cable path) closer to the lever pivot, usually by turning in a leverage-adjustment screw (Fig. 7.9), by removing some inserts under the cable hook, or by moving the position of an adjuster screw (Fig. 7.11).

Move the levers inboard on the handlebars so that the tip of the lever is under your forefinger. The lever will bypass your second finger and let you pull it to the grip, rather than losing some range by hitting your finger(s). Hold the handlebar with three fingers (and your thumb), and pull the lever with your forefinger. Make sure you pull on the end of the lever, because that is where the leverage is. You will find that you can grip the handlebar better, and your arms will stay more relaxed when braking. In addition, it will be comfortable to simply rest your forefingers on the levers so that you will be ready to brake at any time. I suggest placing the levers of powerful disc brakes in this position too.

Note that it is easy to move the brake lever inboard far enough with twist shifters and with Shimano integrated brake and shift levers, but it may not be easy with trigger shift levers that have a separate band clamp. The band clamp usually goes inboard of the brake lever, and it may prevent the lever from moving inboard enough for a rider with large hands (and bar ends taking up some handlebar real estate) to get unimpeded one-finger braking. The shifter band clamp may hit the bulge or curve of the handlebar and stop before it has moved inward enough that the brake lever clears the second finger. And even though wider handlebars are back in fashion, the bends in a riser bar may be too far outboard to allow the shifter and the brake lever to move inboard as far as you might wish. Try putting the trigger shifter outboard of the brake lever, and see if you can get the function and finger clearance you desire.

---

for cantilever brakes in §vii-23, coupled with the pad offset described in step 3 here.

1. **Roughly adjust each pad.** Loosen the pad nut, push the arm toward the rim, and tighten the pad nut with the pad flat against the rim.

2. **Determine the proper amount of pad offset from the brake arms.** While holding the pads against the rim, measure the space between the end of the link and the inside edge of the opposite brake arm (Fig. 7.26); this length should be at least 39mm. If it is less than 39mm, the end of the noodle may hit the opposite arm when the brake is applied, particularly as the pads wear. Obviously, this placement would prevent the brakes from grabbing the rims, which is not what you have in mind when you apply the brakes.

3. **Set the pad offset.** Ensure that the length in Figure 7.26 is ≥39mm by interchanging concave washers of various thicknesses nesting over convex washers on either side of the mounting tab (Fig. 7.27). By interchanging taller and shorter concave washers from one side of the mounting tab to the other,

you set the pad offset so that (a) the space between the end of the link and the inside edge of the opposite brake arm (Fig. 7.26) is at least 39mm, and (b) the top of each brake arm is a little outside of vertical relative to the brake mounting bolt when the brake is applied (i.e., the arms are approximately parallel).

4. **Finalize the pad-to-rim adjustment.** On brakes with vertical return springs such as in Figure 7.26, flip the springs off their retention pins and connect the tops of the arms with a rubber band to lightly hold the pads against the rim. Otherwise, hold the pad against the rim or put a rubber band around the brake lever after you have connected the cable.

5. **Loosen the pad anchor nut, and then tighten the pad-fixing nut with the pad held flat against the rim.** The pad's top edge should be about 1mm below the edge of the rim. Applying toe-in to the pads (Fig. 7.34), so that the front end of the pad hits the rim before the rear end, is not necessary in many cases, but it is recommended if the brakes squeal. To get just a bit of toe-in, slip a paper clip between the tail of the brake pad and the rim, and then hold the pad against the rim and tighten it down.

6. Rehook the return springs behind the retention pins.

NOTE: *On high-end "parallel-push" V-brakes, the linkage attached to the pad-mounting bracket keeps the pad moving horizontally as it contacts and leaves the rim surface (Figs. 7.24 and 7.26–28). When interchanging wheels with these brakes, there is usually no need to adjust the pads if the rim width varies; the only necessary adjustment is to the cable length.*

c. Threading of the cable to the brake through the curved alloy guide pipe (the "noodle")

For the rear brake, of the two supplied noodles pick the one whose curvature and length best fit the frame for a smooth cable path. Bend the noodle if need be. Hook the head of the noodle into the notch in the horizontal link.

1. **Slip the rubber accordionlike dust boot onto the cable, big end first, and over the tip of the noodle** (Fig. 7.24). If you are using Gore-Tex RideOn cables, you can dispense with the boot and use Gore's little "Grub" seal instead. The Grub seals the end of the Gore plastic sheath, which should be cut to terminate halfway between the guide-pipe tip and the cable anchor bolt.

2. **Connect the cable to the anchor bolt on the opposite arm.**

3. **Set the cable length so that there is 1–1.5mm of space between each pad and the rim.** Tighten the cable anchor bolt with the lever barrel adjuster screwed out one turn. Make sure the wheel is centered in the frame or fork.

d. V-brake centering and/or spring-tension adjustment

- Some V-brakes use a vertical return spring (Fig. 7.26) adjusted by a screw at the mounting pivot on each arm (Fig. 7.24); turn the screw clockwise to move the arm farther from the rim, and vice versa. A quick way to increase spring tension or center the brakes on the trail without fooling with the screws is to bend one or both vertical springs outward after pulling them off the retention pins on the back of the arms as in Figure 7.26, and rehook them behind the retention pins. Hold the spring with your thumb near its base while bending it outward at the top to avoid breaking the plastic adjuster housing.

- Dia-Compe 747s use a spring adjuster cam rotated by a 5mm hex key; turn the cam toward the imprinted "H" or "L" for more or less spring tension.

- Avid Arch Supremes have an innovative (and very quick) way to set the spring balance. While lightly squeezing the lever so that the pads touch the rim, loosen and retighten the plastic knob at the top of the arch. The W-shaped spring passes through the knob and hooks on the arms; it automatically finds its balance point when the knob is loosened.

If the V-brake springs do not adjust with any of these three methods, look at spring-tension adjustment for cantilever brakes, §vii-25, because any of the spring configurations used in cantilevers could be built into a V-brake.

IMPORTANT: *Regardless of the type of brake you have, after these adjustments squeeze the brake lever hard a number of times to stretch the cable and make sure it does not slip at the anchor bolt.*

NOTE: *If a brake arm does not turn freely on the boss, the boss may be damaged. Bulging or mushroomed bosses can be filed and sanded smaller; bent or broken ones must be replaced (with luck they are the bolt-on type; otherwise new ones must be welded on).*

ANOTHER NOTE: *Parallel-push V-brakes (Fig. 7.24) often do not hold their pad-centering adjustment and may rub the rim after a ride in which they began centered. This is because any bit of grit in any of the numerous pivots will change the return friction on one side relative to the other side, especially as the pivots break in.*

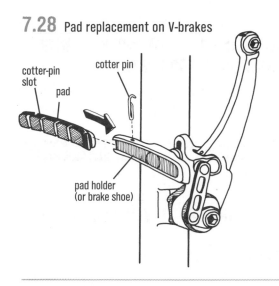

cotter-pin slot

cotter pin

pad

pad holder (or brake shoe)

3. **Slide in the new pad.** Pay attention to the "R" and "L" markings for right and left and the forward direction arrow, if present.

4. **Replace the cotter pin, and check that the pad is secure in the holder.**

NOTE: *Pads meant for straight grooves are not interchangeable with most pad holders that have a curved groove. The pads are flexible enough that they can be jammed into each other's holders in a pinch, but the outer curvature of the pad will no longer match that of the rim.*

vii-19
REPLACING A PAD ON V-BRAKES WITH A ONE-PIECE PAD AND THREADED POST

1. **Note how the washers are stacked on the pad post** (Fig. 7.27).
2. **Unscrew the shoe anchor nut, and remove the old pad and post from the arm.**
3. **Replacing the concave and convex washers as they were, bolt the new pad to the arm.** The convex washers are placed on either side of the brake arm with flat sides facing each other (Fig. 7.27). The concave washers are placed adjacent to the convex washers so that the concave and convex surfaces meet and allow angular adjustability of the pad.
4. **Follow the pad-adjustment procedure in §vii-17b.**

vii-18
REPLACING V-BRAKE PADS IN PAD HOLDERS

 LEVEL 1

It is only on high-end brakes that you will find removable pads that slide in and out of permanent pad holders.

1. **With a pair of pliers, remove the cotter pin from the top of the pad holder** (Fig. 7.28).
2. **Slide the old pad out of its groove in the pad holder** (Fig. 7.28).

vii-20
REPLACING A PAD ON V-BRAKES WITH UNTHREADED PAD POSTS

Follow pad replacement and adjustment procedures for cantilever brakes, §vii-22 and §vii-23.

CANTILEVER BRAKES

vii-21
INSTALLING CANTILEVER BRAKES

 LEVEL 1

If you have the installation directions that came with the brakes, follow them. If not, follow the general installation instructions below. Make sure to install the brakes with all of the parts in their original order. Return springs are not interchangeable from left to right and will often be of different colors to distinguish them.

1. **Grease the brake posts** (Fig. 7.29).
2. **Install the bushings, if applicable.** Each arm may have a separate inner sleeve bushing; if so, slip one onto each brake post.

3. **Determine the type of return-spring anchor.** If the brake arms have either no spring-tension adjustment or a setscrew on the side of one of the arms for adjusting spring tension, continue to step 4. Such brakes anchor the spring in a hole at the base of the brake post. If the brake arms instead have a large nut for adjusting spring tension behind or in front of the brake arm (Fig. 7.29), skip to step 7.
4. **Slip the brake arm and return spring onto the brake post.** Insert the lower end of the spring into the hole at the base of the post (if there are three holes, try the center hole first; use a higher hole to make the brake snappier, a necessity with lower-quality or old brakes). Ensure that the top end of the spring is inserted into its hole in the brake arm as well.
5. **Install and tighten the mounting bolt into the cantilever post.**
6. **Skip the next three steps.** They are only for brake arms with tension-adjustment nuts.
7. **Slip the brake arm onto the cantilever boss.**

7.29 Cantilever brake assembly

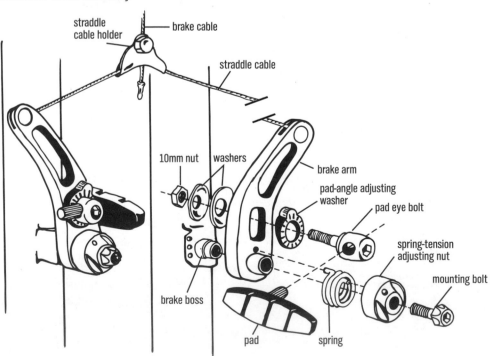

straddle cable holder — brake cable
straddle cable
10mm nut   washers
brake arm
pad-angle adjusting washer
pad eye bolt
spring-tension adjusting nut
mounting bolt
brake boss
pad   spring

8. **Install the spring.** One end inserts into the hole in the brake arm and the other inserts into the hole in the adjusting nut.

9. **Install and tighten the mounting bolt** while holding the adjusting nut.

vii-22
REPLACING CANTILEVER PADS

1. **Remove the old pad.**

2. **Install the new pad.** Most cantilevers rely on an eye bolt with an enlarged head and a hole through it to accept the pad post (Fig. 7.29). Some cantilevers instead have a slotted clamp with a hole for the pad post (Fig. 7.30). A few cantilevers use a threaded pad post that passes through a slot in the brake arm (Fig. 7.31), as on a V-brake.

vii-23
ADJUSTING CANTILEVER PADS

LEVEL 1

There are five separate adjustments that must be made for each pad (labeled "a" through "e" in Figs. 7.32–34):

(a) Offset distance of the pad from the brake arm (extension of the pad post) (a, Fig. 7.32)

(b) Vertical pad height (b, Fig. 7.33)

(c) Pad swing in the vertical plane for mating with the rim's sidewall angle (c, Fig. 7.32)

(d) Pad twist to align the length of the pad with the rim's curvature (d, Fig. 7.33)

(e) Pad swing in the horizontal plane to set toe-in (e, Fig. 7.34)

Cantilevers that feature a cylindrical brake arm are by far the easiest to adjust (Fig. 7.30). Pad adjustment is simple because the pad is held to the cylinder with a clamp that offers almost full range of motion. Other cantilevers employ a single-pad eye bolt to hold all five adjustments (the eye bolt and washers are exploded in Fig. 7.27 and are seen from above in Fig. 7.34). It requires a bit of manual dexterity to hold all five adjustments simultaneously while tightening the bolt.

With all types of cantilevers:

1. **Lubricate the pad anchor threads.**

2. **Set the pad offset** (a, Fig. 7.32). Loosen the pad-clamping bolt, and slide the post in or out of the clamping hole. The farther the pad is extended away from the brake arm, the greater the angle of the brake arm from the plane of the wheel. A benefit of this is that leverage is increased (see straddle-cable angle in Figs. 7.37–38). The drawbacks are that the brake feels less firm because less

7.30 Cylindrical clamp cantilever brake

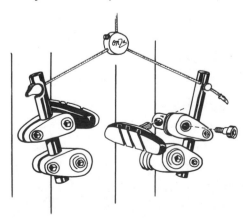

7.31 Threaded-post cantilever brake

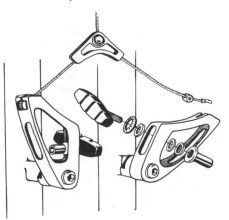

7.32 Distance of pad to fixing bolt (a) and angle against rim (c)

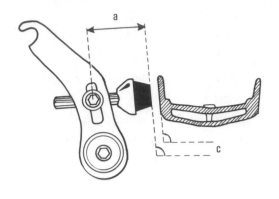

7.33 Up and down (b) and twist (d)

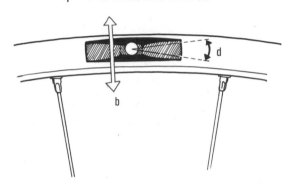

7.34 Brake pad toe-in (e)

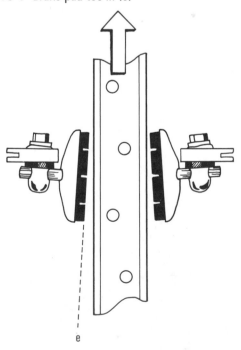

force is required to pull the lever, and clearance between the rider's heels and the rear brake arms is reduced, particularly for small frames. A good initial position is with the post clamped in the center of its length.

NOTE: *With threaded-post pads (Fig. 7.31), set the pad off-set with washers between the brake arm and pad.*

3. **Roughly adjust the vertical pad height** (b, Fig. 7.33). Slide the pad-clamping mechanism up and down in the brake-arm slot. With cylindrical-clamp brakes (Fig. 7.30), loosen the bolt clamping the pad holder to the brake arm, and snug the bolt back up once the rough adjustment is reached. With all other types, leave the pad bolt just loose enough so that you can move the pad easily, and continue.

4. **Adjust pad swing in the vertical plane** (c, Fig. 7.32). Make the face of the pad meet the rim flat with its top edge 1–2mm below the top of the rim. Fine-tune this adjustment by simultaneously sliding the pad up or down while rotating it to meet the rim flat.

5. **Adjust the pad twist** (d, Fig. 7.33). Make sure the top edge of the pad is parallel to the top of the rim. Modern pads are quite long and require precision with this adjustment. With cylindrical-clamp brakes (Fig. 7.30), the pad-securing bolt may now be tightened.

6. **Finally, adjust the pad toe-in** (e, Fig. 7.34). The pad should either be adjusted flat to the rim or toed-in so that when the forward end of the pad touches the rim, the rear end of it is 1–2mm away from the rim.

If the pad is toed-out, the heel of it will catch and tend to chatter, making for a grabby feel and squealing noise. If the brake arms are not stiff, or if they fit loosely on the cantilever boss, the same thing will happen when flat. Toe-in is a must with flimsy brake arms and will need to be adjusted frequently as the pads wear to keep them quiet.

NOTE: *If the bike shudders under hard braking, add more toe-in. If that doesn't fix the shudder and the bike does not have a suspension fork, there's too much flex in the fork steering tube, thus pulling the cable tighter when the pads grab the rim. Replacing the front cantilever brake with a V-brake (Figs. 7.24–25) will fix this problem. The shudder will also probably disappear if you use a cable hanger bolted onto the fork crown, rather than a cable hanger above the headset as in Figures 7.5–6.*

On cylindrical-arm brakes with two anchor bolts (Fig. 7.30), the toe-in is adjusted by loosening the bolt that holds the vertical height adjustment of the pad. Because you have already tightened the other bolt that holds the pad in place, simply loosen this second bolt and swing the pad horizontally until you arrive at your preferred toe-in or flatness setting. Tighten the bolt again, and you are done with pad adjustment.

With any brake using a single bolt to hold the pad as well as control its rotation, you now have the tricky task of holding all the adjustments you have made and simultaneously tightening the nut. Most eye-bolt systems are tightened with a 10mm wrench on the nut on the back of the brake while the front is held with a 5mm hex key. Help from someone else to either hold or tighten is useful here. Probably the trickiest brake to adjust has a toothed or deeply notched washer between the head of the eye bolt and a flat brake arm (Fig. 7.29). The adjusting washer is thinner on one edge than on the other, so rotating it (by means of the tooth or notch) toes the pad in or out. With this type, you must hold all the pad adjustments as you turn this washer and then keep it and the pad in place as you tighten the nut. It's not an easy job, and the adjustment changes as you tighten the bolt.

The other common type has a slotted brake arm with a convex or concave shape, and cupped washers separate the eye-bolt head and nut from the brake arm (Fig. 7.35). The concave-against-convex surfaces allow the pad to swivel, and tightening the bolt secures everything. Again, you may not get it on the first try. Threaded posts (Fig. 7.31) also employ such washers.

NOTE: *Some curved-face brakes do not hold their toe-in adjustment well; you may need to sand the brake-arm faces and washers to create more friction between them.*

Brakes with a cylindrical arm and a clamp secured only by the pad eye bolt are adjusted functionally in the same way as the curved-face ones with cupped washers. A rare but simple-to-adjust type (Campagnolo, Fig. 7.36) has a ball joint at each pad eye bolt.

vii-24
ADJUSTING STRADDLE CABLE

The straddle cable should be set so that it pulls on the brake arms in such a way as to provide optimal braking. This is not always the adjustment that produces the highest leverage, for sometimes brake feel (i.e., stiffness when pulling the lever) is improved when leverage is reduced because you are doing more of the work. In general, I recommend setting the straddle cable for high leverage and reducing it from there to improve lever feel.

7.35 Curved-face cantilever brake

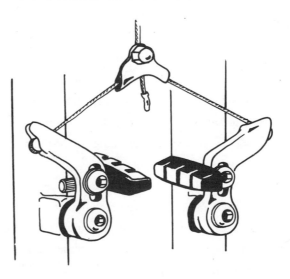

7.36 Ball-joint cantilever brake

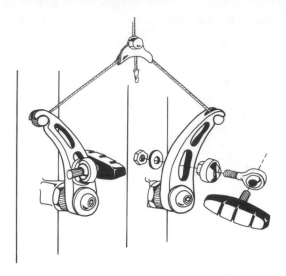

7.37 Cable angle when open

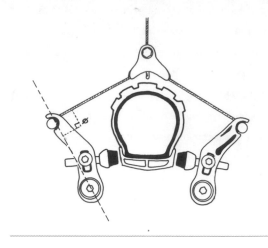

With any lever arm, the mechanical advantage is highest when the force is applied at right angles to the lever arm. For general purposes, set the straddle cable so that it pulls as close to 90 degrees to the brake arm as possible (Fig. 7.37). An esoteric and more precise argument is that once the pad hits the rim, the actual lever arm is the line from the face of the pad to the cable attachment point on top of the arm (because the pad, not the brake boss, now becomes the fulcrum). If you set the straddle cable at 90 degrees from this line, the leverage is maximized (Fig. 7.38). Pull the cable to the desired position with pliers, and tighten the nut on the straddle-cable hanger with a wrench (Fig. 7.39).

With low-profile brake arms, a 90-degree straddle-cable angle results in a short straddle cable set very low and close to the tire. Make sure that you allow at least an inch of clearance over the tire to prevent mud, or a bulge in the tire, from engaging the brake.

The straddle cable has a metal blob on at least one end (Figs. 7.40–42). The blob fits into the slot atop one brake arm and acts as a quick-release for the brake. The other end of the straddle cable is fixed to the opposite brake arm.

7.38 Cable angle when closed

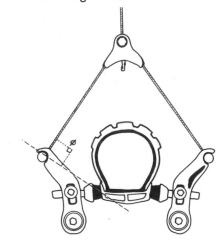

7.39 Tightening straddle-cable holder to brake cable

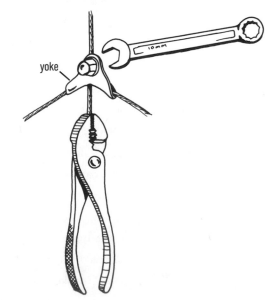

yoke

On Shimano cantilevers built since 1988, the brake cable connects directly to the cable clamp on one brake arm, and a link wire hooks to the other arm. On post-1993 Shimano cantilevers, the cable passes through a link-wire holder accommodating not only a link wire but also a fixed length of cable housing (Fig. 7.42). The brake cable passes directly through the link-wire holder and housing segment to the cable clamp on the brake arm. The mechanic has no choice of straddle-cable settings; the setting is predetermined.

From 1988 to 1993, Shimano brakes did not have the housing segment on the link-wire holder; instead the holder was clamped to the brake cable. For this type, simply set the cable length from the link-wire holder to the brake arm the same on both sides.

Some brakes do not have a cable clamp on either brake arm; both arms are slotted to accept the blob on the end of a straddle cable or link wire. In this case, a small cylindrical clamp forms a second blob on the end of the straddle cable (Fig. 7.41), or a link-wire holder that holds two separate link wires is used.

With any straddle cable, after its length is set, the position of the straddle-cable holder is set by loosening the bolt (Fig. 7.39) or setscrews (Fig. 7.41) that hold it onto the end of the brake cable and sliding it up on the brake cable. Tighten it in place. It is set properly when the brake engages quickly and the lever cannot be pulled closer than a finger's width from the handlebar. Some cable slack can be taken up with the barrel adjuster on the brake lever (Fig. 7.1).

The lateral position of the straddle-cable holder can be changed with setscrews as well. The holder should generally be centered on the straddle cable, but sometimes the brake cable pulls asymmetrically as it comes around the seat tube. In these cases, the straddle-cable holder may need to be offset for the brakes to work (Fig. 7.43).

7.40–7.42 Straddle cables

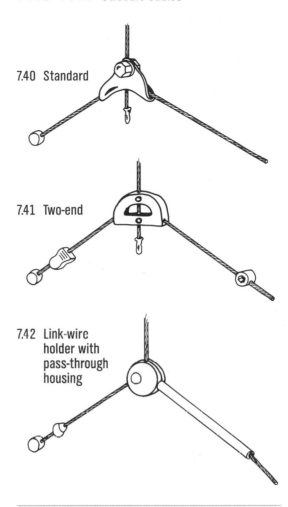

7.40 Standard

7.41 Two-end

7.42 Link-wire holder with pass-through housing

vii-25
ADJUSTING SPRING TENSION

The spring-tension adjustment centers the brake pads about the rim and also determines the return spring force. There is only one adjustment to make on brakes with a single setscrew on the side of one brake arm. Turn the screw (Fig. 7.44) until the brakes are centered and the pads hit the rim simultaneously when applied. Higher spring tensions can be achieved by moving the spring to a higher hole in the brake boss.

Some brakes rely on a large tensioning nut in front of (Fig. 7.29) or behind the brake arm and do not use the holes in the brake bosses as anchors. On these, the tensioning nuts may be turned

7.43 An offset straddle-cable stop requires an offset straddle hanger

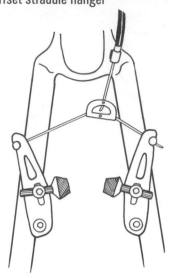

7.44 Adjusting return-spring tension with a setscrew

7.45 Adjusting return-spring tension with tensioning nut

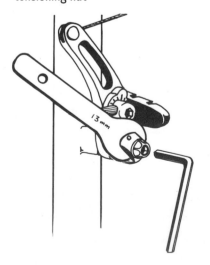

on both arms to get the combination of return force and centering you prefer. You must loosen the mounting bolt while holding the tensioning nut with a wrench. Turn the nut to the desired tension, and while holding it in place with the wrench, tighten the mounting bolt again (Fig. 7.45).

On really old brakes without a tension adjustment, centering is accomplished by removing the brake arm and moving the spring to another hole on the boss. It is a rough adjustment at best, and some bosses do not have more than a single hole. When this adjustment fails, you can twist the arm on the boss to tighten or loosen the spring a bit. That, of course, is an even rougher adjustment.

NOTE: *If the brake arms do not rotate easily on the brake post, there is too much friction. Remove the brake, and check that the post is not bent or split, in which case a new one needs to be screwed in or welded on. If not bent, the post is probably too fat to slide freely inside the brake arm, owing to either paint on it or bulging or mushrooming of the post because of overtightening of the brake mounting bolt. In this case, if it's the replaceable type, screw a new post into the frame or fork. Otherwise, file and sand around the post to reduce its diameter. File and sand uniformly, only a little at a time; avoid making the post too thin.*

vii-26
LUBRICATING AND SERVICING CANTILEVER BRAKES

The only lubrication necessary for cantilever brakes is on the cables, levers, and brake arms. This should be performed whenever braking feels sticky. Lever and cable lubrication is covered in §vii-5. Cantilevers can be lubricated by removing them, cleaning and greasing the pivots, and replacing them (§vii-21).

HYDRAULIC RIM BRAKES

This section applies to brakes that are fully hydraulic and are mounted on the cantilever bosses. The most common type is Magura (Fig. 7.46), and these instructions, while possibly applicable to others, focus on Maguras.

The Magura brake has great stopping power, is practically maintenance-free, and is simple to adjust. The system is completely sealed from dirt, and there are no cables and housings to wear. Pads are replaced simply by pulling them out by hand and pushing new ones in. A screw on the lever adjusts pad-to-rim spacing as easily as turning a barrel adjuster on a cable-actuating lever.

vii-27

INSTALLING AND ADJUSTING MAGURA RIM-BRAKE CALIPERS ONTO CANTILEVER-BRAKE BOSSES

⚙ LEVEL 1

1. Snap a C-shaped plastic ring around each wheel cylinder.

2. **Assemble the adapter brackets around the plastic ring on each wheel cylinder.** Use the supplied 4mm bolts, installing the L-shaped elbow behind the top bracket hole (Fig. 7.48). Right and left wheel cylinders are normally determined by orienting the crossover hose connecting the cylinders toward the bike (Fig. 7.46)—that is, the hose from the lever and the bleed hole are away from the fork or seatstay.

NOTE: *The adapter brackets (Fig. 7.46) are asymmetrical and can be reversed from left to right to move the slave cylinder closer to the rim or vice versa. Normal mounting is with the bracket imprinted with "Magura" on the right when facing the brake.*

3. **Slide the included D-shaped washer onto the cantilever boss.** The flat side of the washer is on top. A thick washer with a setscrew must be used with some suspension forks to clear the fork brace.

4. **Bolt the adapter bracket to the cantilever boss with a bolt and washer.** If mounting a bracket with the quick-release feature, first screw the mounting bolt with the spool-shaped head a few turns into the brake boss. Slide the QR unit over the mounting slot on the adapter bracket (Fig. 7.47). Push the bracket onto the brake boss so that the spool-shaped

---

7.46 Magura hydraulic brake

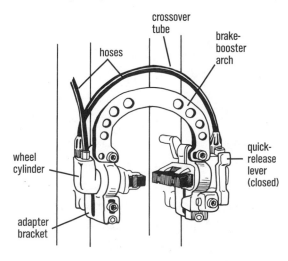

7.47 Magura brake-pad installation and quick-release operation

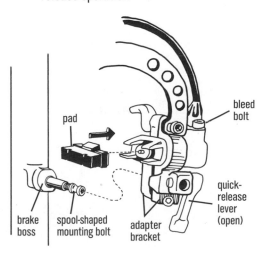

7.48 Installing and/or adjusting elbow

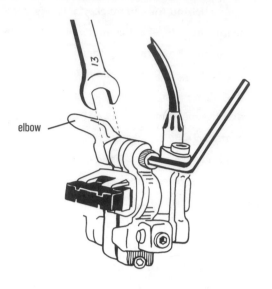

7.49 Installing hydraulic brake hose

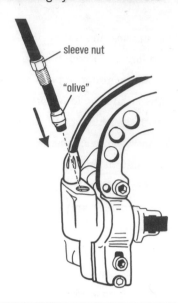

sleeve nut

"olive"

mounting bolt head comes through the hole in the quick-release unit. Flip the QR lever up to its closed position. Tighten the mounting bolt with a 5mm hex key. You can now remove this side of the brake by merely flipping the quick-release lever down and pulling the bracket straight off (Fig. 7.47). To install, push the bracket onto the boss so that the bolt head sticks out through the hole in the QR unit, and flip the lever up.

NOTE: *The QR unit is installed properly when the quick-release lever's pivot pin is above the spool-shaped mounting bolt, not below it.*

5. **Set the pad position.** Slide the adapter bracket up and down to adjust the height of the wheel cylinder. Loosening the mounting bolt and the other bolt (or bolts) holding the bracket together (Fig. 7.48) allows the cylinder to be slid in or out and rotated. Using these adjustments in tandem, set the pad-to-rim contact so that the pad hits the rim flat about 2mm below its upper edge. See to it that the pad holders do not drag on the tire. When retracted, the pads should sit 2–3mm away from the rim.

7.50 Bleeding and/or filling Magura brake hoses

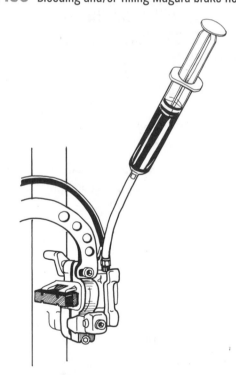

6. **Position the elbows** (Fig. 7.48). They support the brake and simplify repositioning after removal. Loosen the bolt above the wheel cylinder. With a 13mm open-end wrench, rotate the elbow until it contacts the inner side of the seatstay or fork leg, and tighten the bolt

(Fig. 7.48). Aftermarket elbows are available to better fit certain suspension forks.

7. **If you have the "brake booster" arch** (Fig. 7.46), **loosely bolt it onto the right bracket adapter.** Its oval mounting hole goes on the right. Swing the arch over the wheel, and slide it laterally until the booster's bottom left hole lines up with, and slips over, the bolt head on the left bracket. Tighten the top bolt on the right bracket to fix the booster in place. When releasing the brake, pull the left side of the booster off the bolt head, and leave it attached to the right cylinder when pulling it off.

8. **If the hose is not connected, attach it** (Fig. 7.49). See §vii-13e for hydraulic hose routing and cutting.

9. **If the brake is not firm when you pull the lever, bleed it.** See §vii-29.

10. **Fine-tune pad-to-rim spacing by turning the adjustment screw on the lever.** Some systems take a 2mm hex key; the screw is under the lever. Newer systems have a finger-operated knob on the front of the lever.

vii-28
REPLACING THE MAGURA PADS

Pad replacement is very simple:

1. **Remove the wheel.**
2. **Grab the pad and pull it straight out** (Fig. 7.47).
3. **Push the new pad in.** Pay attention to the rotation-indicator arrow on it.
   That's it!

vii-29
BLEEDING MAGURA RIM BRAKES

 LEVEL 2

A spongy feeling at the lever indicates the need to bleed air from the lines. Bleeding is a mainte-nance operation that also clears out dirt that has crept in and should be done every 500 miles or so. If the oil inside comes out clean, you will know you can wait longer next time. There is rarely a need to bleed due to air bubbles, because air does not get in unless the system is opened or gets damaged. That said, any air bubbles will rise toward the highest point in the system, so they should be up in the lever after any ride, mean-ing that it will not take much new fluid to drive them out.

1. **Back out the lever adjustment screw(s).** Older models have a 2mm microadjustment screw under the lever and a 2mm reach-adjustment screw on top of the lever. Newer models have a single knob on the front of the lever.

2. **Remove the bleed bolt on the right brake wheel cylinder** (Fig. 7.47).

IMPORTANT: *Never squeeze the lever while the system is open; fluid will squirt out.*

3. **Fill the Magura syringe with Magura brake fluid.** The syringe has a tube with a barbed fitting on the end (Fig. 7.50).

4. **Invert the syringe, and push any air up and out with the plunger.**

5. **Screw the fitting into the bleed hole on the wheel cylinder** (Fig. 7.50). (In a pinch, a squirt bottle of fluid can be used instead of the syringe, but it is easy to allow air in this way. You will need another person to hold the bottle tip tightly in the bleed hole and squeeze the bottle while you open and close the lever bleed bolt.)

6. **Tip the bike or rotate the lever on the handle-bar so that the lever bleed bolt is at its high-est point.**

7. **Remove the bleed bolt from the lever.**

8. **Screw in a piece of tubing with a barbed fit-ting into the lever bleed hole.** Have the tube drain into a bottle of fluid hanging from the handlebar (Fig.7.20).

9. **Push fluid into the wheel cylinder with the syringe** (Fig. 7.50). Let it push fluid out of the lever and into the catch bottle.

10. **Reinstall the bleed bolt at the lever and tighten it.** Make sure the bolt and washer are free of grit.

11. **Remove the syringe or bottle from the wheel cylinder.** Leave a dome of fluid bulging from the hole.

12. **Put the bolt back in and tighten it.** Again, the bolt and washer must be free of grit.

13. **Squeeze the lever.** If the bubbles have been driven out, the brake will no longer feel spongy. Repeat until the sponginess is gone. You may need to bleed the system again after riding; the bubbles will have collected at the lever.

14. **Adjust the pad spacing and lever reach to your liking.** Use the two 2mm bolts or the single knob on the lever.

LINKAGE BRAKES

There are so many vastly different linkage brakes (Fig. 7.51) besides V-brakes floating around on older bikes that including them all in detail is not possible here. Linkage brakes are often quite similar to cantilevers or V-brakes and are adjusted, centered, and mounted in much the same way. If in doubt, refer to specific instructions from the manufacturer.

U-BRAKES

vii-30
INSTALLING U-BRAKES

 LEVEL 1

U-brakes (Fig. 7.52), once very popular under the chainstays of mountain bikes, mount on the same bosses that roller-cam brakes (Fig. 7.53) do,

7.51 Linkage brake

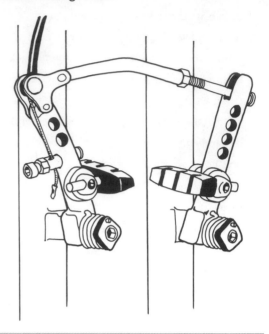

but at a greater distance from the hub than cantilever bosses. Like roller-cams, U-brakes cannot be mounted on cantilever bosses, as the pads would hit the tire rather than contact the rim.

1. **Grease the pivots.**

2. **Slide the arms onto the pivots.**

3. **Screw in the mounting bolts.**

4. **Tighten the straddle-cable yoke to the brake cable** (Fig. 7.39).

5. **Attach the straddle cable to the cable clamp on one arm.**

6. **With a chainstay-mounted U-brake, set the position of the straddle-cable yoke the easy way.** Loosen the straddle-cable bolt and squeeze the lever to the grip after slipping the yoke up against the bottom-bracket cable guide. Then tighten the bolt. This is the highest position on the cable and allows for the longest possible straddle cable.

vii-31
ADJUSTING U-BRAKES

1. **Set the position of the rear straddle-cable yoke as outlined in step 6 in the previous**

7.52 U-brake (usually under chainstays)

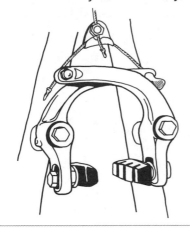

section. On a front brake, set the position about 2 inches (5cm) above the brake.

2. **Tighten the straddle cable while pulling the brake cable tight with pliers** (Fig. 7.39). Make sure you have tightened the anchor bolt enough that the cable does not slip.

3. **Check that you cannot pull the lever closer than a finger's width from the grip.** Tension the cable as needed with the straddle-cable yoke or the lever barrel adjuster (Fig. 7.1).

4. **Set the spring tension.** Release the straddle cable, loosen the mounting bolt, and swing the pad away from the rim; then tighten the mounting bolt. Center the brake by setting the spring tension on one arm first, followed by the other arm in the same fashion. If the brake has a small hex-head setscrew on the side of one arm, use it to make fine spring-tension adjustments.

vii-32
REPLACING AND POSITIONING U-BRAKE PADS

U-brakes rely on brake pads with threaded posts. Install them with the original spacers in their original orientation. The pads should hit the center of the braking surface and should have a small amount of toe-in. There is no adjustment for spacing from the brake arm. Hold the pad in place

with your hand while tightening the nut with a wrench. As the pads wear, they tend to slide up on the rim and hit the tire, so check this adjustment frequently. You should also regularly clear hardened mud from inside the brake arms; it can build up here on U-brakes and abrade the tire sidewalls.

ROLLER-CAM BRAKES

vii-33
REMOVING AND INSTALLING ROLLER-CAM BRAKES

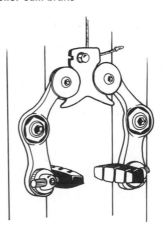 **LEVEL 1**

Roller-cam brakes (Fig. 7.53) mount on U-brake bosses attached to the fork and either the chainstays or the seatstays. These brakes are mounted farther from the hub than cantilever bosses, and, like U-brakes, they will not work on standard cantilever bosses.

Roller-cams are removed by first pulling the cam plate out from between the rollers on the ends of the arms. Remove the mounting bolts, and pull the arms off the bosses.

Installation is performed in reverse: Grease the bosses and the inside of the pivots as well as the edges of the cam plate and the mounting bolts.

7.53 Roller-cam brake

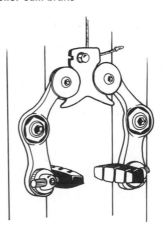

vii-34
ADJUSTING ROLLER-CAMS

1. **Check that the pulleys spin freely.** Loosen them with a 5mm hex key on the front and an open-end wrench on the back. The pulleys should rest on the narrow part of the cam (Fig. 7.53), which gives the greatest mechanical advantage when the brakes are applied. Change pad spacing by changing the location of the cam on the cable.

2. **Center the brake.** Use a 17mm wrench on the nut surrounding the mounting bolt to adjust spring tension. Loosen the mounting bolt, make small adjustments to the 17mm nut, and tighten the mounting bolt again.

3. **Tighten the cam onto the cable.**

vii-35
REPLACING AND POSITIONING ROLLER-CAM PADS

The pad eye bolt is held on the front with a 5mm hex key. The bolt in the back is adjusted by using a 10mm open wrench. The pads should be toed-in slightly. As the pads wear, they tend to slide up the rim and rub the tire, so check this adjustment periodically.

TROUBLESHOOTING BRAKES

The first thing to check with any brake is that it stops the bike!

1. **While the bike is stationary, pull each lever.** See that it firmly engages the brake while the lever is still at least a finger's width away from the handlebar grip. If not, skip to §vii-2 to §vii-4 for tensioning cable, §vii-13 to §vii-14 for adjusting and bleeding hydraulic disc brakes or adjusting mechanical disc brakes, or §vii-27 to §vii-29 for adjusting and bleeding hydraulic rim brakes.

2. **Moving at 10 mph or so, apply each brake one at a time.** By itself, the rear brake should be able to lock up the rear wheel and skid the tire, and the front brake alone should come on hard enough that it will cause the bike to pitch forward. Careful. Don't overdo it and hurt yourself testing your brakes!

If you can't stop the bike quickly, you must make some adjustments and perhaps do a little cleaning. A brake works by forcing the brake pads into contact with the rim (or disc) to create friction. Anything that reduces the friction compromises braking. With this principle in mind, it should be obvious that these surfaces need to be clean and dry, that they should line up well with each other, and that the mechanism to pull them into contact should move freely and pull at an angle that offers high mechanical advantage.

That said, here is a general brake-inspection list:

1. **Check cable length.** Ensure that the cable is short enough to pull the pads against the rims or rotors without the levers contacting the handlebar grips, but long enough to allow the wheels to turn without dragging on the pads once the pads are centered. See §vii-2 to §vii-4 to adjust.

2. **Clean the rims (or rotors).** Remove any grease or glaze buildup on pads and brake tracks. Remove grease with rags and solvent, and lightly buff aluminum or steel rim surfaces with sandpaper to remove glaze. Solvent residues on pads, rims, and discs cause brake squeal; remove such residues with soap and water. Clean disc-brake rotors and pads with isopropyl alcohol. You can also clean disc-brake pads by using a file or by rubbing them together.

3. **Check pad wear.** Ensure that the pads are not excessively worn (Fig. 7.54); if they have

7.54 Worn brake pad

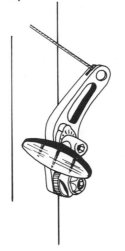

7.55 Removing dirt from brake pad

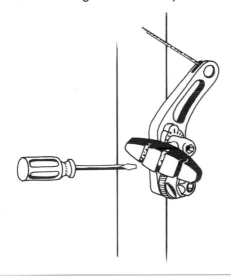

crosswise wear-indicator grooves, make sure these are not worn off. Make sure the pads contact the rims effectively (Figs. 7.26 and 7.32–34). Dig out any rocks or pieces of aluminum that are embedded in the pads to prevent rim damage (Fig. 7.55). Beware of lip formation on the top edge of the pad over the rim edge as the lower part of the pad wears away; this lip can prevent the pad from releasing from the rim. On disc-brake pads, make sure the friction material is at least the thickness of a dime (1.2mm). Replace or

adjust pads as needed, and adjust the brake (refer to the section that applies to your brake) to get the desired response. Buy good pads; poor-quality pads can wear quickly and may require more than twice as much distance to stop as good ones!

4. **Check cable wear.** Check the cables for fraying, wear, and free movement, and check that the angle at which the cable meets each cantilever brake arm is close to 90 degrees (pulling at right angles generates the most leverage [Figs. 7.37–38]). If replacing cables, see §vii-6. Recognize that cables, housings, and pads are maintenance items; replace them frequently with good-quality ones. On hydraulic brakes, check the hoses for damage and wear.

5. **Check centering.** Ensure that the brakes are centered (the pads are spaced equally from either side of the rim or disc rotor) and that they apply and return easily. Readjust as needed (see adjustment section for your brake).

6. **Check toe-in.** If rim brakes squeal and the rims and pads are clean (steps 2 and 3), toe-in the pads so that the forward edge of each pad touches the rim while the trailing edge is 1mm or so away from it (Fig. 7.34). See pad adjustment under your brake type. The flimsier the brake arms are, or the looser they are on the brake bosses, the more toe-in is required.

7. **Check brake-boss flex.** If the seatstays or fork legs are too flexible, applying rim brakes will bow them outward and decrease braking pressure. This tendency can be counteracted by attaching a horseshoe-shaped "brake booster" connecting the brake mounting bolts and bridging over the tire. These boosters are available for V-brakes, cantilevers,

hydraulic rim brakes (see Fig. 7.46), U-brakes, roller-cams, and other linkage brakes.

8. **Check disc-brake howl or rub.** Clean the rotors with alcohol, check mounting bolt tightness, replace pads and bed them in carefully (§vii-11), check for hydraulic fluid leaks (step 11, §vii-14b), check rotor tightness (§vii-13a), check rotor trueness (§vii-16), check caliper centering (§vii-13b or §vii-13c), check pad spacing (§vii-13f), and check frame stiffness (check that suspension pivots are not loose).

CRANKSETS

If you don't have time to do it right the first time, you must have time to do it over again.

—Anonymous

The crankset, your bike's power center, consists of a pair of crankarms, a bottom bracket (aka BB), and chainrings (Fig. 8.1), all attached together by chainring bolts and crank bolt(s). A bottom bracket is a spindle supported by bearings. However, on modern, integrated-spindle (aka "two-piece") cranksets (Fig. 8.2), it's less clear where the bottom bracket ends and the crank-arms begin, because the spindle is integrated as a single piece with the right crankarm. The bearings are thus usually called the "bottom bracket" on a two-piece crank.

CRANKARMS AND CHAINRINGS

viii-1
REMOVING AND INSTALLING CRANKS

Most modern cranks are easy to remove with a single hex key. The two-piece (Fig. 8.2) design means that only the left arm needs to come off; the spindle pulls out of the bearings along with the right crankarm.

NOTE: *"Right," in this chapter and generally throughout this book, refers to the drive side of the bike, and "left" refers to the nondrive side.*

To remove a traditional three-piece crankset (Fig. 8.1), you will need either a thin-wall 14mm (sometimes 15mm or 16mm) socket wrench or a large 8mm hex key in order to remove the crank bolt. You may or may not need a crank puller (Fig. 8.6) to take off the crankarms.

Removal

a. Integrated-spindle cranks with two pinch bolts on the left arm

⚙ LEVEL 1

1. **Unscrew the cap from the left arm completely.** This takes a special splined tool for Shimano; others require a hex key.
2. **Loosen the two pinch bolts holding the arm onto the spindle** (Fig. 8.3). Use a 5mm hex key.
3. **Pull off the left arm.**
4. **Pull the right arm (and attached spindle) straight out.** You may need to tap the end of the spindle with a rubber mallet to get it started. If there is a bearing seal stuck on the spindle, leave it there; when you install the crank, the seal will go back against the bearing.

TOOLS

5mm, 6mm, 7mm, 8mm, and 10mm hex keys or socket drivers

Torx T30 wrench or socket driver

14mm socket wrench

3⁄8-inch drive ratchet or torque wrench

3⁄8-inch drive extension

chainring nut tool

external-bearing bottom-bracket wrench or socket

Shimano TL-FC16 splined left arm cap installation tool or equivalent

internal bottom-bracket splined socket with large opening for ISIS/ Octalink

snapring pliers

crank puller with ends for square-taper and splined spindles

continued

8.1 Square-taper crankset, exploded view

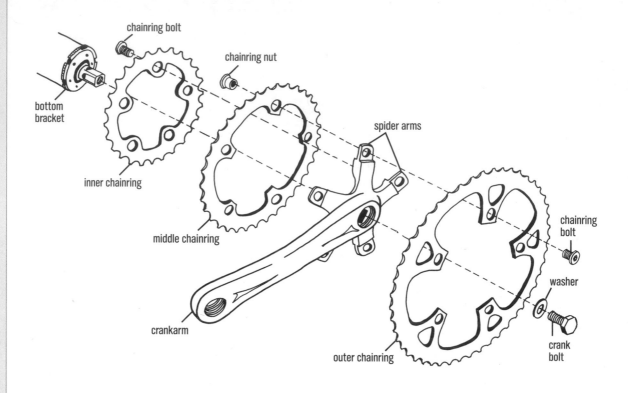

8.2 Integrated spindle (aka "two-piece") crankset, exploded view (2003–2005 Shimano XTR FC-M960 shown)

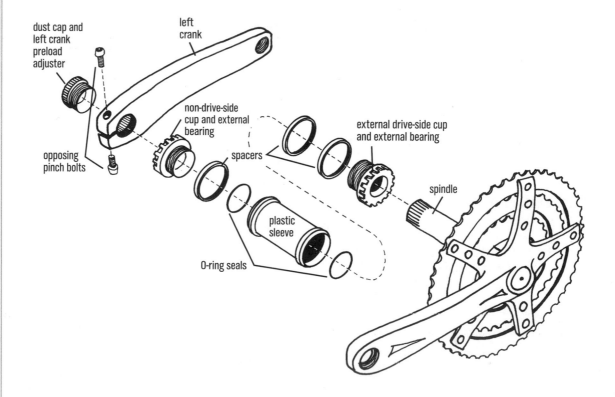

8.3 Removing and installing left two-bolt crankarm (Shimano HollowTech II shown)

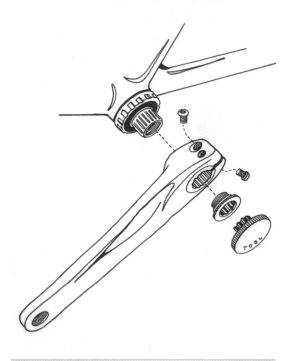

2. Pull the right arm (and attached spindle) straight out. Tap the end of the spindle with a mallet if it's stuck. If a bearing seal comes off with the arm, you can clean it in place or pull it off and put it back on the bearing.

NOTE: *Race Face X-Type cranks are the opposite of other integrated-spindle cranks; the left arm is fixed to the spindle. The drive-side arm comes off with an 8mm hex key.*

c. Three-piece cranks (square taper, Shimano Octalink, and ISIS)

⚙️ ⚙️ LEVEL 2

1. **Remove the dust cap covering the crank bolt if present.** This requires either a 5mm hex key, a two-pin dust cap tool, or a screwdriver.

2. **Remove the crank bolt with the appropriate wrench** (Figs. 8.4–5). Make sure that you extract the washer (Fig. 8.1) with the bolt. If you leave it in, you will not be able to pull the crank off.

NOTE: *Some cranks that accept a hex key in the crank bolt are self-extracting and don't require a crank puller (Fig. 8.6). The crank bolt is held down by a retaining ring threaded into the crank; as the bolt is unscrewed, its lip pushes on the ring and pushes the crank off.*

b. Integrated-spindle cranks with a single crank bolt

⚙️ LEVEL 1

1. **Unscrew the crank bolt as in Figure 8.3, except with a large hex key.** The arm will come right off. Do not unscrew the cap that surrounds and partially covers the bolt (it takes a pin tool or a 10mm or larger hex key to get it off); that cap traps the bolt head so that the arm comes off simply by unscrewing the bolt.

NOTE: *The 2007–2010 Shimano XTR (FC-M970) cranks (Fig. 8.5) don't have this self-extractor cap and require a separate tool for crank extraction. Unscrew the plastic ring around the bolt head—it unscrews clockwise(!) because it has left-hand threads. Thread the TL-FC35 tool shown in Figure 8.5 into the arm (counterclockwise) to hold the bolt head in; tighten it in as far as it will go, at least 3.5 turns. Now unscrew the bolt; it will push the arm off.*

8.4 Removing and installing a crank bolt

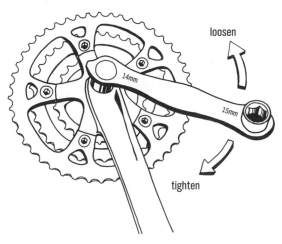

"Square taper," "Octalink," and "ISIS" are three different bottom-bracket and crankarm interface standards. Square-taper bottom-bracket spindles are square on the end (Figs. 8.1, 8.18, 8.21–23) and fit into a square hole in the crankarm. The spindle ends are tapered (at a 2-degree angle) to tighten into the crank as the arm is pushed into the spindle. ISIS (Fig. 8.19) and Shimano Octalink (Fig. 8.20) are both oversized hollow spindles (aka "pipe spindles") with longitudinal splines on the ends.

3. **Unscrew the crank puller's** (Fig. 8.6) **center push bolt so that its tip is flush with the face of the tool.** Make sure the flat end of the push bolt is the right size for the bottom bracket; the push bolt end is much smaller for a square-taper spindle than for an ISIS or a Shimano Octalink splined spindle.

4. **Thread the crank puller into the hole in the crankarm.** Be sure that you thread it in (by hand) as far as it can go; otherwise, you will not engage sufficient crank threads when you

tighten the push bolt, and you will damage the threads. Future crank removal depends on those threads being in good condition.

5. **Tighten the push bolt clockwise** (Fig. 8.6) **until the crankarm pulls off the spindle.** Use a socket wrench or the included handle.

6. **Unscrew the puller from the crankarm.**

Installation

a. Integrated-spindle cranks with two pinch bolts on the left arm

LEVEL 1

1. **Grease the spindle tip and the bore of each bearing.**

2. **Push the spindle (which is attached to the right crankarm) in through the bearings from the drive side.**

3. **Slide the left arm onto the end of the spindle.** Check that the crank is at 180 degrees from the right arm.

8.5 Removing and installing a Shimano 2007–2010 XTR FC-M970 crankset

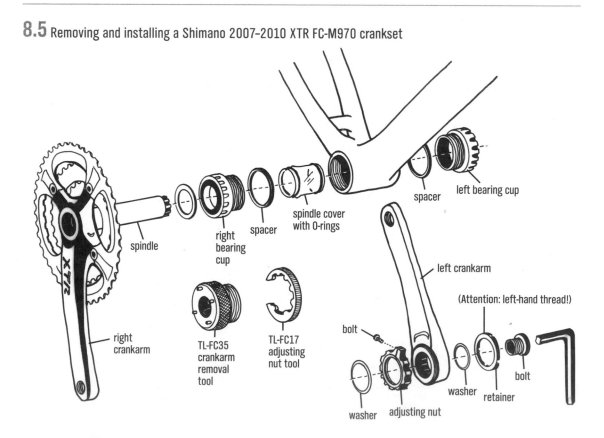

spindle

right bearing cup

spacer

spindle cover with O-rings

spacer

left bearing cup

right crankarm

TL-FC35 crankarm removal tool

TL-FC17 adjusting nut tool

left crankarm

(Attention: left-hand thread!)

bolt

washer

adjusting nut

washer

retainer

bolt

4. **Gently tighten the left-side dust cap** (Fig. 8.3). Use the special plastic splined cap tool for Shimano or a hex key for FSA. Torque is not tight—0.4–0.7 N-m—just enough to pull the right and left cranks over against the bottom-bracket cups.

5. **Tighten the two opposing (greased) pinch bolts** (Fig. 8.3). Using a 5mm hex key, alternately tighten each bolt one-quarter turn at a time. Torque is 10–15 N-m.

6. **Recheck the torque after one ride as the crank may settle in and the bolt will need retightening.**

b. Integrated-spindle cranks with a single crank bolt

LEVEL 1

1. **Grease the spindle tip and the bore of each bearing.**

2. **Push the spindle (which is attached to the right crankarm) in through the bearings from the drive side.**

3. **Slide the left arm onto the end of the spindle.** Check that the crank is at 180 degrees from the right arm.

4. **Tighten the crank bolt with an 8mm hex key.** Torque is high; see Appendix D.

5. **Recheck the torque after one ride as the crank may settle in and the bolt will need retightening.** Periodically check the torque from then on.

NOTE: *These instructions also apply to Race Face X-Type cranks except with left and right interchanged, because the left Race Face crankarm is integrated with the spindle.*

ANOTHER NOTE: *Installation of FC-M970 (2007–2010 Shimano XTR; Fig. 8.5) follows the previous instructions with these exceptions: Before installing the left crankarm, tighten the adjustment ring to eliminate the gap between it and the crankarm. Install the arm. Adjust the bearing play by turning the adjustment ring with the TL-FC17, and then tighten its pinch bolt with a 2.5mm hex key. Screw in the crankarm cap counterclockwise with the TL-FC35. When new, the crankarm cap is already installed; check that it is tight with the TL-FC35.*

c. Three-piece cranks (square taper, ISIS, and Octalink)

LEVEL 1

1. **Slide the crankarm onto the bottom-bracket spindle.** With square-taper spindles, clean off all grease from both parts. Grease may allow the soft aluminum crank to slide too far onto the spindle and deform the square hole in the crank. With an ISIS or a Shimano Octalink splined spindle, however, do grease the parts. With ISIS and Octalink cranks you must be careful to line up the crank splines with those on the spindle before tightening the crank bolt.

2. **Install the crank bolt.** Apply grease to the threads and tighten (Fig. 8.4). Apply titanium-specific antiseize compound for titanium spindles and for titanium crank bolts. If you

have aluminum or titanium crank bolts, first tighten the cranks with the greased steel bolt to the specified torque; then replace the steel bolt with the lightweight bolt, and tighten it to spec.

NOTE: *Here is where a torque wrench comes in handy; tighten the bolt to about 32–49 N-m (300–435 in-lbs), and as high as 59 N-m for some steel oversized bolts in ISIS spindles (see Appendix D). If you're not using a torque wrench, make sure the bolt is really tight, but don't muscle it until your veins pop.*

3. **Replace the dust cap.**

4. **Check the front-derailleur adjustment (see §v-5).** Removing and reinstalling the right crankarm could affect chainring position and hence shifting.

5. **Recheck the torque after one ride as the crank may settle in and the bolt will need retightening.** Periodically check the torque from then on.

---

viii-2
MAINTAINING CHAINRINGS

The chainring teeth should be checked periodically for wear, the chainring bolts should be checked periodically for tightness, and the chainrings themselves should be checked for trueness—watch them as they spin past the front derailleur.

1. **Wipe the chainring down and inspect each tooth.** The teeth should be straight and uniform in size and shape. If the teeth are hook-shaped (Fig. 8.7), the chainring needs to be replaced. The chain should be replaced as well (see §iv-5), because a worn chain causes hook-shaped teeth, and this tooth shape will effectively change the spacing between the teeth and accelerates wear on a new chain.

CAUTION: *Don't be deceived by the seemingly erratic tooth shapes designed to facilitate shifting; if such*

teeth repeat regularly, that's probably what they are. Shifting ramps located on the inner side (Fig. 8.8) that are meant to speed chain movement between the rings often look like cracks on cheaper chainrings, because they are pressed into the ring rather than being a separate piece riveted on, as on better chainrings.

NOTE: *Another wear evaluation method is to lift the chain from the top of the chainring; the greater the wear of either part is, the farther the chain separates. If it lifts more than one tooth, at least the chain, and perhaps the chainring, need to be replaced.*

2. **Remove minor gouges and small burrs in the chainring teeth with a file.**

3. **If an individual tooth is bent, try bending it back carefully with a pair of pliers or an adjustable wrench.** It will likely break off; heed the message and buy a new chainring.

4. **While slowly turning the crank, watch where the chain exits the bottom of the chainring.**

8.7 Worn chainring teeth

8.8 Chainring shifting ramps and asymmetrical teeth

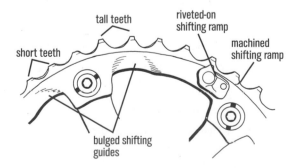

tall teeth

riveted-on shifting ramp

short teeth

machined shifting ramp

bulged shifting guides

See if any of the teeth are reluctant to let go of the chain. That can cause chain suck. Locate any offending teeth, and see if you can correct the problem. If the teeth are really chewed up or cannot be improved with pliers and a file, the chainring should be replaced.

viii-3
TIGHTENING CHAINRING BOLTS

Check that the bolts are tight by turning them clockwise while holding the nut on the backside from turning. Most chainring bolts take a 5mm hex key on the bolt and a two-pronged chainring-nut tool on the nut (Fig. 8.9). It's now common for chainring bolts to take a Torx T30 star-shaped tool and chainring nuts to take a 6mm hex key. Grease or threadlock compound on the bolts can prevent creaking.

viii-4
FIXING WARPED CHAINRINGS

Looking down from above, turn the crank slowly and see whether the chainrings wobble back and forth relative to the plane of the front derailleur. If they do, make sure there is no play in the bottom bracket by adjusting the bottom bracket (§viii-10, step 15). It is normal to have a small amount of chainring wobble and flex when you pedal hard, but excessive wobbling will compromise shifting. Small, localized bends can be straightened with an adjustable wrench (Fig. 8.10). If the chainring is really bent, replace it.

viii-5
REPAIRING BENT CRANKARM SPIDERS

If you installed a new chainring and are still seeing serious back-and-forth wobble, chances are good that the spider arms (Fig. 8.1) on the crank are bent. If the crank is new, this is a warranty item, so return it to your bike shop for replace-

8.9 Removing and installing chainring bolts

8.10 Straightening a bent chainring

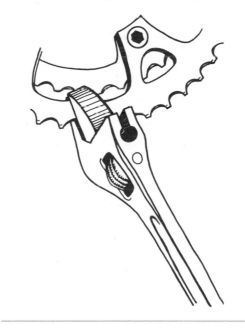

ment. If the crank is used, you will still need to visit the shop, because correcting the problem on a crankset with aluminum spider arms requires special equipment (not all shops will have the bending tools and surface plate required; you may need to find a shop that specializes in repairs). If the crank has carbon-fiber spider arms, the problem cannot be corrected and the crank will have to be replaced.

viii-6
REPLACING A CHAINRING

a. Replacing either of the two largest chainrings

 **LEVEL 1**

1. **Unscrew the chainring bolts** (Fig. 8.9). You'll need either a 5mm hex key or a Torx T30 wrench. Hold the nut on the backside if it turns. The nut will take either a pronged chainring-nut tool (a thin screwdriver in a pinch) or a 6mm hex key.

2. **Install the new chainrings.** The outer chainring has a protruding pin meant to keep the chain from falling down between it and the crankarm. Make sure this pin lines up under the crankarm and faces away from the bicycle. The middle and inner rings each have a little bump protruding radially inward that is also to line up under the crankarm. The chainring bolt holes will have recesses for the heads of the chainring bolts and nuts; make sure that these recesses face away from the spider arm tabs. If the chainrings are rotated relative to the crank or inverted, the shift ramps (Fig. 8.8) will not work.

3. **Lubricate the bolts and tighten them** (Fig. 8.9).

NOTE: *Whenever you change the outer chainring size, you must reposition the front derailleur for proper chainring clearance, as described in §v-5.*

b. Replacing the innermost chainring (aka "granny gear")

  **LEVEL 2**

1. **Pull off the crankarm** (§viii-1).

2. **Remove the bolts securing the chainring.** These bolts are threaded directly into the crankarm (Fig. 8.1) and take either a 5mm hex key or a Torx T30 wrench.

8.11 Outer and middle chainrings

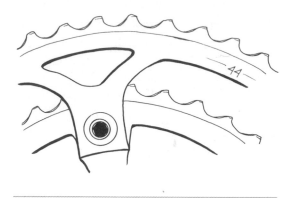

3. **Install the new chainring.** Its little bump protruding radially inward lines up under the crankarm. Make sure that the chainring is oriented so that the recesses for the heads of the chainring bolts receive those parts and are not facing inward toward the spider.

4. **Lube and tighten the bolts.**

NOTE: *Some cranks do not accept separate chainrings; the chainrings come on and off as a set, or they are not removable. The 1996–2002 Shimano XTR and 1997–2003 XT cranks rely on a slip-on spider system that spins off all three chainrings from the crankarm as a single unit (Fig. 8.12). After removing a circlip (by prying it off with a screwdriver), use a special lockring tool to loosen the chainring-spider-securing lockring; a female-threaded tool that goes on the crank bolt holds the lockring tool in place (Fig. 8.12). Once the spider is off, you can interchange chainrings within the set or simply pop on a whole new set.*

Economical cranks often have chainrings riveted to the crank or riveted to each other and bolted to the crank as a unit. In either case, if you want to replace a chainring, you must replace either the entire crank or the chainring set.

5. **Replace the crankarm** (§viii-1).
   Go ride your bike.

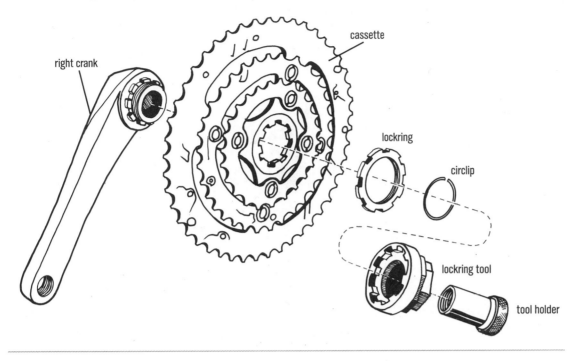

BOTTOM BRACKETS

LEVEL 2

Traditionally, bottom brackets thread into the frame's bottom-bracket shell. Originally, these were square-taper bottom brackets (Fig. 8.13), and the cranks were separate from the bottom-bracket spindle (three-piece cranks). External-bearing bottom brackets (Fig. 8.14) for two-piece (integrated-spindle) cranks (Fig. 8.2) then took over.

Now, however, the trend is toward frames with unthreaded bottom-bracket shells into which the bottom-bracket bearings are pressed. There are a number of different widths and diameters of these.

Bottom-bracket bearings tend to be fairly well sealed toward the outside but not toward the inside, and water can come in around the seatpost. So if your frame's bottom-bracket shell does not have a drain hole in it, I recommend drilling one to let water out (this goes for any bottom-bracket shell, not just BB30). Drill it as close to straight

8.13 Bottom-bracket assembly

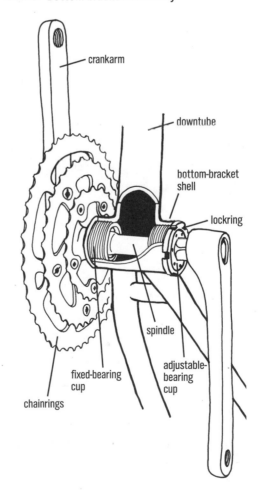

8.14 Removing and installing external-bearing cups; note left-hand threads on drive side

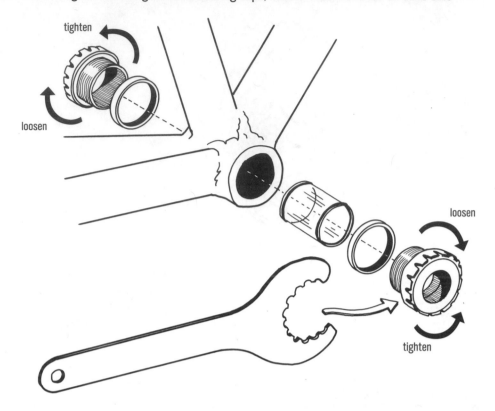

tighten

loosen

loosen

tighten

under the bottom when the complete bike is standing upright, but place it so that it will not be covered by the plastic screw-on derailleur cable guide.

a. Threadless bottom brackets

Eliminating bottom-bracket threads can reduce factory machining and assembly time and may allow the use of full-carbon bottom-bracket shells, so threadless bottom brackets with press-in bearings (Figs. 8.15–17) are bound to be the wave of the future. However, there is so far no standard for width or diameter of the frame's bottom-bracket shell. Apart from some early designs with small bearings for three-piece cranks, threadless bottom brackets take integrated-spindle cranks, but that spindle can be either 24mm or 30mm.

b. BB30 and PF30

Both BB30 and Press Fit 30 (aka "PF30") cranks have 30mm-diameter bottom-bracket spindles and will pass through 30mm inside diameter (ID) bearings.

On BB30 mountain bikes, the bearings press into a 68mm- or 73mm-wide bottom-bracket shell and are prevented from going in further by snaprings seated in grooves in the inner diameter of the shell (Fig. 8.15).

PF30 bearings are the same size as BB30 bearings (42mm outside diameter [OD], 30mm ID), but they are housed inside 46mm-diameter plastic sleeves (Fig. 8.16) that press straight into the bottom-bracket shell without any need for snaprings.

c. BB92 and BB95

A number of road and mountain bike systems, called variously "BB86," "BB90," "BB92," and "BB95," are named for the width of the bottom-bracket shell. BB86 and BB92 are often called the "Shimano press-fit system" standards for road

8.15 BB30 crankset, exploded view

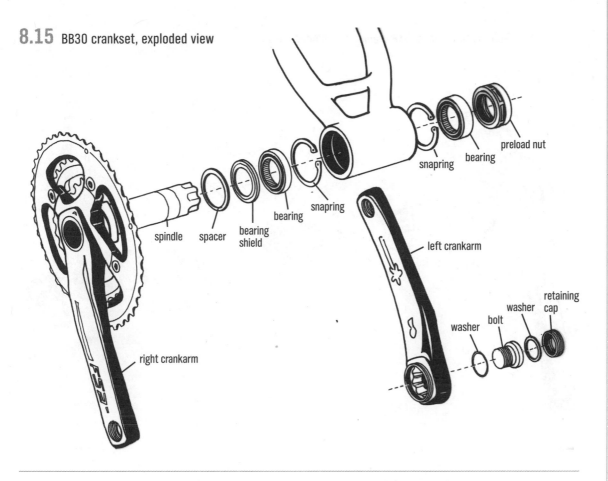

spindle   spacer   bearing shield   bearing   snapring

snapring   bearing   preload nut

left crankarm

washer   bolt   washer   retaining cap

right crankarm

8.16 PressFit 30 (PF30) bottom bracket

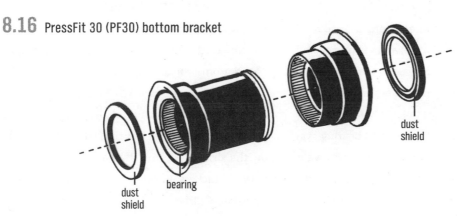

dust shield   bearing   dust shield

and mountain bikes, respectively, even though other crank manufacturers make bottom brackets for this standard as well. For simplicity and symmetry with PF30, I'll call the Shimano system "Press Fit 24," or PF24, because the spindle diameter is 24mm. PF24 bottom brackets accept standard integrated-spindle cranks for external-bearing bottom brackets (Fig. 8.2).

A BB86 road shell is 86.5mm wide, whereas a BB92 mountain bike shell is 91.5mm wide. Both bottom-bracket shells have a 41mm ID. The PF24 system is similar in principle to PF30 (Fig. 8.16); like PF30, the bearings for BB86 and BB92 are incorporated into plastic sleeves that press into the bottom-bracket shell. On PF24, however, the bearings have a 37mm OD, and the sleeves have

8.17 Trek BB95 with Truvativ GXP crankset, exploded view

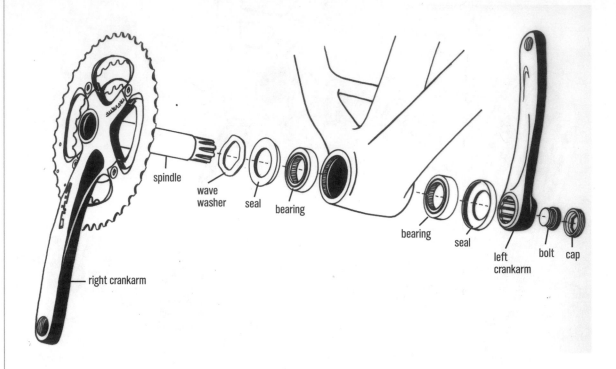

spindle

wave
washer

seal

bearing

bearing

seal

left
crankarm

bolt

cap

right crankarm

a 41mm OD. Each sleeve's shoulder is 1.75mm wide, creating a 90mm overall width for road BB86 (86.5mm + 1.75mm + 1.75mm) and a 95mm overall width for mountain BB92, making the width from bearing face to bearing face exactly the same as on the Trek systems.

BB90 and BB95 are Trek's slip-fit bearing systems for road and mountain bikes, respectively. The road bottom-bracket shell is 90mm wide, whereas the mountain bottom-bracket shell is 95mm wide. Both BB90 and BB95 shells have a 37mm ID for the bearing seat, which is molded directly into the frame (Fig. 8.17). The 37mm OD × 24mm ID bearing is the same as you would find inside the threaded cup of any external-bearing system, and it is compatible with any of the standard external-bearing/integrated-24mm-spindle cranksets (Fig. 8.2). Trek supplies bearing sets for all cranksets, and the bearings slip into place with finger pressure alone.

d. Threaded bottom brackets

ISO (aka "English" or "BSA") threads are standard on threaded mountain bike bottom brackets. The bottom-bracket cups are usually engraved "1.370 × 24," denoting a 1.370-inch thread diameter and a thread pitch of 24 threads per inch. It is important to remember that left-hand threads on the drive side are standard on English/ISO bottom brackets. In other words, you tighten the right-hand (drive-side) cup by turning it counterclockwise (Fig. 8.28). Meanwhile, the threads on the left cup are right-hand threads and are therefore tightened clockwise.

ISO-threaded mountain bike bottom-bracket shells come in two widths: 68mm (older) and 73mm. Bottom brackets generally have stamped or printed numbers such as "73–118" (meaning that the shell is 73mm wide and the spindle is 118mm long). Many external-bearing bottom brackets are designed to work for both shell widths by means of

2.5mm spacers added on either side between the bearing cups and the shell faces.

e. Two-piece threaded cranksets

With the bearing cups of integrated-spindle, external-bearing cranksets (Fig. 8.2) being external to the bottom-bracket shell (Fig. 8.14), the bearings and spindle can be far larger (and hence stiffer) than prior designs (whose bearings are contained within the bottom-bracket shell). The external bearings can also be right up against the crankarms (Fig. 8.3), adding more stiffness.

For integrated-spindle bottom brackets to work properly, the threads on both sides of the frame's bottom-bracket shell must be aligned, and the end faces of the shell must be parallel. If you are installing an expensive bottom bracket and have any doubts about the frame, it is a good idea to have the bottom-bracket shell tapped (threaded) and faced (ends cut parallel) by a qualified shop possessing the proper tools. These tools are pictured in Figure 1.4. This procedure will improve durability and freedom of movement and will reduce the likelihood of creaking while pedaling.

f. Three-piece threaded cranksets

For three-piece cranks, the most common type of bottom bracket is probably the cartridge type (Fig. 8.18 or 8.19); it has cups that accept the splined removal tool shown in Figure 8.19. These bottom brackets can have a square-taper spindle (Fig. 8.18), an ISIS splined spindle (Fig. 8.19), or a Shimano Octalink splined spindle (Fig. 8.20).

Although most Octalink bottom brackets are the cartridge type, the first generation of Shimano XTR Octalink bottom brackets had four sets of loose, adjustable, and overhaulable bearings: two sets of tiny ball bearings and two sets of needle bearings (Fig. 8.20).

NOTE: *Shimano has two noninterchangeable Octalink standards: Octalink 1 and Octalink 2. Octalink 1 (Fig. 8.20), found only on XTR and on some Shimano road models, has eight (hence "Octa") spline ridges that are 2.2mm wide separated by 5mm-long valleys. Octalink 2 works with Shimano XT, LX, and Deore cranks, and its spline ridges are 2.8mm wide, while its valleys are 9mm long.*

The most common mountain bike bottom bracket prior to the 1990s was the square-taper cup-and-cone style with loose ball bearings (Fig. 8.21). As discussed previously regarding external-bearing two-piece cranks, the bottom-bracket shell for cup-and-cone bottom brackets must be threaded concentrically, and the faces of the shell must be "faced" parallel to each other and perpendicular to the spindle. Otherwise, the bearings will drag and wear excessively.

Another older bottom-bracket type has cartridge bearings secured by an adjustable cup and lockring at either end (Fig. 8.22).

8.18 Shimano cartridge, square-taper bottom bracket

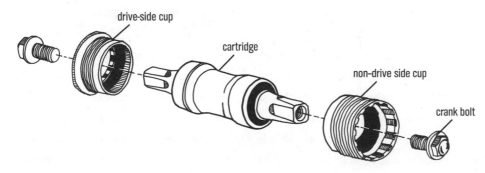

drive-side cup

cartridge

non-drive side cup

crank bolt

8.19 ISIS cartridge bottom bracket

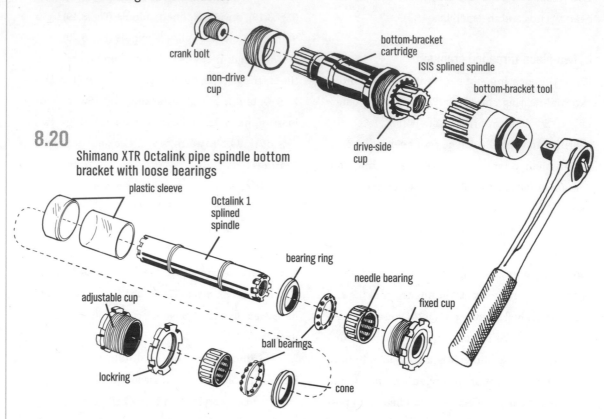

bottom-bracket cartridge

ISIS splined spindle

crank bolt

non-drive cup

bottom-bracket tool

drive-side cup

8.20

Shimano XTR Octalink pipe spindle bottom bracket with loose bearings

plastic sleeve

Octalink 1 splined spindle

bearing ring

needle bearing

fixed cup

adjustable cup

ball bearings

lockring

cone

8.21 Standard cup-and-cone, loose ball bearing, square-taper bottom bracket

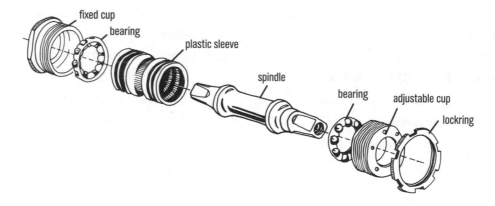

fixed cup

bearing

plastic sleeve

spindle

bearing

adjustable cup

lockring

Some square-taper bottom brackets do not thread into the bottom-bracket shell. One type, found on old Fisher, Klein, and Fat Chance frames, uses cartridge bearings held into an unthreaded bottom-bracket shell by snaprings in machined grooves. Another type, made first by Mavic and then by Stronglight, includes a cartridge that is externally threaded on each end (Fig. 8.23). It slips into the bottom-bracket shell and is held in place by tapered lockrings threaded onto the cartridge. The lockrings have a convex 45-degree taper to bind against the bottom-bracket shell, which is machined with a matching 45-degree concave taper on its ends.

The most important item in bottom-bracket installation is to put the correct bottom bracket in.

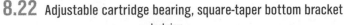

8.22 Adjustable cartridge bearing, square-taper bottom bracket

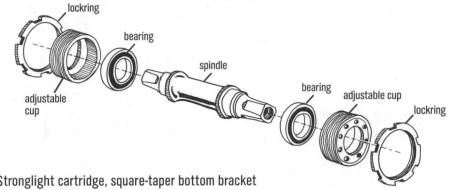

8.23 Mavic/Stronglight cartridge, square-taper bottom bracket

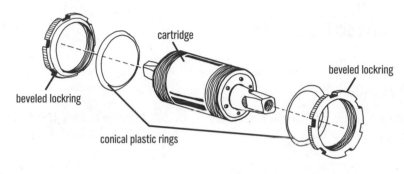

If a bike has a bottom-bracket spindle of the wrong length, the chainrings will not line up well with the rear cogs. The center ring should be in line with the center of the cogset; this is called the chainline (see Fig. 5.49). No amount of fiddling with the derailleurs will get a bike with a chainline that is way off to shift properly. Get a bottom bracket with the proper spindle length, thread, and cartridge width for the frame, crank, and bottom-bracket shell width. Before installing a new bottom bracket of a different brand and model than the crank, see Figure 5.49 and read §v-48.

viii-7
INSTALLING A THREADED EXTERNAL-BEARING BOTTOM BRACKET

 LEVEL 2

1. **Add spacers as required.**

    (a) 68mm bottom-bracket shell: On Shimano, FSA Mega Exo, and Race Face X-Type,

put two of the three supplied 2.5mm spacers over the thread of the right cup and the remaining one on the thread of the left cup (Fig. 8.2); on Truvativ GXP, put one spacer on the right cup and one on the left cup (Fig. 8.14).

    (b) 73mm bottom-bracket shell: With Shimano and FSA, slip one spacer on the right cup and none on the left; use no spacers for Truvativ.

    (c) E-type front derailleur (Fig. 5.15): Instead of placing a spacer adjacent to the right cup's flange, insert the front-derailleur bracket. This derailleur will not work with a GXP crankset.

NOTE: *A removable plastic sleeve (Fig. 8.14) keeps contamination away from the backside of the bearings. Keep the sleeve on the right cup when installing the cup.*

2. **Grease the threads.**

3. **Start the cups by hand.** Turn the right (drive-side) cup counterclockwise and the left cup clockwise.

4. **Tighten the cups.** Use the splined tool designed for the purpose (Fig. 8.14). Torque is high (35–50 N-m), so yank on the tool pretty hard, because for this task you are not likely to have a splined tool that works with a torque wrench.

5. **Install the spindle and crankarms.** Follow the instructions in §viii-1a, b, or c, depending on type.

viii-8
INSTALLING A THREADLESS BOTTOM BRACKET

 LEVEL 2

Threadless bottom-bracket installation is similar to threadless headset installation (§xi-22).

a. BB92 (PF24) and BB95 (24mm integrated spindle)

1. **Clean and grease inside the ends of the bottom-bracket shell.**

2. **Press in the bearings and install the spindle and crankarms.** Follow one of these procedures, depending on the bottom-bracket shell and the crank type.

    (a) On a Trek frame with a 95mm-wide bottom-bracket shell (BB95):

    i. For Shimano HollowTech II, FSA Mega Exo, and other non-GXP cranksets, simply push the bearings in by hand (Fig. 8.24) and place the Trek-supplied seals over them (Fig. 8.17). Trek does have a plastic bearing-installation tool for its BB90/BB95 frames, but it's not a necessity. Install the spindle and crankarms, following the instructions in §viii-1a, b, or c, depending on type.

    ii. For Truvativ GXP, push the bearings in by hand (Fig. 8.24), making sure that you put the one with the smaller bore (22mm rather than 24mm) in the left side with its

8.24 Pressing in a Trek BB95 by hand

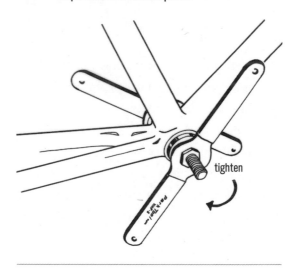

8.25 Pressing in BB92 (PF24), BB30, or PF30 cups with a headset press

tighten

protruding inner bearing-ring lip facing inward. Place the flat, rubbery bearing seal against the right bearing, and slip the wavy washer onto the crankarm (Fig. 8.17). Push in the (greased) spindle from the drive side, place the metal bearing cover over the spindle and left bearing, and engage the left arm on the (greased) spindle splines. Tighten the crank bolt to 50–57 N-m.

(b) On a frame with a 92mm-wide bottom-bracket shell (BB92 [PF24]):

Using a headset press, press in each 41mm OD PF24 plastic (or aftermarket aluminum) bearing cup, with or without the bearing in it (Fig. 8.25); doing one cup at a time ensures proper alignment. If the bearings are in the cups, use bushings in the bearings like the ones that come with the Park BBT-39 tool; in a pinch, the flat faces of the headset press will also work. Ensure that both bearing cups are seated fully. If the bearings were not in the bearing cups, push them into the cups with the headset press and Park BBT-39 bushings or the like, or an old bearing, against the bearings. Place the manufacturer-supplied seals over them. Install the spindle and crankarms, following the instructions in §viii-1a, b, or c, depending on type.

b. BB30 (30mm spindle)

1. **Clear the bottom-bracket shell of any metal chips or other detritus.**

2. **Grease the contact surfaces.** Apply a thin layer of grease to the snapring grooves and surfaces outboard of them and to the snaprings themselves.

3. **Insert the snaprings.** If the snapring has a hole (eye) on either end, push the tips of the snapring pliers into the holes, squeeze the handles to reduce the snapring's diameter, and install the snapring into the groove inside one end of the bottom-bracket shell (Fig. 8.26). If the snapring does not have holes, compress the ring by pushing it into the shell, push the ring's square-cut end to the groove in the shell so that the ring edge drops into the groove, and work around, pushing the rest of the ring into place. Check that the snapring is fully engaged in the groove all the way around. Repeat for the other snapring in the other end. (To remove a snapring with holes on the ends, compress it with snapring pliers and pull it

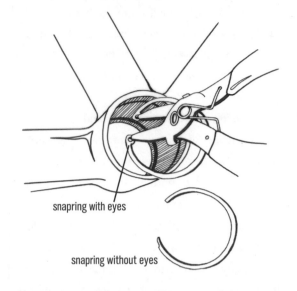

snapring with eyes

snapring without eyes

out. To remove a snapring without eyes, slip a screwdriver blade under the pointed end of the snapring, push the blade inward beyond the groove, and keep pushing on the screwdriver blade, working from that end toward the square-cut end until the snapring is free.)

4. **Press in the bearings.** Beg, borrow, or buy tool bushings for BB30 bearings (FSA, Park, and Cannondale sell such bushings). With a headset press, press in both bearings simultaneously or one bearing at a time (Fig. 8.25) depending on the bushings you have. Obviously, you are pressing both bearings in until they stop at the circlip. Without a headset press, if you're careful and have BB30 tool bushings, you should be able to press the bearings in straight using a large bench vise.

5. **Grease the backside of each bearing.** This protects it from water trapped in the shell.

6. **Place the supplied aluminum bearing shields against the bearings.** Their machined grooves face inward toward the bearings.

7. **Push the spindle in from the drive side.** Lightly grease the spindle bearing areas, splined end, and threads first. You'll probably

need a mallet, because BB30 spindles are designed to be a light interference fit.

8. **If supplied, put a wavy washer on the left end of the spindle.** It goes between the bearing shield and the crankarm and takes out lateral play.

9. **Push on the left crankarm and tighten the crank bolt.** Ideally, use a torque wrench (8mm or 10mm hex driver) to torque spec (torque is often less than with external-bearing cranks; see Appendix D for torque specs).

10. **Check the wavy washer.** It should be compressed somewhat, but not flattened. If it is not slightly compressed, remove the crank, add as many spacers against the bearing shields as are required to fill the space so that the wavy washer will be slightly flattened when the crankarm is on, and reinstall the crankarm.

11. **If the bearings fit loosely or creak, they need Loctite.** Remove them (§viii-13), smear a thin layer of Loctite 609 retaining compound where they sit inside the bottom-bracket shell, and reinstall them. Allow the Loctite to cure as specified in the directions or, if you do not have the instruction sheet, at least 24 hours.

c. PF30 (30mm spindle)

1. **Clean and grease inside the ends of the bottom-bracket shell.**

2. **Press in the plastic bearing cups.** Using a headset press, press in each 46mm plastic cup with the bearing inside, one at a time (Fig. 8.25). Ideally, use bushings in the bearings like the ones that come with the Park BBT-39 tool; the flat faces of the headset press will also work. Ensure that both bearing cups are seated fully. Place the manufacturer-supplied seals over them.

3. **Install the spindle and crankarms.** Follow the instructions in §viii-1a, b, or c, depending on type.

d. Square-taper press-in

Small-diameter unthreaded bottom-bracket shells with snapring grooves can be found on Fisher, Klein, and Fat Chance frames from the 1980s. Two snaprings retain the bearings in the shell, and the spindle has a square taper. If the shell is bored to the correct diameter, you can probably seat the cartridge bearings by hand. If not, you can press them in with a vise or a headset press, using a large socket or other flat-ended cylindrical object as a drift pushing against the bearing, as long as whatever you use is just slightly smaller in diameter than the OD of the bearing. The inboard bearing stops are usually shoulders or snaprings on either end of the axle.

If the bearings will go in by hand, install one snapring with snapring pliers into the groove in one end of the shell. Push the entire assembly of axle and two bearings in from the other side of the bottom-bracket shell. Install the other snapring, and you're done.

If you can't press them in by hand, press one bearing in as far as the snapring groove by using one vise jaw or headset-press face against the shell face, the other against first the bearing, until it reaches the shell, and then the drift to push the bearing into the bottom-bracket shell's bore. Install the snapring. Install the spindle, and push the other bearing in the same way until you can install the other snapring.

---

viii-9
INSTALLING A THREADED CARTRIDGE BOTTOM BRACKET

 LEVEL 2

Cartridge bottom brackets can have a square-taper axle (Fig. 8.18); a large, splined ISIS axle (Fig. 8.19); or an Octalink (Fig. 8.20) axle.

1. **Thread the left cup (clockwise) in three to four turns by hand.**

2. **Slide the cartridge into the bottom-bracket shell.** Pay attention to the right and left markings on the cartridge. The cup with the raised lip and left-hand thread is the drive-side cup (the cup shown on the left in Fig. 8.18 and on the right in Fig. 8.19).

(a) Add a 2.5mm spacer. If you have a 68mm-width bottom-bracket shell (yes, measure it!) and are using a bottom bracket designed for both 73mm and 68mm bottom-bracket shells, add at least one spacer on the drive side. Install the arms (§viii–1b), and check that they are centered about the chainstays; if not, add or remove spacers.

(b) If you are using a Shimano E-type front derailleur, it takes the place of one spacer. An E-type front derailleur's bracket mount, shown in Figure 5.15, slips between the shell and the cup lip. Some ISIS bottom brackets will accept only an E-type front derailleur with a 68mm shell, because there is room only for a single spacer with 68mm and there is no spacer room with a 73mm. Some Shimano bottom brackets are designed to accept an E-type front derailleur on either a 68mm or a 73mm shell; with these, you install either two 2.5mm spacers or one spacer and the E-type bracket between the right cup and a 68mm shell. With a 73mm shell, you install either the E-type front-derailleur bracket or a single 2.5mm spacer against the shell.

3. **Tighten the right (drive-side) cup.** Tighten it counterclockwise with a splined cup installation tool like the one depicted in Fig. 8.19; tighten with an open-end wrench, a torque wrench, or a standard socket wrench (as shown in Fig. 8.27, except on the drive side) until the lip seats against the face of the bottom-bracket shell. Recommended torque is high (see Appendix D).

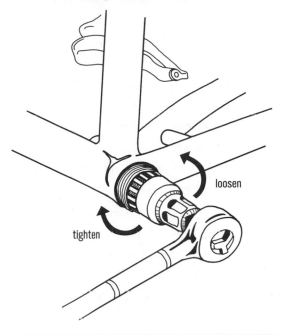

4. **Tighten the left (nondrive) cup.** With the same tool, tighten the cup clockwise against the cartridge (Fig. 8.27) to the same torque as the right cup. There is no adjustment of the bearings to be done; you can put on the crank now (§viii-1b).

viii-10
INSTALLING CUP-AND-CONE BOTTOM BRACKETS

⚙️ ⚙️ LEVEL 2

In cup-and-cone bottom brackets (Figs. 8.20–21), ball bearings ride between cone-shaped bearing surfaces on the spindle and cup-shaped races in the threaded cups. The "fixed cup" (the left-hand cup in Figs. 8.13 and 8.21 and the right-hand cup in Fig. 8.20) has a lip on it and fits on the right (drive) side of the bike (Fig. 8.28). The opposite, "adjustable cup" is held in position by a lockring threaded onto the cup against the bottom-bracket shell. A retaining cage usually holds the individual ball bearings together.

Again, it is a good idea to have the bottom-bracket shell tapped (threaded) and faced (ends cut parallel) by a qualified shop possessing the proper tools (Fig. 1.4).

1. **Unless you have a shop fixed-cup tool, have a shop install the fixed cup for you.** The shop tool ensures that the cup goes in straight and tight. The tool pictured in Figure 8.28 can be used in a pinch, but it may let the cup go in crooked and will slip off before you get it really tight. The fixed cup must be very tight (see Appendix D for torque) so that it does not vibrate loose. Remember that English-threaded fixed cups are tightened counter-clockwise (Fig. 8.28).

2. **Wipe the inside surface of both cups with a clean rag.**

3. **Put a medium layer of clean grease on the bearing surfaces.** The balls should be half covered; any more is wasted and attracts dirt.

4. **Wipe the axle with a clean rag.**

5. **Figure out which end of the axle is toward the drive side.** The drive side may be marked with an "R," or choose the longer end (when measured from the bearing surface). If there is writing on the spindle, it will usually read right side up for a rider on the bike. If there is no marking and no length difference, the spindle orientation is irrelevant.

6. **Slide one set of bearings onto the drive-side end of the axle** (Fig. 8.29). Make sure you orient the retainer cage correctly. The balls, rather than the retainer cage, should rest against the axle-bearing surfaces. Because there are two types of retainer cages with opposite designs, you need to be careful to avoid binding, as well as smashing, the cages. If you're still confused, there is one easy test: If the retainer cage is installed correctly, the axle will turn smoothly; if the retainer is installed the wrong way around,

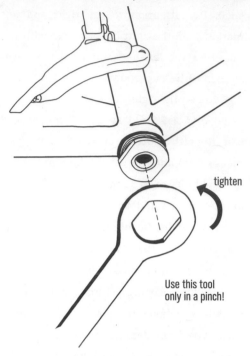

8.28 Drive-side fixed cup; note left-hand threads

tighten

Use this tool
only in a pinch!

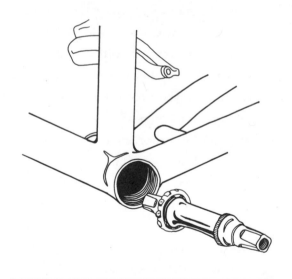

8.29 Placing the axle in the bottom-bracket shell

it won't. If the bottom bracket has loose ball bearings with no retainer cage, stick them into the greased cup. Most rely on nine balls; you can confirm that you are using the correct number by inserting and removing the axle and checking to make sure that they are evenly distributed in the grease and are

8.30 Tightening lockring

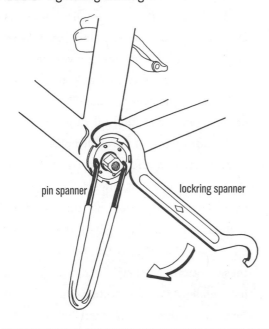

pin spanner

lockring spanner

neither piled up (indicating you have too many) nor gapped for more balls. The XTR loose-bearing bottom bracket in Figure 8.20 requires the installation of a bearing ring, a set of ball bearings, and a needle-bearing set on the spindle.

7. **Slide the axle into the bottom-bracket shell.** Push the bearings into the fixed cup (Fig. 8.29). Use your pinkie to stabilize the end of the axle from the fixed-cup end as you slide it in.

8. **Insert the protective sleeve.** The plastic sleeve shown in Figures 8.20–21 keeps dirt and rust from falling from the frame tubes into the bearings, so if you don't have a sleeve, get one. Push it against the inside edge of the fixed cup.

9. **Place the second bearing set into the greased adjustable cup.** If there is a bearing retainer, make sure it is properly oriented. On an XTR loose-bearing BB (Fig. 8.20), install the bearing ring, ball bearings, and needle bearings on the spindle as you did on the other end.

10. **Screw in the adjustable cup.** Leaving the lockring off, turn the cup clockwise, ensuring

that it is going in straight over the axle. Screw the cup in as far as you can by hand, ideally all the way until the bearings seat between the axle and cup.

11. **Locate the appropriate tool for tightening the adjustable cup.** Most cups have two holes that accept the pins of an adjustable cup wrench called a "pin spanner" (Fig. 8.30) or a splined end for a tool like the one in Figure 8.19. Another type of adjustable cup has two flats on which you may use an adjustable wrench. The XTR loose-bearing BB in Figure 8.20 requires a toothed lockring spanner or the lockring tool shown in Figure 8.12.

12. **Carefully tighten the adjustable cup against the bearings.** Do not overtighten. Turn the axle periodically with your fingers to ensure that it moves freely. If it binds up, you have gone too far; back it off a bit. Overtightening can force the bearings to dent the bearing surfaces of the cups, and the axle will never turn smoothly again.

13. **Screw the lockring onto the adjustable cup by hand.**

14. **Tighten the lockring against the bottom-bracket shell.** Use a lockring spanner that fits the lockring while holding the adjustable cup in place (Fig. 8.30). If you turn the bicycle upside down, you can pull down harder on the wrenches.

15. **Check for play.** As you snug the lockring against the bottom-bracket shell, wiggle the bottom-bracket spindle periodically. Because the lockring pulls the cup out of the shell minutely, it loosens the adjustment. The spindle should turn smoothly without free play in the bearings. I recommend installing and tightening the drive-side crankarm onto the drive end of the spindle (Fig. 8.4) at this time so that you can push the crank from side to side to check for free play. Adjust

the cup so that the axle play is just barely eliminated.

16. **While holding the cup, fully tighten the lockring** (Fig. 8.30). To prevent the bottom bracket from coming out of adjustment during a ride, tightening it as tightly as you can is about right (recommended torque is in Appendix D). You may have to repeat this step a time or two until you get the adjustment just right.

viii-11
INSTALLING OTHER TYPES OF BOTTOM BRACKETS

 **LEVEL 2**

A couple of ever more rare variations are worth mentioning:

(a) On cartridge-bearing bottom brackets with adjustable cups on both ends (Fig. 8.22), simply install the drive-side cup and lockring, slide the cartridge bearing in (if it is not already pressed into the cup), slip the spindle in, and then install the other bearing, cup, and lockring. Tighten each lockring while holding the adjustable cup in place with a pin spanner (Fig. 8.30); the cup could also take a splined cup tool like the one in Figure 8.12 or 8.27. Adjust for free play as described in §viii-10, steps 11–15.

   i. The advantage of having two adjustable cups is that you can center the cartridge by moving it from side to side in the bottom-bracket shell. If the chainrings end up too close or too far away from the frame (see Fig. 5.49 and §v-47), you can move one cup in and one out to shift the position of the entire cartridge.

   ii. Sometimes cartridge-bearing bottom brackets bind up a bit during adjustment and installation. A light tap on each end of the axle usually frees them.

(b) Mavic or Stronglight cartridge-bearing bottom brackets (Fig. 8.23) require both ends of the bottom-bracket shell to be chamfered at an angle to seat the convex tapered lockrings. You need to go to a shop equipped with the Mavic tool for this. Once this is done, simply slip the cartridge into the shell, slide on one of the angled plastic rings from either end (pictured in Fig. 8.23), and screw on a lockring, angled side inward, from either side. Holding the cartridge with a pin spanner, tighten the lockring on either side (Fig. 8.30). The beauty of these bottom brackets is that they work independently of the bottom-bracket shell threads, so they can be installed in shells with ruined threads or with nonstandard threads. Mavic stopped producing them in 1995, after which Stronglight temporarily took over the design.

OVERHAULING THE BOTTOM BRACKET

A bottom-bracket overhaul consists of cleaning or replacing the bearings, cleaning the axle and bearing surfaces, and regreasing them. With any type, both crankarms must be removed (§viii-1).

viii-12
OVERHAULING INTEGRATED-SPINDLE BOTTOM BRACKETS

 **LEVEL 1**

1. **Remove the crankarms** (§viii-1).
2. **Remove the rubber cover seal covering the bearing.** To get this seal off to reveal the bearing, slip a blade under the edge and pry it up (Fig. 8.31), possibly working around the outside with a thin screwdriver for FSA and Shimano cover seals that extend inside the

bearing bore. In many cases, the drive-side cover seal stays stuck on the crank spindle and pulls off with the right crank.

3. **Pry out the circular seal between the bearing's inner and outer rings.** With a razor blade or knife blade, get under the edge of the seal and pry it off (Fig. 8.32).

4. **With solvent and a clean toothbrush, scrub dirty grease out of the bearing.**

5. **Blow the bearing out with compressed air.** Wear safety glasses.

6. **Repack the bearing with clean grease.**

7. **Replace the bearing seal and the bottom-bracket cover seal.**

8. **Reinstall the crankarms (§viii-1).**

You can't get at the other side of the bearing without removing it from the cup with a special bearing puller (see §viii-13), but do the best you can to flush the bearing out and dry it out afterward.

If the bearings still do not turn well after this or are gritty, they will have to be replaced; see §viii-14.

viii-13
REPLACING BEARINGS IN THREADLESS OR THREADED EXTERNAL BOTTOM BRACKETS (STEEL OR CERAMIC BEARINGS)

⚙️ ⚙️ ⚙️ LEVEL 3

You can replace the bearings with the same type, or you can make the axle spin better than ever by replacing the bearings with upgraded steel ones or with the ultimate: ceramic bearings. Ceramic bearings are expensive, but they deliver such a performance advantage that no top pro cyclist will ride without them. Ceramic ball bearings are lighter, smoother, 2.5 times rounder, 2.5 times harder, and 50 percent stiffer than steel balls and are less affected by heat.

8.31 Pry bearing cover seal from external bearing with a box-cutter blade

8.32 Pry bearing seal from external bearing with a box-cutter blade

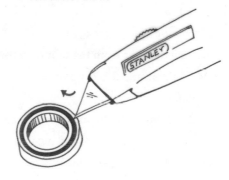

a. Interchanging the bearings (with ceramic or steel bearings) inside external-bearing cups

⚙️ ⚙️ ⚙️ LEVEL 3

An expensive tool is required to pull the bearings out of external-bearing cups, so in most cases replacing or upgrading the bearings means replacing the entire cups with new ones containing new bearings. SRAM, FSA, and others offer cups with ceramic bearings inside. Instructions for installing the new cups are in §viii-7; removal is just the opposite after you have removed the cranks as in §viii-1.

If you have the required tool and want to upgrade the bearings inside external-bearing cups, first select the bearings from your bike shop or a source such as WheelsMfg.com, EnduroForkSeals.com, CeramicSpeed.com, or BocaBearings.com.

Make sure the bearings are correct for the crank-set. Even though the spindle is 24mm, not all manufacturers use bearings with a 24mm ID. Stock FSA and Shimano bearings are 25mm ID; a thin plastic shim integral with the outer bearing cover (making the cover shaped like a top hat) brings the bore down to the 24mm diameter of the spindle (it's visible in Fig. 8.31). If you are simply replacing the bearings and reusing the stock seals, get 25mm ID bearings. Otherwise, Enduro's Shimano/FSA replacement kit uses a 24mm ID bearing and a thin outer silicone cover seal instead of the stock one.

1. **Remove the crankarms** (§viii-1).
2. **Unscrew the cups from the frame** (§viii-7, Fig. 8.14). Remember, the drive-side cup will be left-hand-threaded.
3. **Remove (or not) the bearing cover seals.** Slip a razor blade under the edge (I mean the seals covering the face of the outboard cup, not the actual seals on the cartridge bearings) and pry it up (Fig. 8.31), possibly working around the outside with a thin screwdriver blade for FSA and Shimano cover seals that extend inside the bearing bore. You can leave them on, and when you push out the bearings in the remover tool, the bearings will push the cover seals off.
4. **Get a specialty tool for removing and installing bearings from external-bearing cups.** It must ensure complete bearing insertion and proper alignment. Enduro has a nice one (made by Sonny's Bike Tools), as does Phil Wood. The key to the external bottom-bracket bearing puller is a two-piece collet. These instructions are for the Enduro tool; the Phil Wood tool is slightly different.
5. **Drop the collet down into the bearing from the inboard side.**
6. **Push a rounded-nose cylindrical "collet expander" into it.** It will spread the collet

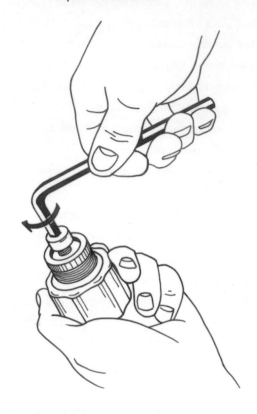

8.33 Press new bearing into external-bearing cup with Enduro tool

inside the bearing bore so that its lips will catch the back of the inner bearing race. Many bearing cups have an internal shelf that would prevent you from pushing the bearing out if you did not have this collet.

7. **Put the bearing cup's outboard end facedown into the tool's cup holder.**
8. **Push the bearing out by applying pressure on the collet expander.** With the Enduro tool, you accomplish this by running a big bolt through the expander and tightening the bolt. This often takes considerable force, and especially in the case of Truvativ/SRAM GXP, the bearing finally comes free with a loud pop.
9. **Determine bearing orientation.** Think ahead about maintenance before determining the orientation of the bearings. Even though ceramic balls cannot rust and are more than twice as hard as steel balls, the races are

still steel, can rust, and need maintenance. Ceramic cartridge bearings, like most steel cartridge bearings, have bearing retainers that separate the balls from each other. This reduces friction by preventing neighboring balls, whose adjacent sides are turning in opposite directions, from rubbing each other. The bearing retainer may be asymmetrical, so when you remove the bearing seals with a razor blade (Fig. 8.32), you'll see the balls on one side and you'll see only the retainer from the other side. Proper maintenance requires cleaning out the bearing and pumping new grease into it, so before you press the bearings in, determine which side the bearing retainer is closed on and make sure that side faces inboard. That way, you can pry off the bearing covers and clean and grease them easily as in §viii-12. Truvativ/SRAM recommends a service interval of 100 hours for the ceramic bearings in its XX crankset. Service interval will obviously depend on how you use the bike.

10. **Place the bearing on an insert that fits snugly in the bearing's ID.** One end of the insert is 24mm in diameter, and the other is 25mm.

11. **Place the insert and bearing inside the bore of the tool's cup holder, facing upward.**

12. **Place the bearing cup over the bearing, and put a support ring atop it.**

13. **Run the bolt through and tighten the bolt.** Tighten with an 8mm hex key until it hits a dead stop (Fig. 8.33).

14. **Check that the bearing is in as far as the old one was.** If not, flip the bearing cup over, with the insert still inside the bearing bore, and put the cup back into the tool's cup holder with the cup's threaded section down inside. Reinstall the bolt and tighten it until it stops. This second pressing step is always necessary with Truvativ and SRAM GXP cranks (24mm ID bearings), because the replacement bearing (a standard size, 7mm thick) is 1mm narrower than the (proprietary) bearing employed by Truvativ.

15. **On a non–drive side Truvativ/SRAM GXP bearing, install its sleeve.** GXP cranks require an 11.5mm-wide, 1mm-thick sleeve that stops the non-drive shoulder of the GXP spindle and establishes the side-to-side position of the crankset. Use the special GXP insert in the tool to install the sleeve.

16. **Install the cups as in §viii-7 and the crankarms as in §viii-1.** Spin them.

b. Interchanging the bearings in threadless bottom brackets

BB95

LEVEL 1

With Trek's BB95 (Fig. 8.17) system, the bearings will usually come out with only minor persuasion: pulling them out with your finger. If need be, walk the bearing out a bit at a time by placing a big hex key against it from the opposite side and gently tapping it with a hammer as you move the hex tip around from side to side on the backside of the bearing.

Put the new bearings in as described in §viii-8a.

BB30

LEVEL 2

With a BB30 crank (Fig. 8.15), you'll need a special bearing puller. Enduro has a removal/installation tool that works similarly to the tool described in §viii-13a. As in §viii-13a, you insert the collet and collet expander into the bearing and drive it out by tightening the tool's center bolt.

The following instructions are for Park's BBT-39 T-shaped BB30 bearing puller (actually, it's a pusher-outer).

1. **Angle the BBT-39's T-end in through one bearing, and push it straight in against the other bearing** (Fig. 8.34). Make sure the tool does not hit the snapring's eyes (Fig. 8.14).

2. **Center the BBT-39 shaft with the dummy bearing insert in the near side.**

3. **Smack the handle with a hammer.** The bearing on the far side will pop out.

If you don't have the correct tool, you'll probably want to have a shop do this to avoid mauling the inside of the bottom-bracket shell, but if you're careful, you can reach in against the backside of the opposite bearing (not against the snapring!) with a rod or big hex key that you tap with a hammer. Work a little bit on each side of the bearing, moving the end of the rod or wrench from side to side and around the bearing as you tap it to slowly walk the bearing out.

Install the new bearings as in §viii-8b.

PF30 and BB92 (PF24)

 **LEVEL 2**

These instructions apply to Press Fit systems for both 30mm and 24mm spindles.

1. **Insert the bearing remover.** On PF24 (BB92), use the Park BBT-90 tool, which is simply a slimmer version of a headset cup remover. As in §xi-20, slide the remover tool in, narrow end first (Fig. 11.36), and pull it out from the other end until its wings snap outward behind the bearing. On PF30, use the BBT-39 and follow the instructions for BB30, except that the tool pushing against the bearing will pop out the entire plastic cup with the bearing still inside.

2. **Push the old bearing out.** Smack the remover with a hammer (Fig. 11.37).

3. **Repeat for the other bearing.**

4. **Install the new bearings as in §viii-8a, step 2b for PF24 and as in §viii-8c for PF30.**

viii-14
OVERHAULING CARTRIDGE BOTTOM BRACKETS (OR NOT!)

Standard cartridge bottom brackets (Figs. 8.18–19) are sealed units and cannot be overhauled. They must be replaced when they stop performing properly. Remove the cranks as in §viii-1. Remove the bottom bracket by unscrewing the cups with

8.34 Push out BB30 bearing with Park BBT-39 tool

POP!

the splined cup tool (Fig. 8.27), and install a new bottom bracket as directed in §viii-9.

viii-15
OVERHAULING CUP-AND-CONE BOTTOM BRACKETS

⚙ ⚙ LEVEL 2

Cup-and-cone bottom brackets (Figs. 8.20–21) can be overhauled entirely from the nondrive side after you have removed the crankarms as described in §viii-1.

1. **Remove the lockring.** Use a lockring spanner as in Figure 8.30, except the lockring spanner and the rotation direction will be reversed.

2. **Remove the adjustable cup.** Use a tool that fits the particular cup (usually a pin spanner like the one in Fig. 8.30).

3. **Leave the fixed cup in place.** Check that it is tight in the frame by putting a fixed-cup wrench on the cup and trying to tighten it counterclockwise (Fig. 8.28).

4. **Clean the cups and axle with a rag.** There should be no need for a solvent unless the parts are glazed.

5. **Clean the bearings with a citrus-based solvent.** Don't remove them from their retainer cages. A simple way to clean them is to drop the bearings in a plastic bottle, fill it with solvent, cap it, and shake it. A toothbrush may be required afterward, and a solvent tank is certainly handy if you have access to one. If the bearings are not shiny and in perfect shape, replace them. Balls with dull luster and/or rough spots or rust should be replaced.

6. **Wash the bearings in soap and water.** This removes solvent and remaining grit.

7. **Dry the bearings.** Towel them off and let them thoroughly air-dry. An air compressor is handy here.

8. Install the bottom bracket as in §viii-10.

9. Install the crankarms as in §viii-1 and Figure 8.4.

viii-16
OVERHAULING OTHER TYPES OF BOTTOM BRACKETS

⚙ ⚙ LEVEL 2

If any cartridge-bearing bottom bracket becomes difficult to turn, the bearing seals must be removed (Fig. 8.32) and the bearings scrubbed and flushed with solvent, dried, and regreased. If that doesn't fix the problem, the bearings must be replaced. If they are pressed into cups, then you may also have to buy new cups. Be doubly sure to get the correct size.

1. **Reverse the installation procedure outlined in §viii-11a to remove the bottom bracket.**

2. **Replace the bearings and cups.**

3. **Reinstall the bottom bracket (§viii-11a) and crankarms (§viii-1).**

TROUBLESHOOTING CRANK AND BOTTOM-BRACKET NOISE

viii-17
CREAKING NOISES

Mysterious creaking noises can be enough to drive you nuts. Just as you think you have your bike tuned to perfection, a little noise comes along to ruin your ride, and these annoying little creaks, pops, and groans can be a bear to locate. Pedaling-induced noises can originate from almost anything connected to the crankset, such as movement of the cleats on your shoes, movement of the crankarms on the bottom-bracket spindle, loose chainrings, or poorly adjusted bearings. Of course, noises can also originate from seemingly unrelated components, such as the seat, seatpost, frame, wheels, or handlebar.

Creaking occurs when parts that are supposed to be fixed together instead move against each other. Insufficient tightening of fasteners or lack of grease between parts is often the cause.

Before spending hours overhauling the drivetrain, spend some time trying to isolate the source of the noise. Try different pedals, shoes, or wheels. Pedal out of the saddle, and pedal without flexing the handlebar. If the source of the creak turns out to be the saddle, seatpost, wheels, or handlebar, turn to the appropriate chapter for directions on correcting the problem.

If the creaking is in the crank area, do the following:

1. **Check to make sure that the chainring bolts are tight, and tighten them if they are not** (Fig. 8.9).

2. **If that step does not solve the problem, make certain that the crankarm bolts are tight** (Figs. 8.4–5). If they are not, the resulting movement between the crankarm and the bottom-bracket spindle is a likely source of noise. If the crank is of a different brand than the bottom bracket, check with the manufacturer or your local shop to make sure that they are recommended for use together. Incompatible cranks and spindles will never properly join.

3. **If the fit is not ideal, apply Loctite.** Bearings may sometimes move inside threadless bottom brackets and creak. Remove the bearings (§viii-13), smear a thin layer of Loctite 609 retaining compound where they sit inside the bottom-bracket shell, and reinstall them.

4. **Apply grease if the cartridge moves inside the cup.** Rust, and alternating wet and dry cycles, can break down the glue bond that holds the cup(s) onto a cartridge bottom bracket (Figs. 8.18–19). If the cartridge can move within the cup, it will creak. Fix it by removing the bottom bracket (§viii-14 and Fig. 8.27) and slathering grease inside the cup(s) and around the outside of the cartridge where the parts meet. Grease the cup threads too, because the cup can also make noise as it moves against the bottom-bracket shell. Tighten the bottom bracket back into place (Fig. 8.27).

5. **If the creaking persists, recheck the adjustments and inspect the bottom bracket threading and facing.** The bottom bracket can creak owing to improper adjustment, lack of grease, cracked bearings, worn parts, or loose cups. All of these things require adjustment or overhaul via the procedures outlined in §viii-12 through §viii-16. Many integrated-spindle designs (Fig. 8.2) are very sensitive to the bearings being out of parallel, and creaking may occur if the bottom-bracket shell is not perfectly tapped and faced. This is a job for a good bike shop.

6. **Now for the bad news.** If creaking persists, the problem could be rooted in the frame. Creaks can originate from cracks in and around the bottom-bracket shell, so be sure to check that area. The threads in the bottom-bracket shell could also be worn to the point that they allow the cups to move slightly. Neither of these is a good sign, unless, of course, you were hoping for an excuse to buy a new frame.

viii-18
CLUNKING NOISES

1. **In the case of crankarm play, grab the crankarm and push on it from side to side.**

    (a) If there is play, tighten the crankarm bolt (Figs. 8.3–5; torque spec is in Appendix D).

    (b) If there is still crankarm play with a cup-and-cone bottom bracket (Figs. 8.13, 8.20, and 8.21) or a cartridge-bearing bottom bracket with a lockring on either side (Fig.

8.22), adjust the bottom-bracket spindle end play (§viii-10, steps 11–15).

(c) If bottom-bracket adjustment does not eliminate crankarm play, or if the bike has a nonadjustable cartridge bottom bracket (Figs. 8.18–19 or 8.23), the bottom bracket is loose in the frame threads, and you should tighten it up. With a cup-and-cone bottom bracket, you can go back to §viii-10 and start over, making sure that the fixed cup is very tight. A cheater bar (extension tube) may need to be used on the fixed-cup wrench to tighten it to high enough torque. Adjustable-cup lockrings need to be equally tight (Fig. 8.30) once the spindle end play is adjusted properly.

The lockrings and fixed-cup flanges must be flush with the bottom-bracket shell all the way around; if they are not, the bottom bracket must be removed, and the bottom-bracket shell must be faced (cut parallel) by a shop equipped with a facing cutter.

(d) If the crankarm play persists, the hole in the crankarm could be worn-out. This is a common problem with square-taper bottom brackets (Figs. 8.18 and 8.21–23) if the bike was ridden without the crankarm bolt properly tightened. You will have to buy another crankarm. Make sure you tighten this one to the correct torque spec (Appendix D) and keep it tight.

(e) If the bottom-bracket fixed cup or lockring will not tighten completely or keeps coming loose, then either the bottom-bracket cups are stripped or undersized, or the frame's bottom-bracket shell threads are stripped or oversized. Either way, it's an expensive fix, especially the frame-replacement option! Get a second opinion if you reach this point. If you can find a Mavic-style bottom bracket (Fig. 8.23), you can still use the frame.

2. **In the case of pedal end play, grab each pedal and wobble it to check for play.** If either is loose, see Chapter 9.

viii-19
HARD-TO-TURN CRANKS

If the cranks are hard to turn, overhaul the bottom bracket (see §viii-12 through §viii-16)—unless you want to continue intensifying your workout or boosting the egos of your cycling companions. The bottom bracket may be shot and need to be replaced.

viii-20
INNER CHAINRING DRAGS ON CHAINSTAY

If you hear noise because the inner chainring is dragging on the chainstay, either the bottom-bracket spindle is too short, you need a spacer between the bottom-bracket shell and the drive-side external-bearing cup (only applies to a 68mm-wide bottom-bracket shell), the square hole in the crankarm is deformed so that the crank slides on too far, the frame is bent, or you have switched to a larger inner chainring. If the bottom-bracket spindle is too short, you need a new one of the correct length. If you have a 68mm-wide bottom-bracket shell with external bearings and don't have a spacer on the drive side, you need at least one 2.5mm spacer between the shell and the external-bearing cup (Shimano requires two spacers or one spacer along with the bracket of an E-type front derailleur); see §viii-9, step 2. If the square hole in the crank is badly deformed, you need a new crankarm; otherwise it will continue to loosen up and cause problems. If the frame is bent, refer to §xiv-13 to check on it and then decide what to do based on those instructions. If the chainring is too large, you need to get a smaller one.

With an adjustable cartridge-bearing bottom bracket with a lockring on either end (Fig. 8.22), the entire bottom bracket may be offset to the left. To move it to the right, screw the left cup in farther, back the right cup out some, adjust out the end play, and tighten the lockrings back down (Fig. 8.30).

NOTE: *See §v-48 (Fig. 5.48) on chainline to establish proper crank-to-frame spacing. The chainring might not be rubbing the frame, but the crank is still too far inboard if the derailleur cannot move inward far enough to shift to the granny gear. The mechanism on a Shimano "top-swing" front derailleur in particular can hit the seat tube and stop before the chain drops onto the inner ring. The problem is compounded with an oversized seat tube. And if the bottom bracket is too long, you may have the opposite problem. The front derailleur will not reach the large chainring.*

PEDALS

9

To everything, turn, turn, turn . . .

—The Byrds

To best serve its purpose, a bicycle pedal needs only to be firmly attached to the crankarm and provide a stable platform for the shoe. A simple enough task, but you'd be amazed at the different approaches that have been taken to achieve this goal. Of the two basic types of mountain bike pedals, the standard cage-type pedal, with or without a toeclip and strap (Fig. 9.1), is the simplest and cheapest. The "clip-in" pedal (Fig. 9.2), found on most mid- to high-end cross-country and trail mountain bikes, has a spring-loaded shoe-retention system, much like a ski binding. Clip-in pedals are also called "clipless" pedals because they have no toeclip.

Cage-type pedals are fairly common on lower-end bikes. They are relatively unintimidating for the novice rider, and the frame (or "cage") that surrounds the pedal provides a large, stable platform (Fig. 9.1). For doing stunts and gravity-driven mountain biking, many riders prefer "flat" pedals to clip-in pedals, that is, standard pedals with a broad platform and often little steel pins sticking up to provide more traction with the shoe sole. Without a toeclip, the top and bottom of a stan-

9.1 Cage-type pedal with toeclip and straps

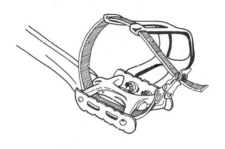

9.2 Clip-in pedal

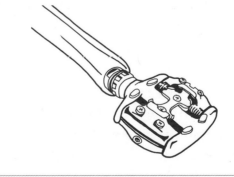

dard or flat pedal are the same, and you can use just about any type of shoe. Using a toeclip without a strap can keep your foot from sliding forward and still allow easy release in almost any direction. When you add a toe strap and use a stiff-soled

TOOLS

15mm pedal wrench

small and large
  adjustable
  wrenches

3mm, 4mm, 5mm,
  and 6mm hex keys

screwdriver

pliers

knife

grease

oil (chain lubricant)

FOR OVERHAULING PEDALS

7mm, 8mm, 9mm,
  10mm, 17mm, and
  18mm open-end
  wrenches

Shimano or Look
  splined tool
  (depending on
  pedal)

snapring pliers for
  some Time pedals

13mm cone wrench

8mm socket wrench

bench vise

225

mountain bike shoe with aggressive tread, the combination works well to keep your foot on the pedal while you are riding even the roughest singletrack. When tightened, the strap allows you to pull up on the upward part of the pedal stroke, giving you more power and a more fluid pedal stroke. Of course, as you add clips and straps, the pedal becomes harder to enter and to exit, especially with boots or shoes with aggressive tread designs.

Clip-in models offer all the efficiency advantages of a good clip-and-strap combination, yet allow easier entry and exit from the pedal. These pedals are more expensive and require special shoes and accurate mounting of the cleats. Your choice of shoes is limited to stiff-sole models that accept cleats for your particular pedal. Once you have them dialed in, you will find that clip-in pedals waste less energy through flex and slippage and allow you to transfer more power directly to the pedals. This greater efficiency combined with low weight explains their universal acceptance among cross-country mountain bike racers. Referring to the shoe sole, most clip-in mountain pedals are "SPD" compatible, where SPD stands for Shimano Pedaling Dynamics. Shimano produced the first successful clip-in mountain pedal in the mid-1980s (Fig. 9.2) and set the shoe standards. "SPD compatibility" indicates that the cleat mounts with two side-by-side M5 screws, spaced 14mm apart, screwing into a movable, threaded cleat-mounting plate on a shoe with two longitudinal grooves in the sole (Fig. 9.6). However, SPD compatibility does not necessarily mean that one company's cleat will work with the pedal of another company.

NOTE: *Some pedal cleats do work with other brands of pedals, but it's best to assume that they do not and just stick with cleats and pedals of the same brand and type. Some cleats and pedals do not mix and match, and you might find yourself unable to disengage at a most inopportune moment.*

This chapter explains how to remove and replace pedals, how to mount the cleats and adjust the release tension with clip-in pedals, how to troubleshoot pedal problems, and how to overhaul and replace spindles on almost all mountain bike pedals. Incidentally, I use the terms "axle" and "spindle" interchangeably, as both terms are used by manufacturers and bike shops.

REMOVING AND INSTALLING PEDALS

🔧 LEVEL 1

Note that the right pedal axle is right-hand threaded and the left is left-hand (reverse) threaded. Both unscrew from the crank in the pedaling direction.

a. Removal

1. **Engage the wrench.** Slide a 15mm pedal wrench onto the wrench flats of the pedal axle (Fig. 9.3). Or if the pedal axle is designed to accept it, you can use a 6mm or 8mm hex key from the backside of the crankarm (Fig. 9.4). This design is particularly handy on the trail, because you probably won't be carrying a 15mm wrench. But if you are at home and the pedal is on really tight, it will probably be easier to use the standard pedal wrench. Some pedals have no wrench flats and can

9.3 Removing or installing pedal with a 15mm wrench

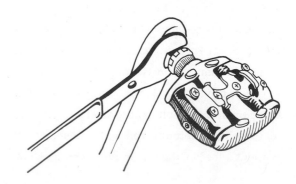

9.4 Removing or installing pedal with a hex key

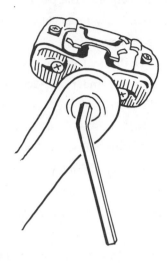

be removed only with a 6mm or 8mm hex key (Fig. 9.4).

2. **Unscrew the pedal in the appropriate direction.** The right (or drive-side) pedal unscrews counterclockwise when viewed from that side. The left-side pedal is reverse-threaded, so it unscrews in a clockwise direction when viewed from the left side of the bike. Once loosened, either pedal can be unscrewed quickly by turning the crank forward with the wrench engaged on the pedal spindle and the rear wheel positioned off the ground so that it can turn.

b. Installation

1. **Use a rag to wipe clean the threads on the pedal axle and inside the crankarm.**

2. **Grease the pedal threads.**

3. **Start screwing the pedal in with your fingers.** Turn clockwise for the right pedal, counterclockwise for the left one.

4. **Tighten the pedal.** Use a 15mm pedal wrench (Fig. 9.3) or a 6mm or 8mm hex key (Fig. 9.4). This can be done quickly by turning the cranks backward with the wrench engaged on the pedal spindle.

Setting up clip-in pedals involves installation and adjustment of the cleats on the shoes and adjusting the pedal-release tension.

ix-2
INSTALLING AND ADJUSTING PEDAL CLEATS ON THE SHOES

⚙ LEVEL 1

The cleat is important because its position determines the fore-and-aft, lateral (side-to-side), and rotational position of your foot. If your feet aren't properly oriented on the pedals, you could eventually develop hip, knee, or ankle problems.

9.5 Removing rubber cover concealing the cleat holes

before

9.6 Cleat setup on an SPD-compatible shoe

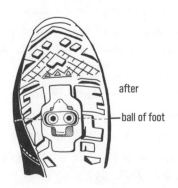

after

ball of foot

1. **If the shoe has a precut piece of rubber covering the cleat-mounting area, remove it.** Cut around the cover's outline with a knife, pry an edge up with a screwdriver (Fig. 9.5), and yank it off with some pliers. If the rubber is hard to pull off, warm it up with a hair dryer to soften the glue.

2. **Put the shoe on, and mark the position of the ball of your foot.** It's the big bump behind your big toe; mark on the side of the shoe toward the crankarm. This will help you position the cleat fore and aft. Take the shoe off, and continue drawing the line straight across the bottom of the shoe (Fig. 9.6).

3. **If there are threaded holes in the shoe sole to accept cleat screws, skip to step 4.** If there are no threaded shoe holes, you must install the backing plate and threaded cleat plate that came with the pedals. Remove the shoe's sock liner, put the rectangular backing plate inside the shoe over the two slots, and put the threaded plate on top of it with the threaded protuberances sticking out through the slots, rather than up at your foot.

4. **Screw the cleat that came with the pedals onto the shoe.** Lube the cleat screw threads first, and use a 4mm hex key to install the screw. Make sure you orient the cleat in the appropriate direction. Some cleats have an arrow indicating forward (Fig. 9.6); if yours do not, the instructions accompanying the pedals probably specify which direction the cleat should point. Also note if the right and left cleats are different (see note under next step).

5. **Position the cleat.** Put it in the middle of its lateral- and rotational-adjustment range, and line up the center of the cleat over or (preferably) 1cm behind the mark you made in step 2 (Fig. 9.6). It is actually the position of the ball of the foot relative to the pedal spindle you are interested in, and with some

systems the center of the cleat is not actually at the center of the pedal. Adjust these cleats accordingly to establish your desired relationship between the pedal spindle and the ball of the foot (usually you want the spindle directly under or 1–2cm behind the ball of the foot).

NOTE: *Cleats for Time ATAC pedals (Figs. 9.14 and 9.22), Crank Brothers pedals (Eggbeater [Fig. 9.21], Candy, Acid, and Mallet), and Look 4 × 4 pedals have no lateral or rotational adjustment; just set the screws at your mark and tighten the cleat down, making sure the arrow on the Time cleat points forward. Crank Brothers and Look 4 × 4 cleats are symmetrical, so mount either end forward. Put the Time cleat with the imprinted stars (or the "G/L" imprint) onto the left shoe for less float range and earlier (13-degree) release angle; put it on the right shoe for more float and wider (17-degree) release angle. Conversely, put the Crank Brothers (or Look 4 × 4) cleat with the imprinted circles onto the right shoe for less float range and earlier (15-degree) release angle; put it on the left shoe for more float and wider (20-degree) release angle. You may now tighten the screws, skip the remaining steps, and go riding! (Incidentally, the older-model Time TMT pedal, of which few were sold, also had only fore-and-aft cleat adjustment, but the only shoe you could use with it was Time's mountain shoe. The ATAC pedals work with any SPD-compatible shoe.)*

As for the positioning of cleats for release angle, I recommend setting either system, especially Crank Brothers and Look 4 × 4 cleats, for the earlier release angle. That way, you are more likely to get out in a hurry when you need to. There is no spring-retention adjustment on Crank Brothers, Look 4 × 4, or pre-2004 Time pedals (Time ATAC XS pedals, introduced in 2004, do have a spring-tension adjustment), so the only way to get more retention is to increase the release angle. If you find yourself pulling out before you want to, for instance when descending fast on rocky terrain, interchange the cleats to increase the release angle.

6. **Snug down the screws enough that the cleat won't move when clipped in or out of the pedals.** Don't tighten fully yet. Follow the same steps with the other shoe.

7. **Set the lateral cleat position.** Put the shoes on, sit on the bike, and clip into the pedals. Ride around a bit. Notice the position of your feet. Pedaling is more efficient the closer the feet are to the plane of the bike, but you don't want them in so far that they bump the cranks. Take off the shoes and adjust the cleats laterally, if necessary, to move the feet side to side. Get back on the bike and clip in again. (Some cleats have no lateral adjustability.)

8. **Set the rotational cleat position.** Ride around some more. Notice whether your feet feel twisted and uncomfortable. You may feel pressure on either side of your heel from the shoe. If necessary, remove your shoes and rotate the cleat slightly. Some pedals offer free-float, allowing the foot to rotate freely for a few degrees before releasing. Precise rotational cleat adjustment is less important if the pedal is free-floating.

NOTE: *For Speedplay Frogs (Fig. 9.16), angle the cleat slightly toward the outside of the shoe, and tighten the mounting screws just enough that the cleat can still turn. Clip into the pedal, and rotate the heel inward until it just touches the crankarm. Tighten the cleat in this position. Frogs have no inward release; this procedure sets the inward stop.*

9. **Once cleat position feels right, trace the cleats with a pen or scribe.** That way, you can tell if the cleat stays put.

10. **While holding the cleat in place, tighten the bolts down firmly.** Hold the hex key close to the bend so that you do not exert too much leverage and strip the threads.

11. **If the cleat holes are open to the inside of the shoe, seal them.** Remove the insole, place a waterproof sticker over the opening inside, and replace the insole.

12. **When riding, take the 4mm wrench along.** You may want to fine-tune the cleat adjustment over the course of a few rides.

13. **Check cleat bolt tightness every few months.** You don't want to lose a screw (or a cleat) while riding. You may have to pick dirt out of the screw head and hammer the 4mm hex key into the hex hole so that the wrench won't slip. Ideally, use a torque wrench (4–5 N-m) with a hex bit.

ix-3
ADJUSTING THE RELEASE TENSION ON CLIP-IN PEDALS

 **LEVEL 1**

If you find the factory release-adjustment setting to be too loose or too restrictive, you can adjust the release tension on most clip-in pedal brands; exceptions are Crank Brothers, Look 4 × 4, Speedplay, and pre-2004 Time. The adjusting screws are usually located at the front and rear of the pedal (Fig. 9.7). The screws affect the tension of the nearest set of clips. The adjusters are usually

9.7 Release tension adjustment

3mm hex key

operated with a small (usually 3mm) hex key. Old Onza H.O. (Fig. 9.8) and Look SL-3 (Fig. 9.15) pedals are adjusted differently; see §ix-4.

Before starting, clean the shoe cleats and the pedal clips. Lubricate the clip edges and cleat ends with dry lubricant (so that you don't track it onto your carpet) and the pedal springs with wet chain lube (Fig. 9.24). Whenever you have trouble getting in or out, start with this step.

1. **Locate the tension-adjustment screws.** They are usually on either end of the pedal, fore and aft; you can see the screw in Figures 9.7 and 9.9–13. Time ATAC XS (2004 and later) spring-adjustment screws are located on the outboard side at the front and back of the pedal.

2. **Loosen or tighten the release tension as you see fit.** To loosen the tension adjustment, turn the screw counterclockwise, and to tighten it, turn it clockwise (Fig. 9.7). It's the standard "lefty loosey, righty tighty" approach. There usually are click stops in the rotation of the screw. Tighten or loosen one click at a time (one-quarter to one-half turn), and go riding to test the adjustment. Many types include an indicator that moves with the screw to show relative adjustment. Make certain that you do not back the screw out so far that it comes out of the spring plate.

NOTE: *With early Ritchey, Scott, Girvin, Topo, Wellgo, and other dual-rear-clip–dual-rear-spring pedals, you will decrease the amount of free-float in the pedal as you increase the release tension.*

ix-4
ADJUSTING THE TENSION OF OTHER TYPES OF PEDALS

 LEVEL 1

(a) Time (pre-2004, Figs. 9.14 and 9.22), Crank Brothers (Fig. 9.21), and Look 4 × 4 pedals

9.8 Onza H.O. clip-in pedal, pre-1997

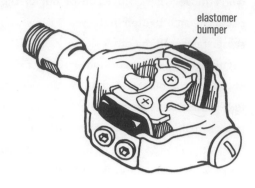

elastomer bumper

have no tension adjustment. They offer high retention and lots of float, yet they require low entry and release force and therefore require no adjustment. As mentioned in §ix-2, you can change retention by interchanging the right and left cleats to obtain a wider or narrower release angle.

(b) Original double-sided Look mountain pedals have a single 5mm bolt that adjusts both sides. It has a large window with a pointer to show the relative adjustment. The even older, one-sided Look models that resemble Look road pedals have a small slotted screw in the center to adjust the tension. Look SL-3 pedals (Fig. 9.15) have a 3mm adjustment screw with spring tension indicator on either side that is reached through a hole in the top of the rear clip. Current Look mountain pedals, dubbed 4 × 4, which are Crank Brothers Eggbeaters (Fig. 9.21) with Look axles and bearings, are adjusted like Crank Brothers Eggbeaters—you alter retention by interchanging the right and left cleats to obtain a wider or narrower release angle.

(c) Old Onza H.O. clip-in pedals (Fig. 9.8) rely on elastomer bumpers to provide release tension. Adjust them by changing the elastomer. Bumpers of varying hardness are included with the pedals. Onza's black bumpers are the hardest, and the clear ones are the softest. There are several grades in between. The harder the bumper, the greater the release tension. To replace bumpers, unscrew the two hex bolts holding each bumper on (Fig. 9.23). Pull the old bumper out and put in the new one. While you are at it, make sure that the Phillips screws that hold in the cleat guides are tight, because they have a tendency to loosen and fall out. In fact, it wouldn't hurt to put a small dab of Loctite on the threads while you're checking them.

(d) Speedplay Frogs (Fig. 9.16) have no tension adjustment; ease of release can be adjusted by rotating the cleat on the shoe sole to change the release angle.

OVERHAULING PEDALS

⚙️ ⚙️ LEVEL 2

Just like a hub or bottom bracket, pedal bearings and bushings need to be cleaned and regreased regularly. Most pedals have a lip seal around the axle where it enters the pedal. Pedals without one get dirty inside very quickly.

First remove the pedal from the bike (§ix-1a, Figs. 9.3–4) and inspect it to figure out which section of directions to follow for overhauling.

There is wide variation in mountain bike pedal designs. This book is not big enough to go into great detail about the inner workings of every single model. In general, pedal guts fall into two broad categories: those that have cartridge bearings and/or bushings (Figs. 9.13–9.16 and 9.23), and those that have loose ball bearings (Figs. 9.11–12 and 9.18).

Many pedals are closed on the outboard end and have a nut surrounding the axle on the inboard end (Figs. 9.9–13). The axle assembly installs into the pedal as a unit and is accessed by this inboard nut. The axle assemblies on other pedal designs are accessed from the outboard end by removing a dust cap (Figs. 9.18 and 9.21–23).

Before you start, figure out how the pedal is put together so that you will know how to take it apart; the following paragraphs and the illustrations on subsequent pages should help. In a few cases, what the pedal guts are like may not be clear until you have completed step 1 in the overhaul process.

Shimano pedals usually have two sets of loose bearings and a bushing that comes out as a complete axle assembly (Figs. 9.11–12). You will see the tiny ball bearings at the small end of the axle (Fig. 9.17).

Many clip-in pedals use an inboard bushing and an outboard cartridge bearing (Figs. 9.13 and 9.21–23). Some also have an additional needle bearing between the two. Some of these pedal guts are accessed from the crank side; others are accessed via an outboard dust cap. Speedplay pedals also have cartridge bearings and bushings; they differ in that they are opened like a clamshell (Fig. 9.16).

All pre-2002 Look, plastic-body Time ATAC, and Time TMT mountain pedals have an inboard cartridge bearing and an outboard needle bearing (Figs. 9.14–15). The axle assembly is accessed from the crank side.

Some pedals—even clip-in models (older Tioga models come to mind)—have no bearings at all. Instead, they just use bushings inside a plastic axle sleeve.

ix-5
OVERHAULING PEDALS CLOSED ON THE OUTBOARD SIDE

⚙️ ⚙️ LEVEL 2

1. **Remove the axle assembly.** This requires either an open-end wrench, a splined tool designed for the pedal, or snapring pliers.

9.9 Removing the axle from a Shimano clip-in pedal

9.10 Removing the axle from a Scott pedal

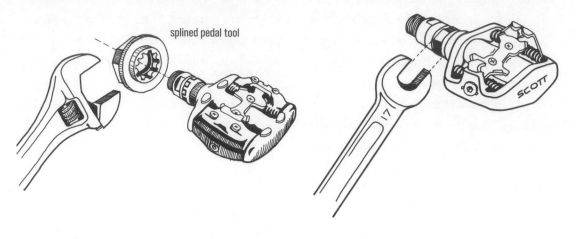

splined pedal tool

On most varieties, removal is accomplished by unscrewing the nut surrounding the axle where it enters the inboard side of the pedal (Figs. 9.9–10). See note under (a) regarding thread direction. High-end pre-2004 Time ATACs with carbon-filled plastic bodies, later butterfly-shaped Ritcheys and current Ritchey V3 Pros, and old Time TMTs use a different approach. These pedals mostly rely on a snapring on the inboard end (Fig. 9.14) that must be removed with snapring pliers (Fig. 1.3). In place of the snapring, 2000–2003 Time ATACs with carbon-filled plastic bodies have an aluminum cup threaded onto the inboard end of the pedal.

(a) Shimano (except M959), pre-2002 Look, and Exus take a plastic splined tool, but the Look tool is not compatible with the other two. Use a large adjustable wrench to turn the tool (Fig. 9.9). Most other closed-end pedals (including Shimano M959) take a 17mm or 18mm open-end wrench (Fig. 9.10). The nut is often plastic and can crack if you turn it the wrong way, so be careful. Hold the pedal body with your hand or a vise while you unscrew the assembly. The fine threads take many turns to unscrew.

NOTE: *The threads inside the pedal body are reversed from the crankarm threads on the axle; the internal threads on the drive-side pedal are left-hand threaded, and vice versa. That means the right axle assembly unscrews clockwise and the left axle assembly unscrews counterclockwise. It's confusing, but like bottom-bracket threads, pedal bodies are threaded so that pedaling forward works to unscrew the assembly.*

(b) All pre-2002 Look, recent high-end Ritchey, and pre-2004 high-end Time mountain pedals have a large inboard cartridge bearing and an outboard needle-bearing cartridge. These bearings tend to stay very clean and seldom require overhaul.

(c) Axles in original Time plastic-body ATACs, recent high-end Ritchey, and old Time TMTs are removed via a snapring on the crank side (Fig. 9.14). Popping the snapring out requires inward-squeezing snapring pliers. Now skip to step 3 with any of these. On 2000–2003 Time ATACs with carbon-filled plastic bodies, unscrew the aluminum cup from the inboard end of the pedal body. You can try an adjustable pin tool on the small pinholes on its face, or you can carefully clamp the cup in a vise or grab it with pliers. Skip to step 3.

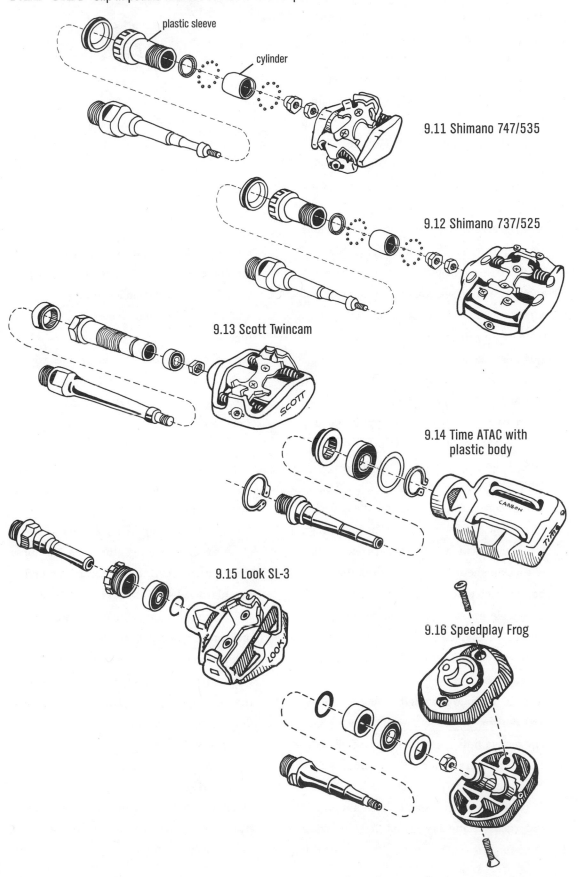

plastic sleeve

cylinder

9.11 Shimano 747/535

9.12 Shimano 737/525

9.13 Scott Twincam

9.14 Time ATAC with plastic body

9.15 Look SL-3

9.16 Speedplay Frog

(d) There are five versions of Look clip-in mountain pedals. The oldest models, marketed under the Look and Campagnolo names, clip in only on one side and resemble Look road pedals in design and function. The next Look models resemble original Shimano double-sided mountain clip-in pedals (Fig. 9.12) and take a large steel cleat. Look SL-3s (Fig. 9.15) take smaller cleats. Look 4 × 4 mountain pedals are Crank Brothers Eggbeaters (Fig. 9.21) on a Look axle assembly. Current Look Quartz pedals roughly resemble original Time ATACs (Fig. 9.14). Axle assemblies in the single-sided model are accessed with an 18mm open-end wrench, whereas double-sided Looks (Fig. 9.15) require a special splined tool that is purchased separately.

(e) Speedplay Frogs have a cartridge bearing and a needle bearing, which can be regreased without opening the pedal. Remove the Phillips screw from the outboard end of the pedal body, and squirt grease in with a fine-tip bicycle grease gun (Fig. 1.2) until it comes out the axle end. If you decide to open a Frog (reminds you of junior-high biology, doesn't it?), the pedal comes apart like a clamshell when you unscrew the single bolt on each side with a 2.5mm hex key (Fig. 9.16). Before you put the pedal back together, put a thin bead of automotive gasket sealer all the way around the edge of one pedal half to seal water out.

2. **Inspect the axle bearing/bushing assembly, and remove the nuts.** You will notice either one or two nuts on the thin end of the axle. These nuts serve to hold the bearings and/or bushings in place.

(a) If the axle has just a single nut on the end (Figs. 9.13 and 9.16), simply hold the axle's

9.17 Tightening a Shimano locknut

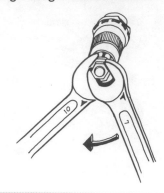

large end with a 15mm pedal wrench and unscrew the little nut with a 9mm wrench (or whatever size fits it). The nut may be very tight, because it has no locknut.

(b) If the axle has two nuts on the end, they are tightened against each other. To remove them, hold the inner nut with a wrench while you unscrew the outer nut with another wrench (Fig. 9.17). Shimano and older Tioga pedals use two nuts in this fashion. On Shimanos, the inner nut acts as a bearing cone, so be careful not to lose the tiny ball bearings as you unscrew the cone.

3. **Clean all the parts.**

(a) If the bearings are loose, use a rag to clean the ball bearings, the cone, the inner ring that the bearings ride on at the end of the plastic sleeve (it looks like a washer), the bearing surfaces on either end of the little steel cylinder, the axle, and the inside of the plastic axle sleeve (Figs. 9.11–12). To get the bearings really clean, wash them in the sink in soap and water with the sink drain plugged; the motion is the same as washing your hands, and it results in both the bearings and your hands being clean for a sterile reassembly. Blot dry.

(b) If, on a pedal with a cartridge bearing (Figs. 9.13–16), the bearing is dirty or worn-out, clean it if you can; otherwise replace it. These bearings often have steel bearing covers that cannot be pried off without damaging them, nor can the covers be replaced. If the pedal has plastic bearing covers, pry them off with a razor blade (Fig. 6.32), clean the bearing with solvent, let it dry, and repack it with grease.

(c) Needle bearings (Time, pre-2002 Look, recent Ritchey, and Coda) can be cleaned with a solvent and a thin bottlebrush slipped inside the pedal-body bore.

(d) On a bushing-only pedal, such as older Tioga, just wipe down the axle and the inside of the bushings.

4. **Lightly grease everything and reassemble the parts as they were.** This is a simple process with bushings, cartridge bearings, and needle bearings—not so simple with loose bearings!

(a) With a loose-bearing pedal, it is exacting work to place the bearings on their races and screw the cone on while keeping them in place. On a Shimano (Figs. 9.11–12), grease the bushing inside the plastic axle sleeve, and slide the axle into the sleeve. Slide the steel ring, on which the inner set of bearings rides, down onto the axle and against the end of the sleeve. Make sure that the concave bearing surface faces out, away from the sleeve. Coat the ring with grease, and stick half of the bearings onto the outer surface of the ring. Slip the steel cylinder onto the axle so that one end rides on the bearings. Make sure that all of the bearings are seated properly and that none are stuck inside of the sleeve.

(b) To prevent the bearings from piling up on each other and ending up inside the sleeve instead of on the races, grease the cone and start it on the axle a few threads. Place the remaining half of the bearings on the flanks of the cone. Being careful not to dislodge the bearings, screw the cone in until the bearings come close to the end of the cylinder but do not touch it. While holding the plastic sleeve, push the axle inward until the bearings seat against the end of the cylinder. Make sure that the first set of bearings is still in place. Screw the cone in without turning the axle or cylinder. Tighten it with your fingers only, and loosely screw on the locknut.

5. **Adjust the axle assembly.** Skip this step for Time, recent Ritchey, and Look pedals.

(a) Pedals with a small cartridge bearing and a single nut on the end of the axle, such as Exus, Coda, VP, Wellgo, Topo, Girvin, Speedplay, and Scott, simply require that you tighten the nut against the cartridge bearing while holding the other end of the axle with a 15mm pedal wrench. This approach secures the inner ring of the cartridge bearing against the shoulder on the axle, and proper adjustment is ensured.

(b) On pedals with two nuts on the end of the axle, hold the cone or inner nut with a wrench and tighten the outer locknut against it (Fig. 9.17). Check the adjustment for freedom of rotation, and be sure there is no play. Readjust as necessary by tightening or loosening the cone or inner nut and retightening the locknut.

6. **Replace the axle assembly in the pedal body.**

(a) Smear grease on the inside of the pedal hole; this will ease insertion and act as a barrier to dirt and water. Screw the sleeve back in place with the same wrench you used to remove it (Figs. 9.9–10).

NOTE: *Pay attention to proper thread direction (see note in step 1). Tighten carefully; it is easy to overtighten and crack the plastic nut.*

9.18 Loose-bearing pedal, exploded view

bearings
cone
lock washer
nut
dust cover

(b) On original Time plastic-body ATACs, recent Ritcheys, and old Time TMTs, after replacing the axle assembly, pop the snapring back into its groove just inside the inboard lip of the pedal body. For 2000–2003 Time plastic-body ATACs, screw the aluminum retaining cup back onto the pedal body to hold the axle assembly in place.

7. **Put the pedals back on your bike.** Go ride.

ix-6

OVERHAULING LOOSE-BEARING PEDALS WITH AN OUTBOARD DUST CAP

 **LEVEL 2**

NOTE: *Many non–clip-in pedals are not worth the effort to overhaul, and not all economical pedals are accessible to overhaul. Assess the value of the pedals and your time before continuing.*

1. **Remove the dust cap with the appropriate tool.** This could be a pair of pliers, a screwdriver, a coin, a hex key, an adjustable pin tool, or a splined tool made especially for your pedals. Different dust cap styles are shown in Figures 9.18 and 9.21–23 (although not all on loose-bearing pedals), and it should be easy to figure out which tool is needed to

9.19 Replacing the ball bearings

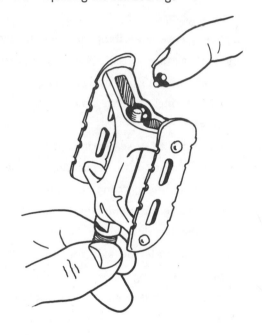

remove the cap. If you see a cartridge bearing inside rather than loose balls, skip to §ix-7.

2. **Unscrew the locknut.** Hold the inboard end of the axle with a pedal wrench or hex key, and use the appropriate size socket wrench (as shown in Fig. 9.20) on the locknut.

3. **Unscrew the cone.** Hold the pedal over a rag to catch the bearings. Keep the bearings from the two ends separate in case they differ in size or in number. Count them so that you

can put the right numbers back in when you reassemble the pedal. The guts should look like Figure 9.18.

4. **With a rag, clean the parts.** Wipe off the bearings, cones, and bearing races. Clean the inside of the pedal body by pushing the rag through with a screwdriver. If there is a dust cover on the inboard end of the pedal body, either clean that in place or after popping it out with a screwdriver.

5. **To get the bearings really clean, wash them in a plugged sink with soap and water.** The motion is the same as washing your hands, and it results in both the bearings and your hands being clean for a sterile reassembly. Blot dry.

6. **If you removed it, press the inboard dust cover back into the pedal body.**

7. **Replace the inboard-side bearings.** Smear a thin layer of grease in the inboard bearing cup first. Once all the bearings are in place, there will be a gap equal to about half the size of one bearing.

8. **Replace the outboard-side bearings** (Fig. 9.19). Drop the axle in and turn the pedal over first so that the outboard end is up, and smear grease in that end.

9. **Bring the cones to the bearings.** Screw the outboard cone in until it almost contacts the bearings, and then push the axle straight in (from the outboard end) to bring the cone and bearings together; this prevents the bearings from piling up and getting spit out as the cone turns down against them. Without turning the axle (which would knock the inboard bearings about), screw the cone in until it is finger-tight.

9.20 Removing or tightening the locknut on an Onza H.O. pedal

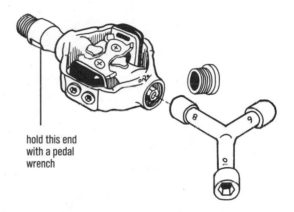

hold this end with a pedal wrench

9.21 Crank Brothers Eggbeater

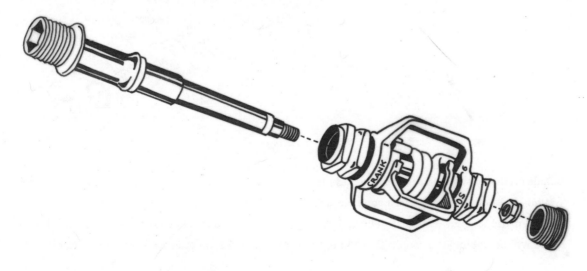

9.22 Time ATAC Alium or Alium HP, exploded view

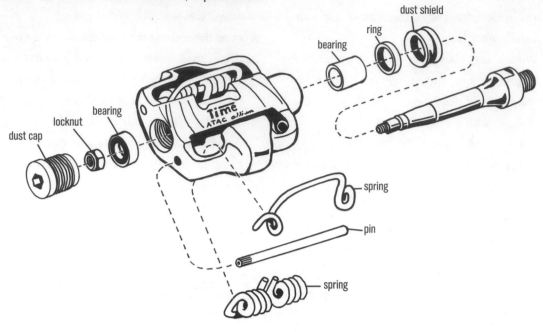

9.23 Onza H.O. clip-in pedal, exploded view

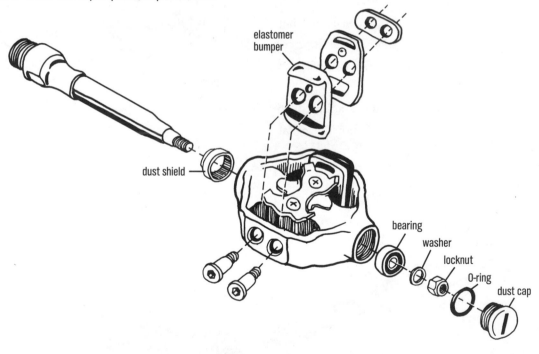

10. Slide on the washer and screw on the locknut. While holding the cone with a cone wrench, tighten the locknut (similar to Fig. 9.17, but you will be holding the cone with a 13mm or so cone wrench, not a 10mm standard open-end wrench).

11. Check that the pedal spins smoothly without play. Readjust as necessary by loosening the locknut, tightening or loosening the cone, and retightening the locknut.

12. Replace the dust cap.

ix-7
OVERHAULING CARTRIDGE-BEARING PEDALS WITH AN OUTBOARD DUST CAP

⚙️ ⚙️ LEVEL 2

Aluminum-body Time ATAC Alium, Alium HP (Fig. 9.22) and Z Control, and all 2004 (and later) carbon-composite-body ATACs (ATAC XS), Crank Brothers (Eggbeater, Candy, and Mallet), Look 4 × 4, older Ritchey, Onza H.O. (Figs. 9.8 and 9.20), some Wellgo, some VP, Nashbar, and Norco, among others, have an axle-end nut accessed from the outboard end by removing the dust cap. Inside is a sealed cartridge bearing on the outboard end and a brass or composite bushing on the crank side.

NOTE: *Crank Brothers pedals (Eggbeater, Candy, and Mallet models) have a lengthwise grease hole down the center of the axle. You can regrease the pedal without disassembly simply by removing the dust cap and screwing in the plastic knurled grease-adapter cap with a hole in the end (supplied with most aftermarket models and available from Crank Brothers). By using a fine-tip grease gun (Fig. 1.2), squirt grease into the hole. When done, replace the dust cap.*

1. **Take off the dust cap.** Some take a 5mm or 6mm hex key, others require a coin or a screwdriver, and Time ATAC XS takes a pin spanner (Fig. 1.2, lower right-hand corner) with tiny pins (you can file the pins down to make them fit).

2. **Unscrew the outboard nut** (Fig. 9.20). Use a socket wrench (usually 8mm, 9mm, or 10mm). Hold the crank end of the axle with a 15mm pedal wrench.

3. **Push the axle out the inboard end.** This frees the outboard cartridge bearing. The guts should look similar to Figures 9.22–23.

4. **Clean and regrease the axle and the inside of the pedal body hole.** Replace the cartridge bearing if necessary. On Ritcheys, Time Aliums, Alium HPs, and Z Controls, the brass bushings inside the pedal body are also replaceable, but you need a special (unavailable) tool, so it's a factory job.

5. **Reassemble the pedal.** Push the axle back into the pedal body, slip the cartridge bearing onto the outboard end of the axle, and thread on the end nut.

6. **Tighten the little end nut down against the cartridge bearing.** Hold the crank end of the axle with a 15mm pedal wrench or a hex key to keep it from turning.

NOTE: *Ritcheys will still have side play at this point; the dust cap is an integral part of the assembly. Once it is tightened down, the play goes away.*

7. **Replace the dust cap.**

ix-8
UPGRADING THE PEDAL SPINDLE

You may want to lighten the pedals with titanium spindles. Another reason to replace the axle is to use a shorter or longer one to decrease or increase the pedaling stance (distance between the feet when pedaling). With some pedals, you may be able to buy a separate axle that you can install into the same sleeve, bushings, and bearings as the axle it replaces. Other manufacturers sell axles only as a complete assembly, including the axle, sleeve, bushings, and bearings.

If you are going to install a lightweight and/or different-length aftermarket axle or axle assembly into the pedals, make sure that you purchase one intended for the pedal brand and model you have. If all you are doing is replacing the axle, go ahead and follow the overhaul procedures outlined in §ix-5 to §ix-7. If you bought the entire assembly, just take out the old assembly. Again

9.24 Lubricating the release mechanism

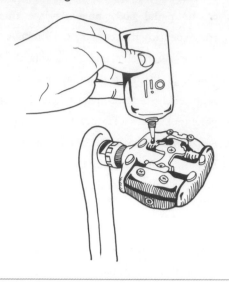

(I obviously feel the need to say this often), pay attention to the direction of the threads (see note in §ix-5, step 1). Following the procedures in §ix-5 to §ix-7, install the new assembly.

Reinstall the pedals (Fig. 9.3 or 9.4). You'll be amazed how much lighter your bike feels . . . or is that your wallet?

TROUBLESHOOTING PEDAL PROBLEMS

ix-9
CREAKING NOISE WHILE PEDALING

1. **The shoe cleats are loose, or they are worn and need to be replaced** (see §ix-2).
2. **Pedal bearings need cleaning and lubrication** (see §ix-5 to §ix-7).
3. **The noise is originating from somewhere other than the pedals** (see Chapter 8, "Troubleshooting Crank and Bottom-Bracket Noise").

ix-10
TOO EASY OR TOO HARD RELEASE OR ENTRY WITH CLIP-IN PEDALS

1. **Release tension needs to be adjusted** (see §ix-3).

2. **Pedal-release mechanism needs to be cleaned and lubricated.** Clean off the mud and dirt, and then drip chain lubricant onto the springs (Fig. 9.24) and dry lubricant onto the cleat contacts on the clips.
3. **The cleats themselves need to be cleaned and lubricated.** Clean off dirt and mud, and put a dry chain lubricant or a dry grease (such as pure Teflon) on the contact ends of the cleats.
4. **The cleats are worn out.** Replace them (§ix-2).
5. **The knobs on the shoe sole that contact the pedal might be so tall that they prevent the cleat from engaging.** Install a shim or two under the cleat. Alternatively, locate where the pedal edges contact the sole, and trim some of the rubber with a knife.
6. **The clips on the pedal are bent down.** Straighten them if you can, or replace them. If you can't repair or replace the clips, you may have to replace the entire pedal.
7. **If it is hard to clip in, check the metal cleat guide plate at the center of the pedal.** It is held on with two Phillips screws, and they may be loose or may have fallen out.
8. **Time ATAC spring clips can get bent and not hold the cleat as well.** They are replaceable by driving out the pin with a hammer and a punch (see Fig. 9.22).

ix-11
KNEE AND JOINT PAIN WHILE PEDALING

1. **Cleat misalignment often causes pain on the sides of the knees** (see §ix-2).
2. **You need more rotational float.** Pedals that offer the most are the Time ATAC and Speedplay Frog.
3. **If your foot wants to roll inward (pronate), but your shoe and pedal force your foot to roll outward,** then there is likely to be an

increase in the tension on the iliotibial band, the tendon connecting the hip and calf. This will eventually cause pain on the outside of the knee. You need to see a specialist, because you will probably need custom foot beds (insoles) to correct the problem.

4. **Fatigue and improper seat height can also contribute to joint pain.** Pain in the front of the knee right behind the kneecap can indicate that the saddle is too low. Pain in the back of the leg behind the knee suggests that the saddle is too high. (See Appendix C for seat-height guidelines.)

CAUTION: *If any of these problems result in chronic pain, consult a specialist. If you experience foot pain, a specialist can make custom foot beds to fit inside your shoes. Custom foot beds can also correct leg misalignments emanating from the foot.*

SADDLES AND SEATPOSTS

Even if you're on the right track, you'll get run over if you just sit there.

—Will Rogers

TOOLS

4mm, 5mm, and 6mm
  hex keys

screwdriver

grease

OPTIONAL

soft hammer

securely mounted
  vise

penetrating oll

hacksaw

flex hone

electric drill

cutting oil

After a few hours on the bike, I can pretty much guarantee that you will be most aware of one component on your bike: the saddle. It is the part of your bike with which you are most . . . uh . . . intimately connected. Nothing can ruin a good ride faster than a poorly positioned or badly designed saddle.

The seatpost connects the saddle to the frame. It must hold the saddle firmly in the proper position without letting it tilt or slide down or back. Some have shock-absorbing systems that cushion the ride.

x-1
CHOOSING A SADDLE

Most bike saddles are made up of a padded and covered flexible plastic shell suspended like a hammock between rails that attach at the tip and tail (Fig. 10.1). There are countless variations on (and a few notable exceptions to) this theme. Some have extra thick foam or high-tech gel pads. Some have depressions, holes, or splits in the shell to reduce pressure in sensitive areas.

10.1 Modern lightweight saddle

Some have rails made of titanium, hollow chromoly steel, or even aluminum or carbon fiber. Others have leather, synthetic leather, or Kevlar covers. You can expect to spend anywhere from $20 to more than $300 for a saddle, and price may not be the best indicator of what makes a saddle really good—namely, comfort.

You have a lot of choices in saddles. My best advice is to ignore price, weight, fashion, and looks and instead choose a saddle that is comfortable. I could go on for pages about high-tech gel padding, scientifically designed shells that flex in just the right places at just the right moment, and all sorts of factors that engineers consider when designing a saddle. None of it would count for squat if, after reading it, you ran out and bought a saddle that turned out to be a giant pain in the rear. Saddles are different because people are different. Try as many as you can before buying one.

The marketing war raging over saddles designed to prevent male impotency (Fig. 10.2) can limit a consumer's ability to select appropriately. If you buy a saddle out of fear and it is uncomfortable, you have done yourself a disservice. Don't take it on faith or scientific studies that your saddle is protecting you. If it hurts, or you get numb while riding on it, it isn't working for you. What works for one person won't necessarily work for another.

Determine which saddle shape and design are the most comfortable for your body, and then—and only then—start looking at titanium rails, fancy covers, and all the other things that improve a saddle and add to its cost. I know a lot of people who need 300g or 400g saddles with tons of thick padding to feel comfortable on even a short ride. I know others who can ride for hours on a skinny little sub-100g saddle. It's a matter of preference. Any decent bike shop worth its weight in titanium should let you try a saddle for a while before locking you into a sale.

Brooks and Idéale saddles have no plastic shell, foam padding, or cover. They are simply constructed from a single piece of thick leather attached to a steel frame with large brass rivets (Fig. 10.3). This was the main type of saddle up until the 1980s. Brooks still makes them and even offers them with titanium rails these days. This sort of saddle requires a long break-in period and frequent applications of a leather-softening compound that comes with the saddle or from a shoe store. Like a lot of old bike parts, you either love 'em or hate 'em. If you're not familiar with them by now, go out and buy a modern saddle (Figs. 10.1–2).

A saddle with a plastic shell and foam padding requires little maintenance except keeping

10.2 Saddle designed to not contact the perineum

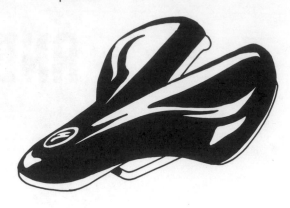

10.3 Brooks leather saddle

it clean; check periodically that the rails are not bent or cracked (a good sign that you need to replace the saddle).

x-2
POSITIONING THE SADDLE

Even if you have found the perfect saddle, it can still feel like some medieval torture device if it isn't properly positioned. Saddle placement is the most important part of finding a comfortable riding position. Not only does saddle position affect how you feel on the bike, but also you become a much better rider with the saddle in the right place. There are three basic elements to saddle position: tilt, fore-and-aft, and saddle height (Fig. 10.4).

See Appendix C, §C-3, for a detailed explanation of setting saddle and handlebar position. The following are some short guidelines.

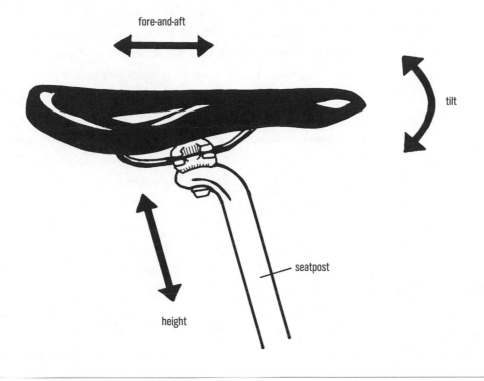

fore-and-aft

tilt

seatpost

height

Proper saddle height (Fig. 10.4) is key to transferring good power to the pedals. The ideal saddle height for cross-country mountain bike racing places your leg in a 90–95 percent extension (knee bend of 25–30 degrees) when your foot is at bottom dead center when you are riding (Fig. 10.5). However, you may find this position to be too high for riding technical singletrack, and it is way too high for gravity-driven mountain biking.

Make sure the seatpost is inserted deeper than the limit line.

To improve your balance and center of gravity when riding a descent, bring the saddle height down—how far depends on you and the kind of riding you do. Pro downhill racers prefer very low saddle heights when compared with pro cross-country racers. You can also use a seatpost that goes up and down at the release of a lever, so that you can pedal efficiently on nontechnical sections and can drop the seatpost lower for technical descending.

10.5 Knee bend at bottom dead center should be 25–30 degrees from straight for cross-country riding.

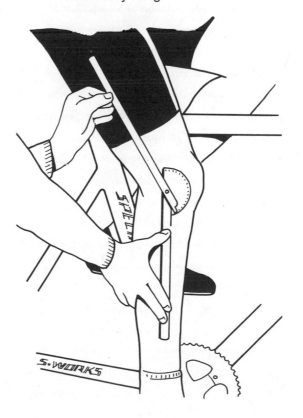

A common cause of numb crotch and butt fatigue (and even sore arms and shoulders) is an improperly tilted saddle (Fig. 10.4). The general rule of thumb is that you should keep the saddle level when you first install it, although it may take a slight downward tilt (maximum of 2 degrees) at the nose to accomplish this—the long seatpost extensions on many mountain bikes mean that there may be enough flex in the seatpost and saddle such that a saddle with a 2-degree downward slope becomes level when you sit on it. After a while, some people find that they prefer a slight upward or downward tilt to their saddles. Other than perhaps for downhill riders, I strongly discourage making that tilt difference between nose and tail much more than ¼ inch (6mm) in height. Too much upward tilt places too much of your body weight on the nose of the saddle. Too much downward tilt will cause you to scoot down the saddle as you ride. That puts unnecessary pressure on your back, shoulders, and neck.

Fore-and-aft position (Fig. 10.4) determines where your butt sits on the saddle, the position of your knees relative to the pedals, and how much of your weight is transferred to your hands. Regardless of manufacturer, all saddles are designed to have your butt centered over the widest part. If this is not where you sit, reposition the saddle. You want to position the saddle so that you have a comfortable amount of bend in your arms without feeling too cramped or stretched out. If you find that your neck and shoulders feel tighter than usual and your hands are going numb, try redistributing your weight by moving the saddle back. Fore-and-aft saddle position also affects how your legs are positioned relative to the pedals. Ideally, your fore-and-aft position should be such that your knee pushes straight down on the forward pedal when the crankarms are in a perfectly horizontal position. If the saddle will not go back as far as you wish and you have a short-length women's saddle, try replacing it with a standard-length men's model.

Butt pain is intimately connected to handlebar position, as are other aches and pains. The shorter the upper-body reach and higher the handlebar, the more weight will go on the butt. The longer the reach and lower the handlebar, the more the top of the pelvis rotates forward and moves the saddle pressure point from the sit bones to the soft tissue of the perineum and genital area. As a general rule, a novice rider will want a shorter reach, a higher handlebar, and perhaps a correspondingly wider saddle than will an experienced rider. Once again, consult Appendix C.

X-3
MAINTAINING THE SEATPOST

A standard seatpost requires little maintenance other than removing it from the frame every few months. When you do that, wipe it down, regrease it, dry out and grease the inside of the frame's seat tube (turn the bike upside down to pour out any trapped water), and then reinstall the seatpost. Also do this after any ride in the rain. This maintenance keeps the seatpost clean and moving freely for the purposes of adjustability. It also should prevent the seatpost from getting stuck in the frame (a very nasty and potentially serious problem), and will prevent a steel seat tube from rusting out from the inside. The procedures for installing a new seatpost are in §x-8, and those for removing a stuck seatpost are in §x-11.

To be extra sure of not getting the seatpost stuck in the frame, run a thin bead of silicone bathtub sealer around the base of the seatpost where it enters the seat tube as well as up the slot in the seat tube. Do this every time you remove or reposition the seatpost to prevent water from entering the seat tube.

Suspension seatposts require periodic tune-ups (see §x-9). Regularly check any seatpost for

Carbon seatposts

Carbon-fiber seatposts are susceptible to breakage if the seatpost-clamping mechanism digs in and cuts some fibers or makes a notch in the post. Point-loading on a thin carbon part is not a good idea. Unless you have a special seatpost binder clamp intended for carbon seatposts, you should reverse the binder clamp so that its slot is not lined up with the seat-tube slot. That way, it will pull more evenly around the circumference and not push the slot into the seatpost (Fig. 10.6). And if you have a slotted seat-tube shim tube that some bikes have to fit the seatpost, you should offset that slot from the other two slots as well. You can imagine how the top corners of the slot could dig into the back of the seatpost (where the load on it is also highest) if you crank down on the bolt with the slots of the binder clamp and seat tube and perhaps a seat-tube shim all stacked up there. This is where carbon seatposts break.

Carbon seatposts often slip down because the clear coat layer on the outside is soft and gets compressed by the clamping pressure. This of course also leads to the user tightening the bolt more, thereby increasing the probability of it snapping off. If the post slips, use some carbon assembly paste or spray on it (Fig. 10.6). This stuff works because the small plastic spheres in the solution press back against the clamp to increase

the pressure uniformly and avoid point-loading. In the absence of carbon assembly paste, try not greasing the post. Unlike an aluminum or a steel seatpost, a carbon post itself cannot corrode, so grease to prevent seizure is less of an issue. However, corrosion of a surrounding aluminum seat tube or seat-tube sleeve can nonetheless seize the post, so the best solution is carbon assembly compound.

10.6 Spraying CarboGrip carbon assembly compound on a carbon post

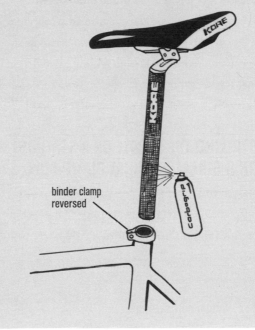

binder clamp reversed

cracks or bends so that you can replace it before the seatpost breaks with you on it.

If your bike has a carbon seatpost, make sure to read the Pro Tip on this subject.

x-4
INSTALLING THE SADDLE

 LEVEL 1

Remember the heavy steel posts with the skinny section on top on kids' bikes (or on cheap adult

bikes)? Those seatposts have a separate saddle clamp that slides down over the seatpost shaft, and a single horizontal bolt that pulls together a number of knurled washers with ears to hold the saddle rails. They are cheap to make, being simply a steel tube with some washers and a bolt, but they do not hold up well to adult use.

Much more secure (and generally lighter) is a seatpost with an integrated saddle clamp. Most posts have either one or two bolts for clamping the saddle.

A single-bolt seatpost can have either a vertical bolt or a horizontal bolt. The vertical bolt pulls two clamshell clamp halves together (Figs. 10.4 and 10.7). The horizontal bolt pulls two ears of the clamp toward each other to clamp the rails, and the ears may even slide down on angled ramps so that tightening the bolt pulls the rails down onto the saddle cradle as well as against it from the sides.

The two-bolt posts can rely on one of three systems. In one system, the two bolts work together, pulling the saddle rails into the clamp (Fig. 10.8). In the second system, such as the American Classic post, a smaller second bolt works to offset the force of the main bolt (Fig. 10.9). In the third system, two side-by-side bolts hold the saddle clamp together.

No matter which type you have, it is reasonably easy to figure out how to remove, install, and adjust the saddle.

x-5
INSTALLING THE SADDLE ON A SEATPOST WITH A SINGLE VERTICAL CLAMP BOLT

Systems with a single vertical bolt (Fig. 10.7) usually have a two-piece clamp that fastens onto the saddle rails. On most single-bolt mod-els, moving the clamp and saddle along a serrated curved platform controls saddle tilt. Before you tighten the clamp bolt, make sure there is no second, much smaller bolt (or setscrew) that adjusts seat tilt. If you find a second bolt, skip to §x-6.

1. **Loosen the bolt.** Loosen until there are only a couple of threads holding the upper clamp.

2. **Turn the top half of the clamp 90 degrees, and slide in the saddle rails.** Slide the saddle in from the back where the space between the rails is wider. You might need to remove the top of the clamp from the bolt completely if the clamp is too large. If you do disassemble the clamp, pay attention to the orientation of the parts so that you can put them back together the same way.

3. **Install the saddle.** Set the seat rails into the grooves in the saddle cradle piece, and set the top clamp piece on top of the rails (Fig. 10.10). Slide the saddle to the desired fore-and-aft position.

4. **Tighten the bolt and check the seat tilt.** Readjust if necessary.

10.7 Single-bolt seatpost

10.8 Two-bolt seatpost

x-6
INSTALLING THE SADDLE ON A SEATPOST WITH TWO EQUAL-SIZED CLAMP BOLTS

This type of post is illustrated in Figure 10.8.

1. **Loosen or remove one or both of the bolts.** Loosen the bolts until you can open the clamp enough to perform step 2.

2. **Install the saddle.** Slide either the top clamp piece or saddle cradle piece out, set the saddle rails in their grooves in the piece remaining on the post, and then slide the piece you removed back in from the side.

3. **Slide the saddle to the desired fore-and-aft position.** Tighten down one or both of the clamp bolts completely.

4. **Set the saddle tilt.** Loosen one clamp bolt, and tighten the other to change the tilt of the saddle (Fig. 10.11). Repeat as necessary. Complete by tightening both bolts.

x-7
INSTALLING THE SADDLE ON A SEATPOST WITH A LARGE CLAMP BOLT AND A SMALL SETSCREW

This type of post is illustrated in Figure 10.9 and used to be much more common.

1. **Loosen the large clamp bolt.** Loosen until the top part of the clamp can either be removed or rotated out of the way so that you can slide the saddle rails into place.

2. **Install the saddle.** Place the saddle rails into the grooves in the cradle, and set the grooves of the top clamp piece down over them. Slide the saddle to the desired fore-and-aft position. Tighten the large bolt.

3. **Adjust the saddle tilt.** Loosen the large clamp bolt, adjust the saddle angle as needed by turning the tilt-adjustment bolt, and retighten the clamp bolt. Repeat until the desired adjustment is reached.

10.9 Single-bolt seatpost with small adjusting bolt

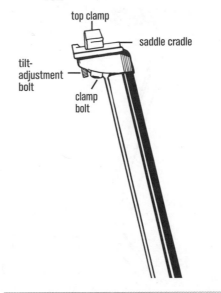

10.10 Saddle installation on a single-bolt seatpost

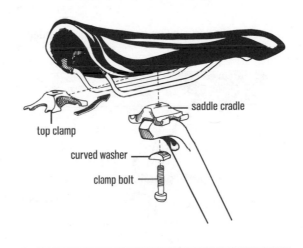

10.11 Saddle installation on a two-bolt seatpost

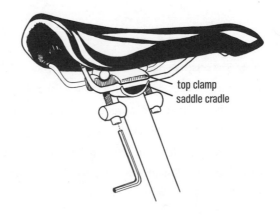

SADDLES AND SEATPOSTS

10.12 Seatpost installation into the frame

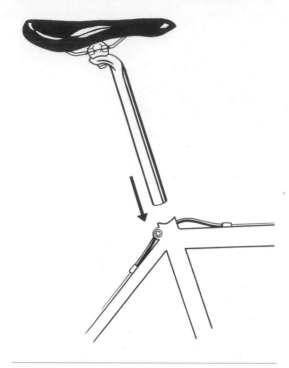

10.13 Closing a quick-release seatpost binder

NOTE: *The setscrew may be vertical or horizontal. With a vertical setscrew (Fig. 10.9), the screw is usually adjacent to the clamp bolt. A horizontal setscrew is usually positioned at the top front of the seatpost, pushing back on the clamp. With such a setscrew, push down on the back of the saddle with the clamp bolt loose to make sure the clamp and setscrew are in contact.*

x-8

INSTALLING THE SEATPOST INTO THE FRAME

1. **Check for irregularities, burrs, and other problems inside the seat tube.** Check visually and manually with your finger; if there are some, you may need to sand or otherwise clean out the inside of the seat tube. It may be necessary for a bike shop to ream the seat tube if a seatpost of the correct size will not fit.

2. **Grease the seatpost, the inside of the seat tube, and the binder bolt.** If you are using a sleeve or shim to adapt an undersized seatpost to fit the frame, grease it inside and out, and insert it.

3. **Insert the seatpost (Fig. 10.12) and tighten the seat binder bolt.** Some binder bolts are tightened with a wrench (usually a 5mm hex), and some have a quick-release lever (Fig. 10.13). To tighten a quick-release, flip the lever open so that it is directly in line with the body of the bolt—in other words, about halfway open. Finger-tighten the nut on the other end, and then close the lever. It should be fairly snug, about tight enough to leave an impression in the heel of your hand for a few seconds. Open the lever, reposition the end nut, and close the lever again as necessary to get the right closing force.

4. **Adjust the seat height to your desired position.** It is a good idea to mark this height on the post with an indelible marker or a piece of tape. This way, if you remove the seatpost, you can just slide it right back to the proper place.

IMPORTANT: *As mentioned in §x-3, periodically remove the seatpost, invert the bike to drain water out of the seat tube, and let it dry out. The frequency depends on the conditions you are riding in; certainly do it after a ride in pouring rain. For a steel frame, spray oil (or better yet, JP Weigle Frame Saver) into the seat tube to arrest the rusting process; this might help with oxida-*

10.14 Suspension seatpost

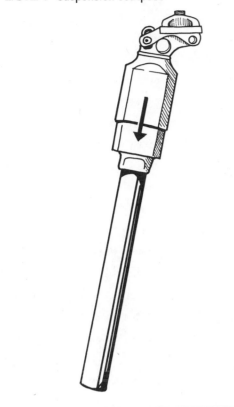

tion inside aluminum and magnesium frames as well. Regrease the post and the inside of the seat tube, and reinstall the post.

x-9
ADJUSTING SUSPENSION SEATPOSTS

Shock-absorbing seatposts come equipped with some sort of spring—either a steel coil, an elastic polymer ("elastomer"), or an air cushion. The telescoping, elastomer spring type (Fig. 10.14) is probably the most common. Some seatposts have linkages that swing the saddle on an arc, rather than up and down.

To adjust the "boing" in most suspension seatposts, either change the amount of preload on the elastomer spring or replace the elastomer(s). With telescoping seatposts (Fig. 10.14), and even with some parallelogram-linkage posts, you must first pull the seatpost out of the frame.

If you look up inside a telescoping seatpost from the bottom, you will usually see a large slotted screw threaded into the walls of the post. If you tighten the screw clockwise, you will increase the preload on the spring and hence stiffen the seatpost. If you loosen the screw (counterclockwise), you will reduce the preload and soften the ride.

To change springs, remove the screw and then the spring completely, make the switch (remember to grease the elastomers!), and replace the screw. You will find that as you change preload or elastomer combinations, the height of your saddle changes, so expect to slide the seatpost up and down in the frame to adjust for this.

Some parallelogram-linkage posts can be adjusted by turning a preload screw behind the saddle clamp and/or pushing the elastomer out from the side and replacing it (or interchanging small elastomer plugs into a larger elastomer).

There are other suspension-seatpost designs available as well, and it is difficult to provide instructions that apply to all of them. Fortunately, most shock-absorbing seatposts are tuned as described here, and the others usually come with extensive instructions.

I recommend following the same regular maintenance procedures you would use for a standard seatpost (§x-3), in addition to maintenance of the suspension components.

IMPORTANT: *See the "Important" note under §x-8.*

x-10
ADJUSTING HEIGHT-ADJUSTABLE TELESCOPING SEATPOSTS

Seatposts such as the Maverick SpeedBall, the Crank Brothers Joplin (same as the Maverick; Fig. 10.15), and the GravityDropper allow the rider to vary seat height with the flip of a lever, the push of a button, or the pull of a knob. These seatposts generally have two positions: a high saddle for pedaling efficiency and a low saddle

10.15 Maverick SpeedBall/Crank Brothers Joplin
height-adjustable seatpost overhaul

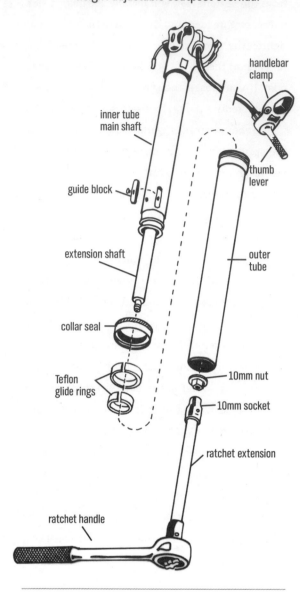

inner tube
main shaft

guide block

extension shaft

collar seal

Teflon
glide rings

ratchet handle

handlebar
clamp

thumb
lever

outer
tube

10mm nut

10mm socket

ratchet extension

for safe descent of technical trails, although some have multiple positions into which they can lock.

To raise the saddle, push and hold the button or lever or pull the knob while standing up off the saddle; release the lever, knob, or button when the saddle reaches its high position. Some posts require you to be sitting down when initially operating the lever, button, or knob to release the mechanism and then stand up. To lower the

saddle, push and hold the button or lever or pull the knob while sitting on the saddle; release the lever, knob, or button when the saddle reaches its low position.

I recommend following the same regular maintenance procedures you would use for a standard seatpost (§x-3), and wipe and lube the extending inner seatpost shaft after every ride or two on Maverick and Crank Brothers height-adjust posts. The GravityDropper has a rubber boot over it, but it and the shaft are easy to remove for a quick lube. Here's how to do it:

1. **Lift the lower portion of the rubber boot.** The post must be in the up position.

2. **Remove the top cap.** An open-end or adjustable wrench will do the trick.

3. **Push the handlebar switch or pull knob and hold it.**

4. **Gently pull out the inner post.**

5. **Thoroughly clean and lubricate.** Use a light lithium grease.

6. **Push the handlebar switch or pull knob and hold it.**

7. **Reinstall the inner post and tighten the top cap.**

Maverick/Crank Brothers posts should be overhauled every 50–100 hours of riding. Here's how to do it:

1. **Remove the seatpost from the bike.** There's no need to remove the saddle.

2. **Remove the threaded collar seal.** Unscrew the seal by hand (you may need to carefully break it free with a pipe wrench or pliers), and slide it up the inner tube.

3. **Remove the nut from inside the bottom of the outer tube** (Fig. 10.15). Use a 10mm socket on an extension to reach the nut.

4. **Slide the inner tube out of the outer tube.**

5. **Clean the components thoroughly.** Use a light solvent/degreaser and/or a clean rag. Push

the clean rag down into the outer tube with a dowel.

6. Apply a slick petroleum-based grease (**Slick Honey** works well). Smear it all around on the main shaft, extension shaft, guide block, and Teflon glide rings (Fig. 10.15).

7. **Insert the inner tube back into the outer tube.**

8. **Thread the 10mm nut onto the compression shaft.** Tighten it to 4 N-m (35 in-lbs) of torque.

9. **Put the seatpost in the lowered position.**

10. **Screw on the collar seal.**

Worn parts can be replaced if the seatpost develops excessive rotational or fore-and-aft play. These seatposts are such niche products that I won't take the space to describe how to replace them; you can find instructions online.

However, I have a few words of caution. First, be careful of stripping bolts. Replacing the cable from the handlebar button or lever (or even adjusting its length) is more delicate than replacing, say, a derailleur cable, mainly because the cable-fixing bolts are so small and can easily be stripped.

Second, watch out for the post's main spring. The GravityDropper has a coil spring, and the Maverick and Crank Brothers posts have an air spring; either type of spring can be dangerous if you are not careful, so get out of the way when working on it. You can fully deflate the SpeedBall/Joplin air spring through its Schrader valve (at the center of the 10mm nut mentioned previously), but to get all of the air out, you must cycle the spring up and down using the release lever while the post is upside down. Once the block that guides the post has been removed, don't touch the release lever in case there is still air inside. On the GravityDropper, unscrew the bottom cap slowly, and keep your face away from the end of the tube where the spring will shoot out.

IMPORTANT: *See the "Important" note under §x-8.*

⚙ ⚙ ⚙ LEVEL 3

The seatpost can get stuck when you do not follow the "Important" note in §x-8. This is a level 3 task because of the risk involved. This may be a job best done by a shop, because if you make a mistake, you run the risk of destroying the frame. If you're not 100 percent confident in your abilities, go to someone who is—or at least to someone who will be responsible if he or she screws it up.

1. **Remove the seat binder bolt.** Slide the binder collar up the seatpost. Easy enough.

2. **Squirt ammonia around the seatpost, and let it sit overnight.** Ammonia dissolves aluminum oxide; automotive antifreeze or Coca-Cola (yes, the soft drink) often will as well; penetrating oil will work only with a steel seatpost in a steel frame. To get the most penetration, remove the bottom bracket (Chapter 8); turn the bike upside down; pour ammonia, antifreeze, or Coke in from the bottom of the seat tube; and let the bike sit upside down overnight.

3. **Stand over the bike and twist the saddle.**

4. **If step 3 does not free the seatpost, use thermal expansion/contraction.** The idea is to get either the seatpost to shrink and pull away from the seat tube, the seat tube to expand and pull away from the seatpost, or both. But you must be aware of the relative Coefficient of Thermal Expansion (CTE) of the materials the seatpost and seat tube are made of. The CTE of aluminum (and of magnesium) is about double that of steel, and the CTE of carbon is almost zero.

(a) If you have a carbon-fiber seatpost stuck in a frame made out of any of these materials, warm up the seat-lug area with a hair dryer (or even a heat gun, if you're careful) to expand it.

(b) If you have an aluminum seatpost stuck inside a carbon or steel frame, cool the seatpost down. If there is a big enough hole from the bottom-bracket shell into the seat tube after you've removed the crankset, drop in small hunks of dry ice, and let the post get really cold. From the outside, discharge the entire cartridge of a tire inflator at the joint of the seatpost and the seat collar to freeze the seatpost and shrink it. (Alternatively, cool the exposed seatpost with a plastic bag filled with dry ice.)

(c) If both parts are made of the same metal, you can still try to cool the post rapidly while you heat the seat lug in hopes they'll shrink and expand in opposite directions.

(d) Now try twisting as in step 3.

5. **If step 4 does not free the seatpost, you will need to move into the difficult and risky part of this procedure:**

(a) Clamp the top of the seatpost into a large bench vise that is bolted to a very secure workbench. Remove the saddle and all the clamps from the top of the seatpost first, and turn the bike upside down above the vise. You have just ruined your seatpost. Don't ever ride it again.

(b) Perform the thermal expansion/contraction trick from step 4.

(c) Grab the frame at both ends, and begin to carefully apply a twisting pressure. Be aware that you can easily apply enough force to bend or crack the frame, so be careful. If the seatpost finally releases, it often makes such a large "pop" that you will think you have broken many things!

6. **If that did not work, take the bike to a car repair shop.** Ask a mechanic to smack the underside of the seatpost clamp with an air impact hammer. If this maneuver works, it will take seconds and won't damage the frame. Be forewarned, however, that the action is loud and violent.

7. **If step 6 fails, cut off the seatpost a few inches above the seat lug.** There are a number of things you can try now:

(a) Warm up the seat-lug area with a hair dryer to expand it. Discharge the entire cartridge of a tire inflator down inside the seatpost to freeze and shrink it. Now clamp what's left of the seatpost in a vise, and try twisting as in step 5.

(b) Get your hands on a slide hammer; borrow or rent one from an auto body–related business. This is a tool for pulling dents out of car bodies and consists of a long rod with a heavy cylindrical weight (5-pound is a good size for this) that slides along it. The end of the rod can be attached to what you are pulling by a number of means, and when you rapidly slide the weight toward the handle, it pulls the whole rod forcibly in the direction of the handle when it hits the handle. To attach the slide hammer rod end to the seatpost, either clamp vise-grip pliers to the post or drill a transverse hole through it. Assemble the slide onto the slide hammer rod, and attach its end to either the pliers with clamping jaws or into the holes via hooks that point inward toward each other. Have someone hold the frame (the inertia of the frame makes it easy to hold even when you are in the act of freeing the post), and slam the weight toward the end away from the frame. Chances are, it will pop right out.

(c) Drill a ½-inch (13mm) hole transversely through the seatpost, insert a long steel rod through it, have somebody hold the frame, and twist on it as hard as you can. The post will make a huge noise if it comes free.

8. **If the seatpost is still not free, try one of two (completely undesirable) alternatives:**

   (a) Go to a machine shop and get the remaining seatpost reamed out of the seat tube. The chances of the shop managing to line everything up perfectly so that the cutter does not make a hole in the seat tube are not good.

   (b) Cut the remaining seatpost out by hand. Sit down and think for a while before you take on this job, and then proceed carefully, because there is a risk of completely trashing the frame. Here's how to do it:

   i. Cut the seatpost off a little more than an inch above the seat lug on the frame. Use a hacksaw.

   ii. Remove the blade from the saw, and wrap a piece of tape around one end of the blade. You're making a handle with which to grab the blade.

   iii. Hold on to the taped end, and slip the other end into the center of the post.

   iv. Carefully (very carefully) make two outward radial cuts about 60 degrees apart. Your goal is to remove a wedge from the hunk of seatpost stuck in the frame. Be careful—this is where many people cut too far and go right through the seatpost and into the frame. Of course you wouldn't do that, would you?

   NOTE: *A much faster but also more dangerous method is to use a reciprocating handheld jigsaw with a long blade for wood. It will go through an aluminum seatpost very quickly. The question is, what will it do to your frame? On a steel or titanium frame, the wood blade may only polish the inside of the seat tube where it hits the tube. The blade will probably go through a carbon, aluminum, or magnesium frame just as easily as it goes through an aluminum seatpost, though.*

   v. Work the remaining piece out. Once you've made the cut, pry or pull this piece out with a large screwdriver or a pair of pliers. Be careful here, too. A lot of over-enthusiastic home mechanics have damaged their frames by prying too hard. Curl in the edges with the pliers to free more and more of the seatpost from the seatpost walls. The seatpost should eventually work its way out.

9. **If all else fails, dissolve the seatpost.** If you happen to be someone with access, a metal such as gallium that is liquid at near room temperature will dissolve aluminum. But if the frame is aluminum, then you're stuck. And whatever the frame is made out of, you'd better get a chunk of that material and put some of the liquid metal on it first to see what happens before you go near the frame with it.

IMPORTANT: *Once the seatpost is out of the frame, remember to go back and reread §x-3 outlining the regular maintenance procedures required for a seatpost. In other words, take the seatpost out and apply grease every once in a while. You don't want to have to do this again, do you?*

TROUBLESHOOTING PROBLEMS IN THE SEAT AND SEATPOST

x-12
LOOSE SADDLE

Check the seatpost clamp bolts. They are probably loose. Reestablish your fore-and-aft saddle position (§x-2) and your saddle tilt, and tighten the bolts. Check for any damage to the clamping mechanism, and replace the post if necessary. If you need help, look up the instructions that apply to your seatpost.

x-13
STUCK SEATPOST

A stuck seatpost can be a serious problem. Follow the instructions in §x-11 carefully. Otherwise, you might damage your frame.

x-14
SADDLE SQUEAK WITH EACH PEDAL STROKE

The problem comes from the smooth leather or plastic moving against metal parts or from grit in the rail attachments.

1. **Lubricate the contact points of the saddle with the clamp and rails.** On saddles that extend low on the sides, contact of the leather overlapping the saddle shell with the seatpost clamp or rails is likely the culprit. Greasing or powdering the contact area with talcum will eliminate the noise. Also, roughing up the leather at the point where it contacts metal will quiet it down, because smooth leather sliding on metal can squeak.

2. **Try squirting chain lube into the three points where the rails are inserted into the plastic shell of the saddle** in case some grit working at the rails is making the noise.

3. **Grease the rails where they sit in the channels in the seatpost clamp.**

x-15
CREAKING NOISES FROM THE SEATPOST

A seatpost can creak from movement of the clamp that holds the saddle, or movement of the shaft against the sides of the seat tube while you ride. A dry seatpost can also cause creaks, so first try greasing it.

1. **On frames with an internal collar, shorten the seatpost.** Some frames have an internal collar to adapt the seat tube to a certain seatpost diameter. Remember that the internal diameter of the seat tube is larger below the collar. I have seen bikes that creaked because the bottom of the seatpost rubbed against the sides of the seat tube below the extension of the collar. You can solve that problem by shortening the seatpost a bit with a hacksaw. If you do saw off the seatpost, make sure that

you still have at least 3 inches of seatpost inserted in the frame for security.

2. **If movement among the frame, sizing shims, and post is causing creaking, grease all these parts well.**

3. **If the creaking originates from the seatpost head where the saddle is clamped, check the clamp bolts.** Lubricate the bolt threads, and you will be able to tighten them a bit more.

4. **If shock-absorbing seatposts squeak as they move up and down, try greasing the sides of the inner shaft.** Grease the elastomers inside too.

x-16
SEATPOST SLIPPING DOWN

1. **Tighten the frame binder bolt.**

2. **If the seatpost still slips, try using some carbon assembly paste or spray, especially if it is a carbon seatpost** (see Pro Tip earlier in the chapter). Grease and sand, or valve-grinding compound, on the seatpost is a poor second alternative.

3. **Check the seatpost diameter.** If the seat-binder lug is pinched closed, and you still can't get the post to not slip down, even with assembly paste, you may be using a seatpost with an incorrect diameter, or the seat tube on the bike is oversized or has been stretched. Try putting a larger seatpost in the frame, and replace if you find one that fits better. If the next size up is too big, you may need to shim the existing post. Cut a 1 × 3–inch piece of aluminum from a pop can. Pull the seatpost out, grease it and the pop-can shim, and insert both back into your frame. Bend the top lip of the shim over to prevent it from disappearing inside the frame. You may need to experiment with various shim dimensions until you find a piece that will go in with the seatpost and also prevent slippage. Go ahead—pop cans are cheap.

HANDLEBARS, STEMS, AND HEADSETS

The great thing in this world is not so much where you stand, as in what direction you are moving.

—Oliver Wendell Holmes Jr.

On a bike, you maintain or change your direction largely by applying force to the handlebar. If everything works properly, variations in that pressure will result in your front wheel changing direction. Pretty basic, right? Right. But there is a somewhat complex series of parts between the handlebar and the wheel that makes that simple process possible. The parts of the steering system are illustrated in Figure 11.1. In this chapter, we cover most of that system by going over handlebars, stems, and headsets. The explanations in this chapter start at the outside of each end of the handlebar and move toward the middle.

BAR ENDS

xi-1
INSTALLING BAR ENDS

 **LEVEL 1**

Bar ends are meant to provide a powerful hand position while you are climbing, as well as an alternative stretched-out position while you are riding on smooth roads. They are not meant to

be positioned vertically to provide a higher hand position. If you want your hands higher, get a taller, more vertical stem and a riser handlebar that has a double bend to elevate the ends. This way you still have easy access to the brake levers.

1. **Slide the shifters, brake levers, and grips inward.** This makes room at the end of the handlebar for the bar end. See §xi-3 for instructions on moving the grips and Chapters 5 and 7 for moving shifters and brake levers, respectively.

2. **Loosen the bolt on the bar-end clamp.** This bolt usually accepts a 5mm hex key.

3. **Slide the bar end onto the handlebar** (Fig. 11.2).

4. **Tighten the clamp bolt enough that it just holds the bar end in place.** Rotate the bar ends to the position you like (see Appendix C, §C-3e, for position recommendations).

5. **Tighten the clamp bolt.** Make sure it is snug. (Recommended torque is in Appendix D.)

NOTE: *The ends of some superlight handlebars can be damaged by bar ends and therefore come equipped with small, cylindrical, aluminum inserts that provide support under the bar ends when inserted at*

TOOLS

4mm, 5mm, and 6mm hex keys

headset wrenches (two) sized to headset

bike stand

hammer

screwdriver

hacksaw

flat file

round file

glue stick

electrical tape

grease

isopropyl alcohol

scissors, tin snips, or knife

OPTIONAL

star-nut installation tool

threadless saw guide

carbon-specific hacksaw blade

carbon assembly paste or spray

continued

11.1 Steering assembly (shown without brakes for clarity)

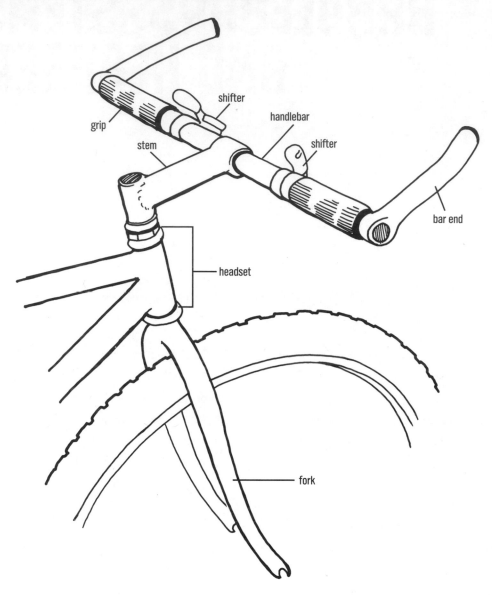

11.2 Grip and bar-end assembly, exploded view

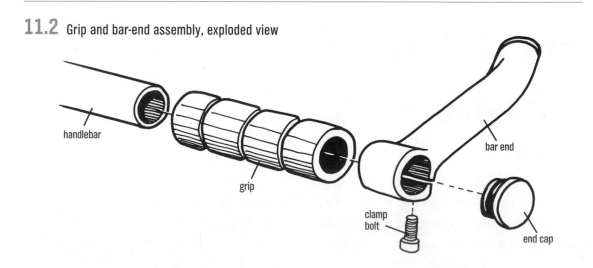

the ends of the handlebar. Similarly, some composite handlebars have aluminum reinforcements at their ends to add support under the bar end. These types of handlebars cannot be shortened, as the bar ends will not have the support that they need.

xi-2
REMOVING BAR ENDS

1. **Loosen the bolt on the bar-end clamp.** This bolt usually accepts a 5mm hex key.
2. **Pull the bar end off** (Fig. 11.2).

GRIPS

xi-3
REMOVING THE GRIP

 LEVEL 1

If the grip is shot, just cut it off with a knife. Otherwise, do the following:

1. **Remove the bar end and bar-end plug** (Fig. 11.2, §xi-2) **if installed.**
2. **Roll back an edge of the grip on itself.**
3. **Squirt rubbing alcohol on the handlebar and the underside of the exposed grip** (Fig. 11.3). Flip the rolled-up edge back down, and repeat steps 2 and 3 on the other end of the grip.
4. **Starting at the ends, twist the grip back and forth as you pull outward on it** (Fig. 11.4). The wet sections will slip easily, and the dry middle section will start moving as the ends twist. Pull the grip off.

xi-4
INSTALLING THE GRIP

1. **Squirt rubbing alcohol inside the grip.** This is usually not necessary with a lock-on grip (it will have a clamping collar with a binder bolt on either end of the grip). Rubbing alcohol lubricates well and dries quickly (immediately with a blast of compressed air!). Water

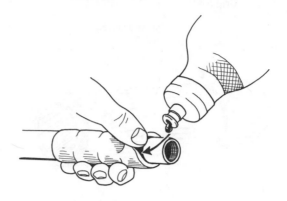

11.4 Grip removal

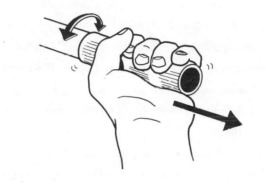

dries slowly, so the grip slips for a few days. Hairspray and spray adhesives can be used to prevent grip slippage, but they are bad to breathe, and they can set up permanently, thereby thwarting subsequent removal and repositioning.

PRO TIP

Grip removal

A syringe can be used to inject rubbing alcohol under the grip. The needle can be slipped under the grip from the end, and it can even be pushed through the grip. With alcohol underneath, the grip will slide off in seconds.

2. **Slide and twist the grip onto the handlebar.**

NOTE: *Some grips have a closed end. If you are going to use bar ends, you will need to cut off the closed*

HANDLEBARS, STEMS, AND HEADSETS

11.5 Trimming grip to accommodate bar end or Grip Shift

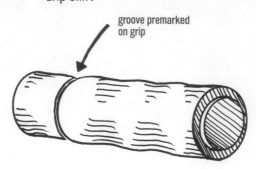

groove premarked on grip

11.6 Clamp-type stem for threadless headset

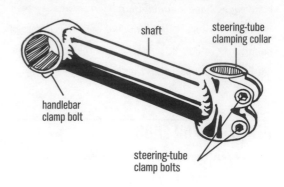

shaft

steering-tube clamping collar

handlebar clamp bolt

steering-tube clamp bolts

end; you may also want to shorten the grip to adjust to your hand size or to adapt to a twist shifter. Some grips have a groove that marks where they are meant to be cut with a pair of scissors (Fig. 11.5). Otherwise, you can cut them off anywhere you wish with scissors, tin snips, or a knife. If you have a thin, lightweight handlebar, you can easily cut off the end of the grip by hitting the end of the grip with a mallet or hammer after it is installed on the handlebar. The handlebar will cut a nice hole in the grip end like a cookie cutter! **ANOTHER NOTE:** *Grips used alongside Grip Shift and other twist shifters are shorter than standard grips, as part of the hand is sitting on the twist grip. Grips specifically designed for Grip Shift shifters are readily available in bike shops. If you can't find them, just cut the grips you have to the proper length.*

3. If this is a lock-on grip, tighten the screws on the collar on each end.

HANDLEBARS

xi-5
REMOVING THE HANDLEBAR

 LEVEL 1

1. **Remove the bar ends and grips** (Fig. 11.2), **followed by the brake levers and shifters.** Instructions for removal of bar ends and grips are in §xi-2 and §xi-3, for brake levers in Chapter 7, and for shifters in Chapter 5. If

you are going to replace the same handlebar (for instance, if you're removing the bar to ship your bike), you need remove only a grip, shifter, and brake lever from one side, or not at all if you have a front-opening stem (Fig. 11.7). It is easier to remove grips when the handlebar is clamped into the stem than when it is sitting on a workbench; therefore, if you are moving the parts to another handlebar, remove them while the handlebar is still on the bike.

2. **Loosen or remove the stem's handlebar clamp bolt(s).** With a single-bolt stem (Fig 11.8), just loosen that bolt. This bolt usually takes a 5mm hex key. With a front-opening stem, completely remove the front cap by removing the two, three, or four bolts that hold it on, with a 4mm or 5mm hex key.

3. **Pull the handlebar out.**

xi-6
INSTALLING THE HANDLEBAR

1. **Loosely mount the handlebar in the stem clamp.** With a single-bolt stem, remove the stem clamp bolts, grease the threads, and reinstall the bolt. Grease the inside of the stem clamp, and grease the clamping area in the center of the handlebar. With a front-opening stem, place the front cap over the handlebar and replace the bolts.

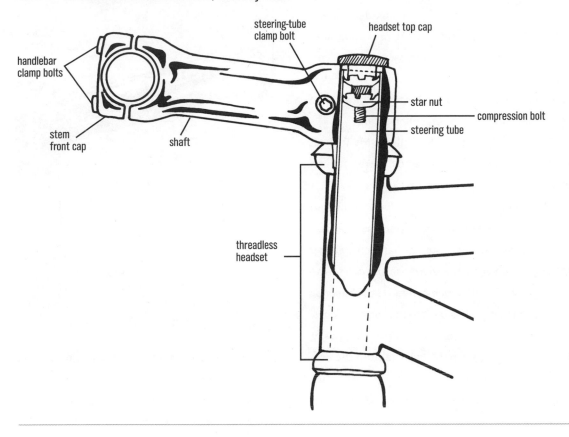

11.7 Threadless headset and stem, cutaway view

2. **Twist the handlebar to the position that you find most comfortable.** Usually, this is with ends pointed up and back, but the exact position is a matter of personal preference.

3. **Tighten bolts that clamp the handlebar to the stem.** Tighten to the recommended torque (Appendix D). The torque applied is particularly important with expensive, lightweight stems and handlebars. You can pinch, and thereby weaken, a lightweight handlebar by overtightening, and the high-strength tubing will crack right by the stem. Light stems come with small bolts with fine threads, and overtightening can strip the threads inside the aluminum (or magnesium, etc.) stem. If you don't have a torque wrench and you do have a lightweight stem with small bolts (e.g., M5 or M6 bolts, which take 4mm and 5mm hex keys, respectively), use a short hex key so that you can't get much leverage. Proper torque is even more important with carbon-fiber handlebars.

4. **Check the gaps at the stem clamp.** Make sure that there is the same amount of space between the stem and either edge of the front plate on a front-opening stem. Any stem whose clamp gap(s) gets pinched until touching when tightened around the handlebar needs to be replaced, along with the handlebar. This is because overtightening has stretched the stem cap and deformed and weakened the handlebar.

xi-7
MAINTAINING AND REPLACING THE HANDLEBAR

A bike cannot be controlled without a handlebar, so you never want one to break on you. Do not

HANDLEBARS, STEMS, AND HEADSETS

look at the handlebar on your bike as a permanent accessory. All aluminum handlebars will eventually fail. If titanium, steel, or carbon-fiber handlebars are repeatedly stressed above a certain level, they will eventually fail as well. What that level is depends on the particular handlebar. The trick is not to be riding when it fails.

Keep the handlebar clean. Regularly inspect it for cracks, crash-induced bends, corrosion, and stressed areas. If you find any sign of wear or cracking, replace the handlebar. Never straighten a bent handlebar—replace it! If you crash hard on your bike, consider replacing the handlebar even if it looks fine. If you have had a crash and can see no problems with the handlebar, remove the bar ends and check whether it is bent at the bar-end edges. A carbon-fiber handlebar can be broken internally, and the damage may not be visible from the outside. If the bar has taken an extremely hard hit, it's a good idea to replace it rather than gamble on its integrity. This is especially true with lightweight handlebars; the high hardness of the materials used may prevent visible bending, but they may be so weakened that they will soon shear off.

Some manufacturers recommend replacing stems and handlebars every four years. If you rarely ride the bike, this is overkill. If you ride hard and ride often, every four years may not be frequent enough. Do what is appropriate for you, and be aware of the risks.

STEMS

The approximately horizontal stem connects to the approximately vertical steering tube of the fork (which is either 1, 1⅛, or 1¼ inches in diameter) and clamps around the handlebar, which has one of two diameters: 25.4mm or 31.8mm. Stems come in two basic types: (1) threadless steering tubes (Fig. 11.7) or (2) threaded steering tubes (Fig. 11.9). Some stems have shock-absorbing

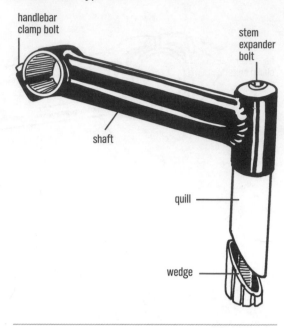

11.8 Quill-type stem

handlebar clamp bolt

stem expander bolt

shaft

quill

wedge

mechanisms with pivots and springs to provide suspension (Fig. 11.10).

Stems for threadless steering tubes (Fig. 11.6) have a clamping collar for the fork steering tube. Because the steering tube has no threads, the top headset cup slides on and off. In this case, the stem plays a dual role: It clamps around the steering tube to connect the handlebar to the fork, and it also keeps the headset in proper adjustment by preventing the top headset cup from sliding up the steering tube (Figs. 11.7 and 11.11). If you have an old 1-inch-diameter steering tube (the old standard) and a stem for a 1⅛-inch steering tube (the current standard), you can get a slotted aluminum reduction bushing (normally supplied with a new stem) to allow the stem to be used with the steering tube.

Stems for threaded steering tubes (Fig. 11.8) were the standard until the mid-1990s. They have a vertical "quill," which extends down into the steering tube of the fork and binds to the inside of the steering tube by means of a wedge-shaped plug pulled up by a long bolt that runs through the quill (Fig. 11.9).

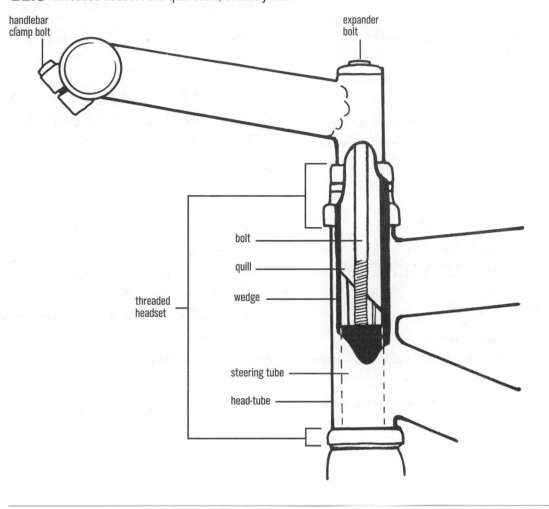

handlebar
clamp bolt

expander
bolt

bolt

quill

wedge

threaded
headset

steering tube

head-tube

11.10 Suspension stem, quill type

spring

quill

wedge

11.11 Threadless headset cup held in place
by stem

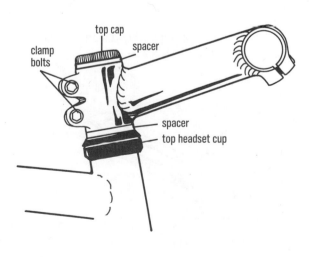

top cap

clamp
bolts

spacer

spacer

top headset cup

Suspension stems used to be quite popular and were made for both threadless and threaded steering tubes. The Softride stem (Fig. 11.10) uses a parallelogram system with four pivots to prevent the handlebar from twisting as it moves up and down. Others have a single pivot around which the handlebar swings in an arc. The spring is usually a steel coil or an elastic polymer ("elastomer"). Some suspension stems also come with a hydraulic damper to control the speed of movement.

xi-8
REMOVING A CLAMP-TYPE STEM FROM A THREADLESS STEERING TUBE

LEVEL 1

1. **Loosen the horizontal bolts clamping the stem around the steering tube.** This should take about two or three turns.

2. **Remove the adjusting bolt in the top cap covering the stem clamp** (Fig. 11.12). Unscrew it with a 5mm hex key. Removing this bolt will allow the fork to fall out, so hold the fork as you unscrew the bolt.

3. **With the bike standing on the floor to keep the fork from falling out, pull the cap and the stem off the steering tube.** Leave the bike standing until you replace the stem, or slide

the fork out of the frame, keeping track of all headset parts.

4. **If the stem will not budge, see §xi-14a.**

xi-9
INSTALLING AND ADJUSTING THE HEIGHT OF THE STEM ON A THREADLESS STEERING TUBE

LEVEL 2

Installing and adjusting the height of a stem on a threadless fork are much more complicated than installing and adjusting the height of a standard stem in a threaded fork. On a threadless fork, the stem is an integral part of the headset (Fig. 11.7), so any change to the stem position alters the headset adjustment. That's why this procedure carries a level 2 designation.

1. **Stand the bike up on its wheels so that the fork does not fall out.**

2. **Grease the parts.** Grease the top end of the steering tube if it is steel or aluminum, but leave it dry if it is carbon fiber. Loosen the stem clamp bolts and grease their threads.

3. **Slide the stem onto the steering tube.**

4. **Set the stem height to the desired level.** If you want to place the stem in a position higher than directly on top of the headset,

11.12 Loosening or tightening compression bolt on a threadless headset

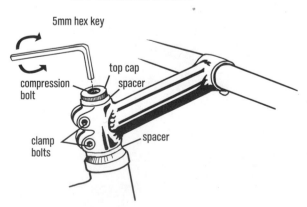

5mm hex key

compression bolt

top cap

spacer

clamp bolts

spacer

11.13 Steering-tube overlap

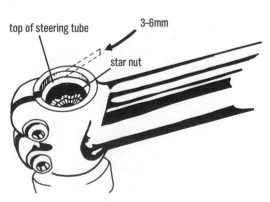

top of steering tube

3–6mm

star nut

you must put some spacers between the bottom of the stem clamp and the top piece of the headset. No matter what, there must be contact—through direct contact or through spacers (and including the top crown on a double-crown fork)—between the headset and the stem. Otherwise, the headset will be loose.

5. **Check the steering-tube overlap.** To adjust the threadless headset, the top of the stem clamp (or, ideally, spacers placed above it) should overlap the top of the steering tube by 3–6mm (⅛–¼ inch) (Fig. 11.13). If it does, skip ahead to step 8.

NOTE: *I recommend always having one spacer above the stem, especially with a carbon steering tube. If you add the spacer, measure the 3–6mm overlap from the top of the spacer, not from the stem. That way, the entire stem clamp is clamped onto the steering tube, and there is no chance for the upper part of the clamp to pinch the end of the steering tube.*

6. **If the steering tube is too short, move spacers or replace the fork:**

   (a) If the top spacer or the top of the stem clamp overlaps the top of the steering tube by more than 6mm (¼ inch), the steering tube is too short to set the stem height where you have it. If you have spacers below the stem, remove some until the top edge of the stem clamp (or spacer above it) overlaps the top of the steering tube by 3–6mm. If you cannot lower the stem any farther, or do not want to, get either a fork with a longer steering tube, a stem with a shorter clamp, or a stem that is angled upward more to attain your desired handlebar height. The stem is cheaper and easier to replace than the fork.

   (b) On many old suspension forks, you could simply replace the steering tube and fork-crown assembly with a longer one and bolt the existing fork legs into it. But

nowadays, to get a longer steering tube, you must replace the fork.

7. **If the steering tube is too long, move spacers or cut the tube:**

   (a) If the top of the steering tube is less than 3mm (⅛ inch) below the top spacer or the top edge of the stem clamp (or if the steering tube sticks up above the top of the stem clamp), you have a choice. If you want the option to raise the stem for a higher handlebar position, stack some headset spacers on top of the stem clamp until the spacers overlap the top edge of the steering tube by at least 3mm.

   (b) If, however, you are sure you will never want the stem any higher, then go ahead and cut off the excess tube. First, mark the steering tube along the top edge of the spacer above the stem clamp or the stem clamp itself (if you are not heeding my advice to always have at least a single thin spacer above the stem). Remove the fork from the bike. Make another mark on the steering tube 3mm below the first mark. Place the steering tube into a padded vise or bike-stand clamp.

   (c) There is a star-shaped nut that is inserted inside the steering tube (Fig. 11.7). The bolt through the top cap screws into it to adjust the headset bearings. If the star nut is already inside the steering tube and it looks like the saw will hit it, move the star nut down—see step 8 for instructions to do that.

   (d) Make your cut straight. Mark it straight by wrapping a piece of tape around the steering tube and cutting along the edge of the tape. If you are not sure your cut will be straight, start it a little higher and file it down flat to the tape edge. If you really want to be safe, use a tool specifically designed to help you make a straight cut. Park Tool's "threadless saw guide" will do the trick. Remember that you can always shorten the steering tube a little more, but you cannot make it longer! So apply the old adage "measure twice, cut once." Use a round file on the inside of the tube and a flat file on the outside to remove any metal burrs left by the hacksaw or cutter.

(e) When you have completed cutting and deburring, put the fork back in, replacing all of the headset parts in the way that they were originally installed (Figs. 11.18–20). Return to step 1.

NOTE: *If you are cutting a carbon-fiber steering tube, cut three-quarters of the way through and then turn the steering tube over and cut from the other side to meet your prior cut. This will prevent cutting all the way through and peeling layers of carbon back in the process.*

8. **Check that the edges of the star-shaped nut are at least 12mm below the top edge of the steering tube.** The nut must be far enough down that the bottom of the headset top cap does not hit it once the adjusting bolt is tightened. In the case of a steel or aluminum steering tube, if the nut is not in deep enough, you need to drive it deeper into the steering tube after removing the stem. In the case of a carbon steering tube, to anchor the top cap and to prevent crushing the carbon steering tube with the stem clamp, set an expander plug inside the steering tube under the stem clamp, usually by tightening its bolt with a hex key.

(a) Driving the star nut deeper into a metal steering tube is best done with a star-nut installation tool (Fig. 11.14). The tool threads into the nut, and you hit it with a hammer until it stops; the star nut will now be set 15mm deep in the steering tube. If you do not have this tool, go to a bike shop and have the nut set for you. If you insist on doing it yourself, follow the steps to push the star nut

11.14 Setting the star nut in the steering tube

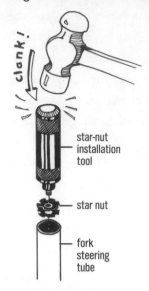

in deeper as outlined in (b). Just remember that it is easy to mangle the star nut if you do not tap it in straight.

(b) To push the star nut in farther without the proper tool, put the adjusting bolt through the top cap and thread it six turns into the star nut. Next, if the star nut is not already inside the steering tube, set it over the end of the steering tube and tap the top of the bolt with a mallet. Use the top cap as a guide to keep it going in straight. Finally, tap the bolt in until the star nut is 15mm (⅝ inch) below the top of the steering tube.

NOTE: *The wall thickness of steering tubes differs depending on whether they are made of steel or aluminum, the grade and heat treating they have, and the usage the fork is designed for. Therefore, the stock headset star nut may not fit in, and it will just bend when you try to install it. Even pros sometimes ruin star nuts. This is not a big problem, because replacements can be purchased separately. If the star nut goes in crookedly, take a long punch or rod, set it on top of the star nut, and drive it all the way out of the bottom of the steering tube. Dispose of the star nut and get another.*

Standard ID is 22.2mm (⅞ inch) for a 1-inch steel steering tube, 25.4mm (1 inch) for a 1⅛-inch steel steering tube, and 28.6mm (1¼ inches) for a 1¼-inch steel steering tube. If the steering tube is aluminum, its ID will be undersized. If the stock star nut from the headset does not fit, get one that is the correct size. Fork manufacturers often supply one with each fork. In a pinch, you can make an oversized stock star nut fit by bending each pair of opposite leaves of the star nut toward each other with a pair of Channel-lock pliers to reduce the nut's width. Now you can insert the nut; be aware that it may not grip as well as a properly sized one.

9. **Install the headset top cap on the top of the stem clamp or spacer(s) above it.** Grease the threads of the top-cap adjusting bolt, and thread it into the star nut inside the steering tube (Fig. 11.12).

10. **Adjust the headset and stem before tightening the stem bolts.** Line the stem up straight with the front wheel. Headset adjustment is explained in §xi-16.

11. **Tighten the stem bolts.** Tighten to the recommended torque (see Appendix D).

xi-10
REMOVING A STANDARD QUILL-TYPE STEM FROM A THREADED FORK

 LEVEL 1

1. **Loosen the stem anchor bolt on the top of the stem.** Unscrew it three turns or so. Most stem bolts take a 6mm hex key.

2. **Tap the top of the bolt down with a hammer** (Fig. 11.15). This disengages the wedge from the bottom of the quill. If the bolt is recessed in the stem so that a hammer cannot get at it, leave the hex key in the bolt and tap the top of the key until the wedge is free.

3. **Pull the stem out of the steering tube.** If the stem will not budge, see §xi-14b.

xi-11
INSTALLING AND ADJUSTING THE HEIGHT ON A QUILL STEM IN A THREADED FORK

1. **Lube all contacting parts.** Grease the stem quill, the bolt threads, the outside of the wedge or conical plug (Fig. 11.8), and the inside of the steering tube.

11.15 Freeing the stem wedge

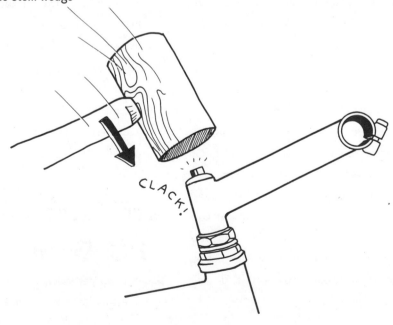

CLACK!

2. **Tighten the bolt until it just pulls the wedge or plug into place.** Don't tighten the bolt enough to prevent the stem from inserting into the steering tube.

3. **Slip the stem quill into the steering tube** (Fig. 11.9) **to the depth you want.** Make sure the stem is inserted beyond its height-limit line.

4. **Line the stem up with the front wheel, and tighten the bolt.** It needs to be tight, but don't overdo it. You can overtighten the stem bolt to the point that you bulge out the steering tube on the fork, so be careful. Recommended torque is in Appendix D.

xi-12
MAINTAINING AND REPLACING THE STEM

A bike cannot be controlled if the stem breaks, so make sure yours doesn't break. Because aluminum has no fatigue limit, all aluminum parts will eventually fail. Steel and titanium parts that are repeatedly stressed more than about one-half of their tensile strength will eventually fail as well. Stems and handlebars are not permanent accessories on your bike. Replace them before they fail on you.

Always clean the stem regularly and examine it for corrosion, cracks, bends, and stressed areas. If you find any, replace the stem immediately. If you crash hard on your bike, especially hard enough to bend the handlebar, replace the stem and possibly the fork. It makes sense to err on the side of caution. Lightweight, expensive stems, in particular, need to be replaced after a violent impact, even if you see no visible signs of stress. The hard, thin material is not likely to bend, but it may be so weakened that it will break soon.

Some manufacturers recommend replacing stems and handlebars every four years. If you rarely ride the bike, this is overkill. If you ride hard and ride often, every four years may not be frequent enough. Do what is appropriate for you, and be aware of the risks.

xi-13
SETTING STEM AND HANDLEBAR POSITIONS

Complete treatment of this subject is in §C-3. Here are some brief suggestions:

- At least initially, set the handlebar twist so that the bends in the handlebar are pointed up and back. I also recommend setting the bar ends, if installed, so that they are horizontal or tipped up between 5 and 15 degrees from horizontal (§C-3e).

- Setting handlebar height and reach is very personal. Much depends on your physique, your flexibility, your frame, your riding style, and a few other preferences. Again, this subject is covered in depth in Appendix C.

- Because I do not know anything about you personally, I will leave you with a few simple guidelines:

  (a) If you climb a lot, you will want the handlebar lower and farther forward to keep weight on the front wheel on steep uphill trails.

  (b) If you descend technical trails a lot, you will want the handlebar higher and with less forward reach.

  (c) If you ride a lot on pavement, a low, stretched-out position is better aerodynamically. A low position means that the handlebar grips are about 7–12cm (2¾–4¾ inches) lower than your saddle. A stretched-out position would place your elbow at least 2 inches (5cm) in front of your knee at the top of the pedal stroke.

xi-14
REMOVING A STUCK STEM

⚙ ⚙ ⚙ LEVEL 3

A stem can get stuck onto, or into, the steering tube because of poor maintenance. Periodically regreasing the stem and steering tube will keep them sliding freely, and the grease will form a barrier against sweat and water getting in between the two. If the stem is really stuck, be careful; you may ruin the fork as well as the stem and headset while trying to get the stem out. In fact, you're better off having a shop work on removing the stem, unless you really know what you are doing and are willing to accept the risk of destroying a lot of expensive parts.

a. Removing a stuck stem from a threadless fork

1. **Remove the top cap** (Fig. 11.12) **and the bolts clamping the stem to the steering tube.**

2. **Spread the stem clamp.** Insert a coin into the slot between each bolt end and the opposing threadless half of the binder lug (Fig. 11.16). Turn the bolts around, install them from the opposite direction, and tighten each bolt against each coin so that the clamp slot opens wider. The stem should come right off the steering tube.

NOTE: *If the stem is the type that comes with a single bolt in the side of the stem shaft ahead of the steering tube (Fig. 11.7), loosen the bolt a few turns and tap it in with a hammer to free the wedge. It might also require some penetrating oil, and perhaps some heat to expand it, to free this type of stem from around the steering tube.*

11.16 Sticking a coin in the crack to spread the stem clamp

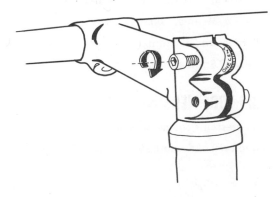

3. **If the stem still will not come free,** pour ammonia, automotive antifreeze, or Coca-Cola in around the stem clamp to dissolve the aluminum oxide sticking the parts together and let the stem sit—overnight if need be. If it is still stuck, use thermal expansion and contraction to free the parts: Try heating the stem clamp with a hair dryer and discharging a tire inflation cartridge inside the steering tube. Still no luck? You may have to hold the crown in a vise, following instructions 8 to 10 in §xi-14b on freeing a quill-type stem. Failing that, your last resort is to saw through the base of the stem clamp and the steering tube and replace the stem and fork.

b. Removing a stuck stem from a threaded fork

1. **Unscrew the expander bolt on top of the stem three turns or more.**

2. **Smack the bolt (or the hex key in the bolt) with a hammer** (Fig. 11.15). Do this until the bolt drops down, indicating it has completely disengaged the wedge.

3. **Grasping the front wheel between your knees, twist back and forth on the handlebar.** Don't use all of your strength, because you can ruin a fork and a front wheel this way.

4. **If the stem didn't budge, squirt ammonia around it where it enters the headset.** Let the bike sit for several hours, and add more ammonia every hour or so. (This assumes it's an aluminum stem; ammonia or Coca-Cola dissolves aluminum oxide, whereas penetrating oil dissolves steel rust.)

5. **Turn the bike over, and pour ammonia, automotive antifreeze, or Coca-Cola into the bottom of the fork steering tube.** Let it run down around the stem quill for several hours, and add more every hour or so. Note that penetrating oil works only on steel parts.

11.17 Clamping the fork crown in a vise

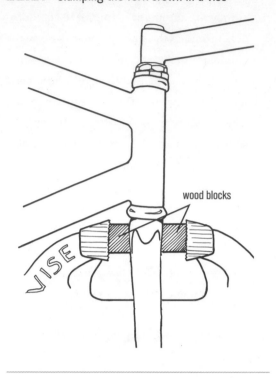

wood blocks

VISE

6. **Repeat step 3.** Still stuck? Continue with step 7.

7. **Discharge a tire inflation cartridge inside the quill shaft to chill and shrink it.** Remove the stem expander bolt to allow access.

8. **If the stem doesn't come free, use a heavy-duty vise.** Is it solidly mounted? You'll need it to be.

9. **Remove the front wheel** (Chapter 2) **and the front brake** (Chapter 7).

10. **Clamp the fork crown into the vise between wood blocks** (Fig. 11.17). If you have an old suspension fork with crown clamp bolts, remove the inner fork legs from the crown by loosening the crown bolts and yanking the legs out.

11. **Repeat steps 3 and 7.** If this doesn't work, you may need to saw off the stem just above the headset and have the bottom of the stem reamed out of the steering tube by a machine shop.

HEADSETS

HEADSET TYPES AND HOW TO DETERMINE FIT TO A GIVEN FRAME AND FORK

There are three basic types of threadless headsets: traditional (aka "external" or "TR," Fig. 11.18), cupless internal (aka "integrated" or "IS," Fig. 11.19), and press-in internal with lipped cups (aka "semi-integrated," "zero stack," "low stack," or "ZS," Fig. 11.20). Older mountain bikes have threaded steering tubes with threaded headsets (Fig. 11.21); these always have traditional external cups.

FORK MEASUREMENT

Headsets come in many sizes for mountain bikes, and the size refers to the diameter in inches of the fork steering tube. However, in these days of tapered steering tubes, you need to measure the diameter of the steering tube both at its base (crown race seat diameter) and at its top (stem clamp diameter). Standard mountain bike sizes are 1 inch, 1⅛ inches, 1¼ inches, 1½ inches, and a combination of two of these sizes. The diameter of the crown race seat will be 1–2mm larger than the headset size, whereas the steering-tube diameter at the top will be exactly the headset size. For instance, the steering-tube diameter of a fork for a 1⅛-inch headset will measure 28.6mm (1⅛ inches) at its top and approximately 30mm at its base; the steering-tube diameter of a fork for a 1½ -inch headset will measure 38.1mm (1½ inches) at its top and approximately 39.8mm at its base; and the steering-tube diameter of a fork for a 1½ /1⅛-inch "tapered" headset (Fig. 11.22) will measure 28.6mm at its top and approximately 39.8mm at its base.

HEAD-TUBE MEASUREMENT

You determine the headset size as above from the diameter(s) of the fork steerer, and you determine

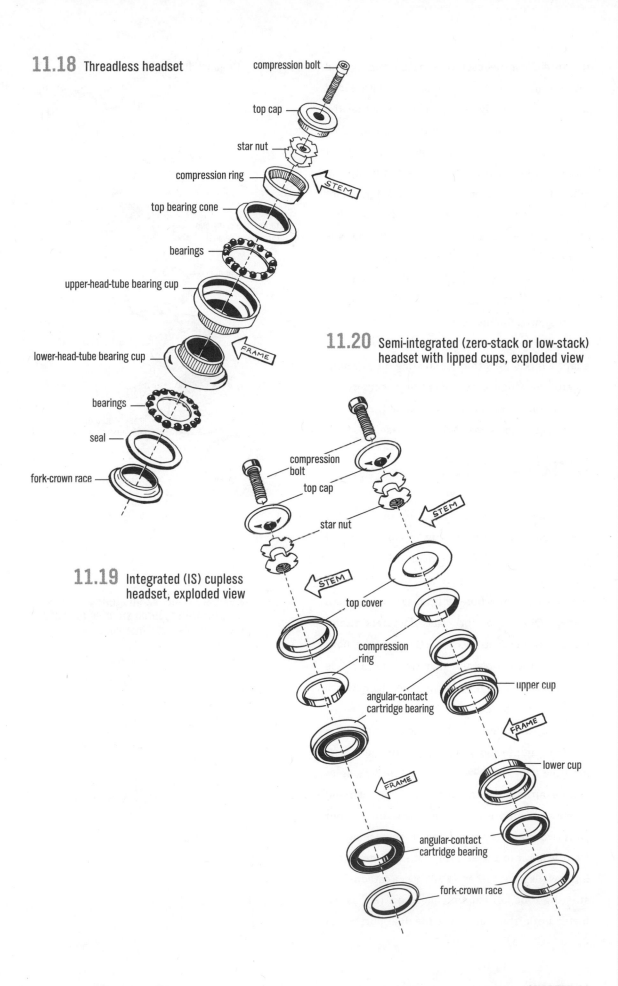

11.18 Threadless headset

compression bolt

top cap

star nut

compression ring

top bearing cone

bearings

upper-head-tube bearing cup

STEM

lower-head-tube bearing cup

FRAME

bearings

seal

fork-crown race

11.20 Semi-integrated (zero-stack or low-stack) headset with lipped cups, exploded view

compression bolt

top cap

star nut

STEM

STEM

11.19 Integrated (IS) cupless headset, exploded view

top cover

compression ring

angular-contact cartridge bearing

upper cup

FRAME

lower cup

FRAME

angular-contact cartridge bearing

fork-crown race

the threadless headset type by examining and measuring the inside of the head-tube (threaded headsets are simply determined by whether the fork has a threaded steerer or not). If the inside of the head-tube is cylindrical and uniform (except for perhaps a small cut edge a few centimeters in where the reamer stopped), then it is intended for a press-in cup—either a traditional (TR) or semi-integrated (zero stack or low stack). If, however, there is a raised and chamfered (angled) surface ringing the inside of the head-tube anywhere from 5mm to 25mm in, then it most likely takes an integrated (IS) headset.

Note that you can get reducer headsets to adapt a fork with a thinner steering tube or non-tapered steering-tube to a head-tube that's meant for a steering tube that is either larger throughout or is tapered and larger only at its base.

THREADLESS HEADSETS

Threadless headset systems (Figs. 11.18–20) are lighter than threaded ones because they lack the stem quill, bolt, and wedge (Fig. 11.9) of a threaded headset (Fig. 11.21). The connection between the handlebar and the stem is also more rigid than the type of connection with an expanding stem wedge. Of course, fork manufacturers prefer threadless headsets because they do not have to thread their forks and they can offer a single steering-tube length; steering-tube diameter is now the only variable.

On a threadless headset, the top cup and a conical compression ring slide onto the steering tube (Figs. 11.18–20 and 11.22–24). The stem clamps around the top of the steering tube and above the compression ring. A star-shaped nut with two layers of spring-steel teeth sticking out from it fits into the steering tube and grabs the inner walls (Figs. 11.7 and 11.23). On a carbon-fiber steering tube, an expandable insert (Fig. 11.25) instead of a star nut serves the dual purpose of

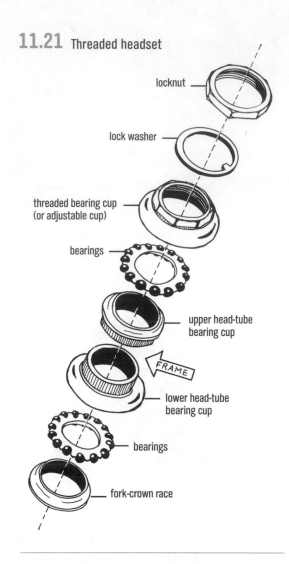

11.21 Threaded headset

locknut

lock washer

threaded bearing cup (or adjustable cup)

bearings

upper head-tube bearing cup

FRAME

lower head-tube bearing cup

bearings

fork-crown race

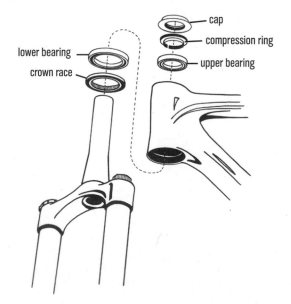

11.22 Trek/Gary Fisher E2 integrated cupless headset with tapered steering tube and differentially sized bearings

cap

compression ring

upper bearing

lower bearing

crown race

11.23 Semi-integrated (zero-stack or low-stack headset system), cutaway view

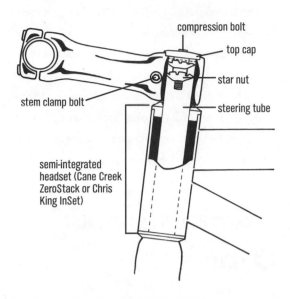

compression bolt

top cap

star nut

steering tube

stem clamp bolt

semi-integrated headset (Cane Creek ZeroStack or Chris King InSet)

11.25 Inserting an expandable support/anchor plug into a carbon-fiber fork steering tube

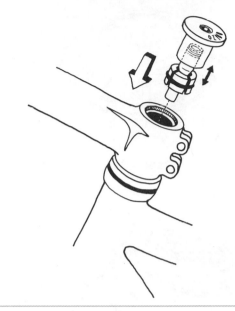

11.24 Integrated headset with drop-in bearing cups (Campagnolo shown), exploded view

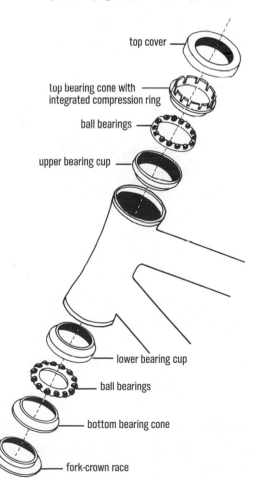

top cover

top bearing cone with integrated compression ring

ball bearings

upper bearing cup

lower bearing cup

ball bearings

bottom bearing cone

fork-crown race

anchoring the top cap and protecting the steering tube from being crushed by the stem clamp.

A top cap sits atop the stem clamp and pushes it down by means of a long bolt threaded into the star nut to adjust the headset (Figs. 11.12 and 11.23). The stem clamped around the steering-tube holds the headset in adjustment (Fig. 11.11).

The next generation of threadless headsets are internal, or integrated, headsets, concealed inside the frame's steering-tube (Figs. 11.19–20 and 11.22). Where traditional threaded and threadless headsets have bearing cups that are pressed into the head-tube (Figs. 11.18 and 11.21), integrated headsets have bearings seated inside the head-tube. The bearings either rest on a chamfered platform within the head-tube itself (Figs. 11.19 and 11.24) or have semi-integrated press-in cups with thin flanges that extend out to the edges of the head-tube (Figs. 11.20 and 11.23). Otherwise, the headset is identical to, and is adjusted in the same way as, the traditional threadless systems shown in Figures 11.7 and 11.18.

Prior to the 1990s, practically all headsets and steering tubes were threaded. The top bearing cup

11.26 Needle bearings

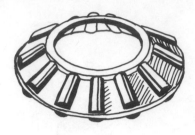

11.27 Lower parts of cartridge-bearing headset

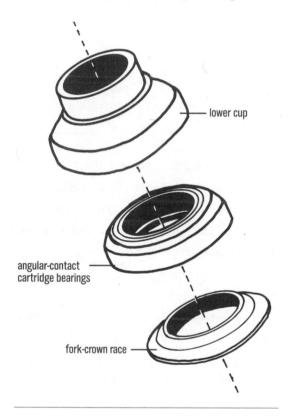

lower cup

angular-contact
cartridge bearings

fork-crown race

on a threaded headset has wrench flats, a toothed washer stacked on top of it, and a locknut that covers the top of the steering tube. That locknut tightens against the washer and top cup (Fig. 11.21). A brake-cable hanger (Fig. 7.6) and extra spacers may be included under the locknut.

Traditionally, headsets, whether threaded or threadless, used ball bearings held in some type of steel or plastic retainer (or "cage") (Figs. 11.18, 11.21, and 11.24) so that you did not have to chase dozens of separate balls around when you worked

on the bike. A variation on this design (Stronglight, some Ritchey models) has needle bearings held in conical plastic retainers (Fig. 11.26) riding on conical steel bearing surfaces.

Cartridge-bearing headsets are now the standard and generally employ "angular-contact" bearings (Fig. 11.27), because normal cartridge bearings cannot take the side (axial) forces encountered by a headset. Each bearing is a separate sealed, internally greased unit.

xi-15
CHECKING HEADSET ADJUSTMENT

⚙ LEVEL 1

If the headset is too tight, the fork will be difficult to turn or at least will feel gritty when you do. If the headset is too loose, it will rattle or clunk while you ride. You might even notice some play in the fork as you apply the front brake.

1. **Check for headset looseness by holding the front brake and rocking the bike forward and back.** Try it with the front wheel pointed straight ahead and then with the wheel turned at 90 degrees to the bike. Feel for back-and-forth movement (or play) at the lower head cup with your other hand. If there is play, you need to adjust the headset because it is too loose.

NOTE: *This task is more complicated with a suspension fork and even with many rim brakes. There is always some side-to-side play in any suspension fork, as well as in many brakes; this makes it hard to isolate whether the play you feel is from the headset, the fork, or the brakes. You must feel each part as you rock the bike, and you may have to make some trial-and-error headset adjustments.*

If the headset is loose, skip to the appropriate adjustment section, xi-16 or xi-17.

2. **Check for headset tightness by turning the handlebar back and forth.** Feel for any bind-

ing or stiffness of movement. Also, check for the chunk-chunk-chunk movement to fixed positions characterizing a pitted headset (the pits are indentations in the bearing surfaces made by overtightening the bearings, forcing the balls to make dents); if you feel this, you need a new headset (skip to §xi-20). Lift the front wheel off the ground, and lean the bike to one side and then the other to see how easily the headset turns and allows the front wheel to steer (be aware that cable housings can resist the rotation of the fork). Lift the bike by the saddle so that it is tipped down at an angle with both wheels off the ground. Turn the handlebar one way and let go of it; then repeat the other way. See if it returns to center quickly and smoothly on its own. If the headset does not turn easily on any of these steps, it is too tight, and you should skip to the appropriate adjustment section, xi-16 or xi-17.

3. **With a threaded headset, try to turn either the top nut (the locknut) or the threaded cup by hand.** They should be so tight against each other that they can be unscrewed only with wrenches. If you can tighten or loosen either part by hand, you need to adjust the headset; go to §xi-17.

xi-16
ADJUSTING A THREADLESS HEADSET

 **LEVEL 1**

Adjusting a threadless headset, whether it is a modern integrated type (Figs. 11.19–24) or the traditional type (Figs. 11.7 and 11.18), is much easier than adjusting the threaded style. It is a level 1 procedure and usually takes only a 5mm hex key.

1. **Check the headset adjustment** (§xi-15). Determine whether the headset is too tight or too loose.

11.28 Loosening or tightening the compression bolt on a threadless headset

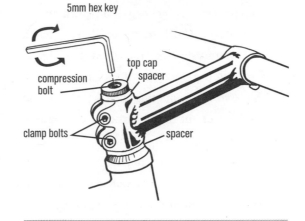

2. **Loosen the bolt(s) that clamp(s) the stem to the steering tube.**

3. **If the headset is too tight, loosen the bolt on the top cap.** Unscrew it about one-sixteenth of a turn with a 5mm hex key (Fig. 11.28). Recheck and repeat as necessary.

4. **If the headset is too loose, tighten the bolt on the top cap.** Tighten it about one-sixteenth of a turn with a 5mm hex key (Fig. 11.28). Be careful not to overtighten it, thereby pitting the headset. If you're using a torque wrench, 22 in-lbs is a recommended setting. Recheck the adjustment and tighten or loosen further as necessary.

(a) If the cap does not move down and push the stem down, make sure the stem is not stuck to the steering tube. If it is, refer to §xi-14a.

(b) Another hindrance occurs if the conical compression ring shown in Figures 11.18–20 and 11.22 is stuck to the steering tube, preventing adjustment via the top cap bolt. With the stem off, gently tap the steering tube down with a mallet, and then push the fork back up to free the compression ring. Grease the ring and the steering tube and reassemble.

(c) If neither the stem nor the compression ring is stuck, yet the cap still does not push the stem down, the steering tube may be so long that it is hitting the lip of the top cap and preventing the cap from pushing the stem down. The steering tube's top should be 3–6mm below the top of the top edge of the stem (Fig. 11.13) or of the spacers above the stem. If the steering tube is too long, add a spacer, or cut or file some off the top (see §xi-9, step 7).

(d) Another thing that can thwart adjustment is when the star nut is not installed deeply enough and the cap bottoms out on the star nut. The highest point of the star nut should be 12–15mm below the top of the steering tube. With metal steering tubes, tap the nut deeper with a star-nut installation tool (Fig. 11.14), or put the bolt through the top cap, thread it five turns into the star nut, and gently tap it in with a soft hammer while using the top cap to keep it going in straight (see §xi-9, step 8). With carbon steering tubes, loosen the aluminum expander (Fig. 11.25) with a hex key, move it down, and retighten it.

(e) With a double-crown fork (Fig. 13.18), you must loosen the clamp bolts on the upper crown. There are three of them—one clamps the steering tube, and the other two each clamp one upper fork tube (stanchion). If the headset is loose and these bolts are still clamped, tightening the headset compression bolt cannot push the stem and top crown down more. After the headset is adjusted properly, retighten the bolts to the torque specified by the fork maker.

(f) Once you have fixed the cause of the adjustment problem, return to step 1.

5. **Tighten the stem clamp bolts.** Tighten to the recommended torque, given in Appendix D.

6. **Recheck the headset adjustment.** Repeat steps 2–4 if necessary.

With some integrated headsets, you may need a shim under the bearing cover so that its edges do not drag and scrape on the top end of the head-tube.

If the headset is adjusted properly, make sure that the stem is aligned straight with respect to the front wheel, and then go find something else to do, because you are done.

xi-17
ADJUSTING A THREADED HEADSET

 LEVEL 2

The secret to good adjustment is simultaneously controlling the steering tube, the adjustable cup, and the locknut as you tighten the latter two together.

NOTE: *Perform the adjustment with the stem installed. Not only does it give you something to hold to keep the fork from turning during the installation, but also there are slight differences in adjustment when the stem is in place as opposed to when it is not. Tightening the stem bolt can sometimes bulge the walls of the steering tube very slightly (Fig. 11.9), just enough for it to shorten the steering tube slightly and throw your original headset adjustment off.*

1. **Once you determine whether the headset is too loose or too tight, follow the steps outlined in §xi-15.**

2. **Put a pair of headset wrenches on the headset's nuts.** Headset nuts come in a wide variety of sizes, so make sure you have the proper sizes of wrenches. Place the wrenches so that the top one is slightly offset to the left of the bottom wrench. That way you can squeeze them together to free the nut (Fig. 11.29).

NOTE: *People with small hands or a weak grip will need to hold each wrench at the end in order to get enough leverage.*

3. **Hold the lower wrench in place, and turn the top wrench counterclockwise to loosen**

11.29 Loosening a headset locknut

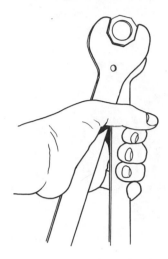

11.30 Tightening a headset locknut

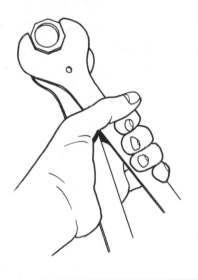

the locknut. It may take considerable force to break the locknut loose, because it needs to be installed very tightly to keep the headset from loosening.

4. **Depending on whether the headset was too loose or too tight, do one of the following:**

    (a) If the headset was too loose, turn the lower nut (the threaded cup) clockwise about one-sixteenth of a turn while holding the stem with your other hand. Be very careful when tightening the cup; overtightening it can ruin the headset by pressing the bearings

into the bearing surfaces and making little indentations. The headset then stops at the indentations rather than turning smoothly, a condition known as a "pitted" headset.

    (b) If the headset was too tight, loosen the threaded cup counterclockwise one-sixteenth of a turn while holding the stem with your other hand. Loosen the cup until the bearings turn freely, but be sure not to loosen to the point that play develops.

5. **Holding the stem, tighten the locknut clockwise with a single wrench.** Make sure that the threaded cup does not turn while you tighten the locknut. If the cup does turn, either you are missing the toothed lock washer separating the cup and locknut (Fig. 11.21) or the washer you have is missing its tooth. In this case, remove the locknut and replace the toothed washer. Put it on the steering tube so that the tooth engages the longitudinal groove in the steering tube. Tighten the locknut again.

NOTE: *You can adjust a headset without a toothed washer by working both wrenches simultaneously, but it is trickier to adjust and often comes loose while riding. But if the steering tube is cut too short to accept a washer in the headset, you may have to do without one.*

6. **Check the headset adjustment again.** Repeat steps 4 and 5 until the headset is properly adjusted.

7. **With wrenches on both nuts, tighten the locknut (clockwise).** Snug it firmly against the washer(s) and threaded cup to hold the headset adjustment in place (Fig. 11.30).

8. **Check the headset adjustment again.** If it is off, follow steps 2–7 again. If it is adjusted properly, make sure the stem is aligned with the front wheel.

NOTE: *If you constantly get what you think to be the proper adjustment and then find it to be too loose after you tighten the locknut and threaded cup against*

HANDLEBARS, STEMS, AND HEADSETS

each other, the steering tube may be too long, thereby causing the locknut to bottom out. Remove the stem and examine the inside of the steering tube. If the top end of the steering tube butts up against the top lip of the locknut, the steering tube is too long. Remove the locknut and add another spacer.

If you don't want to add another spacer, file off 1 or 2mm of the steering tube. Be sure to remove any burrs both inside and out. Avoid leaving filings in the bearings or steering-tube threads. Replace the locknut and return to step 5.

xi-18
OVERHAULING A THREADLESS HEADSET

🗲 🗲 LEVEL 2

These instructions apply to both integrated (Figs. 11.19–20 and 11.22–24) and traditional (Figs. 11.7 and 11.18) threadless headsets.

Just like any other bike part with bearings, headsets need periodic overhauls. If you use your bike regularly, you should probably overhaul a loose-bearing (Figs. 11.18 and 11.24) or needle-bearing (Fig. 11.26) headset once a year. Headsets with cartridge bearings (Figs. 11.19–20 and 11.22) need less frequent maintenance; some angular-contact bearings can be disassembled and cleaned, and some cannot. With those that cannot, if a bearing fails, either replace the bearing or, if it has pressed-in bearings (Fig. 11.31), replace the entire cup (§xi-20).

1. **Mount the bike upside down in a work stand.** Alternatively, be ready to catch the fork when you remove the stem.

2. **Disconnect or remove the front brake** (Chapter 7), **unscrew the top cap bolt** (Fig. 11.28) **and stem clamp bolts, and remove the top cap and the stem.** If you have a double-crown fork (Fig. 13.18), loosen the bolts on the top tube (i.e., stanchion) and pull the top crown off.

3. **Remove the top headset cup, sliding the top cup, conical compression ring, and any other**

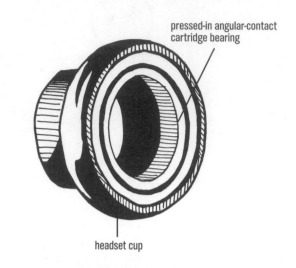

11.31 Cartridge bearing pressed into headset cup

pressed-in angular-contact cartridge bearing

headset cup

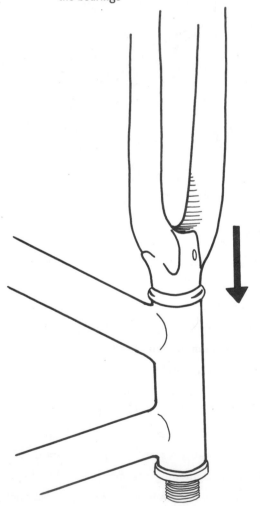

11.32 Setting the fork in the head tube to seat the bearings

spacers above it off the steering tube (Figs. 11.18–20, 11.22, and 11.24). It may take a tap with a mallet on the end of the steering tube, followed by pushing the fork back up, to free the compression ring.

4. **Pull the fork out of the frame.** The lower bearing and seal may come with it.

5. **Remove any bearing seals that are present.** Remember the position and orientation of each.

6. **Remove any bearings remaining in the head-tube or cups.** Be careful not to lose any. Separate the top and bottom sets if they are of different sizes.

7. **Clean or replace the bearings:**

    (a) With either ball-bearing (Figs. 11.18 and 11.24) or needle-bearing (Fig. 11.26) headsets, put the bearings (leave the balls or needles in their retainers) in a jar or old water bottle along with some citrus-based solvent. Shake. If the bearings from the top and bottom are of different sizes, keep them in separate containers to avoid confusion. Blot the bearings dry with a clean rag. Plug the sink, and wash the ball bearings (whether separate or held in retainers) in soap and water in your hands, just as if you were washing your palms by rubbing them together. Your hands will get clean for the assembly steps as well. Rinse bearings thoroughly and blot them dry. Air-dry completely.

    (b) Some cartridge bearings (Fig. 11.27) can be pulled apart and cleaned. Hold the bearing over a container (to catch the balls) so that the beveled outer surface that fits into the cup faces down, and push up on the bearing's inner ring. The bearing should come apart—the inner ring will pop up and out with the bearings stuck to its outer surface. It may take a little rocking of the inner ring as you push up. If the bearing does not come apart, first pry off the plastic seal covering the bearings with a knife or razor blade (as shown in Fig. 6.32), and then try again. Wipe the bearings, bearing rings, and seals with a clean rag.

    (c) If the bearings are the type that will not come apart, check to see if they turn smoothly. If they do not, buy new ones and skip to step 8.

8. **Wipe all of the bearing surfaces and areas the bearings might touch with clean rags.** Wipe the steering tube clean, and wipe the inside of the head-tube clean with a rag over the end of a screwdriver.

9. **Inspect all of the bearing surfaces of loose-ball headsets for wear and pitting.** If you see pits (separate indentations made by bearings in the bearing surfaces), replace the headset; skip to §xi-20.

10. **Grease all bearing surfaces.** If you are using cartridge bearings, apply grease conservatively.

    For the angular-contact cartridge bearing that you have disassembled, smear grease around the outside of the inner bearing ring, and stick the balls into the grease in the channel around the ring. With the outer ring sitting beveled side down on the table, push the inner ring (which has the balls attached) down into it (the internal bevel on the inner ring should be facing up, opposite the bevel on the outer ring). Snap the bearing seals back into place.

11. **Replace the lower bearing.** The bike should be upside down in the bike stand.

    (a) For a cupless integrated headset (Figs. 11.19 and 11.22), set a bearing into the chamfered seat in the bottom of the head tube itself. For an integrated headset with drop-in cups (Fig. 11.24), place the lower cup into its chamfered seat in the bottom of the head-tube.

    (b) With loose-ball headsets, make sure you have the bearing retainer right side up

HANDLEBARS, STEMS, AND HEADSETS

but also prevents grit from falling into the bearings as you put the cup on.

15. **Slide the (greased) compression ring and top cover onto the steering tube.** Ensure that the narrower end of the compression ring slides into the conical space in the top of the top cup (Figs. 11.19 and 11.22) or into the bearing of a cupless headset (Fig. 11.21). If you have a double-crown fork (Fig. 13.18), slide the top crown onto the steering tube and the upper fork tubes.

NOTE: *On a Campagnolo integrated headset (Fig. 11.24), which appears on some Cannondale mountain bikes, there is a plastic biconical compression ring inserted into the top bearing cone (Figs. 11.24 and 11.33), and like a normal split compression ring, it centers the top cone in the bearings. The upper edge of the plastic compression ring is notched like a turreted castle tower. Above this part comes the top bearing cover, whose inner edge is beveled for the turreted top conical edge of the plastic compression ring. To preload the bearings, you must first install the top bearing cover upside down (Fig. 11.33) and then push down on it. This preloads the bearings by pushing the top cone down. If you install the top bearing cover in its standard orientation before the cop cone and plastic compression ring are slid down far enough to preload the bearings, the beveled inner edge of the top bearing cover will pinch the turreted upper conical edge of the plastic compression ring in place and not allow it to slide down farther. Once you have pushed the bearing cone down fully in this manner, flip the top bearing cover right side up and put it in place over the cone and compression ring (Fig. 11.34).*

16. **Replace the stem and spacers.** Slide on any spacers you had under the stem. Slide the stem on, and tighten one stem clamp bolt to hold it in place.

17. **Turn the bike right side up in the bike stand.**

18. **Check the steering-tube overlap.** The stem clamp or, ideally, the top spacer above the

11.33 Seating Campagnolo threadless headset, part 1

11.34 Seating Campagnolo threadless headset, part 2

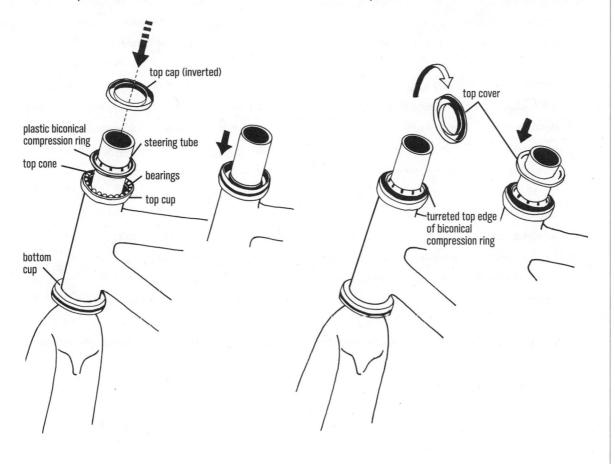

stem should extend 3–6mm above the top of the steering tube (Fig. 11.13).

(a) If the overlap is correct, install the top cap on the top of the stem clamp and steering tube, and screw the bolt into the star nut inside the steering tube (Fig. 11.28).

(b) If the steering tube is too long, remove the stem. Add a spacer or file the steering tube shorter until the stem clamp, or spacer above it, overlaps it by 3–6mm. If the steering tube is too short, remove spacers from below the stem if there are any. If there are no spacers to remove, try a new stem with a shorter clamp. Install the top cap on the top of the stem clamp, and screw the bolt into the star nut (Fig. 11.28).

19. Adjust the headset, following the instructions in §xi-16.

xi-19
OVERHAULING A THREADED HEADSET

 **LEVEL 2**

Just like any other bike part with bearings, headsets need periodic overhauls. If you use your bike regularly, you should probably overhaul a loose-bearing (Fig. 11.21) or needle-bearing (Fig. 11.26) headset once a year. Headsets with cartridge bearings (Fig. 11.27) need less frequent overhaul; some angular-contact bearings can be disassembled and cleaned, and some cannot. With those that cannot, if a bearing fails, you either replace the bearing or, if it has press-in bearings (such as Chris King and Dia-Compe's "S" series, Fig. 11.31), you replace the entire cup (§xi-20).

1. **Disconnect the front brake** (Chapter 7).

2. **Remove the stem.** Loosen the stem bolt three turns, tap the bolt down with a hammer to free the wedge (Fig. 11.15), and pull the stem out.

3. **Remove the headset locknut.** Place one headset wrench on the locknut and one on the threaded cup. Loosen the locknut by squeezing the wrenches together, which will turn the locknut counterclockwise (Fig. 11.35). Unscrew the locknut from the steering tube.

4. **Mount the bike upside down in a work stand.** Alternatively, be ready to catch the fork when you remove the threaded cup.

5. **Remove the threaded cup.** The headset washer(s) will slide off the steering tube as you unscrew the cup.

6. **Pull the fork out of the frame.**

7. **Remove any seals that surround the edges of the cups.** Make a point of remembering the position and orientation of each cup.

11.35 Loosening a headset locknut

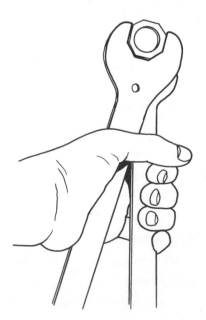

8. **Remove the bearings from the cups.** Be careful not to lose any. Separate the top and bottom sets of bearings if they are of different sizes.

9. **Clean or replace the bearings:**

    (a) With standard ball-bearing (Fig. 11.21) or needle-bearing (Fig. 11.26) headsets, put the bearings in a jar or old water bottle along with some citrus-based solvent. Shake. If the bearings from the top and bottom are of different sizes, keep them in separate containers to avoid confusion. Blot the bearings dry with a clean rag.

    (b) Some cartridge bearings (Fig. 11.27) can be pulled apart and cleaned. Hold the bearing over a container (to catch the balls) so that the beveled outer surface that fits into the cup faces down, and push up on the bearing's inner ring. The bearing should come apart—the inner ring will pop up and out with the bearings stuck to its outer surface. It may take a little rocking of the inner ring as you push up. If the bearing does not come apart, first pry off the plastic seal covering the bearings with a knife or razor blade (as shown in Fig. 6.32), and then try again. Wipe the bearings, bearing rings, and seals with a clean rag.

    (c) If the cartridge bearings will not come apart, check to see if they turn smoothly. If they do not, buy new ones and skip to step 11.

10. **Plug the sink, and wash the ball bearings in soap and water in your hands.** Wash as if you were washing your palms by rubbing them together. Do this with loose balls as well as with balls held in retainers. This helps keep your hands clean for the assembly steps as well. Rinse bearings thoroughly and blot them dry. Let them air-dry completely.

11. **Wipe the bearing surfaces and other places the bearings might touch with clean rags.** Wipe the steering tube clean, and wipe the

inside of the head-tube clean with a rag over the end of a screwdriver.

12. **Inspect all the bearing surfaces of loose-ball headsets for wear and pitting.** If you see pits (separate indentations made by bearings in the bearing surfaces), you need to replace the headset. If that's the case, skip to §xi-20.

13. **Grease all bearing surfaces.** A thin film will do, especially with cartridge bearings. For the angular-contact cartridge bearing that you have disassembled, smear grease around the outside of the inner bearing ring, and stick the balls into the grease in the channel around the ring. With the outer ring sitting beveled side down on the table, push the inner ring (which has the balls attached) down into it (the internal bevel on the inner ring should be facing up, opposite the bevel on the outer ring). Snap the bearing seals back into place.

14. **Install the bearings in their cups.** The bike should be upside down in the bike stand.

    (a) Place a set of bearings in the top cup and a set in the cup on the lower end of the head-tube.

    (b) With loose-ball headsets, make sure you have the bearing retainer right side up so that only the bearings contact the bearing surfaces (note the different upper cup styles and bearing orientations in Figs. 11.18 and 11.21). If you have installed the retainer upside down, it will come in contact with one of the bearing surfaces, and the headset will not turn well. This is a bad thing, because assembling and riding it that way will turn the retainer into jagged chunks of broken metal. To be safe, double- and triple-check the retainer placement by turning each cup pair in your hand with the bearing in between before proceeding. Some loose-ball headsets have the bearings set up identically for both top and bottom (Fig. 11.21), where

the top piece of each pair is a cup, the bottom piece is a cone, and the bearing retainer rides the same way in both sets. Many headsets, however, place both cups (and hence the bearing retainers) facing outward from the head-tube (Fig. 11.18). Also, watch for asymmetry in ball size; some headsets have smaller balls on top than on the bottom.

NOTE: *Stronglight and Ritchey needle-bearing headsets come with two pairs of separate conical steel rings. These are the bearing surfaces that sit on either side of the needle bearings (Fig. 11.26). For each set of conical rings, you will find that one is smaller than the other. Place the smaller one on the lower surface of each pair: the fork-crown race and the cup on top of the head-tube.*

    (c) If the ball bearings are loose with no bearing retainer, stick the balls into the grease in the cups one at a time, making sure that you replace in each cup the same number that you started out with.

    (d) With angular-contact cartridge bearings, the beveled end faces into the cup (Fig. 11.27).

15. **Reinstall any seals that you removed from the headset parts.**

16. **Slide the steering tube of the fork into the head-tube.** Ensure that the lower headset bearing seats properly (Fig. 11.32).

17. **Screw on the top cup, with the bearings in it, onto the steering tube.** Keeping the bike upside down at this point not only keeps the fork in place, but also prevents grit from falling into the bearings as you thread the cup on.

18. **Slide on the toothed washer** (Fig. 11.21). Align the tooth in the groove going down the length of the steering-tube threads. If you have one, install the brake-cable hanger (Fig. 7.6) the same way. Screw on the locknut with your hand.

19. **Turn the bike over.**

20. **Grease the stem quill and insert it into the steering tube** (Fig. 11.9). Make certain that it is in deeper than the imprinted limit line.

21. **Line the stem up with the front wheel, and tighten the stem bolt.** See Appendix D for recommended torque.

22. **Adjust the headset as described in §xi-17.**

xi-20
REMOVING THE HEADSET

🪚 🪚 🪚 LEVEL 3

1. **Open the headset and remove the fork and bearings.** Follow steps 1–6 of §xi-18 or 1–8 of §xi-19, depending on headset type (i.e., threadless or threaded).

    (a) If you have a cupless integrated headset with bearings seated on steps machined into the head-tube itself (Figs. 11.19, 11.22, and 11.24), skip to step 5.

    (b) If you have a headset with cups pressed into the head-tube, continue with step 2.

2. **Slide the solid end of the headset-cup remover (aka "headset rocket") through the head-tube** (Fig. 11.36). As you pull the headset-cup remover through the head-tube, the splayed-out tangs on the opposite end of the tool pull through the cup and spread out.

3. **Strike the solid end of the cup remover with a hammer.** Smack it until you drive the cup out (Fig. 11.37). Be careful: The cup may go flying, and so might the headset rocket.

4. **Remove the other cup.** Slide the cup remover in through the opposite end of the head-tube, and repeat steps 2 and 3 on the opposite end of the end tube.

5. **Remove the fork-crown race.**

    (a) With a suspension fork (or a rigid fork with a broad crown), getting the fork-crown race off can be a bear. Clamp the steering tube into a vise, or turn the fork upside down

11.36 Inserting a cup-removal tool

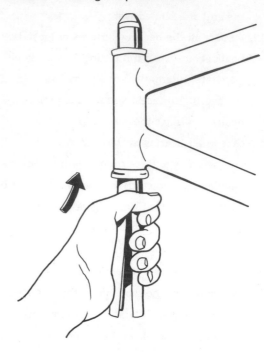

11.37 Removing a lower headset cup

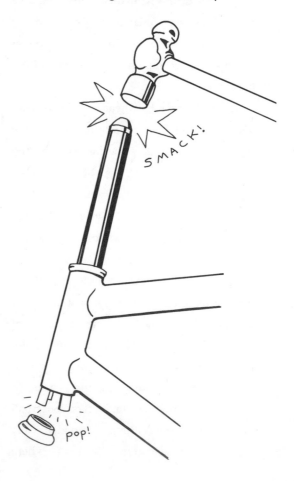

11.38 Removing a fork-crown race with a screwdriver

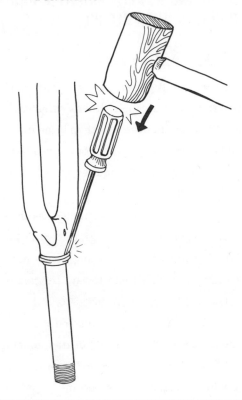

11.39 Removing a fork-crown race with a crown race remover

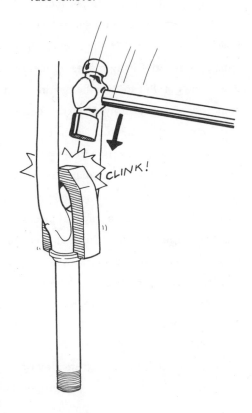

CLINK!

so that the top of the steering tube is sitting on the workbench. If you find a notch on the front and back of the fork crown under the fork-crown race, place the blade of a large screwdriver that you don't care very much about into the notch on one side of the crown so that it butts against the bottom of the headset fork-crown race. Tap the handle of the screwdriver with a hammer to drive the race up the steering tube a bit (Fig. 11.38). Move the screwdriver to the groove on the other side, and tap it again to move that side of the race up a bit. Continue in this way, alternately tapping either side of the race up the steering tube, bit by bit, until it gets past the enlarged section of the steering tube and slides off. With luck, the screwdriver will not be damaged, but be prepared to relegate it to use on similar jobs in the future.

(b) If there is no notch and there is not enough to the fork-crown race's edge protruding over the crown to get a screwdriver against it, get the race to start moving up by using a sharp chisel or box-cutter blade. Tap the chisel or box-cutter blade with a hammer when its edge is between the race and the fork-crown edge. Once the crown race has moved up a bit, start using a broad screwdriver as previously described to "walk" the race off the steering tube's enlarged base.

(c) If you are fortunate enough to have a Park Universal crown-race remover tool (Fig. 1.4), use it! Using the finger-tightened screws at the bottom, tighten the blades in under the fork-crown race until they stop. Then tighten the top screw to slide the race up the steering tube.

(d) If you have an old, narrow rigid fork, you can get the fork-crown race off as in (a), (b), or (c), but you can also do it more elegantly with a crown-race remover or an appropriately sized

11.40 Removing a fork-crown race with a vise

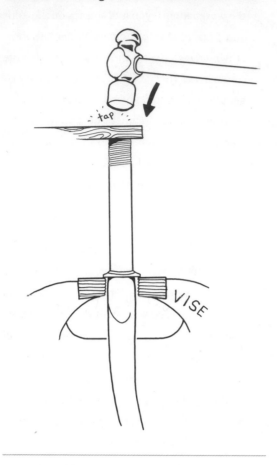

xi-21
PREPARING A FRAME AND FORK PRIOR TO INSTALLING A HEADSET

LEVEL 3

You can install a new headset yourself if you have the necessary tools. Otherwise, get a shop to do it. You should head to a shop if the frame has not been properly prepared for the headset prior to installation; the job requires special tools that only some shops possess.

If this is a frame with chamfered bearing seats for an integrated headset (Figs. 11.22 or 11.24), you shouldn't need to do anything except drop the bearings in, beveled end toward the head-tube seat, and follow the steps in §xi-16.

With a headset with cups—be it semi-integrated (Figs 11.20 and 11.23) or traditional (Figs. 11.18 and 11.21)—on a new frame (or on one on which headsets have become pitted in the past), make sure that the head-tube has been reamed and faced. If not, you will need a bike shop equipped with the proper tools to do it for you. Reaming makes the head-tube ends round inside and of the correct diameter for the headset cups to press in. Facing makes both ends of the head-tube parallel so that the bearings can turn smoothly and uniformly. A head-tube reaming-and-facing tool is shown in Figure 1.4.

The base of the steering tube also needs to be turned down to the correct diameter for the fork-crown race. The crown-race seat on top of the fork crown must be faced in a way that places the race parallel to the head-tube cups. This is generally only a concern with rigid forks; suspension forks usually come with the tube properly machined to accept the fork-crown race. But you do have to make sure that the fork-crown race is the right size for the fork.

The fork steering tube (threaded or threadless) must also be cut to the proper length.

bench vise. Stand the fork upside down on the top of the steering tube. Place the U-shaped crown-race remover so that it straddles the underside of the fork crown and its ledges engage the front and back edges of the fork-crown race. Smack the top of the crown-race remover with a hammer to knock the race off (Fig. 11.39).

(e) To remove the crown race with a bench vise, flip the brakes out of the way and slide the fork in, straddling the center shaft of the vise. Tighten the vise so that its faces lightly contact the front and back of the fork crown with the lower side of the fork-crown race sitting on top of the vise faces. Put a block of wood on the top of the steering tube to pad it. Strike the block with a hammer to drive the fork down and knock the race off (Fig. 11.40).

11.41 Setting a fork-crown race

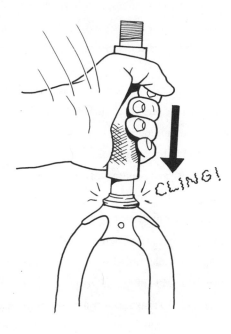

CLING!

11.42 Measuring the amount of steering tube to cut

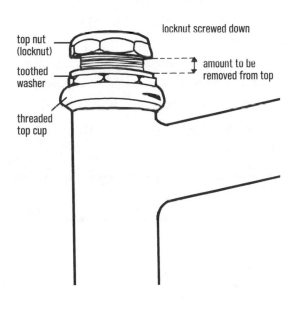

top nut (locknut)

toothed washer

threaded top cup

locknut screwed down

amount to be removed from top

Remember, you can always go back and cut more off, but you can't add any, so be careful! You can wait until the headset (and stem, in the case of a threadless headset) is installed. Or you can figure out the length first.

The safest way to make sure you don't cut the steering tube too short is to install the headset first (§xi-22). Determining the steering-tube length for an already installed threadless headset is detailed in §xi-9. Once a threaded headset is installed, measure the excess length as shown in Figure 11.42, remove the top nut, and cut that much off the top. Saw it down to length, and file off the burrs that the hacksaw left on the inside and outside edges of the steering-tube end.

xi-22
INSTALLING A HEADSET

⚙ ⚙ ⚙ LEVEL 3

1. **Install the fork-crown race.** Slide the (greased inside) fork-crown race down on the fork steering tube until it hits the enlarged section at the bottom. Slide the crown-race slide punch up and down the steering tube, pounding the race down until it sits flat on top of its seat on the fork crown (Fig. 11.41). Some crown-race punches are longer and closed on the top and are meant to be hit with a hammer rather than to be slid up and down by hand. Check if installation is complete by holding the fork up against the light to see whether there are any gaps between the fork-crown race and the crown. For an integrated headset (Figs. 11.19, 11.22, and 11.24), you can skip the rest of this section and install and adjust the bearings as described in §xi-18 and §xi-16.

NOTE: *Extra-thin fork-crown races can easily be bent or broken by the crown-race punch. Chris King and Shimano both make support tools that sit over the race and distribute the impact from the punch.*

2. **Grease where the cups will go.** Put a thin layer of grease inside the ends of the headtube.

3. **Prepare the headset press and cups for installation.** By hand, place the headset cups

11.43 Pressing in headset cups with a headset press

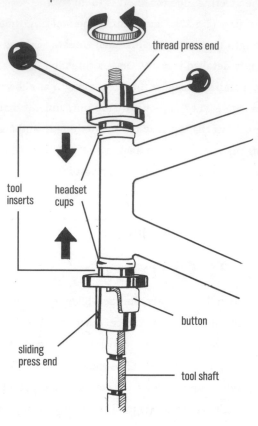

the cups are not touching the precision surfaces that the bearings roll in!

NOTE: *Some headsets have cartridge bearings that are permanently pressed into the cups (Fig. 11.31). If you use a headset press that pushes on the center of the cups, you will ruin the bearings. You need a press or an insert on the press that pushes the outer part of the cup and does not touch the bearings.*

4. **Press in the cups.** Hold the lower end of the headset-press shaft with a wrench. That will keep the tool from turning as you press in the cups. Tighten the press by turning the handle on the top clockwise (Fig. 11.43). Keep tightening the tool until the cups are fully pressed into the ends of the head-tube. Examine them carefully to make sure that they are pressed in square so that there are no gaps between the cups and the ends of the head-tube.

NOTE: *You can easily crush thin headset cups with a flat-surface headset press when it is used without inserts, so be careful and stop when the cups reach the head-tube.*

5. **Grease all bearing surfaces.** If you are using cartridge bearings (Fig. 11.24), a thin film will do.

6. **Assemble and adjust the headset.** Follow the instructions in §xi-18 and §xi-16 for a threadless headset and in §xi-19 and §xi-17 for a threaded one.

TROUBLESHOOTING STEM, HANDLEBAR, AND HEADSET PROBLEMS

xi-23

HANDLEBAR SLIPS

Tighten the pinch bolts on the stem that holds the handlebar, but not beyond the maximum allowable torque (see Appendix D). With a front-opening stem, make sure that there is the same amount of space between the stem and the front plate on both edges of the front plate. With any stem, if the clamp closes against itself without holding the handlebar securely, be sure to check that

into the ends of the head-tube. Slide the headset-press shaft through the head-tube. Press the button on the sliding end of the tool, and slide it onto the shaft until it bumps into one of the cups (Fig. 11.43). This same method, and often the same press, can be used for semi-integrated (Figs. 11.20 and 11.23) and traditional (Figs. 11.18 and 11.21) headsets. The press has separate inserts that may be appropriate to put into the cups before sliding the press into place.

NOTE: *Make sure that the press and any installed press inserts make contact only with the outer cup flange and not with the bearing seat.*

Find the nearest notch on the tool's shaft, and release the button to fix the detachable press end in place. Whatever you do, be certain that the parts that make contact with the handlebar is not deformed and that the stem clamp is not cracked or stretched; replace any questionable parts (replace lightweight stems and bars if the clamp edges touch each other). You can slide a shim made out of a beer can between the stem and handlebar to hold it better if you have a heavy stem and handlebar, but don't try this with lightweight parts. Replacing parts is a safer option—there is always a reason that parts that are meant to fit together no longer do! With super-light stems and handlebars, you cannot just keep tightening the small clamp bolts as you can the larger bolts on heavy stems because you will strip threads and/or cause handlebar and stem failures.

xi-24
CREAKING HANDLEBAR NOISES

Loosen the stem clamp first. Then grease the area of the handlebar that is clamped in the stem, slide the handlebar back in place, and tighten the stem bolt. Also, sanding the hard anodized surface inside the stem clamp and on the clamping area of the handlebar can eliminate creaking.

xi-25
SLIPPING BAR END

Tighten the bar-end clamp bolt. If you have to go beyond the specified torque, the handlebar or the bar end may be damaged and may need to be replaced.

xi-26
STEM NOT POINTED STRAIGHT AHEAD

Loosen the bolt(s) securing the stem to the fork steering tube, align the stem with the front wheel, and tighten the stem bolt(s) again. With

a threaded headset, the bolt you are interested in is a single vertical bolt on top of the stem. Loosen it about two turns, and tap the top of the bolt with a hammer to disengage the wedge on the other end from the bottom of the stem (Fig. 11.15). With a threadless headset, there are one, two, or three horizontal bolts pinching the stem around the steering tube (Figs. 11.6–7) that need to be loosened to turn the stem on the steering tube. Do not loosen the bolt on the top of the stem cap (Fig. 11.12); you'll have to readjust the headset if you do.

xi-27
FORK AND HEADSET RATTLE

The headset is too loose. Adjust the headset (§xi-16 or §xi-17).

xi-28
STEM, BAR, AND FORK ASSEMBLY NOT TURNING SMOOTHLY

If it does not turn smoothly but instead stops in certain fixed positions, the headset is pitted and needs to be replaced. See §xi-20 to §xi-22.

xi-29
STEM, BAR, AND FORK ASSEMBLY NOT TURNING FREELY

The headset is too tight. The front wheel should swing easily from side to side when you lean the bike or lift the front end. Adjust the headset (§xi-16 or §xi-17, depending on type).

xi-30
STEM STUCK ON OR IN FORK STEERING TUBE

See §xi-14.

WHEELBUILDING

A child of five could understand this. Fetch me a child of five.

—Groucho Marx

TOOLS

spoke wrench

truing stand

wheel dishing tool

13mm, 14mm, and 15mm cone wrenches

17mm open-end wrench (or an adjustable wrench)

spoke-prep compound

OPTIONAL

linseed oil

LEVEL 3

Congratulations. You have arrived at the task most often used to gauge the talents of a bike mechanic. Next to building a frame or a fork, building a good set of wheels is the most critical, and creative, of a bike mechanic's tasks. Despite the air of mystery surrounding the art of wheelbuilding, the construction of a good set of bicycle wheels is really a pretty straightforward task.

Clearly, wheels are the central component of a bike. For any bike to perform well, its wheels must be well made and properly tensioned. Once you learn how, it is quite rewarding to turn a pile of small parts into a set of strong and light wheels that you can bash around with confidence. You will be amazed at what they can withstand, and you will no longer go through life thinking that building wheels is something that just the experts do. With practice, you can build wheels at your house that are just as good as any custom-made set and far superior to those built by machine.

This chapter is not meant to be an exhaustive description of how to build all types of wheel spok-

ing patterns, but you will learn here how to build the five spoking patterns that are used in virtually all mountain bike wheels. (If you are interested in a more comprehensive treatment of the subject of wheelbuilding, I recommend reading *Barnett's Manual* by John Barnett, *The Art of Wheelbuilding* by Gerd Schraner, or *The Bicycle Wheel* by Jobst Brandt.) In this chapter, you will learn how to build wheels in the classic "three-cross" spoking pattern, in which each spoke crosses over three other spokes (Fig. 12.1) for either rim brakes or disc brakes. But that isn't the only spoking pattern to be learned here; §xii-7 details how to build radially spoked wheels; §xii-8 teaches the building of rear disc-brake wheels; and §xii-9 sets out the lacing of two-cross and one-cross wheels. Finally, §xii-10 discusses heavier-duty wheels for big riders.

xii-1
GETTING TOGETHER WHEELBUILDING PARTS

Here are the parts you need: a rim, a hub (make sure that the hub you are using has the same

12.1 The complete wheel with three-cross spoke pattern

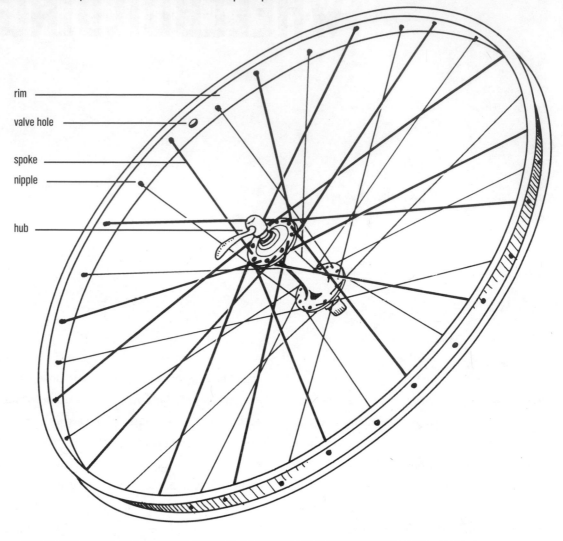

rim
valve hole
spoke
nipple
hub

12.2 Spoke and nipple

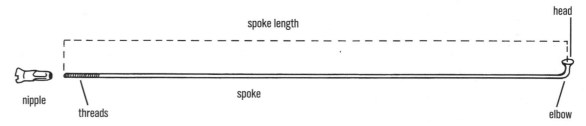

spoke length

head

nipple

threads

spoke

elbow

number of holes as the rim), properly sized spokes, and nipples to match. I suggest getting the spokes from your local bike shop. That way, a mechanic can help make sure you are getting the right spoke lengths (Fig. 12.2) and can counsel you on what gauge (thickness) of spoke to buy, as well as what rim makes sense for your weight, budget, and the kind of riding you plan on doing. You can also use an online spoke calculator to figure out spoke length. Remember: When purchasing spokes or when using a spoke calculator, you must specify that you will be using a "three-cross" spoking pattern (unless you are building a radial wheel [§xii-7] or a one- or two-cross wheel [§xii-9]).

For building disc-brake wheels, I recommend avoiding alloy nipples and superthin spokes unless the rider is small. Brass nipples and 14/15-gauge double-butted spokes (see §xii-10a for more on this) will best take the extra braking loads.

Make sure that you also have a spoke wrench that is the right size for the nipples you are using. And if you are building with UST tubeless rims from Mavic, the rim should come with threaded eyelets you screw into the rim to hold the nipple, as well as the tool needed to grasp their splined heads and screw them in. You also may want to consider longer spoke nipples to avoid losing any inside the rim, which has no access for you to get them out from the tire side.

NOTE: *If you are just replacing a rim on an old wheel, do not use the old spokes. You won't save much money reusing the old spokes, and the rounded-out nipples and weakened spokes will soon make you wish you had gone ahead and bought a new set.*

ANOTHER NOTE: *If you are using thin (1.8mm = 15-gauge) or thinner spokes, there may be some play between the hub holes and the spokes. This will work the spokes over time and bring on premature spoke breakage. DT Swiss sells spoke washers to go between each spoke head and the hub flange to take up this slack.*

xii-2
LACING THE WHEEL

For the sake of brevity and clarity, I do not discuss using spoke-prep compound with every instruction to thread a nipple onto a spoke. Although spoke-prep compound is not mandatory, I think that the wheel is improved if the compound is used. It encourages the nipples to thread on more smoothly, it takes up some of the slop between the spoke and nipple threads, and its thread-locking ability discourages the nipples from vibrating loose. Better yet, use DT Swiss Pro Lock Nipples, which contain a two-component adhesive in the nipple thread to prevent the spoke-nipple connection from loosening under the effect of operating loads (loading and unloading of the wheel during riding), thereby ensuring constant spoke tension.

If you are using spoke-prep compound, apply it to the spoke threads before putting each nipple on. Do not apply too much, or it will be hard to adjust the nipples months and years down the trail; you want the spoke-prep just in the dips of the threads. To get the right amount, dip the threads of a pair of spokes into the spoke-prep compound and then take two more dry spokes and roll the threads of all four spokes together with your fingers. With DT Swiss Pro Lock nipples, you don't have to do any of this, but you also want to complete the wheel in one sitting. Just as with epoxy glue, you will be bursting little beads of the two glue components inside the nipple. So if you get this done while the glue is viscous, the nipples will hold better than if you let the glue harden and then turn the nipples again in ensuing days.

In the absence of spoke-prep compound, at least dip the threads of each spoke in grease. Grease accomplishes everything spoke-prep compound does, save for locking the threads.

1. **Divide the spokes into four separate groups, two sets for each side of each hub flange.** Rubber-band each set together.

IMPORTANT: *If you are building a rear wheel (or a front disc-brake wheel—Fig. 12.26), you should be working with two different spoke lengths, because spokes on the drive side (or brake-rotor side) are almost always shorter, due to different axle spacing and sometimes different hub flange diameters on the two sides. For a rear disc-brake wheel or a radial wheel, skip to §xii-8 or §xii-7.*

2. **Hold the rim on your lap with the valve hole away from you.** Notice that the holes alternate being offset upward and downward from the rim centerline. With an off-center rim (OCR, Fig. 12.3), have the spoke holes offset downward, toward your lap.

NOTE: *If you are building a rear wheel with an off-center drilled rim (e.g., Ritchey OCR, Bontrager ASYM), make sure as you are lacing that you orient the rim so that the spoke holes are offset to the left (nondrive) side (see Fig. 12.3). If you are building a front disc-brake wheel with an off-center rim, make sure as you are lacing that you orient the rim so that the spoke holes are offset to the right (nonrotor) side. The rim is meant to reduce wheel dish by offsetting the nipples to reduce the otherwise very steep angle at which rear drive-side or front disc-side spokes normally hit the rim. The balanced left-to-right spoke tension should increase the lifetime of the wheel, and the lower spoke angle moves the rear drive-side spokes away from the rear derailleur. Also, when using the chain on the dished, titanium, ninth (largest) cog of Ritchey's "2 × 9" drive-train, the derailleur does not snag the spokes because the rim offset moves them farther inboard.*

3. **Hold the hub in the center of the rim, with the right side of the hub pointing up.** In the illustrations, the right side (or the rotor side of a disc-brake front hub—Fig. 12.26) is the one with the nut end of the quick-release on it.

IMPORTANT: *On a rear hub, the right side is the drive side. Standard front hubs are symmetrical; pick a side to be the right side. But if you are building a front disc-brake wheel (Fig. 12.26), I will ask you to call the left side the right side. In other words, follow the lacing instructions to the letter, except substitute the rotor side of the hub (which is actually the left side) whenever the instructions refer to the right side. That way, the spokes on both sides that oppose the braking force on the rotor will come out of the outside of the hub flanges. The wheel will hence be stronger, because*

12.3 OCR laced correctly

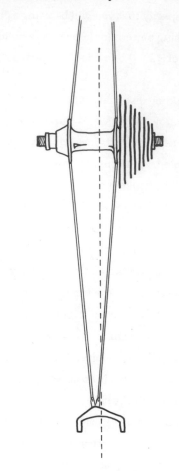

12.4 First half of right-side spokes placed in hub

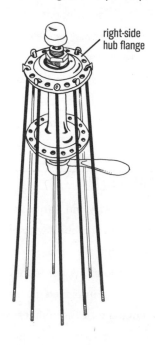

right-side
hub flange

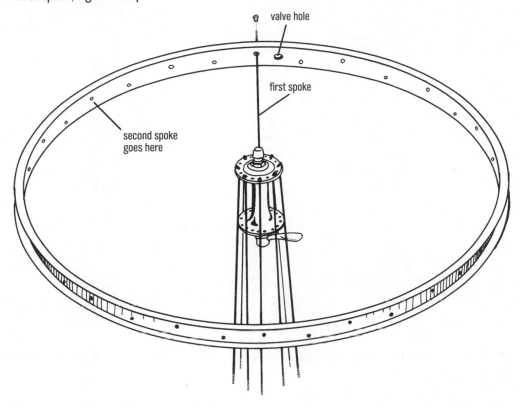

valve hole

first spoke

second spoke
goes here

these *"pulling" spokes come into the rim from a wider angle. If you are building a rear disc-brake wheel, read §xii-9 before continuing.*

a. First set of spokes

4. **Drop a spoke down into every other hole in the top (right-side) hub flange so that the spoke heads are facing up** (Fig. 12.4). If you're using a rear wheel or disc-brake front wheel, make sure to put the shorter spokes on the right (drive) side. On some (older) hubs, half of the holes you are looking at will be countersunk deeper into the hub flange to provide a radius less stressful on the spoke elbow, so don't use those holes—use their neighbors. That said, most hubs today have the same countersinking on all holes so that they can also be used to build a completely symmetrical, radially spoked wheel.

5. **Bring a spoke from the hub into the first rim hole counterclockwise from the valve hole.** Thread the nipple onto the spoke clockwise three turns to secure it yet not tighten the spoke (Fig. 12.5). Notice that this hole is off-set upward (on an OCR, this means that the hole is offset upward from the centerline of the spoke holes, not the centerline of the rim). If the first hole that is counterclockwise from the valve hole isn't offset upward, you have a misdrilled rim, and you must offset all instructions one hole.

NOTE: *With Mavic UST tubeless rims, first slide the threaded eyelet onto the spoke, then thread the nipple onto the spoke clockwise three turns, and then tighten the threaded eyelet into the rim with the special splined tool. Putting some spoke threadlock on the eyelet threads, as well as on the spoke threads, is a good idea.*

12.6 First set of spokes laced

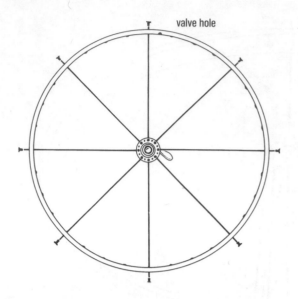

valve hole

12.7 Spoke-hole offset

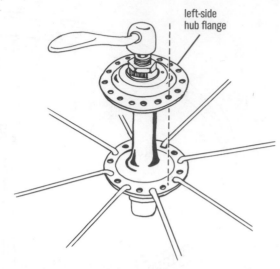

left-side
hub flange

6. **Working counterclockwise, put the next spoke on the hub into the hole in the rim four holes away from the first spoke, and thread the nipple onto the spoke three turns.** There should be three open rim holes between these spokes, and the hole you put the second spoke into should also be offset upward.

7. **Continue counterclockwise around the wheel in the same manner.** You should now have used half of the rim holes that are offset upward, and there should be three open holes between all spokes (Fig. 12.6).

8. **Flip the wheel over.**

b. Second set of spokes

9. **Sight across the hub from one flange to the other flange.** Notice that the holes in one flange do not line up with the holes in the other flange; each hole lines up in between two holes on the opposite flange (Fig. 12.7).

10. **Drop a spoke down through the hole in the top flange that is immediately clockwise from the first spoke you installed** (the spoke that is just clockwise from the valve hole).

If this is a rear wheel or a front disc-brake wheel, you are now using the longer spokes.

11. **Put this new spoke into the second hole clockwise from the valve hole, next to the first spoke you installed** (Figs. 12.8–9). This hole will be offset upward from the rim centerline.

12. **Thread the nipple clockwise onto the spoke three turns.**

13. **Double-check your lacing.** Make sure that the spoke you just installed starts at a hole in the hub's top (left-side) flange, which is half a hole space clockwise from the hole in the lower flange where the first spoke you installed started. These two spokes should be diverging but still nearly parallel (Fig. 12.9).

14. **Drop a spoke down through the hole in the top (left-side) hub flange two holes away in either direction, and continue around until every other hole has a spoke hanging down through it** (Fig. 12.8).

15. **Working counterclockwise, take the next spoke from the hub and put it in the rim hole that is three holes counterclockwise from the valve hole.** This hole should be offset upward

12.8 Lacing second set

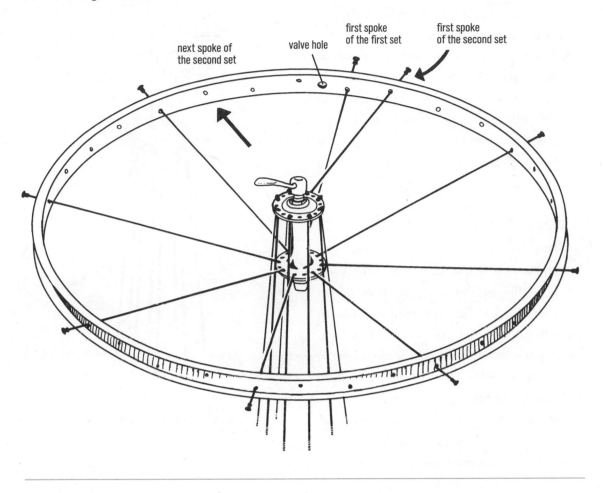

next spoke of
the second set

valve hole

first spoke
of the first set

first spoke
of the second set

12.9 Diverging parallel spokes

12.10 Second set of spokes laced

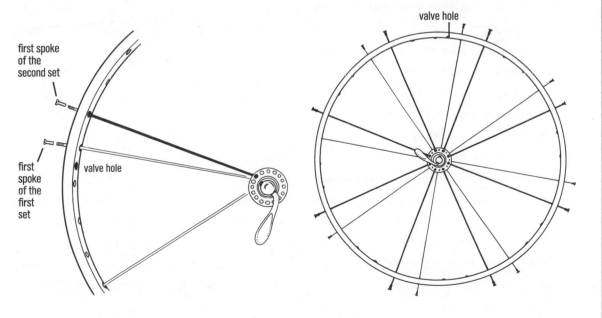

first spoke
of the
second set

first
spoke
of the
first
set

valve hole

valve hole

and four holes counterclockwise from the spoke you just installed. Thread the nipple onto the spoke three turns.

16. **Follow this pattern counterclockwise around the wheel** (Fig. 12.10). You should have now used half of the rim holes that are offset upward, as well as half of the total rim holes. The second set of spokes should all be in upwardly offset holes, one hole clockwise from each spoke of the first set.

c. Third set of spokes

17. **Drop spokes through the remaining holes on the right side of the hub, from the inside of the hub out** (Fig. 12.11). Remember: If you are building a rear wheel or front disc-brake wheel, these should be the shorter spokes.

18. **Flip the wheel over.** Grab the spokes you've just dropped through the hub to keep them from falling out.

19. **Fan the spokes out.** Now they cannot fall back down through the hub holes.

20. **Grab the hub shell and rotate it counterclockwise as far as you can** (Fig. 12.12).

21. **Pick any spoke on the top (right-hand) hub flange that is already laced to the rim.** Now find the spoke five hub holes away in a clockwise direction.

22. **Take this new spoke, cross it under the spoke you counted from (the one five holes away), and stick it into the rim hole two holes counterclockwise from that spoke** (Fig. 12.13). Thread the nipple onto the spoke three turns. Expect to bend the spokes some.

23. **Continue around the wheel, doing the same thing** (Fig. 12.14). You may find that some of the spokes don't quite reach far enough. If that's the case, push down on each one about 1 inch from the spoke elbow to help them reach.

12.11 Placing third set of spokes in hub

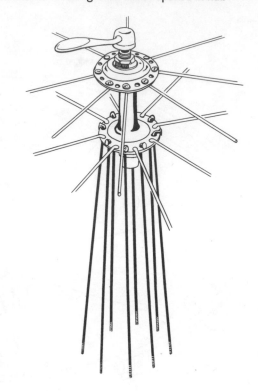

12.12 Rotating hub counterclockwise

24. **Check your lacing.** Make sure that every spoke coming out of the upper side of the top flange (the spokes that come out toward you with their spoke heads hidden from view) crosses over two spokes and under a third.

12.13 Lacing third set of spokes

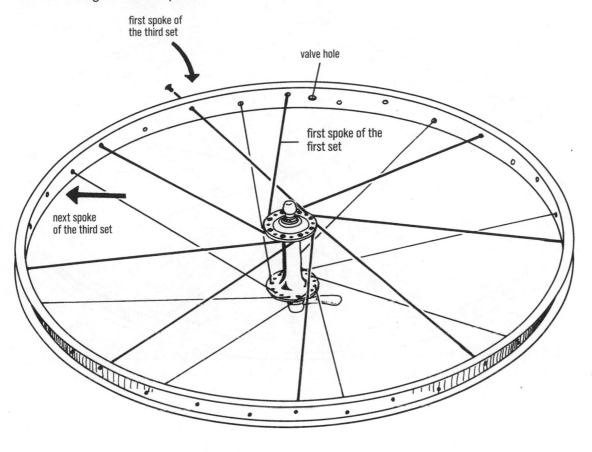

first spoke of
the third set

valve hole

first spoke of the
first set

next spoke
of the third set

All three of these "crossing" spokes come from the underside of the same flange and have their spoke heads facing toward you. These crossing spokes begin one, three, and five hub holes counterclockwise from the spoke that you just inserted into the rim (Fig. 12.14). This is called a "three-cross" pattern because every spoke crosses three others on its way to the rim (over, over, under). Every upwardly offset hole should now be occupied on the rim.

12.14 Third set laced

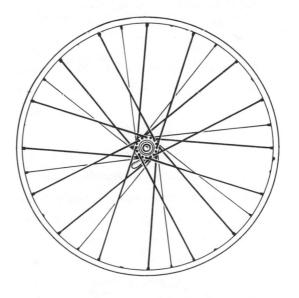

d. Fourth (and final) set of spokes

25. **Drop spokes down through the remaining hub holes in the bottom flange from the inside out.** Do it as shown in Figure 12.11, but

12.15 Lacing fourth set of spokes

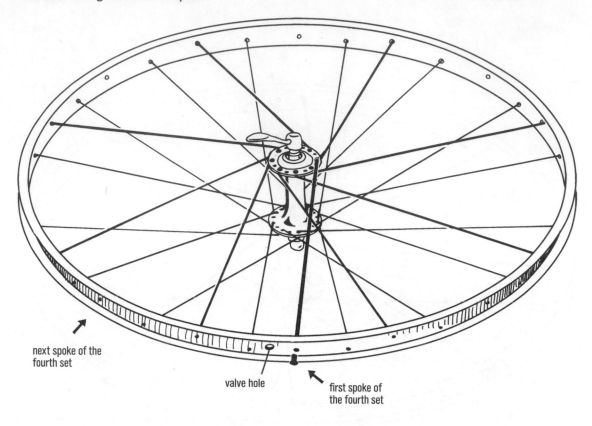

next spoke of the
fourth set

valve hole

first spoke of
the fourth set

with the other side of the hub up. On a rear or front disc-brake hub, these are again the longer spokes.

26. **Flip the wheel over.** Grab the spokes to keep them from falling out.

27. **Fan the spokes out.**

28. **Pick any spoke on the top (left-hand) hub flange that is already laced to the rim.** Now find the spoke five hub holes away in a counterclockwise direction.

29. **Take that spoke, cross it over two spokes and under the spoke you counted from.** Stick the spoke into the rim hole two holes clockwise from the spoke it crosses under (Fig. 12.15). Thread the nipple onto the spoke three turns.

30. **Continue around the wheel, doing the same thing until the wheel is laced as shown in Figure 12.1.** You may find that some of the spokes don't quite reach far enough. If that's

12.16 Converging parallel spokes

valve hole

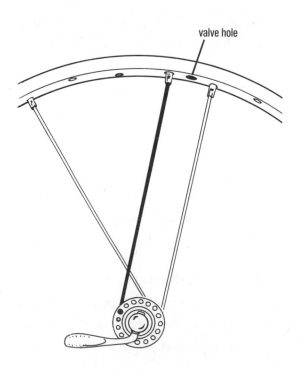

the case, push down on each one about 1 inch from the spoke elbow to help them reach.

31. **Check your lacing.** Make sure that every spoke coming out from the upper side of the top flange (the spokes that come out toward you with their spoke heads hidden from view) crosses over two spokes and under a third (Fig. 12.1). All three of these crossing spokes come from the underside of the same flange, with spoke heads facing toward you. The crossing spokes begin one, three, and five hub holes clockwise from each spoke emerging from the top of the upper (left) hub flange (Fig. 12.1). Every hole should now be occupied on the rim. The valve hole should be between "converging parallel" spokes (Fig. 12.16) to make room for the pump head when you inflate the tire.

IMPORTANT: *If you are building a rear wheel, note that the spokes coming out of the outside of the hub flange on both sides oppose the clockwise twist the chain applies on the cogs. Similarly, if you are building a front disc-brake wheel (Fig. 12.26), you will notice that the spokes coming out of the outside of both flanges oppose the twist the brake pads apply to the rotor. See §xii-6 for more on this.*

xii-3
TENSIONING THE WHEEL

1. **Put the wheel in the truing stand.** If you are using a through-axle hub, you can get adapters for many truing stands that allow you to secure the hub in the stand. And if the wheel is so tall that it doesn't clear the truing stand bed (usually only an issue with 36-inch rims or when a 29er wheel is trued with a big tire on it), you can get extension pieces for the truing stand uprights.

2. **Tighten each nipple with a spoke wrench.** Tighten until only three threads are visible beyond the bottom of the nipple (see Figs. 12.17–20 for rotation direction).

NOTE: *From now on, every time you tighten or loosen a spoke nipple, turn it back in the opposite direction by a one-eighth turn afterward. This process unwinds the twist in the spoke that your tightening or loosening has just caused.*

3. **Press the spokes coming outward from the outer side of the hub flanges down with your thumb at their elbow.** This straightens out their line to the rim. Spokes coming out of the inner side of the flange do not need this adjustment.

4. **Go all the way around the wheel, tightening each nipple a half turn.** Do this uniformly, so that the wheel is not thrown out of true.

5. **Check to see whether the spokes are tight enough to give a tone when plucked.** Squeeze pairs of spokes toward each other, and compare their tension with that of a good wheel with spokes of the same gauge; your wheel should have considerably less tension at this point.

6. **Repeat steps 4 and 5 until the spokes all make a tone but are under less tension than an existing, good wheel.**

xii-4
TRUING THE WHEEL
a. Lateral true

Side-to-side trueness is the most obvious wheel parameter when you spin the wheel.

1. **Make sure the hub axle has no end play.** If it does, adjust the hub (see §vi-15d) to eliminate the end play.

2. **Optional: Put a drop of linseed oil around the top of each nipple.** This lubricates the contact area between the nipple and the inside of the rim hole.

3. **Set the truing-stand feelers so that one of them scrapes the side of the rim at the worst lateral wobble (Figs. 12.17–18).**

4. **Tighten the spokes coming from the opposite side of the hub from the scrape, and**

12.17 Pull rim to the right

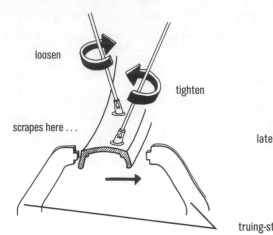

loosen

tighten

scrapes here . . .

12.18 Pull rim to the left

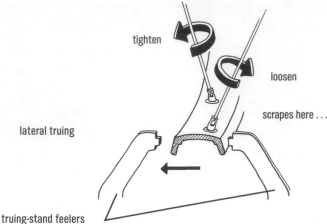

tighten

loosen

scrapes here . . .

lateral truing

truing-stand feelers

loosen the spokes coming from the same side of the hub (Figs. 12.17–18). Make these tightening and loosening adjustments on two or three spokes on either side of the spot where the rim scrapes. Start with one-quarter turn on nipples at the center of the scraping area, and decrease the amount you turn each nipple as you move away in either direction. This process pulls the rim away from the feeler. If your adjustments do the opposite, you are turning the nipples in the wrong direction.

IMPORTANT: *You normally turn something to the right to tighten it and to the left to loosen it, but tightening and loosening spoke nipples at the bottom of the wheel are the opposite of what you would normally do (Figs. 12.17–20). This is because the nipple head is underneath the spoke wrench. This does not apply if you rotate the wheel so that you are looking down on the nipple from the top. Try opening a jar that is upside down, and you will immediately understand the principle involved.*

5. **Work around the wheel in this way.** Bring the feelers in closer as the wheel gets truer.

12.19 Pull rim in

12.20 Let rim out

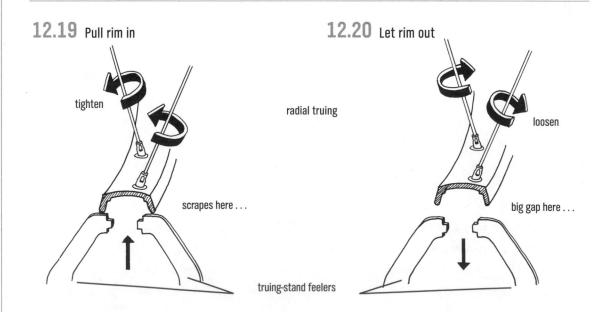

tighten

scrapes here . . .

radial truing

loosen

big gap here . . .

truing-stand feelers

NOTE: *On disc-brake rims, you may need to scrape decals off the rim sides so that they won't hang up on the truing-stand feelers and make it hard to tell where the real wobbles are.*

b. Radial true

Although not as obvious as side-to-side trueness, out-of-roundness is more important to the longevity of the wheel, because "uniformity of tension is the key to durability" (Portia Masterson, formerly of Self Propulsion bike shop in Golden, Colorado).

1. **Set the truing-stand feelers so that they will contact the circumference of the rim, rather than the sides** (Figs. 12.19–20).

2. **Bring the feelers in until they scrape against the highest spot on the rim** (Fig. 12.19).

3. **Tighten the spokes one-quarter turn at the point where the rim scrapes.** This will pull the rim inward. Decrease the amount of each turn (to a one-eighth turn and less) as you move away from the center of the scraping area.

4. **Work around the wheel this way, bringing the feelers up as the wheel becomes rounder.** Loosen the spokes at a dip in the rim (Fig. 12.20). If the spokes are too tight at this point, they will be hard to turn and will creak and groan as you turn them. When the spokes become hard to turn (i.e., the nipples feel on the verge of rounding off), loosen all of the spokes in the wheel one-quarter turn before continuing. Compare the tension with a good wheel with the same-gauge spokes; the tension should still be lower in the wheel you are building.

xii-5
CENTERING (OR DISHING) THE WHEEL

The rim on a good wheel must be centered in the frame or fork (between the brake pads if you have rim brakes). On a rear hub or a disc-brake front hub, one hub flange is set back farther from

12.21 Using the dishing tool to check the centering of the rim relative to the axle ends

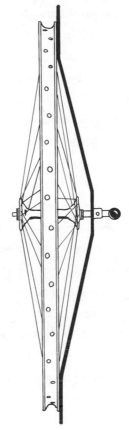

the axle end (and hence from the frame or fork dropout) on that side than is the other flange. Although the wheel in Figure 12.21 (a front wheel for rim brakes) is symmetrical, an end view like this of either a rear wheel or a disc-brake front wheel would show the tighter spokes on the side with either the cogs or disc rotor to be much flatter (i.e., less angle to the rim) than the (looser) spokes on the other side. Thus, the wheel will be dish-shaped when the rim is centered. This is what is meant by "wheel dish."

1. **Place the dishing tool across the right side of the wheel, bisecting the center** (Fig. 12.21).

2. **Tighten or loosen the dishing gauge screw until the gauge contacts the outer face of the axle end nut** (Fig. 12.21).

3. **Flip the wheel over.**

4. **Place the dishing tool across the other side of the wheel.**

5. **Check the gap of the dishing gauge with this axle–end nut face** (Fig. 12.22). Any gap between the dishing gauge and the axle–end nut face indicates the amount that the rim is offset from the centerline of the wheel. If there is no gap, but an overlap instead, reset the dishing gauge on this side (the previously overlapped side).

6. **Flip the wheel over and check the other side.** Repeat steps 4 and 5 on the opposite side.

7. **Put the wheel back in the truing stand.**

8. **Pull the rim toward the center.** By tightening the spokes on the opposite side of the wheel from the axle end that had the gap between the axle–end nut face and the dishing gauge, you will be reducing the gap between the dishing tool and the nut. Tighten a half turn each. If the spokes start getting really tight (they will creak a lot when tightening, the nipples will start rounding off, and the spokes will feel much tighter than the spokes in a comparable wheel), then loosen the spokes on the opposite side of the wheel a half turn each.

9. **Recheck the wheel with the dishing gauge by repeating steps 1–5.**

10. **If the wheel is still off-dish (there is still a gap between the dishing gauge and the end nut when you flip the wheel over), repeat steps 6–8.** Continue until the gap is zero (i.e., the dish is correct).

11. **Prestress the spokes by squeezing each pair of spokes together with your hands** (Fig. 12.23). They will make a "ping" noise as they unwind.

    (a) Leaning on the wheel is a quicker way to prestress the wheel, but this method has the potential to wreck the wheel if you are not careful. To proceed, set the axle end on

12.22 Checking wheel dish on the other side of the hub

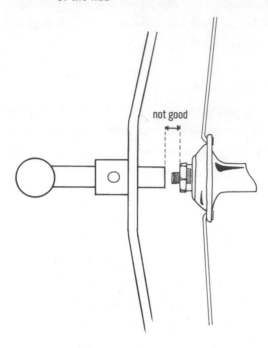

not good

12.23 Relieving spoke tension

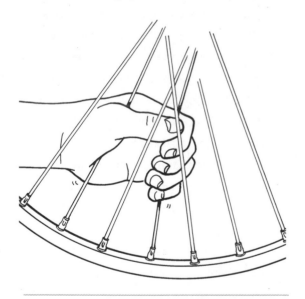

the workbench and carefully press down on the rim with your hands at the 9 o'clock and 3 o'clock positions. This procedure will affect an area of about three spokes on each side, so rotate the wheel three spokes, press down again, rotate three more spokes in the same direction, press down again, and so on.

After you finish one side, flip the wheel over and do the other side. Do not press down with all of your might; although a well-built wheel's lateral strength is impressive, it is still easy to destroy your work with too much pressure.

(b) The amount of readjustment the spokes need to make will be reduced if you have been turning each nipple back a one-eighth turn in the opposite direction after each rotational correction (as directed in §xii-3, step 2). If none of the spokes are twisted, there will be no pinging and readjustment during prestressing.

(c) If prestressing throws the wheel way out of true, the spokes are probably too tight. Loosen them all a one-eighth turn. Some loss of wheel trueness is normal. If the loss is minor, you may overlook it.

12. **Repeat §xii-4, followed by §xii-5, prestressing the spokes frequently as you go.** This will keep improving the accuracy of the build.

13. **Bring up the tension to that of a comparable wheel by making small tightening adjustments to every nipple.** Adjust dish and true after each time around, until the wheel is as you want it.

14. **If the rim is oily, wipe it down with a citrus-based biodegradable solvent.**

Congratulate yourself on building your wheel, and show it off to your friends.

xii-6
REVIEWING THE WHEEL BUILD

Your wheel has some features that you won't find on machine-built wheels. Most significantly, on your rear wheel the pulling spokes are to the outside. In plain speak, this means that you have a spoking pattern that best resists the twisting force on the hub produced by pedaling forces on the chain.

In the rear wheel you have just built, half of the spokes are called "pulling," or "dynamic," spokes, and the other half are called "static" spokes. The pulling spokes are the ones directed in such a way that a clockwise twist on the hub increases the tension in them. If you look at the wheel from the drive side, you will see what I am talking about. You will also see that the static spokes do not oppose a clockwise twist on the hub. In fact, their tension decreases when you stomp on the pedals.

By placing all of the pulling spokes so that they come from the inside of the hub flanges out (i.e., the spoke heads are on the inward side of the flanges), you have made the spokes undergoing the largest tension changes lie across the hub flange and thus better support the spoke elbow. You have also increased their angle to the rim and hence their ability to oppose forces acting on the rim. Similarly, if you just built a front disc-brake wheel (Fig. 12.26), the pulling spokes opposing the braking force on the disc are to the outside of the hub flanges.

If you have chosen the appropriate parts for your weight and riding style and have the proper spoke tension, then you should have a strong wheel that will last you a long time. Congratulations!

xii-7
LACING RADIALLY SPOKED WHEELS

With the advent of stronger rim materials and stiffer rim cross-sections, radially spoked wheels—in which the spokes emanate radially from the hub out to the rim, rather than crossing each other (Fig. 12.24)—are very popular. They are very simple to lace up, and radial spoking offers a number of advantages, but a completely radial wheel can be used only on the front. On the rear, you must still use a crossing pattern on one side (usually the drive side) to oppose the twist on the

12.24 Radially spoked front wheel

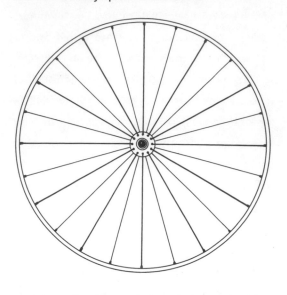

12.25 Radial/three-cross rear wheel

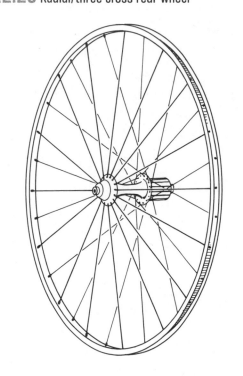

hub caused by the chain (Fig. 12.25). Similarly, you cannot use a radially spoked wheel with disc brakes, as the spokes cannot oppose the torque the brake applies to the brake rotor.

A radially spoked wheel is vertically stiffer than a crossed one because radial spokes allow little opportunity for spokes to absorb energy in the spoking pattern. The radial wheel can be laterally stiffer too because all of the spokes can come to the outside of the hub flange and increase the pulling angle to the rim.

A radial wheel is lighter because the spokes are shorter. Further weight can be removed with fewer spokes, and radial spoking allows any even spoke count to be used (with nonradial patterns, the spoke count must be a multiple of four). And radial spoking allows the use of flangeless direct-pull hubs and nail-head or double-threaded spokes (straight spokes without elbows), eliminating a potential weak spot in each spoke.

Note that the warranty of some hubs is voided when spoked radially. Shimano has this stipulation, for instance. The stress is greater on hub holes with radial spoking because there is less material to resist the tearing of the hub holes when the spoke is pulling straight outward than if it is pulling at an angle along the hub flange.

a. How to lace a radial front wheel

Simply drop all the spokes from the inside of each flange outward, and lace the spokes straight to the rim (Fig. 12.24).

b. How to lace a rear wheel with a radial left side and a three-cross drive side

First lace the drive side following the instructions in §xii-2a, steps 4–7, and §xii-2c, steps 17–24. Now lace the left-side spokes radially outward through the hub flange and straight to the rim (Fig 12.25).

The tensioning and truing steps are the same for radial and radial–three-cross wheels as for standard three-cross wheels, but radial spoke tension should be higher to help prevent the spokes from vibrating loose.

NOTE: *These instructions place the radial spokes to the outside of the hub flange so that their angle to the rim (and hence their ability to oppose lateral forces on it) is highest.*

xii-8
LACING REAR THREE-CROSS DISC-BRAKE WHEELS

NOTE: *If you are building a wheel with a Rohloff or other internal-gear hub, the hub may be too large to build a three-cross wheel, as the spokes would wrap across the other spokes on the hub flange, causing them undue stress. Rohloff says that 26-inch and 700C (29-inch) wheels must always be laced in a two-cross pattern, and 24-inch and smaller wheels must be laced only in a one-cross pattern. See §xii-9 for instructions.*

If you are building a rear disc-brake wheel (Fig. 12.28), you want the drive-side outer spokes opposing the chain force on the cogs, but you also want the left-side outer spokes opposing the braking force on the rotor. This pattern makes for a stronger wheel by having the wider-angle spokes doing more of the work. And, as with all disc-brake wheels, I recommend brass nipples and 14/15-gauge double-butted spokes (see §xii-10a for more on this).

The drive side will be laced in just the same way as described in the lacing instructions in §xii-2, but the nondrive side will be laced in the opposite way that the left-side turns would be laced in §xii-2.

a. First set of spokes

1. Follow §xii-2a, steps 1–5.

b. Second set of spokes

2. Push a spoke up through the hole in the top flange that is immediately clockwise from the first spoke you installed (the spoke that is just clockwise from the valve hole).

3. Follow §xii-2, steps 11–13, and then step 4 here.

12.26 Front disc-brake wheel

12.27 Rear disc-brake wheel: first two sets of spokes completed, first spoke of third set installed

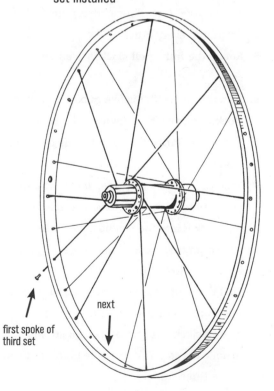

first spoke of third set

next

12.28 Completed rear disc-brake wheel

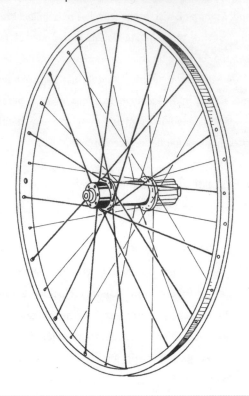

4. **Drop one spoke down through each of the adjacent hub holes on either side of the newly laced spoke.** Skip a hole, and continue around the hub flange, dropping a spoke down into every other hole.

5. **Rotate the hub shell clockwise as far as you can.**

6. **Find the spoke that is five hub holes counterclockwise from the single spoke coming up out of the flange that you installed in steps 2 and 3.**

7. **Take this new spoke, cross it over the spoke you counted from (the one five holes away), and stick it into the rim hole two holes clockwise from that spoke.** Thread the nipple onto the spoke three turns.

8. **Find the next spoke counterclockwise on the hub flange.** Put it in the rim hole four holes counterclockwise from the spoke you just installed in step 7. Thread the nipple onto the spoke three turns.

9. **Continue counterclockwise around the top (brake-side) hub flange until all spokes whose heads stick out of the top flange are one rim hole counterclockwise from the first set of spokes installed in the rim.**

c. Third set of spokes

10. **Follow §xii-2, steps 17–24.** After you complete step 22, the wheel should look like the wheel shown in Figure 12.27 (except the other fanned-out unlaced spokes coming out of the top flange are not shown).

d. Fourth (and final) set of spokes

11. **Pick any spoke on the top (rotor-side) flange whose head is facing up and is already laced to the rim.** Now find the spoke five clockwise hub holes away.

12. **Follow §xii-2, steps 22–24.**

Your wheel is now laced. Note that the drive-side outer spokes oppose the chain pull and the rotor-side outer spokes oppose the braking force on the rotor (Fig. 12.28). Give yourself a big pat on the back, and then begin tensioning and truing your wheel, starting with §xii-3.

xii-9
LACING TWO-CROSS AND ONE-CROSS WHEELS

Two-cross (or one-cross on 24-inch and smaller wheels) is a must for rear wheels with a Rohloff SpeedHub. And reducing the number of spoke crossings on any wheel shortens the spokes. This removes some weight and reduces the vertical compliance of the wheel. Obviously, you will need shorter spokes; this will be accounted for automatically in online spoke calculators when you input the number of crosses.

To lace a two-cross wheel, begin by following the steps in §xii-2a and §xii-2b exactly (or follow the steps in §xii-8a and §xii-8b exactly for a

Rohloff or other rear disc-brake hub). In §xii-2c, steps 21–22, count three hub holes over, not five. And step 24 in the case of a two-cross wheel now becomes the following:

1. **Check your lacing.** Make sure that every spoke coming out of the upper side of the top flange (the spokes that come out toward you with their spoke heads hidden from view) crosses over one spoke and under a second. Both of these "crossing" spokes come from the underside of the same flange and have spoke heads facing toward you. These crossing spokes begin one and three hub holes counterclockwise from the spoke that you just inserted into the rim. This is called a two-cross pattern because every spoke crosses two others on its way to the rim (over, under). Every upwardly offset hole should now be occupied on the rim.

In §xii-2d, steps 25–26, count three hub holes over, not five, and cross over one spoke and under the spoke you counted from. And step 28 in the case of a two-cross wheel now becomes the following:

2. **Check your lacing.** Make sure that every spoke coming out from the upper side of the top flange (the spokes that come out toward you with their spoke heads hidden from view) crosses over one spoke and under a second. Both of these crossing spokes come from the underside of the same flange and have their spoke heads facing toward you. The crossing spokes begin one and three hub holes clockwise from each spoke emerging from the top of the upper (left) hub flange (Fig. 12.1). Every hole should now be occupied on the rim. The valve hole should be between converging parallel spokes (Fig. 12.16) to make room for the pump head when inflating the tire.

With a Rohloff or other rear disc-brake hub, you end up following these changes as well when you follow the steps in §xii-8c and §xii-8d.

And lacing a one-cross wheel reduces by one once again the number of hub holes you count over to and the number of crosses the spoke makes (now each spoke crosses only under one other spoke and crosses over none).

xii-10
BUILDING WHEELS FOR BIG RIDERS

Wheels for heavy and tall riders require greater lateral and vertical stiffness. The weight of the rider can more easily bend and laterally flex the rim, and it creates another problem as well. The heavier rider detensions the spokes at the bottom of the wheel more by making the rim more D-shaped at the bottom as it rolls. If the spokes are under less tension, or if the nipple flanges periodically lose contact with the bases of the rim holes, the nipples may unscrew and the wheel will fall apart. To achieve the necessary higher strength, you can add the several characteristics.

a. Spoke count and thickness

The spoke count needs to be high: Thirty-six or more spokes is highly preferable for riders weighing more than 190 pounds. The spokes need to be heavier, as thicker spokes are less prone to breakage. Although 14/15-gauge (2.0mm, or 14-gauge, on each end, and 1.8 mm, or 15-gauge, throughout the center section), double-butted spokes are thinner than straight 14-gauge spokes, DT Swiss testing has shown that the wheel will probably last longer with them. Because most breakage occurs at the nipple or the elbow and butted spokes are the same thickness there, spoke breakage will not increase. But butted spokes will stretch more, allowing the spoke nipples to better stay in contact with the rim as the rim changes shape while rolling.

b. Nipple type

Brass nipples are preferable to aluminum ones, due to the extra stress a big rider puts on

310

the wheel. The added weight is slight, and the increase in durability can be significant.

c. Rim section and drilling

The deeper the rim is, the higher its hoop strength (vertical stiffness and strength). Very deep V-section rims work with low spoke counts because of this high hoop strength. The strongest wheel would be from a deep-section rim drilled for more spokes. Unfortunately for heavy riders, many deep V-section rims are also thinner to reduce weight and hence lose some strength.

d. Spoking pattern

With 8-, 9-, and 10-speed rear wheels, dish is high (one side of the wheel is flatter than the other), meaning that there is a great tension difference between spokes on the two sides. The loose spokes on the left may unscrew, especially under high pedaling forces, and the tight spokes on the right may break. As the chain twists the cogs clockwise, the spokes opposing the twist (the "pulling spokes") get tighter, while the static spokes are under reduced tension and may unscrew.

An off-center rim, such as a Ritchey OCR, can help by reducing the wheel dish. The rim holes are offset to the left side (Fig. 12.3) so that the drive-side spokes come to the rim at a lower angle and can work with lower tension and more even tension between the two sides. The left-side spokes come to the rim at a higher angle and can be under higher tension without forcing the use of dangerously high tensions on the drive side. Before lacing an off-center rim, make sure you read the note in step 2 of §xii-2.

Using radial spokes on the left side (see §xii-7) can counteract the problem of grossly uneven tension. With a radial left side, the chain twisting the hub forward always tightens all the left-side spokes, rather than loosening half of them as it would with a crossing pattern.

And if the hub shell is stiff enough to carry the drive-force twist from the cog side to the nondrive side, putting radial spokes on the drive side and crossing spokes on the nondrive side can reduce the spoke tension disparity. This occurs because the spokes on the flatter (drive) side are shorter than the spokes coming in from the wider angle on the nondrive side. Thus, their relative angles to the rim are more similar.

FORKS 13

If you come to a fork in the road, take it.

—Yogi Berra

The fork serves a number of purposes. Most obviously, it connects the front wheel to the handlebar. Of course, the fork allows the bike to be steered, and it supports the front brake. The fork also offsets the front hub some distance forward of the steering axis. This offset distance (called the "fork rake"), combined with the angle of the steering axis (the "head angle") and the wheel size, determines how your bike is going to handle and steer.

All forks, suspended (Figs. 13.1–2) or rigid (Fig. 13.3), provide at least a minimum amount of suspension by allowing the front wheel to move up and down. The steering axis angles the fork forward from vertical and the front hub is offset forward, and those two characteristics make it possible for a fork—even a so-called rigid fork—to flex along its length and absorb vertical shocks. Suspension forks add a much greater range of vertical wheel travel.

All mountain bike forks are made up of a steering tube, a fork crown, two fork legs, brake bosses (usually disc-brake mounts and/or cantilever/V-brake posts, but on really old forks you may find roller-cam/U-brake posts), and fork ends (also called "dropouts" or "fork tips"). Figures 13.1–3 illustrate these parts on suspension forks and a rigid fork, respectively.

These days virtually all mountain bikes come equipped with suspension forks (Figs. 13.1–2). Their most distinguishing feature is the spring inside. That spring can be made up of compressed air, steel or titanium coils, elastic polymer bumpers (elastomers), or a combination. Most suspension forks also include a damping system to control how fast the spring compresses and rebounds. The damper acts much in the same way as a shock absorber on a car or a door closer that keeps a door from slamming.

Hydraulic damping systems are the most common, relying on the controlled movement of oil from one chamber to another. That flow is usually regulated by a system of holes that act to slow the rate of flow. Some pneumatic dampers

TOOLS

metric hex keys
metric open-end
  wrenches
adjustable wrench
needle-nose pliers
safety glasses
soft hammer
long screwdriver
nonlithium grease
citrus degreaser

OPTIONAL

torque wrench
ruler or caliper
dropout alignment
  tools
solid bench vise
snapring pliers
shock pump
metric socket
  wrenches
bike stand
medium-strength
  threadlock com-
  pound (Loctite 242
  or similar)

continued

continued

antiseize compound
for titanium bolts

22mm, 24mm, and
26mm sockets

13.1 Disc-brake-specific
air-sprung suspension
fork with 15mm lever-
operated through-axle

13.2 Cantilever/V-brake-specific
elastomer-sprung suspen-
sion fork for 9mm quick-
release axle

13.3 Rigid fork

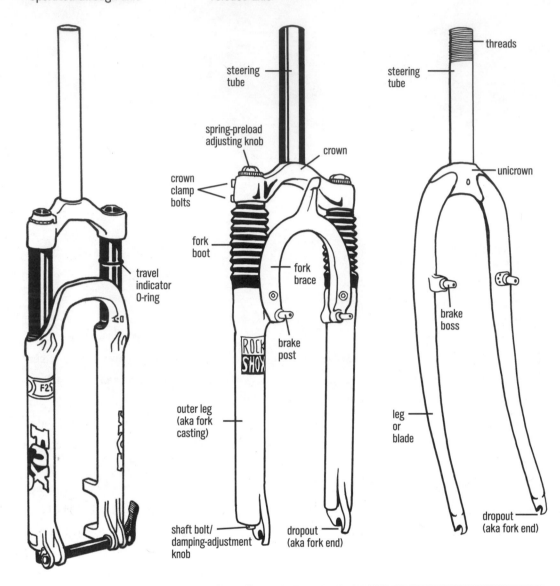

operate on a similar principle with compressed air instead of oil.

The most commonly used suspension-fork design has "telescoping" fork legs that consist of two sections: inner legs attached to the fork crown and steering tube and outer legs attached to the front hub that slide up and down over the inner legs (Fig. 13.4). Although this description applies to the vast majority of suspension forks, there are a number of variations that vie for a small piece of the fork market. Cannondale's HeadShok design incorporates rigid fork legs attached to a single shock unit inside the head-tube, and its "Lefty" fork has only a single telescoping, left leg. "Upside-down" telescoping forks have thinner lower legs sliding up and down inside fatter upper legs. There are also "linkage" suspension forks that use a system of pivots and movable arms attached to the fork legs and controlled via a spring.

13.4 How a suspension fork works

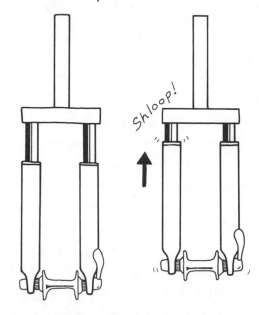

Shloop!

13.5 One messed-up fork

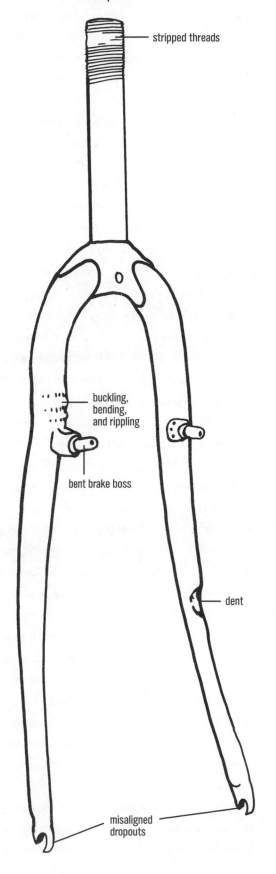

stripped threads

buckling,
bending,
and rippling

bent brake boss

dent

misaligned
dropouts

xiii-1
INSPECTING THE FORK

LEVEL 1

For the most part, forks are pretty durable, but they do break sometimes. A fork failure can ruin your day because the means of controlling the bike is eliminated. Such loss of control usually involves the rapid transfer of your body directly onto the ground, resulting in a substantial amount of pain.

Ever since I first opened my frame-building shop, people have regularly brought me an amazing collection of forks that had broken, sometimes with catastrophic consequences. Some had steering tubes broken either at the fork crown or in the threads. Others had fork crowns that broke or separated (releasing a fork leg or two), fork-crown bolts that broke or fell out, fork legs that folded, cantilever posts that snapped, fork braces supporting the brake cable that broke off, and front dropouts that broke off. Top caps can fly off of coil- or elastomer-sprung forks (and shoot up at your face!), and seals can blow on air-sprung forks; in either case, the fork immediately bottoms out. Pivots on linkage forks can break or fall apart. You can go a long way toward preventing problems such as these by regularly inspecting your bike's fork.

With that in mind, get into the habit of checking the fork regularly for any warning signs of impending failure—bends, cracks, and stressed paint. If you have crashed your bike, give the fork a very thorough inspection. If you find any indication that the fork has been damaged, replace it. A new fork is cheaper than emergency room charges, brain surgery, or an electric wheelchair.

When you inspect a fork, remove the front wheel, clean the mud off, and look under the crown and between the fork legs. Carefully examine all the outside areas. Look for any spots where the paint or finish looks cracked or stretched. Look for bent parts, from little ripples in fork legs to skewed cantilever posts and bent dropouts (Fig. 13.5).

Put the wheel back in, and watch to see if the fork legs twist when you secure the wheel quick-release or axle nuts; twisting indicates bent dropouts. Check to make sure that a true wheel centers under the fork crown. If it doesn't, turn the wheel around and put it back in the fork. That way you can confirm whether the misalignment is in the fork or the wheel. If the wheel lines up off to one side when it is put in one way and off the same amount to the other side when it is put in the other way, then the wheel is off-center (out of dish; see §xii-5) and the fork is straight. If the wheel is skewed off to the same side in the fork no matter which direction you place the wheel, then the fork is misaligned.

I recommend overhauling your bike's headset annually (see §xi-18 and §xi-19), and when you do, carefully examine the steering tube for any signs of stress or damage. Check for bent, cracked, or stretched areas; stripped threads on the steering tube (Fig. 13.5) or inside the cantilever brake bosses or postmount disc-brake bosses (Fig. 13.1); bulges where the stem expands inside (threaded steering tube); or crimping where the stem clamps around the top (threadless steering tube).

With a threaded fork, hold the stem up next to the steering tube to make sure that when the stem quill (Fig. 11.8) is inserted to the depth at which you have been using it, the bottom of the quill is always more than 1 inch below the bottom of the steering-tube threads. If you secure the stem quill by tightening the expander bolt (Fig. 11.9) when it is in the threaded region, you are asking for trouble; the threads cut the steering-tube wall thickness down by about 50 percent, and each thread offers a sharp breakage plane along which the tube can cleave.

On telescoping suspension forks, if the fork has crown clamp bolts (older forks were made this way), check that they are tight (ideally, you should do this with a torque wrench to verify that they are tightened to the figure recommended by the fork manufacturer). If the fork crown has titanium clamp bolts and you do lots of fast and rough downhill riding, consider replacing them annually (or get a new fork without clamp bolts); the heads of titanium fork-crown bolts have been known to snap off. Forks with crown bolts (Figs. 13.11–12 and 13.20–21) are no longer made, which is a good thing.

Check for oil leaks, from either around the top of the outer leg or around the bolt at the bottom of the outer leg. Check for torn, cracked, or missing seals around the top of the outer leg. Check that the air valve and the valve core inside it are tight. If the fork has stripped threads inside the postmount disc-brake bosses (Fig. 13.1), it's more likely that the brake caliper has been attached with bolts that are too short than that the bolts were overtorqued, but you want to be careful to avoid both.

On linkage forks, there are lots of bolts, pins, and pivots that need to be checked regularly. Make sure that all bolts are tight and all pins have their circlips or other retaining devices in place so that they do not fall out. Check for cracks and bends around the pivot points.

If you have any doubts about anything on the fork, take it to the expert at your bike shop. Err on the side of caution—replace it before it fails without warning.

REPAIRING FORK DAMAGE

If your inspection has uncovered damage that does not automatically require fork replacement, here are some guidelines to go by and some means of repair.

a. Dents

Not all fork dents threaten the integrity of the fork. On a rigid fork, particularly a steel one, a small dent usually poses little risk. A large dent (Fig. 13.5), of course, does. On a suspension fork, almost any dent can adversely affect the fork's operation, even if it does not pose a breakage threat. Many suspension-fork parts are replaceable.

b. Fork misalignment

Within limits, a rigid fork made of steel can be realigned if it is slightly off-center (see §xiii-18). Rigid forks made out of any other material and suspension forks cannot be realigned. Don't try!

c. Stripped steering-tube threads

If the threads on the steering tube are damaged (Fig. 13.5) so that the headset slips when you try to tighten it, you need to replace the steering tube. The steering tube alone or the steering tube and fork-crown assembly can be replaced on

some early suspension forks. You don't usually have that option when it comes to rigid forks, so you usually need to replace the whole thing.

d. Obvious bend, ripple, or crease in fork legs

Replace the fork if you feel, or see, ripples and bends in it (Fig. 13.5). The poor handling and potential breakage pose too great a threat to your safety to be worth saving a few bucks.

e. Bent or stripped disc-brake bosses or cantilever bosses

Postmount disc-brake bosses (Fig. 13.1) are threaded inside and can become stripped. If the cause was the use of overly short bolts to mount the brake caliper, you may be able to tap the threads with an M6 tap and install the recommended-length bolts for your brake and fork. Otherwise, you probably need to replace the lower legs or the entire fork. Bent disc-brake mounts, whether they are postmounts (Figs. 13.1 and 7.17) or IS mounts (Fig. 7.16), mandate replacement of the lower legs or the entire fork.

On most suspension forks that have cantilever studs, as well as on some rigid forks, the studs can be unscrewed with an 8mm open-end wrench and replaced. It is a good idea to use a threadlock compound such as Loctite 242 on the threads of the new mount.

A bent or stripped cantilever boss on an old rigid fork (Fig. 13.5) usually means that you must buy a new fork. If you have a frame builder in your area, he or she may be able to weld or braze a new boss onto a steel fork. You will also need to repaint the fork.

MAINTAINING RIGID FORKS

Beyond touching up the paint and performing the regular inspections just described, the only maintenance procedure for a rigid fork (Fig. 13.3) is to check the fork's alignment (§xiii-17) and improve on it (§xiii-18). This is called for if your bike is handling badly. You can perform minor realignment on a steel fork if you find that it is off-center; note that realigning is risky enough to qualify as a level 3 job. Do not try to realign titanium, carbon-fiber, aluminum, or suspension forks. (I know I am repeating myself; I am trying to make sure that you get the message.)

xiii-4
TUNING AND MAINTAINING SUSPENSION FORKS

Suspension forks (Figs. 13.1–2) are now the standard on mountain bikes. They offer a significant performance advantage and increase the versatility of the bike. The market is dominated by telescoping forks with air springs, coil springs, elastomer springs, or a combination of these inside, and any of them above the very cheapest forks are also equipped with hydraulic damping systems. Continual improvements in the science of bicycle suspension have resulted in a proliferation of fork models, rendering older models rapidly obsolete.

I address tuning generally in §xiii-7, but with such a vast and expanding array of fork models out on the trails, detailing the overhaul of every one is impossible here without turning this book into a multivolume encyclopedia. Most telescoping forks share enough similarities that they lend themselves to common basic service steps, but there really is no way to properly service a modern fork without consulting its specific service manual (generally available online), if for no other reason than to obtain recommended oil weights and volumes. Often a different oil weight and oil volume will be required for the upper tube and lower leg of each side of the fork (yes, four different volumes and three, maybe even four, different weights in a given fork); even among different models of the same model line and year of a given fork brand, the volume in a particular section of the fork may vary 20-fold or more! So guessing is a poor idea.

You may be on your own with a linkage-style fork or a fork with aftermarket upgrades; if you can't find online information, I hope you at least kept your owner's manual! Linkage-style forks rely on several pivot points, so there are plenty of places for things to go wrong. Be especially vigilant about inspecting these forks regularly.

An important safety measure you can take is to check periodically online or with your bike shop to make sure that your fork has not been recalled by the manufacturer. If it has, make sure you get the fork to your shop or the manufacturer before riding it again.

xiii-5
GENERALLY MAINTAINING TELESCOPING SUSPENSION FORKS

 LEVEL 1

On old fork models, if you do minor maintenance frequently and keep the inner legs covered with fork boots, you can greatly increase the life of the seals as well as the time between fork overhauls. A dry or dirty dust seal rubbing on a dry or dirty inner leg usually causes stickiness in suspension forks.

1. **Wipe clean the exposed upper tubes and the seal atop each lower leg.** If the fork has protective boots (Fig. 13.2), remove them for these steps if they are the flat type that wraps around and attaches with Velcro; slide them up if they are the rubber bellows type, also known as "gaiters" (Fig. 13.2).

2. **Put a thin coat of Teflon-fortified lubricant on the outside of the seals and inner legs.**

3. **If the fork has boots, put them back into position.** You may need to stretch the bottom of each rubber bellows–type fork boot

with needle-nose pliers to get it in the groove around the top of the outer leg and behind the fork brace.

xiii-6
MEASURING FORK TRAVEL

 **LEVEL 1**

You can't make any useful ride adjustments to a fork (aka "fork tuning") without knowing the fork's total travel, its sag (aka "ride height"), and the amount of its travel used on a given trail.

a. Measure maximum possible travel

The owner's manual should state the total fork travel, but if the fork has internally adjustable travel, you might not know how it's set, depending on whether or not an internal travel spacer (§xiii-16, Fig. 13.29) is installed.

To measure total available travel, do the following:

1. **Measure the distance down the upper fork leg tube from the lower edge of the fork crown to the top of the lower leg.** On forks without adjustable travel, this measurement will usually be close to the total available travel. Pull up on the handlebar to make sure that a negative spring is not preventing the crown from coming up any higher.

2. **Remove the main spring(s).** With an air fork, fully deflate the top spring through the valve atop the fork crown (Fig. 13.6). Push down on the fork while doing so to push out maximum air. With a coil or elastomer fork, unscrew each spring top cap and pull the spring out (Figs. 13.7 and 13.21), or just let the spring stick out the top of the leg. Some top caps are knurled and can be unscrewed by hand (Figs. 13.7 and 13.21), whereas others mandate removal with a 22mm or larger wrench. On older forks that have crown bolts

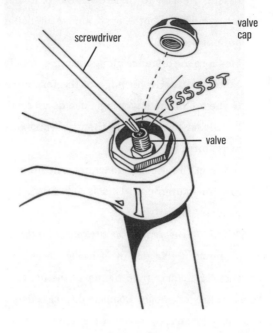

13.6 Deflating the positive chamber in an air-sprung suspension fork

screwdriver · valve cap · FSSSST · valve

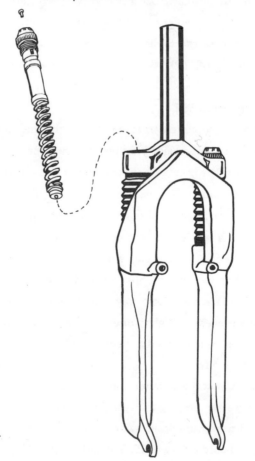

13.7 Removing the spring stack from a Manitou SX suspension fork

and a split crown, loosening the crown bolts makes it easier to unscrew the cap. If there are springs in both legs, remove or deflate both of them.

3. **Measure the distance along the upper fork leg tube from the lower edge of the fork crown to the top of the lower leg.** Push down on the handlebar to make sure the fork won't compress further.

4. **Subtract the second measurement from the first measurement.** This is the fork's total available travel.

IMPORTANT: *To ensure that the tire cannot hit the fork crown during a ride (which is highly undesirable), measure the distance from the top of the tire to the bottom of the fork crown. Compare this measurement to the total fork travel, or remove the springs and push the fork down as hard as you can toward the tire. If the crown can hit the tire on full compression, it can stop you dead (literally!). Use a smaller tire if necessary to ensure that the tire cannot hit the crown. Many fork manuals specify the largest tire you can safely use with a specific fork.*

b. Measure sag

"Sag," also called "ride height," is the amount of fork compression that occurs when the rider sits on the bike without moving. It is a critical measurement you will need in order to properly tune a fork. Although you can measure the sag of a rear shock by yourself, you can't properly measure fork sag without someone else holding you up, so enlist a friend to assist you. If the fork has boots, they must be removed for this procedure (Velcro ones are easy to remove; rubber bellows need to be removed or cut off as in §xiii-11).

1. **Adjust the compression damping to its lightest setting.** If the fork has a lockout lever, make sure it is switched off (turned fully counterclockwise if it's atop the crown, flipped

13.8 Adjusting high-speed and low-speed damping

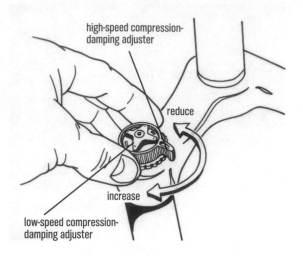

to its open position if it's a remote lever or button on the handlebar). Turn the compression-damping adjuster knob (usually atop the drive-side fork leg) fully counterclockwise until it stops. If the fork has compression-damping adjuster rings for both high-speed (often called lockout) and low-speed damping, turn both of them fully counterclockwise (Fig. 13.8). The same goes for "Gate" settings or other knobs that dictate blow-off force required to overcome the low-speed compression damping that resists fork activity from pedaling inputs.

2. **Establish a way to mark the travel used.** If the fork already has an indicator O-ring around at least one upper tube (Fig. 13.1), you're good to go. If not, smear a ring of dark-colored grease around one upper tube where it comes out of the seat atop the lower leg, or tighten a plastic zip-tie around it (Fig. 13.9), and slide it down against the seal.

3. **Have your friend hold your bike upright while you sit on it.** Wear the full riding gear you normally use, including full water bottles, hydration pack, and tool pack.

4. **Standing on the pedals, rock back and forth to activate the suspension.** Squeeze the brakes to avoid running over or head-butting your friend. If you have an "intelligent" or "pedal platform" fork that automatically distinguishes between bumps and pedaling forces, it may take some time to fully sag. For instance, a Fox TerraLogic F80X or F100X fork is essentially locked out until the tire hits a bump, and you might have the impression that it does not sag. Actually, it just takes a little while, because there is only a small bleed port in the damper that allows oil to pass by the piston. So wait 30 seconds or so for the fork to settle to ride height.

5. **While you're still standing (motionless) on the pedals, have your friend push the indicator O-ring, zip-tie, or grease glob down against the upper seal.** He or she should do this quickly, so neither of you loses balance.

6. **Gently climb off the bike.** Avoid compressing the suspension further; doing so would negate your careful placement of the marker for sag height.

7. **Measure the sag.** Measure the distance between the marker and the top of the seal. You want to have the bike sag to a certain percentage of your fork's total travel, so compare your sag measurement to total travel measured in section a. This is how you determine the main spring setting (see sag recommendations in your owner's manual and/or §xiii-7).

c. Measure travel used

Start your ride with an indicator O-ring (Fig. 13.1), zip-tie (Fig. 13.9), or grease glob on an upper tube pushed down against the top of the outer leg. At the end of the ride, measure the distance from this mark to the top of the outer leg (Fig. 13.9). Compare this to your total travel. This helps you determine the proper spring rate, preload, and

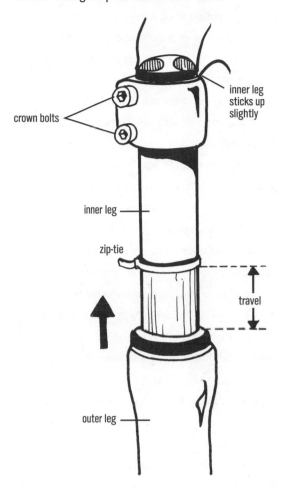

damping to use. If the fork is adjusted properly for the course you are riding, it will bottom out (i.e., use the full travel) at least once on the course; otherwise, you are not using the fork's full potential. The tuning sections (§xiii 7 to §xiii-9) go into more detail on this subject.

xiii-7
TUNING SUSPENSION FORKS

 LEVEL 1

This section sets out what to adjust on a fork and why. Subsequent sections explain how to actually perform those adjustments. Most of this advice applies equally to rear suspension, so use this guide for tuning rear shocks as well.

320

Pick out a short test course with at least 100 meters of rough trail, a hill, and a sharp turn. Go back and forth, climbing and descending, keeping your riding style consistent, to see how each change you make affects performance. A short course is good, because it encourages frequent retesting and you can remember everything that happened.

Make one change at a time, and ride the course in between so that you can isolate the effect of each change. Keep track of your observations immediately after every ride in a notebook that you keep by your bike, rather than waiting until you have time to work on your bike and have forgotten what it was that you wanted to change.

Familiarize yourself with your fork adjustments by riding the test course with each variable at its maximum setting and then at its minimum setting (again, changing one thing at a time), including tire pressure. This allows you to really appreciate what, say, rebound damping does and what it feels like when the damping is too high or too low. The downside is that you'll become so aware of how your fork works that your friends will harass you about always fiddling with it during rides!

Before adjusting the fork, keep in mind these three important caveats (you'll discover the truth of them if you ride your test course with, one at a time, tire pressure, positive spring rate, high-speed compression damping, and rebound damping at maximum or minimum settings):

1. **Tires are your first line of suspension.** Softer tires (up to a point) grant improved traction and lower rolling resistance on rough terrain. The softer the tires are, the lower the small-bump compliance you will need from the fork and rear suspension. And once you find a tire pressure you like, ride it that way until you decide to retune your shocks, because your suspension will feel different with different tire pressure.

2. **A bottoming sensation (even if the fork is not bottoming) may actually be caused by an overly stiff spring or excessive damping for the bike, the rider, and the terrain.**

3. **A harsh sensation (even if the bike has soft springs) may actually be caused by a spring rate that's too soft or rebound damping that's too high for the bike, rider, and terrain,** causing the suspension to ride with much of the travel compressed (i.e., the fork is "packed up").

After setting tire pressure, adjust the fork in the following sequence:

a. Spring rate

"Rate" is how much length the spring shortens in response to a given force. You change the rate on an air fork by changing the air pressure (Figs. 13.10–11), and you change the rate on a coil or elastomer fork by interchanging springs (Fig. 13.7) and/or varying the spring preload (Fig. 13.12).

Remember the sag measurement you made in §xiii-6b? This is where to use it; you want the fork to settle into a certain percentage of its travel when it is just rolling along on smooth ground. How much depends on what kind of riding you do:

13.10 Adjusting positive air pressure

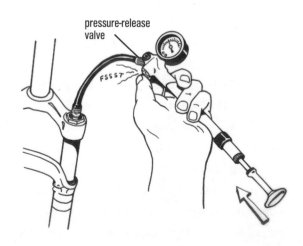

pressure-release valve

13.11 Inflating a RockShox Mag or early SID air-oil fork

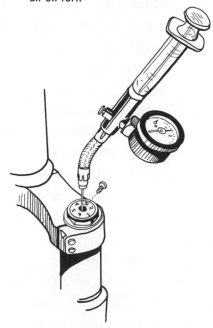

13.12 Adjusting spring preload

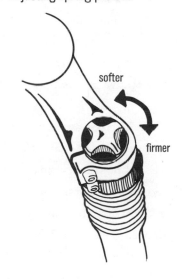

- For cross-country racing, total travel is usually less than 3 inches, and you want it stiff. Set the spring rate so that sag is 5–15 percent of travel.
- Trail bikes with 3–5 inches of travel work well with sag set at 15–20 percent of travel.
- Set all-mountain bikes with 5–7 inches of travel to 25–35 percent sag.

- Downhill and other gravity-driven riding with 7–10 inches of travel benefit from 35–45 percent sag.

1. If the spring rate is too soft, you will easily bottom the fork (i.e., go through its full travel), need high preload (coil and elastomer forks), and have too low of a front end on rough downhills.

2. If the spring rate is too hard, the fork will rarely or never bottom, meaning that you're not absorbing the bumps as you could, costing you energy and comfort.

b. Spring preload (coil-spring and elastomer forks only)

Adjust spring rate before you adjust preload. Ideally, you want to hit the spring rate right on and have minimal preload, because preload makes the spring rate ramp up faster and respond more harshly.

Without springs to interchange, preload is the only spring rate adjustment; use it alone to set sag depth. This setting obviously overlaps with the spring rate.

You can often adjust preload while riding, because the knob(s) is (are) easily accessible (Fig. 13.12). This is how you know how to change it:

1. If the spring preload (or spring rate) is too low, the bike will sag too much, the front end will be too low entering turns, and oversteering will occur.

2. If the spring preload (or spring rate) is too high, the bike will sag insufficiently, the fork will feel stiff and/or harsh, and it will understeer, especially when attempting a tight turn at low speeds.

c. Air volume (air forks only)

Varying air volume in an air fork is similar to varying preload in coil and elastomer forks. Reducing air volume makes the fork stiffen up faster as it moves (that is, the spring rate ramps up faster), and vice versa. For instance, if you find an air pressure that works well through its initial and intermediate travel, but you bottom the fork too often, you can decrease the air volume to stiffen the fork sooner with the same air pressure. On virtually any air fork, you can decrease the volume in an air cylinder by removing the valve and pouring in some oil, but many air forks also have an adjustable piston to vary the air volume.

d. Negative spring rate

The negative spring in an air fork works against the main air ("positive") spring to compress the fork. This makes the fork more compliant over small bumps and makes it behave more like a coil spring throughout its travel. Early air forks did not have negative springs, and riders suffered on stutter bumps.

Air springs have a "progressive spring rate," meaning that as the spring is compressed, the force it takes to move the next increment of travel goes up exponentially, rather than linearly. A coil spring, in contrast, has a "linear spring rate" through much of its stroke; it takes the same increase in force to move 1mm farther, whether you are at the beginning or middle of the spring's compression. Also, the tight air seals in an air fork usually mean it has more "stiction" (the coefficient of static friction, or the force it takes to make the fork move initially) than a coil-spring fork.

Thus, it takes more force to get an air fork to move initially on a little bump, and the force required to keep moving farther into the stroke on bigger bumps ramps up. By pulling the fork down, a negative spring can help the fork react quickly to small bumps. A negative air spring—a separate air chamber—will also start in its fully compressed (hence fully ramped-up) point. As the negative air spring moves through the stroke, its force ramps down rapidly while the main spring's

force is ramping up rapidly, so the net spring rate of the fork is fairly linear.

NOTE: *Because elastomers also are progressive springs, they are often paired with coil springs to yield a more linear overall spring rate (Fig. 13.7).*

The negative spring adjustment is generally via a Schrader valve on either the bottom of the leg or the top, adjacent to the positive spring Schrader valve. Because the negative air chamber pulls the fork down when filled with compressed air, make sure you pump up the positive spring first. If you mistakenly pump up the negative spring first while the positive spring pressure is zero, then as you pump the positive spring, the pressure in the negative spring will go up and up as the fork lengthens. In that situation, you can try pumping the positive spring to a zillion psi, and you still will not get the fork to full length! Some forks fill both the positive and negative spring chambers from a single Schrader valve; both chambers will be pumped to the same pressure.

Instead of an air negative spring, some air forks have a negative coil spring at the bottom of the fork, which may or may not be adjustable.

Many forks with positive and negative spring chambers are designed so that if the pressure in the positive and negative springs is equal, the bump force required to start the fork moving is close to zero, meaning that small-bump compliance is optimized. Consult the fork manual for the recommended starting point for your fork. Once you find the pressure in your positive spring that you like for big hits, tweak the negative spring pressure to get the small-bump compliance you seek. It may take a little going back and forth.

e. Rebound damping

Rebound damping controls the speed of return of the spring. Have you ever checked a car strut (shock absorber) by pushing down on a fender and releasing it to see if the car bounces a single

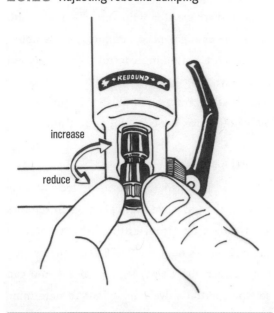

time or if it keeps boinging up and down? That's a check of rebound damping, and you want a single bounce from your bike.

High-end forks generally have a rebound-damping adjuster knob at the bottom of the damper (non-disc-brake) side, and it is usually red in color (Fig. 13.13). Cheap forks have no damping at all. In-between forks have no adjuster knob, and the only way to adjust rebound on a nonadjustable fork damper is to take it apart and change the shim stack or change the oil viscosity (lighter oil = faster rebound).

Back the rebound adjuster out fully (counterclockwise; often it's indicated on the adjuster as turning it toward "faster" versus "slower"). Ride off a curb and check how many bounces you get. Keep tightening the adjuster until you get only a single bounce off the curb.

There is an ideal rebound setting for every type of terrain at a given speed, so feel free to play around with this adjustment. It's an important one for control and comfort.

1. **If rebound damping is set too low, the fork will spring back too fast.** It's set too low if the wheel springs up from the ground after land-ing a jump and it feels as if you're returning from a bungee jump. You will also have trouble maintaining a straight path through rocks, you will understeer, the front wheel will try to climb the berm while cornering, and the ride height will be too high in rough terrain.

2. **If rebound damping is set too high, the fork will not spring back fully after each hit.** When bumps come rapidly, the fork will "pack up"—it will get progressively shorter so that it will have less and less travel available for successive rapid hits. This will feel quite harsh, and the fork will bottom after several successive large hits, even though compression damping and spring rate are correct. The fork will oversteer and won't rebound after landing a jump.

f. Low-speed compression damping

Compression damping in general controls the speed at which the spring compresses, and low-speed compression damping in particular controls the speed at which the spring compresses when the fork shaft is moving slowly (i.e., not hitting a big bump). Low-speed compression damping is added to the fork to help it resist bobbing due to pedaling, and it keeps the suspension up during hard braking and fast, bermed turns, when the G-force would otherwise push the rider and the bike down. If the fork has a separate low-speed compression-damping adjuster, it will generally be a blue ring or knob atop the damper (drive-side) leg paired with the high-speed compression-damping knob or lockout lever (Fig. 13.8).

"Pedal platform" is a distinct type of low-speed compression damping designed to resist low-frequency (not just low-speed) fork-shaft movement. Its effect is the same: Pedal platform keeps the bike riding higher and resists diving when braking.

As with all damping, don't overdo it; use just enough low-speed or pedal platform damping to keep the suspension up when you are braking and pedaling and in when you are riding berms and G-outs.

1. If low-speed compression damping is set too low, the symptoms include bobbing when pedaling, fork dive while braking, and oversteering.

2. If low-speed compression damping is set too high, the ride height is high despite a soft spring and/or little preload, the fork does not absorb stair steps well, and understeering is common.

g. High-speed compression damping

High-speed compression damping is for the big stuff; it controls the speed at which the spring compresses when the fork shaft is moving fast (i.e., hitting a big bump). Without it, the fork would bottom out hard. This adjuster will usually be a blue knob atop the damper (drive-side) leg (Fig. 13.8).

Set the adjuster all the way out unless the fork bottoms out; you want the adjuster set low enough that it absorbs bumps quickly through the system and lets the spring work. Even with the perfect spring rate, if high-speed compression damping is set too high, the piston will move so slowly through the oil that you'll already be past the obstacle before the fork has moved. Your goal in setting compressing damping is to have the fork travel used up when you are at the highest point of the rock you're rolling over.

1. If high-speed compression damping is set too low, the symptoms include bottoming out and instability.

2. If high-speed compression damping is set too high, the fork will not react to small bumps, will feel harsh, and will rarely or never bottom out.

h. Bottoming control damping

Some forks have this adjustment; it's an additional bit of high-speed compression damping. Use as little bottoming control as possible. But if you ride very aggressively and take a lot of big hits yet still want a super-plush ride, this adjustment could give you everything you want.

i. Inertial valve

A fork with a pedal platform or lockout may have an inertial valve that opens when the fork shaft moves fast from hitting a bump hard. If the fork has an adjuster, it will generally be atop the damper (drive-side) leg (Fig. 13.14). You can set the inertial valve adjustment to determine how big a bump it will take to blow open the compression-damping circuit.

Set the adjustment high at first so that it gives you the pedaling performance you want on a smooth climb. Then ride your test course and see how much bump compliance you've sacrificed by setting the inertial valve for high blow-off, and back it off until you find your happy medium.

13.14 Adjusting RockShox inertial-valve blow-off sensitivity

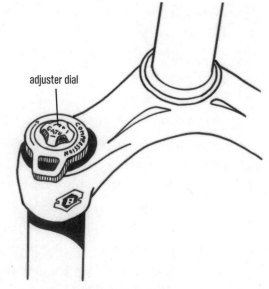

adjuster dial

1. If the inertial-valve adjustment is set too high, the fork will not respond to small bumps.

2. If the inertial-valve adjustment is set too low, the fork will bob when pedaling on smooth surfaces.

j. Travel

If fork travel is adjustable, increase it for rough courses and decrease it for climbing and riding smooth trails or roads. Some forks, both air and coil-spring types, have a knob atop the spring leg to adjust travel, with marks on the outside of the upper tube indicating travel (Fig. 13.15). Other forks require removing the outer legs and repositioning a spacer on the fork shaft above or below a plunger inside the inner leg (Fig. 13.29); see §xiii-16 for directions. The more spacers there are below the plunger, the less travel there is (because the spacers prevent the shaft from extending as far out of the bottom of the inner leg), and vice versa.

A shorter fork is an advantage aerodynamically when you are riding long stretches of road; it helps get you down out of the wind. And when the bike is climbing, a shorter fork keeps the front end down, maintaining more weight on it, so that the front wheel does not become too light for proper steering.

A longer fork is an advantage on big bumps at high speed, as it allows the bump force to be absorbed more completely.

Here are some general fork-tuning guidelines:

- **Speed up:** Because rebound and compression damping are speed-sensitive, don't worry about settings that feel good at low speeds being too light for high speeds; the fork will get stiffer as you hit things faster. At all speeds, you want the fork to pop back as quickly as possible without kicking back, and you want it to compress into the travel as quickly as possible without bottoming.

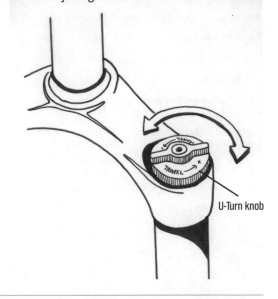

U-Turn knob

- **Heat up:** Damping is temperature-sensitive. Oil is thick and sluggish in the cold, but when the weather gets hot, the fork gets really lively. You will need to adjust accordingly in summer. Choose a stiffer spring rate and firmer damping adjustments.

- **Cool off:** In the cold of winter, overall speeds are slower, the grease and oil in the fork are thicker, and the elastomers and coil springs are stiffer. Consequently, lighten up the spring and damping adjustments. If you're really into taking your fork apart, lighter oil in the damper will help.

Here are some common ride symptoms and some suspension-tuning fixes for them:

Fork too hard	Fork too soft
Decrease compression damping	Increase spring rate
Decrease rebound damping	Increase compression damping
Decrease spring rate	Increase oil viscosity
Decrease oil viscosity	Replace old damper oil
Increase spring rate*	Put oil in (empty) damper
Decrease inertial valve adjustment	

*If you are running a spring rate that is too soft for your weight and ability, you could be misled into thinking *that the spring rate is too stiff. This is because you are using up the fork travel before you begin to ride. Furthermore, the fork is working in a stiffer spring-rate range on smaller hits, giving the impression that the fork is harsh and stiff. This is where the ride-height (sag) adjustment is important.*

Front end understeers/ nervous descending	**Front end "knifes"/ oversteers**
Increase rebound damping	Decrease rebound damping
Decrease spring preload	Increase spring preload
Decrease spring rate	Increase spring rate
Decrease compression damping	Increase compression damping

Front end pushes or washes out in turns	**No response to small bumps**
Increase rebound damping	Decrease compression damping
Decrease spring preload	Decrease spring preload
Decrease spring rate	Decrease spring rate
Decrease compression damping	Increase negative spring rate
	Decrease rebound damping
	Overhaul dirty fork
	Decrease inertial valve adjustment

xiii-8

TUNING COIL-SPRING AND ELASTOMER FORKS

 LEVEL 1

Telescoping coil/elastomer-spring suspension forks (Figs. 13.7 and 13.20) are simple in principle and are generally straightforward to adjust. After you understand how to adjust your coil/elastomer-spring fork from reading this section, you can fully utilize the tuning tips you learned in §xiii-7.

a. Setting spring preload

Spring preload, the amount of compression of the spring at rest, can be adjusted on many coil-spring or elastomer forks, but it should be done only after you have installed the correct spring for you. On many forks, you can adjust the preload simply by turning the adjuster knobs on the top of the fork crown (Fig. 13.12)—even while riding, as you encounter terrain variations. On forks that have springs in only one leg (usually the left leg), there is only one preload adjuster. Note that the "U-Turn" knob (Fig. 13.15) on some RockShox coil-spring models adjusts travel, not preload.

Rotating the adjuster knob(s) clockwise gives a firmer ride by tightening (and thus shortening) the spring stack. Rotating the adjuster knob(s) counterclockwise softens the ride. Make sure the top cap surrounding the knob does not unscrew from the fork crown; you may need to hold it tight with one hand (or a wrench) when you loosen the adjuster knob. Check the top cap occasionally to make sure it is not unscrewed or being forced out because of stripped threads. If its threads seem to be stripped, get a new top cap right away; if the top cap pops off, the spring can shoot up into your face at high velocity.

Preloading uses up some of the spring's length and therefore makes the spring stiffen up faster as the fork moves. Varying the preload changes the fork's sag, and it shortens the life of the spring, as it is being compressed even while the bike is hanging in the garage. It is better to change the spring stack (see xiii-19b) to get the ride you want and minimize preload; use the preload adjustment only as a way to change the fork quickly during a particular ride.

b. Replacing elastomers and coil springs

To make major changes in the fork's spring rate, you must change the springs inside of the fork (Fig. 13.7). Manufacturers usually color-code the elastomers—and often coil springs as well—for stiffness, although you can tell the difference between stiff and soft elastomer bumpers by squeezing them between your fingers. (Some manufacturers refer to the elastomers as "MCUs" for "micro-cellular urethane," referring to small air voids trapped inside the urethane spring.) Extra springs usually come with the fork, or you can buy them from a dealer.

1. **Unscrew the top cap (or caps, if there are springs in both legs) counterclockwise.** On its old, pre-1998 forks, RockShox recommends that you first loosen the crown bolts to relieve inward pressure on the fork legs before unscrewing the caps. On some forks, the top caps can be unscrewed with your fingers, whereas others require a wrench (22mm is common) to unscrew the top cap; sometimes you must remove a knob covering it first. Manitou TPC (Twin Piston Cartridge—Fig. 13.28) and RockShox "Pure" damping systems have springs in one leg.

2. **Pull the spring(s) out of the fork** (Fig. 13.7). Oftentimes, springs will come out attached to the top cap(s), and several springs may be snapped together with plastic connectors. On many older (pre-1996 or so) forks, the top cap is connected to a rod (the "skewer" in Fig. 13.20) that runs through each of the elastomer bumpers. If the springs do not come out with the top caps, turn the bike upside down or compress the fork to get them out.

3. **Clean any old grease off the parts.**

4. **Choose the coil springs and/or elastomers that you intend to use.** If any of the elastomers are misshapen or look squished or worn in any way, replace them. Some manufacturers provide a nominal and replacement length for coil springs and elastomers. Measure the springs and check them!

5. **Apply a new coating of grease to the new parts and everything you just cleaned.** Make sure to grease the outside of the coil springs to reduce the noise of the springs rub-

bing inside the legs. However, in forks with open-bath dampers, hydraulic oil sloshes all around in the spring chamber, so there is no need to grease the springs, but you should replace the oil bath (Fig. 13.25). Pour out the old oil, and replace it with the same volume and weight of new oil (check specs in the fork manual). Make sure you don't let any dirt fall down into the leg.

6. **Put the spring stack in the fork leg** (Fig. 13.7), **and screw the cap down.** Be sure to retighten the crown bolts to the required torque if you loosened them.

c. Adjusting damping

Damping controls the speed at which the spring compresses or extends; the damping system moves oil through or around a piston that is being forced through the oil chamber (in rare cases, compressed air is used instead of oil). Varying the size of the hole or the thickness of the oil varies how easily the piston can move through the oil.

The locations of compression- and rebound-damping adjusters are described in §xiii-7, but on older forks, before the color conventions became established, they were a bit different. The rebound-damping adjuster, if it existed, was at the bottom of the fork leg (same place you'll find it today), whereas the compression damping adjuster would have been at the top of the leg. The knob may have been black (Fig. 13.16) or nonexistent (Fig. 13.17), but, like today's, the adjustment was through the bottom shaft bolt with a thin hex key, whether attached to the knob or not.

Additionally, many forks have a remote lockout button or lever on the handlebar. This is in fact simply a gross compression-damping adjuster.

Some forks have an "inertial valve" (often called "pedal platform") overriding the compression-damping adjustment that distinguishes between

13.16 Damping adjuster knob on a Manitou SX fork

knob

shaft bolt

13.17 Adjusting damping on early RockShox Judy fork

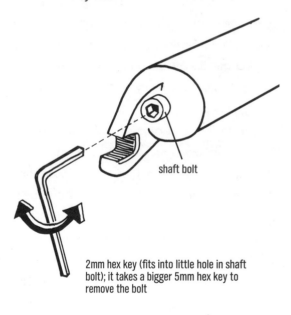

shaft bolt

2mm hex key (fits into little hole in shaft bolt); it takes a bigger 5mm hex key to remove the bolt

pedaling forces and bump forces. The fork will be highly damped until a bump of a certain impact magnitude is encountered, at which point the inertial valve opens and the fork moves freely (within the constraints of the compression-damping adjustments you have set). This threshold impact magnitude required to open the inertial valve is also adjustable on some forks (Fig. 13.14).

xiii-9
TUNING AIR-SPRING FORKS

⚙ LEVEL 1

The lightest forks use compressed air as a spring. It would, after all, be hard to come up with a spring lighter than one made of air!

After you understand how to adjust an air-spring fork from reading this section, you can fully utilize the tuning tips you learned in §xiii-7.

a. Adjusting positive air pressure

Greater air pressure in the positive spring chamber means a stiffer fork, and vice versa. It is a good idea to check the air pressure every couple of weeks; all forks lose pressure over time.

Do not use a tire pump on the fork; the large stroke volume is poor for adjusting low volumes of air at high pressure. The gauge won't tell you how much air is left in the fork, and unless the fork takes a ball-inflation needle, you will lose most of the pressure when removing the pump head. You need a shock pump with a no-leak fitting, as the Schrader valves on air forks can lose air when the pump is removed. Newer shock pumps have a no-leak fitting built into the head (Fig. 13.10) that prevents leakage from any standard Schrader valve.

RockShox Mag-series forks, early SIDs, and the air assist on post-2002 Judys use valves that require a ball-inflation needle (Fig. 13.11). SID forks from 1999 to 2000, and all Marzocchi air forks, require a special adapter that fits down in the recessed Schrader valve and prevents air from escaping as the adapter is removed.

Pump to the pressure needed to give you the desired sag—see §xiii-7a, or consult the fork manual.

IMPORTANT: *If the fork has an air negative spring as well as an air positive spring, always pump the positive spring chamber first. If you pump the negative* spring first, it may pull the fork down (i.e., shorten it) and increase the volume of the negative spring chamber. Then, if you pump the positive spring, it will drive the pressure in both chambers, reaching incredibly high pressure levels and still not bringing the fork up to full length.

The pump for old RockShox Mag forks is just a plastic syringe with a dial gauge on it (Fig. 13.11). The air valve on each leg is located beneath either a Phillips screw or a plastic pry-off cap on top of the compression-damping adjustment knob. Tighten the adjustment knob before inserting the pump needle to avoid pinching the rubber valve on the top of the adjuster rod inside, causing it to leak. Moisten the needle, and insert it into the valve hole (Fig. 13.11).

b. Adjusting the negative spring

The negative spring in an air fork works against the main air spring to actually compress the fork.

The second Schrader valve for an air negative spring will be either at the bottom or the top of the left leg. Again, be sure to pump the positive spring before pumping the negative spring. Some air forks have a coil-type negative spring, and many of these are not adjustable. Early (1998) SID forks have a coil-type negative spring on top of the cartridge shaft under the right-hand piston that is adjustable. There is a circlip constraining the top end of the spring, and you can clip it into any of six grooves to vary the compression of the negative spring. You must take the fork apart and remove the cartridge to do it, though (§viii-13 and §viii-14).

c. Adjusting damping

See §xiii-8c, as it is the same as on coil/elastomer-spring forks.

d. Making other adjustments

Reducing air volume in an air-sprung fork is similar to increasing preload in a coil-spring or elastomer fork; it makes the fork stiffen up faster as it moves (i.e., the spring rate ramps up faster). You can decrease the volume in an air cylinder by removing the valve and pouring some oil into the chamber. Many forks do require a certain volume of oil in each air chamber anyway (be sure to use the specified oil).

On the 1998 RockShox SID, you can change air volume by changing piston height: Increase the volume by tightening the piston deeper into the fork and decrease it by unscrewing the piston. You get at the piston by releasing the air with a ball needle and unscrewing the top nut with an adjustable wrench. Screw the piston in or out with an 8mm hex key.

If you have the fork apart (§xiii-13), you can change oil viscosity (§xiii-14 and §xiii-15) or the shim stack covering the compression- or rebound-damping bleed holes to change the speed of the fork shaft on compression or rebound.

You can also change the blow-off threshold with an inertial valve and/or vary travel on some models (see §xiii-7i and §xiii-7j).

xiii-10
REMOVING FORK LEGS FROM THE FORK CROWN

LEVEL 1

This discussion applies to double-crown (aka "triple-clamp") forks—forks with a crown above and below the head-tube (Fig. 13.18)—as well as to single-crown forks prior to 1998 that have a slotted crown. In most newer single-crown forks, the upper tubes (aka "inner legs" or "stanchions") are pressed into the crown and cannot be removed. If the fork has a slotted crown, pulling the inner legs out of the crown is a more convenient way to add or replace dust boots (which were important back then due to poor seals on the fork legs) than pulling the outer legs off the inner legs (§xiii-13).

When pulling the inner legs out of a single slotted crown or out of both slotted crowns of a double-crown fork, you can leave the fork steering tube and crown in the bike. It is not necessary to remove the fork legs from the crown to replace or adjust springs or dampers.

1. **Disconnect the brake.** Unbolt a hydraulic brake. Disconnect a cable-actuated brake by removing the cable end from the brake lever (the reverse of §vii-6, steps 8–10).

2. **Loosen the crown bolts.** They are shown removed in Figures 13.20–21. If there are two bolts on each side of the fork crown, do not completely undo one bolt while leaving the other fully tightened. Doing so places a great deal of clamping force on the remaining tight bolt, and you could strip the head while you are trying to loosen it. Instead, unscrew one bolt about one-quarter turn and then do the same to the other. Then go back to the first bolt and loosen it by another one-quarter turn. Repeat until the crown is loose enough to free the leg.

3. **Pull both fork legs out of the crown(s) using a gentle rocking motion.**

xiii-11
REMOVING AND INSTALLING FORK BOOTS
⚙ LEVEL 1

Fork boots (Figs. 13.2 and 13.7) keep dirt off the inner legs and the seals at the top of the outer legs. To check the fork's travel (§xiii-7), you will need to remove the boots if installed. Since the 2000 model year, fork boots are generally unnecessary, thanks to effective multiple sealing systems.

1. **Remove the inner or outer legs.** With a pre-1998 slotted-crown fork or a double-crown model, remove the fork legs from the crown (see §xiii-10). Pressed-in legs require you to pull off the outer legs—see §xiii-13, steps 1–7.

2. **Pull the fork boots off.**

3. **Slide the boots onto the inner legs, large end down toward the outer legs.** Make sure that you are using boots designed for the fork.

4. **Pull the lip of each fork boot into the groove in the top of the outer leg.** You may need to stretch the boot with needle-nose pliers to get it to slide over the outer leg behind the fork brace.

5. **Replace the inner or outer legs.** For a slotted crown, see §xiii-10; for a pressed-on crown, see §xiii-13.

xiii-12
INSTALLING INNER LEGS IN A FORK CROWN
⚙ LEVEL 1

This procedure applies only to single-crown forks prior to 1998 as well as to double-crown (or "triple-clamp") forks (Fig. 13.18).

1. **Wipe the upper tubes clean, and make sure that the fork-crown bolts are loose.** If applicable, install the fork boots (§xiii-11).

2. **Insert the upper tubes into the fork crown.**

   (a) Single-crown forks: Some forks have a lip against which the inner leg is supposed to rest. Slide the inner leg up into the crown until it hits the lip. Otherwise, on single-crown forks, push the inner leg through the crown until the top of the leg sticks up no more than 2mm above the top of the crown (Fig. 13.9).

   (b) Triple-clamp forks: Slide the inner legs up through both crowns. Make sure that the upper crown is the right shape and orientation to work with the bike's head-tube length (Fig. 13.18). For instance, the RockShox triple-clamp forks in Figure 13.18 specify that the lower crown must be located so that there are 180mm of exposed upper

13.18 Upper crown height and orientation for head-tubes of different lengths with triple-clamp forks (example shown is for RockShox)

331

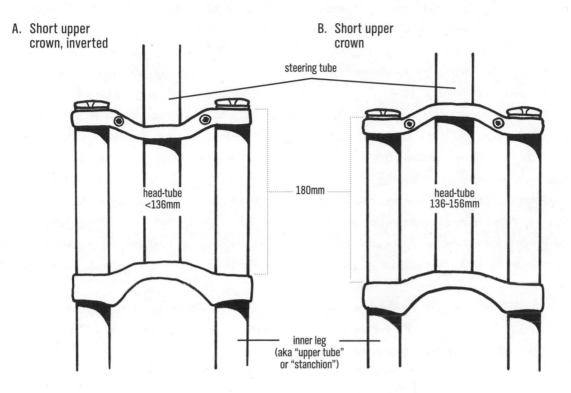

A. Short upper crown, inverted

B. Short upper crown

steering tube

180mm

head-tube <136mm

head-tube 136–156mm

inner leg (aka "upper tube" or "stanchion")

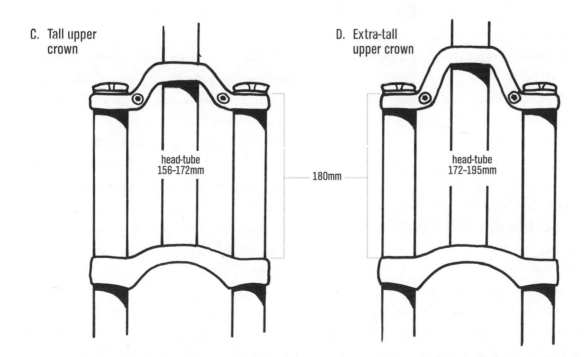

C. Tall upper crown

D. Extra-tall upper crown

head-tube 156–172mm

180mm

head-tube 172–195mm

tubes above the lower crown. Upper crowns come in different heights (i.e., short, tall, extra-tall) for different frame sizes. They can be installed either right side up or inverted so that the crowns clamp the upper tubes just below the top while ensuring that the specified length of upper tube extends above the lower crown (Fig. 13.18).

IMPORTANT FOR DOUBLE-CROWN FORKS: *If more than the manufacturer's specified length of upper tubes is above the lower crown, the lower crown will be too close to the tire and could hit it during large impacts, which can stop you and the bike dead and leave you that way. Furthermore, some triple-clamp forks have shims to be inserted into the lower crown's clamping slots; other triple-clamp forks have reinforcements around the upper tubes under the lower crown. To avoid fork failure, make sure to include whatever the manufacturer intended; consult the fork manual.*

3. **Tighten the crown bolts to the manufacturer's specified torque.** If the crown has paired bolts (Fig. 13.9), alternately tighten the two bolts on each side. If the fork requires shims at the clamps, make sure they're in place. Use an antiseize compound on titanium bolts and a medium-strength threadlock compound on steel bolts.

IMPORTANT: *Fork-crown bolts are critical bolts—make sure to tighten them to the required torque specified in Appendix D.*

xiii-13
OVERHAULING FORKS WITH BOLTS AT THE BOTTOM OF THE OUTER LEGS

 LEVEL 2

Frequent fork overhaul is not generally as necessary with modern (post-2000 or so) forks as it is with rear shocks or with old forks. Modern forks have a large volume of oil compared to rear shocks, as well as far better seals, oil baths, and other lubrication systems that most forks in the 1990s lacked. Nonetheless, this is an important maintenance procedure to keep your bike performing optimally.

The fork needs to be overhauled if, as you gradually lean harder on the handlebar, it is hard to get started moving downward and when the fork finally does compress, it goes down chunk, chunk, chunk, like going down a set of stairs. The fork needs an overhaul and new seals if you constantly have an excessive amount of oil coming out of the fork, and you should overhaul it immediately if it has reached the point where you have no damping—the fork is just acting like a pogo stick. It needs new bushings (which requires taking the fork apart) if the lower legs clunk back and forth on the upper tubes.

Use this section (by itself, at least) only if you cannot get your hands on a service manual specific to the fork you are overhauling. The sheer number of suspension-fork brands and models on the market make a detailed description of the service of them all unrealistic. This section emphasizes forks that were the top models in 2001 and earlier, and even though current high-end forks are overhauled with similar procedures, the details are different (and important). I'm still including this section rather than sending you only to online service manuals, because online service manuals often don't go back to the last century, and the need for service with those old forks is great. The seals and lubrication systems on pre-2001 forks tend to be wanting, and as they are getting long in the tooth now, frequent service is even more necessary. Simpler, lower-end modern forks can often be overhauled by following the instructions in this section as well.

Even if you were to disassemble modern forks following these instructions, you would still need the manufacturer's specifications for the quantity and weight of oil to put in the upper tube and lower leg on each side. Without that, you cannot expect optimal performance and could even damage the fork. And owners' manuals that come with forks generally do not have detailed service information; if printed in six or so languages, they would be massive! But online resources, which hardly existed when the first edition of this book came out in 1996, now offer a wealth of easily accessible information. Go to foxracingshox.com, rockshox. com, manitoumtb.com, marzocchi.com, dtswiss. com, and so on to find service instructions and diagrams for your fork.

On 1999 (and later) Manitou forks with the "Microlube" grease fitting on the back of the leg, you usually do not need to take the fork apart. Just inject the proper Manitou Microlube grease (this type is thinner than most bicycle grease) with a fine-tipped grease gun into the grease fitting. With a few squirts in each leg, the fork will feel smooth again until it really needs an overhaul. It only takes a bit; if you try to fill the fork with grease, you will lock it up! You may, however, take it apart as described in subsequent paragraphs.

These instructions apply to most 1995–2001 or so mid- to high-end forks. The fork must have a bolt head protruding from the bottom of each outer leg (Figs. 13.16–17 and 13.19) to be disassembled in this way. (Forks without bottom bolts are usually either very old or very inexpensive. You can usually get these forks apart too. You need either snapring pliers to remove the snapring at the top of each outer leg or a long hex key to get at the head of the compression bolt way down inside after removing the springs. Keep track of everything, and put all the parts back together the same way after cleaning and lubricating.)

Now, back to overhauling. This is an oily job; wearing rubber gloves is a very good idea.

1. **Disconnect or remove the front brake** (Chapter 7), **and remove the front wheel**

(§ii-2). It is easier if you remove the fork from the bike as well (§xi-18 and §xi-19).

2. **Turn the fork upside down.** This will keep oil from pouring out.

3. **Unscrew the bolts on the bottoms of the fork legs** (Fig. 13.19). Leave a few threads engaged (this is important). If the bolts are not backing out, you are turning the shafts inside the fork along with them. Pump more air into an air fork (Figs. 13.10–11), or tighten the preload adjuster on a coil-spring or elastomer fork (Fig. 13.12) to prevent the shaft from spinning. On some forks, you actually turn this bolt clockwise, rather than counterclockwise, to release the shaft—yet another reason for service instructions specific to your fork.

NOTE: *The bolt size varies, and the bolt is sometimes hidden under a damping-adjustment knob that you must first remove with a screwdriver or yank out (Fig. 13.16), sometimes after loosening a setscrew. Some air forks have a negative spring air valve at the bottom of one leg; after deflating this valve (keep your eyes away from it, because oil will spurt out), unscrew the bolt surrounding the valve with an open-end wrench.*

IMPORTANT: *If there is a small bolt head deep down inside the large bolt head (Figs. 13.16–17), don't unscrew it. That's a damping adjuster, and if you unscrew it past*

13.19 Freeing an inner leg from the lower bushings

TAP!

13.20 1995 RockShox Judy fork, exploded view (inner leg shortened for clarity)

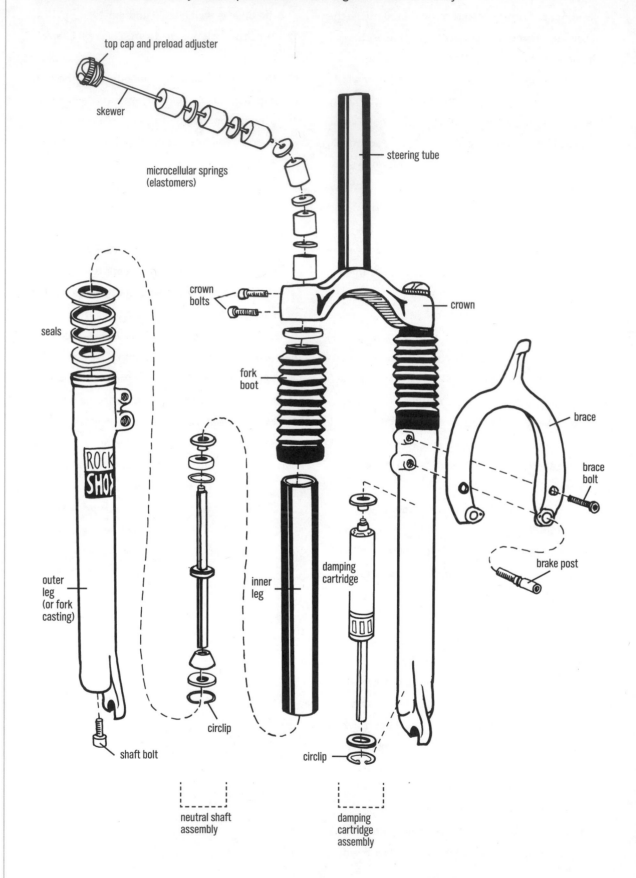

top cap and preload adjuster

skewer

microcellular springs
(elastomers)

steering tube

crown
bolts

crown

seals

fork
boot

brace

brace
bolt

ROCK
SHOX

damping
cartridge

brake post

outer
leg
(or fork
casting)

inner
leg

circlip

shaft bolt

circlip

neutral shaft
assembly

damping
cartridge
assembly

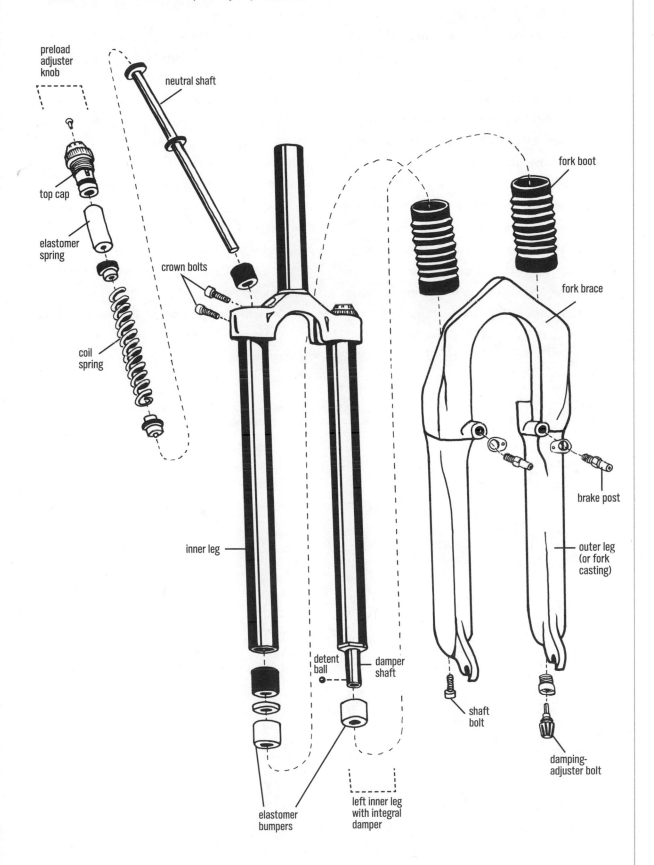

preload
adjuster
knob

top cap

elastomer
spring

coil
spring

neutral shaft

crown bolts

fork boot

fork brace

inner leg

detent
ball

damper
shaft

outer leg
(or fork
casting)

brake post

shaft
bolt

damping-
adjuster bolt

elastomer
bumpers

left inner leg
with integral
damper

its stop, you will break the part. Use the larger wrench size on the large bolt head, and unscrew that.

4. **Tap each bolt with a mallet** (Fig. 13.19). You'll know when the inner leg shafts pop free from the lower legs. If there is an adjuster shaft sticking out the bottom of the bolt or nut, put a socket or valve cap over it so that when you smack the bolt with the hammer, you won't break the little shaft.

5. **Remove the bolts.**

6. **Rotate the fork down with a bucket positioned underneath.**

7. **Pull the lower leg assembly off the inner legs** (Figs. 13.20–21). Let any oil pour out into the bucket. If oil is present, the fork has an oil bath inside (or it has a damping cartridge that has leaked oil inside the leg).

NOTE: *On a fork with a removable fork brace (Fig. 13.2), do not remove the brace.*

8. **With a clean, lint-free rag, clean the inner legs and the shafts sticking out of them.** Check the damper shaft (Figs. 13.20–21) for surface abrasion or bending and for oil leaks. If you want to work on the damper or change internal travel spacers, skip to xiii-14 to xiii-16.

NOTE: *On many older Manitou forks, there is an elastomer around the damper shaft that extends from the inner leg (Fig. 13.21). It is a good idea to clean and grease the shaft, but if you remove it, be ready to catch the steel ball that will fall out. This is the "detent" ball for the damper that puts the clicks in the damper adjustment.*

9. **Clean the wiper seals at the top and the bushings inside the outer legs.** There are two

---

13.22 Cleaning lower bushing

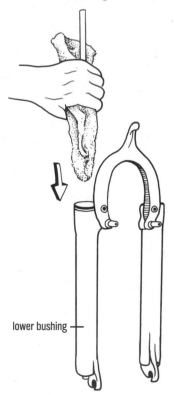

lower bushing

13.23 Greasing lower bushing

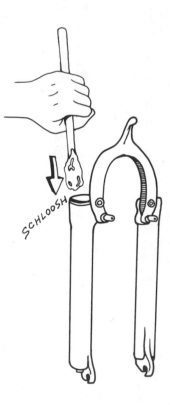

SCHLOOSH

13.24 Greasing inner leg

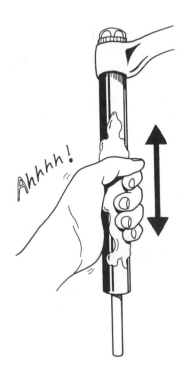

Ahhhh!

Old forks with external shaft bolts

I f the fork does not have an oil bath or the Manitou Microlube system, you can keep it lubricated longer by putting an oil bath in. Squirt 15cc or so of automatic transmission fluid in through the bottom bolt holes before replacing the bolts (Fig. 13.25). This keeps lubricant sloshing around up to the upper bushings as you ride. Use a brass or plastic crush washer under the bottom bolt to reduce leakage.

WARNING: Don't put an oil bath in forks with internal shaft bolts you reach from the top (there is no bolt on the bottom of the outer leg), as you could crack the legs by tightening the bolts down onto trapped oil.

bushings in each outer leg: one at the top and one halfway down. Reach the bottom one with a rag wrapped around a long rod (Fig. 13.22). The top seals can be pried out and cleaned or replaced if need be. If there is a foam ring between two wiper seals, you may want to at least pull that out and clean it well with solvent so that the ring can do its job properly. Be sure to reengorge the foam ring with shock oil prior to reinstallation. If the bushings are shot (indicated by movement of the inner leg wobbling inside the bushings), they may be replaceable with special tools, or you may need to buy new fork lowers.

10. **Smear nonlithium grease (such as Buzzy's Slick Honey lube) on the wipers and bushings in the lower legs.** To grease the lower bushings, slather grease on the end of a long rod, and reach down to the lower bushings with it (Fig. 13.23). It is counterproductive to grease between the upper and lower bush-

ings, so don't do it. In a fork with an oil bath, greasing the bushings is unnecessary.

11. **Smear a thin layer of the same grease on the inner legs** (Fig. 13.24).

12. **Slide the outer legs gently over the inner legs.** Install the fork boots first if the fork has them. Take care not to damage the upper dust seals or the lower bushings. To get the lower legs on completely, it may help to spread the lower leg assembly slightly while you rock it side to side to engage the bushings on the inner legs.

13. **Replace the oil bath** (Fig. 13.25) **if the fork has one inside the outer legs.** This is where you need oil bath specs—oil volume and weight—for your fork.

14. **Put the shaft bolts** (Figs. 13.16–17) **back in the bottom of the outer legs.** Engage the threads in the shaft. If the bolt threads do not engage, push the inner legs in farther.

15. **Tighten the bolts.** See the fork owners' manual or Appendix D for torque specs. You're done!

xiii-14
CHANGING THE DAMPER OIL ON PRE-1998 MANITOU DAMPERS AND REPLACING ROCKSHOX JUDY CARTRIDGES

🔧 🔧 LEVEL 2

As with overhauling the lower leg assembly (§xiii-13), these two damper overhaul sections do not cover all possible damping variations. Consult an (online) service manual for your fork. These sections are useful for a few types of forks from around the turn of the century whose manuals may be hard to find online.

This section applies to Manitou pre-TPC dampers and early RockShox cartridge dampers. Skip to §xiii-15 for Manitou TPC and RockShox "Pure" damping systems. RockShox HydraCoil and Marzocchi open-bath dampers get an oil change whether you want it or not when you pull the fork apart as described in §xiii-13.

1. **Start by taking the fork apart as described in §xiii-13 through step 7.**

2. **Remove the coil-spring or elastomer fork springs (§xiii-8b) or deflate the air spring(s).** If you don't do either, the shaft or cartridge on some forks will shoot out at you when you remove its retainer. The temptation to push the damper shaft up and down will be great, but be very careful. The shaft is meant to be supported in the fork and move straight up and down, and if you put a side load on it, you could allow oil to leak out around the seal.

3. **On an old RockShox, to remove and inspect (or replace) the cartridge and/or neutral shaft** (Fig. 13.20), **remove the circlip at the bottom of the inner leg with inward-squeezing snap-ring pliers** (Fig. 13.26). When you replace the cartridge (or neutral shaft), orient the snap-ring so that its sharp edge faces away from the springs.

   (a) Starting in the 1999 model year, some air-spring models require a special tool for removing the negative spring and the cartridge that is essentially a hollow 15mm hex key. Be careful when you unscrew the cartridge retainer with this special tool—it is left-hand-threaded.

   (b) For an older, non-TPC Manitou damper (Fig. 13.21), unscrew the damper seal nut at the bottom of the leg (Fig. 13.27). Do this with the fork upside down; this will prevent oil from pouring out.

4. **Pour out the old oil.** (We're back to talking specifically about Manitou now.)

5. **Add a little new oil of the weight you want.** Automatic transmission fluid (ATF) is 15-weight and works fine for non-TPC Manitou forks if you don't have fork hydraulic oil. Slosh the ATF around inside to rinse the damper clean, and pour it back out.

13.26 Removing cartridge-retaining circlip from RockShox inner leg

13.27 Hand tighten old-style (pre-TPC) Manitou damper nut with O-ring slipped down around inner leg

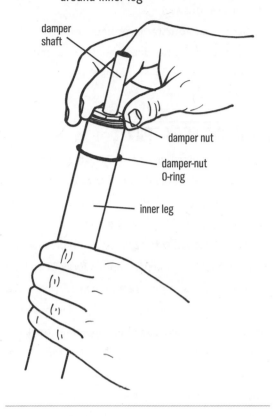

CHANGING OIL IN A MANITOU TPC OR ROCKSHOX PURE DAMPER

 **LEVEL 2**

Again, this is specific to turn-of-the-century forks that you still see around on the trails and whose service manuals are harder to locate. If you can find a service manual online or elsewhere for your fork, use it.

Manitou TPC dampers rarely need oil changes because of the high oil volume keeping them cool and the absence of springs in the oil to grind aluminum into it. But they are easy to service when needed. The RockShox "Pure" damping system, as found in post-2001 SID SL and high-end Psylo forks, is very similar to Manitou TPC, and almost the same instructions apply. If the information is not printed on the outer leg, look for springs (air, coil, or elastomer) in only one leg of the fork; that's a hint that the Manitou is TPC or the high-end RockShox is Pure. (Many 1999–2001 low-end RockShox forks have a single-sided spring with a single-piston cartridge in the other leg, but it's not Pure.)

The springs should be installed (or inflated) in the other leg so that the fork is at its full length.

6. **Fill the non-TPC Manitou damper with new fork oil or ATF to the top of the inverted inner leg.** Stroke the shaft a few times to get the air bubbles out, and top off with oil again.

7. **Slide the nut back down onto the shaft and start it in the threads.**

8. **Roll the rubber O-ring down off the nut so that it surrounds the fork inner leg** (Fig. 13.27).

9. **Tighten the end nut by hand until the O-ring groove is just showing above the tube** (Fig. 13.27). Air and excess oil are vented out through a hole under the nut's lip when the O-ring is not covering it.

10. **Roll the O-ring into its groove in the nut.**

11. **Tighten the nut with a wrench.**

12. **Continue with reassembly of the fork** (§xiii-13, step 8).

1. **Unscrew the adjuster-knob cap on the top of the damper leg.** It's usually on the right side (Fig. 13.28), but early TPC dampers were in the left leg. Keep the fork right side up. You may need to remove the lockout or adjustment lever first. The upper (compression-damping) piston is attached to the cap—jiggle it as you pull the piston up and through the threads (Fig. 13.28).

2. **Pour out the old oil.** If you don't have the fork owner's manual, note the height of the oil below the top of the crown before pouring it out. You will need to fashion a dipstick out of a dowel rod or wire.

13.28 Getting the Manitou TPC's top piston in and out

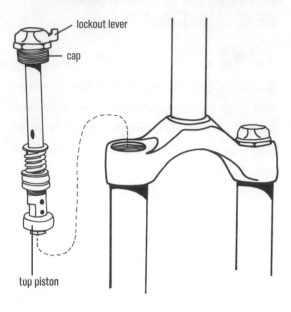

10. **Replace the springs or inflate the other leg to make the fork full length.**

11. **Remove the syringe.**

12. **Screw the adjuster lever back on.** Remember to put the little detent ball back onto its spring in the cap—it makes the lever click.

xiii-16
CHANGING FORK TRAVEL

Changing travel varies from very easy to very complicated. On the easy end is an external knob or lever. On the complicated end are a different damping cartridge, a neutral shaft, and a spring stack (these parts are shown in Figs. 13.20–21). With persistence, you may be able to find parts for old forks. Then take apart the fork as in §xiii-12 and §xiii-13, put in the new pieces, reassemble it, and voilà, different travel. Just make sure that you check the total travel as in §xiii-6a and that there is no way the fork crown can hit the tire when the fork is compressed fully. Although changing travel does not make the crown come down farther, the temptation may be to use a bigger tire with the longer travel.

a. Travel-adjust knob

To change travel, turn the large knob on top of the left leg to increase or decrease travel. On RockShox Coil U-Turn, the big coil spring itself screws down or up along large threads around the outside of a big plastic plunger to shorten or lengthen the fork. You can shorten the fork while riding by turning the U-Turn knob clockwise, but you must take your weight off the spring to turn it counterclockwise and lengthen the fork. RockShox 2-Step Air (only two possible travel settings) and Air U-Turn compensate for the travel change, keeping the same spring rate.

b. Plunger-height screw under the spring

The "Vari-Travel" system on some RockShox Psylo forks simply requires removing the left top

3. **Add a little new 5-weight fork oil.** Both TPC and Pure take 5-weight. Slosh it around inside to rinse the damper clean, and pour it back out.

4. **Pour in new 5-weight oil to the proper level.** If you have the fork owners' manual, fill to the level below the top of the crown as specified. If not, fill to the height it was before. Keep the fork straight up and down.

5. **Slip the piston back in** (Fig. 13.28), **and tighten the cap back on.** That's it for Manitou.

6. **For RockShox Pure, bleed the fork as detailed in steps 7–12.** Bleeding is required to squeeze the air out, because the Pure damper, unlike the TPC, has no air in it.

7. **Half-fill a small plastic syringe (without a plunger in it) with 5-weight fork oil, and stick it into the hole in the top cap.**

8. **Remove the springs from the other leg or deflate it.**

9. **Stroke the fork up and down slowly.** This pushes air bubbles up into the syringe and pulls oil down out of it. Continue until no more air comes up.

cap and removing the coil spring. Reach down inside with a long screwdriver, and turn the screw on the top of the plunger; each turn changes the travel by 1mm.

c. Internal spacers

A common way to change travel is by disassembling the fork (§xiii-13, steps 1–7) and inserting or removing plastic travel spacers. By putting spacers below the plunger on one of the fork's shafts, you can reduce travel, because the shaft cannot extend as far out of the bottom of the inner leg (the spacer hits the cap in the bottom of the inner leg and prevents the plunger from coming as far down—look at Fig. 13.29 to understand the concept). To increase travel, remove spacers from below the plunger. Nowadays, these travel spacers are generally spool-shaped with a slot down one side that snaps onto the shaft. An older type of internal spacer can be found in some RockShox Judy forks. Each plastic All Travel spacer (Fig. 13.29) is tubular with lips

13.29 Changing travel on a RockShox Judy with All Travel

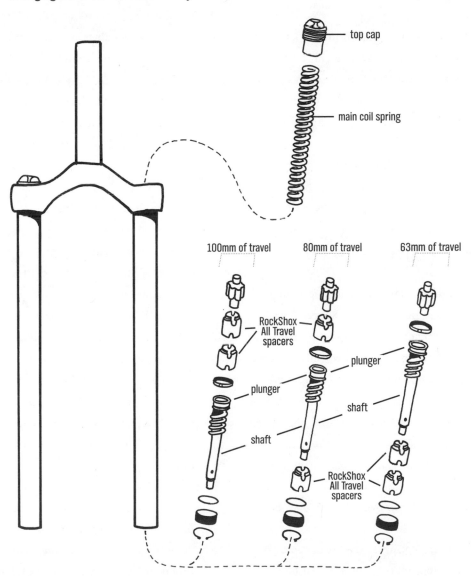

at one end to snap into a spring or insert into another spacer.

This is how to change travel on many forks with internal spacers:

⚙️⚙️⚙️ LEVEL 3

1. Pull the fork apart as in §xiii-13, steps 1–7.

NOTE: *You may be able to just take the top cap off the spring side of the fork crown with a big, flat-end socket and pull out (or turn the fork over and drop out) the spring shaft.*

2. Remove the spring. Remove the coil spring (Fig. 13.29), or release the air from the valve(s)—wear safety glasses, as oil spurts out.

3. Remove the spring shaft from the left inner leg. This can be done by removing a split ring with a screwdriver or a circlip with inward-closing snapring pliers (Fig. 13.26); remove any rings and washers the clip is holding back.

NOTE: *Some RockShox SID forks require a special SID cartridge-removal tool: a hollow 15mm hex key that fits over the shaft and engages the threaded cap at the bottom of the inner leg. Put a 15mm socket or box wrench on the other end of the tool, and unscrew the cap clockwise.*

IMPORTANT: *This SID cap is left-hand-threaded.*

4. Install or remove a travel spacer (or two). Either the spacers will snap onto the spring shaft from the side, or they will slide up onto the shaft (and the lips of the spacers may snap into each other or into the bottom of the small spring attached to the plunger as in Fig. 13.29). If you want to reduce travel by the length of the spacer, snap a travel spacer onto the spring shaft under the plunger. To increase travel, remove a spacer from below the plunger.

5. Reinstall the spring shaft. If you removed it from the top, replace the top cap (and coil spring if applicable). If you removed the shaft from the bottom, replace the split ring (split it open and start one end, rotating it in) or snapring (Fig. 13.26; make sure its sharp edge faces out) to hold everything in.

6. Inflate the fork if applicable.

7. Reassemble the fork as in §xiii-13, starting with step 8.

RockShox SID XC All Travel

This variation of the spacer system requires reversing the neutral shaft. The SID XC packaging includes a single All Travel spacer identical to those on the Judy (Fig 13.29).

1. Pull the fork apart as in §xiii-13, steps 1–7, and release the air from the valves.

2. Remove both shafts from the inner legs using snapring pliers (Fig. 13.26) and a small-blade screwdriver to pry out the snapring. The negative spring shaft is reversible; if you want maximum travel, leave the All Travel spacer out of the fork and set up the shaft so that the end with a circumscribed line around it points down; screw the piston into the opposite end. The scribed end is longer from the glide ring to the end, so having it down allows more shaft to extend out of the inner leg and—voilà!—more travel. The negative spring goes on the longer end, below the glide ring. Once you get it apart, you'll see what I mean.

3. If you want less travel, slide the All Travel spacer up onto the damper shaft (the shaft from the right leg) and snap it into the spring below the piston. Remove and save the thin spring guide that had been snapped into the spring.

4. Unscrew the piston from the short end (without the circumscribed mark) of the left-side shaft. Pull the negative spring off the long end.

5. Screw the piston into the longer, scribed end, and put the negative spring onto the shorter,

unscribed end. The negative spring has a tight-fitting plastic spring guide snapped into the piston end, so it does not slide easily. I find it simpler to snap the spring off the guide and move them separately. With the short end of the neutral shaft down and the All Travel spacer limiting the downward extension of the damper shaft, travel is shortened.

6. Reassemble the fork as in §xiii-13, starting with step 8.

xiii-17

CHECKING FORK ALIGNMENT

🌟 🌟 🌟 LEVEL 3

Checking the alignment may help explain bike-handling problems. You will need a ruler, a true front wheel, and, for a rigid steel fork, dropout-alignment tools (Fig. 1.4). With any type of fork other than a rigid steel one, this procedure is diagnostic only, because you should not try to realign any other type of fork.

If you find the alignment to be off more than a couple of millimeters in any direction with any fork other than a steel, unsuspended one, you need a new fork. If the fork is new, misalignment should be covered as a warranty item.

If a steel fork is more than 8mm off in any direction, you ought to get a new fork. If the dropouts of a steel fork are slightly bent, you can realign them. You can also take a moderately bent (between 2mm and 8mm) steel fork to a frame builder or a bike shop for realignment. Make sure that whoever you take it to is properly equipped with a fork jig or alignment table and is well versed in the art of "cold setting" (a fancy term for bending) steel forks.

1. **Remove the wheel and the fork** (§xi-18 and §xi-19).

2. **Measure the spacing between the faces of the dropouts** (Fig. 13.30). Adult and high-quality children's bikes should have a spacing of 100mm between the inner surfaces of the dropouts. (Some low-end kids' bikes have narrower spacing—about 90mm or so.) Measure the distance between the flat surfaces, not between wheel-retaining bumps. Dropout spacing up to 102mm and down to 99mm is acceptable. Beyond that in either direction means a new fork. If you have a rigid fork made of steel, you can go to a bike shop or frame builder for realignment.

3. **Clamp the steering tube of the fork in a bike stand or a padded vise.**

13.30 Measuring dropout spacing

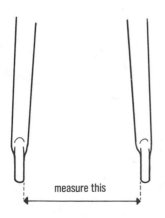

measure this

13.31 Aligning dropout with dropout-alignment tool

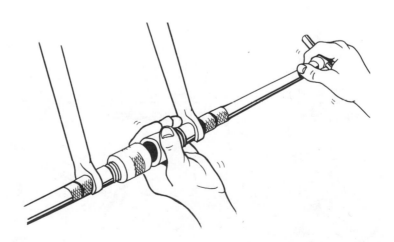

4. **Install the dropout-alignment tools** (Fig. 13.31). The tools are made to be used on either the fork or the rear triangle of the bike, so they have two axle diameters and spacers for use in the (wider-spaced) rear dropouts. Move all the spacers to the outside of the fork ends so that only the cups of the tools are placed inside the dropouts. Install the tool so that the shaft is seated up against the top of the dropout slot. Tighten the handles.

5. **Check how the tool's cups line up.** Ideally, the ends of the cups should be parallel and lined up with each other (Fig. 13.32). The cups of Campagnolo dropout-alignment tools are nonadjustable and are nominally 50mm in length; the ideal space between their ends is 0.1–0.5mm. The cups on Park dropout-aligning tools (illustrated in Figs. 13.31–33) can be threaded in and out so that you can bring the faces up close to each other no matter the dropout spacing. If they are lined up (Fig. 13.32), and the dropouts are spaced between 99mm and 102mm apart, continue on to step 6. If the dropouts on your rigid fork made of steel are not lined up straight across with each other (Fig. 13.33) and are within the 99–102mm spacing range, skip to §xiii-18

to align them; then come back to here after they're aligned.

NOTE: *It is crucial that the fork dropout faces be parallel before you continue with step 6, or the rest of the alignment procedures will be a waste of time. Clamping the hub into misaligned dropouts will force the fork legs to twist, and any measurement of the side-to-side and fore-and-aft alignment of the fork legs with misaligned dropouts will not be accurate.*

6. **Remove the tire from a front wheel.** Make sure the wheel is true and properly dished (§xii-4 and §xii-5).

7. **Install the wheel in the fork.** Make sure the axle is seated against the top of the dropout slot on either side and that the quick-release skewer is tight. Lightly push the rim from side to side to be certain that there is no play in the front hub. If there is play, you must first adjust the hub (§vi-15d).

8. **Check the alignment visually.**

   (a) Look down the steering tube and through the rim's valve hole to the bottom side of the rim (Fig. 13.34). The steering tube should be lined up with this line of sight through the wheel (Fig. 13.35). When you are sighting through the steering tube and the valve hole, you should see the same amount

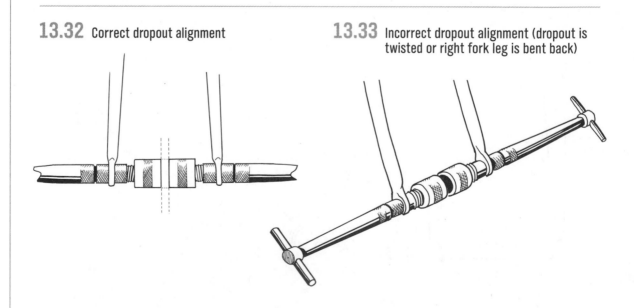

13.32 Correct dropout alignment

13.33 Incorrect dropout alignment (dropout is twisted or right fork leg is bent back)

of space between each side of the rim and the sides of the steering tube while you see the seam side of the rim centered through the valve hole.

(b) Turn the wheel around, and install it again so that what was the right end of the hub is now the left. Sight through the steering tube and the wheel valve hole again. Placing the wheel in the fork both ways corrects for deformation in the axle or any wobble in the wheel. If the wheel is true and properly dished and the axle is in good shape, the wheel should line up exactly as it did before. If it does not line up, but the wheel is off by the same amount to one side as it is to the opposite side when the wheel is turned around, the wheel is off and the fork is fine side to side.

(c) If this test indicates that the fork is up to 2–3mm off to the side, that is close enough; continue on, please. If it is off by more than 3mm, get a new fork or have it aligned by a frame builder (if it is steel, because by now you know that you should not try to align suspension, titanium, carbon-fiber, or aluminum forks).

NOTE: *If you are sighting through the wheel in this way and you cannot see the bottom side of the rim through the valve hole because the hub is in the way, the fork*

13.34 Sighting through the steering tube to check fork alignment

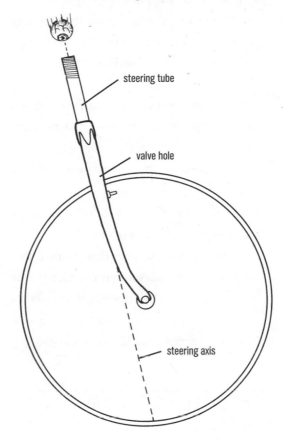

steering tube

valve hole

steering axis

has big problems. *For the bike to handle properly, the front hub must have some forward offset from the steering axis (Fig. 13.34). This offset, or "rake," is usually around 4cm on a mountain bike. If you sight through the steering tube and see the front hub, the*

13.35 Correct alignment of valve hole in a straight fork

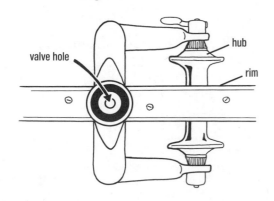

valve hole

hub

rim

13.36 Checking fork alignment with a ruler

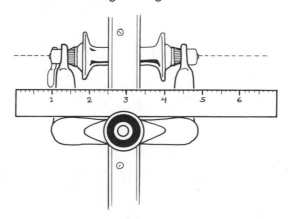

fork is bent backward so much that it has little or no offset. If this is the case, you need a new fork.

9. **Place a ruler on edge across the fork legs just below the fork crown** (Fig. 13.36). Make sure the ruler is perpendicular to the steering tube.

10. **Lift the fork toward a light source so that you are sighting across the ruler and the front hub toward the light.** The ruler's edge should line up parallel with the axle ends sticking out of either end of the hub (Fig. 13.36). This test will tell you if one fork leg is bent back relative to the other. If the axle lines up parallel to the ruler, or very close to that, fork alignment has checked out completely, and you can put it back in the bike. If one fork leg is considerably behind the other, get a new fork or have this one aligned (if it is steel).

xiii-18
ALIGNING DROPOUTS ON A RIGID FORK MADE OF STEEL

⚙ ⚙ ⚙ LEVEL 3

You should do this only with a steel, nonsuspension fork.

Dropouts are easy to tweak out of alignment; simply pulling the bike off a roof rack and failing to lift it high enough to clear the rack skewer will do it. A fork may also have come with misaligned dropouts when new.

NOTE: *If the dropout is bent more than 7 degrees or so, or if the paint is cracked at the dropout where it is bent, bending the dropout back is too dangerous. Replace the fork.*

1. **Install dropout-alignment tools, and check the alignment as in §xiii-17, steps 5–7.** If the tool cups are not lined up with each other (Fig.13.33) and the fork spacing is between 99 and 102mm, continue with steps 2–4 to align the dropouts. If the fork spacing is wider than 102mm or less than 99mm, there is no point in aligning the dropout faces, because you must bend the fork legs as well to correct the spacing. Without an alignment table or fork jig, you cannot do this accurately. Get a new fork or have a qualified mechanic or frame builder align the fork.

2. **Clamp the crown** (or "unicrown," Fig. 13.3) **of the fork very tightly.** Do this between two wood blocks in a well-anchored vise (Fig 11.40).

3. **Bend each dropout until the open faces of the dropout-alignment tools are parallel.** Grab the end of the dropout-alignment tool handle with one hand and the cup of the tool with the other, and turn the tool to bend the dropout (Fig. 13.31). Recheck. Repeat until the edges line up straight with each other (Fig. 13.32).

4. **Remove the tools and continue with §xiii-17, step 6.**

FRAMES

Come to kindly terms with your Ass for it bears you.
—John Muir, *How to Keep Your Volkswagen Alive*

TOOLS

ruler or caliper

string

bike stand

metric wrenches
and hex keys

OPTIONAL

dropout-alignment
tools

derailleur-hanger
alignment tool

metric taps

English-thread
bottom-bracket
tap set

thread-cutting oil

drill and drill bits

16mm cone wrench

Your Volkswagen is not a donkey . . . and your mountain bike is not a Volkswagen. Still, you'd be well served to follow Muir's sage advice and stay on good terms with your bike. In doing so, pay close attention to the frame, because it is the most important part of your bike. It is the one part of your bike that is nearly impossible to fix on the trail if it breaks, and if it does fail, the consequences can be serious. Therefore, get to know your frame. Come to kindly terms with it . . . for it bears your ass . . . or something like that.

xiv-1
DESIGNING FRAMES

The traditional "diamond," or "double-diamond," mountain bike frame design evolved from a combination of postwar cruiser bikes and road-racing bikes. The rigid design of a road bike relies on a "front triangle" and a "rear triangle" (Fig. 14.1); never mind that the front triangle is not actually a triangle—or much of a diamond, for that matter. Although the basic concept is similar, there are some notable differences between road and mountain bike geometries. Mountain bike frames feature a higher bottom bracket for more ground clearance, a longer and wider rear triangle for more tire clearance and a wider rear axle, a shorter seat tube (and correspondingly lower top tube) for more stand-over clearance, brake bosses, and larger-diameter tubing.

In the pursuit of low frame weight and price coupled with high frame strength, durability, comfort, control, and performance, mountain bike frame design has changed radically in the relatively short time since the inception of the sport. Take a look at a modern mountain bike, and compare it to the Marin County Repack-style bikes of the late 1970s or the Crested Butte off-road "cruisers" that popped onto the scene around the same time. The difference is amazing, even if you are just comparing a fully rigid design (Figs. i.3 and 14.1) to one of the early models made from or patterned

347

14.1 Rigid frame

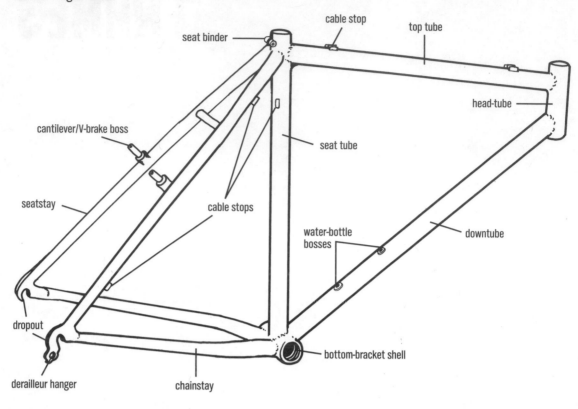

cable stop

top tube

seat binder

head-tube

cantilever/V-brake boss

seat tube

seatstay

cable stops

water-bottle
bosses

downtube

dropout

bottom-bracket shell

derailleur hanger

chainstay

14.2 Frame with rear suspension

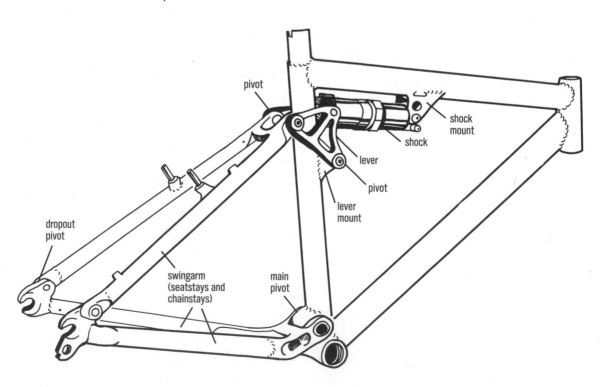

pivot

shock
mount

shock

lever

pivot

lever
mount

dropout
pivot

swingarm
(seatstays and
chainstays)

main
pivot

after circa 1940 Schwinn-style cruisers. Start looking at full-suspension models (Figs. i.4 and 14.2), and you have a whole new breed of animal. And full suspension has now become so common that you even find it on cheap department store bikes.

xiv-2
DESIGNING SUSPENSION FRAMES

Rear suspension (also called "full suspension" because it is usually combined with a suspension fork) involves a design totally different from the traditional double diamond. Most suspension frames have a front triangle and a "rear swingarm" (Fig. 14.2).

There are almost as many rear-suspension designs (and names for them) as there are suspension frame designers. Over the past few years, the changes have been fast and furious, and I'll wager that within another few years there will be a whole new crop of popular designs with a whole new crop of catchy names. Although it would be pointless to go on at length about specifics of current designs, this chapter divides suspension frames into broad categories and gives general maintenance guidelines for them.

xiv-3
REVOLUTIONIZING FRAME MATERIALS

The revolution in bicycle-frame materials has been going on since the birth of the bicycle. Wood was the material of choice for the first bicycles, but that was soon replaced by steel, aluminum, and even bamboo. Aluminum, carbon fiber, steel, and titanium are the materials most commonly used to build mountain bike frames, but magnesium and metal matrix composites account for a tiny share too. Because these materials come in a variety of grades with varying costs and physical properties, assume that I am talking about the highest grades for the materials used in bicycles.

For example, the aluminum used in window frames is a lot different from the heat-treated 6000- and 7000-series aluminum used in high-end bicycle frames.

Steel has the highest modulus of elasticity (a principal determiner of stiffness) as well as the highest density and tensile strength of any of the metals commonly used in frames. The modulus of elasticity, the density, and the tensile strength of aluminum are much lower than those values for steel, and titanium has values between the two. Metal tubing characteristics are maximized for bicycles by (1) butting (i.e., placing thickness where it is needed and not where it adds useless weight), (2) increasing diameter to add stiffness, and (3) heat-treating and alloying to boost certain physical properties of the metal. With intelligent use of materials, long-lasting frames of comparable stiffness-to-weight and/or strength-to-weight ratios can be built out of any of these metals.

Carbon fiber and similar composite frame materials consist of fibers embedded in a resin (plastic) matrix. These materials can be extremely light, strong, and stiff. Bike frames can be built by molding them in a single piece ("monocoque" construction); by gluing large molded carbon sub-assemblies together (also sometimes misleadingly called monocoque; each piece is, of course, a single piece, but the whole is a number of pieces); by bonding "tube to tube" where carbon tubes are mitered to fishmouth around each other and then wrapped with carbon fibers to hold them together; or by gluing carbon-fiber tubes into lugs (usually made of carbon fiber or aluminum). A big advantage of molded carbon composites is that they can be made thicker or thinner in specific areas where extra strength is or is not needed. And contrary to widely held notions, they can be repaired when they break; a number of small carbon frame-building shops offer such a service.

xiv-4
INSPECTING THE FRAME

 LEVEL 1

You can avoid potentially dangerous or at least ride-shortening frame failures by inspecting your bike's frame frequently. If you find damage and you are not sure how dangerous the bike is to ride, take it to a bike shop for advice.

1. **Clean the frame every few rides.** That way, you can spot problems early.

2. **Inspect all tubes for cracks, bends, buckles, dents, and paint stretching or cracking.** Look especially near the joints where stress is highest. If in doubt, take the frame to an expert for advice.

3. **Perform the "coin test" on questionable areas of carbon frames.** Using the edge of a coin, tap on the frame in any area that looks cracked, damaged, or otherwise suspicious, as well as over the rest of the frame for comparison. If, instead of a satisfying "clack" sound consistent over the tubes, you hear a dead "thwap" sound, there may be cracks or delaminated areas hidden within the structure. Take the frame to an expert for analysis.

4. **Inspect the rear dropouts and the welds around the brake bosses and cable stops for cracks.** Check to be sure that the dropouts, the derailleur hanger on the right dropout, brake bosses, and cable stops are not bent. (Check Fig. 14.1 for names and locations of frame parts.) Some derailleur hangers, dropouts, and cantilever/V-brake bosses (Fig. 14.1) bolt to the frame and are replaceable. Otherwise, badly bent or broken dropouts, brake bosses, disc-brake mounts (Fig. 14.3), and cable stops require having a new one welded, riveted, or brazed on; a frame builder in your area may be able to do it.

5. **Look for deeply rusted areas on steel frames.** Remove the seatpost every few months and after every wet ride, invert the bike to let water pour out of the seat tube, and allow it to dry fully before replacing the post. Look and feel for deep rusted areas inside or for rust falling out. I recommend squirting a rust protective spray designed for bicycle frames (Frame Saver), WD-40, or oil inside the tubes periodically (after letting the frame dry out upside down with the seatpost removed). Remember to grease both the seatpost and the inside of the seat tube when you reinsert the seatpost. After sanding off the rust on any external areas where the paint has come off, touch them up with touch-up paint or nail polish (hey, it's available in lots of cool colors, but be advised that it is not as durable as good paint and requires periodic retouching).

6. **On suspension frames, check the swingarm movement and the shock condition.** Disconnect the shock. Move the swingarm up and down, and flex it laterally, feeling for play or binding in the pivots. Check the shock for

14.3 International Standard (IS) disc-brake mount (shown on a sliding dropout for a Rohloff SpeedHub)

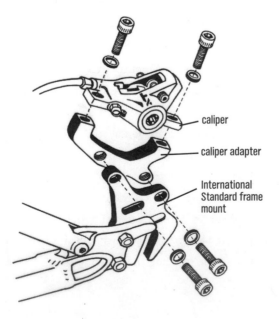

caliper

caliper adapter

International Standard frame mount

leaking oil, cracks, a bent shaft, or other damage. Further shock maintenance is described in §xiv-8.

7. **Check that a true and properly dished wheel sits straight in the frame, centered between the chainstays and seatstays, and lined up in the same plane as the front triangle.** Tightening the hub skewer should not result in bowing or twisting of the chainstays or seatstays.

xiv-5
CHECKING AND STRAIGHTENING THE REAR-DERAILLEUR HANGER

⚙ ⚙ ⚙ LEVEL 3

1. **Thread a derailleur-hanger alignment tool into the derailleur hanger on the right dropout** (Fig. 14.4).

2. **Install a true rear wheel without a tire on it.**

3. **Swing the tool around, measuring the spacing between its arm and the rim all the way around.** The arm of the tool should be the same distance from the rim at all points. Some tools, such as the one in Figure 14.4, have an extension rod extending at right angles from the arm and held by a hand-turned setscrew that you can adjust to check the spacing; others require you to measure it with a ruler or caliper.

4. **If the tool has play in it, keep it pushed inward lightly as you perform all of the measurements.** Otherwise, you will get inconsistent data.

5. **Correct any inconsistent spacing between the tool arm and the rim.** If the tool varies in its lateral proximity to the rim by more than 1mm or so all the way around, carefully bend the hanger by pulling outward on the arm of the tool lightly where it is closest to the rim.

6. **If the derailleur hanger is really bent, be careful.** You may not be able to align it without

14.4 Checking derailleur-hanger alignment

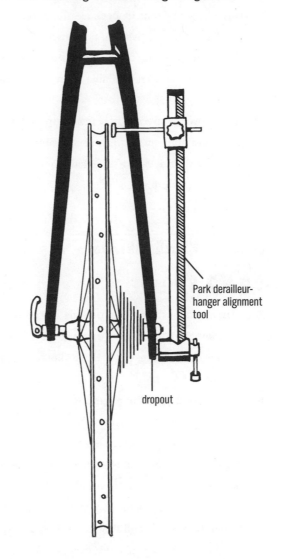

Park derailleur-hanger alignment tool

dropout

14.5 Installing replacement rear-derailleur hanger

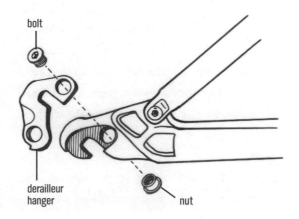

bolt

derailleur hanger

nut

breaking it (you may even have trouble threading the tool in because the threaded hole has become oval-shaped). If the derailleur hanger bolts onto the frame, replace it with a new one, available from your bike dealer (Fig. 14.5).

7. If the threads are really screwed up and the derailleur hanger is not a replaceable style, see §xiv-6 and Figure 14.6 for other derailleur hanger options.

xiv-6
FIXING DAMAGED THREADS

🔧 🔧 🔧 LEVEL 3

A mountain bike frame has threads in the bottom-bracket shell, cantilever brake bosses, some disc-brake bosses, the water-bottle bosses, and the rear-derailleur hanger (Fig. 14.1). Some bikes have a threaded seat binder, and some also have a small threaded hole in the bottom of the bottom-bracket shell onto which a plastic derailleur-cable guide is bolted. Some frames also have a threaded front-derailleur mount or two.

1. Whenever you have to retap any threads, first brush them clean and then use oil on the tap (with titanium threads, use canola oil).

2. If any threads on the frame are stripped or are cross-threaded, try chasing through (retapping) the threads with the appropriately sized thread tap.

3. Except in the case of the left-hand-threaded, drive-side bottom-bracket threads, turn the tap forward (clockwise) a bit, then turn it back, then forward (two steps forward and one back), and so on, to prevent the tap from binding and possibly breaking. Be aware that taps are made of very hard and brittle steel. If you put any side or twisting forces on small taps, they can break off easily. Be care-ful. If the tap breaks, you'll have a real mess, because the broken tap in the hole is harder than the frame, so it's impossible to drill the broken tap out. If you break off a tap in the frame, do not try to get it out yourself. Take the frame to a bike shop, a machine shop, or a frame builder before you break off what little is left sticking out. Unless you put the tap in crooked, breaking one should not be a problem when you retap damaged frame threads, as these threads will be so worn; getting the tap to find any metal to bite into will probably be your biggest problem.

IMPORTANT: *Tapping a bottom-bracket shell takes a good amount of expertise. You really need expert supervision if you have never done it before and still want to do it yourself. In addition to making sure that you place the correct tap in the correct end of the shell, be certain that the taps go in straight. Most bottom-bracket taps have a shaft between the two taps to keep them parallel to each other (Fig. 1.4). They must both be started at the same time from both ends. If you mess it up, you may ruin the frame. If in doubt, ask an expert.*

The following tap sizes are commonly found on mountain bikes:

Water-bottle bosses	M5 (5mm × 0.8)
Bottom-bracket shell hole for shift-cable guide	M5 (5mm × 0.8)
Seat binders and brake bosses	M6 (6mm × 1)
Disc-brake postmounts	M6 (6mm × 1)
Derailleur hanger	M10 (10mm × 1)
Bottom-bracket shells	1.37 inches × 24 tpi*

tpi = threads per inch

NOTE: *Remember, the chain-side bottom-bracket threads are left-hand-threaded; the other side is right-hand-threaded.*

4. Replace the old bolt with a new one, except in the case of a bottom-bracket cup or rear derailleur, as long as its threads look perfect.

5. If tapping the threads and using a new bolt do not work, try these remedies:

(a) For cantilever/V-brake bosses, some brake posts are replaceable. Replaceable posts have wrench flats (usually 8mm) at the base, and they thread into a boss welded to the frame. If they are not like this, you must take your bike to a frame builder to get a new boss welded on.

(b) For disc-brake bosses, international standard mounts (Fig. 14.3) are standard on frames (and postmounts [Fig. 7.17] are standard on forks), and about the only thing that can happen to these robust tabs is that they can get bent. But threaded disc-brake mounts (i.e., postmounts) do exist on some frames, and if the threads are stripped, it is often because overly short bolts were employed to mount the disc brake (generally, 10–12mm of thread engagement is required; this much bolt length should stick through the brake's mounting tab; see Fig. 7.17). If so, you may be able to tap out the threads and use new bolts of the specified length without further problems. Otherwise, the entire dropout, swingarm, or frame may need to be replaced.

(c) For water-bottle bosses and threaded front-derailleur braze-on bosses, some bike shops have a tool that rivets bottle bosses into the frame. Check for this possibility first, because you can avoid a new paint job that way, although such riveted bosses tend to loosen up over time. Otherwise, if the frame is metal, take it to a frame builder to get a new boss welded or brazed on.

(d) For derailleur-hanger threads, if your bike has a replaceable rear-derailleur hanger, bolt a new one onto the frame (Fig. 14.5).

Without that, and if the threads are so badly damaged that an M10 tap won't repair

14.6 Inserting dropout saver

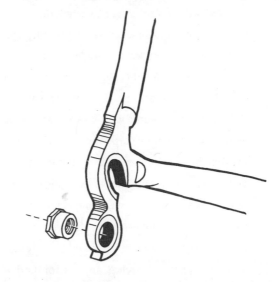

them, another option is to use a "Dropout Saver" derailleur-hanger backing nut (Fig. 14.6) made by Wheels Manufacturing and available at bike shops. A Dropout Saver is simply a sleeve threaded the same as your dropout was, with 16mm wrench flats on one end. Drill out the hole in the damaged derailleur hanger with a $^{15}\!/_{32}$-inch drill bit, push the Dropout Saver in from the backside, and screw in the derailleur. Dropout Savers come in two lengths, according to the thickness of the dropout.

Yet another option is to saw off the derailleur hanger with a hacksaw and use a separate derailleur hanger from a really cheap bike that fits flat against the outside of the dropout and is held in by the hub axle bolts or quick-release. You could also get a new frame or swingarm, or you may be able to have the dropout replaced by a frame builder.

(e) For seat binders with a separate binder clamp, just replace the whole clamp rather than mess with its threads. With a welded-on binder, you can drill it out and use a quick-release or a bolt and nut. Seat binder threads rarely get stripped, however; it is usually the bolt that is the problem.

(f) For bottom-bracket shell threads, you can use a Mavic or Stronglight cartridge bottom bracket (§viii-6, Fig. 8.23), if you can still find one and are using an old square-taper crank that works with its spindle length. This bottom-bracket type does not depend on the threads in the shell to anchor it, but you must have a shop bevel the ends of your bottom-bracket shell with a special cutting tool (which may not be easy to find in a newer bike shop; you may need to seek out an older shop that has one lying around, or find a machine shop that can do the job for you).

(g) For bottom-bracket cable-guide bolt-hole threads, a new hole in the bottom of the bottom bracket can be drilled and tapped, or the stripped hole can be tapped out with larger threads for a larger screw. Make sure the screw you use is short enough that it does not protrude into the inside of the bottom-bracket shell.

xiv-7
REPAIRING CHIPPED PAINT AND SMALL DENTS

Fixing chips is simply a matter of cleaning the area and touching it up. Sand any chipped paint or rust completely away before touching up the spot. Use touch-up paint for your bike, model paint, or fingernail polish.

Small dents can be filled with automotive body putty, but there is little point to filling them if you are doing only a touch-up, because the area probably won't look that great anyway.

There are plenty of frame painters around the country who can fill dents, repaint frames, and even match original decals. Many of them advertise in bike magazines and online.

xiv-8
MAINTAINING THE SHOCK
a. Daily maintenance

Keep the shock shaft, shaft seals, and bottom-out bumper clean. Clean them after every ride (you know—when you wipe down and lube the chain),

14.7 Rear-shock parts and adjustments

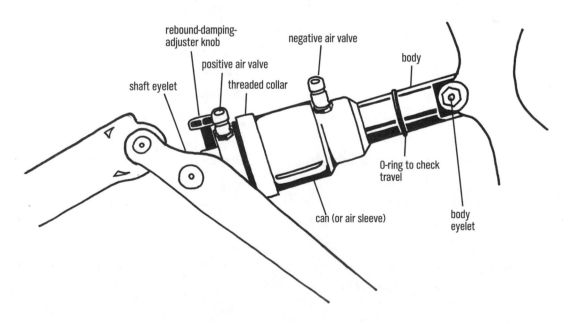

but do not use high-pressure water on them. The pressure can blow the seals inward and contaminate the shock. Lightly lubricate the shaft or shock body (the part that slides in and out).

Keep the bushings in the "eyelets" (mounting holes on either end of the shock—Fig. 14.7) clean and greased.

b. Every-40-hours maintenance: Air-sleeve service

 LEVEL 2

At a minimum, you need to remove the air sleeve (or "can"—see Fig. 14.7) from an air shock after every 40 hours of riding unless you are riding in very clean conditions.

This may seem like a ridiculously frequent schedule of maintenance, but if you think about it for a second, you will see that it makes sense. You don't think twice (or I hope you don't) about changing the oil in your car's engine every 3,000 miles, do you? Well, 3,000 miles is 50 hours of driving at 60 mph, and the engine has a lot of oil volume and an oil filter to keep pulling contaminants out of the oil every time it circulates.

Now consider your bicycle shock. Its piston is constantly going up and down as you ride, it has less than a teaspoon of lubricant in it, and it has no room for an oil filter. Forty hours does not seem so extreme in that context, does it?

You also need to regrease the eyelet bushings once a month and/or after every 40 hours of riding, but of course you will do this anyway while you are reinstalling the shock after doing the air-sleeve service following every 40 hours on the trail. If you don't do the air-sleeve service yourself every 40 hours, have a qualified mechanic do it for you.

Air-sleeve overhaul

Because the air sleeve should be overhauled frequently, I've changed the instructions so that you can do an overhaul in a hotel room or parking lot, without a vise. And even if you do have a vise, you may not be able to push the can on far enough to screw it back on anyway, so reassembling the air sleeve this way, on the bike, may be a must in any case.

1. **Deflate the shock.** Sit on the bike while depressing the Schrader valve pin to release as much air as possible. Removing the valve core with a Schrader valve-core tool (Fig. 1.3) will ensure that all of the air is released, especially if the shock has a second positive air chamber.

2. **While sitting on the bike, grasp the air sleeve with your hands and unscrew it.** Turn it counterclockwise, as if it were a lid on a jar. If you cannot get enough of a grip to twist the air sleeve, wrap an inner tube around it first.

NOTE: *Alternatively, after removing the shock as in step 3, you can clamp the faces of the "shaft eyelet" (the eyelet at the big end of the shock—see Fig. 14.7) between the soft jaws of a vise (Fig 14.8). In the absence of soft jaws, use pieces of wood or aluminum against the jaw faces. If you see that the bushings will be damaged by the vise (or if you're going on to do the damper service in section c, you'll want to remove them first—see step 4, except in this case for the shaft eyelet.*

3. **Remove the shock from the bike.** This can be as simple as removing the two mounting bolts and pulling the shock off. But if the shock doesn't pull out of its mounting tabs when you remove the bolts, there may be a hollow, threaded shaft through the eyelet that overlaps into the holes in the frame tabs. In this case, install one bolt a few threads and tap it inward with a hammer to knock the sleeve out of the near tab. Remove the bolt, and tap the sleeve the rest of the way out with a hex key or the like.

4. **Slide the can (air sleeve) off** (Fig. 14.8). If the shock bushings on the body eyelet are too wide to allow the can to slide off, you'll need to

14.8 DT air shock disassembled in vise for air-sleeve service

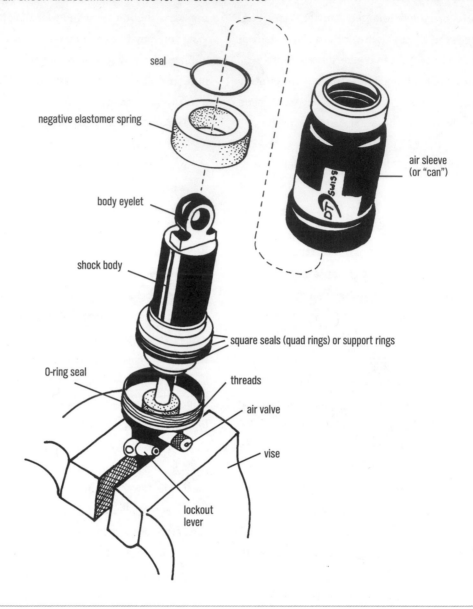

seal

negative elastomer spring

air sleeve (or "can")

body eyelet

shock body

square seals (quad rings) or support rings

O-ring seal

threads

air valve

vise

lockout lever

remove them. This can sometimes be harder than it looks; if the bushings are pressed in too hard, you may not be able to pull them out with your fingers alone, which is the ideal situation to prevent damaging them. There is a special puller tool for removing eyelet bushings, and if you have one, great. Otherwise, if you're careful, you can pull them out with pliers or a vise, or you can use an "easy-out" (a cone-shaped reverse-threaded tool to remove broken bolts) to twist the bushing out.

5. **Clean all seals and contact areas.** With a clean, lint-free rag and perhaps some isopropyl alcohol, thoroughly clean the seals at the narrow end of the can, the seals around the piston, the inside of the can, the threads, and the O-ring atop them (which the can screws up against; visible in Fig. 14.8). Wipe down the piston shaft and the shock body as well.

6. **Inspect the seals and replace if needed.** If any are damaged, or if you have had significant air

or oil leakage, buy a seal kit for the shock, and install those seals. Remove O-rings and rubber square-cross-section seals ("square seals" or "quad seals") from the shock body (piston) by squeezing and pushing them with your thumbs until a loop pops up that you can grab. The glide rings, seal-backing rings, and so on will then pop up and off easily in the same way. Dig the seals out of their grooves in the narrow end of the can with a sharpened pick of some sort. A couple of long nails you sharpened by spinning them in a drill against a belt sander will do fine. Leave one straight, and bend the other one near the tip so that you have some options for digging the seals out of their grooves. Rather than going in under the edge of each seal with your tool, which could scratch the shock's anodized coating and create an air leak, stab each rubber seal and Teflon backing ring with your sharp pick, and stretch the seal up over the lip of its groove and pull it out. Press the new O-rings, rubber square seals, glide rings, seal-backing rings, and so on back in place where the old ones were.

7. **Wipe some Slick Honey grease on all the seals.**

8. **Slip the air sleeve back onto the shock body and, if you can, up against the threads.** If you have the shock in a vise or can do so in your hands, screw it on (clockwise) hand tight, and then you're done. If you can't get the air sleeve screwed on, go to step 9. Not being able to press the sleeve far enough to engage the threads is actually a good sign, indicating the seals are effective at preventing air from getting past them.

9. **Install the shock in the bike.** First grease the eyelets and reinstall the aluminum bushings if you removed them (press them in with a vise if they won't go in by hand alone). Replace any bolts, washers, and hollow threaded through-sleeves you removed.

10. **Sit on the saddle to compress the shock and screw the air sleeve back on.** You build negative-spring pressure behind the piston as soon as the seals engage on the shock body, and using the leverage of the bike to push it together is the most effective way to get the threads on the can and shock body to meet up. While sitting on the saddle, grab the air can and screw it on clockwise, as if it were a lid on a jar. Turn the air can by hand only. There will generally be a seam in the wraparound label on the shock, and that will usually line up behind the shock, adjacent to the frame tube; that's one way to know you have it screwed on all the way.

You're ready to ride another 40 hours!

c. Annual maintenance: Damper oil change

Change the shock oil once a year or so.

Just as in a high-quality suspension fork, a rear shock has a spring to compress and rebound over bumps, and it has a damper to slow the movement of the spring both when it compresses and when it rebounds. Most current forks have the spring in one leg and the damper in the other leg, but because a rear shock has only one leg, both the damper and the spring are in it. You've seen in section b how to take the air can (the spring) off an air shock; the damper is inside the shock body (Fig. 14.8).

The oil inside the shock body degrades over time, reducing damping. If you notice a damping loss, you need an oil change. This is generally a factory operation; send it in during the winter when you're not riding, unless you have a spare shock to substitute. Because special tools are recommended for many shock services, such as replacing air valves, glide rings, shaft bushings, shaft seals, and eyelet bushings, it may not make sense for you to own these tools, in which case a good relationship with a shock-literate shop is in order.

That said, some shocks are friendlier to home mechanic service than others. Following is an example for illustration purposes of a simple-to-service rear shock damper. Unless you have this particular shock, you'll need to download the technical manual from your shock manufacturer's website. This probably won't be in the owners' manual; you will be looking for a "technical manual" or "service guide." You may need to search in the dealer section of the site to find it.

To alter damping, shim stacks (on shock pistons) and oil weight can be changed. Shock shims are thin discs with springs behind them that cover the holes through the damper piston that allow oil to pass. The smaller the piston orifice, the slower the shock movement; thus, if a shim keeps a hole closed longer, damping is higher. Shims vary in flexibility and diameter; oil can force its way past a smaller or more flexible shim much more easily.

Tune kits containing shims, seals, glide rings, springs, valve cores, a piston, and so on, as well as the shock oil you need, can be obtained online and at some bike shops. The specific shim stack and oil weight in the shock will have been selected by the shock manufacturer to meet the requirements of your specific bike frame. In other words, all shocks of a certain length of a given model are not the same; the damper will have been designed to match the leverage ratio of the bike for which it's intended. So unless you really know what you're doing, don't interchange parts inside your shock's damper. Yes, high-end tuning shops can get more performance out of a shock for your specific application by changing the shim stack, but don't try it without expert advice.

Damper service on a RockShox Monarch rear shock

⚙ ⚙ ⚙ LEVEL 3

Since 2010, both the RockShox Monarch and Ario shock dampers have been specifically designed for service by a shop mechanic or a motivated home mechanic. Have your parts kit in hand with replacement seals and valve core before you start.

1. **Open the rebound and the "Gate."** Turn the red rebound adjuster knob all the way counterclockwise (toward the rabbit). Flip open the Gate lever (akin to a lockout lever) if one is present.

2. **Remove the air can.** Follow the instructions in section b through step 4.

3. **Release the air from the damper.** With a standard Schrader valve-core remover (Fig. 1.3), unscrew the little plastic air cap covering the damper air-fill port on the side of the body eyelet. Depress the valve with a pick; wear safety glasses because it is at 250 psi. Remove the valve core with the valve-core remover.

4. **Unscrew the air piston and pour out the oil.** Use a pair of adjustable wrenches, one on the 17mm flats atop the air piston (aka "seal head") and one on the body eyelet (Fig. 14.9). Alternatively, you can clamp the body eyelet in a vise between aluminum or wood soft

14.9 Unscrew seal head from shock body

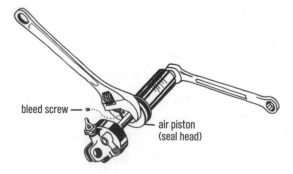

bleed screw —

air piston (seal head)

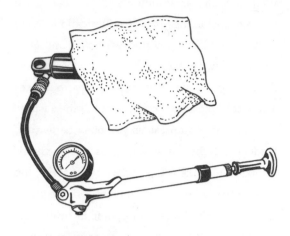

jaws. Break the seal head free from the top of the shock body, unscrew it completely over a bucket or pan, and dump out the oil.

5. **Pump out the internal floating piston (IFP).** Put a Monarch air-fill adapter into a shock pump (Fig. 1.3); the adapter that was required to pump up older Marzocchi Bomber and RockShox SID air forks looks similar but is actually slightly different. Screw the adapter into the air-fill port (where the valve core was in the side of the body eyelet). Drape a rag over the top of the shock body, and pump the IFP (a brass piston) out into the rag (Fig. 14.10).

6. **Remove the plastic compression ball from the seal-head bleed hole.** With a 2.5mm hex key, unscrew the setscrew from the bleed hole atop the air piston (Fig. 14.9), and with a 1.5mm hex key, push the small plastic ball out of the hole from the bottom.

7. **Remove the seals.** To avoid scratching the parts, remove the rubber O-rings, square seals and Teflon glide rings from around the air piston, the "fixed" oil piston at the end of the shaft, and the IFP by squeezing and pushing them with your thumbs until a loop pops up that you can grab. As described in section b, step 6, and without scratching the metal, stab

and remove the air piston's inner seal that seals the top of the body.

8. **Clean the parts.** Use isopropyl alcohol and a clean rag.

9. **Install new seals and glide rings.** Grease them lightly with Slick Honey first.

10. **Install the IFP to the proper depth inside the shock body.** Orient the IFP so that its recessed side is facing you. Measure the outside diameter of the body. Then, using the depth gauge of a digital or dial caliper (Fig. 1.4) in the bottom of the piston's recess, measure to the top of the shock body. If the outside diameter of the body measures 31mm, the IFP should be inserted to a depth of 48mm. Similarly, for progressively larger and longer shocks, the depth for a given body diameter will be 54mm for 38mm OD, 59mm for 44mm OD, 65mm for 51mm OD, 70mm for 57mm OD, 76mm for 63mm OD, and 78mm for 66mm OD.

11. **Install a new Schrader valve core into the damper air-fill port.** Use the Schrader valve-core remover to do so.

12. **Fill the damper with oil.** Clamp the body eyelet in a vise, and stand the shock body vertically. Fill it to the brim with 7-weight suspension oil. Scrape air bubbles off the oil surface.

13. **Install the shaft.** Push the damper piston (at the end of the shaft) down into the shock body slowly until oil comes out of the hole in the shaft above the piston, and then pull the piston back out, keeping it vertical. Again, the rebound and Gate adjusters must be fully open. Refill the body to the brim with oil, and scrape off the air bubbles. Slide the seal head (air piston) down to the bottom of the shaft against the fixed damper piston. Screw the seal head into the shock body, and tighten it with a 17mm or adjustable wrench; oil will come out of the bleed hole atop the seal head. Make sure that the shaft does not

slide down, because if the fixed damper piston moves away from the seal head now or at any point during the rest of the assembly process, it will displace oil from the shock body. If you have a torque wrench and a 17mm crowfoot socket (Fig. 1.4), with the crowfoot turned at 90 degrees from the torque wrench handle in order not to multiply the torque, tighten the seal head to 250 in-lbs.

14. **Install a new compression ball.** Insert the new ball into the bleed hole atop the seal head. Follow it with the setscrew, and tighten with a 2.5mm hex key until you feel the setscrew just touch the ball. Tighten the setscrew an additional one-half turn.

15. **Pressurize the damper.** Using the shock pump with the Monarch air-fill adapter on it, pump air into the damper air-fill valve (Fig. 14.10). The pressure will be 250 psi for all Monarch and Ario shocks except the Ario 3.2, the pressure for which will be 500 psi. Ideally, you'd fill the damper with pure nitrogen (air is 78 percent nitrogen), but you'd need specialty shock fill equipment for that.

16. **Replace the air-fill port cap.** Use the Schrader valve-core remover to do so.

17. **Complete the air-sleeve (can) service.** Return to section b, step 5.

xiv-9
MAINTAINING THE SUSPENSION FRAME

⚙️ ⚙️ LEVEL 2

⚙️ ⚙️ ⚙️ LEVEL 3

Because suspension frames vary in complexity, so does the level of necessary maintenance. In addition to the regular inspections described early in this chapter, maintenance is needed on the shock and the pivots.

a. Evaluation of the condition of the suspension

While the bike is standing still, you can tell if the suspension needs some lubrication. Stand next to the bike, apply the rear brake, and push down lightly on the saddle. Gradually increase the pressure. Notice how much pressure it takes before the bike finally compresses. If the suspension does not compress as you push harder and harder, and then it finally goes down, chunk, chunk, chunk, like going down a set of stairs, you have a dry system. Clean and lubricate the pivots and the shock. There is no point in tuning the suspension until you have it moving smoothly.

If the swingarm begins compressing smoothly under a relatively gentle push, then you have a pretty clean, well-lubricated system.

Also remove the rear wheel and the shock, and lift the swingarm and let it drop. If the swingarm falls under its own weight, the pivots are not sticky. If you must forcefully move the swingarm through its travel, you had better get to work on those pivots. New frames usually take a little force to move until the pivot bushings and bearings work in; if your frame is like this and there is no noticeable lateral wiggle to the swingarm, the pivots are in decent shape.

b. Pivot maintenance

The pivots on any suspension frame require periodic attention. Pivots usually rely on cartridge bearings or bushings (usually steel or brass, but some are made of ceramic or plastic). They are held together by through-bolts, by clamps with pinch bolts surrounding the pivot shaft, or by pins secured with cotters or snaprings. High-quality bushings often let you know they are wearing by getting sticky before they get loose. Crummy bushing material just wears thinner and gets loose. Bearings fail if the seal fails, allowing the bearings to get dirty or lose their lubricant, or they get overloaded. Side loads, in particular on a

bearing not designed to take forces from the side (as opposed to radial), can wreck a bearing. This is more likely to happen on installation or removal than on usage on the bike, however, unless some suspension members are way out of alignment.

The shock also pivots at its "eyelets" at either end (Fig. 14.7) on brass bushings or on bearings.

Plan on cleaning and greasing pivot bushings on the order of every 40 hours of riding. Inspect them for wear frequently. Check for wear by feeling for lateral play and binding with the shock deflated or disconnected. If the rear end is loose from side to side, or if it is so sticky that you can hardly move it, go through the system by taking the linkage apart one piece at a time (this usually just requires removing screws and bolts). Test each joint for wiggle and bind once you have isolated it from the other joints. Check the bushings for scoring and deformation into an oval shape, and lubricate any squeaky ones. Be careful about using solvents on plastic bushings, as some materials can swell. Bearings usually wear longer than bushings, as long as they are kept greased. If not yet ruined, they can be opened and repacked with grease as is done for other cartridge bearings (Fig. 14.11). When they are worn-out, they can be replaced, and unlike most bushings found in bike frames, pivot bearings are often of stock sizes that you can find at an automotive bearing store.

If there are grease fittings on any of the pivots, by all means put a grease gun on them fre-

quently and pump some grease in (you can spoon bicycle suspension grease into the grease gun). For suspension grease, Buzzy's Slick Honey is one that seems to work well.

To replace worn bushings and bearings, you will need to push them out of the holes in the ends of the linkage arms in which they are seated. This requires some socket wrenches and perhaps box-end wrenches and even a hammer and a punch.

1. **Push the old bushing or bearing out.**

   (a) If the linkage member has a through-hole of the same size on both sides (i.e., the bushing or bearing can go in from either side), then you can push out the bearing or bushing with a vise and a socket. Select a socket just slightly smaller than the outer diameter of the bushing or bearing, and set it against the bushing or bearing between the jaws of a vise (Fig. 14.12). Never apply

14.12 Pushing out a swingarm bearing or bushing with a vise, using a socket as a drift and a box wrench for clearance

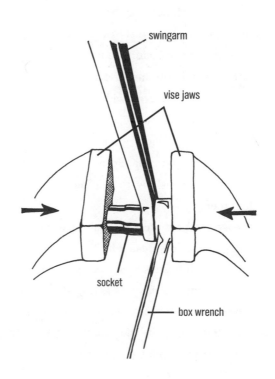

swingarm

vise jaws

socket

box wrench

pressure to the inner bore or against the seals of a cartridge bearing (at least one you want to keep—the old trashed one you may treat as you like); the socket should be against the outer ring of the bearing. Against the opposite jaw of the vise, place the box end of a wrench just bigger than the bushing or bearing so that it surrounds the bushing or bearing up against the face of the linkage member (Fig. 14.12). Alternatively, you can employ a second socket, open end toward the bushing or bearing, whose inner diameter is just larger than the bushing or bearing. Tighten the vise until it pushes the bushing or bearing out (into the box wrench or larger socket).

(b) If the bushing or bearing is up against a seat in the linkage arm—in other words, the hole is not the same diameter on both sides as the bushing or bearing but instead is bored in from one side such that the bushing or bearing has a pocket (it seats against the flat bottom of the hole)—you must employ a different technique. On the other side there is only a small hole for the pivot bolt to pass through. In this case, get the bushing or bearing out by placing a punch, screwdriver, or bolt against its inside diameter from the side of the link arm with the small hole. Support the link arm adjacent to the bushing or bearing somehow (perhaps on a socket just bigger than the bushing or bearing), and tap the bushing or bearing out with a hammer.

2. **Grease the hole the new bushing or bearing will go into, and press it in.**

(a) On link arms that have parallel faces at the bushing or bearing hole, just place the bushing or bearing against the hole in the link arm, and press it in with the flat jaws of the vise; put aluminum plates against the vise

14.13 Pushing a cartridge bearing into a swingarm eyelet with a vise, using a socket as a drift

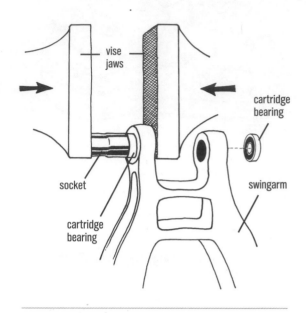

jaws if they do not have smooth faces. Place the old bushing or bearing (or a socket just smaller than its OD—Fig. 14.13) against the new one if it needs to be pressed in farther than flush with the link in the arm's face.

(b) You must press in the bushing or bearing with an appropriately sized socket on link arms that have deep bearing pockets or that do not have parallel faces at the bushing or bearing hole. Obviously, a flat vise cannot push a bearing into a configuration like this; you need to place something behind the bearing, such as a socket, that can enter the pocket and still be pulled back out. (You could perhaps use the old bearing to push the new one in, but then you might have a problem getting the old bearing out of the pocket.) Select a socket the size of or slightly less than the outer diameter of the bearing. Squeeze the bushing or bearing with one (smooth) jaw of the vise against the back of the link-arm eyelet pocket and the other jaw against the socket (Fig. 14.13).

xiv-10
MAINTAINING A PIVOTLESS SUSPENSION FRAME

⚙ LEVEL 1

Suspension frames without moving pivots fall into two categories: beam bikes, and bikes with a shock that depends on the flex of the chainstay rather than on pivots.

The principal beam suspension used on mountain bikes is the Softride beam, and Softride, Breeze, Otis Guy, and Ritchey are some of the frame brands that have used it. Inspect the beam-mounting points on the frame periodically for indications of fatigue (stretched, bulged, or cracking metal or paint). Note that Softride beams are fairly maintenance-free.

One of the simplest and lightest rear-suspension designs relies on a small shock behind the seat tube and flexing chainstays. Beyond checking the chainstays for indications of fatigue (stretched, bulged, or cracking metal or paint), you really need only to keep the shock serviced as described previously and tuned to your weight and riding style as described next.

xiv-11
TUNING THE REAR SUSPENSION

⚙ ⚙ LEVEL 2

There are three main variables in the setup of the rear-suspension system: sag, compression damping, and rebound damping.

The four main types of shocks are air-oil (Figs. 14.7 and 14.14), air-air, coil spring (or "coil over"), and elastomer (or "elastomer over"). In both air-oil and air-air shocks, compressed air acts as the spring. Coil-over and elastomer-over shocks use either a coil spring or an elastomer spring surrounding a damper cylinder (the coil or elastomer fits "over" the damper—thus the name).

Most shocks rely on the flow of oil through a small opening separating two chambers to slow the suspension movement. The oil provides the damping, and there is often pressurized gas behind an additional, movable piston pushing against the oil chamber. Nitrogen is commonly used as the gas in shock dampers, as it is less likely to emulsify if it mixes with the oil. Air-air shocks, however, operate on the same basic principle as a hydraulic damper but damp the suspension through the movement of compressed air, rather than oil, through metering holes in a piston.

Air-oil and air-air shocks are tuned for the spring rate by varying the air pressure. You must have a shock pump with a no-leak head (Fig. 14.14). When a pump that has a no-leak head is removed, the head backs out far enough to release the valve pin so that the valve can seal before the head allows any air to escape. A pump like this is a must for pumping air into these or even for checking the air pressure, because the air volume is so small and the air pressure is so high that the slightest leakage dramatically reduces internal air pressure.

14.14 Shock adjustments on Fox RP23

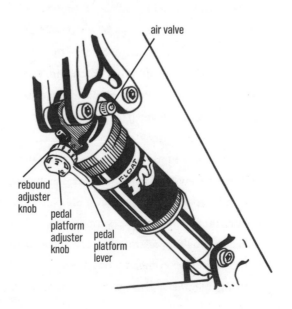

air valve

rebound adjuster knob

pedal platform adjuster knob

pedal platform lever

You can change the spring rate of most coil-over and elastomer-over shocks by turning a threaded preload collar around the shock body or by replacing the spring.

Start with the air pressure, coil, or elastomer (or spring preload) recommended by the bike manufacturer for your weight, and experiment from there. Because the shock location, leverage ratio, and pressure requirements vary from bike to bike, the recommendations will come from the bike manufacturer and not from the shock manufacturer. The leverage ratio is the amount the rear axle moves vertically with a given amount of shock movement. For instance, a 2:1 leverage ratio indicates that the rear wheel will move up 2 inches if the shock compresses 1 inch (or 6 inches of rear-wheel travel with 2 inches of shock compression). Obviously, the lower the leverage ratio, the lower the spring rate you can use and get similar performance.

On rear shocks with hydraulic (or compressed-air) damping systems, damping is adjusted by varying the size of the orifices through which the oil (or compressed air) flows; this is accomplished by changing the shims (thin steel discs of varying diameter and flexibility) that cover the holes in the piston and are held in place by a spring or by changing the viscosity of the oil (or the air pressure in the damper). On many models, the damping orifices are adjusted with knobs (Fig. 14.14). Many shocks have a "pedal-platform" lever (Fig. 14.14) or a lockout lever (Fig. 14.8). Tuning techniques vary from shock to shock, so be sure to read the owners' manual that came with yours.

Please review §xiii-8 and §xiii-9 for an explanation of suspension spring rates, preload, compression damping, rebound damping, and other considerations—they are the same for rear suspension. The same recommendations found in §xiii-7 for setting up forks apply to rear suspension too.

The recommendations that follow apply to cross-country, full-suspension bikes as well as to downhill versions, although more specific downhill considerations are found in §xiv-12.

a. Setting sag

"Sag," or "ride height," is the amount the bike compresses when you just sit on it. You want the bike to sag so that the shock is preloaded and forces the rear wheel into the ground when the bike is unweighted over bumps, thus increasing tire contact and traction in rough terrain. Ride height is not dependent on damping because there is no movement involved; it is dependent only on the spring rate and preload.

Sag is affected by changes to the spring and/or spring preload adjustment. A good rule of thumb is to set the spring so that sag uses up one-quarter of the bike's travel, but consult §xiii-8 and §xiii-9 for more specific recommendations based on your riding style.

Measure the shock shaft length or the eye-to-eye length of the entire shock when you are off the bike. Have someone else measure it again when you are sitting on the bike. The difference between the measurements is the sag.

For an air shock, measure the travel and sag with an O-ring or zip-tie wrapped around the shock body (Fig. 14.7). Find the shock's full travel length by deflating the shock and sitting on the saddle (and deflating it more while sitting on it). Set the O-ring position against the end of the air sleeve, and then inflate the shock and measure from the O-ring to the end of the air-can seal. To find the sag, sit on the bike, push the O-ring against the air can, and then carefully get off. Measure from the O-ring to the end of the air-can seal, and divide by the full travel length to get the percentage of sag. Some rear shocks have sag values inscribed on the shock body.

Adjust the sag in an air shock by adjusting the air pressure with a pump with a no-leak head (Fig. 14.14). If you have a negative air spring (Fig. 14.7), make sure you pump the positive spring first (see §xiii-9).

If, say, you're going for a sag that is 25 percent of travel on a coil or elastomer shock, if less than 75 percent of the shaft length is still showing, increase the preload or the spring rate. (You can do this by changing the spring.) If more than 75 percent of the shaft length is showing, decrease the preload or spring rate. In both of these systems, the preload is usually set by turning a threaded collar surrounding the shock body that compresses the coil spring or the elastomers. Depending on the shock and the spring used, if you have used more than two to six preload turns of the spring collar to reach 25 percent travel usage in ride height, you need a stiffer spring.

IMPORTANT: *Excessive preload on a soft shock can cause the shock to fail. "Coil bind" ruins coil-over shocks; if you must preload the shock more than two full turns to set the sag, you are in danger of coil bind and need a stiffer spring. Coil bind means that there is no space between coils—each loop of the coil is stacked up against the next one. Consider, for instance, if the bottom-out of the rear suspension occurs at 2 inches of shock travel and the shock has 2⅜ (2.375) inches of total travel. If you tighten the preload collar down more than 0.375 inch, the coil will bind and stop the shock before the swingarm bottoms out. Coil bind puts tremendous stress on the shock and breaks important parts that you would like to keep. It is more of an issue with stiffer springs and occurs at fewer preload-collar turns, because the thicker wire of the spring leaves less space between coils.*

On steep downhill courses, more of your weight will be shifted to the front of the bike, so more sag in the rear is a good idea.

b. Checking the front-rear balance

You want to have the front and rear suspension balanced so that everything works together like a beautiful symphony in motion. Check the front-rear balance by standing next to the bike on level ground, lightly applying the front brake, and stepping straight down on the pedal closest to you while the crankarm is at bottom dead center. If the top tube doesn't tip forward or backward as the suspension is compressed, the spring rates are well balanced. Next, sit on the bike in riding position. If one end drops noticeably more than the other, you need to increase the spring preload and/or the spring rate on the end that dropped farther (or soften the spring on the end that dropped less).

c. Adjusting rebound damping

If adjustable, set the rebound damping as low as you can without causing the bike to "pogo" (bouncing repeatedly after a bump). Do the "curb test," starting with the rebound fully open (the rebound knob turned counterclockwise until it stops). Ride off the curb, and note how many times the shock bounces. You want only one bounce. Turn the rebound knob (Fig. 14.14; rebound knobs are usually red) clockwise one-quarter turn, and ride off the curb again, repeating until you get only one bounce. Record the number of turns (i.e., clockwise) of the knob it took.

If you can adjust rebound on the fly and have no lockout lever, turn the rebound damping up when you climb. It does not need to throw you up as much when you hit things, as you are going much slower anyway. You will climb faster this way. Of course, if there is a lockout lever, use it on smooth climbs. Remember to reduce the rebound damping or open the lockout when you head back down.

d. Adjusting compression damping

If the shock has a compression-damping adjustment, set it as light as possible without bottoming out the shock more than once or twice on the course. You want to absorb the bumps with the springs as much as you can.

e. Setting the inertial valve

Some modern shocks have an "inertial valve" on the compression-damping system designed to distinguish between bump forces and pedaling forces (Fig. 14.14; compression adjusters are usually blue). Such a system is often said to provide a pedal platform for the rider to push against while pedaling without bobbing up and down. Depending on manufacturer, acronyms for these pedal platform systems include ProPedal (Fox: Fig. 14.14), SPV (Manitou), Brain (Specialized), Motion Control (RockShox), HVR (DT Swiss), TST (Marzocchi), and CV/t (5th Element).

The threshold bump force magnitude required to open the inertial valve and make the shock fully active is adjustable on some shocks, either with a lever that you can flip on the fly like a lockout lever (Fig. 14.14), with a knob, or with a change in the air pressure in an air chamber behind the valve. If adjustable, set the threshold as low as you can (so it blows open most easily when hitting a bump), yet high enough that when you pedal aggressively on a smooth surface the rear suspension does not bob up and down.

To adjust the Fox ProPedal knob shown in Figure 14.14, do the following:

1. **Turn the ProPedal lever to the PROPEDAL position.** If you are looking at the lever from the front, turn it clockwise, the same as you would any lockout lever.
2. **Pull the ProPedal knob out toward you.**
3. **Turn the ProPedal knob to the setting you want.** There are three numbers on the knob: 1 = light (lower bump threshold to make the shock compress), 2 = medium, and 3 = firm. Turn the knob clockwise until the number you want lines up with the ProPedal lever. As the ProPedal knob turns, it clicks twice per setting: It clicks as you leave the current setting, and it clicks into the new setting.
4. **Push the ProPedal knob in.** This locks in the setting.

f. Adjusting shock mounts

Some shocks have adjustable attachment positions. Usually, these have a number of different mounting holes for one eye of the shock, but some frames mount the body end of the shock via a threaded collar that can be turned to vary the position of the shock. Varying the shock position varies the head angle, bottom-bracket height, and ride height of the bike, and it may change the rear travel length as well.

Some frames also have adjustable head angles to accomplish similar things. A shallower head angle makes the bike more stable at high speed and gets the front wheel farther out ahead for steep drops.

g. Riding and tweaking

Again, see §xiii-8 and §xiii-9, and follow the guidelines about picking a test course and taking notes. You want to bottom out a couple of times on the front and rear on a course. If the suspension is never bottoming out, the spring is too stiff or the compression damping is too high.

Change settings in small increments. It is easy to overadjust. Make only one adjustment at a time. Also, once you have balanced the front and rear ends, any adjustment you make to the front you should also make to the rear, and vice versa. Read the bike manual as well as the shock manual for adjustment methods and recommendations.

Suspension tuning is affected by (1) rider weight, (2) rider ability, (3) riding speeds, (4) course conditions, (5) rider style, (6) rider position on the bike, and (7) temperature. If any of these things change, so should the tuning.

Use the softest springs you can with little preload; you want to bottom out occasionally, but not frequently. If you are bottoming out too much, you need to change the compression damping or the spring rate. If the compression is slow, yet you are still bottoming out, the spring is too soft. You will feel beaten up on the intermediate hits, or when you are bottoming out on a big hit it will be harsh through the entire stroke. Stiffen the spring rate, and lighten the compression damping. The ride height (sag) you've chosen dictates some of the spring rate.

Preload makes the spring rate ramp up faster. If you can use a stiffer spring and back off on preload, you will be a lot happier.

Set the compression damping to blow off quickly; your plush spring won't bottom out harshly anyway! The compression damping should be set high enough that on big hits you use up all the travel, but the saddle shouldn't smack you in the butt when you hit bottom. Tighten up compression damping if you blow through the stroke and get bounced too hard.

Decrease the rebound damping to return quickly without the pogo effect. You want a lively rebound, because a sluggish return will allow the suspension to pack up (as you go over stutter bumps, water bars, or closely spaced rocks, the bike will ride lower and lower).

Again, if you have no damping adjuster, change the oil viscosity (§xiv-8c).

Tighten up the rebound damping if the bike springs back too fast. The rebound should not be so quick that you are getting bounced (remember the curb test—§xiv-11c). Tighten the rebound up for climbs if you have a quick adjuster or lockout lever.

Damping is speed sensitive. Don't worry about settings that feel good at low speeds being too light for high speeds; the shock will get stiffer as you hit things faster. At all speeds, you want the shock to pop back as quickly as possible without kicking back.

If you have an adjustable pedal platform (i.e., inertial valve), set it as low as possible to get the amount of firmness you want when pedaling aggressively on smooth surfaces (a high setting gives the firmest, locked-out feel). The low threshold setting will allow the shock's compression-damping system to open up and move freely on smaller bumps.

Damping is also temperature sensitive. Oil is thick and sluggish when cold, but when it gets hot, the shock gets really lively. You will need to adjust accordingly in summer, with a stiffer spring and firmer damping adjustments. And in the cold of winter, when overall speeds are slower, the grease and oil in the shock are thicker, and coil and elastomer springs are stiffer, you can lighten up the spring and damping adjustments.

If there is no damping adjuster, you can vary the oil viscosity. Look up the stock oil weight in the shock tech manual. Heavier oil slows the shock; lighter oil speeds it up. And replacing the oil in the shock periodically is a good idea, even if you like its performance, because oil breaks down with use and has little worn bits of the shock floating in it. For most people, this is a shop service; see §xiv-8c.

xiv-12
ADJUSTING WHEN RIDING DOWNHILL COURSES

Everything in §xiv-11 applies, with a few additions here. Again, you are looking for a setup in which the front and rear shocks bottom out on the biggest bump on the course, but make sure you are riding at race speed before making adjustments.

On rougher courses, increasing the spring rate (or preload) will keep you from bottoming out so much. Compensate for small bumps by reducing rebound damping to keep the shock from packing in on successive hits. If the bike is bucking, increase damping a bit.

NOTE: *Too much damping, not just too little, will sometimes cause bucking. Heavily damped shocks will respond so slowly that they will pack in over repeated bumps, giving you a rigid bike and low ride height (i.e., the suspension will be fully compressed and won't return).*

On smooth courses, try decreasing the spring rate (or preload) and increasing damping. Negotiating turns will usually be the major challenge, and the lower ride height (sag) provided by the softer spring will keep you closer to the ground. The greater sag will also increase the available amount of negative fork travel (the amount the wheel can go down), which will help maintain tire traction when the bike is turning and when it is braking. Higher compression damping, although making the shock absorption slower, will still be fast enough to deal with isolated bumps and will eliminate the harshest bottoming-out. Higher rebound damping will reduce the bouncing of the bike after the isolated bumps.

Where there is no general rough or smooth characterization of the course, set up the suspension to perform best on the sections in which you have the most trouble for the most elapsed time. In other words, don't set the suspension for a tricky section you get through in a couple of seconds; set it up for a challenging section on which you will spend half a minute.

xiv-13
CHECKING FRAME ALIGNMENT AND ADJUSTING DROPOUT ALIGNMENT

⚙️ ⚙️ ⚙️ LEVEL 3

These are inexact methods for determining frame alignment. If the alignment is way off, these methods will tell you. If you find alignment problems, other than perhaps moderately bent derailleur hangers (§xiv-5) or dropouts, do not attempt to correct them. Adjusting frame alignment is a difficult and delicate task; if it can be done at all, only someone who is practiced at aligning frames should perform this task with an accurate frame-alignment fixture.

1. **Stretch a string from dropout to dropout around the head-tube.** With the frame clamped in a bike stand, tie the end of a string to one rear dropout. Stretch it tightly around the head-tube, and tie it symmetrically to the other dropout (Fig. 14.15).

2. **Measure from the string to the seat tube on either side** (Fig. 14.15). The measurement should be at least within 1mm of being the same on both sides.

14.15 Checking frame alignment with a string

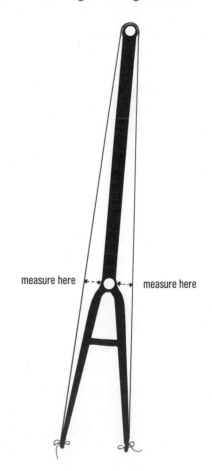

measure here   measure here

14.16 Measuring dropout width (or axle overlock dimension)

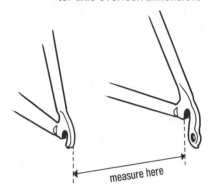

measure here

14.17 Using dropout-alignment tools on rear dropouts

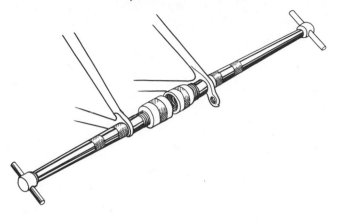

3. **Put a true and properly dished rear wheel in the frame, and check that it lines up in the same plane as the front triangle.** Make certain that the wheel is centered between the seatstays and chainstays (or swingarms). The hub should slide in easily without requiring you to pull outward or push inward on the dropouts. Tightening the hub quick-release should not result in bowing or twisting of frame members.

4. **Remove the wheel, and measure the spacing between the dropouts** (Fig. 14.16). On most mountain bikes made since 1990, this spacing should be 135mm, but wider spacings are common on downhill and freeride bikes. Mountain bikes made between 1984 and 1990 or so should have a rear spacing of 130mm. Mountain bikes made prior to 1984 are likely to have a rear spacing of 125mm. Measure the width of the rear hub with a caliper to see what the rear-end spacing of the frame should be. No matter what the nominal measurement for the frame should be, if it is between 1mm less and 1.5mm more than the nominal, it is acceptable. For instance, for a frame whose rear spacing should be 135mm, acceptable spacing is 134–136.5mm.

5. **If you have dropout-alignment tools, put them in the dropouts so that their shafts are fully seated into them** (Fig. 14.17). Arrange the tool spacers (and the cups if they are adjustable) so that the faces of the cups are within 1mm of each other. Tighten the handles on the tools. The tool cups should line up straight across from each other, with their faces parallel. If the tools do not line up with each other, one or both dropouts are bent. If the frame has replaceable bolt-on dropouts, go ahead and replace them. If the frame has a composite or bonded rear triangle and the dropouts are off, there is nothing you can do about it if the bike is not equipped with replaceable dropouts. If the frame has a steel rear triangle, you can align the dropouts by bending them carefully with the dropout-alignment tools. Hold the cup of the tool with one hand, and push or pull on the handle with the other. Aluminum or titanium rear dropouts can sometimes be aligned, but it is something you should have a shop do. Titanium is hard to bend because it keeps springing back, and you run a great risk of breaking aluminum by bending it.

6. **On suspension frames, check for smooth swing-arm movement without play.** See §xiv-10.

APPENDIX A
TROUBLESHOOTING INDEX

This index is intended to assist you in finding and fixing problems. If you already know wherein the problem lies, consult the Table of Contents for the chapter covering that part of the bike. If, however, you are not sure which part of the bike is affected, this troubleshooting index can be of assistance. It is organized alphabetically, but because people's descriptions of the same problem vary, you may need to look through the entire list to find your symptom. If more than one symptom applies, you will need to examine all possible causes.

This index can assist you with a diagnosis and can recommend a course of action. Following each recommended action is a list of chapter numbers to which you can refer for the repair procedure to fix the problem.

Table A.1	Troubleshooting Bike Problems		
SYMPTOM	LIKELY CAUSES	ACTION	CHAPTER
bent wheel	misadjusted spokes	true wheel	6
	broken spoke	replace spoke	6
	bent rim	replace rim	12
bike pulls to one side	wheels not true	true wheels	6
	tight headset	adjust headset	11
	pitted headset	replace headset	11
	bent frame	replace or straighten	14
	bent fork	replace or straighten	13
	loose hub bearings	adjust hubs	6
	tire pressure really low	inflate tires	2, 6
bike shimmies at high speed	frame cracked	replace frame	14
	frame bent	replace or straighten	14
	wheels overly flexible	replace wheels or tighten spokes	12
	wheels are out of true or dish	true wheels	6
	loose hub bearings	adjust hubs	6
	headset too loose	tighten headset	11
	flexible frame/heavy rider	replace frame	14
	poor frame design	replace frame	14
bike vibrates when braking	see "chattering and vibration when braking" under "Strange Noises"		
brake doesn't stop bike	misadjusted brake	adjust brake	7
	worn brake pads	replace pads	7
	wet rims	keep braking	7
	greasy rims	clean rims	7

Table A.1	Troubleshooting Bike Problems, continued		
SYMPTOM	LIKELY CAUSES	ACTION	CHAPTER
brake doesn't stop bike (continued)	sticky brake cable	lube or replace cable	7
	steel rims in wet weather	use aluminum rims	12
	brake damaged	replace brake	7
	sticky or bent brake lever	lube or replace lever	7
	air in hydraulic brake	bleed brake	7
	worn disc-brake pads	replace pads	7
	brake pads missing	install pads	7
brake rubs on rim (see also "bent wheel")	brake misaligned	adjust brake	7
chain falls off in front	misadjusted front derailleur	adjust front derailleur	5
	chainline off	adjust chainline	8
	chainring bent or loose	replace or tighten	8
chain jams in front between chainring and chainstay ("chain suck")	dirty chain	clean chain	4
	bent chainring teeth	replace chainring	8
	chain too narrow	replace chain	4
	chainline off	adjust chainline	8
	stiff links in chain	free links, lube chain	4
	thick inner chainring teeth	use thinner chainring	8
chain jams in rear	misadjusted rear derailleur	adjust derailleur	5
	chain too wide	replace chain	4
	small cog not on spline	reseat cogs	6
	poor frame clearance	return to dealer	14
chain skips	tight chain link	loosen tight link	4
	worn-out chain	replace chain	4
	misadjusted derailleur	adjust derailleur	5
	worn rear cogs	replace cogs and chain	6, 4
	dirty or rusted chain	clean or replace chain	4
	bent rear derailleur	replace derailleur	5
	bent derailleur hanger	straighten hanger	14
	loose derailleur jockey wheels	tighten jockey wheels	5
	bent chain link	replace chain	4
	sticky rear shift cable	replace shift cable	5
chain slaps chainstay	chain too long	shorten chain	4
	weak rear derailleur spring	replace spring or derailleur	5
	terrain very bumpy	ignore noise	n/a
derailleur hits spokes	misadjusted rear derailleur	adjust derailleur	5
	broken spoke	replace spoke	6
	bent rear derailleur	replace derailleur	5
	bent derailleur hanger	straighten or replace	14
knee pain	poor shoe-cleat position	reposition cleat	9
	saddle too low or high	adjust saddle	10
	clip-in pedal has no float	get floating pedal	9
	foot rolled in or out	replace shoes or get orthotics	n/a

Table A.1	Troubleshooting Bike Problems, continued		
SYMPTOM	**LIKELY CAUSES**	**ACTION**	**CHAPTER**
pain or fatigue when riding, particularly in the back, neck, and arms	incorrect seat position	adjust seat position	10
	too much riding	build up miles gradually	n/a
	incorrect stem length	replace stem	11
	poor frame fit	replace frame	14
	incorrect handlebar height	adjust stem height or get stem with different angle	11
pedal entry difficult (with clip-in pedals)	mud in cleat or pedal	clean cleat and pedal	9
	spring tension set high	reduce spring tension	9
	shoe sole knobs too tall	trim knobs	9
	loose cleat	tighten cleat	9
	dry cleat and pedal	lubricate cleat and pedal clips	9
	cleat guide loose or gone	tighten or replace	9
pedal moves laterally, clunks, or twists while pedaling	loose crankarm	tighten crank bolt	8
	pedal loose in crankarm	tighten pedal to crank	9
	bent pedal axle	replace pedal or axle	9
	loose bottom bracket	adjust bottom bracket	8
	bent bottom-bracket axle	replace bottom bracket or axle	8
	bent crankarm	replace crankarm	8
	loose pedal bearings	adjust pedal bearings	9
pedal release difficult (with clip-in pedals)	spring tension set high	reduce spring tension	9
	loose cleat on shoe	tighten cleat	9
	dry pedal spring pivots	oil spring pivots	9
	dirty pedals	clean and lube pedals	9
	bent pedal clips	replace pedals or clips	9
	dirty cleats	clean, lube cleats	9
	worn cleat	replace cleat	9
pedal release too easy (with clip-in pedals)	release tension set too low	increase release tension	9
	cleats worn-out	replace cleats	9
rear shifting poor (see also "chain jams in rear" and "chain skips")	misadjusted derailleur	adjust derailleur	5
	sticky or damaged cable	replace cable	5
	loose rear cogs	seat and tighten cogs	6
	worn rear cogs	replace cogs	6
	worn/damaged chain	replace chain	4
resistance while coasting or pedaling	tire rubs frame or fork	adjust axle and/or true wheel	2, 6
	brake drags on rim	adjust brake	7
	tire pressure very low	inflate tire	2, 6
	hub bearings too tight	adjust hubs	6
	hub bearings dirty/worn	overhaul hubs	6
	mud packed around tires	clean bike	2
resistance while pedaling only	bottom bracket too tight	adjust bottom bracket	8
	bottom bracket dirty/worn	overhaul bottom bracket	8
	chain dry/dirty/rusted	clean/lube or replace	4
	pedal bearings too tight	adjust pedal bearings	9
	pedal bearings dirty/worn	overhaul pedals	9
	bent chainring rubs frame	straighten or replace	8
	chainring rubs frame	adjust chainline	8

Table A.1	Troubleshooting Bike Problems, continued		
SYMPTOM	LIKELY CAUSES	ACTION	CHAPTER
stiff steering	tight headset	adjust headset	11
suspension problems, front or rear	fork needs tuning	tune fork	13
	fork needs overhaul	overhaul fork	13
	rear suspension misadjusted	tune rear shock	14
	rear shock dirty	overhaul rear shock	14
	suspension pivots worn/dirty	overhaul pivots	14
tire loses air or is flat	deflated tire	pump tire	6
	hole in tube	patch or replace tube	6
	bad valve	replace tube or valve	6
	hole in tubeless tire	patch or replace tire	6
	leaky seal around tubeless tire	seal, replace, or add sealant	6

STRANGE NOISES: Weird noises can be hard to locate; use this list to assist in locating them.

chattering and vibration when braking	bent or dented rim	replace rim	12
	loose headset	adjust headset	11
	brake pads toed-out	adjust brake pads	7
	brake pads worn-out	replace brake pads	7
	bent or scratched rotor	straighten or replace rotor	7
	loose rotor	tighten rotor mounting bolts	7
	wheel out of round	true wheel	6
	loose wheel spokes	tighten spokes	12
	greasy sections of rim	clean rim	6
	oily disc-brake rotor or pads	clean rotor and pads/replace pads	7
	loose caliper mounting bolts	tighten brake mounting bolts	7
	rim worn-out, ready to collapse	replace rim ASAP!	12
	cracked seatstay	replace frame or seatstay	14
clicking noise	cracked shoe cleats	replace cleats	9
	cracked shoe sole	replace shoes	9
	loose bottom bracket	tighten BB	8
	loose crankarm	tighten crankarm	8
	loose pedal	tighten pedal	9
clunking from fork	headset loose	adjust headset	11
	suspension-fork bushings worn	replace bushings	13
creaking noise (see also "squeaking noise")	dry handlebar/stem joint	grease handlebar and inside stem clamp	11
	hard-anodizing of stem and handlebar	roughen stem clamp interior with sandpaper	11
	dry stem/steering-tube joint	grease steering tube and inside stem clamp	11
	cartridge BB moves inside cup	grease inside cup	8
	loose seatpost	tighten seatpost	10
	loose shoe cleats	tighten cleats	9
	loose crankarm	tighten crankarm bolt	8
	cracked frame	replace frame	14
	dry, rusty seatpost	grease seatpost	10

Table A.1	Troubleshooting Bike Problems, continued		
SYMPTOM	LIKELY CAUSES	ACTION	CHAPTER
rubbing or scraping noise when pedaling	crossed chain	avoid extreme gears	5
	front derailleur rubbing	adjust front derailleur	5
	chainring rubs frame	longer bottom bracket or move bottom bracket over	8
rubbing, squealing, or scraping noise when coasting or pedaling	tire dragging on frame	straighten wheel	2, 6
	tire dragging on fork	straighten wheel	2, 6
	brake dragging on rim	adjust brake	7
	mud packed around tires	clean bike	2
	dry, dirty hub dust seals	clean dust seals	6
squeaking noise	dry hub or BB bearings	overhaul hubs or BB	6, 8
	dry pedal bushings	overhaul pedals	9
	squeaky saddle	grease leather-rail contact and oil rail attachments	10
	dry suspension pivots	overhaul suspension	13, 14
	rusted or dry chain	lube or replace chain	4
	dry suspension fork	overhaul fork	13
	dry suspension seatpost	overhaul seatpost	10
squealing noise when braking	brake pads toed-out	adjust brake pads	7
	greasy rims	clean rims and pads	7
	loose brake arms	tighten brake arms	7
	flexible seatstays	use brake booster plate	7
	oily disc-brake rotor	clean rotor and pads	7

APPENDIX B
GEAR DEVELOPMENT

The gear tables on the following pages are based on 26-inch (66cm) and 29-inch (72cm) tire diameters. Your gear-development numbers may be slightly different if the diameter of your bike's rear tire—at inflation, with your weight on it—is not 26 or 29 inches. However, these numbers will be very close—unless, of course, your bike has 20-inch, 24-inch, or 650B wheels or some other nonstandard size. Gear inches for 650B wheels (27.5-inch, or 69cm tire diameter) will be approximately halfway between the numbers for 26-inch and 29-inch wheels, so you can interpolate between the two charts to get the value for a 650B wheel. For other sizes, use the measurement system detailed on the next page.

If you want to have totally accurate gear-development numbers for the tire on your bike at a specific inflation pressure, you can measure the tire diameter very precisely following the procedure in Figure B.1 and the steps on the next page. You can then create your own gear chart by plugging your tire's diameter into the gear-development formula above the chart on page 379, or by multiplying each number in the first (26-inch) chart by the ratio of your tire's diameter (in inches) divided by 26 inches (the tire diameter we used in the first gear chart).

Here are the steps to measure the diameter of the tire (have someone assist you in making the marks):

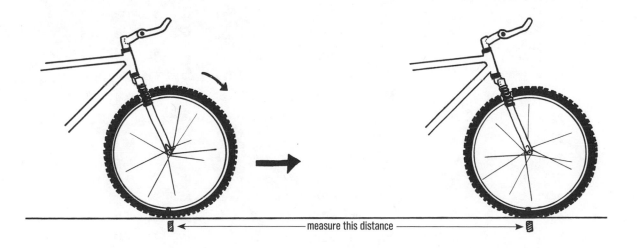

measure this distance

B.1 Rolling out the wheel to measure its circumference. For gear development, measure the rear wheel. For cyclocomputer setup, measure the front wheel.

1. Sit on the bike with the tire pumped to your desired pressure.
2. Mark the spot on the rear rim that is at the bottom, and mark the floor adjacent to that spot.
3. Roll bike forward one wheel revolution, and mark the floor again where the mark on the rim is at the bottom (Fig. B.1).
4. Measure the distance between the marks on the floor; this is the tire circumference at pressure with your weight on it.
5. Divide this number by π (π = 3.14159) to get the diameter.

NOTE: *This roll-out procedure is also the method used to measure the wheel size with which to calibrate your bike's computer, except that most computers use the front wheel for data.*

Table B.1		Gear Development for 26-inch Wheels													
		CHAINRING GEAR TEETH													
		20	21	22	23	24	25	26	27	28	29	30	31	32	33	34
REAR HUB COGS	11	47	50	52	54	57	59	61	64	66	69	71	73	76	78	80
	12	43	45	48	50	52	54	56	58	61	63	65	67	69	71	74
	13	40	42	44	46	48	50	52	54	56	58	60	62	64	66	68
	14	37	39	41	43	45	46	48	50	52	54	56	58	59	61	63
	15	35	36	38	40	42	43	45	47	49	50	52	54	55	57	59
	16	32	34	36	37	39	41	42	19	45	47	49	50	52	54	55
	17	31	32	34	35	37	38	40	41	43	44	46	47	49	50	52
	18	29	30	32	33	35	36	38	39	40	42	43	45	46	48	49
	19	27	29	30	31	33	34	36	37	38	40	41	42	44	45	46
	20	26	27	29	30	31	32	34	35	36	38	39	40	42	43	44
	21	25	26	27	28	30	31	32	33	35	36	37	38	40	41	42
	22	24	25	26	27	28	30	31	32	33	34	35	37	38	39	40
	23	23	24	25	26	27	28	29	31	32	33	34	35	36	37	38
	24	22	23	24	25	26	27	28	29	30	31	32	34	35	36	37
	25	21	22	23	24	25	26	27	28	29	30	31	32	33	34	35
	26	20	21	22	23	24	25	26	27	28	29	30	31	32	33	34
	27	20	20	21	22	23	24	25	26	27	28	29	30	31	32	33
	28	19	19	20	21	22	23	24	25	26	27	28	29	30	31	32
	29	19	19	20	21	22	22	23	24	25	26	27	28	29	30	30
	30	18	18	19	20	21	22	23	23	24	25	26	27	28	29	29
	31	17	18	18	19	20	21	22	23	23	24	25	26	27	28	28
	32	16	17	18	19	19	20	21	22	23	24	24	25	26	27	28
	33	16	17	17	18	19	20	20	21	22	23	24	24	25	26	27
	34	15	16	17	18	18	19	20	21	21	22	23	24	24	25	26
	35	15	16	16	17	18	19	19	20	21	22	22	23	24	24	25
	36	14	15	16	17	17	18	19	19	20	21	22	22	23	24	25
	37	14	15	15	16	17	18	18	19	20	20	21	22	22	23	24
	38	14	14	15	16	16	17	18	18	19	20	21	21	22	23	23

GEAR FORMULA

Gear development = (number of teeth on chainring) × (wheel diameter) ÷ (number of teeth on rear cog). To find out how far you travel with each pedal stroke in a given gear, multiply the gear development by π (3.14159265).

							CHAINRING GEAR TEETH									
35	**36**	**37**	**38**	**39**	**40**	**41**	**42**	**43**	**44**	**45**	**46**	**47**	**48**	**49**	**50**	**51**
83	85	87	90	92	94	97	99	102	104	106	109	111	113	116	118	120
76	78	80	82	84	87	89	91	93	95	97	100	102	104	106	108	110
70	72	74	76	78	80	82	84	86	88	90	92	94	96	98	100	102
65	67	69	71	72	74	76	78	80	82	84	85	87	89	91	93	95
61	62	64	66	68	69	71	73	74	76	78	80	81	83	85	87	88
57	58	60	62	63	65	67	68	70	71	73	75	174	78	80	81	83
53	55	57	58	60	61	63	64	66	67	69	70	72	73	75	76	78
51	52	53	55	56	58	59	61	62	64	65	66	68	69	71	72	74
48	49	51	52	53	55	56	57	59	60	62	63	64	66	67	68	70
45	47	48	49	51	52	53	55	56	57	58	60	61	62	64	65	66
43	45	46	47	48	49	51	52	53	54	56	57	58	59	61	62	63
41	43	44	45	46	47	48	50	51	52	53	54	56	57	58	59	60
40	41	42	43	44	45	46	47	49	50	51	52	53	54	55	56	58
38	39	40	41	42	43	44	45	47	48	49	50	51	52	53	54	55
36	37	38	39	41	42	43	44	45	46	47	48	49	50	51	52	53
35	36	37	38	39	40	41	42	43	44	45	46	47	48	49	50	51
34	35	36	37	38	38	39	40	41	42	43	44	45	46	47	48	49
32	33	34	35	36	37	38	39	40	41	42	43	44	45	45	46	47
31	32	33	34	35	36	37	38	39	39	40	41	42	0	44	45	46
30	31	32	33	34	35	36	36	37	38	39	40	41	42	42	43	44
29	30	31	32	33	34	34	35	36	37	38	39	39	40	41	42	43
28	29	30	31	32	32	33	34	35	36	37	37	38	39	40	41	41
28	28	29	30	31	31	32	33	34	35	35	36	37	38	39	39	40
27	28	28	29	30	31	31	32	33	34	34	35	36	37	37	38	39
26	27	27	28	29	30	30	31	32	33	33	34	35	36	36	37	38
25	26	27	27	28	29	30	30	31	32	32	33	34	35	35	36	37
25	25	26	27	27	28	29	29	30	31	32	32	33	34	34	35	36
24	25	25	26	27	27	28	29	29	30	31	31	32	33	34	34	35

GEAR FORMULA

Gear development = (number of teeth on chainring) × (wheel diameter) ÷ (number of teeth on rear cog). To find out how far you travel with each pedal stroke in a given gear, multiply the gear development by π (3.14159265).

Table B.2	Gear Development for 29-inch Wheels													
	CHAINRING GEAR TEETH													
	20	21	22	23	24	25	26	27	28	29	30	31	32	33	34
11	51	54	56	59	62	64	67	69	72	74	77	79	82	85	87
12	47	49	52	54	56	59	61	63	66	68	70	73	75	78	80
13	43	46	48	50	52	54	56	59	61	63	65	67	69	72	74
14	40	42	44	46	48	50	52	54	56	58	60	62	64	66	68
15	38	39	41	43	45	47	49	51	53	54	56	58	60	62	64
16	35	37	39	41	42	44	46	21	49	51	53	55	56	58	60
17	33	35	36	38	40	41	43	45	46	48	50	51	53	55	56
18	31	33	34	36	38	39	41	42	44	45	47	49	50	52	53
19	30	31	33	34	36	37	39	40	42	43	45	46	47	49	50
20	28	30	31	32	34	35	37	38	39	41	42	44	45	47	48
21	27	28	30	31	32	34	35	36	38	39	40	42	43	44	46
22	26	27	28	29	31	32	33	35	36	37	38	40	41	42	44
23	25	26	27	28	29	31	32	33	34	36	37	38	39	40	42
24	23	25	26	27	28	29	31	32	33	34	35	36	38	39	40
25	23	24	25	26	27	28	29	30	32	33	34	35	36	37	38
26	22	23	24	25	26	27	28	29	30	31	33	34	35	36	37
27	22	22	23	24	25	26	27	28	29	30	31	32	33	34	35
28	21	21	22	23	24	25	26	27	28	29	30	31	32	33	34
29	20	20	21	22	23	24	25	26	27	28	29	30	31	32	33
30	19	20	21	22	23	23	24	25	26	27	28	29	30	31	32
31	18	19	20	21	22	23	24	25	25	26	27	28	29	30	31
32	18	18	19	20	21	22	23	24	25	26	26	27	28	29	30
33	17	18	19	20	21	21	22	23	24	25	26	26	27	28	29
34	17	17	18	19	20	21	22	22	23	24	25	26	27	27	28
35	16	17	18	19	19	20	21	22	23	23	24	25	26	27	27
36	16	16	17	18	19	20	20	21	22	23	23	24	25	26	27
37	15	16	17	18	18	19	20	21	21	22	23	24	24	25	26
38	15	16	16	17	18	19	19	20	21	22	22	23	24	24	25

REAR HUB COGS

CHAINRING GEAR TEETH

35	36	37	38	39	40	41	42	43	44	45	46	47	48	49	50	51
90	92	95	97	100	103	105	108	110	113	115	118	120	123	126	128	131
82	85	87	89	92	94	96	99	101	103	106	108	110	113	115	117	120
76	78	80	82	85	87	89	91	93	95	98	100	102	104	106	108	111
70	72	74	77	79	81	83	85	87	89	91	93	95	97	99	101	103
66	68	70	71	73	75	77	79	81	83	85	86	88	90	92	94	96
62	63	65	67	69	70	72	74	76	78	79	81	189	85	86	88	90
58	60	61	63	65	66	68	70	71	73	75	76	78	80	81	83	85
55	56	58	60	61	63	64	66	67	69	70	72	74	75	77	78	80
52	53	55	56	58	59	61	62	64	65	67	68	70	71	73	74	76
49	51	52	54	55	56	58	59	61	62	63	65	66	68	69	70	72
47	48	50	51	52	54	55	56	58	59	60	62	63	64	66	67	68
45	46	47	49	50	51	53	54	55	56	58	59	60	62	63	64	65
43	44	45	47	48	49	50	51	53	54	55	56	58	59	60	61	63
41	42	43	45	46	47	48	49	51	52	53	54	55	56	58	59	60
39	41	42	43	44	45	46	47	48	50	51	52	53	54	55	56	58
38	39	40	41	42	43	44	46	47	48	49	50	51	52	53	54	55
37	38	39	40	41	42	43	44	45	46	47	48	49	50	51	52	53
35	36	37	38	39	40	41	42	43	44	45	46	47	48	49	50	51
34	35	36	37	38	39	40	41	42	43	44	45	46	0	48	49	50
33	34	35	36	37	38	39	39	40	41	42	43	44	45	46	47	48
32	33	34	35	35	36	37	38	39	40	41	42	43	44	45	45	46
31	32	33	33	34	35	36	37	38	39	40	41	41	42	43	44	45
30	31	32	32	33	34	35	36	37	38	38	39	40	41	42	43	44
29	30	31	32	32	33	34	35	36	36	37	38	39	40	41	41	42
28	29	30	31	31	32	33	34	35	35	36	37	38	39	39	40	41
27	28	29	30	31	31	32	33	34	34	35	36	37	38	38	39	40
27	27	28	29	30	30	31	32	33	34	34	35	36	37	37	38	39
26	27	27	28	29	30	30	31	32	33	33	34	35	36	36	37	38

APPENDIX C
MOUNTAIN BIKE FITTING

If you are buying a new bike, get one that fits you properly. Fit should be the primary consideration when selecting a bike; you can adapt to heavier bikes and bikes not painted your favorite color, but your body will eventually protest on one that doesn't fit. The simple need to protect your more sensitive parts should keep you away from a bike without sufficient stand-over clearance (Fig. C.1), but there are a lot of other factors to consider as well. You need to make certain that your bike has enough reach to ensure that you don't bang your knees on the handlebar. You also need to check that your weight is properly distributed over the wheels so that you don't end up going over the handlebar on downhill stretches or find yourself unweighting the front end on steep climbs. An improperly sized bike is both inefficient and terribly uncomfortable. Therefore, take some time and find out how you can pick the properly sized bike.

I've outlined two methods for finding your frame size. The first is a simple method of checking your fit on bikes at your local bike shop. The second is a bit more elaborate, as it involves taking body measurements. This more detailed approach will allow you to calculate the proper frame dimensions whether the bike is assembled or not.

C.1 Bike height

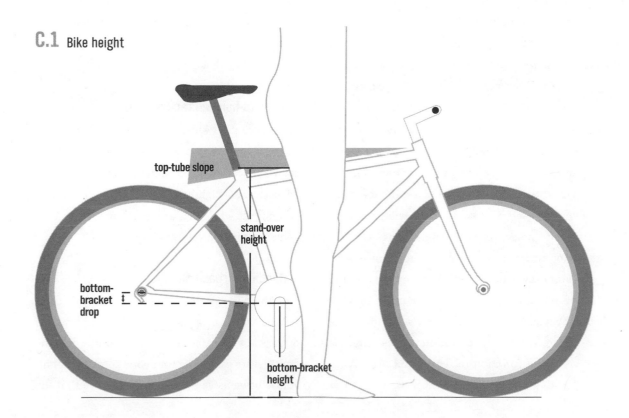

top-tube slope

stand-over height

bottom-bracket drop

bottom-bracket height

C-1

SELECTING THE CORRECT SIZE OF AN ASSEMBLED BIKE

a. Stand-over height

Stand over the bike's top tube and lift the bike straight up until the top tube hits your crotch. The wheels should be at least 2 inches off the ground to ensure that you can jump off the bike safely without hitting your crotch. There is no maximum dimension here. Though it may seem like a lot, 5 inches or more of stand-over height is fine, as long as the top tube is long enough for you and the handlebar height can be set properly for you.

NOTE: *If you have 2 inches of stand-over clearance on one bike, you should not assume that a bike from a different manufacturer with the same listed frame size will also offer you the same stand-over clearance. Manufacturers often measure frame size in different ways. They also slope and/or curve their top tubes differently and use different bottom-bracket heights (Fig. C.1), all of which affect the final stand-over height.*

All manufacturers measure the frame size up the seat tube from the center of the bottom bracket, but the top end of the measurement varies. Some measure to the center of the top tube ("center-to-center" measurement), some measure to the top of the top tube ("center-to-top" measurement), and others measure to the top of the seat tube (also called "center-to-top" measurement), even though there is wide variation in the length of the seatpost collar above the top tube. Obviously, each of these methods will give you a different frame size for the same frame.

No matter how the frame size is measured, the stand-over height of a bike depends on the slope of the top tube and the bottom-bracket height (Fig. C.1). Top tubes that slant up to the front are common, so stand-over clearance is obviously a function of where you are standing. With an up-angled top tube, straddle it 1 or 2 inches forward of the nose of the saddle, and then lift the bike up into your crotch to measure stand-over clearance.

A bike with a 125mm–travel suspension fork will have a higher front end than a bike with an 80mm– or 100mm–travel suspension fork, or a bike with a rigid fork, because the suspension fork has to allow for travel. And a full-suspension bike is automatically even taller, because the pedals need to be higher off the ground (higher bottom bracket) to ensure that they still clear obstacles when the suspension compresses. Complicating it even more are different wheel sizes. For instance, a 29er bike (bike with 29-inch wheels) will have a higher front end than a 26er with the same fork travel. All of this makes it difficult to compare listed frame sizes from even the same manufacturer to determine stand-over height. Unless the manufacturer lists the stand-over height in its catalog or on its Web site and you know your inseam length, you need to actually stand over the bike.

NOTE: *If you are short and cannot find a frame size small enough for you to get at least 2 inches of stand-over clearance, consider a bike with 24-inch wheels instead of 26-inch wheels.*

b. Knee-to-handlebar clearance

Make sure your knee cannot hit the handlebar (Fig. C.2). Check this while standing out of the saddle as well as when seated and with the front wheel turned slightly. Be certain that your knees will not hit when you are in the most awkward pedaling position you might use.

c. Handlebar reach and drop

Ride the bike. See whether the reach feels comfortable when you are holding the handlebar grips or the bar ends. Make sure that you can grab the brake levers easily and that your knees do not hit your elbows as you pedal. Check to see that the

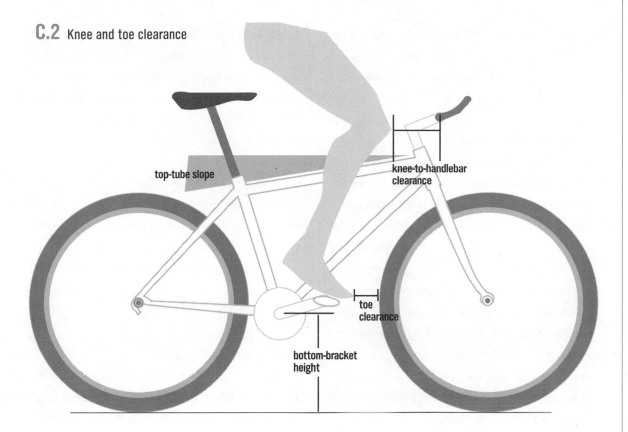

top-tube slope

knee-to-handlebar clearance

toe clearance

bottom-bracket height

stem can be raised or lowered enough to achieve a comfortable handlebar height.

NOTE: *Threadless headsets (the standard on all bikes today) allow very limited adjustment of stem height (§xi-9). Large changes in height require a change in stems.*

ANOTHER NOTE: *If you are tall and cannot find a bike with the handlebars as high as you need, consider a bike with 29-inch wheels instead of 26-inch wheels.*

d. Pedal overlap

"Pedal overlap" is a common bike-shop term, but it is a misnomer because you are actually interested in whether your toe, not the pedal, can hit the front tire when you are turning sharply at low speeds. Sitting on the bike with the crankarms horizontal and your foot on the pedal, turn the handlebar and check that your toe does not hit the front tire (Fig. C.2). Toe overlap is to be avoided for any kind of slow-speed, technical riding, as pedaling up rocky terrain slowly can often result

in the front wheel turning sharply back and forth as the feet pass by. Toe overlap is not an issue for most other riding, because at higher speeds, turning the bike does not require turning the front wheel at enough of an angle to hit the foot.

C-2
CHOOSING FRAME SIZE FROM YOUR BODY MEASUREMENTS

You will need a second person to assist you. This method is for cross-country and trail bikes; bikes for gravity-driven riding (downhill, freeride, dual slalom, four-cross, jumping, etc.) need to be considerably smaller.

By taking the three easy measurements shown in Figure C.3, most people can get a very good frame fit. The procedure I use when I design a custom frame for a client is more complex than this, involving more measurements, but the following method works well for picking an off-the-shelf bike. To avoid the trouble of making these calculations yourself, go to the free "Take Your Measurements" page at zinncycles.com; it will automatically calculate your frame size from these measurements.

a. Measure your inseam

Spread your stocking feet about 2 inches apart, and measure up from the floor to a three-foot carpenter's level or broomstick held level and pulled firmly up into your crotch with one hand in front and one in back. You can also use a large book and slide it up a wall to keep the top edge horizontal—as you pull it up as hard as you can—into your crotch. You can mark the top of the level, broomstick, or book on the wall and measure up from the floor to the mark. With the book, it is harder to pull up enough to compress the soft tissue up against the bottom edge of the pelvis than with a broomstick—so pull up hard.

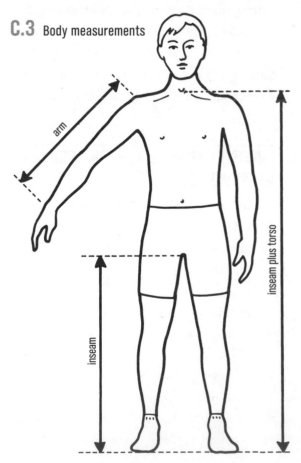

C.3 Body measurements

b. Measure your inseam-plus-torso length

Hold a pencil horizontally in your sternal notch, the U-shaped bone depression just below your Adam's apple. Standing up straight in front of a wall, mark the wall with the horizontal pencil. Measure up from the floor to the mark.

c. Measure your arm length

Hold your arm out from your side at a 45-degree angle with your elbow straight as shown in Figure C.3. Measure from the sharp bone point directly behind and above your shoulder joint (the lateral tip of the acromion) to the wrist bone on your little finger side.

d. Find your frame size

Subtract 36–42cm (13.5–16.5 inches) from your inseam length. This length is your frame size measured from the center of the bottom bracket to the top of a horizontal top tube; subtract another ¾ inch to get an approximate center-to-center size. If the frame you are interested in has a sloping top tube (most mountain bikes do), you need a bike with an even shorter seat-tube length. With a sloping-top-tube bike, project a horizontal line back to the seat tube (or seatpost) from the top of the top tube at the center of its length (Fig. C.4). Mark the seat tube or seatpost at this line. Measure from the center of the bottom bracket to this mark; this length should be 36–42cm less than your inseam measurement. Also, if the bike has a bottom bracket higher than 29cm (11½ inches), subtract the additional bottom-bracket height from the seat-tube length as well.

Generally, smaller riders will want to subtract closer to 36cm from their inseam, while taller riders will subtract closer to 42cm. However, full-suspension bikes generally have higher bottom brackets, which reduces stand-over height, so the more suspension travel you have, the shorter the seat-tube length you will want. There is considerable range here. The top-tube length (next step) is more important than a specific frame size, and if you have a short torso and short arms, you can use a small frame to get the right top-tube length, as long as you can raise your bars as high as you need them. Be aware that interrupted-seat-tube configurations of some full-suspension frames make measuring frame size challenging.

You really want to be sure that you have plenty of stand-over clearance, so do not subtract less than 36cm from your inseam to obtain your seat-tube length. If you are short and cannot find a bike small enough to get at least 2 inches of stand-over clearance, look for one with a curved top tube, or consider one with 24-inch wheels instead of 26-inch wheels. And if you are tall and cannot find a bike big enough for you without installing a superlong seatpost that will cantilever you out over the rear wheel, causing you to wheelie on climbs, consider one with 29-inch wheels instead of 26-inch wheels.

NOTE: *A step-through frame (i.e., "women's frame," "mixte frame," or "girl's bike") having a steeply up-angled top tube meeting near the bottom-bracket shell makes seat-tube length for stand-over clearance nearly irrelevant. With a step-through bike, the only considerations will be horizontal and vertical reach to the bars.*

e. Find your top-tube length

To find your torso length, subtract your inseam measurement (found in step a) from your inseam-plus-torso measurement (found in step b). Add this torso length to your arm-length measurement (found in step c). To find the top-tube length, multiply this arm-plus-torso measurement by a factor in the range between 0.47 and 0.5. If you are a casual rider, use 0.47; if you are a very aggressive rider, use 0.5; if you are in between, use a factor in between.

The top-tube length is measured horizontally from the center of the seat tube (or seatpost) to the center of the head-tube (Fig. C.4). Obviously, the horizontal top-tube length is greater than the length found by measuring along the top tube on a sloping-top-tube bike, so don't just measure

C.4 Bike dimensions

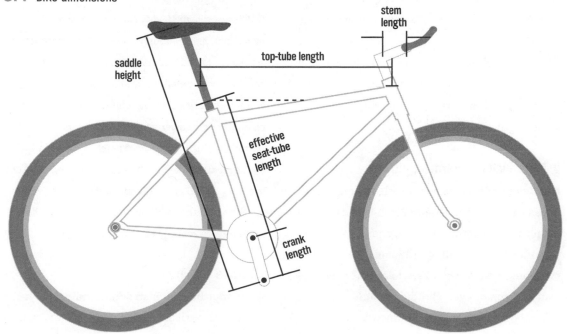

along a sloping top tube. Your body position is dictated by the horizontal distance of your hands reaching forward from your butt. Measuring along a sloping line does not give you useful information.

NOTE: *Full-suspension bikes with an interrupted seat tube often have a seatpost clamp that angles the seatpost back sharply along a line that would not intersect the bottom bracket. If you are tall and prefer to have your seat high, your seat would end up far back from where it normally would be on a bike of that size, and vice versa. You need to account for this shallow seatpost angle by estimating where the center of your virtual seat tube would be by extrapolating a line from the center of the saddle to the center of the bottom bracket. Measure from this imaginary line horizontally forward to the center of the head-tube to find your top-tube length.*

f. Find your stem length

Multiply the arm-plus-torso length you found in step e by a factor in the range between 0.085 and 0.115 to find the stem length. A casual rider should multiply by 0.085 or so, while an aggressive rider should multiply by closer to 0.115. This is a starting stem length. Finalize the stem length once you are sitting on the bike and see what feels best.

If you will have to accept a top-tube length different from one that is ideal for you, you will need to make a corresponding adjustment of stem length.

g. Determine crankarm length

Most mountain bikes come with 175mm cranks (measured hole to hole—see Fig. C.4), and it is rare to find another crank length on one. But tall riders will often be better off with 180mm crankarms or even longer custom cranks, while short riders will want 170mm or even shorter custom cranks; see more about crank length at zinncycles.com.

POSITIONING OF YOUR SADDLE AND HANDLEBAR

The frame fit is only part of the equation. Except for the stand-over clearance, a good frame fit is relatively meaningless if the seat setback, seat height, handlebar height, and handlebar reach are not set correctly for you.

a. Saddle height

When your foot is at the bottom of the pedal stroke, lock your knee without rocking your hips. Do this sitting on your bike with someone holding you up, or do it with your bike mounted on a stationary trainer stand; have someone else observing. Your foot should be level, or the heel should be slightly higher than the ball of the foot.

A second way to determine seat height uses your inseam measurement (Fig. C.3), found in step a under section C-2 above. Multiply your inseam length by 1.09; this is the length from the center of the pedal spindle (when the pedal is down) to one of the points on the top of the saddle where it contacts your butt bones (ischial tuberosities) (Fig. C.4). Adjust the seat height (Chapter 10) until you get the proper height.

NOTE: *These two methods yield similar results, although the measurement-multiplying method is dependent on shoe sole and pedal thicknesses. Both methods yield a biomechanically efficient pedaling position, but if you do a lot of technical riding and descending, you may wish to have a lower saddle for better bike-handling control. Or you may at least want to install a quick-release seat binder, a GravityDropper, or a Crank Brothers Joplin (Fig. 10.15) adjustable-height seatpost, and then drop the saddle down when you are about to negotiate a technically challenging descent.*

b. Saddle setback

Sit on your bike on a stationary trainer with the crankarms horizontal and your foot at its normal angle when pedaling at that point. Have a friend drop a plumb line from the front of your knee below your kneecap. You may use a heavy ring or washer tied to a string for the plumb line. The plumb line should touch the end of the crankarm (thus placing the center of rotation of the knee over the center of rotation of the pedal) or pass up to 2cm behind it (Fig. C.5); you will need to stick your knee out (away from the bike) to get the string to hang freely. A saddle positioned fore-and-aft in this manner encourages smooth pedaling at high revolutions per minute, while 2cm farther back encourages powerful seated climbing. You may also wish to experiment with a saddle position farther forward; this can keep the front wheel on the ground on steep climbs.

You also will want to make sure that your cleat position (§ix-2 in Chapter 9) is set properly. Generally, you will want your foot deep enough into the pedal that the ball of the foot is right over the pedal spindle or up to 2cm ahead of it. Riders with big feet will want their cleats farther back, often as far back as possible, while riders with short feet will often want to move the cleats far forward.

Slide the saddle back and forth on the seatpost (Chapter 10) until you achieve the desired fore-and-aft saddle position. Set the saddle level or very slightly tipped down at the nose so that it comes to level with seatpost and saddle flex when you're sitting on it (downhill racers and big-air free-riders sometimes tip their saddles up steeply at the nose, but their saddles are set very low, and you cannot pedal in an efficient, high seat position this way). Recheck the seat height in step a above, as fore-and-aft saddle movements affect seat-to-pedal distance, too.

c. Handlebar height

Measure the handlebar height relative to the saddle height by measuring the vertical distances of the saddle and handlebar up from the floor (Fig. C.5)

C.5 Saddle and stem position

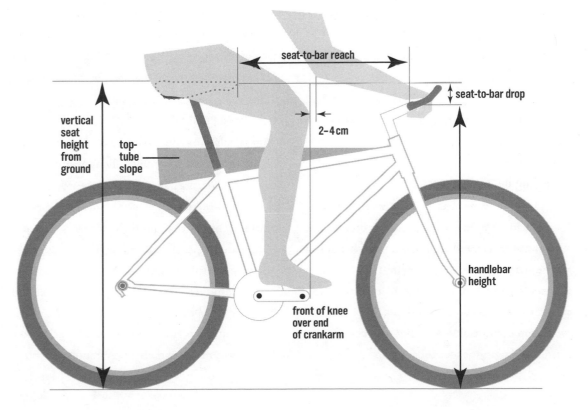

and subtracting one from the other. How much higher you set the saddle than the handlebar (or vice versa) depends on your flexibility, riding style, overall size, and the type of riding you prefer.

Aggressive and/or tall cross-country riders will prefer to have their saddle at least 10cm higher than their bar. Shorter riders will want proportionately less drop, as will less aggressive riders. Riders doing lots of downhill stretches will want their bars higher; handlebars on downhill and dual-slalom bikes are commonly considerably higher than the saddle. Generally, people beginning mountain bike riding will like the bars high and can lower them as they become more comfortable with the bike, with faster speeds, and with riding more technical terrain.

If in doubt, start with 4cm of drop for general cross-country riding and vary it from there. The higher the bar, the greater the tendency of the front wheel to pull up off the ground when climbing, and the more wind resistance you can expect, while, up to a point, the more comfort and control you will have going down technical terrain with drop-offs. Change the handlebar height by raising or lowering the stem (Chapter 11), or by switching stems of different angles and/or bars of different bends.

Again, threadless headsets allow only limited handlebar-height adjustment without substitution of a different stem or handlebar.

d. Setting handlebar reach

The ideal reach from the saddle to the handlebar is also dependent on personal preference. Aggressive riders will want a more stretched-out position than will casual riders. This length is subjective, and I find that I need to look at the rider on the bike and get a feel for how he or she would be comfortable and efficient before suggesting a length for handlebar reach.

A useful starting place is to drop a plumb line from the back of your elbow with your arms bent in a comfortable riding position. This plane determined by your elbows and the plumb line should be 2–4cm horizontally ahead of each knee at the point in the pedal stroke when the crankarm is horizontally forward (Fig. C.5). Select a position you find comfortable and efficient; pay attention to what your body wants.

Vary the saddle-to-handlebar distance by changing stem length (Chapter 11), not by changing the seat fore-and-aft position, which is based on pedaling efficiency (step b above) and not on reach.

NOTE: *There is no single formula for determining handlebar reach and height. I can tell you that using the all-too-common method of placing your elbow against the saddle and seeing if your fingertips reach the handlebar is close to useless. Similarly, the oft-suggested method of seeing whether the handlebar obscures your vision of the front hub is not worth the brief time it takes to look, as it largely depends on elbow bend, the inclination of your neck, and the front-end geometry of the bike. Another method, involving dropping a plumb bob from the rider's nose, is dependent on both the handlebar height and elbow bend and thus does not lend itself to a prescribed relationship for all riders.*

e. Bar-end position

Bar ends are an optional item, have largely fallen out of favor, and generally only appear on cross-country bikes, if at all. Performance riders using them should position the bar ends in the range between horizontal and 15 degrees up from horizontal (Fig. C.6). Bar-end angles in this range allow powerful pulling on the bar ends when you're climbing out of the saddle, because the bar ends are perpendicular to the forearms when you're standing. This bar-end angle also makes for a lower, more extended position when you're

C.6 Bar-end angle for performance riders

15 degrees

C.7 Bar-end angle for casual riders

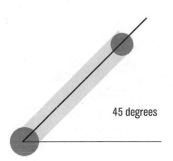

45 degrees

seated and grabbing the hooks of the bar ends. Use the bar-end position you find comfortable for pulling against when climbing standing or seated and for pedaling on extended paved stretches while seated.

Casual riders often prefer a higher angle (Fig. C.7) in order to pull with a straight wrist and closed fist while seated. Leave the bar-end mounting bolts a bit loose, sit on the bike, and grab the bar ends comfortably. Tighten them down in that position.

NOTE: *Bar ends are not to be used to adapt a poor-fitting bike. Do not use the bar ends to raise your hand position by pointing them straight up. If you want a higher hand position, get a taller or more up-angled stem and/or a higher-rise handlebar. Bar ends are not meant to be positioned straight up and used for cruising along while you're sitting up high, because steering is compromised and you will not be able to reach the brakes when you need them.*

APPENDIX D
TORQUE TABLE

One of the single biggest sources of mechanical problems (and breakage risk) is the overtightening or undertightening of fasteners, particularly on lightweight equipment. It is great to have the "feel" for what is tight enough, but many people do not have this sense, and, in any case, "feel" should only supplement torque measurement. With some parts, particularly today's superlight stems and handlebars, it is important to tighten them to exact torque specifications; otherwise, they could break while you are riding, resulting in an immediate and terrifying loss of control of the bicycle. Even "old guard" mechanics, with their "feel" from years of practice, often overtighten the small, light bolts on lightweight stems.

That said, I do recommend that you develop a sense of proper bolt tightness. When tightening small bolts, choke up on the wrench (even if you are using a click-type torque wrench) so you can feel with your fingers how hard you are twisting it. Torque = force × radius, and when you choke up, you reduce the radius at which you apply the force and thus have to apply more force to get the same torque on the bolt, which in turn makes you more aware of the effort it takes. You don't get this sensation when tightening a small bolt by pulling from the end of a long lever where it takes little force to apply a lot of torque. Don't worry about throwing off the torque reading by choking up, as long as you are pulling smoothly. Most torque wrenches have a spring inside to balance the torque on the square bit drive, and this spring action is independent of hand position (the spring pulls from the end of the

wrench, and it is the tension on this spring that determines the reading measured by the wrench, irrespective of where you grab the wrench as long as you don't grab its head).

There is also a danger in undertightening fasteners. The handlebar in an undertightened stem clamp can come loose and twist, or an undertightened brake cable can pull free when you really yank hard on the brakes. Also, an undertightened bolt suffers more fatigue during use than one that is preloaded.

The standard method of calculating torque specifications is to load the fastener to 80 percent of its yield strength. When you have a rigid joint, this method works very well. High bolt preload ensures that the fastener is always in tension to prevent metal fatigue in the fastener. However, many bike parts are not rigid, and high torques can overcompress or crush components. This is especially important when you are using parts of different brands, eras, or materials together. For instance, a stem manufacturer's torque specification for a handlebar clamp may not have anticipated that a carbon handlebar would be used, and what would work for an aluminum handlebar could crush the carbon one. There is no springback in a rigid joint, but if parts flex under tightening (a handlebar is a good example), that flex may provide the preload that the bolt needs at a considerably lower torque setting than if it were bolted around a solid steel part.

Flex-head torque wrenches (Fig. 1.3) usually have a twist knob at the base of the handle to adjust tension on the internal spring. You read the torque setting on a vernier scale or against a line on an indicator window on the side of the handle. When the set torque is reached, the head of the wrench snaps over to the side to alert you. Alternatively, a beam-type torque wrench (Fig. 1.3) has a needle arm parallel to the wrench shaft that moves across a scale.

You actually need two torque wrenches for working on bikes. The big one cannot measure torques accurately for small bolts. The little one cannot tighten a bottom bracket or crank bolt sufficiently because it does not have a long enough handle, and its scale does not go up high enough.

Using a torque wrench is not a guarantee against a screwup; it simply reduces the chances of one. First, you must make sure that the torque setting you are using is the one recommended for the bolt you are tightening. The torque table in this appendix includes a lot of bolts, but it obviously cannot include all bolts from all manufacturers, so consult your owners' manual when possible.

Second, lubrication of the bolt, temperature, and a wide variety of other variables will affect torque readings as well. Bicycle bolts generally assume lubrication or the application of thread-lock compound (which provides lubrication before it dries) on the threads, but often not under the bolt head. Lubricating under the bolt head allows the bolt to turn farther at the same torque setting than the same bolt would turn without lubrication under the head, and it thus increases the tension on the bolt.

Third, the torque reading will depend on whether the bolt is turning or you are starting a stationary bolt into motion, because the coefficient of static friction will be higher than the coefficient of dynamic (sliding) friction. If you try to determine the torque of a bolt by checking which torque setting is required on the handle to unscrew the bolt, you will have estimated a higher torque than the actual one, particularly if the bolt has been in place for some time and has corrosion or dirt around it.

Fourth, the reading on the torque wrench assumes that the head is centered over the bolt; the torque reading will be low if you have a radius multiplying the torque. For instance, measuring tightening torque on a pedal axle (if not using a 6mm or 8mm hex key in the hex hole in the axle end) requires a "crowfoot" 15mm open-end wrench attachment on a torque wrench. The crowfoot (Fig. 1.4) creates an offset between the axle centerline and the tool head centerline, which, if lined up straight with the torque wrench, multiplies the torque setting displayed on the wrench handle (i.e., it will make the wrench—the radius in the torque equation—effectively longer). The decimal by which you must multiply the torque reading on the wrench to determine the actual torque applied to the bolt will usually be imprinted on the crowfoot. If, however, you tighten the pedal with the crowfoot at a bit less than 90 degrees to the wrench handle, the setting on the handle is approximately accurate.

Finally, torque wrenches are not 100 percent accurate, and their accuracy changes over time with wear on the internal spring. Most torque wrenches can be calibrated; there will be a bolt attached to the spring that can be screwed in or out to adjust the reading on the wrench to match a known torque. This is generally a factory service.

Ultimately, your feel and common sense are also necessary to ensure safety. A good mechanic tightens a bolt as much as is needed to secure the part, keeping even tension on paired bolts, and doesn't exceed the maximum recommended torque.

It will be worth your while to review §ii-17b in Chapter 2 to help you develop a feel for bolt tightness. Whether or not you have "the touch," a torque wrench is a wonderful thing, as long as you know how tight the bolt is supposed to be.

Listed below are tightening torque recommendations of many bike component manufacturers. Where there is only one number listed and not a range, the number indicates the maximum torque allowable. You can assume minimum torque is about 80 to 90 percent of that number.

Most torques are for steel bolts; where possible, aluminum and titanium bolts are described as such in the table. Note that it is particularly important to use a copper-filled lubricant such as Finish Line Ti-Prep on titanium bolts to prevent them from binding and galling.

CONVERSION BETWEEN UNITS

The following table is in inch-pounds (in-lbs), Newton-meters (N-m), and foot-pounds (ft-lbs); I find Newton-meters easiest to use, because the numbers tend to be nice, round one- or two-digit figures. Divide in-lb settings by 12 to convert to foot-pounds (ft-lbs). Multiply in-lb settings by 0.113 to convert to Newton-meters (N-m).

BOLT SIZES

M5 bolts are 5mm in diameter and take a 3mm or 4mm hex key (except on derailleurs, where they often take a 5mm hex key or an 8mm box wrench).

M6 bolts are 6mm in diameter and generally take a 5mm hex key.

M7 bolts are 7mm in diameter and generally take a 6mm hex key.

M8 bolts are 8mm in diameter and generally take a 6mm hex key (or 8mm for crank bolts).

M10 bolts are 10mm in diameter and on bikes will likely take a 5mm or 6mm hex key (rear-derailleur mounting bolt).

The designation "M" in front of the bolt size number means millimeters and refers to the bolt shaft size, not the hex key that turns it; an M5 bolt is 5mm in diameter, an M6 is 6mm, and so on, but it may not have any relation to the wrench size. For instance, M5 bolts on bicycles can be found that accept 3mm, 4mm, or 5mm hex keys or an 8mm box wrench. M5 bolts attach bottle cages to the frame, and although many accept a 4mm hex key, others have a rounded cap head and take a 3mm hex key. The M5 bolts that clamp a front derailleur around the seat tube, or that anchor the cable on a front or rear derailleur, generally take either a 5mm hex key or an 8mm box wrench. And M5 disc-brake-rotor bolts often take a Torx T25 key.

Conversely, the big single-pinch bolts found on old stems usually take a 6mm hex key, but they may be M6, M7, or even M8 bolt size.

Generally, tightness can be classified in three levels:

1. **Snug (10–30 in-lbs, or 1–3 N-m):** Small setscrews (such as Grip Shift mounting screws), bearing-preload bolts (such as on threadless-headset top caps), and screws going into plastic parts need to be snug.

2. **Firmly tightened (30–80 in-lbs, or 3–9 N-m):** This refers to small M5 bolts, such as shoe-cleat bolts, brake and derailleur cable-anchor bolts, derailleur band-clamp bolts, small stem faceplate or steering-tube clamp bolts, and brake-rotor mounting bolts. It also refers to many bigger M6 bolts, especially when threaded into aluminum or magnesium, such as brake- and shift-lever clamp bolts and some disc-brake-caliper mounting bolts. M6 brake-arm mounting bolts and some M5 and M6 seatpost clamp bolts need to be firmly tightened.

3. **Tight (80–240 in-lbs, or 9–27 N-m):** Wheel-axle nuts, old-style single-bolt stem bolts (M6, M7, or M8), some M6 disc-brake-caliper mounting bolts, seatpost binder bolts, and seatpost saddle-clamp bolts need to be tight.

4. **Really tight (280–600 in-lbs, or 31–68 N-m):** Crankarm bolts, pedal axles, cassette-lockring bolts, and bottom-bracket cups are large parts that need to be really tight, or they could creak or loosen due to the high pedaling loads placed on them.

Table D.1	Mountain Bike Fastener Torque Table				

(Unit conversion factors are at end of table)

GENERAL TORQUE SPEC FOR STEEL BOLT THREADED INTO AN ALUMINUM PART	in-lbs		N-m		ft-lbs	
M5 bolt	60		7		5	
M6 bolt	120		14		10	
M6 bolt clamping a carbon part	100		11		8	
M7 bolt	180		20		15	
M8 bolt	220		25		18	
BOTTOM BRACKETS AND CRANKS	**min**	**max**	**min**	**max**	**min**	**max**
Bontrager Big Earl ISIS crankarm fixing bolts, M12		420		55		35
Bontrager chainring fixing bolt, aluminum	50	70	6	8	4	6
Bontrager chainring fixing bolt, steel	70	95	8	11	6	8
Bontrager Select, Race, Race Lite Earl ISIS crank bolts, M15		420		55		35
Bontrager square-taper (Sport) crankarm fixing bolts, M8	320	372	36	42	27	31
Campagnolo chainring fixing bolt		71		8		6
Campagnolo/Fulcrum Ultra-Torque crank fixing bolt	372	531	42	60	31	44
Campagnolo/Fulcrum Ultra-Torque external bearing cups		310		35		26
Campagnolo square-taper crankarm fixing bolt (M8 steel)	283	336	32	38	24	28
Campagnolo square-taper cartridge bottom bracket cups		619		70		52
Easton chainring fixing bolt		40		4.5		3.3
Easton external bearing cups	301	363	34	41	25	30
Easton left crankarm fixing pinch bolts (M5)		105		12		9
FSA M8 steel crankarm fixing bolt	304	347	34	39	25	29
FSA M12 steel crankarm fixing bolt	434	521	49	59	36	43
FSA M14 steel crankarm fixing bolt	434	521	49	59	36	43
FSA M14 aluminum crankarm fixing bolt	391	434	44	49	33	36
FSA M15 steel crankarm fixing bolt	434	521	49	59	36	43
FSA M15 aluminum crankarm fixing bolt	434	521	49	59	36	51
FSA M18 bearing preload bolt, MegaExo	4	6	0.4	0.7	0.3	0.5

Table D.1 — Mountain Bike Fastener Torque Table, continued

BOTTOM BRACKETS AND CRANKS, continued	in-lbs		N-m		ft-lbs	
	min	max	min	max	min	max
FSA M18 bearing preload bolt, BB90, BB86	6	13	0.7	1.5	0.5	1.1
FSA M5 pinch bolt, split aluminum crankarm, MegaExo	106	115	12	13	9	10
FSA M5 pinch bolt, split aluminum crankarm, BB90, BB86	97	133	11	15	8	11
FSA M17 crankarm fixing bolt, carbon crank, BB90, BB86	398	487	45	55	33	41
FSA M18 crankarm fixing bolt, carbon crank, MegaExo	398	487	45	55	33	41
FSA BB30 crankarm fixing bolt	345	434	39	49	29	36
FSA steel Allen chainring fixing bolt	80	106	9	12	7	9
FSA aluminum Allen chainring fixing bolt		87		10		7
FSA aluminum Torx chainring fixing bolt		104		11		9
FSA aluminum cartridge bottom bracket cups	347	434	39	49	29	36
FSA MegaExo bottom bracket cups	345	434	39	49	29	36
Race Face X-Type crankarm fixing bolt	363	602	41	68	30	50
Shimano chainring fixing bolt, steel	70	95	8	11	6	8
Shimano crankarm fixing bolt (Octalink/ Hollowtech)	305	435	35	50	25	36
Shimano Hollowtech 2 left crankarm fixing pinch bolts (M5)	88	132	12	14	7	11
Shimano integrated-spindle (Hollowtech 2) bearing cups	305	435	35	50	25	36
Shimano left crankarm bearing preload cap (Hollowtech 2)	4	6	0.5	0.7	0.3	0.5
Shimano loose-ball-bearing bottom bracket fixed cup	609	695	69	79	51	58
Shimano loose-ball-bearing bottom bracket lockring	609	695	69	79	51	58
Shimano square/Octalink cartridge bottom bracket cups	435	608	50	70	36	51
Shimano square-taper crankarm fixing bolt (M8 steel)	305	391	34	44	25	33
Shimano XTR FC-M960 left crankarm bearing preload cap	6	13	0.7	1.5	0.5	1.1
Shimano XTR FC-M960 left crankarm fixing pinch bolts (M5)	106	132	12	15	9	11
Shimano XTR FC-M970 adjustment nut	9	13	1.0	1.5	0.7	1.1
Shimano XTR FC-M970 adjustment nut fixing bolt	9	10	1.0	1.2	0.8	0.9
Shimano XTR FC-M970 crankarm fixing bolt (8mm hex key)	392	479	44	54	33	40
Truvativ aluminum chainring bolts	71	80	8	9	6	7
Truvativ GXP left crank bolt	416	478	47	54	35	40
Truvativ GXP self extractor cup (16mm hex key)	106	133	12	15	9	11
Truvativ GXP external bearing cups	301	363	34	41	25	30

Table D.1 — Mountain Bike Fastener Torque Table, continued

BOTTOM BRACKETS AND CRANKS, continued	in-lbs min	in-lbs max	N-m min	N-m max	ft-lbs min	ft-lbs max
Truvativ Howitzer ISIS external bearing cups	301	363	34	41	25	30
Truvativ ISIS cartridge bearing cups	301	363	34	41	25	30
Truvativ M8 crank bolts, square taper	336	372	38	42	28	31
Truvativ M12 crank bolts, ISIS	381	425	43	48	32	35
Truvativ M15 crank bolts, ISIS	381	425	43	48	32	35
Truvativ self-extractor cup, ISIS or square taper (10mm hex key)	106	133	12	15	9	11
Truvativ steel chainring bolts	106	124	12	14	9	10
Zinn Zinn-tegrated external bearing cups	301	363	34	41	25	30
Zinn Zinn-tegrated left crank bolt	400	450	45	51	33	38
Zinn Zinn-tegrated self extractor cup (10mm hex key)	106	133	12	15	9	11

BRAKES	in-lbs min	in-lbs max	N-m min	N-m max	ft-lbs min	ft-lbs max
Avid Arch Supreme arch-mounting bolt	35	40	4	5	2.9	3.3
Avid split-clamp lever-mounting bolts	28	36	3	4	2	3
brake arm–mounting bolt, M6	40	60	5	7	3	5
brake-cable anchor bolt, M5	50	70	6	8	4	6
brake-lever clamp bolt, M6	50	70	6	8	4.2	5.8
brake-lever clamp—slotted screw	22	26	3	3	2	2
cantilever brake pad bolt	70	78	8	9	6	7
Shimano V-brake leverage-adjuster bolt	9	13	1.0	1.5	0.8	1.1
straddle-cable yoke nut	35	43	4	5	3	4
V-brake pad nut	50	70	6	8	4	6
Magura hydraulic rim brake:						
M6 center bolt		52		6		4
M5 housing clamp bolt		35		4		3
bleed screws		35		4		3
brake-line sleeve nuts		35		4		3

DISC BRAKES	in-lbs min	in-lbs max	N-m min	N-m max	ft-lbs min	ft-lbs max
Avid/SRAM disc brake:						
banjo bolt	50	55	5	6	4	5
banjo bolt	50	55	5	6	4	5
cable-fixing bolt	40	60	5	7	3.3	5
caliper adapter–mounting bolts, M6	80	90	9	10	7	8
CPS caliper-mounting bolts to adapter or post mount, M6	70	90	8	10	6	8

Table D.1 — Mountain Bike Fastener Torque Table, continued

DISC BRAKES, continued	in-lbs		N-m		ft-lbs	
	min	max	min	max	min	max
Avid/SRAM disc brake, continued:						
old rear caliper adapter–mounting bolts, M6	40	60	5	7	3	5
rotor-mounting bolts, M5, TORX		55		6		5
single-lever clamp bolt	30	40	4	5	2.5	3.3
two-bolt lever clamp bolt	2.5	3.0	0.3	0.3	0.2	0.3
Coda disc brake:						
caliper-mounting bolts, M6	69	78	8	9	6	7
hose sleeve	69	78	8	9	6	7
lever clamp bolt	72	108	8	12	6	9
rotor-mounting bolts, M5	40	50	5	6	3.3	4.2
DiaTech disc brake:						
mounting pins	62	80	7	—	5	7
Formula disc brake:						
caliper-mounting bolts, M6	76	84	9	9	6	7
rotor-mounting bolts, M5	42	47	5	5	4	4
valve couplers	101	111	11	13	8	9
Hayes disc brake:						
caliper bleeder	25	35	3	4	2	3
caliper-bridge bolts	100	120	11	14	8	10
caliper-mounting bolts, 74mm caliper w/ mount bracket M6	100	120	11	14	8	10
caliper-mounting bolts, 74mm caliper w/ post-mount forks M6	75	85	8	10	6	7
lever pins	14.0	20.0	1.6	2.3	1.2	1.7
master cylinder bleeder	18	22	5	6	2	2
master cylinder jam nut	45	55	5	6	4	5
master cylinder pivot set screw	12.0	16.0	1.4	1.8	1.0	1.3
pad pin (Ryde)	10	14	1.1	1.6	0.8	1.2
reservoir cap screws	4.3	5.3	0.5	0.6	0.4	0.4
rotor-mounting bolts, M5	45	55	5	6	4	5
master-cylinder (brake-lever) clamp bolts:						
98/99, DH Purple (1-pc clamp)	15	20	1.7	2.3	1.3	1.7
handlebar master cylinder clamp screw	25	35	3	4	2	3
HFX-9, Sole (1-pc clamp)	30	35	3.4	4	2.5	2.9
Mag, Mag plus, EC, HFX-9 (2-pc clamp)	15	20	1.7	2.3	1.3	1.7

Table D.1	Mountain Bike Fastener Torque Table, continued					
DISC BRAKES, continued	**in-lbs**		**N-m**		**ft-lbs**	
	min	max	min	max	min	max
master-cylinder (brake-lever) clamp bolts, continued:						
hose connections:						
caliper—G1	40+1 turn		4.5 + 1 turn		3+1 turn	
caliper—G2	55	65	6	7	5	5
master cylinder (HFX-9, Sole, El Camino, Stroker, and later)	55	65	6	7	4.6	5.4
master cylinder (HFX-Mag, Mag Plus)	40+1 turn		4.5 + 1 turn		3+1 turn	
Hope disc brake:						
rotor-mounting lockring		310		35		26
RockShox disc brake:						
cable-guide hardware		50		6		4
caliper-mounting bolts, M6		50		6		4
rotor-mounting bolts, M5		50		6		4
Magura disc brake:						
caliper hose fitting, 0-degree		51		6		4
caliper hose fitting, 90-degree (banjo bolt)		51		6		4
caliper mounting bolts, M6		51		6		4
master cylinder (brake-lever) clamp bolts		34		4		3
master cylinder hose fitting		34		4		3
master cylinder reservoir cover screws		5		1		0
rotor mounting bolts, M5		34		4		3
Shimano hydraulic disc brake, old 4-piston XT type:						
banjo bolt	44	60	5	7	4	5
caliper bleed nipple	27	44	3	5	2	4
caliper mounting bolts, M6		55		6		5
lever clamp bolt		70		8		6
pad axle bolt	20	35	2	4	2	3
reservoir screws	3	5	0.3	1	0.2	0.4
rotor-mounting bolts, M5	18	35	2	4	2	3
Shimano hydraulic disc brake, 2-piston LX/XT/XTR type:						
banjo bolt	44	60	5	7	4	5
caliper bleed nipple	35	53	4	6	3	4
caliper mounting bolts, M6	53	69	6	8	4	6
lever clamp bolt	53	69	6	8	4	6
lever hose-sleeve nut	44	60	5	7	4	5

Table D.1 — Mountain Bike Fastener Torque Table, continued

DISC BRAKES, continued	in-lbs		N-m		ft-lbs	
	min	max	min	max	min	max
Shimano hydraulic disc brake, 2-piston LX/XT/XTR type, continued:						
rotor-mounting splined lockring		350		40		29

CHAIN GUIDES	in-lbs		N-m		ft-lbs	
	min	max	min	max	min	max
Truvativ M5, Box Guide		40		5		3
Truvativ M6, Box Guide		71		8		6
Truvativ M6, Box Guide		97		11		8

DERAILLEURS AND SHIFTERS	in-lbs		N-m		ft-lbs	
	min	max	min	max	min	max
Shimano Rapidfire shifter clamp bolt, M6	53	69	6	8	4	6
Shimano rear derailleur cable anchor bolt, M5	44	60	5	7	4	5
Shimano rear derailleur mounting bolt, M10	70	90	8	10	6	8
Shimano rear derailleur pulley center bolts, M5	27	34	3	4	2	3
Shimano thumb shifter clamp bolt, Allen, M6	53	69	6	8	4	6
Shimano thumb shifter clamp bolt, slotted screw	22	26	3	3	2	2
Shimano thumb shifter parts anchor screw	22	24	3	3	2	2
Shimano XT/XTR lever cable-access screw cover	3	4	0	1	0	0
SRAM 3.0 front derailleur clamp bolt, M5		70		8		4
SRAM front derailleur cable anchor bolt, M5		44		5		4
SRAM Grip Shift lever-mounting screw		17		2		1
SRAM X-Gen front derailleur clamp bolt, M5	44	62	5	7	0	6
SRAM rear derailleur cable anchor bolt, M5	35	45	4	5	4	5
SRAM rear derailleur cage-stop screw		13		2		2
SRAM rear derailleur mounting bolt, M10	70	85	8	10	3	4
SRAM rear derailleur pulley center bolts, M5		22		3		7
SRAM trigger lever-mounting bolt		44		5.0		3.7

HUBS, CASSETTES, QUICK-RELEASES	in-lbs		N-m		ft-lbs	
	min	max	min	max	min	max
bolt-on steel skewer		65		7		5
bolt-on titanium skewer		85		10		7
Cannondale Lefty front-axle bolt		133		15.0		11
Mavic cassette cog lockring		354		40		30
nutted front hub		180		20		15
nutted rear hub		300		34.0		25
quick-release axle locknut	87	217	10	25	7	18
Shimano cassette cog lockring	261	434	30	50	22	36

Table D.1 — Mountain Bike Fastener Torque Table, continued

HUBS, CASSETTES, QUICK-RELEASES, continued	in-lbs		N-m		ft-lbs	
	min	max	min	max	min	max
Shimano freehub cassette body—mounting bolt	305	434	35	50	25	36
Shimano hub quick-release lever closing	43	65	5	7	4	5

MISCELLANEOUS PARTS	in-lbs		N-m		ft-lbs	
	min	max	min	max	min	max
AheadSet bearing preload, M6		22		3		2
fender to frame bolts, M5	50	60	6	7	4	5
water-bottle cage bolts, M5	25	35	3	4	2	3

PEDALS AND SHOES	in-lbs		N-m		ft-lbs	
	min	max	min	max	min	max
Crank Brothers pedal axle to crankarm	301	363	34	41	25	30
Crank Brothers shoe-fixing cleat bolt, M5	35	44	4	5	3	4
pedal spindle into Truvativ crankarm	186	301	21	34	16	25
Shimano pedal axle to crankarm	304	355	34	40	25	30
Shimano shoe-fixing cleat bolt, M5	41	52	5	6	3	4
shoe spike, M5		34		4		3
Speedplay Frog spindle nut	35	40	4	5	3	3
Time pedal axle to crankarm		310		35		26
toeclips to pedals, M5	25	45	3	5	2	4

REAR SHOCKS	in-lbs		N-m		ft-lbs	
	min	max	min	max	min	max
Manitou:						
air canister	13	21	2	2	1	2
Schrader valve stem	4	9	1	1	0	1
RockShox						
Air-can lockring	55	75	6	8	5	6
Damper seal head		250		28		21
Schrader valve core	8	12	1	1	1	1
Schrader valve housing	25	35	3	4	2	3
Shaft-eyelet assembly	100	110	11	12	8	9
U-Turn air-can assembly	60	70	7	8	5	6

SEATPOSTS AND SEAT BINDERS	in-lbs		N-m		ft-lbs	
	min	max	min	max	min	max
Campagnolo seatpost saddle-rail clamp bolt, M8		194		22		16
Easton seatpost saddle-rail clamp bolts	95	105	11	12	8	9
ITM Forged Lite, all series M7	62	71	7	8	5	6
ITM K-Sword M6 (for GWS system)	88	97	10	11	7	8
ITM K-Sword Special Bolts (saddle clamp bolt)	88	97	10	11	7	8

| Table D.1 | Mountain Bike Fastener Torque Table, continued |

SEATPOSTS AND SEAT BINDERS, continued	in-lbs		N-m		ft-lbs	
	min	max	min	max	min	max
Oval Concepts M6 saddle-rail clamp bolts		133		15		11
Ritchey saddle-rail clamp bolt: Comp, Old Pro, M8		400		45		33
Ritchey saddle-rail clamp bolt: WCS, New Pro, M6		165		19		14
seatpost saddle rail–clamp bolt, M8	175	345	20	39	15	29
seat tube clamp binder bolt, M6	105	140	12	16	9	12
Selcof saddle-rail clamp bolt, M6		71		8		6
Selcof saddle-rail clamp bolt, M8		177		20		15
steel seatpost band–clamp bolt	175	345	20	39	15	29
Thomson saddle-rail clamp bolt, M6		60		7		5
Truvativ M6 two-bolt		62		7		5
Truvativ M8 single bolt		80		9		7
two-piece seat binder bolt, M6	35	60	4	7	3	5

STEMS AND BAR ENDS	in-lbs		N-m		ft-lbs	
	min	max	min	max	min	max
3T M5 bolts (front clamp, steering-tube clamp)		80		9		7
3T M6 bolts (single steering-tube clamp)		130		15		11
3T M6 bolts (two-bolt front-clamp plate)		130		15		11
3T Bono M6 bolts (two-bolt front-clamp plate)		120		14		10
3T M8 bolts (single steering-tube clamp; expander)		175		20		15
3T M8 bolts (single handlebar clamp)		220		25		18
bar end M6 bolt	120	140	14	16	10	12
Bontrager M8 steering-tube clamp bolts		200		23		17
Deda M5 steel bolts (bar clamp, steering-tube clamp)		90		10		8
Deda M5 titanium bolts (bar clamp, steering-tube clamp)		70		8		6
Deda M6 bolts (bar clamp, steering-tube clamp)		160		18		13
Deda M6 old-model hidden steering-tube clamp bolt		130		15		11
Deda M8 bolts (quill expander)		160		18		13
Dimension one-bolt handlebar clamp, M8 bolt	205	240	23	27	17	20
Dimension two-bolt face-plate bar clamp, M6	80	90	9	10	7	8
Dimension two-bolt steering-tube clamp, M6	80	90	9	10	7	8
Easton EA50, 70 bar and steering-tube clamp bolts	60	70	7	8	5	6
Easton EM90 (single M8) steering-tube clamp bolt	70	80	8	9	6	7
Easton MG60, EM90 bar clamp bolts	50	60	6	7	4	5

Table D.1 — Mountain Bike Fastener Torque Table, continued

STEMS AND BAR ENDS, continued	in-lbs min	in-lbs max	N-m min	N-m max	ft-lbs min	ft-lbs max
Easton MG60 (two M6) steering-tube clamp bolts	50	60	6	7	4	5
FSA M5 titanium bolts—use Ti prep		68		8		6
FSA M5 chromoly bolts		78		9		7
FSA M6 chromoly bolts		104		12		9
FSA M8 chromoly bolts		156		18		13
ITM M5, 2 bolts (bar clamp, steering-tube clamp)	62	70	7	8	5	6
ITM M5, 4 bolts (bar clamp)	35	44	4	5	3	4
ITM M6 aluminum bolts in magnesium stem	44	53	5	6	4	4
ITM M6 bolts (fork collar)	88	105	10	12	7	9
ITM M7 bolts (single-bolt front clamp)	106	120	12	14	9	10
ITM M8 bolts (single-bolt clamp or expander)	150	160	17	18	13	13
Oval Concepts titanium M5 faceplate (alloy bars)		84		10		7
Oval Concepts titanium M5 faceplate bolts (carbon bars)		49		6		4
Oval Concepts M6 faceplate bolts for alloy bars		93		11		8
Oval Concepts M6 faceplate bolts for carbon bars		58		7		5
Oval Concepts titanium M6 clamp bolts for alloy steering tubes		84		10		7
Oval Concepts titanium M6 clamp bolts for carbon steering tubes		53		6		4
Oval Concepts M6 clamp bolts for alloy steering tubes		93		11		8
Oval Concepts M6 clamp bolts for carbon steering tubes		58		7		5
Ritchey WCS M5 faceplate bolts for alloy bars	26	52	3	6	2	4
Ritchey WCS M5 faceplate bolts for carbon bars		35		4		3
Ritchey WCS M6 clamp bolts for alloy steering tubes	52	86	6	10	4	7
Ritchey WCS M6 clamp bolts for carbon steering tubes		78		9		7
Salsa one-bolt handlebar clamp, M6 bolt		140		16		12
Salsa one-bolt steering-tube clamp, M6 bolt	100	110	11	12	8	9
Salsa SUL two-bolt face-plate bar clamp, M6	120	130	14	15	10	11
single stem handlebar clamping bolt, M8	145	220	16	25	12	18
Thomson Elite, X2, X4 steering-tube clamp bolts, M5		48		5		4
Thomson Elite handlebar clamp bolts, M5		48		5		4
Thomson X4 handlebar clamp bolts, M5		35		4		3
Truvativ M5 bolts		50		6		4
Truvativ M6 bolts—bar		60		7		5

Table D.1 — Mountain Bike Fastener Torque Table, continued

STEMS AND BAR ENDS, continued	in-lbs		N-m		ft-lbs	
	min	max	min	max	min	max
Truvativ M6 bolts—steering-tube		80		9		7
Truvativ M7 bolts		120		14		10
wedge expander bolt for quill stems, M8	140	175	16	20	12	15

SUSPENSION FORKS	in-lbs		N-m		ft-lbs	
	min	max	min	max	min	max
Fox fork torque specs:						
32, 36, 40 top caps (Damper, Preload, Air, TALAS)	160	170	18	19	13	14
Air tank valve	40	50	5	6	3	4
All 32, 36, and 40 bottom nuts	45	55	5	6	4	5
All 32, 36 and 40 rebound knob screws	10	12	1	1	1	1
All rebound piston bolts	50	60	6	7	4	5
Axle pinch-bolts on 36 and 40 lower leg	14	24	2	3	1	2
Base valve assembly to cartridge tube	50	60	6	7	4	5
Base valve bolt R & RL-RLC	50	60	6	7	4	5
brake post	75	85	8	10	6	7
Cartridge Tube to seal head	50	60	6	7	4	5
Crown pinch-bolts on 40 upper and lower crowns	30	0	3	0	3	
DH axle to lower leg on 36 and 40 forx	14	24	2	3	1	2
F80X IV shaft	115	125	13	14	10	10
F80X IV shaft extension	115	125	13	14	10	10
F80X compression cylinder	105	115	12	13	9	10
F80X IV comp. piston bolt 8-32 × .250"	50	60	6	7	4	5
IV body to slim cartridge tube	40	50	5	6	3	4
LW aluminum damper shaft to rebound piston insert & upper insert (all F80-F100X & 05 R-RL-RLC dampers)	50	60	6	7	4	5
LW Al vanilla plunger shaft to upper & lower inserts (Loctite 262)	65	75	7	8	5	6
LW Al float air shaft to lower inserts (Loctite 262)	65	75	7	8	5	6
Lockout threshold knob set screw (RLT & RLC)	10	12	1	1	1	1
Low- & high-speed compression knob set-screw (36, 40)	10	12	1	1	1	1
Rebound adjuster screw to rebound rod	4	6	0	1	0	0
Schrader valve core	3	5	0	1	0	0
Slim cartridge tube to slim sealhead	40	50	5	6	3	4
TALAS ball screw fitting to top cap (Loctite 242)	50	60	6	7	4	5
TALAS base stud (Loctite 242, 1 drop)	50	60	6	7	4	5
TALAS hex fitting (Loctite 242)	17	19	2	2	1	2

Table D.1 — Mountain Bike Fastener Torque Table, continued

SUSPENSION FORKS, continued	in-lbs		N-m		ft-lbs	
	min	max	min	max	min	max
TALAS IFP shaft bolt to ifp shaft (Loctite 242)	50	60	6	7	4	5
TALAS lower piston bolt (Loctite 242, 1 drop)	50	60	6	7	4	5
TALAS M2 screw tank valve to hex adapter (Loctite 242)	4	6	0	1	0	0
TALAS tank valve (Loctite 262, 360 degrees)	35	45	4	5	3	4
TALAS top cap to ifp shaft (Loctite 242, 1 drop)	50	60	6	7	4	5
TALAS T-port end cap (Loctite 242, 1 drop)	4	6	1	1	0	1
Top cap to LW aluminum damper shaft assembly (all F80-F100X & 05 R-RL-RLC dampers)	70	80	8	9	6	7
Top cap to old chrome damper shaft upper insert	70	80	8	9	6	7
Vanilla preload topcap knob screw (inside top cap)	10	12	1	1	1	1
Manitou fork torque specs:						
adjuster caps and top caps	35	50	4	6	3	4
brake post	90	110	10	12	8	9
comp rod screw	13	53	2	6	1	4
damper screw	13	20	2	2	1	2
EFC/Mach 5/SX cartridge bolt	10	30	1	3	1	3
EFC/Mach 5/SX cartridge cap	30	50	3	6	3	4
fork-brace bolt	90	110	10	12	8	9
leg caps	25	35	3	4	2	3
M6 (5mm key) crown clamp bolt		60		7		5
M8 (6mm key) crown clamp bolt	110	130	12	15	9	11
neutral shaft bolt	10	30	1	3	1	3
Marzocchi fork torque specs:						
26mm top caps	80	97	9	11	7	8
brake post	71	88	8	10	6	7
cartridge foot nut and pump rod	80	97	9	11	7	8
Monster cartridge foot nut	204	230	23	26	17	19
upper and lower crown bolts	44	62	5	7	4	5
upper and lower crown bolts–Monster, Shiver	80	97	9	11	7	8
RockShox fork torque specs:						
Air-valve assembly, Schrader type	20	40	2.3	5	2	3
Air valve core, Schrader type	8	12	0.9	1.4	1	1
Axle bolt, Boxxer	40	60	4.5	7	3	5
Axle pinch bolt, Boxxer	20	30	2.3	3.4	2	3

Table D.1 — Mountain Bike Fastener Torque Table, continued

SUSPENSION FORKS, continued	in-lbs		N-m		ft-lbs	
	min	max	min	max	min	max
BlackBox Lever clamp bolt	6	10	0.7	1.1	1	1
Bottom bolt, 8mm, Boxxer	45	75	5	8	4	6
Bottom bolt, 8mm, dual air	35	55	4	6	3	5
Bottom bolt, 8mm, hollow	45	75	5	8	4	6
Bottom bolt, 8mm, solid	45	70	5	8	4	6
Brake post	65	95	7	11	5	8
Crown bolt, Boxxer	50	80	6	9	4	7
Knob screw, 4mm, U-turn/Pure Climb-It knob	10	14	1.1	1.6	1	1
PopLoc clamp bolt	18	22	2	2.5	2	2
Pure compression piston bolt	30	50	3.4	6	3	4
Pure rebound piston bolt	30	50	3.4	6	3	4
Pure remote cable-set clamp screw	6	10	0.7	1.1	1	1
Pure remote knob cable set-screw	6	10	0.7	1.1	1	1
SID upper-tube threaded retainer	45	75	5	8	4	6
Top cap aluminum, all	55	75	6	8	5	6
Top cap, plastic, all	55	75	6	8	5	6
Topcap, U-turn air	115	145	13	16	10	12
RST fork torque specs:						
Mozo brake arch bolt	70	80	8	9	6	7
Mozo fork crown clamp bolt	70	80	8	9	6	7

Conversion between units

- Divide in-lbs settings by 12 to convert to foot-pounds (ft-lbs).
- Multiply in-lbs settings by 0.113 to convert to newton meters (N-m).
- Multiply kgf-cm settings by 0.098 to convert to newton meters (N-m).

GLOSSARY

adjustable cup: the non–drive side cup in the bottom bracket (Fig. 8.9). This cup is removed for maintenance of the bottom-bracket spindle and bearings, and it adjusts the bearings. The term is sometimes applied to the top cup of the headset as well (Figs. 11.19–20).

AheadSet (a trademark of Dia-Compe and Cane Creek; *or* "threadless headset"): a style of headset that allows the use of a fork with a threadless steering tube (Fig. 11.7).

Allen key (*or* "Allen wrench") (*see* "hex key").

all-terrain bike (ATB): another term for mountain bike.

anchor bolt (*or* "cable anchor" *or* "cable anchor bolt"): a bolt securing a cable to a component.

Answer Products: an American bicycle- and motorcycle-component company and the parent company of Manitou.

Avid: a brake manufacturer, subsidiary of SRAM.

axle: a shaft about which a part turns, usually on bearings or bushings.

axle overlock dimension: a length of a hub axle from dropout to dropout, referring to the distance from locknut face to locknut face (Fig. 14.16).

ball bearing: a set of balls, generally made out of steel, rolling in a track to allow a shaft to spin inside a cylindrical part; may also refer to one of the individual balls.

bar end: a short handlebar extension clamped onto the end of the handlebar and extending approximately perpendicular to it (Fig. 11.2).

barrel adjuster: a threaded cable stop that allows for fine adjustment of cable tension. Barrel adjusters are commonly found on rear derailleurs, shifters, and brake levers (Figs. 5.3, 5.26–27, 7.1).

BB (*see* "bottom bracket").

bearing (*see* "ball bearing").

bearing cone: a conical part with a bearing race around its circumference. The cone presses the ball bearings against the bearing race inside the bearing cup (Fig. 6.24).

bearing cup (or "headset cup"): a polished dish-shaped surface inside of which ball bearings roll. The bearings roll on the outside of a bearing cone that presses them into their track inside the bearing cup (Figs. 6.24, 8.5, 11.18).

bearing race: a track or surface the bearings roll on. The race can be inside a cup, on the outside of a cone, or inside a cartridge bearing.

binder bolt: a bolt clamping a seatpost in a frame, a bar end to a handlebar, a handlebar inside a stem, or a threadless steering tube inside a stem clamp.

bonk: (1) v. to run out of fuel for the (human) body so that the ability to continue further strenuous activity is impaired. (2) n. the state of having such low blood sugar from insufficient intake of calories that the ability to perform vigorous activity is impaired.

bottom bracket (BB): an assembly that allows the crank to rotate. Generally the bottom-bracket assembly includes bearings and an axle and on older bikes may include a fixed cup, an adjustable cup, and a lockring.

409

bottom-bracket drop: the vertical distance between the center of the bottom bracket and a horizontal line passing through the wheel-hub centers. Drop is equal to the wheel radius minus the bottom-bracket height (Appendix C, Fig. C.1).

bottom-bracket height: the height of the center of the bottom-bracket spindle above the ground (Appendix C, Fig. C.1).

bottom-bracket shell: a cylindrical housing at the bottom of a bicycle frame through which the bottom-bracket axle passes (Fig. 8.13).

brake: a mechanical device that decelerates or stops the motion of the wheel (and hence of the bicycle and rider) through friction.

brake block (*see* "brake pad").

brake booster: an arch-shaped part bolted to the ends of the brake bosses to reduce the flex of the bosses and seatstays when the cantilever or V-brakes are applied (Fig. 7.46).

brake boss (*or* "brake pivot," "brake post," "cantilever boss," "cantilever pivot," or "cantilever post"): a fork- or frame-mounted pivot for a brake arm (Figs. 13.2–3, 14.1).

brake caliper: a brake part fixed to the frame or fork containing moving parts attached to brake pads that stop or decelerate a wheel (Figs. 7.12–13, 7.19–20, 7.28–29, 7.33–34, 7.43, 7.48–50).

brake pad (*or* "brake block"): a block of rubber or similar material used to slow the bike by creating friction on the rim, hub-mounted disc, or other braking surface (Figs. 7.19, 7.22).

brake pivot (*see* "brake boss").

brake post (*see* "brake boss").

brake shoe: a metal pad holder that holds the brake pad to the brake arm (Fig. 7.27).

braze-on boss: a generic term for most metal frame attachments, even those welded or glued to the frame.

brazing: a method commonly used to construct steel bicycle frames. Brazing involves the use of brass or silver solder to connect frame tubes and attach various "braze-on" items, including brake bosses, cable guides, and rack mounts to the frame. Although it is rarely done, it is also possible to braze aluminum and titanium.

bushing: a metal or plastic sleeve that acts as a simple bearing in pedals, suspension forks, rear shock mounting points, suspension swingarms, and jockey wheels.

butted tubing: a common type of frame tubing with varying wall thicknesses. Butted tubing is designed to accommodate high-stress points by being thicker at the ends of the tube and thinner in other sections to reduce weight.

cable (*or* "inner wire"): wound or braided wire strands used to operate brakes and derailleurs.

cable anchor (*see* "anchor bolt").

cable anchor bolt (*see* "anchor bolt").

cable boss (*see* "cable stop").

cable end cap: a cap on the end of a cable to keep it from fraying (Fig. 5.20).

cable hanger: cable stop on a stem, headset washer, fork, or seatstay arch used to stop the brake-cable housing for a cantilever or U-brake (Figs. 7.4–6).

cable housing (*or* "outer wire"): a metal-reinforced exterior sheath through which a cable passes (Fig. 5.20).

cable stop (*or* "cable boss," "cable-housing stop," or "outer wire stop"): a fitting on the frame, fork, or stem at which a cable-housing segment terminates (Fig. 14.1).

cable-housing stop (*see* "cable stop").

cage: two guiding plates through which chain travels. Both the front and rear derailleurs have cages. The cage on the rear also holds the jockey pulleys. Also, a water-bottle holder.

caliper (*see* "brake caliper" and "measuring caliper").

Campagnolo: an Italian bicycle-component company.

Cane Creek (originally Dia-Compe USA): American bicycle-component company and originator of the threadless headset.

cantilever boss (*see* "brake boss").

cantilever brake: a cable-operated rim brake consisting of two opposing arms pivoting on frame- or fork-mounted posts. Pads mounted to each brake arm are pressed against the braking surface of the rim via cable tension from the lever (Figs. 7.29–31).

cantilever pivot (*see* "brake boss").

cantilever post (*see* "brake boss").

cartridge bearing: ball bearings encased in a cartridge consisting of steel inner and outer rings, ball retainers, and sometimes bearing covers (Figs. 6.23, 6.35, 11.31).

cassette: a group of cogs that mounts on a freehub (Fig. 6.35); also, a group of chainrings that mounts on a spiderless crankarm (Fig. 8.12).

cassette hub (*see* "freehub").

casting (*see* "outer leg").

chain: a series of metal links held together by pins and used to transmit energy from the crank to the rear wheel (Fig. 4.1).

chain link: a single unit of bicycle chain consisting of four plates with a roller on each end and in the center (Fig. 4.7).

chain suck: a dragging of the chain by the chainring past the release point at the bottom of the chainring. The chain can be dragged upward until it is jammed between the chainring and the chainstay (Fig. 4.27).

chain whip (*or* "chain wrench"): a flat piece of steel, usually attached to two lengths of chain (Fig. 1.2). This tool is used to remove the rear cogs on a freehub or freewheel. (*See also* "Vise Whip," a substitute for this tool.)

chainline: an imaginary line connecting the center of the middle chainring with the middle of the cogset. This line should, in theory, be straight and parallel to the vertical plane passing through the center of the bicycle. The chainline is measured as the distance from the center of the seat tube to the center of the middle chainring (§v-47 Fig. 5.49).

chainring: a multiple-tooth sprocket attached to the right crankarm (Fig. 8.1).

chainring-nut tool: a tool used to secure the chainring nuts while tightening the chainring bolts (Fig. 1.2).

chainstay: a frame tube on a bicycle connecting the bottom-bracket shell to the rear dropout and hence to the rear hub axle (Figs. 14.1–2).

chase (*see* "goose chase").

circlip (*or* "Jesus clip" *or* "snapring"): a C-shaped ring that fits in a groove to hold parts together.

clip-in pedal (*or* "clipless pedal"): a pedal that relies on spring-loaded clips to grip a cleat attached to the bottom of the rider's shoe without the use of toeclips and straps (Fig. 9.2).

clipless pedal (*see* "clip-in pedal").

cog: a sprocket located on the drive side of the rear hub (Fig. 6.35).

compression damping: a diminishment of the speed of compression of a spring on impact by hydraulic or mechanical means.

cone: a threaded conical nut that serves to hold a set of bearings in place and also provides a smooth surface upon which those bearings can roll (Fig. 6.24); can also refer to the conical (or male) member of any cup-and cone ball-bearing system (*see also* "bearing cone").

crank bolt (*see* "crankarm anchor bolt").

crank length: the distance between the centerline of the bottom-bracket spindle and the centerline of the pedal axle (Appendix C, Fig. C.4).

crankarm: a lever attached at the bottom-bracket spindle and to the pedal used to transmit a rider's energy to the chain (Fig. 8.1).

crankarm anchor bolt (*or* "crank bolt"): a bolt attaching the crank to the bottom-bracket spindle on a cotterless drivetrain (Fig. 8.1).

crankset: an assembly that includes a bottom bracket, two crankarms, a chainring set, and accompanying nuts and bolts (Fig. 8.1).

cross-three (*see* "three-cross").

crowfoot socket (*see* "crowfoot wrench").

crowfoot wrench (*or* "crowfoot socket" or "crow's foot"): an open-end wrench head with a square hole at its base to accept the drive stub of a socket wrench or torque wrench (Fig. 1.3).

crow's foot (*see* "crowfoot wrench").

cup: a cup-shaped bearing surface that surrounds the bearings in a bottom bracket (Fig. 8.13), headset (Fig. 11.18), or hub (Fig. 6.23) (*see also* "bearing cup").

damper (*or* "damping cartridge"): a mechanism in a suspension fork or shock that reduces the speed of the spring's oscillation movement (Fig. 13.20).

damping: a reduction in speed of the oscillation of a spring, as in a suspension fork or shock.

damping cartridge (*see* "damper").

derailleur: a gear-changing device that allows a rider to move the chain from one cog or chainring to another while the bicycle is in motion (Figs. 5.3, 5.12).

derailleur hanger: a metal extension of the right rear dropout through which the rear derailleur is mounted to the frame (Fig. 14.1).

diamond frame: a traditional bicycle frame shape (Fig. 14.1).

disc brake: a brake that stops the bike by squeezing brake pads attached to a caliper mounted to the frame or fork against a circular disc attached to the wheel (Figs. 7.16–19).

dish (*or* "wheel dish"): a difference in spoke tension on the two sides of the rear wheel (Figs. 12.3, 12.21).

dishing (*or* "wheel dishing"): a centering of the rim in the frame or fork by adjustment of spoke tension in a wheel.

dishing tool: a tool to check the centering of a wheel rim relative to the axle ends.

double: a two-chainring drivetrain setup (as opposed to a three-chainring, or "triple," one).

downtube: a frame tube that connects the head-tube and bottom-bracket shell together (Fig. 14.1).

drivetrain: the crankarms, chainrings, bottom bracket, front derailleur, chain, rear derailleur, and freewheel (or cassette).

drop: (1) the difference in height between two parts (*see also* "bottom-bracket drop"). (2) a terrain discontinuity you may or may not want to ride off of. (3) something not to do with your tools.

dropouts (*or* "fork ends" or "fork tips"): slots in the fork and rear triangle where the wheel axles attach (Figs. 13.2, 14.1).

DT (aka DT Swiss): a manufacturer of spokes, other bicycle components, and tools.

dust cap: a protective cap keeping dirt out of a part.

easy-out: a cone-shaped, hardened-steel tool with coarse, reverse threads to remove broken bolts. To remove a broken bolt with one, a hole is drilled into the center of the bolt, the easy-out is inserted into the hole, and the easy-out is then turned with a tap handle in a counter-clockwise direction.

elastomer: a urethane spring sometimes used in suspension forks and rear shocks (Fig. 13.12); also called an "MCU" for the material and construction (microcellular urethane).

endo: a (usually unintentional) rotation of the bike and rider forward over the front wheel.

expander bolt: a bolt that when tightened pulls a wedge up inside or alongside the part into which the bolt is anchored to provide outward pressure and secure said part inside a hollow surface. Expander bolts are found inside quill stems (Figs. 11.8–9) and some handlebar-end plugs and handlebar-end shifters.

expander wedge (*or* "wedge"): a part threaded onto an expander bolt and usually used to secure a quill stem inside the fork steering tube or handlebar-end plugs or handlebar-end shifter inside a handlebar. An expander wedge is threaded down its center axis to accept the expander bolt and is either cylindrical in shape and truncated along an inclined plane (Figs. 11.8–10) or conical in shape and truncated parallel to its base.

ferrule: a cap for the end of cable housing (Fig. 5.20).

fixed cup: a nonadjustable cup of the bottom bracket located on the drive side of the bottom bracket (Fig. 8.13).

flange: largest diameter of the hub where the spoke heads are anchored (Fig. 12.4).

fork: a part that attaches the front wheel to the frame (Figs. 13.1–2).

fork casting (*see* "outer leg").

fork crown: a crosspiece connecting the fork legs to the steering tube (Figs. 13.1–2).

fork ends (*see* "dropouts").

fork rake (*or* "offset," "rake," or "wheel offset"): perpendicular offset distance of the front axle from an imaginary extension of the steering-tube centerline (*see also* "steering axis").

fork steerer (*see* "steering tube").

fork tips (*see* "dropouts").

fork trail (*or* "trail"): the distance measured on the ground between the vertical line passing through the center of the front-hub axle (i.e., the center of the wheel contact patch) and the extension of the centerline of the head-tube.

frame: a central structure of a bicycle to which all of the parts are attached (Figs. 14.1–2).

freehub (*or* "cassette hub"): a rear hub that has a built-in freewheel mechanism to which the rear cogs are attached (Fig. 6.35).

freewheel: a mechanism through which the rear cogs are attached to the rear wheel on a derailleur bicycle (Figs. 6.35–36). The freewheel is locked to the hub when turned in the forward direction, but it is free to spin back-

ward independently of the hub's movement, thus allowing the rider to stop pedaling and coast as the bicycle is moving forward (*see also* "freehub").

friction shifter: a traditional (nonindexed) shifter attached to the frame or handlebar. Cable tension is maintained by a combination of friction washers and bolts.

front triangle (*or* "main triangle"): the head-tube, top tube, downtube, and seat tube of a bike frame (Fig. 14.1).

FSA (Full Speed Ahead): a bicycle-component manufacturer.

girl's bike (*see* "step-through frame").

goose chase (*see* "wild goose chase").

granny gear: the lowest gear on the bike. In the granny gear the chain is on the inner (of three) front chainrings and the largest rear cog.

Grip Shift: a twist shifter of the SRAM Corporation that is integrated with the handlebar grip of a mountain bike (Figs. 5.29–30). The rider shifts gears by twisting the grip (*see also* "twist shifter").

handlebar: a curved tube, connected to the fork through the stem, that the rider grips in order to turn the fork and thus steer the bicycle. The brake levers and shift levers are attached to it (Fig. 11.1).

head angle: an acute angle formed by the centerline of the head-tube and the horizontal.

headset: a bearing system, consisting of a number of separate cylindrical parts installed into the head-tube and onto the steering tube, that secures the fork and allows it to spin and swivel in the frame (Figs. 11.18–21).

headset cup (*see* "bearing cup").

headset top cap (*see* "top cap").

head-tube: the front tube of the frame through which the steering tube of the fork passes (Fig. 14.1). The head-tube is attached to the top tube and downtube and contains the headset.

hex key (or "Allen key" or "Allen wrench"): a hexagonal wrench that fits inside a hexagonal hole in the head of a bolt (Fig. 1.1A).

hub: the central part of a wheel to which the spokes are anchored and through which the wheel axle passes (Fig. 6.1).

hub brake: a disc, drum, or coaster brake that stops the wheel with friction applied to a braking surface attached to the hub.

Hurricane Components: a bicycle-component company.

Hutchinson: a French tire company.

hydraulic brake: a type of brake that uses oil pressure to move the brake pads against the braking surface (Figs. 7.16, 7.46).

index shifter: a shifter that clicks into fixed positions as it moves the derailleur from gear to gear.

inertial valve (or "pedal platform"): a valve on the compression-damping system on a front or rear shock designed to distinguish between bump forces and pedaling forces to prevent the shock from bobbing up and down during pedaling. The inertial valve is similar to a lockout lever, but unlike a lockout, it allows the shock to be active for bump absorption while engaged.

inner (see "inner leg").

inner leg: on a telescoping suspension fork, a tube, usually clamped into the fork crown (except in the case of an "upside-down fork"), that slides in and out of the larger-diameter outer leg as the fork compresses and rebounds (Fig. 13.21). On a standard (non-upside-down) fork, it is also called an "upper tube," "inner," or "stanchion."

inner wire (see "cable").

integrated headset: a headset in which the bearing seats are integrated into the head-tube (rather than requiring separate headset cups) and the bearings are completely concealed within the head-tube (Fig. 11.19).

Jesus clip (see "circlip").

jockey pulley (see "jockey wheel").

jockey wheel (or "jockey pulley"): a circular, cog-shaped pulley attached to the rear derailleur that is used to guide, apply tension to, and laterally move the chain from rear cog to rear cog (Fig. 5.47).

knobby tire: an all-terrain tire used on mountain bikes (Fig. 6.1).

lawyer tabs (see "wheel-retention devices").

leverage ratio: amount the rear axle moves vertically on a full-suspension bike with a given amount of movement of the shock shaft.

link: a pivoting steel hook on a V-brake arm that the cable-guide "noodle" hooks into (Fig. 7.25) (see also "chain link").

lock washer: a notched or toothed washer that serves to hold surrounding nuts and washers in position.

locknut: a nut that serves to hold the bearing adjustment in a headset, hub, or pedal.

lockout: a valve on the compression-damping system on a front or rear shock that prevents the shock from compressing. Modern shocks usually have a "blow-off" system that will allow the compression-damping circuit to open with a large impact to prevent the shock from being damaged on big hits.

lockring: a large circular locknut. On a bottom bracket, it is the outer ring that tightens the adjustable cup against the face of the bottom-bracket shell (Fig. 8.13). On a rear shock, the lockring is the threaded ring that tightens the coil spring on a coil-over shock or is used to secure the fore-aft position of the shock body on some air shocks. On a freehub, the lockring holds the cogs on (Fig. 6.35). On a Center Lock disc brake–compatible hub, the lockring secures the rotor to the hub shell (Fig. 7.14).

Low Normal (originally, "Rapid Rise"): a style of rear derailleur pioneered by Shimano in which the return spring is connected to the opposite vertices of the rear derailleur's parallelogram linkage elements compared to the setup for a standard rear derailleur. This arrangement results in the derailleur's moving to the low-gear position (the largest, most inboard rear cog) when the cable tension is removed, rather than to the high-gear position (the smallest, most outboard cog), as on a standard rear derailleur.

Magura: a German brake company.

main triangle (*see* "front triangle").

Manitou: an American suspension-fork and component company, subsidiary of Answer Products.

Marzocchi: an Italian suspension-fork and component company.

master cylinder: a piston chamber at the lever end of a hydraulic brake system (Figs. 7.18, 7.46).

master link: a detachable link that holds the chain together. The master link can be opened by hand without a chain tool (Fig. 4.14).

Mavic: a French wheel and bicycle-component company.

MCU (*see* "elastomer").

measuring caliper: a tool for measuring the outside dimensions of an object or the inside dimensions of a hole by means of movable jaws (Fig. 1.4).

Michelin: a French tire company.

mixte frame (*see* "step-through frame").

mounting bolt: a bolt that mounts a part to a frame, fork, or component (*see also* "pivot bolt").

needle bearing: a steel cylindrical cartridge with rod-shaped rollers arranged coaxially around the inside walls (Fig. 8.20).

nipple: (1) a thin nut designed to receive the end of a spoke and seat it in the holes of a rim (Figs. 12.1–2). (2) a flared tip of a hydraulic caliper bleed fitting onto which a bleed hose can be attached (Fig. 7.16).

noodle: a curved cable-guide pipe on a V-brake arm

that stops the cable housing and directs the cable to the cable anchor bolt on the opposite arm (Fig. 7.25).

NoTubes (*or* "NoTubes.com") (*see* "Stan's NoTubes").

NoTubes.com (*see* "Stan's NoTubes).

offset (*see* "fork rake").

outer (*see* "outer leg").

outer leg: in a telescoping suspension fork, a tube, usually cast out of magnesium and attached to the front-wheel axle (except in the case of an "upside-down fork"), that slides up and down over the smaller-diameter inner leg as the fork compresses and rebounds (Fig. 13.2). On a standard (non-upside-down) fork, it is also called the "casting," "fork casting," "outer," or "slider."

outer wire (*see* "cable housing").

outer wire stop (*see* "cable stop").

pedal: a platform the foot pushes on to propel the bicycle (Figs. 9.1–2).

pedal overlap (*or* "toe overlap" *or* "toeclip overlap"): an overlapping of the toe with the front wheel while pedaling (Appendix C, Fig. C.2).

pedal platform (*see* "inertial valve").

pedaling stance: the lateral distance between the feet while pedaling. It's the distance measured between the two vertical planes defined by the inboard side of each shoe at the first metatarsal as they move around the pedaling circle.

pin spanner: a V-shaped wrench with two tip-end pins. The pin spanner is often used for tightening the adjustable cup of the bottom bracket or other lockrings (Fig. 1.2).

pivot: a pin about which a part rotates through a bearing or bushing. The pivot is found on brakes, derailleurs, and rear-suspension systems.

pivot bolt: a bolt on which a brake or derailleur part pivots.

preload (*see* "spring preload").

Presta valve: a thin, metal tire valve that uses a locking nut to prevent air from escaping out of the inner tube or tire (Fig. 1.1B).

Q-factor: the distance from the outer face of one crankarm at the pedal hole to the plane formed by the outer face of the other crankarm at the pedal hole as it spins. Q-factor is measured normal to this plane. In practice, the easiest way to measure Q-factor is to install the two crankarms on the spindle so that they are parallel to each other (at 0 degrees, rather than at 180 degrees from each other) and measure from the outer face of one crankarm at the pedal hole to the outer face of the other crankarm at the pedal hole.

quick-release: (1) a tightening lever and shaft used to attach a wheel to the fork or rear dropouts without using axle nuts (Fig. 6.23). (2) a quick-opening lever and shaft pinching the seatpost inside the seat tube in lieu of a wrench-operated bolt. (3) a quick cable release on a brake. (4) a fixing mechanism that can be quickly opened and closed, as on a brake cable or wheel axle. (5) any anchor bolt that can be quickly opened and closed by a lever.

quill: a vertical tube of a stem for a threaded headset system that inserts into the fork steering tube. It has an expander wedge and bolt inside to secure the stem to the steering tube (Fig. 11.8).

quill stem: a stem with a quill to insert inside a threaded fork steering tube (Fig. 11.8).

race: a circular track on which bearings roll freely (*see also* "bearing race").

Race Face: a Canadian bicycle-component company.

rake (*see* "fork rake").

Rapid Rise (*see* "Low Normal").

Rapidfire shifter: an indexing shifter manufactured by Shimano for use on mountain bikes with two separate levers operating each shift cable (Figs. 5.24, 5.37).

rear triangle: a rear part of the bicycle frame that includes the seatstays, the chainstays, and the seat tube (Fig. 14.1).

rebound damping: a diminishing of speed of return of a spring by hydraulic or mechanical means.

ride height (*see* "sag").

rim: an outer hoop of a wheel to which the tire is attached (Fig. 12.1).

riser bar: a handlebar with a double bend on each side of the stem clamp so that the grips are higher than the stem.

Ritchey: an American bicycle and bicycle-component company.

RockShox: an American suspension-fork and component company, subsidiary of SRAM.

roller-cam brakes: a brake system using pulleys and a cam to force the brake pads against the rim surface (Fig. 7.53).

saddle (*or* "seat"): a platform made of leather and/or plastic upon which the rider sits (Fig. 10.1).

sag (*or* "ride height"): the amount the front or rear shock compresses with the rider's weight static on the bike. Its purpose is to preload the shock so that it forces the rear wheel down into the ground when the bike is unweighted after a bump, thus increasing tire contact and traction in rough terrain.

Schrader valve: a high-pressure air valve with a spring-loaded air-release pin inside (Fig. 1.1B). Schrader valves are found on some bicycle inner tubes and tubeless tires, on air-sprung suspension forks and rear shocks, as well as on automobile tires and tubes.

sealed bearing: a bearing enclosed in an attempt to keep contaminants out (Fig. 6.23) (*see also* "cartridge bearing").

seat (*see* "saddle").

seat angle: an acute angle formed by the center-line of the seat tube and the horizontal.

seat cluster: an intersection of the seat tube, top tube, and seatstays.

seat tube: a frame tube to which the seatpost (and, usually, the cranks) is attached (Fig. 14.1).

seatpost: an element supporting and securing the saddle (Fig. 10.4).

seatstay: a frame tube on a bicycle connecting the seat tube or the rear shock to the rear dropout and hence to the rear hub axle (Figs. 14.1–2).

shim: a thin element inserted between two parts to ensure that they are the proper distance apart. On bicycles, a shim can be a thin washer and can be used to space a disc-brake caliper away from the frame or fork or to space a bottom-bracket cup away from the frame's bottom-bracket shell. A shim can also be a thin piece of metal used to make a seatpost fit tighter inside the seat tube. Shims can also be small, thin discs found inside suspension forks and rear shocks to control suspension movement by permitting or hindering passage of hydraulic fluid through an orifice.

Shimano: a Japanese bicycle-component company and maker of XTR, XT, Saint, LX, and STX component lines as well as Rapidfire (shifters), SPD (pedals), and STI (shifting systems).

sidepull cantilever brake (*see* "V-brake").

singletrack: a trail with a single furrow made for feet or a two-wheeled vehicle, as opposed to a road or "doubletrack," which has a track for each set of wheels on a four-wheeled vehicle.

skewer: (1) a long rod. (2) a hub quick-release (Fig. 6.23). (3) a shaft passing through a stack of elastomer bumpers in a suspension fork (Fig. 13.20).

slave cylinder: a piston chamber in the caliper of a hydraulic brake.

slider (*see* "outer leg").

Slime (*or* "tire sealant"): a brand of tire sealant consisting of chopped fibers in a liquid medium injected inside a tire or inner tube to flow to and fill small air leaks (Fig. 6.18).

snapring (*see* "circlip").

socket: a cylindrical tool with a square hole in one end to mount onto a socket-wrench handle and with hexagonal walls inside the opposing end to grip a bolt head or nut (Fig. 1.2).

socket wrench (*or* "socket wrench handle" or "wrench handle"): a cylindrical wrench handle with a ratcheting square head extending at right angles to the handle onto which sockets or other wrench bits for turning bolts or nuts are installed (Fig. 1.2).

spacer: on a bicycle, generally a thick washer cylindrical in shape intended to maintain a fixed distance between two parts. Spacers can be found between the headset and the stem and between the stem and the top cap on a threadless steering tube and between the upper bearing cup and the top nut on a threaded steering tube. Spacers may also be used to space a bottom-bracket cup away from the frame's bottom-bracket shell.

spanner (British parlance): a wrench.

spider: a star-shaped piece of metal that connects the right crankarm to the chainrings (Fig. 8.1).

spline: one of a set of longitudinal grooves and ridges designed to interlock two mechanical parts (Figs. 6.35, 7.15).

spokes: metal rods that connect the hub to the rim of a wheel (Figs. 12.1–2).

spring: an elastic contrivance that when compressed returns to its original shape by virtue of its elasticity. In bicycle suspension applications, the spring used is normally either an elastic polymer cylinder, a coil of steel or titanium wire, or compressed air.

spring preload (*or* "preload"): an initial loading of a spring so that part of its compression range is taken up prior to impact.

sprocket: a circular, multiple-toothed piece of metal that engages a chain (*see also* "cog" and "chainring").

SRAM: an American bicycle-component company and maker of Grip Shift, Half Pipes, and ESP (derailleurs); owner of Sachs, RockShox, Avid, and Truvativ bicycle-component companies.

stanchion (*see* "inner leg").

stand-over clearance (*see* "stand-over height").

stand-over height (*or* "stand-over clearance"): the distance between the top tube of the bike and the rider's crotch when the rider is standing over the bicycle (Appendix C, Fig. C.1).

Stan's NoTubes (*or* "NoTubes" *or* "NoTubes.com"): a brand of tire upgrade system named after inventor Stan Koziatek that includes a latex-based tire sealant to convert a standard tire to a tubeless tire.

star bolt (*see* "Torx bolt").

star nut (*or* "star-fangled nut"): a pronged nut that is forced down into the steering tube and anchors the headset top cap bolt to adjust a threadless headset (Figs. 11.7, 11.19–20).

star wrench (*see* "Torx wrench").

star-fangled nut (*see* "star nut").

steerer (*see* "steering tube").

steering axis: the imaginary line about which the fork rotates (Fig. 13.34).

steering tube (*or* "fork steerer" *or* "steerer"): a vertical tube on a fork that is attached to the fork crown, fits inside the head-tube, and swivels within it by means of the headset bearings (Figs. 13.1–3). A steering tube can be threaded or threadless, meaning that the top headset cup can either screw onto the steering tube or slide onto it, and the stem can either insert inside the steering tube and clamp with an expander wedge (threaded) or clamp around the steering tube (threadless).

stem (*or* "gooseneck"): a connection element between the fork steering tube and the handlebar (Fig. 11.1).

stem length: the distance between the center of the steering tube and the center of the handlebar measured along the top of the stem (Appendix C, Fig. C.4).

step-through frame (*or* "girl's bike," "mixte frame," *or* "women's frame"): a bicycle frame with a steeply up-angled top tube connecting the bottom of the seat tube to the top of the head-tube. The frame design is intended to provide ease of stepping over the frame and ample stand-over clearance.

straddle cable: a short segment of cable connecting two brake arms together (Figs. 7.40–42).

straddle-cable holder (*see* "yoke").

swingarm: a movable rear end of a rear-suspension frame (Fig. 14.2).

tap (*or* "thread tap"): a threaded tool made of hardened steel to cut threads. It is shaped like a pointed bolt shaft, but it has lengthwise grooves cut across the threads to give the threads cutting edges. The tap has a square head that fits in a handle to provide leverage to turn the tap.

threaded headset: a headset whose top bearing cup and top nut above it screw onto a threaded steering tube (Fig. 11.18).

threadless headset (*see* "AheadSet").

three-cross (*or* "cross-three"): a pattern used by wheelbuilders that calls for each spoke to cross three others in its path from the hub to the rim (Fig. 12.1).

thumb shifter: a thumb-operated shift lever attached on top of the handlebars (Fig. 5.25).

tire bead: an edge of a tire that seats down inside the rim (Fig. 6.8). The bead's diameter is held fixed to established standards by means of a strong, stretch- and tear-resistant material—usually either steel or Kevlar. These strands alone are also referred to as the "bead."

tire lever: a tool to pry a tire off the rim (Figs. 6.5–6).

tire sealant (*see* "Slime").

toe overlap (*or* "toeclip overlap") (*see* "pedal overlap").

toeclip overlap (*see* "pedal overlap").

top cap (*or* "headset top cap"): a round top part of a headset with a bolt passing through it that screws into the star nut to apply downward pressure on the stem to properly load and adjust the headset bearings on a threadless steering tube (Figs. 11.18–20).

top cup: upper headset cup (*see* "bearing cup").

top tube: a frame tube that connects the seat tube to the head-tube (Fig. 14.1).

torque: a rotational analogue of force. Torque is a vector quantity whose magnitude is the length of the radius from the center of rotation out to the point at which the force is applied, multiplied by the magnitude of the force directed perpendicular to the radius. On bicycles, we are primarily interested in the tightening torque applied to a fastener (this value can be measured with a torque wrench—see Appendix D) and the torque applied by the rider on the pedals to propel the rear wheel and hence the bicycle.

torque wrench: a socket-wrench handle with a graduated scale and an indicator to show how much torque is being applied as a bolt is being tightened (Figs. 1.3, 2.15; *see* Appendix D).

Torx bolt (*or* "star bolt"): a bolt with a six-point star-shaped hole in its head.

Torx wrench (*or* "star wrench"): a tool with a star-shaped end that fits in the star-shaped hole in the head of a Torx bolt (Figs. 1.3, 1.5).

trail: (1) where to ride your mountain bike. (2) (*see* "fork trail").

triple: a three-chainring combination (Fig. 8.1) attached to a right crankarm.

Truvativ: a bicycle-component manufacturer, subsidiary of SRAM.

twist shifter: a cable-pulling derailleur control handle surrounding the handlebar adjacent to the hand grip. It is twisted forward or back to cause the derailleur to shift (Figs. 5.28). (*See also* "Grip Shift").

U-brake: a mountain bike brake consisting of two arms shaped like inverted Ls affixed to posts on the frame or fork (Fig. 7.52).

unicrown: a manufacturing method of nonsuspended (i.e., rigid) forks in which the fork legs curve toward each other and are welded directly to the steering tube (Fig. 13.3).

upper tube (*see* "inner leg").

upside-down fork: a suspension fork whose lower legs (attached to the wheel axle) are the inner legs of the forks and move up and down within the upper, outer legs of the fork.

UST: a tubeless-tire system originated by Mavic, Michelin, and Hutchinson in which the tire seals over a " hump" on the ledge inside a rim free of spoke holes on its outer circumference (Fig. 6.8).

V-brake (*or* "sidepull cantilever brake"): a cable-operated cantilever rim brake consisting of two vertical brake arms pivoting on frame- or fork-mounted pivots pulled together by a horizontal cable. A brake pad is affixed to each arm, and there are a cable link and a cable-guide pipe on one arm and a cable anchor on the opposite arm (Figs. 7.9–11).

Vise Whip: a Pedro's tool (designed by the author) with jaws and a Vise-Grip handle used to remove the rear cogs on a freehub or freewheel (Fig. 1.2). (*See also* "chain.")

wedge (*see* "expander wedge").

wheel dish (*see* "dish").

wheel dishing (*see* "dishing").

wheel offset (*see* "fork rake").

wheelbase: the horizontal distance between the two wheel axles.

wheel-dishing tool (*see* "dishing tool").

wheel-retention devices (*or* "lawyer tabs" or "wheel-retention tabs"): cast-in or separate fixtures at the fork ends designed to prevent the front wheel from falling out if the hub quick-release lever or axle and nuts are loose.

wheel-retention tabs (*see* "wheel-retention devices").

wild goose chase (*see* "chase").

women's frame (*see* "step-through frame").

wrench (*or* "spanner," in British parlance): a tool having jaws, a shaped insert, or a socket to grip the head of a bolt or a nut to turn it.

yoke (or "straddle-cable holder"): a part on a cantilever or U-brake attaching the brake cable to the straddle cable (Fig. 7.39); also, the part of a rear-suspension swingarm attached to the main pivot.

Zinn: the author of this book, not to be confused with Zen.

BIBLIOGRAPHY

Barnett, John. *Barnett's Manual: Analysis and Procedures for Bicycle Mechanics*, 4th ed. Boulder, CO: VeloPress, 2000.

Brandt, Jobst. *The Bicycle Wheel*. Menlo Park, CA: Avocet, 1988.

Dushan, Allan. *Surviving the Trail*. Tumbleweed Films, 1993.

Langley, Jim. *Bicycling Magazine's Complete Guide to Bicycle Maintenance and Repair*. Emmaus, PA: Rodale Press, 1994.

Leslie, David. *The Mountain Bike Book*. London: Ward Lock, 1996.

Lindorf, Werner. *Mountain Bike Repair and Maintenance*. London: Ward Lock, 1995.

Muir, John, and Tosh Gregg. *How to Keep Your Volkswagen Alive: A Manual of Step-by-Step Procedures for the Compleat Idiot*. Santa Fe, NM: John Muir, 1969.

Pirsig, Robert. *Zen and the Art of Motorcycle Maintenance*. New York: William Morrow, 1974.

Schraner, Gerd. *The Art of Wheelbuilding: A Bench Reference for Neophytes, Pros, and Wheelaholics*. Denver: Buonpane, 1999.

Stevenson, John, and Brant Richards. *Mountain Bikes: Maintenance and Repair*. Mill Valley, CA: Bicycle Books, 1994.

Taylor, Garrett. *Bicycle Wheelbuilding 101: A Video Lesson in the Art of Wheelbuilding*. Westwood, MA: Rexadog, 1994.

Van der Plas, Robert. *The Bicycle Repair Book*. Mill Valley, CA: Bicycle Books, 1993.

———. *Mountain Bike Maintenance*. San Francisco: Bicycle Books, 1994.

Zinn, Lennard. *Mountain Bike Performance Handbook*. Osceola, WI: MBI, 1998.

———. *Zinn and the Art of Road Bike Maintenance*, 3rd ed. Boulder, CO: VeloPress, 2009.

INDEX

423

ILLUSTRATION INDEX

ABOUT THE AUTHOR

Lennard Zinn is a bike racer, frame builder, and technical writer. He grew up cycling, skiing, whitewater rafting, and kayaking—as well as tinkering with mechanical devices—in Los Alamos, New Mexico. After receiving his physics degree from Colorado College, he became a member of the U.S. Olympic Development Cycling Team. He went on to work in Tom Ritchey's frame-building shop and has been producing custom mountain, road, and triathlon frames, as well as custom cranks and stems, at Zinn Cycles since 1982 (www.zinncycles.com).

Zinn has been writing for VeloNews since 1989 and is the magazine's senior technical writer. Other books by Zinn are *Zinn & the Art of Road Bike Maintenance* (VeloPress, 3rd ed. 2009), *Zinn & the Art of Triathlon Bikes* (VeloPress, 2007), *Zinn's Cycling Primer* (VeloPress, 2004), *Mountain Bike Performance Handbook* (MBI, 1998), and *Mountain Bike Owner's Manual* (VeloPress, 1998).

ABOUT THE ILLUSTRATOR

Todd Telander is a former mechanic and bike racer who devotes most of his time these days to artistic endeavors. He attended the University of California at Santa Cruz, and while earning degrees in Environmental Studies and Biology, he completed a graduate-level program in scientific illustration. He has since studied fine art in several western states and was awarded an artist's residency at Rocky Mountain National Park. In addition to drawing bike parts, he paints and draws wildlife and landscapes for publishers, museums, design companies, and individuals. You can see more examples of his work on his website, www.toddtelander.com.

Also available from VeloPress

Zinn & the Art of Road Bike Maintenance
3rd Edition
Lennard Zinn applies his prodigious powers of mechanical expertise to the art and science of road bike repair. Newcomers and experienced mechanics alike will benefit from the book's hundreds of illustrations (including exploded views of how components go together), its step-by-step instructions for basic and advanced repair, and Zinn's practical, time-saving maintenance tips. Covers new and old bikes alike.

440 pages • $24.95
ISBN 978-1-934030-42-4

Zinn & the Art of Triathlon Bikes
Aerodynamics, Bike Fit, Speed Tuning, and Maintenance
More than a repair manual, *Zinn & the Art of Triathlon Bikes* presents proven techniques to wring more speed from today's triathlon bicycles. With clear advice on bike fit and comfort, getting aero, tuning for speed, and choosing wisely among equipment upgrades, the tips in this book virtually guarantee faster bike splits. Of course, Zinn includes comprehensive maintenance and repair instructions too, accompanied by more than 300 illustrations and step-by-step directions to ensure trouble-free rides.

352 pages • $24.95
ISBN 978-1-931382-97-7

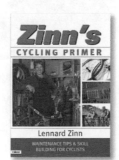

Zinn's Cycling Primer
Maintenance Tips & Skill Building for Cyclists
Drawing upon the research of cycling experts around the world, Zinn's Cycling Primer is a one-stop guide for improving your riding skills. Covering all aspects of road and mountain cycling, Lennard Zinn shows you how to improve your bike fit and bike handling skills, as well as your training and recovery, injury prevention, core strength, and nutrition. Zinn also includes step-by-step instructions for basic road and mountain bike maintenance, repair, and upgrades.

232 pages • $24.95
ISBN 978-1-931382-43-4

YOU BELONG WITH US.

IMBA creates, enhances, and preserves trails for mountain bikers worldwide.

Since 1988, IMBA has encouraged low-impact riding and has built a vast network of trail builders and advocates. We encourage cooperation among different trail user groups and innovative, sustainable trail management solutions.

Principal projects include:

- Subaru/IMBA Trail Care Crew
- National Mountain Bike Patrol
- IMBA Trail Building Schools
- National Take a Kid Mountain Biking Day
- IMBA Epic Rides
- IMBA Trail Solutions Program
- Bike Advocacy at international, national, regional, state, and local levels

As the undisputed expert, IMBA is building the next generation of trail systems right now in communities like yours. We develop trails for all riding styles — from fun, flowing singletrack to challenging downhill trails to Gateway Trail systems that rejuvenate urban areas with dirt jumps and bike parks.

If you ride trails, you belong with IMBA's worldwide network of 32,000 mountain bikers, clubs, retailer members, and corporate partners. Visit www.imba.com to learn about the great benefits members receive, including free gear and discounts. **Visit www.imba.com to learn more.**

FIVE THINGS YOU CAN DO TO GET MORE FROM MOUNTAIN BIKING:

1) Join. Get in touch with local riders and improve your local trails. Join IMBA and learn more about IMBA chapters and affiliated clubs near you at www.imba.com.

2) Speak. Tell land-use and elected officials how important it is to preserve mountain bike access. Visit www.imba.com and sign up for action alerts and talking points.

3) Build. Volunteer for a trail work day. You'll learn a lot and leave with the satisfying experience of building a trail you'll ride for years to come.

4) Respect. Bike bans result from conflict, real or perceived. Be a responsible rider by following IMBA's Rules of the Trail:

- Ride Open Trails
- Leave No Trace
- Control Your Bicycle
- Yield Appropriately
- Never Scare Animals
- Plan Ahead

5) Ride. Get out there and enjoy our sport!